PRIMAL MAN

OTHER BOOKS BY DR. JANOV

The Primal Scream
The Anatomy of Mental Illness
The Primal Revolution
The Feeling Child

Primal Man:
The New Consciousness

ARTHUR JANOV, Ph.D.
and
E. Michael Holden, M.D.

THOMAS Y. CROWELL COMPANY
Established 1834/New York

To

A. S. Neill and Frederick Leboyer

Manufactured in the United States of America

Library of Congress Cataloging in Publication Data

Janov, Arthur.
  Primal man.

  1. Primal therapy. I. Holden, Edward Michael,
1941–   joint author. II. Title.
RC489.P67J36   616.8'914   75–20416
ISBN 0–690–01015–X

  2 3 4 5 6 7 8 9 10

THE CONTRIBUTORS

Arthur Janov, Ph.D., Psychologist, Director of the Primal Institute and President of the Primal Foundation for Education and Research.
E. Michael Holden, M.D., Neurologist, Director of Research, The Primal Foundation.
Bernard Campbell, Ph.D., Anthropologist, Professor of Anthropology, UCLA.
Bernard McInerny, Ph.D., Psychologist, Associate Director of The Primal Foundation.

ACKNOWLEDGEMENTS

Our thanks to Cheryl Faris for her able editing and to Jean Livingston for her hours of manuscript typing. Special thanks to France Daunic for her helpful suggestions and comments on the manuscript.

CONTENTS

INTRODUCTION

Primal Man takes Primal Theory and Primal Therapy far beyond its beginnings as delineated in *The Primal Scream*. All new developments take gestation time and become more sophisticated with time, work and thought. This is certainly true with Primal Theory which we hope to show is far more than an idea about a "Scream."

Primal Man represents the highest development of Primal Theory thus far, although I am sure that in the years to come it will be refined even more. I view books about Primal Theory and Primal Therapy as progress reports; nothing is settled forever. We only hope to share our thoughts and research with the public, both professional and lay, as we go along. This book is the result of more than seven years of observations of Primal patients together with an attempt to fuse those observations with the latest developments in the neurological sciences. I view this fusion as crucial for as I indicate later no psychological theory is worthwhile which does not eventually square itself with what we know about brain function. I believe, therefore, that any diagnosis of mental pathology must be a simultaneous statement about *both* psychological and neurological processes. Neurology, too, must eventually relate itself to *human* functioning, not just brain functions. The purpose, it seems to me, of studying neurology is to gain a better understanding of man's behavior in the world: his sensations, perceptions and cognitions.

I believe that a major contribution of this work lies in the exploration of levels of consciousness: how man processes Pain within three systems of consciousness and how that is related to neurosis and psychosis. Understanding Primal Theory in terms of three levels of consciousness has given us a shorthand to understand and explain what patients go through; it has refined our ability to comprehend where a patient is in his therapeutic progress, and if indeed he is making progress. The discovery of three levels of consciousness has come from the fusion I described above of observation plus neurologic fact. We knew it was possible for patients to Primal on discrete levels of consciousness because we had observed it many times over. The fact that the latest in neurologic research also indicates three discrete levels of pain processing is important. What we have done is relate that processing procedure to specific systems of consciousness.

It is not theory by itself that we are after. We refine the theory for two reasons: to generate testable hypotheses which can then be explored in a research design, and more importantly, to sharpen the therapy in order to be as efficacious as possible in the treatment of patients. The result is that our therapy has changed radically over the years. We have a whole host of new techniques and have discarded many of the original techniques described in *The Primal Scream*. Nevertheless, Primal Therapy is in my opinion exactly what I believed it to be many years ago—the only viable effective treatment for psychophysiologic afflictions. My observations of hundreds of patients over thousands of Primals have only reified my belief that Primal Therapy is the cure for mental illness, if by "cure" we understand it not to be magic by which we reconstitute a totally damaged human being into a perfect specimen, but as a system of making people into feeling human beings so that they no longer suffer neurotic tension, inexplicable psychosomatic symptoms, uncontrolled compulsions, nightmares and the whole panoply of neurotic behaviors.

It is still my belief that there is no other real system of psychotherapy, and our research is beginning to bear this out. We are discovering continuing drops in blood pressure, pulse and body temperature over a long period of time which leads me to believe that we are effecting permanent changes, not just temporary readjustments.

Our brainwave studies also lead us to this conclusion. We chose outsiders to conduct our research as one more means of avoiding bias in the results. This research will continue for years, and I am certain that we have just begun to find out about what real changes are taking place in the systems of our patients. From time to time there will be more books or articles in *The Journal of Primal Therapy* detailing our research results.

This book is written for professionals, graduate students in the mental health sciences and sophisticated lay persons. There may be one or two chapters which can be only fully understood by neurologists or by graduate students in psychiatry and neurology; others can be readily understood by a lay person with some background in psychology, and particularly in Primal Theory and Primal Therapy.

The format of this book is a little different from the usual format. Some chapters were written almost three years apart. I have started with the earlier written chapters and gone from there in order to show the progress in our thinking over the years. I would hope that this would give some insight into how our thinking processes work and how we change in the light of new evidence. In a sense, the reader will make discoveries and change with us as he goes along in the text. Perhaps in this way we can convey some of the excitement of our discoveries.

Each time we open up a neurotic we find Pain; it is our continuing observation that Pain is central to neurosis. Even for those neurotics who had no idea they were in Pain the finding is the same. It is our experience that reliving the traumas of early childhood—the physical damage, the lack of fulfillment of need and the suppression of feelings— resolves and dispels Primal Pain and tension permanently.

The paradigm is really a simple one: Primal Pain produces neurosis and psychosis, and reliving the Pain is resolving. All of the sophisticated theory and research that you will read revolves around that simple paradigm; that has not changed at all in all the years that Primal Therapy has been in existence.

What the reader will find here is a new concept of consciousness, something which has little to do with awareness or many of the other notions of consciousness extant. I believe that we have produced a new quality of consciousness that gives a person total access to his innermost cerebral processes. No longer are his feelings, symptoms, dreams and symbolic behavior a mystery to him. Primal Man is free and at ease precisely because consciousness is the only freedom, and because it is the liberation of Pain which liberates consciousness. Primal Man is relaxed because there are no longer deep buried Pains constantly activating him, keeping him on the go, afflicting him with a variety of symptoms. Primal Man is more intelligent because he is conscious and can lead a more consciously directed intelligent life. His perceptions are opened and his cognitions are broadened. I believe that he is a new kind of person walking the land.

One thing is certain: Primal Theory is not static. As an open, dynamic system it changes in its own terms. It is not a dogma which one simply commits to memory and then goes out to practice. It is not a catechism or a litany chanted by patients in an attempt to get well. It is a scientific system, honed and refined daily so as to better serve a mankind afflicted and bedeviled by Pain . . . Primal Pain.

Arthur Janov
The Primal Institute
Los Angeles, California

CHAPTER ONE

The Nature of Consciousness
Arthur Janov

Introduction

I am going to discuss mental illness as a profound alteration in the state of consciousness. In order to understand what that means we shall need a definition of consciousness: the sum total of the cooperative activities of the structures of the brain as they mediate processes of the body. A definition is essential if we are to understand correctly the nature of mental illness and its cure. It is not simply a matter of semantics which makes such a definition crucial; rather, if we do not properly comprehend the difference between awareness and consciousness, then we shall go astray in our ability to understand and properly treat mental illness.

A. Consciousness and Awareness Defined

Consciousness does not have a "seat," nor is it synonymous with awareness. It is an enduring state of the *entire* organism, not just the brain itself, with fluid access among the various brain structures. A conscious person is one whose brain and body work in harmony, with no section of the brain insulated against any other section. It connotes someone whose body responds wholly to thought and vice versa—someone who thinks what he feels and feels what he thinks. Consciousness is not a brain phenomenon alone, in which the cerebrum exists *in vitro*, excised from its bodily counterparts. *It is a state of the organism.* It is not synonymous with thought, which, like awareness, is a moment-to-moment process which always has a content. When that content is directly related to subconscious processes, I call the phenomenon "consciousness." When the content is unrelated and only symbolically derivative of subconscious processes, I call the phenomenon "awareness." Generally, I use the term "awareness" to denote disconnected thought processes and use "consciousness" when those processes are fully connected. I am using "consciousness" in a very different way than it has been used conventionally. For, in my view, one can be asleep yet be conscious, or be awake and be very unconscious—in the way neurotics and psychotics are unconscious. Neurotics can be very aware but never totally conscious, by definition. This is because neurosis and psychosis (which I shall call "mental illness" hereafter) *are* altered states of consciousness. Painful realities are automatically and reflexively withheld from consciousness by certain structures of the brain, something I shall discuss later.

When certain painful realities are withheld from consciousness, the charge of those impulses being processed unconsciously links up to other areas of the cortex and produces "awareness." Thus, when a young child is totally rejected by his parents, the full experience of rejection may be so shattering that the feeling is shut down and the knowledge is repressed, and instead the child may come to believe that he needs no one. He may rationalize later in life that he can take care of himself. This latter belief is what I term false consciousness. Pain has rendered him unconscious, in the Primal sense.

Such a person may be acutely aware of his surroundings, and because he believes he must totally rely on himself, he may be most perceptive, for the sake of survival, about the world in which he moves. But no act of will can make him conscious of what lies below. His awareness is selective and external. It is not consonant with the underlying Pain which, if liberated, would make him fully conscious.

When one is wholly engrossed in a book, one may be unaware of certain outside realities. But the *potential* for expanded awareness is always present. This is not the case in mental illness. Here the underlying activation produces pseudo-connections so that one is aware of everything but those things which could really expand consciousness.

The differentiation of consciousness from awareness must be made if we are to understand why certain therapies do not work, for *it is always possible to make patients aware but it is not possible to "make" someone conscious.* Patients in some therapies can come to *understand* their needs but to *experience* them as a total psychophysiological event means to be writhing in Pain. To be "aware" of a feeling and to feel the feeling in all its intensity are obviously two different orders of phenomena. That is why in certain kinds of brain dysfunction a person can curse and act angry and not have any idea as to why he is cursing. Or conversely, patients in insight therapy can fully understand their feelings but recognize that they have no way to feel them—and still feel completely shut off emotionally. The point is that the processing of feelings can go on in lower brain centers and in that sense is unconscious. To be conscious of feelings means that certain fundamental connections are being made between lower and higher brain centers (and also between right and left hemispheres, as we shall see later). To be "aware" of these feelings means that certain higher processes are at work (disconnected from the lower processes) which view these feelings as something apart—a so-called objective view. When a patient comes out of a Primal he will say, "I always was aware of my feeling, but I never really knew it." To become aware of the feeling in a Primal is a different experience . . . a total, organic one—consciousness. Awareness is circumscribed by the state of consciousness.

Let us take an example. In Rolfing, where the fascia of the muscles are put under deep massage, there is often a release of feeling. Rolfed patients may cry and may feel that this release has taken them back into their past lives. The patient may be aware of living in Elizabethan times, may see the houses and hear the clatter of hooves on cobblestone pavement. What has happened? With a stored history of Pain there are obvious physical concomitants which operate as part of the defense system. Suppose a young child sees his sister beaten up by his father. He becomes terrified when near his father, tenses up, and has a chronically tense musculature around the stomach. Years later the memory is repressed but the tension remains. It is kneaded and eased by Rolfing. That is, the defense system is mechanically loosened, just as happens in lowering the body temperature with certain drugs. The feelings start to flow, but the overload of Pain involved prevents a proper connection. There is then a "benign misconnection." The patient is driven over the connection into a pseudo-consciousness—past lives. The so-called psychedelic drugs can produce the same sequelae. Pain is released by chemical means, the cortex is flooded beyond its integrative capacities, and rechanneled connections are made: "I'm in an ancient tomb. I see all the slaves in their pretty costumes, etc." What is clear is that the only way to insure expanded consciousness is to begin with it and let it dictate how much it will experience. Defenses are against complete consciousness. To render defenses ineffective is to leave the psyche in a position to be overwhelmed.

It should be clear that the only way to expand consciousness is to bring what is unconscious forward. But it must be done in a slow, orderly fashion so that each stored feeling can be consciously assimilated. This is not possible when the impetus for release is done mechanically and by external means. To flood consciousness with the use of drugs is simply to produce more unconsciousness; this is how mental illness begins in the first place.

A manic mind driven by an overload of Pain due to LSD is not, in my opinion, an expanded consciousness—it is only a more busy one. The psychedelic mind seems to be liberated and open to all sorts of ideas because it is totally fragmented by continuous flooding, so that conscious coherence and discrimination have been lost. Due to overload, the amount of rechanneled connections has proliferated. The drug, by prematurely opening the limbic gate (see *The Anatomy of Mental Illness* by Janov for elaboration of this point), continuously drives the cortex into all sorts of bizarre thoughts because of the liberated (but not liberating) Pain. Whereas tranquilizers can momentarily alter awareness by suppression of activation of certain brain structures (such as the reticular activating system), psychedelics can fundamentally alter the structure of consciousness. That is their danger!

It is my observation after treating a number of post-LSD psychotics that a psychedelic overload can destroy the integrity of consciousness; in that respect LSD is far more dangerous than heroin, which only shuts off the overload. The LSD user often has trouble getting his thoughts together; he will tell long rambling stories without point or conclusion, interrupt or lose his train of thought, and not be able to summarize facts into a cohesive picture. He is truly a split man. I do not think this occurs just while the person is taking the drug. The effects may last for months, for years, or perhaps forever. LSD breaks up neurotic *consciousness* and differs from tranquilizers in that the latter merely alter awareness. If a person has adequate defenses, one "acid trip" may not affect him. But eventually, with enough usage, no matter what the defense structure, serious alterations will take place.

The only consciousness beyond what is real is *unreal* consciousness. A liberated mind can only come about as a result of specific connections being made to one's historic unconscious.

B. *Unconsciousness: Its Form and Cause*

Unconsciousness represents a breakdown in the integrative capacities of the brain as it mediates bodily processes. It occurs when the system is overloaded so that impulses (resulting from action potentials mediated by synapses) which normally have specific innervations with the cerebral cortex to make us conscious, overwhelm the integrative faculties and become shunted into alternate cerebral pathways rendering us, in that sense, unconscious. Curing mental illness means altering consciousness so that awareness and consciousness merge rather than diverge as they do in neurosis and psychosis. This means changing the integrative relationships within the nervous system. *Without that basic and profound change,* I submit, *there can be no cure for mental illness.*

Unconsciousness is not simply an absence of consciousness; it is an active process involving specific brain structures whose function it is to help us survive by rendering us oblivious to catastrophic pains. In short, becoming unconscious is a built-in defense mechanism that has nothing to do with choice or decision making. It is a disconnecting process which occurs when the connection of feeling-centers with knowing-centers would mean overwhelming Pain. The key word is "connection" because it is possible to be aware of Pain without really experiencing it.

An example of my point is fainting. A stimulus such as seeing an auto accident or a violent crime causes someone to faint. Why? Because the stimulus constitutes a neurologic overload resulting in unconsciousness. Here a psychological event becomes immediately translated into internal processes; when the processing breaks down there is a corresponding loss of consciousness.

"Overload" is not simply a matter of how traumatic the stimulus is; on an internal level it must be a stimulus for which "there is no option for escape." When one is hit on the head there are no options. When one is forced to witness a catastrophe there is also no option. But more generally, I believe that overload occurs when our acquired value systems and mores permit no option. Thus someone makes us very angry and we learn we must "turn the other cheek." In a slow and subtle process parents infuse into their children a psychological web which traps feelings and permits no release. As time goes on, this inner rigidity bucking against one's natural impulses can lead to an impasse where perhaps the only release is in the random discharge of an epileptic fit. If nothing a child can do is right for his parents he is left without any adaptive (even neurotically adaptive) responses. The energy of his anguish and frustration will be stored and added to the general pool of Pain, ultimately leading to overload and overflow into symptoms.

While seeing a horrible accident leads to instant overload, the development of a neurotic overload is slower and more subtle but ultimately leads to a similar kind of unconsciousness. The point for now that I am making is that overload is related to unconsciousness both on a physical and on a psychological level.

1. *Physical Unconsciousness*

There are essentially two forms of unconsciousness—one physical, the other psychological. An example of physical unconsciousness is found in an epileptic seizure. It results when the mechanisms ordinarily responsible for consciousness are flooded by nervous activity from lower brain centers, the body convulses from the onslaught, and there is a random, massive discharge of nervous activity. In psychogenic epilepsy (which is what I am discussing) there is usually a stimulus: an argument between one's parents, for example, which produces not just appropriate nervous reaction to the situation, but rather a triggered history of Pain and fear which unleashes a flood of nervous excitation. This excitation coupled with a brain with a subnormal threshold for seizure produces physical unconsciousness. When the brain is strong and healthy, that same random discharge may take place on a sexual level. That is, the person, unable to integrate the meaning of his parents' argument, shuts down against the onslaught of Pain, remains unconscious of his fears and Pain, and later compulsively discharges the energy of the trauma, which has been converted into tension, in a sexual way. A person who has been unable to have either seizures or constant sexual release may find himself in a mental hospital with intractable depression for which he is given electroshock therapy which produces convulsions, random massive discharge, and unconsciousness.* Electroshock acts to prevent the retrieval of unconscious memory into awareness. It reinforces the split, particularly in those cases where the defense system is faltering and unconscious impulses are pressuring for access to awareness.**

The difference between a psychogenic epileptic and other neurotics may be due to certain brain vulnerabilities plus an overarching load of Pain which can be set off by a particularly relevant stimulus. The onset of the epileptic unconsciousness of grand mal begins with vastly increased muscular tension. Often there is an initial scream or cry. The cry usually has an unmistakably emotional flavor to it; it is reflexive, the phonic result of a subcortical process. It is subcortical behavior. The seizure begins,

---

*Depression is a state of high activation with no external release forms.
**See R. R. Miller and A. D. Springer, "Amnesia, Consolidation and Retrieval," in *The Psychological Review,* Vol. 80, No. 1, p. 77.

there is convulsing and writhing, thrashing and unconsciousness . . . and later relaxation. Being "seized" by an overwhelming sexual urge can be the same kind of subconscious process where Pain, perhaps blocked by the limbic system, is rerouted to other brain systems, such as areas of the hypothalamus which in turn lead the cortex to be informed and then presumably to be aware of sexual feeling rather than the original feeling of Pain. The person, in this sense, is truly unconscious even while he is having very conscious sex. And here is the division between awareness and consciousness. The person is "aware" of his sex urge, his sex partner, and sex techniques, but he is completely unconscious of his driving motivation. He is unconscious because there are certain brain areas shut off from facile and proper access to other areas.

There seems to be general agreement that the difference between various kinds of epileptic seizures is due not to different kinds of cerebral mechanisms involved, but to how much brain area, and which area, the discharge involves. With stimulation ranging from slight to massive, there is a corresponding degree of unconsciousness ranging from the partial of the petit mal to the total of the grand mal.

2. Psychological Unconsciousness

The way neurologists have customarily viewed unconsciousness is in terms of the relative inability to respond to stimuli of varying intensity. The more unconscious the person the less "adequate" the stimuli, and the more it takes to rouse him. All of this describes psychological states as well. For in psychosis, a state of maximum unconsciousness, the person may be somewhat in contact or totally out of it so that no one can reach him. That is, no stimuli can rouse him back into the consciousness of the here and now.

In mental illness there is a progressive repression of Pain in childhood, resulting in an accretion of unconsciousness; if what is repressed must be kept out of consciousness it follows that the pool of unconsciousness is enlarged. Unless we are willing to say that each stored Pain memory exists in encapsulated form unconnected to other neurons, we must concede that these unconscious Pains innervate other areas of the brain. When the brain is healthy the underlying action potentials produce a range of psychologic unconsciousness along a continuum from neurosis to psychosis—neurosis being a state of lesser unconsciousness than psychosis because there is a smaller storehouse of Pain. Thus, one way of looking at mental illness is in terms of the amount of unconsciousness present; the more unconscious the person is, the more severe his pathology. Conversely, the deeper and more extensive the Pain, the greater the unconsciousness. When nearly all reality is blotted out because the person is overwhelmed by his Primal Pain we say that he is psychotic. He is just as unconscious as the epileptic, in his own way. The psychogenic epileptic has certain physical vulnerabilities which when overloaded produce a symptom. The psychotic given a similar pressure produces strange ideation, perhaps. We might speculate that the massive discharge of the epileptic helps stave off psychosis by the release of pressure. Is that not what electroshock therapy accomplishes? It helps put the body into a state of shock in which there is not only a release but a mobilization of every physical resource of the body to combat stress.

What is significant about both the psychotic and epileptic reactions is that they are *generalized* responses. The Pain, having lost its specific roots in consciousness, produces generalized results, and the amount of generalization is commensurate with the degree of Pain. Instead of feeling the fear of father when he beat up a sibling, together with the specific feeling of, "He can kill me if I get out of line," there is repressed fear of authority figures. With enough terror that fear can spread to almost any social contact with an adult. The hallmark of mental illness is this generalization process, for it is generalizing a repressed past in the present that makes current reactions inappropriate. There is really no reason to fear social contact with other adults in the present, but the past makes it fearful. The whole point of a curative therapy would be to make present responses *specific* to past events—to tie awareness to the unconscious. So long as consciousness does not know the specific time of and the event related to a Pain, it must remain disconnected and unconscious, exerting a force which mobilizes the system in a diffuse way, producing inappropriate ideas and physical responses. We can define neurosis as *the gener-, alized reaction to unintegrated Primal Pain.*

Relatively little fear can make one fearful only of authority. Sufficiently great fear can make one fearful of almost anyone. Relatively little anger at mother can make one dislike women. Sufficiently great repressed anger can drive one to kill women indiscriminately. A small amount of Pain can make someone imagine that his friend dislikes him. More Pain can make him feel that everyone dislikes him, and still more Pain can produce an idea that everyone is really out to get him. In that case *everyone* becomes symbolic of the person's Pain.

What I am suggesting is that *mental pathology can be thought of in terms of the extent of the unconsciousness and generalization involved.*

Unconsciousness is in direct relationship to Pain. (I use the upper case letter throughout to denote that "Pain" includes both the physical type, such as surgery, and the psychological type, such as humiliation.)

My hypothesis is that the extent of unconsciousness results from the "gating" or blocking which exists on both a vertical and horizontal plane in the brain. In a figurative sense an overload of Pain shuts the gates and redirects the energy elsewhere—from "mother" to "women." It takes energy and activation to keep the gates shut against feelings, so that when we think about Pain and repression we are thinking about a more activated brain. One obvious result of this is insomnia—the inability to shut off the activation which makes the mind race. We would expect to find out about the severity of mental illness by a study of the activation of the brain, both in terms of the frequency and amplitude of the brain waves.

The general assumption is that a healthy person has fluid access to all parts of his brain and body so that the system does less work and can be specific, knowing what the underlying feelings are at all times. The ability to be specific is what stops the generalization process. "Fluid access" is a vague term but I use it to mean that no blocking mechanisms are in constant operation to interfere with normal interconnections between areas of the brain. This means that neural activity in the lower centers which help process feeling is able to have access through intermediate structures to those higher centers which represent feelings into awareness. When that happens, consciousness and awareness merge and are indistinguishable. "Fluid access" also means proper horizontal integration of the two cerebral hemispheres.

The bifurcation of unconsciousness into the physical and the psychological is largely an academic division; we must understand that when we talk about the processing of "psychological" events we are still discussing physiological processes that take place in a brain. Psychological unconsciousness simply means that the stimulus which led to that state was social rather than physical (such as a blow on the head). Psychological unconsciousness means that certain areas of the brain are rendered dysfunctional, but given the right conditions there is the possibility of proper functioning. As we shall see later, I believe that the necessary and sufficient condition for a return to consciousness is a treatment procedure where inhibitory processes preventing the fluid access to certain brain structures are changed. An example of how psychological processes actually alter brain structure is found in rat studies where one group of young rats grew up in a stimulus-deprived environment and another group had a stimulus-enriched one. In the latter group there was a heavier cortex.

One important question about unconsciousness is whether or not early trauma was ever conscious even for a fleeting moment; i.e., were the hurts of our childhood organized completely unconsciously?

For part of the answer let us take a look at some relevant research.* In tests of subliminal perception, where the intensity of the stimulus lay below the conscious threshold, words were flashed to test subjects. One subject responded to a flash with the association "LINE." The stimulus word was "Valparaiso." A week later, given the word "Valparaiso," which he had not *consciously* seen before, he selected "LINE" as the best association to it. His reason was that Valparaiso connoted an ocean *liner* to him, hence the word "LINE." Here is what N. Dixon says about this phenomenon: "That subliminal stimuli may evoke semantically related responses is of great theoretical interest. First, it disposes of the view that subliminal perception is merely a watered down version of normal conscious perception. It thus militates against explaining the phenomenon in terms of consciously perceived parts of the stimulus. In the above experiment it was only when the stimulus energy was increased to threshold level that the subject gave responses that were structurally related to the stimulus. This suggests that at an early pre-conscious stage in cerebral processing, incoming information actually makes contact with memory systems, thereby activating conceptual associations to the applied stimulus." (p. 252) What is relevant for us is that by experimental design it can be shown that when unconscious memories are activated they give rise to conceptual notions, and that this all may take place on an unconscious level.

Research indicates that incoming information can be "received, classified and responded to without a person ever becoming conscious." (Dixon, p. 254) Electroencephalographic recordings from surgical patients with exposed brains, quite awake, indicated clear-cut EEG responses to subliminal stimuli of which the person was "wholly unaware." (*op. cit.,* p. 254) It is Dixon's belief that man's brain can make complex discriminations without the help of those structures upon which consciousness depends—that is, unconsciously. Dixon discusses work with anesthetized cats and concludes: "The existence of two neural systems, one which yields specific information and the other the capacity for conscious ex-

---

*As reported by N. Dixon: *New Scientist*, Vol. 53, No. 781, 3 February 1972, pp. 252-255.

perience of this information, enhances the possibility for subliminal perception." (p. 255)

Dixon reports on one highly significant experiment in which subjects were connected to an EEG while either emotional or neutral words were flashed on a screen either at a subthreshold or a conscious level. The experiment yielded the following results:

1. Conscious thresholds were higher for emotional words. What you see, in short, depends on your state of unconsciousness.

2. Changes occurred on the EEG *prior* to any awareness of the stimulus word. The brain responds even below the level of conscious awareness.

3. The ultimate threshold depended upon the preceding level of cortical activation. The quality of perception depends on the continuous activity of the brain.

Both heart rate and the theta rhythm on the EEG indicated an emotional, unconscious response to critical words prior to any conscious recognition of them. All of this is saying no more than that there is an unconscious level of activity which affects our concepts and our percepts and hence our bodily activities.

C. *Our Dual Consciousness*

There is evidence that we really have two inner worlds—two streams of consciousness, not one, as William James believed. These separate streams involve the two hemispheres of the brain. The dominant or major side (which is the left side in right-handed people) deals with intellectual and conceptual affairs, while the subdominant, minor side is more involved with the consciousness of feeling. It would seem that each hemisphere has its own kind of memories, and perhaps which side a memory is stored on depends upon its content—dates and places go to the major side of the brain, while feelings and Pain go to the minor. A good intellectual memory does not necessarily indicate a good emotional one.

The minor side can express itself non-verbally, while the major side can intellectualize and possibly suppress that expression. In experiments by R. W. Sperry on people whose brains had been surgically divided (a procedure called a commissurotomy), there was the indication that without the action of the dominant hemisphere there was less inhibition of emotional outbreaks. Though the minor side cannot speak, it can swear and sing, which are really feeling functions. I remember finding years ago in my treatment of (psychogenically) stuttering children that they would never stutter when they sang, only when they spoke. I believe that if those children had been feeling human beings with little disruptive intrusion from the dominant hemisphere, they would not have been stutterers. Stuttering, I submit, was the symptomatic result of conflicting impulses generated by two streams of consciousness which were not consonant. I have watched politicians stammering and stuttering whenever they spoke extemporaneously. Perhaps if they were not so occupied with suppressing the truth they could speak with greater fluidity.

It is the subdominant side which processes music, a feeling-evoking stimulus. It is not surprising that my patients who sang did not stutter, for it is the major side which does the talking and the minor one which carries the tune.

The minor side operates more in a relational mode than an analytic one. It is more global in its functions, less specific in its perceptions. It is more adapted to processing a variety of inputs in a total way. What this may mean is that it is the side which can be more insightful because it does see the connection between things and because it can coordinate and integrate, as opposed to dissect and analyze. The minor hemisphere seems to favor feeling because it is the experiential side operating in a non-linear, simultaneous way, which is what feeling feelings is about. The minor hemisphere is timeless, in that sense, and does not keep track of the passage of time.* Freud foresaw this when he described the unconscious as timeless. In his *Interpretation of Dreams,* (Chapter VII, section D) he states: "It is perfectly true that unconscious wishes always remain active. They represent paths which can always be traversed, whenever a quantity of excitation makes use of them. Indeed, it is a predominant feature of unconscious processes that they are indestructible. In the unconscious nothing can be brought to an end, nothing is past or forgotten . . . a humiliation that was experienced thirty years ago acts exactly like a fresh one throughout the thirty years as soon as it has obtained access to the unconscious sources of emotion." I, too, see it as timeless but in a different way, for stored Pain is boundless and continuous on an unconscious level no matter what the higher faculties are doing. It remains unchanged (and in this sense is timeless) irrespective of what is done to the organism.

It is interesting that in both an LSD and a Primal experience (both feel-

---

*There is some evidence that the right-brain also can keep track of time but evidently not as well as the left-brain.

ing-related events) there is that same timeless feeling. One reason for this is that when a person is into the experience of an old childhood feeling, he really is not in "now time." He is back there. A feeling is not something we mark by the clock; it is a total state of the organism.

One wonders if the better integration which I believe occurs in Primal Therapy does not account for enhanced physical coordination. A professional tennis player, for example, found after therapy that he could easily win major tournaments in which he could barely qualify previously. He said that he felt more physically coordinated (and this happens to many of our patients), so that he could react instinctively with less hesitation on his shots. He could also dance better, which means to me that his body could react in a unified way to feeling-evoking stimuli.

The major hemisphere not only does our mathematical calculations, it supplies the language symbols for our dreams. It also supplies the rationales (language again) for our neurotic acts. Visual imagery seems to be a property of the minor side (the term "side" always refers to the brain).

Our neurotic acts seem rational to us because the major side helps make them so. That is its function in neurosis. For example, in one split-brain study (much of the work has been done by R. W. Sperry and by J. E. Bogen) a male subject was speaking aloud about some trivial matter while a photograph of a nude female was presented to his visually isolated minor side. He continued speaking but would intermittently giggle and blush. When asked why he was giggling, he said, "Oh, that machine of yours!" He was obviously having feelings, but the dominant hemisphere incorrectly interpreted them because there was no longer fluid access. In hypnosis, which I see as a packaged neurosis, we can produce the same phenomenon. We can give a subject a post-hypnotic suggestion that a certain woman will be naked but he must pretend not to notice. Later, on cue, he will giggle and blush when the woman enters the room and not know why. He will also rationalize his giggles in some way. Perhaps the hypnotist has done a non-surgical commissurotomy so that one side of the brain does not know what the other side is doing (we shall discuss hypnosis in a moment). Certainly we see this effect in neurosis when a person acts on a feeling, such as by exhibiting himself in public, without any idea what impels him to do so, or under certain stressful situations develops a "splitting" headache.

The fact that the minor side deals with imagery and the major side with language may help us understand the different kinds of psychosis. Perhaps those persons with hallucinations suffer from key early physical traumas, such as events around birth, while those who develop delusions were

overloaded in a psychological way—being humiliated and ridiculed constantly, for example. This is highly speculative indeed. But it would
seem that when physically traumatic events begin their ascent into consciousness, with the use of LSD for example, what would occur would
be a related (though symbolic) *image* of the event rather than an idea
about it. In any case, the symbol would be incorrect due to overload. I
discuss as an example later in this article the seeing of the lights of a flying
saucer as symbolic of being blinded during delivery at birth by fluorescent lights.

If my assumption is correct that hallucinations reflect earlier traumas
than do delusions, then we might assume that hallucinations are indicative
of a deeper psychosis because the overload and shutdown took place sooner in life when the organism was preverbal, as well as more fragile and
vulnerable to stress. The delusional person uses ideation as a defense. His
rationales seem more bizarre than those of a neurotic because they are
further from the actual feeling. There is some tentative and unconfirmed
evidence that a commissurotomy either reduces or eliminates the symbolism in dreams. Or perhaps the person dreams but cannot talk about it.
What is important is that dreams are largely a matter of images (a
right-brain function), with little real conversation going on in them, and
images may be the direct offshoot of feelings, aligned on the same side of
the brain.

For the person who uses ideation as a defense, words become disconnected symbols unto themselves. They become their own reality so that
"Mexico" can mean "mixed-up city" to him. He would then respond
to that symbol and avoid the city because of it—rather bizarre behavior.
On a less bizarre level we find the intellectual who uses words quite
apart from feeling, who quibbles over definitions and makes encounters
in communication a matter of words and phrasing.

Sperry found that the minor side is the one to cause a person to show
displeasure and to wince. When a subject has made a stupid mistake, it
is the subdominant side which makes him show annoyance and disgust.
Sperry believes that insight is not a major-side function as we might
imagine, but derives from the subdominant hemisphere. I would speculate that insight is the direct consciousness of feeling and may be aligned
with its feeling counterpart on the same side of the brain. Pseudo-
insight, the intellectual insight accumulated in some conventional therapies,
would be an unconnected major-side phenomenon (leaving aside vertical
disconnections for the moment) which would not affect the feeling side,
nor would it change it. Pseudo-insight, in my view, would be a neurotic

symbolization of feelings which occurs when there is no integrated access directly to them.

Though the left-brain seems to predominate and to coordinate general behavior from both halves, it is the minor side which sees things in a broader perspective. It sees the context and views the parts of an event as in its gestalt. It is the right-brain which takes the facts perceived by the left-brain and can make proper conclusions (connections) from them. It makes facts "meaningful." When we say that the only real way to understand a Primal is to experience one, we mean it is only with the help of the right-brain that such events are validated, a validation that no amount of "knowing" can achieve. In the split-brain patient, and more importantly in the neurotic, the left-brain does not seem to be aware of the feelings on the other side. When there is full awareness I call it "consciousness." It is this consciousness which I feel may be lacking in the split-brain patient. The split-brain human can cry and feel the pain of a pin prick, for example, but whether he can "feel" and "connect" is another matter. Crying, in short, is not synonymous with feeling. We would be very interested to know (and hope to do research on) whether the split-brain patient can Primal. That is, can he cry deeply and *connect* himself to the origins of his Pain?

It is the disconnected neurotic who often is not aware that he is repressed and disconnected. I believe that it is a step up the ladder from neurosis to at least be "aware" of one's state of repression.

One might well ask at this point whether we have proof that the right-brain is really the feeling one. The answer is that we do not. For now it is an assumption based on meager evidence, such as right-brain musical experience being more feeling than doing mathematics. When Shakespeare said, "That man hath no music in him," he was probably talking about a feelingless person. The evidence we are garnering, however, in our neurophysiologic research may shed more light on feelings and the right-brain. Remembering emotional past scenes seems to galvanize that side into action.

The importance of understanding our dual consciousness is that it is possible to have thoughts which have nothing to do with what one is feeling, and to try to reach and change someone therapeutically through his thoughts and intellectual apparatus alone, without reference to the necessity for connection, is a vain exercise. The left-brain can be quite aware that smoking causes cancer but the person will still pull out a cigarette. The person is aware but not conscious.

D. *Implications of the Split Brain*

The word "dominance" reflects the fact that speech, generated in the major hemisphere, is the basis for conceptual thought—a unique characteristic of *Homo sapiens*. It may be that the neurotic intellectual is someone who has elaborately symbolized his feelings so that he is lopsided on the major side, whereas a normally integrated person would have a balanced hemispheric relationship.

Norman Geschwind has found that the dominant side tends to be five to ten per cent heavier than the minor side, and one wonders if this extra weight is not from the excessive activation required of that side by neurotics to keep feelings repressed, the extra weight being the anatomic result of proliferation of language symbolization.

Language is our symbol system. It is my contention that in neurosis the symbols are often disconnected from their feeling roots, and that unconscious activation can cause seemingly unlimited expansion of this symbolic process, resulting for example in long rambling philosophic discussions about trivia. In this way language becomes the symbol system for the split. The split, however, can certainly occur before the development of language. It would be experienced physically; for example, as a hypersecretion of hydrochloric acid by the stomach—body language. We do not need language to become neurotic but neurotics often use language as part of their defense system.

Geschwind's findings are consistent with the observation that brain development responds to input and the activation that input generates. This is another way of saying that stimulation produces growth, and that uneven growth of the brain may be due to differences in the amount of neuronal activity on each side—again, speculation. But one wonders if cerebral dominance in man occurred because of human neurosis, or in the phylogeny of the human race was it neurosis which produced dominance? It seems that the right-left split is significant in man alone. Monkeys, for example, have little preference for handedness, and once they learn to use one side or the other, they do so with equal facility.

What may be happening to us humans is that we are continuing an evolutionary shift toward the nonfeeling side of the brain, paralleling our increasing lack of humanity toward one another. In a circular bind our inhumanity may help produce this bilateral specialization of the brain and in turn this physical bifurcation perpetuates our inhumanity. It permits us to act against others without a feeling consciousness of what we do.

We are discovering in our current research a trend in post-Primal patients away from dominance toward a more balanced brain. These actual structural-functional changes in their brains add evidence to the assumption that the march of civilization contributed to hemispheric specialization resulting in uncivilized humans. We believe that Primal Therapy may reverse this destructive evolutionary process. Brain research led by a scientist from the UCLA Brain Research Institute indicates a shift in the EEG traces of our patients toward the feeling side; that is, there is evidence of greater processing activity of the right-brain. Follow-up EEG studies at three weeks, three months, and six months indicate evidence of an increased strength of shift to the feeling brain in each study period. His work shows that when questioned about the past, patients change their eye movements while remembering feeling-laden scenes from the dominant side to the subdominant as they proceed in therapy. In tests of counting on their fingers we have seen some instances of change from counting from left to right to counting from right to left.

It is interesting to note that ancient near-Eastern writing was right-to-left, that early cave drawings had faces turned to the right (indicative of left-handedness) and that ancient Chinese writing was from top to bottom, showing no preference for either side. Newborns exhibit no dominance. It is only with the further organization of the brain that dominance appears. It is as though our first period of life recapitulates a phylogenetically ancient past when dominance might not have existed. What this could mean is that dominance was a later development.

Dominance, indicative of our dual consciousness, may have developed when man changed from simple food-gathering to having to kill for survival—and to having to kill others who threatened his survival. Man then had to organize in bands in order to live. He had to give up part of himself, to deny his own needs in deference to the needs of his society. In order to kill animals and other humans he required some kind of shut-off mechanism to allow such acts. Neurosis filled the bill. It allowed killing to become an acceptable part of living, and those who could not do so were the least fit for survival. In this way it was the neurotics who survived. It is no accident that dominance (dual consciousness) is more common among predatory animals.*

As society became more organized there was a division of labor between the classes. There were the physical workers and the mental ones.

---

*For more on this see S. Gooch, *Total Man* (Holt, Rinehart and Winston, N.Y., 1972).

And perhaps in some way our split in consciousness paralleled that process, so that there was a division of labor between the hemispheres into thinking and feeling. With that division of the brain one could think one thing and do another. Feelings could be transmuted into symbolic form—the elaborateness of the ritualistic and symbolic life being commensurate with the amount of loss of self.

Man could then kill for his symbols. He could eliminate others to please the gods, or murder for religious reasons. He could kill others when the state (flag), an abstraction, not himself, was threatened. This is a key point about the relationship between feeling and consciousness. No Primal person could consider the killing of even the lower animal forms.

As man came to defer to higher authority his symbolic and repressive hemisphere (as well as his frontal cortex) became more active. He developed all sorts of ideas and rationales which were out of keeping with his feelings. His concepts outran his body, so to speak, so that he could relate to ideology rather than to himself. The elaboration of the symbolic and false consciousness favored survival.

My hypothesis is: where such transmutation of feeling occurs early in life while the brain is developing, and where continued repression is essential to survival, the structure and functions of the brain will be altered, both phylogenetically and ontogenetically. It would seem that for a brief few moments on this earth we pass through a normal ontogenetic period and then our brains accommodate themselves to the possibility of neurosis. Neurosis became a hereditary legacy to aid the species to survive.

When I discuss the notion of "fluid access," it is precisely the kind of relationships between right and left hemispheres to which I refer. In one sense neurosis can be considered a functional commissurotomy in which the integrating mechanisms of the corpus callosum (the connecting fibers of the two hemispheres) are impaired. This leads to a key hypothesis: an overload of Primal Pain disrupts the smooth unifying functions within the brain and literally produces a split personality—someone with a non-integrated dual consciousness each part of which acts as an independent entity. This split is both horizontal and vertical, and I shall discuss the vertical split in a moment.

The point about the split is that one side of our brain can be feeling something while the other side is thinking something very different. The split person can yell at you and not know why he is doing it, though he will manage to rationalize his acts and put the blame on others.

The neurologic overload was demonstrated in the work of Laitinen.* Laitinen introduced high frequency stimulation to a section of the corpus callosum in patients with intractable tension. It immediately abolished tension. The overload, it seems, produced a temporary commissurotomy.

THE BRAIN—FRONTAL SECTION

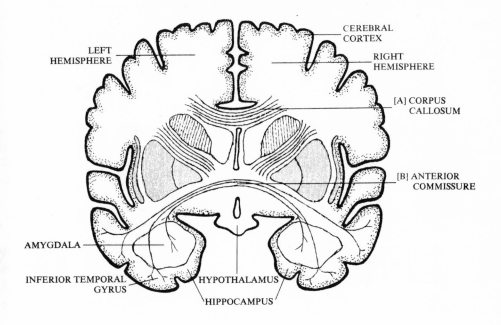

Both [A] and [B] represent key fiber-tract connections between the left and right sides of the brain. *They probably play crucial roles in the development of horizontal neurotic splitting.* As can be seen above, the corpus callosum connects mostly frontal and parietal parts of the brain, whereas the anterior commissure, below, connects temporal *limbic* structures in the region of the amygdala and the hippocampus.

The corpus callosum is more than a connecting group of fibers. It has inhibitory and facilitative functions. The split in consciousness occurs not only from lower to higher brain centers but also between the two sides of the brain. The corpus callosum contains more than two billion nerve cells and is an important structure in the integration of consciousness. Blocks in this area can cause one side not to know what the other side is doing and help to keep us unconscious of our feelings.

---

*Laitinen, L. V., "Stereotactic Lesions in the Knee of the Corpus Callosum in the Treatment of Emotional Disorders," *Lancet,* Feb. 26, 1972, pp. 472-475.

Laitinen states: "It is assumed that in tension the interhemispherical transcallosal . . . pathways are hyperactive." (p. 472)

If the pathways are already hyperactive with tension, why would even more stimulation abolish it? Again, I believe that shutdown as a result of overload is a key process in the human brain. What is interesting is that the formerly tense patients reported a feeling of ease and well-being after stimulation. This ease is a spurious state, I submit; the same kind of subjective phenomenon one sees with meditation, where, when repression is effective, there is a feeling of well-being. The subject, however, cannot differentiate between a true state of ease and one induced by overload. This is why it is so easy to be misled by the various approaches claiming to eliminate anxiety and tension, such as conditioning therapy.

Overload blocks Pain. It would seem that tension is a result of the strain between separate consciousnesses which are not integrated. Or conversely, that consciousness has been divided because of Pain. Once there is this duality, a person then suffers from inexplicable symptoms and dreams. His true feelings become an anathema and he literally can no longer get himself together.

My point is that there are two distinct mental spheres encased in a single body, each with its own perceptions and memories and each having its own experiences. In neurosis the gap between the two is wide enough so that each consciousness is also unconscious of the other, and this accounts for awareness without integrated Primal consciousness. I believe that the state of neurotic unconsciousness is due directly to stored Pain. The mentally healthy person has fluid access, not only from left to right but from lower to upper parts of the brain as well.

The significance of the differential workload between hemispheres is that it permits man to be conscious, as animals are conscious, of external stimuli, but also to be conscious that he is conscious—to be self-aware. It is this introspective faculty that separates him from the animals. Man can be self-conscious and take himself as object. But he can only be objective about that self when he is not separated from it and from his emotions—i.e., when he is truly integrated. I foresee the day when we will be able to tell whether a judge can be objective about those who parade before him in court by testing to see if he has an integrated brain. I will speculate that an excessively high frequency and an inordinate amplitude of his alpha waves are indicators of lack of integration and therefore of a lack of objectivity. We have already done some experiments on a new applicant to the Primal Institute who claimed to have been Primaling and feeling for months prior to his arrival. He was anxious to speed up his therapy and enter training earlier. Our tests indicated that he was not feeling. Though he disagreed at first, it did not take long in his therapy for him to realize how far from feeling he was. Our tests were better indicators than his subjective appraisal, simply because he was not integrated.

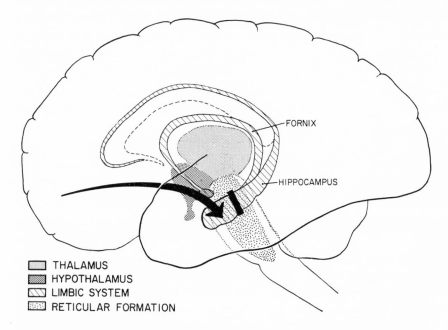

THALAMUS
HYPOTHALAMUS
LIMBIC SYSTEM
RETICULAR FORMATION

The transmission of underlying Pain to consciousness has been blocked by hippocampal inhibition. The aroused feelings continue to have access to lower brain centers which stimulate the body and the cortex in a general way. The painful feeling is rechanneled to other brain centers where it is projected, rationalized, and/or misinterpreted, resulting in a constricted awareness without Primal consciousness.

E. *Limbic System and Frontal Cortex—The Vertical Split*

I have indicated in previous writings how a split in consciousness may have come about also between higher and lower brain centers—between the old reptilian brain, now called the limbic system, and the neocortex. Essentially, it seems to be the responsibility of the limbic system to integrate higher and lower centers and to filter out Pains which cannot be integrated cortically. It is the limbic system, particularly the hippocampus and amygdala with their direct connections to the frontal cortex, which acts as a "gate to consciousness." This system rechannels blocked Pain, diffusing its energy and routing it to a variety of other cortical pathways. This rerouting is what accounts for a false consciousness. The person may become a mathematician absorbed by his symbolic world as a means of retreating from reality. Or, given enough Pain, the person may become delusional and lost in his symbols. Though still "aware" of his surroundings he is unconscious (and crazy because of it). He sees a reality—a man on a street corner, but misinterprets it as "He's laughing at me" because of the intrusion of unconscious stored feelings upon his perceptions. The limbic system is the central storehouse and processing agency for feelings.

F. *The Reticular Activating System*

The limbic system funnels its output into a structure down in the brainstem called the reticular activating system. This system then produces generalized activation of the entire forebrain. It galvanizes the entire cortex in a diffuse, non-specific manner. It has many fibers leading to the thalamus (a relay station) and from there directly to the neocortex. Stored Pain, then, activates this system which then mobilizes the cortex into action.

The limbic system also receives impulses from the reticular system and can send back messages modifying activation. It is the limbic system which integrates inputs from both the reticular system and the frontal cortex. Though the reticular system can "control" the amount of activity of the cortex, there are only certain areas of the cortex which can exert any control over the activity of the reticular system. One of these is the frontal cortex. Because the frontal cortex (discussed in full in a moment) is heavily connected to the limbic system, a good fronto-limbic connection can stop the reticular activation. That is, when a below-conscious feeling keeps us stirred up, the only way to stop that activation permanently is to make a proper connection to the subconscious feeling.

It may be that the frontal cortex affects the *chronic* activation passing through the limbic system, while other cortical fields affect the momentary arousal of the reticular system. In other words, some cortical areas can affect only current situations (inhibiting or stimulating arousal as the moment calls for it), while stored childhood Pain residing in the limbic system can be defused only by a frontal connection. This means that rearranging a symbolic (non-frontal) consciousness in therapy has no real effect on chronic subconscious activation by Primal Pain. Thus, while a male homosexual can be taught to stop acting out and to "tell himself" that he really does not need men, the need for a father (a need stored as Pain due to deprivation-overload and repression) would still produce constant subconscious activation. The person would then smoke or eat twice as much, and he would be just as sick. An addict could be forced away from drugs, but activation by the reticular system would still keep him tense and in need of some tranquilizer to reduce reticular action. It is the activating system which provides the "energy" of feeling, and when disconnected from higher centers this energy is experienced as amorphous tension. It is the nature of the reticular system to diffuse its output.

The assumption that the frontal cortex alone affects long-term chronic activation has implications for impulse control, whether it be of drinking, raping, exhibiting oneself, or whatever. The impulse-ridden person may be acting out a multitude of Pains from his early childhood. Those Pains keep his behavior out of control—control by the frontal cortex. No matter what *thoughts* the person has about the consequences of his acts, such as, "I will die of cirrhosis," "I will go to jail," etc., they will have only momentary *suppressive* effects on the impulsive conduct.

Without frontal connection to the Pain *impulses* which coalesce to make an impulse-ridden person, there can be no downward thrust of control. Control over feelings unfolds and evolves from the "bottom up," as it were, and not from the "top down." It is only when feelings rise to be made frontally conscious that we can say that there is true control.

What is happening on a subcortical level is that the reticular system is continuously galvanized to fight off the threats of shattering Pain from the limbic system. It activates the neocortex so that it may aid in its own defense. Strange ideas and philosophies, then, would be part of the overall defense system recruited by the reticular system for use in the battle to keep Pain locked away. It is only when the Pain can be accepted and felt that there is no need for symbolic channels, and then direct frontal connections can be made.

It is not just the brain that is being activated by the reticular system. It has connections to structures such as the hypothalamus which affect the functioning of the body. Thus, stored Pain leads to reticular arousal which then stimulates or inhibits hypothalamic output, changing hormone balance and our physical systems in a profound way. For example, blocked thyroid output can lead to a general depletion of energy and a change in consciousness such that the person feels overwhelmed by the slightest stressful situation and rationalizes to himself, "I'm just not a fighter." People take advantage of him, and he produces thoughts to make such events palatable.

The fact that limbic Pain keeps the reticular system activated means that the heart is under constant stress, and without correct connections to high centers there is nothing that will stop the activation. No intellectual insight will change it a scintilla. It will only make the feeling and the connection more inaccessible. We have seen this activation in experiments (discussed in full later) with Primal patients in which the beginning liberation of Pain may send the pulse to as high as 240 beats per minute. Once the Primal is finished there can be a drop of 160 beats per minute from the pre-Primal peak. Our research indicates a permanent drop in pulse rate in our patients.

G. *The Frontal Cortex*

Though feelings begin their life in the diencephalon, it is the frontal cortex (more precisely, the fronto-limbic cortex) which represents those feelings in symbolic form—*correct* symbolic representations if the person is mentally healthy. Without the participation of the frontal cortex there is no human feeling, from the Primal point of view. Just as the limbic system alone cannot be considered the "seat of feeling," the frontal cortex cannot be considered the "seat of consciousness." There is no "seat" as such, since it takes fluid interconnections among the various levels of the brain to make a full consciousness—reticular, limbic, *and frontal*. But, nevertheless, the frontal cortex is a key structure in bringing unconscious material into full consciousness.

The frontal area integrates the responses to the major sensory modalities (such as smell, touch, and sight) with input from our internal world. It receives information from outside and from the limbic system and coordinates this information, translating Pain memories stimulated by external events into consciously connected responses.

It is Pain which raises the threshold of the frontal cortex to sensory input, thus keeping us unaware of reality—this is the real meaning of "insensitivity." A heightened threshold wards off reality, both external and internal. It blocks out anything from the outside which could trigger shattering Pain inside. Thus, the neurotic must misperceive in certain areas of his life to keep Pain at bay. Or, he must rationalize in such a

way as to soften any hurt. For example, on television tonight was an interview with a woman whose husband was the last man killed in Vietnam before the cease-fire. She told the reporter that her husband was "selected"
for death in order that the "message" get across to the people. She found a
way not to feel the horror of it all.

Repression of feeling means repression of both what is inside and
what is coming from outside. There must be misperception when something is repressed, for it is our unconscious storehouse which shapes what
we see and hear. The brain "selects its input," as shown in a number
of experiments, including those by Pribram and Spinelli.*

Because repression takes in both the inner and outer milieus we may
find someone who has denied a need to be cared for by his mother later
developing a philosophy about the need to stand on one's own feet. His
perceptions of welfare recipients will be shaped by his early Pains. He will
be unconscious of others' needs because he is unconscious of his own.

For a child to perceive that his parents do not want him around is
overwhelming, so he misperceives in order not to be overwhelmed by
inner Pain. As one patient put it, "I had to pretend that my mother
wanted me so that I could cling to her. How could I cling to someone
I knew hated me?"

What is important to understand about the limbic system is that it is
much older than all the neocortex piled on top of it, and in that sense
we could say that feelings precede intellect. But once intellect became a
property of *human* life, it had to be considered as part of the feeling chain
—as a function evolving from feeling; that is how we must see consciousness, true consciousness—as something which evolves from our
feelings. You do not just "lose your head" in order to feel. You "find
your head" in the sense of finding the right connections. Consciousness,
then, is determined by horizontal access and by the fluidity of connections between the limbic system and the frontal cortex. The smaller the
amount of Pain the lower the threshold against input and the higher
the state of consciousness. There is no higher state of consciousness than
that—no supra-consciousness, achieved by means such as meditation,
which somehow rides above neural interconnections.

The importance of the frontal cortex to feelings is underscored when
someone has undergone a frontal lobotomy, in which connections between the orbito-frontal cortex and lower centers have been severed.

---

*As reported by R. E. Ornstein, *The Psychology of Consciousness* (W. H. Free-
man Co., San Francisco, 1972), page 35.

Though he can still think, the person seems to have lost his "soul." He has lost his human consciousness.

So while the frontal area mediates responses to form the junction point of major sensory modalities and is crucial to the highest levels of consciousness in man, to his ability to abstract and conceptualize, it has no real significance unless we see it in its relationship to other brain structures. Indeed, there are neurophysiologists who believe that the frontal area is part of the limbic system—an end point where Primal memories make their hook-up to their conscious counterparts. When the frontal cortex is engaged in the suppression of those ascending impulses instead of their connection, the result is some degree of unconsciousness. The person is not just "unaware." Structural changes have occurred which make conscious efforts to become aware impossible—such as trying to retrieve memories of events that happened at age two.

The frontal cortex acts very much like a switchboard which inhibits feelings and rechannels disconnected Pains to other association areas of the cortex, producing a symbolic consciousness. Lesions in this area make people more responsive to their feelings and less responsive to learned prohibitions. Conventional insight therapy generally is involved in rearranging the symbolic consciousness; it is my position that without frontal connection there is no basic change. The frontal area alone has major pathways directly to the hypothalamus (and limbic system), so that when there is fluid access there will be control over the hypothalamic hormone secretions of the body. Rearranging symbolic consciousness produces no control because the disconnected segment of Primal feelings remains to alter hypothalamic output. There must be a *reconnection* via the frontal cortex to lower centers. Once that proper frontal connection is made, neurotic symbolic consciousness is dispelled. That means that when a person has a feeling such as "I am all alone and abandoned," he will feel it in certain life situations where he has been left alone, rather than, for example, running to the refrigerator to eat his feelings away. So long as those feelings remain disconnected, he will think about food instead of thinking what he is feeling.

Let us take an example of symbolic consciousness: instead of feeling that "Mother was never there for me," the thought is, "Women are useless and to be ignored." How bizarre the symbolism will be depends on the charge value of the Pain which is trying to gain access to the frontal cortex. With more underlying Pain (and need) there is a greater electrical "pressure," as it were, producing a heavier overload which drives the impulse that much further away from its proper coupling point. Thus, instead of feeling again, "Mother was never there for me," given enough deprivation the person may come to hate women and be hostile to and suspicious of them in general. He has lost a specific consciousness and generalized to a class of beings. Women, then, in his awareness are symbols upon which is projected a past, lost consciousness.

Penfield's work indicates a possibility that the extent of the symbolism may be literally a case of the amount of distance in the brain from the "feeling site" (see *The Anatomy of Mental Illness* for more on this). Penfield cites a case of brain surgery in which he placed an electrode on one point in the temporal cortex and got "I feel like robbers are after me." When he placed it directly on the feeling site it elicited the memory "I remember when my brother held a gun on me." It seems to me that psychotics get stuck one step removed from actual feeling sites and create derivative symbolic images thereafter.

There are some aspects of Penfield's work relevant to our considerations. His surgery was on diseased brains, largely ones with temporal lobe abnormalities. What he found was that stimulation of this area produces an *experiential* response, but the patient (awake, since the operation is done with local anesthesia of the scalp) recognizes that the memory being run off is something from his past. That is, he has at one moment a dual consciousness—reliving a past event and being aware that he is on an operating table reliving that event. After electrode stimulation the patient "could discuss his double awareness and express his astonishment, for it seemed to him that he was with his cousins at their home . . . sight, sound, and personal interpretation—all were recreated for him by the electrode."*

Penfield points out that his surgical patients never look upon the experiential response as "remembering." Instead, it is "living-through moments of past time."** Penfield stresses that a flashback into a stored history is made conscious by (electrode) stimulation. This is the point of Primal Therapy—to render defenses ineffective and stimulate locked-up history through various means. It is no accident that Penfield reports that fear is the commonest emotion evoked by electrode stimulation. For epileptics this was translated as a pre-fit aura; that is, stimulated Pain became transmuted into a signal for a seizure.

Penfield states, "[The patient] has a double consciousness. He enters

---

*W. Penfield and L. Roberts: *Speech and Brain Mechanisms,* Princeton (N.J.) U. Press, 1959, pp. 50-51.
**Op. cit., p. 52.

the stream of the past, and it is the same as it was in the past, but when he looks at the banks of the stream he is aware of the present as well."*

Here are Penfield's conclusions: "Every individual forms a neuronal record of his own stream of consciousness. Since artificial reactivation of the record, later in life, seems to recreate all those things formerly included within the focus of his attention, one must assume that the reactivated recording and the original neuronal activity are identical. Thus, the recorded pattern of neuronal activity may be considered much more than a record, for it was once *used as the final stage of integration to make consciousness what it was.*"** (emphasis mine)

My point is that neurosis is embedded in those stored memories and drives present behavior. Unless unresolved painful memory circuits (and past feelings *are* memories) are integrated, neurosis will not be cured.

Let us take another example of false consciousness—the sighting of the lights of an Unidentified Flying Object. I had a patient who believed he saw those lights, and this notion persisted in his mind for many months—until he had a birth Primal of coming out of the womb into the blinding fluorescent lights of the delivery room. This trauma remained unconscious but later was given life via an hallucination about UFO lights. After the Primal he no longer believed in those lights. That is, after the Pain was properly connected to consciousness there was no longer a need for symbolic derivatives. He could not make that early trauma conscious until a number of other traumata had been connected. As the unconscious Pain overload was reduced it became possible to make a direct conscious connection to that birth experience.

H. *Two-way Split Consciousness*

Thus far I have tried to show how consciousness is split both vertically and horizontally. Since there are structures *below* the corpus callosum involved in feeling, we may have to assume that the vertical split has precedence. That is to say, there are "gates" from the lowest levels of the brain which permit or prohibit access to higher levels at each step of the way to consciousness. It may be possible to determine the level of consciousness of a person by finding out how far down in the brain gat-

*Op. cit., p. 45.
**Op. cit., p. 54.

ing or blocking exists. Thus, a person operating on a "cerebellar level" (a structure far down in the brain) may be a rigid catatonic psychotic, in which case the level of his consciousness is at a minimum.

It is possible in the deepest states of hypnosis, for example, to produce total bodily rigidity in subjects, so much so that the person can be stretched between two chairs with someone standing on his chest without affecting the rigid state. Someone who is a "vegetable," who operates on only the barest vegetative levels and performs only automatic functions, can be said to be deeply unconscious.

Because there may be many gates in the brain regulating feelings on their way to the frontal cortex, possibly we may determine in the future how mentally ill someone is by discovering how far down in the brain ascending feeling impulses are blocked. The assumption is that the greater the Pain, the greater the disconnection.

It is possible that information coming into the brain is stored holographically, so that each scene and its feeling is represented and rerepresented in different areas all at the same time. Each area, however, would process that representation differently: the limbic would add emotional quality, the frontal cortex the ideation, and the reticular system the amount of energy. It would take the entire brain with all its representations to make a complete picture—consciousness. When we consider that the great areas of the neocortex are evolutionary developments from the older lower centers (limbic and frontal cortex), we can see how events can be represented on many different levels of the same chain. As a disconnected neurotic it is possible to know about one's deprivations and feel nothing, or to be tense and anxious from those deprivations and not know why.

It may be that the right-left split constitutes a backup system for a vertical overload. Thus, when vertical gating no longer can suffice, there is horizontal gating along the corpus callosum. This again is speculation. But in any case, the horizontal split seems to be a later developmental one in the organization of feeling. The cerebellum, for example, looks like the cerebrum except that it has no laterality.

There is some evidence that the limbic system is split along right-left lines. M. S. Gazzaniga has been working with split-brain monkeys, and his initial work seems to indicate that the limbic system may be divided. In tests of smell (processed limbically) with human subjects, it was found that rotten-egg odor fed to the right-brain could not be distinguished by the other side. It is much too soon to tell about this kind of split, but it does offer interesting possibilities. For example, certain early memories may be stored on one side (right) and fed to the same side cortex. These stored memories may have different access to lower structures such as the hypothalamus. Thus, Pain would have more facile access to body channels uncontrolled by left-brain activity. There would be uncontrolled bodily stimulation because of the functional split.

Once we understand the split we can comprehend the origin of any number of neurotic symptoms. For example, let us assume that the fear of a tyrannical mother is stored on the right-lower side. The person might grow up with *macho* ideology (left-brain) in which he tries to make it with women but is impotent. No matter how much sex education he has, his impotency would not be affected. The unconscious fear would intrude into each sexual relationship. The man's body would be responding to real, unconscious fears, no matter what his left-brain was saying. The hidden truth would be prepotent over anything the man tried to do sexually, and his body would respond not to what was going on outside but to what was buried inside. Until there was a proper connection, there would be a fear of women (a generalized response which occurs because specific connections have not been made) and impotency.

Or, let us suppose that a man has stored a need for a father on the right-lower side. He would try to make it with women (left-brain ideation) but would fail. His need-Pain would intrude unconsciously. That is, he would have latent homosexual tendencies which would prevent proper heterosexual relationships. Latent homosexual tendencies mean only that he has a general need for male love which takes precedence.

He may have to fantasize very strong masculine women or actually fantasize men while engaging in heterosexual acts. Thus, the stored need-Pain would dominate the images in his mind (fantasies) no matter what he did. He would have *general* needs for men because they were symbolic of a specific need for a father—too painful to accept and feel consciously. His fantasies would be an example of a false symbolic consciousness generated by a real but hidden need—the need for a father. Often the person acts out a left-right compromise; he becomes involved with masculine women.

The blocked need, existing in the form of diffuse activation with access to lower centers regulating sex, would result in an erection and so-called sex drive rather than the experience of Pain. With frontal-right-left connections there would be a Primal Pain experience and the sex drive would diminish radically. The unconscious would become conscious, rerouted activation would cease, and the person would have a truly expanded consciousness.

Until there is a connection to unconscious Pain, a neurotic would need his fantasies in order to have some kind of access, however tenuous, to his feelings. It is these fantasies which would arouse him because they trigger the real arousal—need for father—but unfortunately the aroused Pain is automatically and unconsciously rechanneled into sex. Fantasy is a symbol created out of memory and is as impelling and automatic as a recurring dream.

We can see that if there is an unconscious (right-stored) fear of mother, impotence would result with heterosex. We can understand frigidity if left-brain ideation dominates the feeling side. While the "aware head" tries to make it with men, the body responds to a stored ideology about sex being bad. The body responds to its unconscious input and is an excellent index of what is unconscious.

There may be tendency to think that it is the right-brain which is the unconscious and the left-brain the conscious. However, it should be obvious that real consciousness means an integrated right-left brain. For when feelings are buried, the ideas about those feelings will also be buried (and probably on the left side). A right-brain dominated person is not feelingful; he is impulsive. He cannot *properly* analyze events and cannot evaluate the consequences of his acts. He is left-brain deficient. It takes two to tango.

I. *Hypnosis and Symbolic Consciousness*

Hypnosis is a good example of how to produce a disconnected consciousness. Studying hypnosis is a short-cut way of learning about neurosis. It shows us, for example, how someone can be directed by his unconscious and why neurotics do not learn from their experience. Hypnosis shows us how our bodily processes are controlled unconsciously, and how unconscious impulses can generate certain modes of thought.

It is possible to make a person unconscious in hypnosis so that he is unaware of the experiences of his body—being pricked by a pin, for example. The "real person" is obviously not there. Rather, consciousness has been narrowed by the intervention of another person solely by psychologic means so that the subject is literally rendered unconscious, in my sense of the term. He is predominantly unconscious because a major part of his awareness is constricted and focused on the hypnotist. The person may not later remember what is transpiring while in this state; he is having experiences of which he is unaware, experiences which may later direct behavior—viz, the post-hypnotic suggestions given to him while he was "unconscious."

The hypnotic subject can be made into Sinatra; he will act and sing like him. If you asked him his name, he might say it was Frank Sinatra. His real consciousness has been temporarily replaced by a false one. In neurosis this replacement is not so temporary, but I think that the dynamics of both hypnosis and neurosis are similar. In childhood our parents subtly take away our perceptive, alert, feeling consciousness ("My teacher is bad and I hate her") and substitute homilies and platitudes ("I must not think evil thoughts"). Neurotic parents change our consciousness so delicately that we often do not know what is happening. We grow up believing that the consciousness we carry around, including our ideas and perceptions, is real.

Let us pursue the point about the similarity between hypnosis and neurosis. It is more difficult to see how parents infuse an unreal consciousness into their children not only because it is done subtly but also because it is done over many years. Hypnosis offers us a quick look-in at this process. The hypnotist has substituted his cortex for the subject's. That is, the subject's lower brain centers respond to the consciousness of the hypnotist instead of his own. So when there is an input, a suggestion, the patient reacts as if his own brain has perceived something. If the hypnotist suggests a lower blood pressure and/or suggests indirectly relaxing situations that might in real life lower blood pressure, then the blood pressure will drop in the hypnotic subject. Contrarily, if the hypnotist suggests that the subject has repressed fury, the pressure may well rise. It is possible to decrease body temperature by hypnotic suggestion, but only temporarily of course.

The neurotic has been programmed in more subtle fashion but in the same manner as the hypnotic. He has been told to "Shut up! Don't sass!" Although he has been frustrated, his parents may caution him not even to think anger. Slowly as the child "buys" the program so as to feel loved, his consciousness really becomes that of his parents. The child's body responds to "their" ideas now in the head of the child, in the same way that a hypnotic subject responds to the hypnotist's notions. So the neurotic child has an elevated blood pressure because these ideas now internalized do not allow for proper release of feelings. It is their ideas (parent-hypnotist's) which dictate how the subject's body will react.

This duality of consciousness is a peculiarly human trait which allows man to symbolize his experiences and finally to become enmeshed in symbolism so that he is abstracted from real life. This is what has happened to the hypnotic subject. His consciousness has been largely eradicated and replaced with selective awareness. His unconscious projections become reality. He really "sees" bugs crawling on his arm and is terrified, if that has been suggested by the hypnotist. If he is given the notion of bugs crawling on him as a post-hypnotic suggestion, then later when the hypnotist brings him into awake awareness and produces a proper cue such as waving a handkerchief, the subject will again "see" bugs. He will perceive out of his unconscious.

The experience of suggestion during hypnosis becomes embedded in the unconscious and later impels behavior just as early childhood traumata do. For example, an overeater is told under hypnosis that she hates sweets and will not eat them again. She wakes up and for a few days avoids sweets. But if this is not reinforced by more hypnotic suggestion it will wear off and she will eat sweets again because the valence of the unconscious experience (of the suggestion) is weak in comparison to an unconscious early childhood filled with deprivations of love. Pain will ultimately win.

In our current research on hypnosis with Drs. Jacques Vidal and Marshall Buck of the Computer Science Department of UCLA, an obese subject was hypnotized and age-regressed. We took her back to the age of five where she is eating and playing with her doll. When asked why she is eating she says she is not sure. And then she adds, almost incidentally, that her daddy is gone and is not coming back, and that her mommy said it is her fault. She is sad with this memory. Then I instruct the hypnotist to ask, "Do you miss your daddy?" The patient begins crying deeply, says yes, and begins talking and crying about how she never had him; all she had was grandpa and he was too old to play with her. It would have been possible at that point to make her awake, tell her that she would remember what she just said, and lead her into a Primal by making her call for daddy. But when awake with defenses reinstated she might not have been able to do so, or if she had tried she might have been overloaded (not yet ready for such trauma) and have automatically shut off. If a Primal patient had gone through this and was ready he would go directly from the memory into a Primal when awake.

What happened instead with this hypnotic subject was that she was brought out of it and told she would forget it all upon awakening. She did. She woke up smiling and oblivious to what had just happened to her. That is because she had had an unconscious experience. She had had the beginnings of the feeling—the affect, as it were, without the connection which would have turned it into wracking Pain . . . and true consciousness. Suggesting in hypnosis to this woman twice a week that she did not want to eat still left those buried needs upon which her symptom rested, intact.

The hypnotist, by lulling critical and evaluative consciousness, has direct access to the unconscious. He can, through suggestion (and his authority) remove acquired mores and inhibitions so that a person can sing and dance more freely and get into repressed scenes almost instantaneously. *But no suggestion can remove unconscious memories.* It is similar to what alcohol does by inactivating frontal lobe (and maybe major hemisphere) restraints on responses. In hypnosis the hypnotist can temporarily produce a false consciousness—"I hate sweets and don't like to eat." Real consciousness comes from feeling the Pain of "I have no daddy and I like to eat to soothe my hurt." There is quite a difference.

While sitting with a post-hypnotic subject there is no way to tell that he is still in a partial hypnotic-unconscious state until someone produces the right cue (waving a handkerchief) and then we see irrational behavior. Otherwise, the person seems totally conscious, discussing politics, economics, or what have you.

In neurosis the cues are more subtle and the valence of the unconscious memory stronger. A man failing to help his wife with her chair may set off her wrath, possibly because her parents never cared about her or her comfort. Her reactions are unconscious even though properly rationalized by, "A gentleman always helps a lady." To see her neurosis we need the proper cues. Once they are there the unconscious force becomes inexorable. It always will be until the right connection to her past is made: "Daddy, why don't you care about me?" Connection means proper symbolic representation of feeling. To project her wrath at her husband is incorrect symbolization. The connection must be made from "inside-out"; when it is offered by a brilliant and insightful therapist it is incorporated only into the *disconnected* awareness of the patient.

Hypnosis quickly shows us how crucial it is to make an unconscious experience conscious if we wish to resolve it. Will power is defenseless against the unconscious onslaught. We must take care to rigorously define "to make conscious." For surely, one might argue, the analysts make certain things conscious for their patients. But I would call that being made "aware." Consciousness to me is something organic, evolving out of the unconscious. It is that consciousness which finally permits the hook-up of past scenes with current miseries and compulsions. In Primal

Therapy we do not ruminate about the past and "select" past scenes that might affect our current state. We experience that past and consciousness evolves from it. Here is an example: a patient has a Primal about a certain scene in which his father has left and a new boyfriend for his mother has moved in. This boyfriend dislikes the young boy and makes his life miserable. In his Primal he relives the time when his father returns to visit him and he suddenly senses his father's weakness and inability to protect him from the boyfriend. The Primal feeling is, "Be strong for me, Daddy!" He comes out of the Primal with the insight that he has had a constant fear of men since the time when his father left him unprotected. His consciousness spreads as he sees how this fear has dictated his life and made him non-functional around men: why he could not concentrate with male teachers, why he was so anxious at parties when his girlfriend talked to other young men, and so on. These insights went on for almost an hour as his consciousness was liberated. It was blocked feeling that held down that consciousness and unblocked feeling which freed it. For most of his life he had acted *unconsciously* around men and these unconscious acts had constituted much of his social behavior.

Regression in hypnosis is instructive, for by bringing a subject back to long-forgotten scenes in his childhood we demonstrate that it is still all there lying in the unconscious. No act of conscious will could make a person remember what he remembers while he is hypnotically unconscious. A lifetime accumulation of defense mechanisms prevents that. Primal Therapy dismantles the defense structure so that the past surges upward to consciousness for connection. It does this in an ordered, measured way —the patient by feeling increasingly intense past Pains finally can allow deep buried hurts to arise. The reason for the defense structure in the first place is to repress Pain. Once the Pain is felt the defense structure dissolves. Thus, Primal Therapy can be thought of as an increasing spread of consciousness which continues until the day the patient is entirely conscious in the full sense of that term.

It is consciousness which finally conceptualizes and interprets those deep Pains and makes sense of them. It is the *conscious* connection which makes the hurt so excruciating that it results in waves of screams and groans.

The minor side of the brain does not initiate ideas; it can only mimic them. I suggest that on one level hypnosis produces a dysfunction in the major side of the brain allowing only imitative behavior which responds only to outside cues. It is as though the hypnotist's brain blocks frontal evaluative functions and becomes the major side for the subject, supplying all the ideas. It is then the hypnotist who "conceptualizes" feelings for the subject because it is the major side which conceptualizes feelings. The hypnotist simply misconceptualizes them. He offers the rationales for whatever feelings the subject is having. If he suggests a sad scene, the subject may cry just as he might cry over a scene in a movie, when not hypnotized. The tears would be unreal in that they do not correspond precisely to the past scenes which produced them. Both the suggested scene and the movie scene are symbolic rationales for real feelings. These rationales occur because real consciousness has been diverted away from what is real inside. The person really believes that he is crying over what happens in those scenes. In hypnosis, the hypnotist "paints" the scene for the subject, while in the movie the scene is flashed on a screen. The scenes are symbolically derivative; what is real are the feelings they evoke. What is unreal is the rationale for the feelings, a rationale which permits the subject to remain unconscious of the underlying realities. So long as the cues come from outside, rather than inside, the conceptualizations will be wrong and consciousness will be false.

You can brainwash people into believing falsehoods only when awareness has been divorced from the unconscious. Then that consciousness, grounded in externals rather than in the feelings of the person, capable only of mimicry rather than creativity, can be twisted and turned at will, and the person will believe almost any nonsense. We are heading into an era of Babbitry and robotry because of the neurotic split. It is the Babbit who is a danger because he only parrots ideas taught to him: "There must be no peace without honor," when he has no idea what that really means. The danger is of a mass unconsciousness like that in Hitler's Germany where the people in that unfeeling society were literally mesmerized by Hitler, believing the "Big Lie" which had not an iota of reality to it. They became the apocalyptic figures of Alphaville, thinking and doing only what they were told because they could not feel. They were unconscious because they could not feel. In this state of unconsciousness people respond to words (left-brain) rather than to other more real perceptions. They do not see the insincerity on someone's face or sense the falseness in the tone of the voice. They become symbol-dominated.

What I am suggesting is that hypnosis, like neurosis, severs consciousness along both vertical and horizontal planes. The processing of Pain requires that all neural interconnections are fluid and working smoothly. In frontal lobotomy, where the *connections* of higher and lower centers are severed, there is still the processing of painful feelings subcortically but the frontal cortex no longer "reads" it. It is indifferent to the unconscious. Too many neurotics are functionally lobotomized, indifferent to their Pain, claiming it does not exist. Hypnosis demonstrates that by psychologic means radical alterations can be brought about in brain functioning, and by indirection this indicates that the early psychological environment surrounding a fragile human organism can certainly do the same.

On a horizontal level hypnosis produces a functional disconnection between hemispheres so that they each operate independently. With the frontal cortex and corpus callosum relatively inoperative one loses critical, reflective consciousness. What is missing is the ability to introspect—to feel oneself and to see oneself in action. If I were a Freudian I would say that the superego has been knocked out so that it no longer judges and blocks feelings.

In hypnosis as in mental illness the person is "in" his dream without a separate consciousness of that state. When awareness exists, he either wakes up out of the dream or comes out of his hypnotic state.

In one experiment a heater was put next to the right arm of a hypnotic subject. The suggestion by the hypnotist was that it was a cold-air fan. The subject responded as if he were cold on that arm. As he was put into a deeper trance (under the same conditions) in which actual sleep was induced, he later reported a dream of being against a cold wall. What is clear many times over is that you can fill a person's head with ideas that run counter to his experience, and he will continuously respond to those ideas instead of to his real experience. In this sense, reality becomes meaningless in terms of its effect on the person.

The symbolization that goes on between stimulus and response under hypnosis is determined unconsciously. In sleep there can be a noise of garbage cans outside producing a dream of clattering hooves, not of garbage cans. The experience was unconsciously rewoven in terms of the unconscious of the person. This is what I am suggesting is the mechanism of neurosis. There is a stimulus—someone says something, and then, instead of a real and direct response, there is a symbolic interweaving by the neurotic and an unreal response: the person decides that the speaker really meant to say something against him. That response is unconsciously determined. How bizarre the symbolism is will depend on the level and amount of Pain in the unconscious. What makes some people so unpredictable is the Primal eruption between stimulus and response. A person can say, "Is my car ready?" calling for a simple direct reply, and the neurotic may answer, "Stop rushing me!" He is responding, perhaps,

to being rushed and demanded of as a child. Because of the Primal eruption, the neurotic is not aware of the reality.

Hypnosis and sleep are two different orders of phenomena and are
not parts of the same continuum. During induction of hypnosis the EEG
(electroencephalographic) tracings are far different from what one sees
in deep sleep. Indeed, there is an *increase* in mental activity as indicated
by more alpha and beta wave tracings. This same augmentation of the
alpha wave is also seen in yoga and Zen meditation, indicating to me
that all three processes involve repression and disconnection. The person may feel relaxed due to the efficacy of said repression, but his
mind has become busier.* So we have a situation in hypnosis in which
the person is quite unconscious yet has an active "awake" brain, again
reiterating the difference between unconsciousness and awareness. In
hypnosis the person may seem aware but is largely unconsciously directed.

In sleep a person can be conscious in my sense of the term (having
easy intercerebral access), but this is not the case in hypnosis where,
by definition, access is inhibited. A fully conscious person has few unfathomable dreams because his symbols are a direct outgrowth of his feelings. The same can be said about physical symptoms. He suffers no inexplicable psychosomatic afflictions because there is no redirected energy
affecting organ systems. When the body and mind are one, events of
the body are directly reflected mentally.

An example from my own life to clarify this point: I recently had a
dream that I was an underwater aquanaut testing out the atmosphere in
a new machine. It was a large washing machine and I was wrapped around
the middle core, sliding through the liquid when something went wrong
with my waterproof helmet and I woke up gasping for air, my heart
pounding. I woke up with the exact sensations of an experience occurring
more than forty years before—a birth trauma. I became awake and
aware before I could become conscious. Had I remained unconscious
(and had the amount of Pain permitted) I might have become conscious.
If I had felt all of it I would have been conscious; as it was I had to settle
for awareness, so that I could remain unconscious and defended.

We can see by this discussion that a conscious person is a feeling one,
and vice versa. "Feeling" *means* to be consciously connected. Feeling
post-Primal patients seem to become "smart" and perceptive as they

*Research in hypnosis carried out by G. A. Ulett, S. Akpinar, and M. Turan,
"Quantitative EEG Analysis During Hypnosis," *Electroencephalography and
Clinical Neurophysiology 33*, 1972, pp. 361-368.

never were before, having learned not from books but from their bodies and their previously unconscious past experiences.

It is crucial that we do not confuse awareness with consciousness. Surely the President sees children and youths burned by the bombs he has ordered to be dropped and is aware of what he has done, but he is not conscious of his acts, for if he were he would be driven mad by the *ineffable* horror of it all. He must remain split and therefore unconscious of what he is doing, and his unconsciousness allows him to go on doing it. He rationalizes his behavior in much the same way that a post-hypnotic subject will rationalize when you ask why he has suddenly done something which was suggested to him while he was under hypnosis. They both make their acts "plausible" so that they can seem rational. But he feels no more than the hypnotic subject who has been told "You will feel nothing," and then indifferently watches someone hold a lighted match to his hand. If he cannot experience his own Pain he certainly is not going to be empathic about anyone else's.

Since a feeling person is conscious, it follows from my hypothesis that a non-feeling person is to some extent unconscious. So it is not that a hypnotist can render anyone unconscious; he can only work with those who are already unconscious, already split and disconnected from their true selves. It is because of this already vast unconsciousness that a total stranger such as a hypnotist can come up to him, say a few words, and render him more completely unconscious. Hypnosis is a transient, encapsulated neurosis, and neurosis is a semi-permanent hypnosis. That is why a patient after Primal Therapy can look back and say, "Where was I during my youth? I must have been unconscious. I did so many things that I never understood." Or, "I can't believe that I never saw the suffering of my children. How could I have been so unconscious?" Those individuals neither saw nor heard in very much the same way a hypnotic subject neither sees nor hears except what he has been programmed to perceive.

We see this in our patients who were so-called sexual perverts, who exhibited themselves in public and felt during those events that they were largely unconscious—running off some ritual, the causes of which were never understood. Lance Rentzel, the football player, writes about his exhibitionism: "I drove past a park, and there I saw two young girls . . . What had I done? I knew and I didn't know . . . I had a strange sensation of detachment. I had no idea where I was going or why."* Mr.

---

*Rentzel, Lance, *When All the Laughter Died in Sorrow* (Saturday Review Press, 1972, N.Y.), pp. 116-117.

Rentzel was in a coma—unconscious, programmed by his past and triggered by specific cues (say, losing a football game or dropping a pass), so that he did things of which he was unaware. Those "cues" put him into a hypnotic state just as waving a handkerchief at a post-hypnotic subject can do.

Both Mr. Rentzel and the hypnotic subject were unconscious but not asleep. They were both tied to consciousness with a slim thread, but that thread separates the sleeping from the unconscious. Unconsciousness is a necessary condition for sleep, but sleep is not a necessary condition for unconsciousness. Primal patients may be almost as conscious while asleep as a severely neurotic person is while awake. The severely neurotic and psychotic do not see reality because they are lost in their unconsciousness and what they see are symbols of that state. We have all had the experience of driving a car while daydreaming so that we wonder how on earth we made it across town. We were effectively unconscious while driving a ton-and-a-half of machinery for miles. We had but a slim tie to consciousness, and instead of consciousness being in the forefront paying attention to what was on the street, it was peripheral and in the background.

We effectively hypnotize ourselves by our daydreams; that is, an unconscious Primal force intrudes itself through symbolism and suffuses awareness so that it takes a strong cue (such as a loud horn) to bring us out of it. There is not much difference between hypnosis and living in the fantasy and temporary unconsciousness of daydreaming. The unconscious Pain of neurosis blankets awareness. Indeed, once certain deprivations take place in our childhood we are impelled to act out dreams based on those deprivations—for fame, power, or whatever, depending on the nature of the deprivation. We act out those dreams with our children, making them achieve for us, and we are unconscious of what we do precisely because we act out the dreams instead of feeling what impels them.

A person can be totally rational in many areas of his life, yet be irrational when it comes to a choice of a spouse, for example. Unconscious need determines the choice and that buried need blocks an accurate perception of what kind of a person the spouse is. So, for example, a woman who grew up with a fear of her tyrannical father may later have to select weak men to marry because any strong man might trigger off the terror again. Therefore she maneuvers her life so as not to reawaken her fears and constantly selects passive men. She is unhappy because she also wants a strong man who can take care of her, but it does not happen.

Her unconscious need is like an automatic landing beam for aircraft; it guides her irrespective of her general brilliance and perceptivity.

J. *The Effects of Psychotherapy on Consciousness*

It is possible in some forms of psychotherapy to change personality and attitudes by altering the pseudo-consciousness of the neurotic and rerouting it into other channels. So perhaps a person has been encouraged by his therapist no longer to think of himself as a "shit." Or he decides to change his outlook and see the bright side of things. If we understand that we are only rearranging the false consciousness of the person, then we can see how this change is specious. For if we have not connected him to his underlying Pain, we have not made him conscious —and without this consciousness there *is* no profound and lasting change.

The patient, however, may sincerely believe that he has been changed and helped by anything from meditation to psychoanalysis because he has been able to use some new ideology or mantra as a tranquilizer, diffusing and suppressing the Pain. So long as he is not feeling his Pain, he is bound to believe in what makes him feel more at ease, even when that state of ease is a spurious one as indicated by stress measures of the body such as pulse rate and blood pressure. What about the ideology of Primal Therapy? Isn't that tranquilizing as well? There is no ideology to be learned in Primal Therapy, no jargon containing notions like "castration anxiety," "id," or "superego." In Primal Therapy we put patients *into* intense Pain; we do not take them out of it. If feeling that Pain were not making profound changes, I doubt that any patient would last more than a few days.

In other forms of psychotherapy such as Conditioning or Behavioral Therapy one rearranges the symbolism so that the homosexual patient no longer thinks "cock" and goes on homosexual quests; he now thinks "women." Or the person no longer thinks "food" but instead thinks "cigarette." We have not changed his consciousness; we have modified his symbolic ideation. According to the Behaviorist, a neurotic is simply responding *inappropriately,* becoming fearful and tense when the situation does not call for it. He is trained to relax instead of becoming fearful, for example, in such a situation by presenting the situation (a dog) or a picture of the stimulus (a nude woman to homosexual males) paired with relaxing instructions. He is being deconditioned. What is overlooked, in my opinion, is that neurotic fears *are often appropriate in the context of the past.* My fears of the dark never went away until I had a birth Primal of coming into the light after an inordinately long and hard labor. In childhood I had to have the light on as a *symbol* of safety. There was terror in that canal for me at birth although I never knew it. Later, the dark was frightening because it was symbolic of (and appropriate to) that early trauma. The light was also symbolic of the end of the terror. To have conditioned away my fears of the dark would have been meaningless without that Primal experience which made me truly conscious.

What is being conditioned is the symbolic behavior, not the reality. The Behaviorist is dealing with those fears that the patient is *aware* (rather than conscious) of. Because he is dealing with derivative consciousness, bypassing frontal connections, no profound change can occur. The stored fear will simply find another symbolic outlet once the presenting fear has been conditioned away (which often means being only "beaten down" by mild shocks paired with the stimulus—e.g. pictures of naked men presented to male homosexuals).

In biofeedback techniques that same symbolic fear would be "brought under control" by learning to produce those brain waves which aid in repression. There is no need to labor the point; stored Pain innervates the brain and body, overactivating them until such time as there is a true Primal connection. The key condition for profound change is Primal consciousness.

Let us see what Freud said about all of this back in 1915.* "What is repressed exercises a continuous straining in the direction of consciousness, so that the balance has to be kept by means of a steady counterpressure. . . . The mobility of the repression, incidentally, finds expression also in the mental characteristics of the condition of sleep which alone renders the dream-formation possible. With a return to waking life, the repressive cathexes which have been called in are once more put forth." (p. 90)

Symbolic dreams are the hallucinations of sleep. Most of us while awake can repress feelings enough to squelch their symbolic derivatives. The psychotic is too overloaded for that. The hallucination is just as unconscious as a dream and both are identical processes, the difference being that one takes place in sleep. The psychotic acts out his dream while walking down the street, shouting what the dream characters would

---

*Freud, Sigmund, *Collected Papers, Volume 4* (Basic Books, N.Y., 1959), pp. 86-125.

shout, engaging in bizarre inner conversations, etc. He is unconscious of the world in which he moves, and most of his actions are as automatic as breathing. He is subcortically dominated and whatever cortex he is using is engaged in psychotic symbolization rather than reality. Freud uses the term "primal repression," I have recently discovered (*op. cit.,* p. 86), to denote the processes by which "instincts" are denied entry into consciousness. Primal repression is accompanied by a "fixation" of ideation which "persists unaltered from then onwards." (*op. cit.,* p. 86)

It would not take much recasting to put Freud's work into the Primal matrix, or vice versa. There are some fundamental and profound differences in the views about consciousness and I shall deal with them in a moment, but let us listen to what he said almost sixty years ago: "It is not correct to suppose that repression withholds from consciousness all the derivatives of what was primally repressed. If these derivatives are sufficiently far removed from the repressed instinct-presentation, . . . they have free access to consciousness." (*op. cit.,* p. 88) In short, what is allowed into consciousness is that which is not an immediate reminder of the instinct; in Primal terms, of course, we do not focus on instincts but rather on repressed feelings and memories. But the basic Freudian notion still holds. Freud believed, "The resistance of consciousness against them [instincts] was in inverse proportion to their remoteness from what was originally repressed." He believed that the way to open up the unconscious was to analyze the resistance. I think that such an analysis becomes one more defense but one step removed. Analyzing the resistance *is* resistance. It mobilizes more cortex in the service of repression. I believe that it is Pain which seals events into the unconscious and that feeling Pain in titrated doses opens up the unconscious.

But if the Freudians had read Freud correctly they would have seen that there was more to it than analysis of the resistance. "If we communicate to a patient some idea which he has at one time repressed but which we have discovered in him, our telling makes at first no change in his mental condition . . . There is no lifting the repression until the conscious idea, after overcoming the resistances, has united with the unconscious memory-trace." (*op. cit.,* p. 108) A pure Primal statement with the exception of the idea about overcoming resistance.

Freud stressed that only by bringing the memory trace into consciousness was the possibility of change achieved. This fact seemed to be lost on his later adherents who preferred analysis over the recouping of losses of memory. Freud states, "It is the essence of a feeling that we should feel it, i.e. that it should enter consciousness." (*op. cit.,* p. 110) He knew very well that ideas were ultimately "cathexes of memory traces," (*op. cit.,* p. 111), and that it was no good enmeshing the analyses in those ideas. The *affect memory* was crucial. What he also knew was that the derivative symbolic idea itself became a method of repression. It was used as a defense against proper ideation which would lead to the unconscious material. In this way even the brightest of people could use their rationalizations and pseudo-philosophies to protect themselves against reality. Freud said, "The substitutive idea now plays the part of an anti-cathexis for the *system conscious* by securing that system against an emergence into consciousness of the repressed idea." Though he spoke about feelings, it was usually an *idea* that was repressed for Freud. Later he began speculating about the various systems which were involved in repression, including the preconscious. He would give a "will" to repressive acts and would say that consciousness withdraws its cathexis from this or that and replaces it elsewhere. He did so, I believe, only because the state of neurology at that time would not permit him to do otherwise.

What Freud calls the transfer of cathexes I call rechanneled neural impulses. He understood that the pressure created by repression could discharge its energy in the body, producing what he called conversion symptoms. He falsely believed that if that pressure were brought to the surface via free association of ideas, it would be possible to "overcome the objections of censorship . . . and abrogate repression." (*op. cit.,* p. 125)

Freud knew that "becoming conscious is no mere act of perception, but is probably also a hypercathexis." And by that I believe he meant that consciousness means a proper connection between structures involved with unconscious memory traces and those responsible for their hook-up to higher brain centers.

Freud would certainly eschew the modern-day Behaviorists, for nowhere in their theoretical schemata does consciousness play a significant part. Indeed, some of them seem to think that change can take place unconsciously, as it were, by associating one stimulus (the feared one) with another (a pleasant one), without the annoying interruption of the patient's consciousness. I submit that you cannot leave out the whole interactive nature of the brain and produce change. This is my criticism of the body therapies of the Reichians. Reich had a superb theory, despite its shortcomings and later mysticism. All that was lacking in his schema was the brain.

But even those therapies which deal with consciousness, or at least awareness, such as Reality Therapy, cannot produce profound change, in my opinion, so long as they neglect unconscious motivating forces. Reality Therapists believe that producing a new idea, "I don't need the world's love," will eradicate neurotic ideas and make a person well. It probably does eradicate (or submerge) old ideas, but disconnected new ideas will hardly make anyone well; they only help rationalize the sickness better. Reality Therapists fail to understand the profound subcortical processes which give birth to those neurotic ideas in the first place. You can go on trimming off the top, but the Primal roots will continue to sprout neurotic weeds of one kind or another.

The symbolic level of functioning becomes emphasized when a patient goes to therapies such as the Jungian, where the therapeutic focus is often on dreams and their symbols. This focus solidifies the symbolic consciousness, reinforces intellectual defenses, and makes feelings *more* inaccessible, and without those feelings there never will be true consciousness. In these therapies the cortex is used as a defense rather than an integrator of feelings. The ideation involved does not evolve from feeling; rather it springs from the cortex of someone else's head—the therapist's. In any case, *analyzing* feelings is not the same as feeling them. If we were to analyze the behavior of an animal we certainly would not equate it with therapy. Why do we do so with humans?

What might be happening in therapies such as the Jungian and Freudian, at least on one level, is a "cure" of one side of the brain—the intellectual-repressive segment. While the person is becoming more insightful and aware he is falling deeper into unconsciousness. It would seem that while the insight therapy deals with the left-brain, hypnotherapy deals with the right-brain. The problem, of course, is that the therapies do not facilitate the getting together of the two sides of the brain.

What I am indicating is that all other forms of psychotherapy neglect the split or deal with aspects of it. Connection is the key to unlocking the secrets of neurosis, and any method which neglects the split cannot succeed, in my opinion, just as any psychological theory which neglects need and Pain as its cornerstone is *automatically* led to a reactionary method. If we overlook what it is that makes us human, how can we possibly find ways back to that humanity?

Discussion: Implications of Primal Therapy for Mankind

Freud's great discovery was of the unconscious. If there were a single most significant discovery in Primal Theory it would be of the conscious; that is, that there is no unconscious—immutable, timeless, genetic and universal. There is only blocked consciousness, and it is theoretically possible for a person to have *no unconscious* in the sense discussed herein. It is likely that in the future a real culture will be a conscious one, and there will be no need for an unconscious. I see this in advanced Primal patients now. Some can have a dream, slip down into the feelings of the dream while asleep, make the connections, and remain asleep. Notice! They are making conscious connections while unconscious, because conscious and unconscious has merged. As one patient put it, "I go to sleep to rest my body, not to keep myself unconscious."

What is significant about this is that for the first time people can control their unconscious instead of being controlled by it. So, for example, such things as exhibitionism in conscious people would be unthinkable. Conscious individuals simply would not be driven to do irrational things and would instead produce and maintain a sane, conscious culture.

Primal patients have a different sleep pattern and one patient likened it to that of a dog: very alert with a thin separation between conscious and unconscious, so that with even a slight stimulus during sleep there is immediate consciousness. The sleep is restful yet alert. These patients' dreams are no longer in the past. That is because *their feelings* are no longer in the past. Here is a good example of symbols matching the Pain. Past Pain—past symbol, so that the person dreams of his early schools, homes, etc. He is a child in his dreams because that is where he is in his feelings. We see here how feelings determine our consciousness.

Primal patients become more right-brain determined; the result is less ambition. That is, they are not time-bound, planning and setting long range goals. There is very little they want to work toward. Living in the present is sufficient. But time-bound neurotic man may see this as sickness, since the lack of goals is out of the cultural mode. The very fact that in Primal Therapy there is no clock to work by militates toward the experience of feeling; conversely, those therapies that are time-bound militate against it.

One has to ask about the meaning of the shift to the right-brain in Primal patients. When such a finding is taken alone, all we have is another correlate of the observed change we see in them. But when this is coupled with a consistent drop in blood pressure, pulse, and body temperature, we can make different statements. For now we see that becoming more feeling as a person *means* to be less tense, in terms of the measures of tension we now have. In short, we can make a more definitive argument for the relationship of tension to feeling—namely, that tension is blocked feeling, and as that feeling becomes unblocked there is a drop in tension. Here, too, we can see the relationship of Pain to tension. For as patients feel Pain in Primal Therapy they become more feeling and less tense as indicated by our measures. So, again we see that tension is *unfelt* Pain—an unfeeling state.

In terms of the shift to the feeling side of the brain in Primal patients, it is highly significant that the research team studying the children born in completely non-traumatic ways with the methods of Frederick Leboyer of France found that one hundred percent of these children were ambidextrous! (See *Birth Without Violence* by F. Leboyer, Alfred Knopf, 1975. N.Y.)

What this means to me is that without catastrophic Pain around birth the hemispheres tend to be equalized and working in harmony. That being dominant in one hand or the other is not a natural state but a neurotic one. Further, this lack of dominance not only makes a statement about handedness; it indicates the possibility and probability of a more total emotional integration—and this is what the research team has found with these children, some of whom are now nine years old. Indeed, these children are described just as one might describe Primal Man. So when Primal Therapy produces a shift toward greater equalization of brain hemispheres it adds corroboration to our observations that advanced Primal patients are more integrated emotionally. The Leboyer findings provide dramatic evidence that trauma at birth literally produces a split in the system.

Primal man has a consciousness that resembles non-analytic, relational cultures such as that of the Tobriand Islanders. Primal man lets others be. He no longer evaluates his children's drawings and asks, "What is it?" He just enjoys the experience of viewing them. He is not analyzing himself and dissecting his feelings; he is feeling them. His consciousness is global.

We can see how a comprehension of the nature of consciousness affects philosophical questions regarding the nature of "free will" and "will power." These concepts have been subjects for philosophical polemic for centuries. However, in a unified, conscious person free will and will power are extraneous concerns. For the conscious person there can be no dualism, no split, no involvement with an aspect of consciousness that operates separately from the totality of the organism. There can be no one agency that acts freely, unfettered by past experiences. The notion of a free will is applicable only to normals, who are conscious and have access to themselves in a total way, but they are the ones who are not concerned with such a notion. Neurotics usually think about free will in terms of "acting" in free ways, which usually means "neurotic acting-out."

We are total organisms and every bit of us is affected by our past. Each decision we make is determined by it; there can be no mystical élan which can conquer it, just as no single "aspect" of ourself is free from its influence.

One has to ask, "Where is the free will of the hypnotic subject who under post-hypnotic suggestion behaves in certain ways on cue no matter what he 'wills' about it?" Here it is clear that there is a lack of free will due to disconnection. What will free the hypnotized person is connection. He cannot transcend himself and have free will; rather, he must descend into himself. Again, where is the free will of the person under brain surgery who finds himself reliving the past when an electrode is placed in certain areas of his brain no matter what he "wills" about it? He is a prisoner of those memory circuits just as any neurotic is.

When we think about free will, we usually mean "will power," the ability to control ourselves despite our circumstances. It is the normal, alone, who can control himself because being totally himself, he *is* that control. Normal babies, for example, automatically select a properly balanced diet which best serves their needs. They do not exert "will power." They are in touch with themselves and their needs.

My hypothesis is that there is no power, "will" or otherwise, which rises above our physiology; no special forces which transcend our brains and their stored history. When the body is no longer a mystery to our minds, then we *are* conscious, and truly free: free to fulfill that body properly, which is the only meaningful way to think about free will. "Free will" is just another way of *thinking about* consciousness.

K. *Projected Research*

We have a number of research projects concerned with consciousness underway. We are investigating hypnosis to see what structures are active as the person becomes unconscious. We want to know which side of the brain is lulled first. Later we will investigate which side of the brain goes to sleep first and which side wakes up first.

We have been measuring the frequency and amplitude of the brain waves for several years. Our evidence points to a less active brain after Primal Therapy. Thus, Primal (connected) consciousness means the elimination of a great deal of subcortical activation. Amplitude and frequency of the waves seem to diminish as therapy proceeds; our research here continues.

We are investigating shifts in laterality, and our preliminary evidence is that Primal Therapy produces a shift to the "feeling side" of the brain. Primal Therapy may reduce dominance. In this sense making a connection in Primal Therapy may be an event which literally produces more balanced interconnected hemispheres. Perhaps it is not that we reduce dominance in Primal Therapy so much as equalize the two sides through the liberation of blockages. In any case, our evidence is beginning to indicate that a "Primal connection" is no mere intellectual insight, but a profound, far-reaching cerebral phenomenon. We are finding new relationships between the frontal and occipital parts of the brain which indicate that not only is there a right-left and top-bottom split, but also a front-back one as well.

My colleagues and I hope to develop a matrix of observable neurophysiological parameters which will delineate degrees of repression (and therefore of unconsciousness). Tension, then, will show itself to us in terms of certain EEG parameters. We shall correlate these with certain well-validated psychological tests (such as the Kahn Test of Symbol Arrangement) and attempt to develop a general profile of repression and unconsciousness. We expect the level of unconsciousness to be commensurate with the degree of symbolic abstraction, both from the world and the self.

When there is fluid access among brain structures we expect this to be reflected in both the psychologic and physiologic dimensions, so that, for example, we would find decreases in the amplitude of alpha waves and a corresponding correctness of symbolization on the Kahn test. We hope to develop a number-index of degrees of unconsciousness and therefore of the relative severity of the mental pathology.

We will discover if other therapies produce the kinds of consciousness of which I speak. We will find out if insight given by a therapist can ever make a real change in a patient. We hope to produce scientific standards by which the efficacy of any psychotherapy can be measured. It will no longer be a matter of guesswork or personal preference as to which therapy makes real change.

We expect to see significant changes in our highly intellectual patients whose level of abstraction seems to have frozen out their feelings. We have already begun to note shifts of power to the minor hemisphere. Some of our intellectuals, brilliant scientists aware of our stars and galaxies, were truly unconscious; the level of their symbolic involvement may have risen with the amount of repression going on.

We expect that our research will provide observable data for the kinds of inner changes our patients report. We will learn about the concomitants of change. We know many times over that we produce feeling people; we now want to be more precise about what that means in terms of their internal functioning.

We will want to measure the effects of certain drugs on laterality: to discover the differential effects of various tranquilizers and also to investigate laterality changes with the use of hallucinogens, morphine, and heroin. There is already evidence (in the work of E. A. Serafetinides at UCLA) that the tranquilizer chlorpromazine changes the voltage amplitude on the left side of the brain in schizophrenics. That is, there is a left-side gain in voltage in these patients.

We have found that Primal patients are self-regulating in terms of the use of drugs and tranquilizers. As their tension decreases they find it less possible to use drugs of any kind, and in the advanced stages of the therapy their bodies reject the use of drugs completely. The use of marihuana, for example, is no longer fun; if there is Pain that is what rises immediately. A patient can feel "wired" on one or two cups of coffee. There are no longer inner defenses to block or modify the action of drugs on the system. There may be a way to predict all this by continuous measures of tension. That is, we may know the reaction to drugs based on the amount of residual tension in the patient as shown by our tension index.

We plan to study the various anesthetics in terms of their sites of action. We hope to discover if our tension index can predict how much anesthetic a surgical patient will require. That is, for a more activated brain we would expect the dose required to be higher. We may find that the best way to determine anesthetic dosage is by brain-wave tests before surgery.

There are so many avenues for research. For example, one of our nurses believes that cerebral strokes are predominantly left hemisphere; we wonder if this is true and if it might be due to the increased pressure (activity) on that side to repress Pain. Or, better put, we may hypothesize that strokes result from the strain on the whole brain system occasioned by the antagonism between the hemispheres and between higher and lower centers.

We will want to know if eye tics are more of the left eye rather than the right. We have observed that there are often marked differences in breast size between left and right in women. Is there one particular side that is universally underdeveloped? Is that side more apt to develop cancer? The point is that a split in consciousness is not solely a phenomenon of the brain; it is reflected throughout the body. Our patients have noticed that their left eyelid is more apt to droop. And in the observation of all of our photographs we have noticed a marked difference in the sides of the face—one side may be more aggressive-defensive, while the other side is sensitive and hurting (and it is usually the left side that is the sensitive one). It has occurred to me that inner integration shows itself in the harmony of the face, and that is one reason why post-Primal people look so much better.

Another avenue of investigation will be with the chemical serotonin, a natural tranquilizer produced by the body and found heavily concentrated in the limbic system, where repression takes place. What is significant about this kind of study is that serotonin plays a role in both deep sleep and neurotic repression; indicating, perhaps, that the nature of physical and psychological unconsciousness is very much the same—mediated by the same structures and chemical processes. There is evidence of the hypnotic effects of L-tryptophane, a serotonin precursor.* "Hypnotic" is a key word because we see the similarity of neurosis (and neurotic repression) and hypnosis, at least on a chemical basis. That is, the neurotic is hypnotized and suffers the same kind of unconsciousness as the hypnotic. We are already studying serotonin changes in Primal patients.

We will want to test creativity to see if somehow less-lateralized brains are more creative. Is there an inverse correlation between creativity and brain-wave amplitude and frequency? How does the laterality and other measures of creativity of artists differ from engineers and accountants, for example? What is the disease rate for those with lesser scores on the tension index? We expect it to be significantly lower. Is there a correlation between the depth of repression and the severity of physical illness? So, for example, is the cancer patient more repressed than the colitis patient? And is the person with neurodermatitis less repressed than the other two? Is there a direct correlation between how deep the symptoms are in the body and the depth of repression?

Are amplitude and frequency of brain waves reciprocals? My assumption is that they are, so that in neurotics when the frequency is artificially slowed there should be an increase in amplitude.

*Hartmann, E., Chung, R., Chien, C., "L-Tryptophane and Sleep," *Psychopharmacologia 19*, pp. 114-127, 1971.

The importance of our tension index for psychosomatic disease should not be underestimated, for we may find that when lowered body temperature and blood pressure are accompanied by high amplitude waves, it is a sign not of relaxation, but of inner pressure (one index of which is hypothyroidism). When temperature and blood pressure are low and brain wave amplitude is low, these facts connote relaxation.

What about validity studies into Primal Therapy? We know by observation and by experience that the therapy is valid. We need to account for the resulting changes in patients in terms of brain functioning. What we find will be the correlates of change; as whole man changes, we will discover what mechanisms are associated with the process. We will not say that change was "produced by," for example, decreases in brain-wave amplitude or decreases in blood plasma cortisol. Rather, changes in consciousness are accompanied by multifaceted alterations in physical functioning because body and mind are a unity.

What is implied for brain physiology is that neurotics are people in Pain who act as though they were not. We need some precision about how to account for this. Because neurosis has its beginnings so very early in life, we are going to have to investigate more primitive mechanisms in the brain and search out their involvement. Because the neocortex does not reach its full development until later on in childhood, we assume that the shut-off mechanisms involved in neurosis are significantly subcortical, and this alone indicates that early trauma is organized subconsciously before the infant knows what is happening to him. He later acts out this stored trauma without any awareness that it took place.

What our evidence points to now is that it is the *normal mechanisms* of the brain which provide for neurosis; it is not necessary to assume structural defects, etc., to account for mental illness. Becoming mentally ill is a natural result of Pain and the action of gating mechanisms in the brain.

Because of what has been discussed thus far, it seems clear to me that the validation of Primal Therapy will have to take a different route than the usual procedures for evaluating other therapeutic methods. We produce a different kind of human being, out of the cultural mode, so that culture-bound tests are not valid. Its central validity is in the experience, which is the ultimate validity. No one could ever tell me that birth Primals were possible, no matter how many I had seen, until I had one. Observing such a bizarre event did no good for someone who was not in a psychological position to accept it.

The final validity in the theory is whether it can predictably help people. We sometimes lose sight of the fact that all the research done on the brain, all of the facts uncovered are for the purpose of making a better life for each other. If facts remain *in vitro,* never tied to a viable therapeutic system which can utilize them, then they are ultimately worthless. Our contribution is not facts, but a theory which can make use of them for the benefit of mankind.

L. *Summary and Conclusions*

We have seen consciousness redefined and differentiated from awareness. Such a differentiation is crucial to an understanding of how to make basic change in mental illness, for without a fundamental alteration in the structure of consciousness there can be no cure for mental illness. I have indicated that many therapies heretofore have concentrated on changing awareness but leaving neurotic consciousness intact. Primal Therapy produces a new consciousness—Primal consciousness, which results in the alteration of the relationships between cerebral hemispheres and between higher and lower brain centers. A feeling person is a conscious one with fluid access among the structures of the brain as they mediate processes of the body.

What all this means is that the state of consciousness shapes the flow and pattern of brain functioning—and brain functioning shapes the state of consciousness. It is a true dialectic—an interpenetration of opposites. "Mind" does not produce "brain," and "brain" does not produce "mind." They are one. The form of brain interaction shapes the content, and the content circumscribes the form. The psychological field of forces is ultimately physical, and the physical state of the brain yields psychological events. We will never discover the secrets of the brain-mind by microscopic analysis of nerve cells, for they are but elements of a gestalt. We are never going to localize consciousness because it is a product of our *total* beings. Though it is possible to select and localize certain kinds of awareness with the electronic probing of brain cells, no individual neuron can tell us about human feelings. Feelings, however, may help us understand the action of neurons. To reiterate: the reason we cannot localize consciousness is that it is not a "thing," but both a cause and result of the *organization* of living systems. One does not alter consciousness without an alteration in that organization. Each part of our system belongs to that organization and must be studied in reference to it.

It is the state of consciousness which shapes perceptions and restricts entry into consciousness of those perceptions in the interest of survival. Though the perception of danger is itself a survival function, there are times in our childhood when those perceptions endanger psychological integration and threaten survival. It is my view, following Darwin, that the mere fact of survival of humans over the centuries has produced those mental mechanisms which favor survival, and that our perceptual abilities, upon which we depend for life, warp and bend and distort what we perceive when necessary for continued integration.

The separation of mind and body has flawed our study of man. We have been able to investigate man's brain waves in minute detail without reference to their relationship to such parameters as blood pressure, pulse, and body temperature. We have neglected the whole interactive nature of body and brain.

The mind-body problem which has plagued philosophers and psychologists for centuries is a spurious one—the product of a split, neurotic mind. It has occurred because people were divided into body and mind, and specialists were created to treat each separate from the other. An integrated, whole person never would pose questions about the relationship of mind and body because to him they are one.

BIBLIOGRAPHY

BOOKS

Langworthy, Orthello R., M.D., *The Sensory Control of Posture and Movement*. Baltimore, Williams & Wilkins Company, 1970.

JOURNALS

Aggernaes, A., "The Experienced Reality of Hallucinations and Other Psychological Phenomena." *Acta Psychiatrica Scandinavica*, Vol. 48, No. 3 (1972), pp. 221-38.

Assael, Marcel I., "Petit Mal Status Without Impairment of Consciousness." *Diseases of the Nervous System*, Vol. 33, No. 8 (1972), pp. 526-28.

Bindra, Dalbir, "The Problem of Subjective Experience: Puzzlement on Reading R. W. Sperry's 'A Modified Concept of Consciousness'." *Psychological Review*, Vol. 77, No. 6 (1970), pp. 581-84.

Gelhorn, Ernst, M.D., Ph.D., and Kiely, William F., M.D., "Mystical States of Consciousness: Neurophysiological and Clinical Aspects." *Journal of Nervous and Mental Disease*, Vol. 154, No. 6 (1972), pp. 399-405.

Gulbrandsen, Grete Bryhn; Kristiansen, Kristian; and Ursin, Holger, "Response Habituation in Unconscious Patients." *Neuropsychologia*, Vol. 10, No. 3 (1972), pp. 313-319.

Heath, Robert G., M.D., D.M.Sci., "Pleasure and Brain Activity in Man." *Journal of Nervous and Mental Disease*, Vol. 154, No. 1 (1972), pp. 3-18.

Johnson, Laverne C., "A Psychophysiology for All States." *Psychophysiology,* Vol. 6, No. 5 (1970), pp. 501-16.

Mark, Vernon H.; Barry, Herbert, M.D.; McLardy, Turner, M.D.; and Ervin, Frank R., M.D., "The Destruction of Both Anterior Thalamic Nuclei in a Patient with Intractable Agitated Depression." *Journal of Nervous and Mental Disease,* Vol. 150, No. 4 (1970), pp. 266-72.

Marshall, John R., "The Expression of Feelings." *Archives of General Psychiatry,* Vol. 27 (1972), pp. 786-90.

Okuyama, Yasuo, "Sensory Deprivation and EEG in Normal Subjects and in Depressive and Schizophrenic Patients with Special Reference to the Level of Consciousness." *Tohoku Journal of Experimental Medicine,* Vol. 102, No. 3 (1970), pp. 209-23.

Shallice, Tim, "Dual Functions of Consciousness." *Psychological Review,* Vol. 79, No. 5 (1972), pp. 383-93.

Sperry, R. W., "A Modified Concept of Consciousness." *Psychological Review,* Vol. 76, No. 6 (1969), pp. 532-36.

Sperry, R. W., "An Objective Approach to Subjective Experience: Further Explanation of a Hypothesis." *Psychological Review,* Vol. 77, No. 6 (1970), pp. 585-90.

Weingarten, Seth M., M.D., "Dissociation of Limbic and Neocortical EEG Patterns in Cats Under Ketamine Anesthesia." *Journal of Neurosurgery,* Vol. 37, No. 4 (1972), pp. 429-33.

CHAPTER TWO

The Development of the Brain and Consciousness: The Tripartite Brain
E. Michael Holden

"And if our insight were not clouded by mischievous metaphysical traditions we should find that the problems concerning the relation of mind and body offer no difficulties which are fundamentally different from those regarding the relation of any organ and its function, of any object and its properties. The body-mind problem, then, resolves itself into an inquiry into the peculiarities of this relationship, its mechanism and modus operandi." [1]

C. J. Herrick

Traditionally, consciousness has been considered as consisting of degrees of awakeness along a spectrum from fully alert to deeply comatose. This schema has practical application in clinical neurology, and distinctions between "lethargy," "delirium," "stupor," "semi-coma," and "coma" are important to recognize in reaching an accurate diagnosis of a patient's condition. Even within the category "awake" there are qualitative differences in vigilance, awareness, and attentiveness which may provide important information about an individual's cerebral function. Thus, for instance, in dementing illness ("senility") one may recognize individuals who are vigilant, alert, and attentive, but who act "inappropriately," as if awakeness had become dissociated from full consciousness.

In dementia the separation is literal, based on cortical neuronal loss or impaired function, whereas in emotional illness a similar separation may occur in individuals without structural changes in the brain.

Psychology and psychiatry have directed attention to qualitative divisions of consciousness, noting the partial consciousness associated with dreaming, hypnosis, and activities of the "subconscious." Overlap occurs in levels of consciousness in sleepwalking, intoxication states, and the "dreamy states" seen in temporal lobe epilepsy, postencephalitic parkinsonism, and other disorders altering "consciousness."

The studies of Wilder Penfield and others make it clear that memories may exist beyond willful recall, and suggest that although our recall is limited, large portions if not all of our life experiences are encoded in our brains. Certain forms of focal epilepsy produce episodes which are preceded by the sudden appearance of a very early memory as an "aura." The limiting or selective aspect of memory has practical utility for us. If we were obligated to recall simultaneously all of our life experiences our cerebral activity would be chaotic. (Just driving in heavy traffic, what a burden it would be to have obligatory recall of all the license plates, car colors, street signs, etc., that one has seen.) Thus, normal adult cerebration utilizes memory with selective recall.

For the purposes of this chapter, "levels of consciousness" refers to different degrees of selective awareness in relation to the three fundamental "zones" of our bodies: the viscera within the body wall, the body wall itself, and the space beyond the body. "Consciousness" changes almost day by day in infancy and childhood, often observably. Levels of consciousness are difficult to observe definitively in adults but are clearly numerous and variable. Certain neurological disorders make such observations easier but only a small number of "levels" are distinctive enough to name or describe.

Relationships Between Neurobiology and the Primal Formulation

The intent of this chapter is to present evidence in support of the hypothesis that the Primal formulation is remarkably congruent with a biological approach to mental illness in humans. From the viewpoint of a clinical neurologist who is interested in human behavior, the conventional psychotherapies bear little meaningful relationship to the scientific findings which are pertinent to the embryology, the structure, or the function of the human brain. The Primal formulation is based on observations and a careful description of these without a theoretic "leap" to a dimly related hypothesis.

The deficit in other approaches to mental illness is that the hypotheses go far beyond the observations made, often to the point of producing hypotheses which by their construction are only partially or negligibly testable. Additionally, hypotheses have characteristically been advanced consonant with the premise that psyche and brain function represent different orders of phenomena, only partially interrelated; a premise which appeals to a form of mysticism, untenable to a serious biologist. The "bridge" between neurobiology and the Primal formulation is the neurology of pain and its processing, about which, even just in neurology per se, a great deal is known.

It is Dr. Janov's contention that neurosis and psychosis in humans (in the absence of known organic structural cerebral disorders) bear a necessary, obligatory relationship to previously experienced psychic pain.[2,3] His hypothesis receives strong support from the phenomena reported to occur during and after Primal Therapy. The term "psychic pain" is subjectively known to all, within the framework of daily human life in society. Psychic pain is a phenomenon in human, subjective, mental life and is no less real an entity if it is acknowledged that a precise, physicochemical basis for it has not yet been described.

Psychic vs. Physical Pain

Psychic pain and physical pain share the common denominator of being subjectively experienced as adverse or unpleasant. If pain stimuli are adequate to elicit any response at all, the nature of the response bears a significant, probably obligatory relationship to the intensity (and frequency) of the stimulus. These relationships for physical pain stimuli are well known and a matter of everyday observation. The lure of teleology should be approached with caution, if at all, but in passing it should be noted that *response* amplitude and quality bear an obligatory relationship to *stimulus* amplitude and quality as a manifestation of evolutionary process. Failure to maintain such a relationship as a living action system in an unpredictable natural world would soon lead to extinction of individuals; later, if continued, to extinction of species. Stimuli capable of destroying life forms, partially or totally, must be avoided if such forms are to persist, evolve, and endure as individuals and species. (A converse dialectic applies to the graded, appropriate responses causing an organism to *approach* stimuli which support life and lead to perpetuation of individuals and species.)

These relationships of physical pain to behavior are less likely to be disputed than the (analogous) relationships between psychic pain and behavior. The thresholds of psychic pain vary in humans in relation to age and to the context of such stimuli; they probably reflect individual variation as well. Psychic pain per se is not easy to measure or quantitate, and the ability to measure it at all is only possible if parameters of endocrine, visceral, or behavioral (muscular) change accurately reflect an outward expression of feelings. If one chose to measure only those manifestations of psychic pain which were actually expressed by a particular individual or group of individuals, one would not be much closer to an actual definition of psychic pain. A general definition would be too general, and a specific definition would at present be inaccurate. What can be noted is that psychic pain is a component of human subjective mental life in relation to the adequate stimuli which elicit it. As such it is similar in kind to other components of subjective human mental life.

There is no need to leave a biological frame of reference in considering the properties of psychic pain. Like symbolic mentation itself, psychic pain is a manifestation of human brain function. There are quite probably receptive fields for its appreciation, but (as with the phenomenon of psychic pain itself) these are only partially defined. To elicit psychic pain (by a patient's report) in the process of a deep cerebral electrode study provides important additional information but does not define psychic pain. If indeed psychic pain in human mental life is a symbolic version of physical pain, and considering that it is outwardly manifest in words, postures, facial expressions, tones of voice, and visceral and endocrine changes, then it may fairly be said that psychic pain is an experience of the entire organism, reflected outwardly by characteristic responses and mediated by the entire brain.

The response to pain involves all portions of the brain and the zones of the body functionally integrated by the brain. It is probable that a painful experience is similarly processed whether of psychic or physical origin. The similarities between psychic pain and other components of human subjective mental life become apparent in relation to C. J. Herrick's presentation, which analyzes the nature of nervous system function, especially *cortical* brain function.[1] A theme repeatedly emphasized is that cortical brain function is different *in kind* from subcortical brain function in relation to qualitative differences in morphological organization, and that human cortical function is different in kind from that in apes and infrahuman mammals.

"Reflex responses usually follow immediately upon presentation of their adequate stimuli, and their central adjusting mechanisms are elaborated within the relatively direct lines of conduction employed (medulla oblongata, midbrain, thalamus, corpus striatum, etc.). But cortical functions are in larger measure delayed reactions and individually acquired controls redirecting and recombining the innate reflex and instinctive patterns. The introduction of large masses of higher correlation tissue concerned with delayed reactions within the innate reflex apparatus would tend to distort the reflex patterns and interfere with their prompt and efficient independent action when this is desirable. The addition of associational tissue outside of these deeper centers leaves their local activities unimpaired no matter how extensively the overlying cortical fields are developed. . . ."[1]

Separation of cortical activities in space from the neuraxis below the thalamus, developing along with an increasing option to delay responses to stimuli, are two fundamentally important elements of mammalian, and particularly human, brain function. That is to say, the option to delay responses reflects an inhibitory process by which several immediate possible responses are not made. This gives one more time to consider the nature of a stimulus. After the pause a selected response will be made, appropriate to the stimulus situation in the context of previous similar responses. The option to pause is prerequisite for learning from experience. Brain lesions interfering with the option to delay responses almost always interfere with recent memory functions (subfrontal, temporal, anterior limbic, or hippocampal lesions). This is relevant to the Primal formulation. An option to pause, to consider the nature of the stimulus, is a sufficient condition for a behavioral response which is selected. Such a selection, if adequate stimuli for psychic pain exist, could lead to a response involving *symbolic* withdrawal from the stimulus, *with or without* physical withdrawal from it.

In Dr. Janov's terminology, if responses are made without regard to internal state in response to painful external stimuli, then the sufficient condition exists for the development of a "dual consciousness": the development of an "unreal self." [2,3] The organization of the human cortex does not present a necessary organization for a dual consciousness, only a sufficient one. Simply stated, the human cortex allows a very young child to make responses to environmental stimuli with a lower threshold (more readily) than the "natural" responses, which normally would be in relation to visceral stimuli. Thus, human cortical function is sufficient to mediate responses with relative disregard of visceral imperatives. This occurs with the obligation to process painful external stimuli. Without such (disproportionately) noxious stimuli in the environment there would be no sufficient cause to disregard one's visceral imperative, and responses would be made accordingly, with no cause for or development of a dual consciousness. Young children have the sufficient neurological capacity to eat when they are not hungry, to "potty" when there's no need, to use a spoon at mealtimes when fingers are preferred, to "shush" when they would otherwise cry or scream, to sit still when they would otherwise be exuberantly running, to be polite when dislike exists, and so forth, ad infinitum.

If external stimuli are sufficiently intense, then disregard of the visceral imperative may occur to very extreme degrees. Extreme anorexia, extreme obesity, excessive cigarette smoking, alcoholism, drug abuse, and numerous other examples of human personal "self abuse" are seen in the clinical practice of medicine with a dismaying regularity. The human cortical ability to symbolize in relation to external stimuli may, and by observation often does, mediate responses with limited or negligible personal, visceral relevance.

Dr. Janov has called attention to the operational, qualitative similarities between hypnosis and neurosis in his discussion of dual consciousness. Herrick also recognized the similarities, and has written:

"It is a familiar fact that in dream and reverie there is in perfectly normal people more or less of isolation or dissociation of certain chains of experience from the remainder of the conscious life, a process which may be carried so far in pathological or hypnotic conditions as to result in complete dissociation of certain components or complexes of experience which among themselves form perfectly coherent units that remain quite outside the knowledge of the normal personal consciousness. When this is carried to the extreme, we have the remarkable cases of dual personalities or co-consciousness which have been described by Morton Prince (1914) and many others."[1]

An adversive environment surrounding an infant creates the obligation to respond to the pain experienced. The more adversive the surroundings, the greater the obligation. Dealing with pain and its poignancy becomes one of the high priorities of the brain, and in the struggle the visceral self is partially neglected. The subcortical-visceral insult resulting is registered in the brain and body, and later the registration may be excluded from consciousness as a by-product of dealing with early pain.

Brain Maturation, Visceral Motility, and Psychosomatic Illness

A component of the Primal formulation which seems incongruent with everyday experience is the observation that memories in humans apparently start much earlier in life than is commonly believed. The apparent incongruence is rooted in the dogma that memories can only have a language or verbal representation. Thus it is argued that considering the time course of language development, memories before the age of three are impossible. The concept of "body memories" will be explored in the following section, with comment on their probable relationship to psychosomatic illnesses. There is an orderly development of the human brain such that its phylogenetically older portions are fully functional, and fully adequate, first. It is this observation, and the histological correlates of this information, which make it quite certain that "body memories" are real phenomena. A prenatal or newborn child is adequate in the central portion of his body and the central portion of his brain, and the two, not surprisingly, are corresponding portions.

One can simplify this by referring to the brain as organized in three concentric spheres: an inner sphere, a middle sphere, and an outer sphere,[4,5] and these spheres of nerve cells and their fibers were called by C. J. Herrick the "neuropils," [6] the different "zones" of the brain, organized quite concentrically in the human brain. Not surprisingly, the inner portion of the human brain mediates responses which are in the anatomic midline, the responses which are necessary for the maintenance of the life process itself. Thus the heart, the respiratory muscles, the bladder, the movement of the bowel, the contraction of the stomach, the gastric secretion of hydrochloric acid, hormonal regulation, and the blood forming organs are already adequate at the time a child is born, and probably even before a child is born.

There is limited information about prenatal adequacy except from indirect observations, like the fact that a seven-month-old child *in utero* can hiccup: a documentation of the fact that the medulla is functional and performing adequately, at least in its simple functions. It makes common sense and follows directly from neuroembryological observations that if an individual were exposed to painful experiences very early in life, say before three months of age, that the nervous system *could only* respond through its adequate pathways.

The inner portion of the brain, functionally adequate at birth, corresponds approximately to the median zone of the forebrain. This median zone is not a simple circle as implied by the "concentric" model, but may be thought of more precisely as that portion of the forebrain (forming the inner neuropil) which lines the ventricular cavities.[4,6] Thus the margins of these cavities represent phylogenetically the most ancient portions of the forebrain, and are responsible almost exclusively, along with the activities of the brainstem and spinal cord, for what Dr. Yakovlev called "anabolic visceration." [4,5]

The viscera and innermost brain are the structures which act to *increase* the energy state of the organism. The motilities in the body wall and in all activities in which the body performs work (mental or physical); all utilize energy, and decrease the energy of the entire organism.

To be sure, at any age there is an interface between external, extra-personal space, the space beyond the body, and the inner zone. There must be, because children are thrust out into an external world and must have a capacity to react to it. However, with regard to memories and their position in the body, they need not be verbal as many believe. In fact, almost surely they are *not* verbal until a child is about three-and-one-half or four. If a painful stimulus of some variety were experienced by a three-month-old child, it would be most unlikely that such an individual would represent that pain in overcontraction of his lumbosacral muscles or with a constant frowning expression on his face, because the muscles of facial expression and the movements of the body wall (the sacrospinal muscles, the truncal muscles, the proximal limb muscles) are mediated by a portion of the brain which is not yet fully adequate in its function, either afferently or efferently, at the age of two to three months. One would expect that trauma of that vintage, that is, in a two- or three-month-old child, would be represented somewhere in the midline, in the form (for instance) of stomach pains, oversecretion of hydrochloric acid, colonic spasm, cardiac arrhythmia, or intractable anemia. Thus there is a certain logic, a certain dialectic, regarding the adequacy of specific parts of the brain at a given time and the portion of the body and brain within which a memory will be coded.

Regarding myelination (in the brain), it should be recalled that even in an adult the median zone is made up of nerves which are quite sparsely myelinated, so that a paucity of myelin in *this* zone in infancy is *not* a basis for rejecting functional adequacy of a newborn's brain. The multi-synaptic nerves of the median zone are interconnected, not serially or in parallel, but "ablaterally," [4,5] i.e., without regard to (symmetry and) direction. The "model" one may use for thinking about this is that of a dense three-dimensional spider web. Indeed the idea of neuropil itself is the idea of a "feltwork," something which is connected in a three-dimensional mesh of extremely thin nerve fibers.[4,6]

One can postulate what sort of neurological function could derive from this kind of a network, but importantly one can know that certain kinds of activity simply could not emanate from this variety of (structural) network. The median zone simply does not have the mechanical-structural specificity to allow for such a thing as typewriting (or handwriting for that matter).

One of the most important principles of neurological organization is that neurological function is *not* an "all or nothing" thing; it is a representation of reactivity; mediator of a stimulus-response relationship which is modified with increasing age, sophistication, and (functional) addition to the nervous system. Thus our capacity to make any movement in, say, the fingers, is represented at the level of the spinal cord, but importantly it is rerepresented in the medulla, again in the pons, again in the very complicated relay systems within the mesencephalon, and elaborated extensively by the basal ganglia. Then further modification, fragmentation, and selective inhibition take place at the level of the cortex.

Regarding the age of a child and the type of symptom he or she might have at the time of most severe (Primal) trauma, it could be known, for instance, in an individual with a constant frown on the face or with lumbosacral muscle spasm that such an individual had the bulk of his/her trauma at a time *later than* the time when only the median zone is adequate in its responses. This refers to the maturation and elaboration of responses by the middle brain. Dr. Yakovlev's term "mesokinesis" [4,5] is a well chosen one; he states it is quite simply "the outward expression of the internal state." [4,5]

The very word "emotion" derives from the two Latin words "ex motion" (from motion).[4,5] Feeling states by themselves do not have a movement correlate *except* in the viscera, whereas emotions have their movement correlate at the level of the body wall. One way of thinking about this is that the human body is made up of three "tubes": an inner tube which is the gut and all the viscera; a middle tube which is the body wall itself, including the muscles of facial expression and the tone of voice; and a third or outer tube which is actually the environment (extrapersonal space). The inner brain mediates the activities of the inner body, the middle brain mediates the activities of the middle body, the body wall; and the outer brain, the cortex, mediates the activities and the perceptions that relate to the space beyond the body, extrapersonal space.[4,5] Thus, "mesokinesis" becomes "the message behind the message" that is used by anyone who is interested in knowing something about what another individual is *feeling* (in terms of "feeling state ex motion").

Dr. R. B. Livingston has summarized evidence from deep cerebral electrode studies regarding affective components of stimuli in terms of their anatomic location (in the median and limbic zones).[7] Within the forebrain it appears that along the course of the medial forebrain bundle are cells which concern themselves primarily with pleasurable feeling states, the septal nuclei being the prototypic cell groups in this regard. "The most distinctive sites for negative reinforcement lie in the dorsolateral part of the mesencephalon and a bifurcating zone of the diencephalic brain stem. The most distinctive areas of positive reinforcement are the limbic system and the ventromedial hypothalamus. Regions of positive reinforcement are several times as extensive as those for negative reinforcement." [7]

Accordingly, there is support for the idea in Dr. Janov's book *The Anatomy of Mental Illness*[3] that the diencephalon is the place where feelings have first conscious representation. This follows quite directly from the results of cerebral electrode studies (Olds, Milner, Heath, Delgado, Roberts, and others, see[7]). These studies have been extended in recent years by the first researchers and by others employing stereotactic electrodes to study brain functions. The floor of the third ventricle appears to be an important "first" relay station for the representation of pain- and pleasure-feeling states. This is part of the anatomic and physiologic "substrate" that is concerned with the type of response to a stimulus, i.e., whether it should be facilitated or repressed. This is especially applicable when novel stimuli are presented.

Another embryological contribution to the understanding of how behavior changes with age is a knowledge of which nerve pathways myelinate at which time. This topic has been extensively and carefully studied, and the onset and duration of myelination in different fiber systems has been determined with considerable accuracy.[8,9] There is an obvious relationship between the maturation of behavior and the sequential myelination of the fiber pathways of the brain.

In fact, there is no "mind-body problem"; there is no mind without its anatomic and physiologic substrate. The daily practice of neurology confirms this assertion repeatedly, but actually just simple observation of the phenomena of life illustrates this. People lose their memory with sufficiently powerful head trauma, electric shock, high fever, etc. Certain portions of the brain become dysfunctional when the insult is great enough.

Thus, the studies of human brain myelination are important because the adequacy of a given system of the brain, such as the visual or the vestibular system, correlates behaviorally almost one-to-one with the degree (thickness) and the extent (distance) of myelination which has taken place in a given pathway. It is not by accident that a child begins to realize the intrinsic option for extension (in body and limb postures) at about the same time (five to eight months) (Langworthy, cited by Yakovlev[8]) that the vestibular pathways become myelinated. Maturation of this subsystem is the underlying basis for our adequate relationship to gravity, and between four months and one year of age it becomes fully myelinated and along with other maturing portions of the brain mediates the ability first to roll over, then to sit up, and finally to stand.

It is also not just by accident that the *explorations* of a child are entirely (one-to-one) correlated with the embryology of the child's nervous system. Thus, the newborn baby explores the mouth, the midline, and the genitals, and little else. At about three-and-a-half to four months of age the child begins other explorations: of the toes, of the ears, of the body wall itself; the fingers playing with one another (left hand and right hand). The child is increasingly aware of the space of the body wall itself, and thereafter of the space beyond the body.

Thus, one may be wounded (in the Primal sense) and have painful memories which are on a "timetable" in accord with what portions of the brain are adequate at a given stage of development. One would intuitively think (considering the above) of an individual who experiences chest wall pains or certain varieties of headache (especially those that are mediated by vasodilatation of blood vessels on the scalp or the side of the face) that such an individual had (Primal) trauma in infancy later than someone who presents with psychosomatic illness in the form of an ulcer. This follows upon consideration of where these symptoms lie in relation to the "tubes" of the body. It also follows from consideration of the developmental criteria mentioned above, i.e., what portions of the brain were adequate at a given time.

Dr. Janov's concept of psychic "overload" appears to be very useful. When applied to, say, the hurt of a criticism from an acquaintance, it probably presents an "overload" with regard to (Primal) trauma which occurred after the age of three or four, inasmuch as it is an *idea* which is linked to (psychic) pain. "Degrees of neurosis" quite probably have a concentric relationship within the body, going from the midline outwards, and once stimuli are from extrapersonal space then ideas or concepts alone may be adequate to create "overload" and lead to neurotic symptomatology.

There is an orderly maturation and development of functional adequacy of the brain and body, from within outwards.[4,5] The processing of painful stimuli in infancy and childhood will be done by the portions of the brain adequate to do this, in relation to the stage of maturation. Whereas an adult has functional adequacy in all three fundamental body zones, this is not so for an infant. An infant has integrated, adequate functions only in the viscera, later is adequate in the somatic musculature and noise-making operations, and lastly (much later) becomes adequate in relation to extrapersonal space and concept formation. *It follows then that symptom formation in neurosis will reflect the maturational stage at which one experienced (Primal) trauma.* Early trauma will be registered and later be manifested in relation to visceral (dys)function. Somewhat later trauma will be manifested in postural, muscular, and speech disorders, and trauma after language adequacy is obtained will be manifested by disordered interpersonal life.

Regarding the question of painful memories associated with the birth process itself, to those who hold that a newborn's brain is "too primitive" for such operations one must quickly ask, "Too primitive for what?" A brain which is truly "too primitive" cannot mediate even anabolic visceration, and death follows. A normal newborn child, carrying on normal anabolic visceration, is an action system with a considerable array of talents and capabilities. This makes a pertinent commentary about what portions of the brain are then adequate, are then fully functional. Under consideration are those responsible for the utilization of energy, and in terms of the movements involved, primarily concerned with the movements of cells on cells.[4] (Although even the newborn child does have some body motility involving contractions of the body wall itself.) Regarding the myelination of the brain near the time of birth, Dr. Yakovlev has written:

"At term, most of the intrinsic fiber systems of the nucleated neuronal aggregates in the mantle zone of the spinal cord and brain stem are myelinated.

"During the postnatal development of the nervous system, maturation processes unfold mainly (although not exclusively) in the marginal zone of the neuraxis, the cerebral cortex. This marginal zone becomes the cortical plate, of a characteristic strati-laminate pattern of neuronal assembly."[8]

Simply stated, at the end of gestation developmental criteria document a functional inner brain, a partially functional middle brain, and an outer brain which is starting its definitive function. Receptors and effectors within the body and within the body wall are at a high level of adequacy by the time of birth, thus there is no a priori reason to reject the notion that a newborn child could register significant bodily stimuli. This would be all the more possible if the stimuli were visceral: hunger, thirst, breathing difficulty, visceral pain, etc., but still true if the skin surface were involved (if the skin were, e.g., cold, wet, hot, in pain).

It may be that a majority of human memories are coded in the cortex, but to assert that subcortical memories cannot occur would contradict observed modifiable behaviors in animals with little or no cortex. Lashley (cited in [1]) observed that rats with ablated visual cortices could learn visual brightness discriminations, on the jumping stand apparatus, as rapidly as rats with intact cortices, thus demonstrating subcortical learning even in this simple mammal. This also demonstrates the principle of functional representation at different levels in the nervous system.

Relevant to the formation of cortical memories, the fornix, an important subcortical projection system believed to play a major role in the integration of cortical memories, shows "stainable myelin in the second postnatal month, myelination rapidly gaining momentum in the third and fourth months." [8]

There is a disproportionately great relevance of visceral stimuli in all human activities at all ages. Dr. R. B. Livingston has written, "A priority of physiological goals involves control of respiration, temperature regulation, water balance, nutrition, provision of sleep—in that order—and other goals relating to sex, esthetics, curiosity, novelty and freedom (absence of restraint). Unmet needs challenge the priorities of all other goals." ([7], p. 502) These sentences comment on the hierarchy of needs. Visceral needs declare themselves more urgently than somatic needs which in turn are more urgent than social conceptual needs. As an example, a student trying to write an essay cannot sit comfortably if very thirsty, hungry, or with a very full bladder; nor can the essay be written if his posture and position are sufficiently uncomfortable.

Biologically, it is probably true that strictly speaking, there are no "body-wall needs" or "intellectual needs". They are apparent needs only. In a *biological* sense the postural "needs" and cognitive "needs" are actually "derived". They are re-representations of inner brain (diencephalic) needs. Thus, there is no "need to write" as such, no "need to paint", no "need to compose music". In other words the derived "needs" of man are actually elaborations of the basic needs we share in common with lower vertebrates. Writing and creativity are response options in human endeavor, but are not basic, biological needs. This means that human "needs" have not fundamentally changed through the millennia of evolution. What have changed are the sophisticated ways man has gone about meeting his needs. These ways have become so elaborate that people have come to believe that they have a separate existence.

Because EEG evaluation suggests that the newborn or infant's brain is "electrically immature," some would argue that such brains are "too electrically immature" to register birth memories or early postnatal memories. Again one must ask, "Too immature for what activities?" A newborn child can nurse, can cry out, can urinate and defecate, can cough, hiccup, gag, choke, gasp, and vomit. All of these responses are associated with characteristic (if somewhat difficult to describe) feeling states. If adversive (like severe choking, coughing, or vomiting), such stimulus situations are of utmost personal relevance, and are likely candidates for integration into one's memories.

An infant is in relationship to an external environment from the moment of conception onwards. The extrauterine environment is relatively harsh compared to the intrauterine environment. If sufficiently adversive, external stimuli mediate obligatory responses, even in a newborn child. These responses are most adequate in the viscera, less so in the body wall, and least adequate in relation to the space beyond the body.

Crying, choking, gasping, vomiting, etc., are "simple" responses but they are organismic; the entire body participates. They do not occur in isolation or in a vacuum of potential expression, but participate in behavioral patterns which may mediate the life or death of the individual. These responses are the "protectors" of anabolic visceration, upon which all life and the activities of life depend.

Regarding an adult's ability to describe his or her birth, or events in the first three years of life, all that is *operationally* required is the utilization of the language capability (learned later) to describe the reexperience of visual, auditory, tactile, and painful episodes witnessed and experienced earlier. Just because a newborn cannot speak does not necessarily imply that he cannot register and record memories prior to the development of language. Memory is a selection function and little is known of the criteria for adequate recall, and one cannot argue that very early memories are impossible just because most people cannot recall their birth, infancy, and early childhood.

Information available on the subject of memory registration suggests that one forms memories in relation to stimuli of greatest *personal* relevance. However, it is common knowledge that we register more than we can recall. Dr. Janov's observations suggest that one of the parameters profoundly limiting recall is psychic pain.[2,3] He has written that during and after Primal Therapy recall is markedly facilitated, especially for very early memories.[2,3]

Another variable influencing recall is indicated by the disorders of apraxia, in which individuals can make motor responses to verbal commands only under stimulus conditions of greater intensity than is normally required. (Thus, an individual who is dominant for language in the left hemisphere, following a stroke therein may only be able to "blow out a match" when a lit match is brought near his mouth, apparently unable to do this to a verbal command alone or to the stimulus of a command and a pretended match.) Importantly, apractic individuals always perform *most* adequately to a given stimulus when the response employs structures *closer to the anatomic midline.* (People stand and sit better than they salute, better than they pretend to hold a screwdriver, etc.)

These observations support the Primal formulation, considering that *midline* motor responses are the first to mature in infancy. Simply stated, midline motor responses are learned and integrated very early in life and *are registered with a permanence and durability which is greater than subsequently learned and integrated behaviors, and are still demonstrable even after extensive cortical brain damage.* We scream before we communicate with sounds. We communicate with sounds before we speak words. We speak words before we know their meaning. The prototypic behaviors are the oldest ones, in the anatomic midline.

As noted above, at the time of birth the midline portions of the body represent a functioning action system with an adequate (deep neuropil) portion of the nervous system to perfectly integrate its activities. Sucking, swallowing, breathing, choking, gagging, gasping, crying, digesting, vomiting, and eliminating wastes are among the repertoire of activities available to the newborn child. Additionally, some adequacy of the intermediate neuropil is also in evidence, inasmuch as newborns cry if their skin is too cold or too hot or if they are traumatized. Newborn children move their entire bodies infrequently, but especially in response to adverse stimuli such as hunger, thirst, wet diapers, or trauma as slight as an accidental pinprick; this demonstrates a fairly powerful axial muscular reactivity. As noted in Dr. Purdon Martin's book on the basal ganglia and posture, Dr. André Tomas was able to demonstrate the capacity of newborns to "walk" if the stimuli for so doing were adequate, a capability related to the topic of apraxia previously mentioned. The apparent function of the nervous system, to integrate responses between our internal and external environments, is not a function which starts with the development of language, but one which starts much earlier, *in utero.* Consider for the moment the integration of hiccupping, or total-body moving which is known to occur during gestation, or what is even more familiar, the kicking done by children during the third trimester of pregnancy.

Can a child transiently asphyxiated by an umbilical cord around his neck, or by a compressed loop of umbilical cord, form a memory of it? The reported responses of patients during Primal Therapy suggest that such memories are formed.[2,3] The relationship of asthma or stuttering to such an event is quite congruent with the adequacy of the neural structures integrating the functions of the trachea, respiration, and the larynx in the newborn. Each body part is woven into integrated function by the action of the nervous system. It would be nonrational to say that the trachea "remembers" transient strangulation during birth, but there is neuro-embryological evidence that the functioning unit of trachea and newborn nervous system is a reactive, adequate system; one potentially capable of "learning" from an exceedingly intense stimulus.

A child being born cannot cry out "I'm choking!" but the experience probably is represented in the infant's nervous system. As an adult, using language learned at a later time, he or she might well have access to the representation of such an event. The midline structures have receptors to their adequate stimuli. A painful or adversive stimulus has maximal biological relevance for an organism and there is no reason to doubt that a response to it, and a "memory" of it, would occur in relation to "that which hurts." If children did not cry out when seriously hurt, or in confrontation with a stimulus which could kill them, they would not survive.

Responsiveness is a characteristic of the behavioral repertoire of a newborn child. More controversial is the question of whether a very painful stimulus at or near the time of birth can be the basis for an enduring memory trace. The reported observations of people undergoing Primal Therapy suggest that birth trauma can be remembered, later re-experienced, and somatically may be represented by some degree of visceral dysfunction, especially if one is ever again confronted with a related or similar stimulus.

During the first year of life there is increasing adequacy of the inter-mediate and superficial neuropils and the (spatially) related motilities integrated by them. The most adequate body-brain system, however, is still the inner one, near the anatomic midline: the first to mature, phylo-genetically and ontogenetically. The entero-receptors and the responses to their (adequate) stimulation are themselves adequate at the time of birth, and it is probable that the adequacy of this reactive-responsive sys-tem (further) improves during the early months of postnatal life. Aware-ness and responsiveness of an infant emerge "out of the midline"[4]: an infant explores his mouth before his fingertips, his fingertips before a toy, and a toy nearby before a toy at a distance. All three neuropils continue to mature after birth, but the inner one matures first, is reactive first, and integrates its component of behavior (endokinesis[4]) first.

The topic of maturation in the brain and body bears an obvious relationship to psychosomatic illnesses. These are characteristically visceral dysfunctional disorders involving structures close to the anatomic midline. Tension headache, migraine headache, neurotic rhinorrhea, neurotic sneezing, globus hystericus, asthma, hyperventilation syndrome, some varieties of cardiac arrhythmia, tachycardia with emotional stress, gastric acid hypersecretion, gastric hypermotility, some varieties of gastric and duodenal ulcer, ulcerative colitis, diarrhea, constipation, and perhaps (idiopathic) hypertension are among the visceral disorders, comprising a large fraction of disease, which bring people to medical attention. These are real organic illnesses, but they are apparently different in kind from those diseases which bear much less observable relationship to one's extrapersonal environment. The relationship to environmental stress of an asthma attack, a relapse of duodenal ulcer, or recurrence of migraine headache is often an obvious one.

Other disorders may well reflect reaction to environmental stress, but if so, the relationship is much less obvious. Traditionally the "psychosomatic illnesses" have been those with a more easily observed relationship to environmental, particularly emotional-environmental, stress. *As more becomes known about symptom formation in relation to the maturational stage at which one experienced Primal trauma, quite probably many "organic" illnesses will be added to the list of "psychosomatic illnesses."*

The hypothesis is that psychosomatic illnesses have their causal origins in very early childhood. This is not a certainty, for the visceral reactivity possessed by an infant is quite similar to the visceral reactivity of an adult. Attention should be directed, however, to the differences in options for response in infants and in adults. When an adult (or three-year-old for that matter) is hungry, food is sought and obtained; similarly with thirst and other visceral needs. It is the *dependence* of an infant on its extrapersonal environment for need satisfaction which puts it potentially at risk for lack of such satisfaction. An adult, or older child, can feed himself; an infant cannot. An infant when hungry may cry to alert the members of its environment that something is wrong, but the signal is nonspecific (although urgent) in kind. At the very least an infant must accept a certain latency (time) between need and satisfaction of that need which is often longer than such a latency for an older child or adult.

In the event, accidental or malevolent, that the latency between need and satisfaction for an infant is very long, what can the *infant* do about it? What system of motility can he respond with? The answer is obvious: the midline system, the visceral system, the adequate one. More gastric acid and more gastric muscle contraction may occur, but if food or milk is not forthcoming, then a "visceral insult" of sorts occurs. Undoubtedly hunger, thirst, near-asphyxiation, being too cold, being too warm, being in pain is subjectively experienced as adversive and unpleasant, even by an infant.

The principle emerges then that infants *can* only respond to adversive stimuli with crying and visceral motility. They depend on adults to perfectly satisfy their visceral needs with the objects in the environment which can meet those needs. By the amount that this does not occur, the response of the environment is inadequate; inadequate to maintain a homeostatic relationship between the child's needs and the satisfaction of those needs. It is this "confinement" of an infant's motility (visceral motility) in relationship to the external environment which seems to be the common denominator in psychosomatic illness. Adults with psychosomatic disorders respond to external environmental stress by manifest dysfunction of visceral motility as part of their overall reaction.

It is increasingly clear that the responses to early psychic traumas do not occur in isolation; they are mediated by the functionally adequate portions of the nervous system and the body zones integrated by them. Severe early trauma is registered by, and later manifested as dysfunction of, the viscera. As the middle brain becomes adequate in function, symptom formation may occur in the body wall structures or in relation to speech, and with cortical adequacy symptoms become referable to dysfunctional concept formation and cognitive and social activities.

Discussion

The physiologic changes which correlate with the stages of transition from neurotic to post-Primal give clues regarding the underlying mechanisms, but these are correlates of change rather than actual mechanisms.

Nature provides us with some models which may help clarify the mechanisms. Neurotic adults, as they become demented with one of the several dementing illnesses such as Alzheimer's disease, appear to "lose" their neurosis and to become "like infants" again. Indeed, dementia has been referred to by many neurologists as "a second childhood." Such models suggest that having a well developed *cortex* is then a sufficient, but not a causal, basis for neurosis.

For *mechanisms* of neurosis development and an understanding of their reversal in humans with Primal Therapy, it will almost surely be necessary to consider brain mechanisms which are "old"—i.e., phylogenetically "old"—and concerning the development of an individual, early or more primitive brain functions. The *capacity* to *become* neurotic does not happen at age five, ten, or fifteen for the first time. Developmentally, cortical brain function is hardly in evidence in infants, using criteria of language development, capacity for abstract thought, capacity for highly controlled distal movements in fingers, etc. Although the cortex is anatomically present, it is anatomically (due to a paucity of dendritic connections[10]) and physiologically (considering criteria of spontaneous behavior) "primitive." It is likely that phylogenetically and ontogenetically, *early* brain mechanisms provide the sufficient capacity to become neurotic. Thus, subcortical mechanisms almost surely participate in the process of becoming neurotic.

In humans, physical or psychic defense mechanisms become increasingly graded, sophisticated, and appropriate as individuals mature from infancy to adulthood. Simply, normal brain mechanisms are used in the process of neurosis.

Apparently, neurosis involves a distorted learning process in which individuals avoid things they *naturally* would approach and approach things which *naturally* they would avoid, in relationship to early psychic pain.

The phenomena reported during Primal Therapy make it a virtual certainty that this approach-avoidance distortion is dependent upon pain as a necessary, causally related basis for its development, and that its reversal is also painful.[2,3] Literally then, in relation to a harsh environment, the function of the brain becomes abortive, in that the *natural* relationship to stimuli changes. What is implied for brain physiology is that in neurosis, individuals make responses *as if* they were no longer in pain. (Primal Therapy discloses that they *are* in pain, but it is sequestered in some way, so that distorted responses can and do continue.)

The capacity to sequester painful memories, so that behavior proceeds in a distorted way, quite probably requires cortical mechanisms, since children and physically ill or demented adults demonstrate in varying degrees a more natural, less neurotic, relationship to stimuli: approaching life-supportive ones and avoiding painful ones. This is actually the manifestation of an important clinical principle in neurology: with organic brain disorders and systemic disorders affecting the brain the first cerebral capacities to be lost are the ones most recently acquired prior to the disorder. The more extreme the cerebral insult, the more profound the loss of acquired functions. In adults this occurs in other parameters of cortical brain function. Such insults as the ingestion of several cocktails, a fever of 103°, or mild hypoglycemia return neurotic adults to a more natural (less neurotic) response pattern. Stated differently, sick or demented adults respond *more* according to their actual needs than in accord with *learned* personal past experience.

The actual mechanisms which allow one to develop a distorted relationship to stimuli (approaching those that hurt and avoiding those that feel good) are mechanisms normally present in normal brains but being used in a distorted way in neurosis.

It is likely that, as with convulsing (epilepsy), neurosis is "something the brain can do" in response to sufficient environmental stimuli. In neurosis normal brain mechanisms are utilized to distorted ends.

The brain and body can function with a high threshold to pain regarding responses which are made. Primal Therapy reportedly lowers that threshold.[2,3] (One might ask, "What part of the brain sets the threshold for pain?", but almost surely the answer is, "The whole brain.")

The more general principle emerges, however, that responsiveness to stimuli is an inherent property of all creatures. Those with nervous systems make responses with greater speed and more apparent appropriateness than those without nervous systems. Fish have more sophisticated responses than jellyfish, jellyfish more than protozoa, and so on. Human responses may not be more rapid than those of other mammals but show a qualitative appropriateness and selectivity not seen in responses of infrahuman mammals.

Not unexpected is the ontogenetic, maturational counterpart of this phylogenetic progression. The responses of newborn and infant children are very stereotyped initially, reflecting species-specific behavior,[4] and with maturation of the nervous system the responses become individuated in relation to personal past experience.

Responses which show *individual* variation, in response to low-intensity stimuli of variable biological relevance and reflecting personal past experience, will characteristically be mediated by phylogenetically newer portions of the nervous system, in particular the cerebral cortex. The homotypical association cortex is probably the portion involved. This portion is the "secondary association cortex" of C. J. Herrick, with almost exclusively cortico-cortical connections (it receives fibers from the midline and intralaminar nuclei of the thalamus but not from thalamic *relay* nuclei). "Three general association areas are recognized: (1) a frontal, (2) an anterior temporal, and (3) a parietotemporal-preoccipital area. These cortical regions are phylogenetically recent, showing especially marked development in the primates, and become myelinated later than the primary sensory and motor areas." [11] Consideration of ontological maturation patterns and neuroembryology, and their behavioral correlates, makes it quite likely that the sufficient capacity to become mentally ill, with a dual consciousness, is present from the time of birth onward.

ACKNOWLEDGMENTS

The author acknowledges with gratitude the kindness and inspired teaching provided him by Dr. Simeon Locke and Dr. Paul Yakovlev.

BIBLIOGRAPHY

1. Herrick, C. J.: *Brains in Rats and Men.* A Survey of the Origin and Biological Significance of the Cerebral Cortex. Chicago, University of Chicago Press, 1926. (Printed by Hafner, New York, 1963.)

2. Janov, A.: *The Primal Scream.* Primal Therapy: The Cure for Neurosis. Dell Publishing Co., New York, 1970.

3. Janov, A.: *The Anatomy of Mental Illness.* The Scientific Basis of Primal Therapy. G. P. Putnam's Sons, New York, 1971.

4. Yakovlev, P. I.: "Motility, Behavior, and the Brain." Stereodynamic organization of neural coordinates of behavior. *J. Nerv. Ment. Dis.* 107, 313, 1948.

5. Yakovlev, P. I.: "The Structural and Functional 'Trinity' of the Body, Brain, and Behavior." *Current Research in Neurosciences,* ed. H. T. Wycis, Topical Problems in Psychiatric Neurology, Vol. 10, pp. 197-208 (Karger, Basel/New York, 1970).

6. Herrick, C. J.: *The Brain of The Tiger Salamander* (Amblystoma Tigrinum). Chicago, University of Chicago Press, 1948.

7. *The Neurosciences.* A Study Program Planned and Edited by G. G. Quarton, T. Melnechuk, and F. O. Schmitt. Published by Rockefeller University Press, 1967, Sections 5 and 6 (pp. 499-772).

8. Yakovlev, P. I.: "Morphological Criteria of Growth and Maturation of the Nervous System in Man." *Mental Retardation* Vol. XXXIX: Research Publications, A.R.N.M.D., 1962, p. 29.

9. Yakovlev, P. I. and Lecours, A.-R.: "The Myelogenetic Cycles of Regional Maturation of the Brain." International Conference on Regional Maturation of the Nervous System, Paris 1964; in A. Minkowski: *Regional Development of the Brain in Early Life,* pp. 3-70 (Blackwell, Oxford, 1967).

10. Conel, J.: *The Postnatal Development of the Human Cerebral Cortex,* Vols. I-VI, Harvard University Press, Cambridge, Mass., 1939-1960.

11. T. C. Ruch, H. D. Patton, J. W. Woodbury, A. L. Towe: *Neurophysiology.* Reprinted from *Medical Physiology and Biophysics.* Eighteenth edition of the Howell Textbook of Physiology, edited by T. C. Ruch and J. F. Fulton. (W. B. Saunders Co., 1961; reprinted 1962.)

Additional References (not specifically cited):

Coghill, G. E.: *Anatomy and The Problem of Behavior*. First published 1929. Reprinted by permission of Cambridge University Press, by Hafner Publishing Co., Inc., 1964.

Herrick, C. J.: *Neurological Foundations of Animal Behavior*. Reprinted by arrangement, by Hafner Publishing Co., Inc., 1962.

Yakovlev, P. I.: "Anatomy of the Human Brain and the Problem of Mental Retardation." Reprinted from *Mental Retardation*. Proceedings of the First International Conference on Mental Retardation. P. W. Bowman and H. V. Mautner, Eds., Grune and Stratton Inc., 1959.

Yakovlev, P. I.: "Telencephalon 'Impar,' 'Semipar,' and 'Totopar' (Morphogenetic, Tectogenetic, and Architectonic Definitions)." *International J. of Neurology* Vol. 6, Nos. 3 and 4, pp. 245-265, 1968.

Yakovlev, P. I.: "A Proposed Definition of the Limbic System." In *Limbic System Mechanisms and Autonomic Function*, edited by Charles H. Hockman (Charles C. Thomas, Publisher, 1972, pp. 241-283).

Denny-Brown, D.: *The Cerebral Control of Movement*. The Sherrington Lectures VIII, Chapter II, 1966. Charles C. Thomas, Publisher.

Langworthy, O. R.: *The Sensory Control of Posture and Movement*, A Review of the Studies of Derek Denny-Brown. Williams and Wilkins Co., Publishers, 1970.

Sherrington, C. S.: *The Integrative Action of the Nervous System*. New Haven, Yale University Press, 1906.

Physical Trauma as an Etiological Agent in Mental Retardation. Proceedings of a Conference on the Etiology of Mental Retardation, Oct. 13-16, 1968. C. A. Angle and E. A. Bering, Eds., U. S. Dept. of Health, Education, and Welfare P.H.S., N.I.H., N.I.N.D.S., 1970.

Magoun, H. W.: *The Waking Brain*. Second edition, Charles C. Thomas, Publisher, 1963.

Physiological Correlates of Emotion. Perry Black, Editor. Academic Press, 1970.

Mark, V. H.; Ervin, F. R.; Yakovlev, P. I.: "Correlation of Pain Relief, Sensory Loss, and Anatomical Lesion Sites in Pain Patients Treated by Stereotactic Thalamotomy." *Transactions of the American Neurological Association*, pp. 86-90, 1961.

CHAPTER THREE

The Levels of Consciousness
Arthur Janov

Preface

Dr. Holden presents a neuroanatomical analysis of pain and neurosis. He discusses the development of consciousness as coterminous with the development of the brain and relates levels of consciousness to specific developmental adequacies of the brain. Part of what he says has significant implications for the area of psychosomatic ailments, and I would like to elaborate some of his points, perhaps beyond what he might do.

Dr. Holden has introduced a new notion about the specificity of an affliction as related to a specific time of trauma. In other words, how which organ systems later become affected by stress depends on prototypic events occurring very early in life, in a way associated with the maturation of the brain.

Thus, the newborn is "adequate" in the areas of respiration, coronary response, and other life-sustaining processes. These are integrated by the innermost portion of the brain in the anatomic midline. Traumas at this stage of life (from *in utero* to the age of approximately one year) constitute what I call "first-line traumas."

A fetus strangling on the cord at birth has a limited repertoire of possible responses; certainly he cannot intellectualize his trauma but his body can respond. His heart can speed up enormously, for example. Heart rate increase could become a prototypic response to any later life-threatening situation (including the loss of parental love). The person may respond to any kind of later stress in terms of palpitations. After decades of this kind of reaction he is likely to have a coronary attack. It is my belief that nothing short of reliving the prototypic first-line trauma will prevent the possibility of that heart attack, because the initial trauma has been locked into the system (frozen in time, as it were) and will be reactivated by any later life-threat such as parental rejection or disapproval.

Dr. Holden's discussion of three central tubes making up the human brain-body system is a schematic way of visualizing the body. He suggests that the middle tube (or second line) mediates responses of the body wall, including, e.g., facial expression and voice production. It provides the outer expression of inner feeling states. The inner tube integrates the viscera and inner body, mediating gastric secretions, for example. According to Dr. Holden's formulations a second-line trauma involves activities mediated by the middle brain. Thus, a speech trauma (e.g., forcing early speech) leading to stuttering would be second-line. Facial tics would also be symptomatic of second-line traumas. Obviously a newborn cannot stutter under stress because of the lack of adequate pathways mediating body wall expressions. Second-line pathways become adequate between the ages of three months and two years.

Third-line traumas (and these are my extrapolations, not necessarily Dr. Holden's) would be a later development of the whole system; they would be extrapersonal, socially oriented, and would include such things as school phobias. Clearly, a newborn cannot feel "humiliated" and cannot avoid situations as an eight-year-old who has been "made fun of" by his school teacher might.

It may help to understand symptoms of the various levels by visualizing where the movement of excess energy (which is disconnected Pain experienced as tension) is directed. If there is chronic lip-smacking, or rapid eye-blinking, or a grinding of the teeth, then we know that there is involvement of the second-line. If the movement of the energy is against the viscera (colitis, e.g.) it is first-line. If it is directed socially and extrapersonally, such as in constant fighting, it is third-line. If a second-line symptom is present we may assume that the key overload and split occurred in a period after the first few months of life.

What is important for those of us who are doing Primal Therapy is that when we see a patient with a particular bodily symptom, we can relate it to the age at which he experienced the traumatic event (or events). For example, if we see a patient with a constant frown on his face, we know that the trauma is not first-line, since the pathways adequate for the prototypic frown-response are not developed in the first few months of life. Further, the severity of mental illness may well depend on the extent and severity of first-line traumas—someone with mainly first-line traumas may be considered sicker than someone with a majority of second-line ones.

Thus, an anxious patient with many physical afflictions—asthma, heart palpitations, bowel dysfunctions, etc.—can be seen as one with first-line traumas which must be reexperienced and resolved. Persons who are physically healthy but suffer from more social symptoms such as exhibitionism or transvestism would be considered third-liners. The very severely neurotic person suffers traumas all along the developmental way. This kind of situation results in what I call "compounding"; one Pain laid on top of another in sequence.

Depression, for example, may be a failure to conceptualize first-line hurt. The necessary and sufficient condition for full-blown depression later in life, however, may have been an oppressive atmosphere where no feelings were allowed to be expressed. Most of us suffer to some extent from an inability to conceptualize first-line hurt, but what makes one person prone to a depression and another not is the compounding events later on. Fighting to get out of the canal at birth may make us prototypically outgoing rather than prone to depression, so that later repression at home by parents may result in acting out, being bad, ditching school, and so forth. If the fetus is strangling on the umbilical cord, so that movement means death, then passivity is the key response alternative, and that response later becomes fixed, so that in an oppressive home the person becomes prone to depression.

First-Line Traumas

The reason that first-line traumas are so critical and have such devastating effects is that they are often near-death situations, which is usually not the case later on. Individuals whose life circumstances trigger first-line traumas often have a feeling of impending doom, and that inchoate feeling is the harbinger of the near-death feeling. Doom is truly impending, not in the current life circumstance of the person but in the reality locked away in his brain.

When a person with a near-death first-line trauma stored in his brain takes a plane trip, he may be plunged into terror because there is an element of the possibility of death in the situation. That element, however slight, sets off the real possibility of death which occurred years before, a possibility never experienced fully and resolved. He is afraid of dying because he is afraid of dying not from an air crash, but from a near-death event that is still very much alive in his brain. It is that Primal reality which is prepotent.

The obsession with death may be due to a locked-in memory circuit involving near-death in the birth process. Death has become a preoccupation for this person because his whole system is truly occupied by that hidden memory of impending doom. It is possible that death (suicide) becomes fixed as a solution to any current agony because it is seen as the only way out; indeed, for the neonate struggling in the canal the only way to stop the agony *was* death. The point is that near-death is a *memory* of the system having been close to death, and that memory continually offers up symbols (e.g., "I am going to die in an air crash") as the top-level conscious representations for buried first-line Pains.

It may not be that a brush with death while coming into life would alone account for suicide as an obsession, but that a first-line experience plus second- and third-line repressions (such as being reared in a military household or a Catholic one) might combine to produce that obsession. The total amount of repression would result in the inability to express any Pain other than by suicide. There are neurotics who can express their Pain in some way: shouting at everyone, for example. In the suicide we may be dealing with Pain which occurred before expression was possible. (A baby can at least cry out his hurts, but a fetus in the canal can do nothing.) This plus a childhood milieu where repression was the order of the day sets the stage for suicide. It is not so much that the suicide wants to die; he does not want to live any more in agony.

When we see an ulcer patient, for example, with a hypersecretion of hydrochloric acid, we would think of the possibility of first-line prototypic trauma. We would look for very early hurts which occurred when the person could respond only prototypically viscerally. Certainly a person can respond at any age with an overflow of hydrochloric acid, but it is my contention that excess hydrochloric acid may well be typical of a first-line trauma (say of being four months old and starving in the crib due to "scheduled" feeding), so that all later stress sets off that "gut" response. With enough years of that kind of response there is sufficient wear and tear to produce a lesion.

If we take this paradigm far enough, we arrive at the reason why some of us have hormonal afflictions. We know that thyroxine begins to be manufactured in the fetus at about twenty weeks after conception. Stress to the mother which is transmitted to the fetus at that time may interfere with thyroxine output. The child may be born with slightly depressed thyroid function which only shows up later under continued social pressure. That is, there would be a first-line prototypic thyroid vulnerability so that *any* later stress might affect thyroid output (perhaps subclinically) until the time arrived when there was a serious deficiency. None of this is meant to deny the contribution of heredity to the susceptibility of target organs, for certainly a long history of thyroid dysfunction in a family may already make that response more likely in the offspring when stress occurs.

When we see a patient in therapy with spastic colon, we need to think about the possibility of traumas in the first months of life. We might assume that the final resolution of that symptom involves freeing the organism of the locked-in memory of a trauma which has fixed a certain response to all later stress. We may infer from all of this the possible prognosis for the patient in treatment: how difficult it will be and how long it may take.

The nature of our defenses, then, is unique to the stage of brain development when traumas occurred. Those who had a relatively good first three years of life are not likely to become psychotic even if they are exposed to a neurotic atmosphere later on. But for those who are severely traumatized in the first months, a continued neurotic atmosphere later on may result in psychosis. This means that first-line traumas predispose people toward psychosis; if we have three good years in which to build viable defenses we are more likely to absorb later trauma without cracking.

Even with a relatively stable first three years, later psychosis is possible because of significant second-line and third-line traumas such as being sent away to boarding school at six years of age, having both parents die, having parents involved in a bitter divorce when five, and so on. Ordinarily, however, when we see psychosis the possibility of severe first-line traumas is to be expected.

Dr. Holden's formulations now enable us to understand some of the chronic adult symptoms we see, such as globus hystericus (a constant lump in the throat). Being choked by the cord at birth may make the throat a target area for later symptoms. Excessive pressure to talk may produce a stutterer, not because of the social pressure by parents for speech alone, but because that pressure reactivates first-line traumas to the target area such as strangulation by the cord. Together the valence of all the Primal pressures produces an overload resulting in a symptom such as stuttering. We need to keep in mind part-whole relationships here, for stuttering is not a viable, independent problem, but one which evolves and becomes elaborated out of a developing brain and organism.

The cortex of the newborn is functioning and has a specific electroencephalographic pattern. It is not well developed, however, so that massive input from first-line traumas cannot be circumscribed and contained by words or other symbolic representations even though the Pain may be *registered* cortically. The tremendous input from first-line traumas produces chaos in the baby brain, which is as yet inadequate to conceptualize its experience. The physical counterpart of that mental chaos is random, generalized, chaotic bodily reactions. When first-line traumas are triggered later in life, we see exactly those reactions for which the brain was adequate when the trauma was laid down. Thus, the person under adult stress becomes confused, mixed up, and disoriented—all part of the chaotic reaction of the infant. Or, he may constantly seek out sex. Whether he realizes it or not he is in search of a convulsive release for built-up inner pressure which he believes is sexual, but which in reality may be the build-up of first-line tension. He is using his body for relief of body Pain.

The key point here is that whenever a Pain is triggered not only is the hurt activated, but also *the exact early reaction to that hurt becomes reactivated*. This is because one's life experiences are registered in a sequential, orderly, maturation-dependent way. The *response* is part of the early memory circuit. When something happens that is shattering to us as adults we can be thrown back to how a baby felt under the onrush of inexplicable, unconceptualized Pain. The baby cannot say to himself, "I am going crazy." He is simply awash in confusion and chaos over what is happening to him. It is only the adult who can intellectualize and say, "I feel like I am going to lose my mind"; and he is. He is about to lose the mind that verbalizes, explains, and controls; it defers to a baby mind which is just all mixed up. The descent from the third- to the first-line part of the brain *means* loss of one's normal adult mind. Not only is the Pain a latent experience forevermore, but also the *reaction* to that experience becomes a chronic, latent, stereotyped tendency.

Confusion is a first-line reaction to blocked first-line Pain. A person who is easily mixed up, who gets lost while driving, who cannot handle normal everyday input, is in a chronic first-line reaction state. Similarly, many of us cannot concentrate when upset. Our mind seems to flit here and there. This again may be because first-line Pain "blows" our mind, so to speak, because we are suffering from something which cannot be focused on. Instead, our mind flits over several things trying to pinpoint a cause for an upset that has no words and predates conceptual mental life. Perhaps some forms of mental retardation are, in fact, extreme states of confusion in people who are locked into their traumatized baby brains. Also, traditionally, some forms of schizophrenia are considered as "thought process disorders" marked by confusion, lack of here-and-now orientation, and so forth.

Paranoid reactions are attempts to focus on the source of hurt. Since

the first-line Pain is inaccessible, the hurt is imagined to be external—
"they" are doing it. To a baby caught in agony, there is no "they" and there
is no focus. "They" is manufactured later when words and concepts
become available for use. In a sense, how crazy a person is depends on
how far he is from integrating his early Pain. If he thinks it is all in the
present, he is likely to be sicker than someone who at least understands
that his problem lies in the past in some way. True insanity means that
inaccessible Pain becomes one's total reality by constricting consciousness
to a very large degree.

What I am indicating is that there are two possible reasons for unconsciousness. The first is that events take place in an infant brain which as
yet has no higher consciousness to make them symbolically explicable.
The second is that events may take place when the higher brain
pathways are adequate, but due to the load of Pain the events cannot be
fully assimilated. As Primal patients travel back in time in their therapy
they sooner or later arrive at experiences for which there was no higher
cortex physiologically available to make the experiences rational. They
start to "go crazy" because they *now* have a cortex which tries to explain
a tremendous feeling that apparently has no rationale. When they drop
into and feel the experience the craziness vanishes.

One of the key first-line responses of the infant to trauma is sleep.
Patients into heavy early material may constantly fall asleep during their
Primals until enough of the Pain is out of the way so that it can be experienced fully and consciously. Many neurotics use sleep as a defense, and I
believe it is because they are stuck in first-line defenses and characteristically react to any upset by sleeping. Thus, any current situation triggers
the first-line Pain *and its initial reaction* throughout the life of the neurotic.
All of us are stuck in our early Pain and the reactions to it and spend a
lifetime one step removed from the proper connection, acting symbolically
forevermore.

The newborn has a mean brain mass of about 350 grams. By the time
he is one year old its mass is 825 grams. At three years it is 1,115 grams,
and at twenty it is 1,378. By the age of one year, then, the brain has
reached almost sixty percent of its adult weight, and by the age of three
it has reached eighty percent. Ashley Montagu points out in his book
Touching that in the first year the infant's brain grows more rapidly than
it ever will again afterwards.* The point is that the infant's brain is
developing and that a trauma can potentially produce an "imprint" at

---

*Ashley Montagu, *Touching* (Harper and Row, New York, 1971), p. 54.

every stage of development. The developing consciousness is built around this inner imprint and the result is a false consciousness—a consciousness which collects the overload, distributes and reroutes it, and generally is utilized as a defense structure rather than something which has a direct mediating relationship between biologic energy and living.

The first-line imprint, then, may distort the actual development of the cortex just as much as infections of the kidney in infancy affect its later development. The functioning of the cortex may become deranged by its having to deal with the memories of traumas and to defend against their reactivation rather than integrating them. The burdened cortex mediates neurotic intellect—an intelligence which is filtered and selective and used as a *defense* against what the brain already knows rather than something which evolves *out of* that storehouse of experience. The neurotic cannot learn from his key experiences because he has little or no access to them. When this false consciousness is dismantled, what is laid bare is the early encapsulated imprint of trauma in all its pristine clarity.

In other words, the complex circuitry of the adult brain is not only a container of feeling but an elaborated derivative of the baby brain, recruited to handle the early imprinted overloads. The sophisticated later defenses are simply elaborations of that brain finding new networks to enmesh the Pain. The second- and third-line brain mediators become the suppressors rather than the expressors of feeling and act very much like the superego Freud talked about.

What seems to be true is that each developmental level of the brain has its own level of consciousness, and there is an infant consciousness which is buried with the Pain. Consciousness, then, is what completes the circuit and produces the *experience* of Pain. *Because consciousness brings Pain with it, defenses must ultimately be seen as defenses against consciousness.* The *experience* of Pain must therefore be consciousness-expanding. The process of Primal Therapy is one of uncovering layers of imprints so that full (and true) consciousness can occur.

It is the cortex which is mediating the *neurotic* behaving and thinking. The baby brain can only experience; its experiencing of overwhelming Pain influences the entire brain, shaping and warping all manner of activity, from speech to posture and coordination. That is, the neurotic has neurotic speech and posture because the developing brain which deals with those activities has been distorted by early painful imprints, and they become part of the overall defense structure; that is why speech, posture, and coordination change when we dismantle the defenses.

It is first-line feelings that are prototypic and therefore ultimately resolving in a therapeutic way, particularly of those midline ailments which had their start very early in life. Even though colitis, for example, may not show itself until a person's later years, the susceptibility of the colon may have begun at four months.

One of the most recalcitrant and perplexing psychiatric syndromes is known as anorexia nervosa—a nervous loss of appetite. One of our female patients went down to 80 pounds because of this affliction and was in danger of death. (Indeed, some of the individuals who suffer from this problem do die, and it seems refractory to any sort of psychiatric treatment.) After the first months of Primal Therapy she relived the trauma of being forced to eat, and the necessity of her body to reflexively rebel against food. Her affliction was lessened but was not resolved. Later on she began having birth Primals in which she spit up a large amount of phlegm. She relived being drowned in fluid at birth; the tendency to spit up as a lifesaving device was frozen into the associated memory circuit. She came out of that Primal with the insight that she ate compulsively as an adult *so that she could vomit*, which she did many times each day of her life. Eating gave her the "excuse" for spitting up and was her way of relieving the tension of an inaccessible first-line trauma. Vomiting as a result of the inability to keep food down was a symbolic, substitute form of behavior that would have gone on for a lifetime if those crucial connections had not been made. Almost any upset in her adult life had made her want to vomit and she never knew why. The first-line trauma had produced *generalized* reactions, and that is the essence of neurosis—a generalized reaction to Primal Pain.

One patient began to cough when any upsetting situation was discussed. What was happening was that third-line stimuli were triggering first-line responses down the Primal chain. It was only when this patient relived being choked by a bottle with too big a hole in it very early in life that the cough response was eliminated. Until then, slight unconscious upsets produced coughing spasms; that is, they triggered inaccessible first-line reactions which could not be connected. Coughing-up was a prototypic lifesaving defense against choking to death on milk. It was perpetuated in a completely unconscious way. Later traumas were linked to it in a most subtle fashion. For example, brusque orders by a boss produced a coughing fit in the patient because they set off a feeling of being "smothered." That feeling was linked to the prototypic smothering-drowning event in the crib. Only the Primal enabled that connection to be made because the patient was able to descend down the Primal chain during a therapy session and *feel* the basis for his symptom—something no therapist, no matter how brilliant, could ever do for him. *That is why the only possible expert in psychotherapy is the patient.* Neurotics with psychosomatic ailments are in a constant state characterized by uncon-nected first-line Primal Pain.

When I talk about a trip which starts from the perimeter of the defense structure I am using language more than metaphorically. In a gross way the brain is laid down concentrically as it matures, so that those brain areas which deal with survival mature first and are the most undifferentiated. This also means that Pain registered in those areas has the least access to consciousness. In neurosis a third-line trauma often triggers off the innermost defenses, so that with even a slight social rejection later on the system acts as though its survival were threatened, and all its resources become galvanized toward flight or fight. It is only when we penetrate perimeter defenses that we have possible access to the inner storage areas.

Multi-Level Interactions

In the maturation of the brain each new trauma is represented and then rerepresented holographically on higher and higher levels of the brain neuraxis. In this way a Primal chain is developed, with later trauma reactivating related first-line Pains. What this means is that at each stage of brain development an imprint of the trauma occurs, and as the brain develops each imprint joins other related imprints of traumas, the early imprints becoming connected to the later ones. This fusion and representa-tion continues to occur and becomes more elaborate and complex as maturation goes on.

For example, a trauma may occur during birth which affects respiration so that jerky breathing patterns become prototypic on the first line. Then later the child is forced to speak too soon. The respiration pattern is represented on higher levels of the brain and affects speech—respiration being the vehicle which carries vocalization. The net result of the separate traumas may be stammering.

Still later, hand and arm movements join the speech expression pat-terns to give an overall characteristic way a person expresses his feelings. All of this is because of the holographic pattern of brain development. Each new trauma adds a piece to the total imprint; as one descends the chain in Primal Therapy, each reexperiencing of the traumas clarifies a particular aspect of the overall pattern of behavior. One day the person Primals on the first line—feels the trauma of birth as it affected respiration—and then *and only then* can the entire speech pattern that he developed from birth on be altered in a profound way. This should be the meaning of "personality change" as one sees it used in the literature; it should mean a basic and organismic change of *all* aspects of one's functioning, not just one's superficial outward behavior.

This, of course, is the problem with the approaches used by various clinics for the treatment of speech and sex disorders. They are dealing only with the outward, more recently acquired manifestations of a long and deep Primal chain. They are trying to solve a problem that has deep roots which have little directly to do with speech or sex, and they are attempting to solve the problems from the outside in, rather than from the inside out.

For example, frigidity may have its beginnings when the body shuts off against intolerable first-line Pain which has nothing to do with sex. As the brain begins to understand language it starts to conceptualize sexual inhibitions. As maturation goes on, the general repressive atmosphere and attitudes in the home, church, and school similarly become imprinted until the chain is complete and a sexual problem develops. To think that a lecture or demonstration of a special conditioning therapy technique could really undo all that history and solve the problem is to be superficial in the extreme. The Primal chain must be considered because the brain must be taken into account in *all* its complexity. It is the entire brain that is active in some way in each piece of our behavior, and there are three levels to consider in any behavioral response because of the three levels of consciousness in constant interaction.

Part of sex functioning is a sense of time, rhythm, and coordination. These functions are first-line and can be affected by traumas which predate sexual functioning. This serves to show us how every aspect of our brain can be involved in our behavior. There is no way to teach a sense of rhythm to anyone whose natural rhythm has been damaged and distorted in his first days or weeks of life.

I think we have vastly underestimated the prevalence of frigidity in women simply because many women do not have first-line access and as a result have no concept of real sexuality. Even if they can achieve orgasm it is likely to be localized and not encompass the entire body. The final resolution of problems such as frigidity lies in access to first-line consciousness. The reason that frigidity is such a stubborn problem and takes rather long to reverse is just that it takes time to arrive at the first line, when the bodily defenses are finally shaken loose.

Once the major split away from a Primal feeling takes place, later a similar trauma does not evoke a new feeling; rather, it reinforces the original one. An infant may feel alone and terrified just after birth because he has been removed from his mother and placed in a plastic container. This trauma when repeated often enough may produce a first-line prototypic panic at being left alone. Later, being left alone on the first day in a nursery school may evoke that same panic and reinforce the terror. Still later, being dropped by a girl friend may produce fright and panic which combine with the first- and second-line traumas to produce a severe and inordinate reaction to being left alone. The chain is complete. The events bound together by the same feeling are stored together in the lower brain centers and are accessible to consciousness in the reverse order from which they were laid down. The ease of access obviously also depends on the "charge value" of the trauma.

No matter when shattering Pain is laid down, it will not ascend into consciousness until the organism has experienced and resolved other lesser Pains. In Primal Therapy we do not "build up" a Pain tolerance; rather, we systematically reduce the total amount of Pain so that more can be tolerated by consciousness. As a Primal patient begins to feel traumas, descending from third-line to first-line memories and events, he notices that though he is having the same feeling, the experience seems to be deeper and more encompassing. Insights become more profound. He is truly descending into his central core and becoming totally himself.

From this paradigm we can begin to understand such things as the Freudian "separation anxiety." We can see that any overreaction to a current situation is due to a Primal anlage. The "separation anxiety" is an anaphylactic response in which early unconscious memories are triggered by a current event to begin their ascent into consciousness. The anxiety is due to the fright over the possibility of feeling that ascending early catastrophic Pain. No amount of consolation helps an adult who has an exaggerated reaction to losing his girl friend, because one is truly dealing with sequestered first-line panic. In Primal Therapy we use this third-line material as the *via regia* into the second- and first-line memories.

What is clear about prototypic reactions is that they are not symbolically "learned," nor are they undone by "unlearning." A tachycardiac response to a birth trauma is a species-specific behavior, innate and reflexive. Palpitations which occur under later stress, then, can not be undone until one has traveled back down the chain into the prototypic situation which began them. This has implications for the ultimate resolution of the problem of heart disease (as well as many psychosomatic afflictions). Given one heart attack at age fifty the possibility of a second is likely, not only because the heart is now weak and vulnerable but also because it is an historic target organ for stress. In this sense the heart has become part of a representational hierarchy of responses wedded to a concatenation of Primal traumas which are interrelated neurologically.

There is no way to break the neurologic chain of responses. The process of Primal Therapy is based on the assumption that, all things being equal, those traumas involving the least Pain will have the first access to consciousness; each level must be dealt with and resolved before one can move down to another level of experience. Any artificial attempts to break the chain, such as the use of LSD, can lead to disastrous results which I shall discuss in a moment.

On the other hand, it is possible to enter Primal Therapy and immediately plunge into first-line traumas. This can be ascribed to two central factors: (1) the amount of catastrophic early Pain, and (2) the viability of later defenses. Actually these two are interrelated. With constant stress from the beginning there is no chance to manufacture adequate defenses, and the result is constant overt anxiety.

Newly entering patients who plunge directly into very early traumas are usually highly disturbed individuals, the kind who may have been addicted to one kind of drug or another. This is because the Pain has always been just moments away for them and was something they had to deal with each moment of their waking (and sleeping) existences. The "obsessive-compulsive," on the other hand, has reinforced defenses and may literally be years away from first-line material.

The process of Primal Therapy usually proceeds from the perimeter of the defense system to the interior—in an almost literal way in the brain. If one were to schematize the process it might look like this: 333333322-33222322222222122211122111111121111111. The leitmotif of this schema is that the charge value plus the time of occurrence of a Primal Pain determines its accessibility to consciousness. The severity of the neurosis and the strength of one's neurotic compulsions would depend on how far down the chain one has gone in therapy. It is possible to resolve much of second-line Pain and find oneself devoid of some somatic symptoms, but that does not mean that the neurosis has been cured. Rather, the process of Primaling continues, perhaps for years, until most of the first-line traumas have been reexperienced. We would expect that with the resolution of the major second-line Pains the symptoms of the body wall would be removed, leaving intact first-line symptoms such as asthma and colitis, however.

The fact that a patient proceeds immediately to first-line Primals might not necessarily indicate that he is going to get well faster. If the traumas were exceptionally severe the person might be stuck for a very long time on this level. This is particularly true when there is insufficient capacity to integrate the amount of Pain coming up. What happens then is that the person Primals but finds little relief between times; this may go on for many months until the Primal flood opened up by the therapy subsides. During the time that the patient is Primaling over first-line material his second- and third-line defenses may still be operating, so that a male patient may be tempted to dress up in women's clothes, for example, or he may still find himself praying a good deal.

The problem with using an hallucinogen such as LSD is that it provides access to pain stored subcortically and decreases cortical control; the result is that the person using LSD is flooded with out-of-sequence Pains and has insufficient cortical ability to integrate what is coming up. Rather than feel the first-line traumas which have been dredged up by the drug, the person will symbolize the Pain. He will hallucinate colored lights or the lights of a flying saucer rather than feel being temporarily blinded by strong fluorescent lights at birth. The reason LSD is an hallucinogen is simply because it produces flooding of Pain and symbolization rather than a full, true Primal experience. The drug does not *produce* hallucinations, but rather evokes *Pain* which is hallucinated. There are many other ways to express Primal flooding besides hallucinating.

When Pains are felt in sequence in a Primal there is an obvious total integration of them. Consciousness accepts them and the fact that there is Pain and not symbolization means, de facto, that integration is taking place. There is no need for special integration exercises afterwards. There is a tendency to think that feeling heavy Pain has a disintegrating effect and that one must be "put back together" later on. This is a sloppy metaphor resulting from sloppy thinking. The *blockage* of early Pain is a disintegrating process in a literal way, separating one brain area from another, one part of the body from another, and areas of thought and feeling from one another. It is the *Primal* unblocking experience which is integrating; in our research we see that the activities of the right and left brain hemispheres mirror that integration. It is the Primal experience which integrates the mind with the body so that one can now have natural control of all body functions.

It is possible for a person to suffer from some first-line trauma such as starvation in the crib and still develop adequate defenses later on. If parents offer their child a way to get on with them—to be smart or a go-getter, for example—it is possible for the child to cover his early Pain. Later on he still might suffer an ulcer, however, but he probably would not have chronic overt anxiety. Interestingly, the treatment of his ulcer is exactly what he needed in the crib—lots of milk.

There is obviously an overlapping of the levels of Pain. It is often the case with most of us that we are traumatized on all levels. What differentiates us is how extensive and intensive the traumas were and *when* they occurred. There are some children who receive some kind of love in their first few years when they are both cute and helpless. When they develop some kind of negativism—when they decide to try to lead their own lives—the trouble begins. These are the second-liners, with few symptoms of the midline such as colitis, asthma, hemorrhoids, or ulcers but instead with distorted personalities and somatic complaints in the body wall such as tension headaches, tense facial muscles, and low back muscle spasms.

The notion that early Pain is represented on various levels as the brain matures helps us understand why I call Primal Therapy "neurosis in reverse." For, just as the Pain was laid down from inside outward, the cure involves a descent from the periphery inward. With descent to each new level the person becomes more of a feeling human being. Those with only second-line access would be less feeling than those who had experienced and integrated first-line prototypic traumas.

PROPOSED ANATOMIC LOCI FOR THE THREE MAIN COMPONENTS OF CONSCIOUSNESS

1 FOR VISCERAL CONSCIOUSNESS   **2** FOR EMOTIONAL CONSCIOUSNESS   **3** FOR COGNITIVE CONSCIOUSNESS

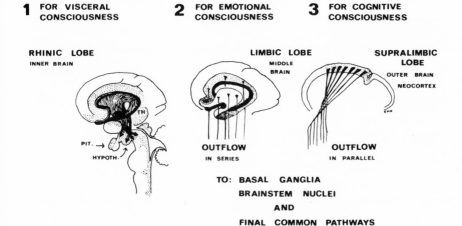

RHINIC LOBE
INNER BRAIN

LIMBIC LOBE
MIDDLE BRAIN

SUPRALIMBIC LOBE
OUTER BRAIN
NEOCORTEX

PIT. →
HYPOTH.

OUTFLOW
IN SERIES

OUTFLOW
IN PARALLEL

TO: BASAL GANGLIA
BRAINSTEM NUCLEI
AND
FINAL COMMON PATHWAYS

(Drawing modified. from Yakovlev, 1948)

One of the ways we corroborate these hypotheses is to observe patients fairly far along in Primal Therapy. As the patient approaches first-line scenes he suffers from transient bizarre sensations and ideation. The patient often feels as though he is going crazy. His responses are more primitive and random, resulting occasionally in hallucinations for a brief moment. As I stated earlier, when the feeling is felt the sensation of impending insanity disappears. In non-Primal persons when these first-line traumas are triggered there may indeed be insanity; the resulting mental breakdown is the fragmentation caused by shattering ascending nonintegrable Pain. Just knowing that it is possible and desirable to re-experience that black, nameless dread or terror which occurred in the earliest months of life helps to stabilize Primal patients, for they know it can be felt with relative impunity. Indeed, feeling is the antidote for the possibility of craziness. The black, empty void is of itself a connected feeling and needs no words of explanation. The fact that a patient is aware that he is in his past, reliving a moment without words or concept, is sufficient connection for a complete Primal. He has "acknowledged" his Pain.

What happens to a person who tries to make sense out of one of these ascending, first-line, preverbal Pains is the development of paranoia—bizarre ideation to rationalize something that has no verbal rationale. Ideation must be strained and unreal because it is being used to explain the unexplainable. This is the reason why the non-initiate feels he is going crazy when he comes close to his first-line Pain. For the first time there *is* no way to "make sense" out of an experience—no formula or frame of reference to make it comprehensible. Feelings and words about feelings, remember, are organized at different levels and in different structures of the brain.

Hallucinations can be considered a more severe form of pathology than paranoid delusions because they are more primitive nonverbal responses. It is my assumption that the more protected (the deeper) the Pain, the more likely it is to produce generalized neurotic behavior, particularly behavior that is prototypic and unlearned. First-line traumas not only have lifelong effects, they also have the most widespread effects on those areas which were functional at the time. As the brain develops and differentiates into its discrete functions, and as it becomes fractionated due to neurosis, then traumas are more compartmentalized, contained, and restricted in their effects.

Another feeling that a Primal patient may have when approaching his first-line Pain is that of an impending seizure. Indeed, the experience of first-line Primals is often convulsive due to the onslaught of great Pain erupting within the system. The body cannot absorb the onrush smoothly due to the relative absence of defenses, and it thrashes and convulses. It is my assumption that psychogenic epilepsy occurs when there is such a total overload of Pain that the system has no more resources for coping in the ordinary ways. Indeed, seizure may be the only thing the brain can do to release its tension. It is a massive random discharge of neurologic tension. Electroconvulsive therapy may produce for patients what they cannot provide for themselves—a massive release. By and large, psychogenic seizures are a result of compounding. Patients who begin to have seizures in Primal Therapy generally are into preverbal experiences which took place before there was a mature cortex to help shoulder the load of Pain. Thus, the physical system starts to discharge the physical trauma.

It is my belief that much of compulsive neurotic sex is an unconscious attempt to produce a first-line discharge. It is one of the only ways a neurotic can bring on a massive convulsive release for himself. Indeed, Primal patients who are fairly advanced in treatment find that convulsive orgasm immediately plunges them into birth Primals. In short, orgasm for the neurotic may well be a discharge of unresolved convulsing Pain, and the reason for the severe convulsions during orgasm must be due to first-line pressure and not to any property of normal sex.

Compulsive sex, then, is a necessary deterrent to the possibility of seizures or of psychosis. It is when the human system becomes rigid, and riddled by internalized moral precepts which preclude free sex, that the first-line discharge moves from the sexual apparatus to the head (seizures). Hospitalized mental patients deprived of sex are also deprived of a chance to discharge tension. It would be far better to teach them the value of sex and masturbation and to help them "let go" with their bodies. It seems almost trivial: a notion that instead of lining up each morning in the hospital for their electroconvulsive shock treatment, patients should be lining up for their morning sex—a seemingly whimsical but deadly serious notion. The problem, of course, is that free sex for mentally ill persons too often brings on more anxiety, not less.

Dreams

It is my assumption that many of our recurrent (often over a lifetime) nightmares occur because sleep has lowered our conscious defense system enough to permit release of first-line Pain. Nightmares also indicate how much pressure we are holding back during the daytime and how hard our systems must be working each day just to keep the Pain at bay. In Primal Therapy we eventually take the patient into that nightmare, so it is no wonder that there is fright. It is a dangerous time in Primal Therapy because as the patient begins to become fully feeling he is going to feel more and more of his horrendous first-line Pain. This is the time he will want to run, but he knows that if he does he will be sick for the rest of his life.

It is possible that our dream life operates on all three levels. If enough old Pains have been evoked during the day, then one is apt to suffer first-line dreams which are nightmares. Milder bad dreams might involve second-line material. Two factors would help indicate on which level the dream operates: the amount of symbolism—how vague or bizarre and removed from reality—and the intensity of feelings inside the dream. Is there terror or just mild apprehension? Are the figures real or shadowy? Are they nonhuman (monsters, animals) or human? The reason that so many of us have inexplicable recurrent nightmares is that they involve inaccessible first-line material which during our waking hours has no egress to consciousness.

It is interesting to note that the feeling (and symbol) during a nightmare is of life and death. We fight for our lives in a nightmare because real life-and-death first-line Pain is ascending. These life-and-death feelings add corroboration to how catastrophic first-line Pain is. We do not arbitrarily "dream up" those feelings: those feelings cause us to "dream up" stories to make them plausible. The feelings are real; only the stories have been changed to protect the person.

We must understand that dreams may become compounded, so that a relatively simple daytime experience may trigger off a second-line feeling which also gathers with it first-line-related Pain. Even when a person has felt the second-line components of a recurrent nightmare he is still apt to have it in attenuated form until its entire first-line basis has been rooted out. Generally there are two ways to differentiate first-line from second-line dreams. The nature of the feeling within the dream—whether it is terrifying or simply somewhat scary—and the complexity of the symbolism. First-line dreams seem to be straightforward, with simple and direct symbolism (e.g., crawling through a dark tunnel into daylight, or being in a room where the walls are closing in). A second-line dream has more of a story, more people, and more elaborate and variegated action. First-line dreams have a simple, direct, strong-action sequence. A person with inadequate defenses who is close to his feelings may suffer continually from nightmares, with almost no triggering necessary. This kind of person is obviously a good candidate for Primal Therapy, since his defense system is already ineffective and therapy is only a matter of helping him feel what is already coming up.

The greater the access to his feelings a person has, the less symbolic will be his dreams. In the absence of defense buffers feelings will come up during sleep and will be tied to very real symbols reflective of those feelings. In neurotics who have little access to their deep Pain the third-line defenses buffer lower-line Pain and must somehow "interpret" feelings. There is obviously going to be distorted symbolism which depends on the nature of the Pain and the density of the defense system. The distance one is from one's first-line Pain will determine the amount of symbolism.

Primal patients have amazingly real, nonsymbolic dreams. When a distorted symbol appears in their sleep they may say to themselves (while asleep), "That is a symbol of a feeling." They will drop into the feeling, make connections, and resolve it all while asleep. The reason that having less symbolic dreams is important is that it is an index of progress in therapy; more consciousness means less symbolism and less neurotic— symbolic—behavior during waking hours. It is consciousness that is the specific antidote for neurosis (symbolic acting-out) whether one is awake or asleep.

Levels of Consciousness

When we talk about "cure" for neurosis the reader needs to understand that there will be unconscious Primal forces impelling a patient's behavior until the major first-line traumas are experienced in Primal Therapy. After much of the second- and third-line material has been resolved we would expect that many of the symptoms—the great compulsions and the acting out—would be eliminated, but that still leaves unconscious forces to produce neurotic behavior, which means that the neurotic is still not free. It is unconsciousness which removes choice and denies freedom. The neurotic is both straitjacketed and impelled by his unconscious. *There is only one freedom—consciousness.* A conscious life is a free one.

What is truly astounding about the human system is that there seems to be a natural sequence of ascension into consciousness of Primal Pain, the most accessible being the first to be connected. As a patient descends into his feelings he finds an interesting phenomenon—each Pain seems deeper and more encompassing, as though there are levels of experience he is passing through. What is happening is that the *same* feeling relived on a third-line level is later experienced on second- and first-line levels with broader implications, deeper insights; in a more all-encompassingly systemic way, since the body is then much more open and has fewer blockages. It must be clear by now that if chronic tension is the result of Primal Pain disconnected from access to consciousness and continuously reverberating on lower levels, then access and connection are what dispel it permanently. Thus, in a real sense it is consciousness that is curative. Neurosis develops in three stages and on three levels and it disintegrates therapeutically in three modes. There is no way to solve first-line problems on a third-line level.

It is often possible for Primal patients to move from third-line to second- or first-line events within a single session. It all depends on how much has previously been resolved and how defended the patient still is. For example, one patient relived a scene in which his grandparents were forcing him to speak at the age of two-and-one-half. Suddenly he was thrown back into a scene at two months when he was in his crib, hungry and crying, and suddenly something was thrust into his mouth (a bottle) in the dark, frightening him terribly. The two traumas to the oral area were on different levels of experience but were quite related. Together they formed the Primal anlage for later stuttering.

Another patient began a Primal with the statement that the room was closing in on her. The reason she complained on that particular day about the room was that a first-line event was pushing toward consciousness. Had she not been in therapy she might have just been tense—feeling "closed in," wanting to get out into the open spaces or go away to a place where she could have "room to breathe." Even though her behavior might seem realistic and appropriate, it would have represented a response to an unresolved old situation. In her Primal she felt the Pain of always having to share her room in childhood and never having enough space for herself. From there she slipped into the first-line Pain of birth when there was not enough room for her —she was a twin.

It may well be that patients reach what I would call "the point of no return" in their therapy, at which time there is fluid access among all levels of Pain. When a patient can descend down the chain within each therapy session, we can expect that he is on an ineluctable course toward health.

It is my hypothesis that there are three distinct levels of consciousness in accordance with how the brain is laid down. Third-line consciousness is the intellectual, topmost level, externally oriented and dealing with the here-and-now. Second-line consciousness is the "feeling consciousness," which includes the Painful scenes of the past; it involves the use of speech but only that which is reflective of feeling.* This is what I have called elsewhere the "limbic consciousness." The first-line level involves an awareness of the body and is a preverbal consciousness. First-line consciousness includes preverbal memories dealing with physical trauma. It involves sensory awareness, a sense of rhythm and of time. It includes the sense of movement and coordination. First-line consciousness is totally inner-directed and deals with all the senses of the body, although primarily the visceral senses.

I believe that there are intermediate or buffer zones (such as the limbic cortex) between the levels of consciousness which control and filter the amount of access between them; this access is largely determined by the amount of Pain on each level. The buffer between levels one and two would be physical defenses, such as a tightening of the muscles, and the buffer between two and three would have to do with words and ideas. I do not mean that the levels are totally exclusive of one another; rather, that there is a predominant zone of operation and we can categorize individuals by the *characteristic* level of functioning. The amount of fluid access within the brain determines the level of consciousness—full consciousness meaning fluid interconnections among all levels.

We must take care to differentiate real from false consciousness, for what the neurotic perceives and reacts to is usually different from the normal. The neurotic may misinterpret a statement by a friend and become angry. He thinks all kinds of revengeful thoughts. The normal does not misperceive and does not clutter his mind with those thoughts. His third-line orientation reflects clear inner channels and is truly a different kind of consciousness from that of the neurotic. The neurotic is continually perceiving out of a storehouse of blocked feelings.

Third-line consciousness involves present hurts. The neurotic may over-react to those hurts without any understanding that his reactions have an overlay from the past. The force of his reactions derives from the blocked

---

*Speech is both a signal system and the vehicle for language, a shared feeling representation between two or more people. Language deals with propositions and symbols and is therefore third-line. A symbol is a mental representation of reality — a higher representation of internal states.

Primal chain. The reaction of the normal does not have that force and is appropriate to the present; the normal is not overly excited by mundane events. The third-line consciousness of the neurotic is solely outer-directed, stimulus-controlled with practically no reflective ability and with little feeling. He is rigid and inflexible and must remain so because he is defended against access down the Primal chain, and it is only that access which ultimately allows for basic change.

Second-line consciousness is feeling-consciousness. Dream consciousness is an example. We use words in our dreams, but they are usually related to a feeling in one way or another. While second-line consciousness provides awareness of feeling, third-line consciousness gives us an awareness of that awareness (through the use of symbols).

Each level of consciousness contributes something different in order to make up a completely represented feeling. The first-line offers the "energy" of the feeling, the force or charge value of it. The second-line produces the quality of feeling and expresses it with emotional responses. The third-line involves the full comprehension of what is being felt and ultimately communicates the feeling symbolically. Thus, energy, quality, and comprehension are the necessary elements that go to make a full feeling. In the neurotic the third-line is expressive of "non-feeling" in ways which tend to become abstract and distorted—an independent awareness disconnected from what is real inside. Because of this disconnection his awareness reflects an unconsciousness, or rather, his awareness of himself *is* a form of unconsciousness. The normal is able to think what he feels and feel what he thinks. When a post-Primal patient talks about something sad he automatically cries, because there is direct coupling between a perception and the feelings which accompany it. It is this access to one's feelings that is the antidote for neurosis and psychosis.

When third-line consciousness is depressed or removed, say by drugs, the condition is known as psychosis. That is, there is no objective appreciation by the higher parts of the brain that one is having a feeling or that what one is perceiving is from the storehouse of memories from the past. That is why I call psychosis the "waking dream." It is the function of the third-line to orient the person in the present, to enable him to acknowledge the past, to sift it and integrate it with what is going on in the present. I have discussed elsewhere a condition in which certain brain injuries produce a person who can say "Shit!" or other feeling-charged words but cannot explain why he said them. In that sense there is an absence of third-line consciousness. Second-line consciousness is emotional consciousness. Individuals with second-line access have access to their feelings, can reflect on the emotional characteristics of their behavior, and can use their past in some manner to direct their current life.

First-line consciousness is apparent in dancing to music. There is an "awareness" of a beat, of rhythm and movement, but no need to explain anything and no need for a storehouse of Pain to make it possible. It is purely physical. Sexual functioning is another example of first-line consciousness. First-line consciousness deals with the energy of our body and can be termed "body consciousness." It is what permits an uncontaminated state I call "ecstasy," in which one can experience the full energy of the body. Ecstasy can only occur when there is full access among all levels, so that a person can completely experience his body in relation to what is going on around him, whether in sex or dancing.

It is possible for neurotics who take drugs such as hashish to blast away third- and second-line consciousness and experience a kind of ecstatic state. The drug has taken the person below the level of pain-connected consciousness into the energy of the first-line which is then directed into producing an ecstatic state. I believe that we never lose the sense of coordination and rhythm characteristic of the first-line, but that what happens is that Pain and the enforced disrhythms of our lives (such as being forced to walk or talk too soon, too early toilet training, etc.) become superimposed on our first-line consciousness and severely distort it. Later, strong measures are needed to regain access to it.

There are some neurotics who cannot function in sex until they hear certain words such as, "I love you." There are others who must hear about the partner's previous sexual exploits. They cannot experience sex on a purely physical level. They cannot give in to the importunings of the body, but instead must stay on a higher level of consciousness and find devious ways to gain access to sexual energies. The route taken depends on the kind of Pain blocked in early life. Their sex experience has nothing to do with relating to a partner; they are relating to their Pain symbolically.

It is the neurotic who must descend through his second-line consciousness in order to gain access to his body; if there is a good deal of second-line Pain, then he is going to be filled with neurotic fantasies during sex. If he grew up hating his mother he may possibly have sadistic fantasies. If his mother was seductive, then his fantasies may be of someone of a different race and color (in order to avoid incestuous feelings arising). In real life, too, he may have to marry someone having a different color, religion, looks, etc., all as a means of not coming close to sexual feelings for his mother. In this case the third-line consciousness selects as a partner someone who is as far away as possible from "mother." It makes a choice based on blocked, inaccessible (and unconscious) second-line Pain. The partner chosen is "symbolic," yet the choice seems rational and well-thought-out; the person chosen may be a very good person, one to whom he can relate, but that does not change the fact that the choice represents symbolic behavior.

Why does sex get so warped? Why does neurosis always show itself so lucidly in sex? Because all behavior for the neurotic is symbolic if it is based on blocked feelings, and sex is just one more type of behavior. But, too, sex is a feeling kind of behavior, and in order to feel anything the neurotic must find a symbolic way to elicit some feeling; this is the function of fantasy. When there is total consciousness, there is no longer a need for symbols; the person is aroused by the real thing, not by pictures (literal symbols) or by stories or fantasies. Being aroused by a picture of a sadistic act (or by the act itself, which is also symbolic) only means that the person has unresolved sadistic feelings from his past. If he were to feel that past the symbol would no longer be arousing.

A sexual ritual such as sadism can be equated to dreams and dream consciousness. The symbols in both represent a *condensation* of a lifetime of critical experiences. These experiences are bound together by the same or similar feelings, so that someone who has been treated cruelly by his parents day in and day out will tend to ritualize it in one way or another. The symbol is tenacious and enduring because it evolves out of those feelings which represent many thousands of experiences. Contained in symbolic form within the ritual or dream, then, is the key unresolved feeling which causes one or the other to continually recur.

Fantasy is not the only way to act out symbolically. If an infant is deprived of adequate nursing, he may block that need later and simply become "excited" at the sight of breasts. As he becomes sexually mature that excitement becomes eroticized and he gets sexually aroused by breasts—with no understanding that it is a rerouted early Pain. The sexual excitement is symbolic of infantile excitement (excitation by need) and there is no extra need for fantasy. In the absence of a real breast, however, the person might use a fantasy in order to become sexually aroused. Even when he is aroused sexually by the "real thing," his behavior is still symbolic because he is relating not to current reality but to past need.

Most of our neurotic thoughts occur at the third-line level; they are the mental residue left after feelings have been filtered through the buffer zones. They become part of the general defense system, reinforcing the barriers against feeling. It is when thoughts can no longer hold back the feelings that we find impulsive acting-out such as exhibitionism. Many exhibitionists report that before they take to the streets they talk to themselves, saying how dangerous it is, how stupid, etc., yet suddenly they find themselves in a "coma-like" state—the second-line has taken over. They are in the dream with third-line consciousness receding into the background. All the third-line arguments will not hold back the tide; the person is unconscious because his third-line, here-and-now cerebration is overwhelmed. The difference between fantasy and actual acting-out, then, depends on the amount of pressure from lower-line Pain and on the strength of third-line defenses. One can slip in and out of fantasy and be back to reality within a few moments, but the acting-out ritual is too consuming and overpowering for that.

It is the third-line apparatus which must deal with the upsurging energies from Pain on the two lower levels. The more lower-line Pain, the more active the third-line becomes, producing, inter alia, insomnia. When the lower-line Pain is excessive, cannot be held back and threatens to break through, then external means are sought by the third-line to quell the Pain and bolster the buffer zone. The use of tranquilizers and heroin is an example of this. There are obviously traumatic events in the present, such as the death of a spouse, which weaken the third-line defense system and permit some egress of the Primal tide. Ordinarily, however, it is the lower energies, the Pains disconnected from third-line knowledge, which constantly innervate top-level consciousness and produce grooved and compulsive acting-out such as exhibitionism. What I am indicating is that full feeling must include all levels of consciousness, because there is a present and a past for each of us, and that past when unresolved is always at work in the present.

The danger of a drug such as LSD is that it blasts open the buffer zones between all levels of consciousness and liberates Primal energies which because of their overload of Pain cannot be controlled. The third-line consciousness must then strain itself to explain what is happening, and bizarre ideation is the result.

The process of Primal Therapy is a matter of *experiencing* what exists on each level rather than of "understanding" it (which would be like the third line comprehending the first). The more Pain experienced, the slimmer the buffer zone and the more feeling the person becomes.

It should be clear that *experience* is a key term, since any kind of intellectual comprehension by the third-line of the second or first means bypassing those lower levels of consciousness, which results in strengthening the buffer zone rather than vitiating it. Intellectual understanding which does not grow out of a feeling experience hardens the defense system. This is because consciousness is an organic, psychophysiologic process and not simply a mental phenomenon. Experience is of the total system. It is neurotic consciousness which becomes inorganic and out of touch with that system, which has thoughts completely at odds with what is going on inside.

The experiencing of each level brings with it its own level of consciousness, so that when a person has descended many times to first-line feelings we can say that he is beginning to "get his body back." No second-line consciousness can do that by itself, although the experiencing of the second-line allows more and more access to first-line Pain and thus paves the way for the repossession of the body. What this means is that *each Pain has its own consciousness.* One has to experience with the first-line infant brain in order to expand consciousness; trying to conceptualize nonconceptual early Pains only serves to make them less accessible and constricts rather than expands consciousness.

As one descends down the Primal chain the entire brain becomes free to do what it never did—to develop *out of* its storehouse of experiences and to utilize those experiences to change one's life. It is that descent into first-line feelings which changes coordination and posture as no third-line activities (such as taking lessons) can do. This is an organismic concept of consciousness and change which enables us to understand why Primal insights, which evolve out of feeling, are the most profound and the most accurate. They are the direct connections of the third-line to the lower levels that replace the misconnections which have occurred before. A "deep" insight means precisely "deep in the brain."

We can often find dramatic evidence of the distinct levels of consciousness in observing patients' Primals. Sometimes a patient will be reliving a first-line Pain, say of birth, and there will be no tears. After a time he will drift into a later memory when the tear ducts were operating, and then his eyes will be flooded with tears. If he should slide into the first-line again, the tears disappear.

Another example of the clear distinction between levels is found in patients who are foreign-born. They will begin their Primals with some current situation and will speak in English. As they recede into an early childhood memory they will automatically revert to their native tongue. The memory code for those early events is clearly interwoven with language; it is as though the foreign language events exist on a stratum of consciousness below the third-line. After the Primal a person may be hard put to speak as fluidly in his early language as he did while in the Primal. Conversely, while in the Primal the person seems to have little access to English, speaking exclusively in his native tongue.

One can observe how organic is consciousness during and just after a therapy session. During the session when a patient has descended to his first line the slightest touch may make him curl up in a ball and start convulsing from not being touched as an infant, yet ten minutes later after the session when the patient is operating on the third-line, here-and-now level of consciousness that same touch will have no effect. This dramatizes how third-line consciousness can operate as a buffer against stimuli, either blocking or distorting their meaning and preventing access to levels of consciousness which could make them meaningful. It also indicates how clear-cut the division between levels of consciousness can be. It illustrates how lower-line consciousness innervates the physical system (in the case above it is the Pain produced by lack of early touches and caresses) and produces physical events such as physical symptoms which are entirely beyond the comprehension of, or control by, higher consciousness. A person totally walled off from his innermost feelings and operating on the third line may not recognize any need for touch but may simply withdraw when it is offered. His system will close up against the early Pain reflexively, because to permit any close touch brings up the Pain of its absence from his early life.

Hypnosis is an example of the loss of third-line consciousness. A hypnotized person can be brought back to an early age level and he seems to be there totally, describing his classroom, friends, and teachers all in perfect detail—something he cannot seem to do when brought out of that state. You can talk to a hypnotized person and he seems to be aware of you, yet he is truly unconscious at that moment; that is, he is on a different level of consciousness. He is more inner-oriented and has momentarily lost his external bearings.

Hilgard has done extensive research on hypnosis and pain.* His find-ings tend to corroborate the existence of discrete levels of consciousness. He hypnotized subjects and subjected them to pain, such as putting their hands in circulating ice water. Generally the subject would report no discomfort, yet when he was given paper and pencil and encouraged in automatic writing (the dissociated part of the self reporting on the other part) it showed that all the pain was being felt somewhere. Hilgard has

---

*Ernest R. Hilgard, "Pain Reduction in Hypnosis." *Psychological Review*, Volume 80, No. 5, Sept., 1973, pages 396-410.

also done similar experiments in which he induced "automatic talking": "By instructing the subject that when the hypnotist's hand is placed on his shoulder he will tell what is going on in the secondary consciousness but will not know that he is talking, similar results to automatic writing are obtained."

Automatic talking is dramatic evidence of the split in consciousness between knowing and feeling. There are many of us who can talk all day and not know which unconscious drives push us to say what we do, and we can say with our every word that we are in Pain but not really "know" it.

Automatic talking demonstrates to me the difference between second- and third-line consciousness; the subject describes the exact pain (due to ice water), where it is felt, yet his topmost consciousness is oblivious to the entire matter. Here is stinging pain, observed by the subject with his own eyes, yet nothing registers into consciousness (third-line consciousness). Many of us walk around with great Pain just under the surface and are unconscious of it. That is the essence of neurosis.

The important point about all this is not just that we should become more conscious, but that unconscious Pains are quietly taking their toll of our systems with the end result being disease and premature death, all without our knowledge. Hilgard found in his subjects that "the cold was as intense as ever but did not hurt." And further, "heart rate and blood pressure rise in the cold water corresponding to those of waking non-hypnosis." It is not just that we felt Pain at age two that matters. It is that *the Pain remains*, keeping our systems distorted and overstimulated. The Pain remains precisely because it has been locked away and prevented from making higher connections which would finally resolve it.

What determines the general level of consciousness of a person is how much Pain he has integrated on each level. Even if he is experiencing first-line Pains there still may be such a storehouse of buried hurts that his consciousness is second-line, not first.

To assume that the experience of first-line traumas such as birth is unnecessary or a "frill" is to literally throw the baby out with the bathwater. To eschew the necessity of reliving such early hurts is to eliminate the possibility of cure, and there are those who practice what I call "mock Primal Therapy" who have done exactly that—they cannot speak about cure because they have robbed the patient of exactly those experiences which are ultimately resolving and curative. Once that has been done the emphasis must shift to third-line, here-and-now activities. Instead of continually descending into themselves, patients have their defenses (and their neuroses) bolstered and are forever condemned to live in the past while falsely believing that they are living in the present.

What is crucial to understand about consciousness is that it is first and foremost of the *self*, not of political systems, economics, psychological theory, etc. These latter (accurate or not) constitute spheres of awareness; they occupy the areas of false consciousness and may exist quite apart from a person's real consciousness. Thus one can be acutely aware of one's world yet totally unconscious of those forces which impel one's daily behavior in that world. One can therefore be "smart" in an intellectual way yet live a stupid life. True intelligence exists when this kind of awareness and self-consciousness coalesce. You do not "raise" consciousness; you "lower" it.

The dialectic of an expanded consciousness is that as it ramifies it becomes more simplified (not simplistic). This means a more simplified life style—fewer needs, demands, ambitions, and neurotic thoughts.

As a concrete example: one patient was asked to leave the apartment she was sharing with her boyfriend. She felt the Pain of this and then went into feelings of being shoved out of her house and sent away to boarding school by her parents; then finally she descended into a birth Primal in which she was shoved out of the canal only to be left all alone —unwanted and unattended. In a single session she descended the chain of Pain. As she did so, she felt how most of her life was occupied with running from the feeling of being alone and unwanted, how all of her waking thoughts were centered around who she would see or visit.

Her level of consciousness expanded as she felt all of the ways she organized her life so as not to have to feel those feelings of being alone and unwanted. She realized that her mind had been occupied with nothing else. Feeling those feelings simplified her life and her thoughts. So long as she had access to only the second-line feelings she would have been less panicky about being alone but some anxiety would have remained. The amount of anxiety left would have been precisely the amount of anxiety occasioned by the repressed first-line trauma. If there had been no first-line Pain, then feeling the second-line trauma would have meant total resolution of the problem.

When a particular Pain has been repressed we might say in a figurative way that it has been "deadened," because it cannot be felt or experienced; the essence of unconscious behavior is that neurotics act out those deadened areas they cannot feel. For example, being treated harshly very early in life may make the infant shut himself off in order to survive the onslaught. Later he may have an abrupt, harsh manner to his personality—

a manner which developed unconsciously and certainly not out of choice. He is acting out something he cannot feel.

A pipe smoker may spend his adult life sucking on a pipe and never feel his early oral deprivation. The pipe is a symbol. The strength of the "adhesion" to the symbol is a direct result of the amount of Pain involved in the deprivation. One might say that the process of Primal Therapy is one of detaching the neurotic from his symbols by defusing the Pain which has forced the adhesion.

Summary and Conclusions

A scream is primordial. It is one of the first behavioral possibilities for the newborn. He can scream long before he can verbalize his needs, and that scream is the way he articulates his early hurts. It is no wonder that patients who relive preverbal events experience "Primal screams." The patient's response while reliving the trauma is in perfect accord with the development of the brain at the time and the available response alternatives. If the patient in therapy were to try to verbalize the problem he had at the age of one, he would not be reliving (and therefore resolving) the trauma.

The scream, then, is a specific and necessary therapeutic event at certain stages of development, both in life and in therapy. To even try to discuss an early, preverbal trauma (as happens in so many therapies) means to be taken *out* of the feeling and into something counterthera- peutic, away from the possibility of final resolution. In this sense we can understand that at certain stages in Primal Therapy the scream *is* curative; it *is* the connection of the early hurt and it is the only possible expression appropriate to the adequacy of the brain at the time of the trauma. Primal patients who simply wail like infants for weeks in therapy some- times feel as though they are not getting anywhere because they are not making any intellectual connections; the baby cries seem endless. But because of the duration of early trauma, screaming is a necessary experience.

Another crucial contribution of this chapter has to do with negative and positive "reinforcement," to use terms from the study of conditioning of responses. There seem to be certain areas of the brain which process pleasurable feelings and others which process Pain (and mediate nega- tive reinforcement). The pleasurable areas are far more extensive in the brain, which may mean, among other things, that we learn better from the positive approach than from situations involving stress and anxiety. Dr. H. J. Campbell has written a book about this point.*

He reported on studies in Sweden with human subjects who had electrodes placed in certain areas of the limbic system. The point was to alleviate mental suffering and mental abnormality by generating more pleasure in the brain. Stimulation of some limbic areas produced pleasure and a desire for more, while stimulation of other limbic areas produced pain.

The first finding of these electrode studies was how very close together the pain and pleasure areas were in the brain. Furthermore, different kinds of pleasure were experienced depending on the area stimulated. Stimulation of one site was described as "about to produce a memory." Stimulating another caused sexual thoughts and the feeling of an imminent orgasm. Yet another produced a "drunk" feeling and the elimination of annoying thoughts. These feelings were subcortically produced; that is, subcortical factors instantly altered the nature and content of the subject's consciousness—something that has been stressed previously.

These studies are reminiscent of W. Penfield's work with epileptic patients undergoing brain surgery. Stimulation of certain temporal lobe sites did indeed produce memories. Just before a seizure some epileptics report this same feeling of an imminent memory, indicating, perhaps, that some seizures are set off when subcortical Primal circuits are activated.

All this indicates how dependent consciousness is on underlying brain activity. What is even more significant is the fact that the underlying activity is not just transient but may be permanent. Campbell: "There is also a chance that the limbic system may contain reverberating circuits in which activation continues after cessation of input, due to nerve impulses travelling round closed loops of nerve fibers." (page 32) This is almost exactly a point made in *The Anatomy of Mental Illness*.

This surely means that first-, second-, or third-line traumas remain as reverberating circuits to shape later consciousness. It is Campbell's belief, after years of research, that all parts of the brain are subservient to the limbic system because that system is ultimately responsible for survival. This is indirectly Holden's point of view as well.

It is my contention that mental illness occurs when the limbic outflow is shut off from other key areas of the brain, producing nonadaptive behavior that may be counter-survival. Further, full consciousness

---

*H. J. Campbell, *The Pleasure Areas* (Eyre Methuen Publishers, London, 1973).

involves the proper integration of all the three "tubes" of the brain. Some of us seem top-heavy with the social-mental component; others are dominated by subcortical forces which result in impulsive behavior. Consciousness in the Primal sense is an *interconnected* event.

Dr. Holden points out that a memory need not be something verbal— something we have stressed over the years. "Memory" is not necessarily linked with "remember." There are many kinds of memory, and the body registers events in a way which can be considered just as important as recalling an event verbally. Indeed, as I have pointed out previously (*Journal of Primal Therapy*, Volume 1, Number 1), a psychosomatic symptom *is* the transmuted body memory of an early trauma.

One final point about memory. There is controversy over the possibility of the memory of birth trauma. We have seen enough reliving of birth memories in Primals to know with certainty about their existence. But perhaps there is a tendency to forget that the brain is made up of cells and that individual cells themselves have a rudimentary form of memory. In an article on longevity by the former Science Editor of Life Magazine there is the point, "If an embryonic cell strain divides, say, twenty times and then is put into the deep freeze for months or even years, it 'remembers' where it left off. After thawing, it divides another thirty times but no more." * Normal cells have a finite limit to their division; in the strain referred to above it was fifty times. The question is, "After thawing, how did the cells 'know' when to stop dividing?" Do they "remember"? No, but there was a memory. The cell "knew" when to stop and was "aware" of how much division had gone on before. It was an *organismic* memory —the same kind of memory which occurs with birth trauma. What is important is to realize that recalling a memory can be something other than an intellectual description. Once that is accomplished we may be less skeptical about the possible imprinting of traumatic memories at birth and before.

It is our experience that Primal Theory and Primal Therapy are understood and accepted by a person to a degree which depends on the amount of access the person has to his Pain. If a person has no hint of the depths of human feeling, then descriptions of Primal feeling states will not affect him. If he has had severe nightmares he knows the depths of feelings which are possible. The fact that he is asleep during those feelings does not change their existence or their intensity.

---

*Albert Rosenfeld, "The Longevity Seekers," *Saturday Review of Science*, Volume 1, Number 2, February 24, 1973, pages 46-49.

If a person operates only with his third-line consciousness, then he will listen only to facts and statistics and will have to be convinced *about feelings* on that level, which of course is almost impossible—all the facts in the world are never really convincing when it comes to feelings. Nietzsche said it in *Ecce Homo*: "[When] a book speaks of nothing but events that lie altogether beyond the possibility of any frequent or even rare experience—it is the first language for a new series of experiences; in that case simply nothing will be heard, but there will be the acoustic illusion that where nothing is heard, nothing is there."

The aim of Primal Therapy is to produce *a system that develops rather than one which compensates*. On a social level, evolution may be a history of compensatory adjustments rather than of smooth development. It may be that our political system is really an elaborate structure which compensates for an economic system based on profit rather than need. Each new measure passed or social program undertaken compensates for some inadequacy in the fulfillment of need.

It is my belief that Primal people represent a new kind of human being, perhaps the first individuals in thousands of years of human life who can feel and who can grasp the meaning of feeling and its relevance to human existence. It is possible that sometime after recorded history began, "civilized" man lost his feelings and lost his understanding of their existence and their nature. The social structures he has erected have been *around* his feelings rather than out of them. For the first time perhaps in thousands of years of human existence we have found a way back to our feelings and our humanity. We have finally grasped the techniques to make man human again and with that to permit the existence of truly human societies without war, exploitation, mental illness, and crime. We know what the techniques are. The question is: Can a society without consciousness—a society where neurotics are the ruling class—utilize those techniques?

CHAPTER FOUR

The Neurophysiology of Consciousness: The Gating of Pain
E. Michael Holden

Neurosis is a potential option of the human brain. It develops in relation to Painful early experiences in a brain with sufficient organization for neurotic development. Corollaries would be that the intensity of Pain experiences are related in amplitude to the severity of subsequent emotional illness, and that an individual who develops (from birth) in a nearly Painfree environment would not develop neurosis, psychosomatic or other emotional illnesses.

The crux of the Primal formulation is that neurosis, a disorder of feelings, evolves in relation to Painful experiences in infancy and childhood which are causal in splitting the three levels of consciousness, one from the other. This occurs, more or less, depending on the intensity (and developmental age) of one's Painful experiences. Implied in this formulation is that brain mechanisms exist which can and do carry out this gating or blocking function such that limited learning results. The neurophysiologic data supporting the existence of a tripartite consciousness and the systems which gate between these will be discussed. Each of the three brain-body zones is associated with a contribution to the total consciousness of the individual.

The partial consciousness resulting from the blocking operations underlies characteristic behaviors (responses) seen in neurosis. When these neurotic behaviors involve responses in the viscera or body wall then the outward expression of neurosis at those levels of neurobiologic organization produce the disorders otherwise called the psychosomatic illnesses.

This essay discusses the development and physiology of pain appreciation in newborns and infants and the dual system of pain representation in the human brain. The third section contains some verifiable data and some hypotheses regarding the gating of pain at a cerebral (hemispheric) level. The most promising features of the Primal formulation as a path to understanding human mental illness are its origin in observations[2,3] rather than speculations, and the ease with which it generates testable hypotheses for future research.

One approach to the understanding of a proposed therapy for mental illness is to ask if it is consistent with the information available regarding the maturation and physiology of the human brain. The premise for such an approach is that mind and behavior are products of brain function in a strict biologic sense. Another asserts that mind and behavior can be analyzed in isolation, separate from neurobiology, seeking to define laws of behavior. My premise is that, strictly speaking, there are no "laws of behavior" per se, only neurophysiologic principles, with external manifestations sometimes mistaken for natural law. Behavior is mediated by brain action via the body itself (the action system which does the behaving). Observing behavior discloses that its organization is not random but is patterned and orderly, often in predictable ways. Many who have studied behavior are familiar with its patterning but have overlooked that they observe a derivative or product of brain activity, mediated by the body, and have mistakenly expressed the lawfulness of these behavioral derivatives as if they themselves were articles of biologic, natural law. Such an approach is limited by the investigator's failure to attend to the brain, rather than to products of its activity.

The essay which follows is in support of the hypothesis that the Primal formulation[2,3] is congruent with information regarding brain maturation and brain function. For that reason the Primal position is more valid than psychological formulations regarding "mind" as a phenomena which can be understood by observing behavior alone.

Neuroembryologic Maturation and the Primal Formulation

Dr. Janov has proposed that neurosis is a process which may start in early infancy, even at or before birth.

To be true, such an assertion must be consistent with the maturational sequence of the human brain. Dr. Janov proposes that psychic or physical pain has obligatory causality in the genesis of neurosis and that a child during its own birth can register the pain and hazards which may occur at that time. One must ask then whether the brain of a full term fetus is mature enough to integrate and register pain at this relatively early state of maturation.

Dr. Yakovlev has discussed brain maturation in detail.[1] The white fatty covering of nerves is called myelin, and the process by which they obtain this myelin sheath is termed myelination. The speed with which nerves can conduct their impulses is a function of this myelin sheath. Myelinated nerves conduct impulses more rapidly than unmyelinated ones. Thus the *sequence* or *pattern* of myelination is a reliable index of brain *maturation*. The brain is organized in three concentric layers, an inner *matrix* zone which is never well myelinated, a middle *mantle* zone, which is next to myelinate and an outer *marginal* zone which myelinates last.

"The progressive myelination of the neuraxis (nervous system) is the most readily observable morphological criterion of maturation . . . In the central nervous system, myelination until term is confined almost exclusively to the fiber systems of the mantle (nuclear) zone in the wall of the neuraxis; . . . It spreads from within out, toward the marginal zone, but the fiber systems which develop in this outermost or cortical zone of the neuraxis, or are derived from this zone, do not begin to myelinate until the end of gestation is reached and the infant is about to face extrauterine life." ([1], p. 16–17) (brackets, mine). Dr. Yakovlev and others have discussed the maturational principle that the human brain and body mature from within, outwards,[4] a principle of significance and relevance to the Primal formulation. Formally speaking, the "anabolic visceration" (Activities of the viscera in which the body's energy stores are increased) capability of the newborn child is mediated by the inner neuropil of the brain and this integrates a set of behavioral options which are fully adequate at birth. ("Neuropil" is the formal term for the dense feltwork of nerve *fibers* in the brain. Each neuropil (inner, intermediate and outer) tends to function as an integral unit.) Were it not so, (inner brain adequacy at birth) newborns would not survive. Anoxia at birth, congenital defects and birth trauma are only several of numerous factors operating, in relation to human birth, which often do interfere with survival. Here we are considering those who do survive. Thus, at term, the inner brain is mature enough to mediate visceral responses and the central nervous system is myelinated in the mantle zone. Does the mantle zone of the brain contain a system of fibers which can register pain? One may answer this question in the affirmative from information presented in the early 1950's from neurophysiologic studies by French and coworkers[6,7,8] which were presented in papers documenting the presence of two pain systems in the brain: a classical, laterally placed one, and a medial (middle) one in the reticular core of the neuraxis. Furthermore, it was shown[8] that the medial, reticular system formed a neurophysiologic basis for the anesthetic state. It is this system which is the most susceptible to general anesthetics.[8]

Recent studies[9] cited by Hilgard[10] that electrical stimulation of cells surrounding the middle of the midbrain (upper brainstem) *abolishes reactions to pain* for the duration of the stimulation (in cats). Also, "these (periaqueductual) cells have been shown to be exquisitely sensitive to morphine and are believed to be the biochemical receptors for this analgesic."[10] The existence of a gate to pain from the periphery, in the middle of the midbrain is supported by the above, and together with other studies cited later[8,16,22] suggest that this region is part of the gating *system* between first and second line components of consciousness.

Considering the above, it may be argued that even the brain of a new-born child is mature enough to transmit and register pain, along the course of a medial reticular pain system. These registrations are transmitted into a forebrain which shows myelination in large portions of the subcortical brain (within the mantle zone, embryologically).

The pattern of subsequent myelination in the cortex, post-natally, shown by the work of Flechsig (cited and discussed by Yakovlev[1], p. 17-32) is relevant in support of the Primal formulation. As a generalization it is true that the brain becomes myelinated from within outwards, but there is also a pattern or sequence of myelination *in the cerebral cortex*, postnatally. "On the basis of his epoch-making studies of the time of appearance of stainable myelin in the white matter of the cerebral hemispheres and in the cortex, Flechsig divided the cortical plate into some forty-five myelogenetic fields (parts of the cortex being myelinated) and numbered them in the order of their progressive myelination."[1] (brackets mine) Three groups of cells acquire myelin on their fibers sequentially over time and Flechsig labeled them the "primordial," "intermediate" and "terminal" myelogenetic fields. The numbers assigned (1-45) indicate *when regions become myelinated* in a sequence, over time. The first cortical region to myelinate is in the precentral gyrus. The second area myelinated is the rhinic lobe (inner brain zone; fibers connecting the temporal lobe with the orbito-frontal regions). Of considerable interest is that primary sensory receptive cortical areas are the next to myelinate in the brain's maturational sequence, and are assigned the numbers three through ten. By the age of six months of postnatal life[1] there is prominent myelination in the cortical areas receiving the sensory data of touch and somesthetic sense (3,6), vision (8) and hearing (10). Of interest is the early myelination medially in the inner "ring" of rhinic lobe cortex (2,5,9). The limbic (middle brain zone) cortex is myelinated next (12,14,20,30), with subsequent myelination spreading out of these primary and medial zones into the zones of secondary association cortex.

Thus even as early as birth to six months of age we are considering a brain with morphological evidence of maturity regarding the reception of primary sensory modalities. The significance of the sensory input is learned later with further maturation, and concomitant myelination in the secondary cortical areas. If now we consider the "adequacy" of stimuli imposed upon a newborn or infant child, one may recall that Sir Charles Sherrington observed pain to be the most adequate of stimuli in terms of a neurologically mediated response to sensory input. Common sense and the events of everyday life tell us pain is the most adequate of stimuli to elicit responses for action, but this relationship has also been well documented repeatedly in neurophysiologic studies of humans and other vertebrates. Thus we need not doubt on maturational grounds that the nervous system of a newborn or infant child can receive, transmit and register pain, as an available behavioral option.

The difficulty of relieving severe physical pain with neurosurgical ablations and sections, and preservation of deep pain even with large brain lesions (areas of damaged nerves) make it clear that pain awareness is one of the major functions of the vertebrate brain, upon which survival of individuals and species may be contingent. Whether at a purely reflexive level or a considered symbolic voluntary level, the responses to pain have very high (the highest) priority for all creatures. One of the brain's major functions is to integrate the stimuli from within the body and body wall with the stimuli from extrapersonal space. Attending to pain stimuli within, on (body wall) and outside the body makes major contributions to the total consciousness. *These physiologic and evolutionary facts generate the hypothesis that human consciousness concerns itself primarily with reactivity to pain.* This doesn't deny the importance of our symbolic and intellectual capabilities but we have *lower thresholds to pain stimuli than to all other modalities of stimuli* and this emphasizes for our consideration the *pre-eminence of reactivity to pain as the major component of human consciousness.*

Maturation of Physiologic Reactivity to Pain in Infancy

Peiper's text[12] discusses the development of reactivity to pain stimuli in newborn and infant children, providing direct observational data pertinent to the present discussion. Responses to intermittent or constant pain stimuli (pin, clothespin) by infants has been studied by several authors (cited in [12]). The minimal response to a local pain stimulus in newborn and infant children is "motor restlessness, which usually starts in the irritated body part but which may involve the whole body. This motor restlessness ceases only when the irritated skin area is inadvertently removed from the pin point."[12] Constant noxious stimulation was effected by pinching skin with clothespins. "Exactly as observed with the previously described stimuli, the simplest response of the infant consists of more pronounced movements of the irritated limb."

There are several important principles illustrated by such studies of pain in newborns and infants:

1. Painful stimuli even in newborns lead to a motor response which is greatest in the painfully stimulated body part;

2. The responses, even by newborns, are appropriate to the stimulus: if a clothespin is attached to the face it is often reached (and removed) by a hand; and

3. The painful stimuli eliciting (albeit clumsy) motor responses were, in a larger perspective, only slightly noxious (compared with extreme hunger, almost choking to death, etc.). Yet, even such slightly noxious pain stimuli (involving small parts of the skin surface) were adequate to elicit appropriate motor responses.

Concerning the maturation of pain stimulus adequacy to elicit a response, Czerny[13] studied the relationship between chronologic age and the sensitivity to primary induction (electric) currents in children one day old to six years of age. He found that chronologic maturation is associated with an increased reactivity to electric current; or viewed conversely, the reactive threshold to electric current falls as a child matures. A six-year-old can recognize and avoid a stimulus with ⅛ th the current amplitude recognized and avoided by a one-day-old child. Considering this progression it should be kept in mind that the testing surface is the skin, the interface between a child and the outside world, not the viscera. *Visceral reactivity is already quite mature at birth* and total body responses to visceral discomfort occur even in premature newborns (re hunger, the need to be burped, thirst, or visceral pain of any sort).

Chronological Age and Sensitivity to Primary Induction Currents

Age of Child	Smallest Current Strength Which Elicits Recognizable Responses Milliamps
1 day	400
6 days	300
11 days	300
17 days	300
23 days	250
3 months	250
9 months	250
2 years	200
3 years	150
4¾ years	150
6 years	50
6 years	50

As emphasized previously,[26] maturity of visceral (midline) reactivity and anabolic visceration[4] at birth argues forcibly that reactivity to pain in infancy is largely confined to this system. This predicts that pain at birth or early infancy will later be manifest by symptoms in the viscera, the midline of the body, integrated by the hypothalamus and median zone (inner neuropil[5]) of the brain. These visceral or first line symptoms form the majority in the psychosomatic illnesses. Examples are neurotic rhinorrhea, globus hystericus, asthma, duodenal ulcer, some forms of cardiac arrhythmia, ulcerative colitis, sexual frigidity or psychic impotence. These first line symptoms are different *in kind* from tension headaches, backaches, and neurotic low back pain (second line), integrated by the intermediate neuropil[5] (maturing later), and also different from delusions, paranoia and phobias (third line) symptoms integrated still later, by the cortex or superficial neuropil.[5]

"Wolowick similarly tested the influence of food intake on the sensitivity of the infant; he measured the threshold to (galvanic) electric current before and during feedings. It was found that the infant became significantly less sensitive during breast or bottle feeding so that considerably stronger currents were needed to elicit a response to the electrical stimulus." ([14], cited in [12]) The observation that feeding a hungry infant produces a calming effect, behaviorally, is a commonplace one. It is not so generally known that pain threshold rises during feeding. The quantity of pain a child integrates is related to need fulfillment for visceral homeostatic needs, and for social-interactional needs. (Provence and Lipton[15] and many other authors have documented the delayed and impaired maturation of mind and body in children whose visceral needs were largely met but whose social-interactional needs were not met.) An increased reactivity to pain, in the face of incomplete need fulfillment in infancy, with subsequent mental and physical illness resulting, supports the Primal formulation which proposes that pain is the causal *raison d'etre* for subsequent mental illness. Dr. Peiper included in his summary, "The pain sense is well developed in the newborn. The reactions have the purpose of withdrawing the irritated skin area from the stimulus. The newborn is very sensitive to tactile and pressure stimuli. A series of reactions characteristic of infancy, such as sucking movements and the tonic palmar and plantar grasp reflexes are elicited in this manner."[12]

The reactivity to pain is a widely and early represented component of human brain function. The myelination studies of Flechsig cited earlier suggest that in normal children at birth the cerebral hemispheres participate in reactions to pain. *However, the reactivity to pain is so extensively represented, even in the lower neuraxis, that virtually all the responses which can be elicited in normal newborns have been observed in newborn children without cerebral hemispheres (anencephalic children,* several references cited in [12], p. 93). This again emphasizes the maturational capability newborns and infants have to react to pain. These reactions are largely confined to the viscera, and registration of insult therein leads to first-line symptoms later. When people are stressed in adulthood, those with painful birth or painfilled infancies will inilude visceral dysfunction in the reaction to stress. This dysfunction reflects obligatory learning of maladaptive visceromotor reactivity in relation to a painful infancy.

It doesn't meet a man's total needs to develop a duodenal ulcer when stressed, but his visceral (first-line) consciousness is so effectively gated from his full awareness that the ulcer may develop despite milk, buffers and tranquilizers. The inaccessibility is well known, and argues for the effectiveness of the gating mechanisms separating the first-line consciousness from the second and third lines. Only a therapy which can change the gating (downward, lower gates) would be expected to truly relieve visceral symptoms of a neurotic first-line consciousness. The accessibility of the first-line symptoms to Primal Therapy is now well documented,[3] and is most physiologically evident by the lowering of pulse, blood pressure and body temperature which occurs (permanently) after Primal Therapy to values more typically seen in children, and by the EEG changes (lower amplitude and EEG power) which also occur during and after Primal Therapy. The initial study of vital signs and EEG changes has been repeated and confirmed[27] for an additional 24 patients.

It is proposed that these physiologic changes serve as the criteria for the non-neurotic state, since behavioral observations alone are (notoriously and) characteristically unreliable as an index of improvement or cure.

In 1965 Melzack and Wall proposed the gate control theory of pain (cited in [16]) which asserts that the pain threshold is not fixed, but is variable. Depending on the nature of the stimulus one may be more, or less, aware of the pain. This model was first proposed in relation to small and larger nerves entering the spinal cord. More recently, Dr. Melzack has emphasized that a gating system exists in the midbrain, activation of which diminishes awareness of pain inputs from the spinal cord (16). It is quite probable that at least one other gating system exists in the cerebral hemispheres as well; (discussed in the next section). The point to emphasize here is that the *phenomena observed in Primal Therapy provide strong support for the gate control theory of pain*. The fact that neurotics in everyday life often function, virtually unaware of early life pain, argues strongly for effective gating systems in the brain. More specifically, when patients in Primal Therapy have *bruises reoccur*, in association with Primals concerning physical trauma at birth or in child-hood, then clearly, gating systems are operating. Similarly, when a Primal patient re-experiences tonsillectomy in a Primal, and has an inflamed bloody pharynx, some form of gating was previously holding back that response in a potential or latent form. Viewed conversely, *before* such bruises or traumas are re-experienced, *where are they*? and how are they *coded* into cells? Primal therapy phenomena such as these argue persuasively for consciousness at the *individual cellular level*, and for powerful gating systems, which in neurosis, keep us virtually unaware of that consciousness. *Primal therapy* is not a "psychotherapy" but *a psychophysiological one*, with access to even cellular registrations of past pains. During a Primal, the *gates* to Pain are lowered markedly giving one *access* to ancient memories, from infancy or birth. One additional point about *gating of pain* is that it appears to be an almost unique example in biological systems of a *positive-feedback system*. Whereas biochemical products, enzyme concentrations, metabolic rate, hormone levels, etc. operate on the principle of *negative* feedback, gating of pain *increases* with the intensity of pain, and *decreases* if the pain intensity decreases. It is, by analogy, as if a dam rose automatically as the water level behind it rose. The overwhelmingly painful stimulus leads to loss of consciousness, the ultimate in gating, short of death itself. Gating operates in neurosis to keep us mercifully unaware of pain from the past.

During a Primal, awareness of a past pain becomes total, and gating is transiently ineffective. Another circumstance, in neurotics which will render gating ineffective, is the abrupt withdrawal of a "pain-killing" analgesic drug. In the rebound phase (withdrawal) one is literally overwhelmed by Primal Pain. The result can be psychosis with extremely high blood pressure and pulse rate. If withdrawal from narcotics occurs in the context of Primal therapy, then one may "plunge" into very early Pain in a first-line Primal. Either way, there is a transient marked decrease in the gating of old Pain. Similarly, whenever one is overwhelmed by the *need to cry*, as when a family member dies, or in a very "emotional" movie, these moments of *access to Pain* occur during transient *decreases* in the *gating* of Pain. One could nearly define neurosis in these terms: *one is neurotic when effectively gated from the severe pains of infancy and childhood.* Primal therapy is an effective cure for neurosis because it decreases the gating of pain in neurotics.

The access to first-line consciousness is one of the major contributions of Primal Therapy to psychiatry. This access means there is no exchange of one symptom for another as so commonly occurs in other therapies. If the registration of infancy pain occurs in the visceral motility integrated by the hypothalamus, then the *source* of the illness resides *there*, not in the second or third lines of consciousness (to which conventional and conditioning therapies have access). It serves no purpose to exchange symbols (in the third line) if the metabolic and physiologic parameters of neuroses are integrated in the first line.

Reactivity to all stimuli is represented and re-represented at multiple levels in the nervous system, and it is generally known that compared with adult sensory reactivity, that of an infant is primitive by comparison. However, the studies cited above document that a newborn human (with mature visceral reactivity) has a nervous system mature enough to react to sensory stimuli, the most adequate of which are pain stimuli. A recent article[25] has provided further evidence of sophisticated responses even in newborns to environmental stimuli. Data was presented documenting a remarkable synchronization between adult speech and the movements of babies hearing that speech. The synchrony was observed with several languages but not with arrhythmic nonsense syllables. Not only does this seem relevant to an infant's learning about speech but literally to learning to move in a human way. (Further implied is possible movement dysfunction in later life—clumsiness, awkwardness—if the auditory input to an infant is jerky, too fast or arrhythmic.)

A Dual Pain System in a Tripartite Consciousness

A brief consideration of the neurology of pain will serve as a basis to later discuss its role in the genesis of neurosis.

Both clinical and neurophysiologic observations during the last fifty years have demonstrated that the appreciation of pain is doubly represented in the mammalian nervous system. The pioneering work of Henry Head (cited in [16]), who sectioned his own superficial radial nerve and studied the qualities of sensory stimuli during nerve regeneration, led him to postulate two systems of fibers mediating two different varieties of pain experience; protopathic pain and epicritic pain sense, is a valid one. Examples from clinical neurology will be cited later. Subsequent neurophysiologic studies have confirmed Head's impression with little need to modify his postulate. The dual pain system has been comprehensively discussed in a recent text ([16], Sec. V). The integration and appreciation of pain is not completely understood but much is known about this modality of sensation. Specific pain receptors have never been convincingly demonstrated. The conclusion that pain appreciation starts at "free nerve endings" may well be true but it is interesting to realize that "free nerve endings" per se have not been demonstrated. ([16], p. 121) The sufficient stimulus to appreciate pain appears to be the destruction or mechanical distortion of body tissues. Tissue destruction is apparently reversible with some stimuli such as hypoglycemia (low blood sugar) or ischemia (inadequate blood flow with decreased oxygen available), but if prolonged leads to cellular death. Pain travels on fibers of large (A-delta) and smaller (C) diameter. These fibers convey different pain qualities[16] but, as will be considered later, the resultant pain appreciation results from an interaction of these two qualities within the central nervous system. Both A-delta and C fibers are scarcely if at all myelinated, *emphasizing that pain appreciation is an ancient and general function in the vertebrate nervous system*, and, we believe, its major function. This is in contrast to the well-myelinated, rapidly conducting, even larger fibers mediating joint position sense and vibration, a phylogenetically newer function. Collins, et al (cited in [16]) "have demonstrated by stimulating exposed peripheral cutaneous nerves in human subjects that stimulation of large fibers produced no pain; stimulation of delta fibers resulted in a sharp, pricking bearable pain, but that unbearable pain was elicited by the stimulations of C fibers." The distribution of fibers mediating unbearable pain is relevant to the Primal formulation and is considered in some detail below. Anterolateral in the spinal cord are the nerve pathways which carry pain information; the *lateral* spinothalamic tract. "Full transection of these pathways always result in loss of pain and temperature sensations on the contralateral (opposite) side, temporarily at least. It has also been shown by direct electrical stimulation of the anterolateral columns in man that *approximately 54% of the fibers carry nociceptive (pain) information* while the remainder are divided between perceptions of warmth (37%)and cold (9%)." (White, et al, cited in [16]) (Brackets mine)

An important paper by Mark, Ervin and Yakovlev[17] documented that stereotactic destruction of the *ventrobasal* (posterior, inferior and laterally located) thalamic nuclei could virtually eliminate the sensation of pinprick on the opposite side of the body *but did not relieve pain* (of cancerous origin). In contrast, the stereotactic destruction of the more medial intralaminar and centrum medianum nuclei was associated with two months of gratifying pain relief *without* sensory loss to pinprick. Thus was created a sensibility which allowed for accurate pinprick localization on the opposite side of the body, together with a brain state which permitted no appreciation of pain (from laryngeal cancer). Even at the level of the thalamus there is (anatomic and physiologic) segregation of protopathic (suffering) and epicritic (discriminative, non-suffering) sensations.

The principle emerges that unbearable agonizing pain sense travels medially in the nervous system. This same paper made a further contribution to understanding the appreciation of unbearable pain by reporting an individual with tongue cancer who underwent surgical destruction of the dorsomedial (upper, midline) nucleus of the thalamus. "This man had a cancer of the tongue with pain in his right jaw, tongue, mouth and side of neck. The major lesion was placed in the dorsal medial nucleus of the thalamus and included and extended into the anterio ventral nucleus of the thalamus. This lesion did not produce a sensory loss or any diminution in the patient's pain. *This man did not, however, mind his pain.* In distinction to the other cancer patients with thalamic lesions who had relief of pain without a relief of suffering, this man's suffering was diminished without obvious pain relief"[17] (italics above, mine). To appreciate the *fact of pain without "minding"* it is analogous to a commentary on the gating of pain; in this example, between the second-line body-feeling component of consciousness and the third-line full comprehension component of consciousness. In a Primal context, this man had a stimulus which normally creates suffering but he did not suffer after the dorso-

medial thalamic lesion. He was *unable to feel*. This is an organic counter-part to the brain state of neurotics; who also *can't feel*. Physiologically, without surgery, a similar gating may be produced with hypnosis. (see [10])
Thus it may be argued that the gating system between the second and third lines of consciousness, between knowledge of pain and suffering with it, includes the dorsal-medial nucleus of the thalamus. This gate can be raised under hypnosis (see [10]) and maximally *closed* with dorsomedial nucleus destruction.

In principle then one may be consciously unaware at the highest level, of body suffering integrated by the subcortical portions of the nervous system. In the Primal context one can be in pain and unaware of it, as long as the gating (in other contexts, defense) exists between the second and third line components of consciousness.

The discussion of the paper[17] presented to the American Neurological Association in 1961 contained several points directly pertinent to this essay and is partially quoted below. Dr. Mark commented, ". . . Stimula-tion of the medial ventral thalamus with the large electrode (in awake alert patients) produced quite a different response than stimulation of the lateral part of the thalamus (associated with stimulation of the sensory nuclei of the thalamus). The stimulation laterally produced a sensation of pins and needles or electric shock-like sensation. Stimulation medial to the ventral posterior medial nucleus of the thalamus, or in one case in the reticular formation of the midbrain; produced a sensation described as 'absolutely terrible' but it couldn't be defined in any specific modality of feeling" (such as warmth, cold, vibration, touch, etc.) (Brackets mine)

The principle emerges that feelings without specific type or content are represented medially in the nervous system, whereas "words about feel-ings" we learn about even into middle life; but *the feelings themselves are integrated from the time of conception onward.* Phylogenetically in evolution and ontogenetically in personal development, we experience feelings years before we develop a symbol system to describe them. *Psychotherapies which deal only with the words about feelings are deal-ing with a symbolic, derived, recently acquired component of brain func-tion, not with the spontaneous, intrinsic brain states called feelings.*

Emotional illness quite obviously is characterized largely by repression of feeling states, states which can exist even in the absence of words which seek to describe them. A therapy for emotional illness, to be effec-tive, must deal with disordered feelings themselves, not with symbolic representations of the disordered feelings. Primal Therapy concerns itself exclusively with disordered feelings. Not unexpectedly, the dual system of pain is cortically represented as well as being evident in the nerves of and below the thalamus. Epicritic pain is projected to the parietal cortex. Lesions in this region, as typically seen in some stroke patients, produce numbness to individual pinprick stimuli on the opposite side of the body. Such patients still can and do suffer, and experience deep unbearable pain on the side of the body affected. This again demonstrates that discriminative pain sense is represented separately from awareness of suffering. The medial system of pain sensibility, represented in the midline thalamic nuclei, is projected forward, largely via the dorsomedial thalamic nucleus, to the orbitofrontal cortex. Lesions in this medial system such as stroke, with destruction of the dorsomedial nucleus, glial tumors of the anterior corpus callosum or frontal pole, or the surgical lesions of orbital undercutting, frontal leukotomy or lobotomy, all produce a change in the response to suffering. Dr. Yakovlev has stated[17]: "Dr. Mark, Dr. Ervin and I were inclined to think that the laterally placed lesions in the thalamus tend to reduce or abolish the public component of a stressful experience, 'the epicritic pain,' conducted through space committed channels of general sensory input. The more medially placed lesions seem to reduce this epicritic component but not the protopathic component of distress (the personal, private component); and the medial-most lesions, if placed rostrally (anterior) in the thalamus, seem to produce the effects comparable to those of frontal leucotomy or anterior thalamotomy" (no suffering, not minding the pain). (Brackets mine)

Suffering, a spontaneous feeling state in relation to pain, is topographically represented in the anterior thalamic projection to the orbitofrontal cortex. The entire frontal lobe, brain anterior to the Rolandic fissure, concerns itself with the final integration of motor responses to stimuli from the body or from extrapersonal space.[4,18] The anterior horn cells of the spinal cord are the "final common pathway"[13] for the body, the action system, but these cells respond to the selections of the frontal (motor) cortex. For any particular stimulus we have a *potential* option to make almost any motor response, but in fact we do not; we make highly selected, *particular* responses from a group of possible ones. Applied to neurosis, one wonders why neurotic people often make (selected) maladaptive responses which often work to their own detriment. In response to frustrating circumstances, some people raise their blood pressure, some increase their gastric acid secretion, some get depressed, some develop migraine or asthma, etc., etc. Why are maladaptive, *substitutive* responses made? How is it that one can feel one way and respond as if feeling another? It seems nearly certain that physical and psychic pain, and the suffering experienced in relation to these, represent the causal basis for the maladaptive responses seen in neurotic people, the major postulate of the Primal formulation,[2,3] based on observations of patients during Primal Therapy.

The Gating of Pain

Dr. Janov has noted the operational similarities between neurosis and hypnosis in several publications.[2,3,20] Quite recently, Dr. E. R. Hilgard published a very interesting paper concerned with the double consciousness observable when deeply hypnotized individuals are exposed to pain stimuli.[10] He observed that the pain of circulating ice water on one hand and arm could be reported as painful by automatic writing with the other hand at a time when there were no outward signs of distress, and for which there was no post-hypnotic memory. Here then is a well-studied clinical situation in which *a person can feel one way and act as if feeling another*. "In the normal non-hypnotic state, she found the experience of the circulating ice water very painful and distressing. In the hypnotic analgesic state, she reported that she felt no pain and was totally unaware of her hand in the ice water; she was calm throughout. All the while that she was insisting verbally that she felt no pain in hypnotic analgesia, the dissociated part of herself was reporting through automatic writing that she felt the pain just as in *the normal non-hypnotic state*." These patients were also unaware of their *visceral* responses to the ice water while hypnotized.

In the practice of clinical neurology one sees some patients with unbearable pain. The "small-nerve" neuropathies of diabetes, leprosy and collagen vasculitis, phantom limb pain, the pain of causalgia, and the spontaneous pain of the "thalamic syndrome" of Dejerine and Roussy are examples of clinical disorders with unbearable pain. In such pain syndromes the lightest tactile stimulus, especially a moving or summated one, on the skin of the involved region suffices to markedly worsen the pain experienced. Has "touch" become "sharp"? No, touch has become very very *unpleasant*. In patients with protopathic pain, there are individual differences along a spectrum from incapacitated, in agony, to stoic and sullen. Similarly, in everyday life there are examples of severe pain stimuli with a wide variation in pain experience and the outward expression of that experience. A skier who skis home with a fractured leg after a fall, apparently unaware of the fracture until his return to the lodge, a soldier wounded in battle who fights on as if not seriously hurt, a patient having teeth extracted with loud white noise received through earphones oblivious of discomfort, the "bearable" labor pains of a woman attending to her respirations (LaMaze method) are some examples of the gating of pain in common experience.

In 1965 Melzack and Wall[20] proposed the gate control theory of pain, a theory which seems valid in the light of subsequent studies utilizing the gating principle to alleviate severe pain syndromes. The gate control theory and its applications has recently been reviewed by Melzack ([16], pp. 153-165). Relevant to this essay is the idea that gating of stimuli occurs *centrally* as well as at the level of (the substantia gelatinosa in) the spinal cord. The observations of Wolowick[14] and Hilgard,[10] cited earlier, provide elegant examples of pain gating in the telencephalon. Another example of gating is seen in some individuals with temporal lobe epilepsy who demonstrate a capacity to carry out complex "high level" behaviors *for which they have no recall*, after the seizure. Cleaning a house, writing a prescription, driving a car, cooking a dinner, are some behaviors reported to this author by family members witnessing patients during temporal lobe seizure episodes. Walking and talking in one's sleep, *for which the participants have no recall*, also represent a type of gating. The relevance of gating to neurosis is the common denominator of a selective awareness with a less-than-fully conscious capacity to make verbal and motor responses. High-level, fairly sophisticated responses for which one later has no recall probably demonstrate a gating operation between the second and third-line components of consciousness. The impulse to respond and the responses actually made (by the body, the action system) are gated from the knowledge of their motive or rationale. In this example gating occurs *during* and presumably in *causal relation to*, an epileptic discharge. Psychomotor epilepsy of the sort cited, with "automatic" responses, occurs with focal discharges. With wider spread of the discharge, leading to a major motor seizure, "automatic" high-level responses are no longer witnessed . . . or possible. Apparently some patterns of focal epileptic discharge, clinically producing psychomotor epilepsy, are capable of biasing the gating system (toward a closed gate) between the second- and third-line components of consciousness. This leads to behaviors which have in common the descriptions: "for which there is no recall." The *localization* of such phenomena is strongly suggested by the studies reported in 1954 by Penfield and Jasper[27]: "Attacks of automatism and subsequent amnesia most often result from a deep sylvian (above and deep to, the temporal lobe) discharge in either hemisphere. The discharge, producing temporal automatism, is usually, perhaps always, in the gray matter of the periamygdaloid region and the circuminsular gutter, (anteriorly, on the inner side of the temporal lobe). This area is bounded by 1. the insula, 2. the auditory gyrus of Heschl, 3. the superior surface of the temporal lobe and 4. uncus." (Brackets mine) Also, these authors make a comment which is relevant to the idea of a gating system operating during automatism with amnesia. "Discharge there does interfere with memory recording and does produce the interference with conscious processes that characterizes automatism. The explanation may well be that this area of cortex is in closer functional relationship with a more distant mechanism, the integrity of which is essential to understanding and to memory recording."[27]*

Does a hard-working executive who finally develops a duodenal ulcer fully comprehend why he works so hard? Do people fully comprehend their attacks of asthma or migraine or stuttering? The answer appears to be that they do not (else the symptoms would not occur), and these phenomena also reflect a variety of gating at a cerebral level.

At present, the exact mechanisms subserving cerebral gating are unknown, but there is some information available. If we consider gating at the lowest level demonstrable in the neuraxis it appears to reside in the dorsolateral gray (substantia gelatinosa) (of the spinal cord and brainstem). Here, the activity ratios of large and small fibers appear to interact in a way which raises or lowers the pain threshold, as originally described by Melzack and Wall.[20] The first (line) gating system then is a column of cells and synapses (junctions between nerves) which can raise or lower the pain threshold between the nervous system and the external environment. Considering the next higher level of gating, the influence of the central area in the reticular formation on the lower gate, Dr. Melzack has written[16]: "Prolonged abnormal activity could also occur at more central levels, which would maintain a continuous descending influence on the spinal gate. Thus, the central (tegmental) area of the reticular formation appears to exert a tonic descending inhibitory influence: stimulation of the area *decreases* the size of cutaneous receptive fields of cells in the spinocervical tract (Taub, cited in [16]). Lesions of the area which would remove inhibition produce hyperaesthesia and hyperalgesia (lowered threshold to pain) in cats. It is conceivable, then, that abnormal

---

* Dr. Penfield adds the footnote, "It may be hypothecated that this periamygdaloid area of gray matter constitutes an essential link between the ganglionic patterns of memory in the temporal cortex and that portion of the centrencephalic system which is devoted to recording of present experience."[27]

reticular activity could reduce the level (or change the pattern) of descending inhibition, thereby opening the gate, and provide the basis for hyperalgesia and hyperaesthesia (increased sensitivity to touch and pin)" (Melzack, et al, cited in [16]) (brackets mine).

Suggesting strongly that the medial reticular formation is in fact the locus of a second gate (between the first line, and the second lines above) are the observations of French, Verzeano and Magoun[7] who showed that intrinsic to the reticular formation, in the pons and midbrain, close to the midline, are cells which demonstrate the unusual neurophysiologic principle of "occlusion." In that paper they demonstrated neurophysiologically the existence of two sensory systems and noted the different properties of each system. They delivered shock stimuli (5 volts, 1 msec) to the divided end of a sciatic nerve (in monkeys) and delivered auditory stimuli (1 msec) to the ears of their experimental animals, and recorded from numerous cortical areas (including the primary auditory receptive cortex) and relevant subcortical sites. "The present study confirms earlier findings in showing that upon peripheral afferent (incoming) stimulation ascending impulses are conveyed to the cortex both in classic sensory paths and through the length of the more central portion of the brain stem. When two stimuli were delivered in rapid succession to different sources, further indications for the lack of segregation of modalities (touch and hearing) in the medial brain stem became apparent. Medially, when the electrodes were placed so as to record potentials from both stimuli, an auditory response was found to be completely eliminated when it followed a sciatic potential by thirteen msec and was markedly attenuated when it succeeded the initial pulse by as long as half a second."[7] This phenomenon, one stimulus blocking another, is the opposite of facilitation, is like the production of a very long refractory period in a cell network, and is a good example of gating at a brainstem level (brackets, mine).

In a brilliant and comprehensive review of the neurophysiology of attention[21] Dr. R. Hernandez-Peon has gathered data and information which strongly supports the idea of a sensory gating function residing in the rostral pons and midbrain. Not only gating of sensory information from the neuraxis below this site but a *gating* contribution to all cerebral sensory analysis including memory, emotions and motivation is discussed. The general principle emerges that the midbrain reticular formation in its reciprocal relationships with neocortex and limbic system serves the strategic function of directing or focusing attention on *particular* sensory inputs, while diminishing attention to irrelevant sensory inputs. The focusing of attention is documented not only by behavioral

criteria but also by electro-physiologic data documenting selective en-
hancement or inhibition of neuronal activity as the basis for directed
attention. Also discussed are some of the biochemical neurotransmitter
substances subserving general vigilance contrasted to those subserving
focused attention. ([21], pp. 173-4). The older concept of the brainstem
reticular formation as simply an alerting system with arousal and hypno-
genic (sleep-inducing) components has been updated in this review,
with the demonstration of its role in the mechanisms of selective attention.
Directly pertinent to the present essay is the discussion[21] of distraction
(especially from pain stimuli) ([21], pp. 159-167). These data argue persuasively for the existence of a second line gating system.

Also, supporting Dr. Janov's assertion that REM sleep is a phenomenon
of second-line consciousness[22] is the demonstration by Hernandez-Peon
that a midbrain gating function can be electrophysiologically demonstrated during REM sleep. ([21], p. 160-3).

This paper[21] provides further support for a system which can perform
a gating function to pain in the midbrain. This second gate appears to
exert a selective influence over information coming to consciousness from
spinal cord inputs. As such it does not gate between peripheral nerves
and the central nervous system. It gates between the spinal cord, medulla
and pons below, and the nervous system above the midbrain. If some
sensory stimuli do not reach the basal ganglia, anterior limbic system of
neocortex, then the midbrain gating system may be postulated to separate
first-line (visceral awareness) consciousness from the second- and third-
line components of consciousness, integrated more rostrally (above).

Before considering the probable locus of the third gate, still higher in
the neuraxis, reference should be made to the *morphine phenomenon*
which vividly illustrates the existence of the third gate and further, suggests that the gates found by electro-physiologic techniques have a biochemical basis, each perhaps with its own neurotransmitter.

"The sudden onset of crushing chest pain" is a grim familiarity in
clinical medicine. In seconds the once-tranquil man is gasping for air,
soaked in sweat, in agony, flexed, writhing, moaning, hurting so much
there are no words to adequately describe his experience. Then, with
fifteen milligrams of morphine given intravenously, in less than a minute,
the hell is leaving. In several minutes the face and body relax, the
breathing becomes deep and regular, the eyes close and the transforma-
tion is complete. One asks, "Are you in pain?"; he answers, "Yes, but it
doesn't bother me . . ." The knowledge of pain (cognito) (third line)
remains but the suffering (dolor) (first and second lines) is gone.

Patients relieved of excruciating suffering like that of a heart attack with morphine enter a brain state similar in its characteristics to the pain-relief state produced by dorsomedial thalamotomy, orbital undercutting, or frontal lobotomy. For these patients, the height of the third gate has been markedly raised, allowing them to *know* pain *without* suffering.

The details are not yet known but there apparently exists a gating mechanism interposed between the thalamus and the cerebral cortex. Some properties of the limbic system suggest that it may be the locus of the third gate. Pertinent to the existence of a third gate, almost surely relevant to the behaviors of neurosis, is the following statement of Dr. Melzack[16]: "Whatever the mechanism, there is now convincing evidence for experimentally induced supraspinal neural phenomena that may last indefinitely. Electrical stimulation of the amygdala or other limbic structures at low current levels (which initially have no pathological behavioral or neural effects) once a day for several consecutive days may produce after-discharges, behavioral convulsions, and a lowering of the stimulus threshold necessary to produce these effects that may persist for months."

The articulate discussion by T.C. Ruch[23] of the interrelationships between cortical association areas and the limbic system (including hypothalamus) strongly suggest that the locus of the third gate can be specified further than "limbic system." The hippocampus, temporal pole and amygdala all receive fibers from the orbital cortex as does the hypothalamus. The orbital cortex also projects to the inner midbrain, the (second) gate[21] referred to earlier. Anatomically the fibers are in a position to influence functions of the recipient neurons, and exert a gating function. Physiologically, destruction of orbitofrontal tissue leads to behavioral *hyperactivity* (therefore the loss of a major inhibitory function), to marked impairment of delayed response performance on standardized tests of same, and, of great importance, loss of anticipatory visceral responses to pain in a conditioning paradigm of shock following a light (O.A. Smith, Jr., cited in 24, p. 470) (see also [24], p. 508, ref. 55).*

Apparently, the orbitofrontal-hypothalamic projection is a "gating system" which can potentially gate between the third-line consciousness, on the one hand, and the first- and second-line components of consciousness, on the other. Another component of Dr. Smith's study pertinent to gating of pain is that prior to orbitofrontal-hypothalamic projection lesions, the

---

*This loss of learned anticipatory visceral response to pain also requires a small lesion in hypothalamus as well as an orbitofrontal lesion. Such is part of the orbitofrontal-hypothalamic projection, however, and is not vital to the visceral response per se, inasmuch as *the actual shock* still induces the rapid heartbeat and increased blood flow, previously seen (no lesions) after the light alone.

light alone (before shock) leads to cessation of lever pressing for food. After the lesions, however, lever pressing continues briskly even after the light is presented. (This recalls the behaviors of humans with orbital undercutting (surgery), the apparent selective blunting of responses to painful situations previously responded to with tension, anxiety and visceral response changes.) "The most likely interpretation is that the frontal areas in this case form a learned link between a light stimulus and the lower centers controling vascular responses, a function shared by the hypothalamus" ([24], p. 471). Applying these principles to human mental illness, "In 1935, Moniz, a Portuguese neurologist, introduced an operation—frontal lobotomy—designed to interrupt most of the connections between the orbitofrontal area and the deeper portions of the brain without completely isolating it from the remainder of the cerebral cortex. The effects of this procedure are most favorable in disorders characterized by emotional tension, e.g. anxiety neuroses, involutional depression and manic-depressive psychosis" ([24], p. 471). Putting this information into the context of the Primal formulation makes it clear that the orbito-frontal-hypothalamic projection exerts a gating operation to pain such that the learned third line associations are in intimate connection with the second line (body musculature, tension, anxiety) and the first line, (rapid pulse, changes in blood pressure, hormonal concomitants). Lesions of this *selective* gate in the orbitofrontal region severs a person's third line (learned cortical associations) from the body wall and second-line consciousness. Also severed is the third-line consciousness from the first-line consciousness, with responses mediated by the hypothalamus and neurons of the median zone of the forebrain. It is hypothesized that the orbitofrontal-hypothalamic projection is a *system*, the function of which is to "gate access" between the third-line and the second-line components, and between the third-line and the first-line components, of the total consciousness. The mammillo-thalamic tract and the projection from the *thalamic* dorsomedial nucleus to the orbitofrontal cortex are probably components of this (third) gate mechanism.

Discussion

The studies demonstrating gating operations to pain stimuli and the phenomenon of impulse occlusion in the brainstem reticular formation provide information pertinent to the postulated existence of a tripartite consciousness. Pain stimuli are of maximal relevance to the organism and its nervous system. Strong painful stimuli, physical or psychic, could potentially (and probably do) establish patterns of neuronal interaction which partially occlude awareness of the entire extra-personal and visceral environment. Expressed very generally, a painful experience raises one's threshold to other (non-painful) stimuli and forces a utilization of brain mechanisms for coping with pain. This is one of the major points of Dr. Janov's formulation; it is the dealing with pains, especially those from early childhood, throughout adult life which determines the perceptions and responses of neurotic individuals. Neurosis is clearly a disorder which limits one's consciousness. When perceptions and responses bear an obligatory relationship to earlier pain, there is an impoverishment of consciousness and a limitation of response options. This impoverishment probably occurs at all levels of the neuraxis. One may be conscious at the functional level of the viscera; it is a consciousness of feeling. One may be conscious at the functional level of the body wall, the outward expression of the internal state (emotion),[4] and lastly one may be conscious in relation to ideas, interpersonal relationship and the sensory environment beyond the body wall (the third line). *There is no biologic "unconscious," only discrete levels of consciousness which, when blocked, (gated) become "unconscious".* The recognition that the human brain is essentially tripartite[4,5] serves as a logical framework upon which to build a greater understanding of physical pain mechanisms and the role of pain in the genesis of emotional illness.

The application of the gating principle, which allows for selective increases and decreases in the awareness of pain, is an application of great potential utility in reaching an understanding of emotional illness. What Dr. Melzack has written about gating and *physical* pain[16] seems to this author directly relevant for *psychic* pain, and is presented as a concluding statement: "Observations that 1. inadequate stimuli may trigger pain, 2. surgical lesions are usually unsuccessful in abolishing these pains permanently; 3. new pains and trigger zones may spread unpredictably to unrelated parts of the body where no pathology exists (consider the exchange of one symptom for another which occurs in conventional psychotherapies) (brackets, mine), and 4. pain may persist indefinitely, cannot be accounted for by the traditional specificity theory of pain. Rather the key to and understanding of these pain states lies in recognizing that injurious stimulation may produce *long-lasting changes* (such as neurosis) (bracket comment, mine) in central nervous system activity. It is more than twenty-five years since W.K. Livingston proposed a memory-like mechanism as their basis, and Nathan, Sunderland, and others (see [16]) have recently supported this view. Yet the concept has failed to gain recognition, partly because so little has been known about long term neural changes.

"The gate control theory of pain permits the proposition that the gate can be biased (upwards or downwards) for long periods of time. The properties of the bias, moreover, can be understood in terms of recent physiological data on mechanisms underlying long term activity in the central nervous system. The extensive speculation about these mechanisms indicates the degree of our ignorance of pain phenomena which, because they represent the worst suffering known to man, should demand our attention" (brackets, mine).

Summary:

The neurology of pain appreciation is organized such that pain mechanisms are almost surely causal in the genesis of neurosis. These mechanisms are postulated to divide the total consciousness into three physiologic components, gating access between them and impoverishing consciousness with the production of neurosis.

This essay is offered in support of the Primal formulation[2,3] which views pain as the obligatory cause of neurosis, and recognizes that pain must be reexperienced if neurosis is to be reversed.

I.   The brain is mature enough in newborn humans to register pain stimuli.

II.   The pain system of the mammalian brain is dualistic, having a lateral component which mediates the knowledge of pain and a medial component which mediates the suffering of pain.

III. There is evidence from studies of hypnotic analgesia and the co-consciousness in some patients with temporal lobe epilepsy that gating of cerebral activity occurs in the telencephalon as well as in the brainstem reticular formation and spinal cord. The orbitofrontal-hypothalamic projection is suggested as the locus for the third gate.

IV.   Neurophysiologic gating functions in the dorsolateral gray of the spinal cord and brainstem, in the medial rostral mesencephalon, and in the orbitofrontal cortex, are postulated to represent the interfaces between the environment and first-line consciousness and between first- and second-line consciousness. At the highest level, between the third-line consciousness and the first and second lines, is the orbitofrontal-hypothalamic projection gating system.

BIBLIOGRAPHY

1. Yakovlev, P. I.: "Morphological Criteria of Growth and Maturation of the Nervous System in Man." *Mental Retardation* 39, Research Publications A.R.N.M.D., 1962.

2. Janov, A.: *The Primal Scream*: Dell Publishing Co., Inc., New York, 1970.

3. Janov, A.: *The Anatomy of Mental Illness*, G. P. Putnam's Sons, New York, 1971.

4. Yakovlev, P. I.: "Motility, Behavior and the Brain," *J. Nerv. Ment. Dis.* 107, 1948, p. 313.

5. Herrick, C. J.: *The Brain of the Tiger Salamander*, University of Chicago Press, Chicago, 1948.

6. French, J. D., F. D. Amerongen and H. W. Magoun: "An Activating System in Brain Stem of Monkey." *AMA Arch. Neurology and Psychiatry*, Nov., 1952.

7. French, J. D., M. Verzeano and H. W. Magoun: "An Extralemniscal Sensory System in the Brain." *AMA Arch. Neurology and Psychiatry* 69, 1963.

8. French, J. D., M. Verzeano, and H. W. Magoun: "A Neural Basis of the Anesthetic State," *AMA Arch. Neurology and Psychiatry* 69, 1953.

9. Liebeskind, J. C., C. Guilbraud, J. M. Besson and J. L. Oliveras: "Analgesia from Electrical Stimulation of the Periaqueductal Gray Matter in the Cat. Behavioral Observations and Inhibitory Effects on the Spinal Cord." *Brain Research* 50, 1973, pp. 441-6.

10. Hilgard, E. R.: "A Neodissociation Interpretation of Pain Reduction in Hypnosis." *Psych. Review* 80, #S. 1973, pp. 396-411.

11. Sherrington, C.: *The Integrative Action of the Nervous System*. Yale University Press, New Haven, original 1906, reprinted 1961.

12. Peiper, A.: *Cerebral Function in Infancy and Childhood*. The International Behavioral Science Series, E. J. Wortis, Consultant's Bureau, New York, 1973.

13. Czerny, A.: "Studies of Pain Thresholds in Infants." (cited in 12) J. B. Kinderhk, 33, 1892, p. 1.

14. Wolowick, A.: (cited in 12) J. B. Kinderhk. 115, 1927, p. 185.

15. Provence, S. and R. Lipton: *Infants in Institutions*. International Universities Press, Inc., 1962.

16. Critchley, M., J. O'Learly, and B. Jennet: *Scientific Foundations of Neurology*. F. A. Davis Co., Sept. 1972, Sect. V.

17. Mark, V., F. Ervin, and P. I. Yakovlev: "Correlation of Pain Relief, Sensory Loss and Anatomical Lesion Sites in Pain Patients Treated by Stereotactic Thalamotomy." *Trans. Amer. Neur. Assoc.*, 1961.

18. Yakovlev, P. I.: "The Anatomy of the Human Brain and the Problem of Mental Retardation." *Mental Retardation*. Proceedings of the First International Conference on Mental Retardation. Eds. P. W. Bowman and H. V. Mautner. Grune and Stratton, Inc., 1959.

19. Janov, A.: "The Nature of Consciousness." *Journal of Primary Therapy* I, No. 1, 1973, p. 7.

20. Melzack, R. and P. Wall: "Pain Mechanisms: A New Theory." *Science* 150, 1965, pp. 971-9.

21. Hernandez-Peon, R.: "Neurophysiologic Aspects of Attention." *Handbook of Clinical Neurology* 3, E. Vinken and Bruyn. John Wiley and Sons, New York, 1969, Chap. 9.

22. Janov, A.: "Sleep, Dreams, and Levels of Consciousness," *Journal of Primal Therapy*, Vol. I, No. 4, 1974 (also see Chapter VIII, this volume).

23. Ruch, Patton, Woodbury, Towe: *Neurophysiology*. W. B. Saunders Co., Philadelphia, 1965, chap. 23.

24. Condon, W. S. and L. W. Sander: "Neonate Movement Is Synchronized with Adult Speech—Interactional Participation and Language Acquisition." *Science* 183 #4120, Jan. 1974, p. 99.

25. Holden, M.: "Levels of Consciousness." Journal of Primal Therapy I, No. 2, 1973.

26. McInerney, B. P. and L. A. Pam: "A Study of the Neurologic and Biochemical Changes of Patients Undergoing Primal Therapy." Partial Fulfullment of requirements for Ph.D. degree, Lawrence University, 1973.

27. Penfield, W. and H. Jasper. *Epilepsy and the Functional Anatomy of the Human Brain*. Little, Brown & Co., Boston, 1954, pp. 832-3.

CHAPTER FIVE

What Happens to the Brain and Body during a Primal?
E. Michael Holden

One of the more perplexing questions in correlating neurophysiology with the phenomenon of a Primal is the straightforward question, "What is a Primal?" From the viewpoint of psychology, Primals have been well described by Dr. Janov[1,2] and related to Primal Pain. From the viewpoint of neurology, what is a Primal?

Primals are spontaneously occurring changes in one's entire physiology and as noted below, present for observation a sequence of phenomena which suggest that they are primarily integrated by the hypothalamus. An exact definition of a Primal cannot be provided at this time but nature has provided us with a model by which we can approach a definition of a Primal, in physiological terms.

Subjective features

Quite consistently, Primal Pain enters one's awareness as a feeling of fright or panic which is most typically experienced as a sensation in the abdomen or chest. Some experience such a sensation in the legs or in the pelvis. Very typically, almost without exception (just before a Primal), the sensation *moves upward* in the body: from pelvis or abdomen to chest to neck to throat, then to the mouth.

With this movement upwards of the feeling there are many components of a sympathetic "mass reaction," listed below:

1. Sudden tachycardia (rapid heart rate) with typical values ranging from 120 to 200 beats per minute.
2. Abrupt rise in blood pressure often into the hypertensive range. Systolic values slightly over 200 mm. Hg have been recorded in many patients.
3. Sudden facial pallor.
4. Sudden "gooseflesh" with hair standing on end.
5. Extreme increases in muscle tension with a usual postural bias *in extension,* with arching and straightening of the back and extension (backwards) of the neck and head.
6. Pupillodilatation.
7. Transient increase in desire to urinate: a sense of urinary urgency.
8. Transient rise in the core body temperature (measured with rectal thermistor), by 1-2° F. most typically.

When the feeling reaches the throat there often occurs a scream, a "cry," indistinguishable in quality from that which may precede a grand mal seizure. Alternatively, one may abruptly start hard, convulsive crying or moaning as if in extreme agony. At this moment of sudden outward expression of the internal feeling, one sees the abrupt start of a predominantly *parasympathetic* mass reaction.

1. The tachycardia diminishes and by the end of the Primal the heart rate is typically slower than the person's usual resting pulse, by 10 to 20 beats per minute. After a (first line) birth Primal a pulse rate of 40-50 beats per minute is not unusual.

2. Blood pressure falls steadily and at the end of the Primal is likewise lower than "normal" for the person, typically 90-110/50-60.

3. Facial pallor is replaced by erythema, "red skin" and profuse sweating.

4. "Gooseflesh" and hair on end cease abruptly.

5. After a Primal, there is a profound decrease in muscle tension. This is demonstrable by EMG pattern but is also obvious by inspection alone. Subjectively there is a sense of profound relaxation in muscles.

6. Crying, the access to tears and the release of the previous high tension state are typically accompanied by decrease in pupil size.

7. Urinary urgency ceases.

8. The core body temperature falls, and after a Primal may be 0.1 to 3.0° F. lower than the person's normal body temperature. The greatest decreases in temperature occur following birth (or other first-line) Primals.

Discussion

I. Neurologists reading the foregoing will immediately recognize that Primals share some features in common both with petit mal and grand mal seizures.* There are some important differences, however:

1. If circumstances require it, a Primal person can voluntarily stop Primalling, as an act of will. Rarely if ever can a patient with a petit mal or grand mal seizure stop voluntarily.

2. Seizures typically include a brief period in coma; Primals do not.

3. Seizures are followed by post-ictal confusion; Primals are followed by post-Primal *clarity* with lucidity of thought.

4. a. Seizures are typically *dis*integrative of neurological function to a far more extreme degree than occurs in Primals; for instance, in seizures (especially grand mal) the righting reflexes are lost and one falls down. It is not possible to remain *standing* during a Primal but Primalling is possible in the sitting position, if necessary.

4. b. During a *seizure,* one does not have normal access to cortical function. During a *Primal,* one is awake and conscious; there is access to normal cortical function. A Primal is a conscious experience.

II. Overlap of Physiological mechanisms manifest during seizures and during Primals.

1. Dr. Yakovlev is best known for his expertise in neuro-embryology and neuroanatomy, but he has demonstrated clinical expertise as well, in several of his many publications. In 1937 he wrote an article, "Neurologic Mechanism Concerned in Epileptic Seizures,"[3] clearly documenting the progression from *sympathetic* predominance to *parasympathetic* predominance, which typically occurs in petit mal and grand mal seizures. Concerning the initial cry and early phase of a grand mal seizure, he wrote, "This inarticulate vocalization possesses an unmistakable emotional quality expressive either of *weird horror or of the excruciating pain of a man in torture.* (italics mine) It is always associated with intense and widespread sympathetic stimulation—dilation of the pupils, protrusion of the eyeballs, bristling of hair and muscular spasm. The patient often

---

*Withdrawal from addicting drugs also usually takes the form of a sympathetic crisis followed by a *para*sympathetic recovery phase, with crying. Addicting drugs are probably addicting precisely because failure to *keep* taking them will bring one very close to Primal Pain or, as we have seen at the Primal Institute, directly to a Primal. Addicting drugs act on cells which mediate suffering, in the medial mesencephalon and medial thalamus, and decreased consciousness of Pain results. *Withdrawal* of these drugs allows such cells to again mediate the fuller awareness of suffering, and this function rebounds (after drug withdrawal) leading to the characteristic transient period during which one is *over*-exposed to Primal Pain.

before falling clenches his hands in a forceful grip on nearby objects. These clinical features suggest that the initial cry of epilepsy is not merely the result of muscular spasm of vocal cords through which air is forced by contraction of muscles of expiration, as is sometimes stated, but is rather a coordinated phonetic reaction of relatively high subcortical (diencephalic) integration.

"The epileptic cry has a close analogy with the so-called chloroform cry, hydrocephalic cry associated with *widespread sympathetic reaction to pain* (italics mine), such as may be induced in experimental animals in which the cerebral hemispheres, including the striatum, are removed (hypothalamic cry)" (reference to Bard cited[3]). Speaking of the recovery phase from a grand mal seizure, we can recognize alterations in homeostasis remarkably similar to those following a Primal. Dr. Yakovlev continued: "Convulsions cease; there are contractions of pupils, increase in salivation, slowing of pulse and respiration, dilation of superficial blood vessels, profuse sweating and fall of blood pressure and temperature." He cites work by Beattie and his associates, and relates the phenomena discussed to hypothalamic function. ". . . there exits in the hypothalamus two functionally distinct mechanisms represented respectively by the anterior and posterior hypothalamic complexes of nuclei and fibers, interlocked by communicating fibers but having separate effector pathways. The anterior complex, through its efferent pathways, appears to be connected with the cranial and sacral parasympathetic system, while the posterior hypothalamic complex is connected with the thoracolumbar sympathetic system. The effects of stimulation of the hypothalamic vegetative mechanism tend to be universal; they reflect on the whole organism rather than on its individual parts; in other words, one or the other mechanism tends to give rise to mass reactions, either prevalently sympathetic or prevalently parasympathetic."[3] Additionally, ". . . one may assume that during the phase of the epileptic seizure proper the sympathetic or posterior hypothalamic mechanism (mammillary body and posterior wall of the third ventricle) is overstimulated, while the parasympathetic or anterior hypothalamic mechanism (tuber cinereum and rostral wall of the third ventricle) is inhibited, this relation being eventually reversed during the phase of recovery."

2. The epigastic aura of epilepsy has been studied by Penfield and Kristiansen (cited in 4). "Such warnings of attack may be described as an *epigastric rising aura,* described below, or an abdominal aura or palpitation in the precordium or epigastrium.

The localizing significance of all these sensations is not strictly accurate, but in general *the origin of discharge has been found in two locations: 1. deep within the Sylvian fissure, and 2. intermediate frontal, especially in the supplementary motor area*"[4] (italics mine).

3. The rise to a crisis or peak which occurs with a Primal is probably integrated by the diencephalon. This is similar in kind to orgasm. For neurotics, orgasm is a mechanism for re-routing and discharging Primal Pain.

4. During a grand mal seizure or a petit mal seizure, the surface EEG clearly indicates seizure activity. This does not occur during a Primal.

Conclusion: A Primal is integrated by a sequence of physiologic changes in the brain following a pattern which is uniform, consistent, and similar in some respects to the patterns seen in epilepsy. The major differences were noted and the main one merits re-emphasis: *Whereas a seizure leads to a transient neural disintegration, a Primal leads to a transient change in neurophysiological state productive of neural integration.* Seizures are followed by post-ictal confusion. Primals are followed by post-Primal clarity and lucidity of thought.

The rise of Primal Pain may, by analogy with focal epilepsy,[4] reflect a depolarization of neurons deep within the Sylvian fissure and/or in the supplementary motor area.

The neurophysiologic overlap between seizure discharges and Primals are partial, but suggesting that at least some cases of epilepsy are neurotic is the fascinating observation that epileptic patients in Primal Therapy become seizure-free, off anticonvulsant medications.

The early neurologists, especially Gowers and Jackson, recognized and studied the order inherent in the patterns of seizures. The studies of Dr. Penfield and his colleagues have further confirmed the order in seizure patterns.

There is another, similar, orderly manifestation of brain activity: the physiologic pattern of Primals.

"It is largely an involuntary act. That scream is felt all over the body. Many describe it as a lightning bolt that seems to break apart all the unconscious control of the body. . . . Suffice it to note here that the Primal Scream is both the cause and result of a crumbling defense system."[1]

III. Within a Primal, What Is a Connection?

At the Primal Institute it is recognized by patients and staff alike that subjectively there are Primals which occur with connection, and pseudo-Primals without connection, constituting only abreaction. This difference should be explored objectively as well. We can state from preliminary observations that there *are* objective, measurable differences between these two modes. Simply stated, "connected" Primals characteristically are followed by vital sign values lower than baseline.

Quite recently, Drs. Penfield and Mathieson have made a brilliant contribution to neurobiology on the subject of memory mechanisms[5] and we feel that their report is quite relevant to, and supportive of, the Primal formulation. Dr. Penfield speculates that "summarizing keys of access" must exist between the scanning functions of hippocampal neurons for cortical memories and the nonverbal components of those memories. Temporal lobe stimulation leads to vivid experiential recall of feelings, emotions and ideas. *The exact same thing occurs during Primals.*

A Primal starts when one is "close" to Primal Pain, signalled to a Primal person by a change in abdominal or chest sensation, as noted previously. Especially, early in Primal Therapy, Primals are elicited by re-creating a past (stimulus) situation which was Painful for the individual. As the patient gains greater and greater access to the Painful stimulus situation in his past, he begins to physiologically totally re-experience it. At this transition is when one sees the start of the sympathetic crisis discussed earlier. In the brain we believe the following circuit is activated. The cognitive memory of a *Painful* past scene or event, or the general theme of the same, is probably registered in the anterior temporal lobe neocortex, as discussed in the chapter on the neurophysiology of feeling.

As a Primal begins, an interface occurs between the rise of the feeling and the mechanisms which normally suppress it, and this is experienced as a threat to the organism. As the experience progresses, however, one sees the buildup of a posterior hypothalamic syndrome, the start of a sympathetic mass reaction. We believe this reflects a *movement of excitation* (neuronal depolarization), perhaps analogous to that in focal epilepsy. The excitation moves from the temporal lobe and insular cortex, eventually to the *hippocampus* (via either the entorhinal cortex or prepyriform cortex). Dr. Penfield hypothesized[5] that the older, earlier memories are "scanned" for by hippocampus neurons more posterior in location. It is thus probable that earlier *Painful* memories have their "keys of access" registered historically, sequentially backwards in the hippocampus. When a person has a third-line Primal, from the present to the relatively recent past, to the *distant* past, *the excitation is probably moving topographically in the hippocampus, from front to back.* From the *hippocampus,* the fornix bundle will carry the excitation to the *mammillary bodies* and (pre-and-post commissural) *hypothalamic nuclei.* There is, from the mammillary bodies, undoubtedly a spread of the excitation to the anterior thalamus and *cingulum* predominantly, but also to other portions of the limbic system such as the amygdala, medial forebrain bundle and orbitofrontal cortex. The cingulum projects widely but one of its important efferent pathways is *back to the hippocampus*. We believe that one of the major determinants for *not* remembering early Painful events in life is the "disconnection" physiologically of those memories from full consciousness. The term used by Dr. Penfield is here poignantly relevant: keys of access. Clearly, part of the *Papez circuit* in the limbic system contains the keys of access to early Primal Pains and early painful memories. It is not enough in a Primal to have a strong feeling and a sympathetic crisis followed by a parasympathetic crisis to gain a true *insight* from the experience. A Primal patient has one or more true *insights* from a Primal only when there is a connection such that one can vividly *feel* and *know* the relationship between an old, early Painful event and a present-day category of neurotic symptomatology. As example, a patient with asthma has true insight into his asthma only when he has fully re-experienced nearly drowning at birth, or having the cord around his neck or whatever is the particular early life causal experience, establishing asthma as one's *prototypic* response to stress. Physiologically, what occurs in the connection? The precise answer is not known. What is clear, however, is that *hippocampal function* changes, for after a connected Primal one has access to an earlier memory registration than before the Primal, and also, there is a concomitant transient change in hypothalamic function (marked drop in core body temperature, as much as 3°F., and marked decreases in pulse, blood pressure and alpha power of the EEG).

The hippocampus is an ancient and vitally important part of the vertebrate nervous system. It is already a prominent structure in primitive vertebrates such as the shark and in reptiles. As a major component of the median telencephalic zone, it is interposed between archicortex and (via its outflow, the fornix) the hypothalamus. The hippocampal plate of the Ammon's horn arises embryologically wholly in the *mantle* layer.[8] As is clearly seen in the developing (fetal) human brain, the hippocampus is interposed between the ancient, median brain, and the phylogenetically newer brain which, in phylogeny and ontogeny, superlaminate or override it anatomically. Its functional role is apparently to adjust the internal environment of the organism in relation to its experience and changing environment. As such it is literally a *sine qua non* for survival. Having keys of access[5] both to one's memories and one's response system for fight or flight, the hippocampus literally connects one's *past* to the system which responds to it. A Painful past leads the neurotic to psychosomatic illness due to re-routing of its effects into and onto the body's homeostasis. By the amount that the hippocampus does this re-routing operation it is functioning *abnormally,* in a biological sense. The *response to Pain* is the issue here. There are two types of response possible. The first is what occurs when the full *experience* and *expression* of Pain occurs. The second is what occurs when the *experience* or the *expression* of Pain is blocked. The question is then, "Can the abnormally functioning hippocampus be restored to normal reactivity?" (so that the experience and expression of Pain occurs fully, without blocking and without re-routing of its force). We can answer in the affirmative. A Primal *is* a full *experience* and *expression* of Pain. We submit that Primals return the hippocampus to its biologically normal function.

To clarify the above, the hippocampus can potentially perform one of three operations in relation to Primal Pain:

1. The effects of Primal Pain can be (inappropriately) directed into and onto the body and its metabolism which causes the internal manifestations of neurosis.

2. The effects of Primal Pain can also be (inappropriately) directed outward to the cortex, resulting in aberrant interpersonal behavior, acting out: the outward manifestation of neurosis.

3. Primal Pain can be fully experienced and expressed. This is the only *biologically* appropriate action of the hippocampus with regard to physical or psychic pain. Ideally, this would occur during childhood, in the present of a child's life. However, if such does not occur *then,* it can occur in the present of an *adult's* life with regard to *childhood* Pain, in Primals. When childhood Pain is re-experienced in adulthood, it is no longer biologically necessary to act *in* or act *out,* and neurosis dissolves.

As Primal Therapy progresses two phenomena occur together: one Primals about *earlier and earlier* Painful events and there is a steady trend toward *lower values of vital signs,* month after month. Thus there are progressive physiologic changes occurring both in the hippocampus and hypothalamus. The natural functions of these brain regions are being restored to biological normal, or in the jargon of neurology, are released from inhibition. Ultimately one has to implicate frontal cortex, perhaps especially *orbitofrontal cortex,* as the inhibitor which is less active in its actions on the hippocampal-hypothalamic circuit (inasmuch as posterior orbital undercutting and infero-medial leukotomy also release the body from the tension and symptoms of neurosis).

In discussing functions of the hippocampus, Carpenter cites the original opinion of Dr. Papez regarding emotional integration: "He expressed the belief that the hippocampal formation and its principal projection system, the fornix, provide one of the main pathways by which impulses from the cortex reach the hypothalamus."[6]

The work of Dr. Kaada[7] is directly pertinent in considering the physiology of a Primal. Birth Primals regularly involve transient periods of respiratory paralysis in the inspiration phase, which probably argues for strong excitation in the anterior cingulum and/or orbitofrontal cortex. Discussing regions which when stimulated inhibit respiration, Dr. Kaada wrote: "The existence of an inhibitory insular and temporopolar field in monkey and man has been confirmed (references cited)."[7] In man, "The (respiration-inhibiting) responses have been produced in patients under light pentothal anesthesia from the anterior cingulate and posterior orbital surface as well as in the conscious patient from the same areas and from the anterior insula and the pentromedial aspect of the temporal pole, particularly in the region of the uncus (references cited)."[7] These same areas are also implicated (by animal studies)[7], p. 1356, in the slow, tonic extensor movements: a prominent feature of deep, first-line Primals.

The anterior cingulate, rostral hippocampal and orbitofrontal regions have also been repeatedly implicated (in animal, especially monkey, studies) as sites which mediate a blood pressure lowering effect, when stimulated ([7], pp. 138,9). Another reason to implicate frontal cortex in this context is that two separate EEG studies done at UCLA Brain Research Institute have shown increased frontal alpha activity and increased frontal non-alpha (2-8cps) activity in the course of Primal Therapy (see chapter on Primal Pain and Aging). There is much less "low voltage fast" activity from the frontal cortex as Primal Therapy progresses. Another way to consider the result of a connected Primal is to view it from the viewpoint of *learned, maladaptive* visceral responses. Consider a common one, the relationship between environmental stress and a rise in blood pressure. As Primal Therapy progresses the hypertensive response to stress becomes separated from environmental stress. The same occurs with headaches, asthma, migraine attacks, flareups of ulcerative colitis, etc. The visceral functions are re-represented in the medial frontal cortex and we believe that Primal Therapy changes the function of that cortex so that it no longer integrates *anticipatory* sympathetic reactions, based on the *old Painful memories*. It changes its function to mediate responses to here-and-now, present day stresses, such as nearly being hit by a car. In the neurotic, both present stress and old Primal-Pain-stress determine the visceral response patterns. Primal Therapy normalizes this reactivity by diminishing Primal Pain, in connected Primals. The pattern of autonomic responses, the vivid return of old memories, and the literal *re-experiencing* of prior events in the entire body during a Primal make it clear that the whole brain participates in a Primal. With *connection in a Primal there is an interface created between old Painful memories and present neurotic symptoms,* an interface which provides true insight. When this occurs, the function of the hypothalamus changes, as noted. The hypothalamic changes are initially transient, after each connected Primal, but after some weeks, a *trend of continuous changes* becomes measurable. This trend, manifested by the changes in vital signs, continues for at least five years (known at present), probably longer. The connection in a Primal is probably a complex pattern of neuronal depolarization between the limbic system and parieto-temporal neocortex. The exact form this takes would be identifiable only with depth electrode studies, and thus will remain unknown (unless an individual with electrodes in the brain *for other reasons* is studied during a connected Primal). The most likely brain regions to definitely change their functions in Primal Therapy are: the posterior hippocampus, the hypothalamus, the anterior cingulum and orbitofrontal cortex, bilaterally. We propose that opening the gates to Pain in Primal Therapy means that the hippocampus is no longer inhibited by orbitofrontal cortical cells. In turn, the *hypothalamus is released* from its keys of access to Primal Pain, and thus returns homeostasis to biological normality, the objective physiologic criterion for the post-Primal state.

Unless a therapy has access to the subcortical and diencephalic structures mediating the neurotic state, then it cannot be effective in curing neurosis.

BIBLIOGRAPHY

1. Janov, A.: *The Primal Scream,* G. P. Putnam's Sons, New York, 1970
2. Janov, A.: *The Anatomy of Mental Illness,* G. P. Putnam's Sons, New York, 1971
3. Yakovlev, P. I. "Neurologic Mechanism Concerned in Epileptic Seizures," Arch. *Neurology and Psychiatry 37,* 1937, pp. 523–554.
4. Penfield, W. and H. Jasper: *Epilepsy and the Functional Anatomy of the Human Brain,* Little, Brown & Co., Boston, 1954.
5. Penfield, W. and C. Mathieson: "Memory: Autopsy Findings and Comments on the Role of Hippocampus in Experiential Recall," *Arch. Neurology 31,* Sept. 1974.
6. Carpenter, M.B.: *Core Text of Neuroanatomy,* Chap. XI, Williams & Wilkins, 1972.
7. Kaada, B. R.: "Cingulate, Posterior Orbital, Anterior Insular and Temporal Pole Cortex" in *The Handbook of Physiology,* Section I: Neurophysiology, Vol. II, Editors: Field, Magoun, Hall, American Physiological Society, Washington, D.C. pp. 1345–1372.
8. Yakovlev, P. I.: "Telencephalon 'Impar,' 'Semipar,' and 'Totopar,'" *International Journal of Neurology,* Vol. VI, #3–4, 1968, p. 255.

CHAPTER SIX

The Sensory Window and Access to Primal Pain
E. Michael Holden

In this chapter access to Primal Pain is discussed.

Suffering is a state of being. It has physical and psychic components or representations in the body. A distinction should be drawn between suffering and being in Pain, for they are not the same. For this discussion, *suffering* is one's state *before* one needs to have a Primal. Being *in Pain* is the total psychophysiological experience of the Pain, occurring within a Primal, when one enters or "drops into" the old feeling. There is a transition between suffering and being in Pain, and in our research we have been learning about its nature. I believe this transition is on a spectrum or continuum. The continuum is that of *access* to Pain. With very little access (much repression in conventional terms), one doesn't suffer, doesn't know one is hurting, and would not seek Primal Therapy or find *The Primal Scream* personally relevant. With more access to Pain, one is suffering, a little or a lot, varying with the individual's personal history and the effectiveness of one's defenses. One who suffers a little would find *The Primal Scream* interesting and might want to know more about Primal Therapy. One who suffers a lot would find *The Primal Scream* deeply and poignantly relevant and would actively seek Primal Therapy. One who suffers tremendously has probably already found relief in another way: heroin addiction, alcoholism, consistent use of (benzodiazepine) tranquilizers, or in some cases, psychosis. Some individuals who are quite open to Pain (but not completely so), who are suffering constantly, will seek to leave their palliative symptomatic Pain-blunting habits and will seek Primal Therapy. Others, perhaps more fatalistic, will stay with their Pain-blunters as the only personally acceptable way to deal with their Pain.

A person who suffers, by definition, is a person quite open to Pain. There are only two ways, before one Primals, the Pain can be dealt with or represented. Pain can be internalized, into the body itself, which leads to psychosomatic illness. Pain can be dealt with by, or re-routed to, the cerebral cortex, in which case it will be externalized. The externalization of Pain leads to outwardly expressed neurotic behavior in interpersonal relationships and includes all forms of acting out. When the interface is between the outer brain (cerebral cortex) and inner brain, the result is a *thought disorder*, or ultimately, *psychosis*. At the Primal Institute we see some people who are suffering only with psychosomatic symptoms or illness. We see some people who have mild thought disorders, who act out their Pain. Probably more common, however, are those who have responded with both modes: those who have psychosomatic symptoms and who also act out their Pain.

The body is our action system, the part which is the final pathway with which we can respond to a Painful past. We know the brain participates, mediates and regulates the responses to Pain, but the body cries, coughs, gets tense, experiences asphyxia, etc., etc.

Early in Primal Therapy, compared with later on, the access to Pain is slight, although the suffering may be quite extreme. The process of Primal Therapy *increases access* to Pain and with one's first Primal one has a new option: to be *in Pain* fully, rather than to be suffering. The option to be *in Pain* fully means that suffering decreases. The brain and body have found the natural way to respond to Pain: completely. Because of that, the biological motive for re-routing Pain into physical symptoms or acting out begins to dissolve. As that occurs, over time, neurosis dissolves. Gradually, sometimes very gradually, but consistently, the physical symptoms go away and the act-outs occur less and less often.

Can access to Pain be measured? I believe it can. The body responds in a predictable, uniform way to increasing access to Pain so one can measure the response pattern. We have been doing this in the Primal research laboratory.

There are two variables to consider in recognizing whether one has little, or much, access to Pain. The first is timing. How long does it take for one to make the transition between suffering and being *in Pain*? People with much access to old Pain make the transition in several seconds (which makes the transition dramatic, sudden and remarkable to observe). People with less access to old Pain make the transition less rapidly; many minutes, or, rarely, more than an hour elapsing before the (characteristic) full response to old Pain occurs.

The second variable which indicates *amount of access* to old Pain is the magnitude of the peak response to it. Sobbing, crying, a pulse of 120/min., no high blood pressure, no EEG response, and very slight change in core body temperature all indicate less than complete access to Pain. By contrast, shrieking, agonized crying, a pulse of 140 to 200 per minute, high blood pressure of about 180/120, elevations of core body temperature and *EEG voltage*, all indicate that *Pain* is beginning to have greater access to consciousness. To summarize, access to Pain is variable and the degree of access can be measured. Also, the greater the access to Pain in a Primal, the greater the fall of the vital sign values *after* the Primal, and the more profound the relaxation after the Primal.

Before considering the subjective and objective features of access to Pain, the concept of the "sensory window" will be discussed. Many authors have written about human sensory experience and perceptions and are familiar with what I am calling here the sensory window. I propose to relate this to Pain access, further on.

We take for granted, from our everyday experience, that our eyes, ears, nose and sense of touch will be appropriately adjusted so that light won't be too bright, sounds won't be too loud, smells won't overwhelm us and touch won't be unpleasant. Part of this adjustment occurs close to the receptor, such as constriction of pupils in bright light, and tensing of the eardrum (by a tiny ear muscle) in response to a loud noise. As long as our sensory window(s) are sufficiently closed then we don't experience sensory input as adverse or unpleasant. Most of the adjustment which closes the sensory window(s) is done *within* the central nervous system.

There exists a balance between *activation* of the brain, almost exclusively a subcortical and brainstem function, and *inhibition* of that activation. For instance, the rage reaction (or "flight-fight" reaction) is one which could potentially occur in us at any time. In fact, however, it does not. It is strongly inhibited most of the time and only a very intense stimulus of life and death magnitude will permit it to occur. When the alarm reaction occurs the (cortical) inhibition is decreased, and the subcortical response is fully expressed, released from cortical inhibition. Sanity and freedom from anxiety, in the present, require a certain ratio between brainstem activation and cortical inhibition.

It is widely recognized that the cerebral cortex exerts an inhibitory force in opposition to brainstem activation. After lesions (sites of damage) in the cortex one sees "release" phenomena which previously were inhibited. Frontal lesions release the sucking, snouting, and forced grasping reflexes normally seen only in infants. Lesions of the motor cortex lead to increased muscle tension and spasticity in the affected limbs, both of which are normally inhibited. Of more interest here, and relevant to the topic of *access to Pain*, some lesions which are *in* or slightly deep to sensory cortex leave an individual with a *sensory window* which is *too open*. This state is intensely unpleasant, and such individuals suffer. The most extreme cases are seen in so-called thalamic syndrome in which touch is appreciated as an agonizingly painful stimulus.

In principle, then, there exists a balance between subcortical activation and cortical inhibition. When this balance is normal the sensory windows are normal and sensory stimuli are not appreciated as painful or unpleasant.

There are two ways this balance can be upset, such that the sensory window is too open, and either will lead to appreciation of ordinary stimuli as painful. This opening of the sensory window occurs *if the function of the cortex* becomes reduced, or *if the activation by the brainstem (reticular formation) is increased*. Either way, the balance of activities changes so that the subcortical:cortical ratio of functions is *increased*.

Pain, Drugs and Craziness

When this ratio is increased, and the sensory window is too open, the individual is biologically organized such that brainstem function is less than normally inhibited by the cortex. This "too open" state is subjectively very unpleasant, and panic commonly occurs. Psychiatrists and psychologists will recognize that this excessively open state is the one which typically precedes either an acute anxiety state or an *acute psychotic episode*. The other way that this excessively open state can manifest itself is not in outwardly expressed psychotic behavior but with *internal visceral* responses, leading to psychosomatic illness. The moderately severe forms of this response are seen in the occurrence of acute flareup of ulcerative colitis, acute decompensation of a gastric or duodenal ulcer, acute asthma attack, acute attack of migraine, or acute attack of angina pectoris, (coronary insufficiency). Dr. Janov and I both believe that when the excessively open state expresses itself internally, viscerally, in severe form, that the result is the start of cancer, or a cardiovascular crisis. In response to being too open, after a lifetime of Pain, we have only two options: to be crazy externally or to be crazy internally. Internal craziness *is* psychosomatic illness. External craziness is psychosis. Furthermore, to clarify, there are two possible ways that one can become too open: either the cortical inhibitory function v.s. the brainstem becomes impaired, or the brainstem activation function becomes excessive. Either way, the brainstem activation is greater than normal.

As newborns and infants, we are biologically adequate only in our inner brains and in the inner body (visceral homeostasis). If traumatized then, Pain is registered in the inner brain and inner body. It has often been observed that birth Primals very early in Primal therapy occur in psychotic or pre-psychotic individuals. This leads to the conclusion that it is *first-line Pains which are psychotogenic*. Expressed differently, psychosis is a disorder which has its causal origins very early in life. There are two major reasons for this. First, the Pains are registered in the brain's inner core, which makes them relatively inaccessible, later on. Second, these Pains occur at a time when the middle and outer portions of the brain are still quite immature and their contributions to repression are not yet fully developed. These early Pains are nearly always life-and-death events and their valence, or charge value, is catastrophic.

With compounding of Pain later in life, on the other levels of consciousness, gating systems become inadequate on the second and third line levels, and there is a constant egress of first line Pain, producing symbolization commensurate with its catastrophic valence_psychosis.

The capacity to suffer is adequate months and years before the capacity to discriminate and understand Pain. We can suffer before we have the capacity to be in *Pain* completely (in a Primal). When catastrophic Pain from infancy surfaces, it cannot be understood or integrated, which leads to the *symbolic*, bizarre perceptions and responses which are *characteristic* of psychosis.

While it is true that cortical impairment often releases psychosis (as with very high fever or with sensory deprivation), it is Pain registered in the *brainstem* which is released. Brainstem function is biologically adequate at the end of gestation and at birth, and can register potentially psychotogenic traumas at that time, for later release. The fact that anti-psychotic medications inhibit collateral fibers of the brainstem reticular formation supports the notion that psychosis has its causal origins in early infancy.

LSD is a drug which opens the sensory window and may lead to acute psychosis or chromosome damage, the latter a possible precursor to cancer.

On the contrary, Thorazine and its analogs are agents which inhibit the [collateral nerves of the] reticular formation in the brainstem, decrease over-activation of the cortex, and are *thus* anti-psychotic in their action.

Thorazine is also effective in the treatment of some psychosomatic physical symptoms. It is an effective agent for treating amphetamine psychosis. The principle is simple and straightforward: psychosis and psychosomatic illness derive from being too open. In response to that excessive openness to sensory input, with a lifetime of accumulated (Primal) Pains, the body or behavior goes crazy. Brainstem stimulants will elicit or worsen the craziness and phenothiazines (Thorazine), butyrophenones (Haldol) or strong analgesics (morphine) will effectively treat the craziness.

A physician working in the Los Angeles County drug rehabilitation program* has made several astute observations on heroin addicts in the methadone maintenance program. These observations strongly support the Primal formulation, and this discussion of the brainstem:cortical relationships in psychosis, and in psychosomatic (visceral) illness.

1. As long as the methadone dose is high enough, then addicts look much younger than their chronologic ages and are remarkably free of psychosomatic illnesses.

2. As the methadone dose is *decreased*, the addicts appear to *age rapidly* and start to develop psychosomatic illnesses, such as ulcer disease, bowel disorders, migraine or asthma.

3. Important and interesting is his observation that the psychosomatic illnesses go away if the methadone dose is again increased. This is a pharmacologic proof that Pain is the basis for psychosomatic illnesses.

Who, among physicians, has treated ulcers, colitis or asthma, with morphine? Has it been tried? This essay proposes that the narcotic analgesics will effectively treat acute psychotic episodes and acute attacks of psychosomatic visceral illness.

Any potent analgesic, such as morphine and its analogs, will treat psychosis or psychosomatic illness *because* it *blocks access* of the cortex and of the body to *Pain*. Morphine allows one to *be suffering and not mind it*. It disconnects suffering from awareness of it. In neurological terms, it markedly raises the gates to Pain.

Perhaps addiction is so feared because *withdrawal* is so unpleasant. I believe, however, that the entire *withdrawal syndrome* is nothing more than abrupt, *overwhelming access to Primal Pain*.

---

*Dr. Charles Starling

In a non-Primal context, withdrawal from narcotics is severe, and may lead to psychosis, and/or a visceral catastrophe, with or without subsequent death. When morphine is withdrawn, *what is released?* The answer is: Primal Pain. With prolonged increased access to an overload of Primal Pain, the mind and the body literally go crazy. This occurs because massive release of brainstem activation overwhelms cortical inhibition.

(Gradual) narcotic withdrawal in a Primal Therapy context gives one a third option: to feel the Pain in small graded increments, *in Primals*: without psychosis, visceral catastrophe or seizures. As the Pain is re-experienced the *biological motive* for morphine (or heroin) addiction dissolves. That is why Primal Therapy is a cure for heroin or other narcotic analgesic addiction.

Consider some pure examples of drug stimulation of the brainstem. Amphetamines accomplish this in a direct pharmacological way. As the dose is increased, one becomes too sensitive to stimuli, and when extreme, this is intensely unpleasant.

High doses of caffeine also open the sensory window and a person experiences this as intensely unpleasant. Very high caffeine doses cause seizures. Strychnine, by its action, inhibits inhibitory nerves throughout the nervous system: it turns on the entire nervous system. Tiny doses of strychnine open the sensory window and it is unpleasant. Higher doses release the seizure response, and still higher doses lead to death.

Impairing cortical function with drugs also leads to unpleasant opening of the sensory window and release of brainstem activation, which is normally inhibited by the cortex. This occurs with general anesthetics, especially when the induction time is slow. (Anesthesiologists give intravenous pentothal to bypass this stage in modern times, but prior to that practice, the phase of excitement and brainstem release was always seen: both as one went under anesthesia, and as one surfaced from it.)

Nature provides us other examples of the sensory window which is unpleasantly too open. When is it that adults feel bombarded or overloaded by ordinary sensory input? Most people have experienced it many times: with fatigue, especially after sleep loss.

Sensory deprivation, if continued long enough, becomes a very painful experience, typically ending in a *panic*. Sensory deprivation opens the sensory window, at least in part, by removing stimuli which keep the cortex functioning normally. This is a variety of cortical impairment. One begins to hear one's own heartbeat as very loud, to hear air on the eardrums as loud and unpleasant in an anechoic (totally soundproof) chamber, and not uncommonly will have visual hallucinations. Some people become transiently psychotic in prolonged sensory deprivation. This is probably related mechanistically to *amphetamine* psychosis. In each case, the brainstem function has predominated over the cortical inhibitory function. Over-activation and a wide open sensory window occur with both, and one experiences this as subjectively very unpleasant. *Panic* is common in both circumstances.

Migraine is the disorder which so commonly is associated with an unpleasantly wide open sensory window that if a person with headache doesn't refer to the phenomena, one doubts the diagnosis. The stereotype of a person with severe migraine is someone in bed with the shades drawn, with a pillow over the ears to diminish sound perception. In this circumstance, normal daylight, or the noise of normal conversation, are perceived as agonizing. The light is "too bright" and the noise is "too loud."

The most important circumstance, for this essay, in which the sensory window is too open is early childhood.

There are dozens of ways we may know with certainty that the sensory window of an infant is "too open."

1. They startle very easily, often in response to a sudden noise, even of low intensity, or to a sudden slight increase in light, like opening a curtain and letting in daylight. Note here that the startle of infants is mechanistically identical to the startle of lower animals, especially reptiles and birds, which have no cerebral cortex, or small mammals, which have little cerebral cortex. They also are wide open to sensory stimuli. In our personal development we pass through the psychophysiologic organizations of our vertebrate ancestors.

2. Infants *cry* very easily, very readily, to a wide variety of stimuli: from a sudden noise, from the need to burp, from having wet diapers, from being thirsty, from being hungry, etc. They have a *low threshold to pain*, a low threshold to all discomforts: they are too open to sensory inputs.

3. The *reflexes* of infancy, like visual and tactile sucking reflexes, like the rooting reflex (turning head toward nipple, touching cheek), the grasp reflex in the hands and toes, and the upgoing toe reflex (Babinski sign), are all reflexes which return in adults who have frontal cortical disease. On neurological (and embryological) grounds, the nervous system of an infant shows a dominance of subcortical over cortical activities. The sensory window is wide open. Sudden or unexpected stimuli are experienced as *very* unpleasant by infants, and in response to their suffering, they cry.

4. The *explorations* of 6-18-month old infants also tell us their sensory windows are wide open. Children of this age perceive in a way which adults seldom experience, except (notably) when on mescaline or LSD trips. I refer here to perceiving one's environment, not overall, but in its most minute detail; whereas an adult walks into a room and perceives the furniture, paintings, carpets, etc., there is much which is seen but not attended to. The infant by contrast (or an adult on LSD, etc.) attends to the minutiae of the environment: the screwhead on the chair, a strand of hair on the rug, a crumb of toast on the floor, etc.

Dr. Simeon Locke illustrates this principle with the anecdote that when a woman loses a ring or small earring, she and older family members are much less likely to find it than the one year old, crawling around on hands and knees, inspecting the house in minute detail.

Infants, then, are neurologically organized in a way which makes them too sensitive to ordinary stimuli. Because this is true they are easily hurt, easily overloaded. For health, they require an environment quite free of sudden noises, sudden changes of light, or sudden tactile stimuli.

Why, then, is it that American birth and delivery practices are truly traumatic? *Everything* is too much and too sudden, and the infant suffers. The cry of the newborn child is not the lusty cry of vibrant life, it is the *cry of agony.* The room is too cold, too noisy, and the light is too bright. The eyedrops and the nasal suction catheter are suddenly applied. All this sudden input is experienced as agonizingly painful because the sensory windows of newborns are extremely open. If obstetricians knew more of an infant's neurological status they would heed the advice of Dr. Leboyer in France* and deliver children more gradually with none of the sudden overloading stimuli the American infant now encounters at birth.

Having briefly considered the sensory window, the next topic to explore is access to Pain in its *subjective* aspects.

When people "need to Primal," what do they experience? How does an individual know he/she is "close to Pain"? Words are notoriously inadequate to describe internal feeling states. The following is a compilation of some of the more common ways people know they are suffering, and need to Primal. There may be the sudden onset of the need to cry. There may be sudden fear, panic, or fear of death; what most neurotics would call "anxiety" and most psychiatrists would call "an acute anxiety attack." There may be sudden or gradual marked increases in muscle ten-

Birth Without Violence—Frederick Leboyer, M.D.: Alfred A. Knopf—1975.

sion, especially in the neck, back or face. There may be extreme sadness with an overwhelming sense of tragedy or loss.

There may be extreme jitteriness, sometimes with tremor of hands or mouth, often with an inner awareness of agitation or restlessness. For some, there is sudden nausea or sudden loss of appetite, or both. There may be a feeling of internal pressure in which one feels, "I'm going to explode." Some experience a change in their thinking as well, feeling "I'm going to lose my mind" or a "spaced-out", "disconnected" mental sense which makes it difficult or impossible to concentrate. Coldness of hands and feet are common, often with cold clammy sweating of palms, and increased underarm sweating. Rarely, but for some people, sudden anger or rage tells them they need to Primal. Depending on one's past habits, some people develop sudden cravings for sweets or for tranquilizers, for alcohol or for a cigarette. Common to all these subjective feeling states which tell people they are close to Pain is a change in abdominal or chest sensations; a change not easy to describe in words but which regularly accompanies the alarm reaction. The sensation of fright in the midline of the body is known to all but only defined by equating it with fear or panic, etc. Also, most people close to Pain experience some feeling of losing control, one of the characteristic accompaniments of panic.

The *objective* features of being close to Pain are readily summarized by recognizing that people are in a state of *sympathetic nervous system overactivation*. Pulse rate and blood pressure and core body temperature are all elevated. The nervous sweating, facial pallor of the sympathetic-excess state are easily observed, as are the moderately or widely dilated pupils which characteristically occur when access to Pain is increased.

Now, in this state of increased access to Pain, what sorts of things will decrease its intensity and take one out of the feeling? For some people, low doses of caffeine (which stimulate the cortex) will decrease Pain access. For sure, moderate doses of tranquilizers, narcotics, nicotine or alcohol will decrease access to Pain. Primal patients also learn that *eating*, especially eating sweets decreases access to Pain. For many, orgasm turns off the feeling. For some people urinating or defecating will decrease access to Pain. Some people can blunt Pain temporarily by talking a lot, or reading, or studying intensely.

There are some paradoxes to mention, such as Primalling immediately after orgasm, or Primalling after a low dose of tranquilizer, nicotine, or alcohol. There is no mystique: the paradoxical response occurs when one was overloaded to begin with, with too much access to Pain. In *that* neurological state, any maneuver which *slightly* blunts Pain brings one closer to, not farther from, effective access to Pain.

So many Primal patients have observed this paradoxical response to Pain-blunting maneuvers that I believe there exists a particular relationship between access to Pain and ability to Primal. The relationship can be expressed in a diagrammatic way, as a diminishing returns curve* which passes through an optimum, a particular zone in which one can Primal. To the left of the optimum, Pain access is too little (as in pre-Primal neurotics) and one cannot Primal. To the right of the optimum, a zone of huge access to Pain, one is overloaded and in that zone cannot Primal either. If one is overloaded, then any maneuver, drug or other, which decreases tension, will paradoxically allow one to Primal soon thereafter. This paradoxical response is thus *not paradoxical at all* but perfectly in accord with the *gating* of Pain.[3] A gate to Pain in the brain is a neurophysiologic function by which our effective access to Pain is decreased. By metaphor, it is like a dam which rises whenever the water level behind it rises, and falls when the water level falls. When one is overloaded, one is in a state of extreme suffering—like five seconds before being hit by a train. It is characteristically a terror state, with or without re-routing of Pain into worsening of a symptom (asthma, headache, colitis, etc.) or an increase in acting out. Thus, the paradox may be someone who needs to Primal, who has a severe headache, but cannot, because the headache is too severe. If the headache is a tension headache, a small amount of alcohol or a tranquilizer will partially relieve it . . . *then* the person can Primal. It may be why someone, when overloaded, has an acute attack of asthma and cannot Primal until *after* some bronchodilator is taken.

To generalize, pre-Primal neurotics have little access to Pain and though they may suffer, they do not feel Pain fully; they do not Primal. They re-route the Pain into symptoms like asthma or hypertension, or act-outs such as alcoholism, drug addiction or compulsive studying, working, etc.

Most Primal patients have appropriate, intermittent, increased access to Pain, and are able to feel the Pain fully in Primals. [Just before Primalling they are suffering and are in a sympathetic nervous system crisis. When the sympathetic crisis ends,they suddenly enter the phase of resolution, the *parasympathetic* phase, with hard crying, increased salivation, profuse sweating increased bronchial secretions (and coughing), sudden decreases in pulse, blood pressure and EEG voltage, and a gradual drop

*See diagram.

in core body temperature. The shift from sympathetic crisis to para-sympathetic recovery phase occurs suddenly, and, by analogy with the same shift which occurs within epileptic seizures,[2] is mediated by the

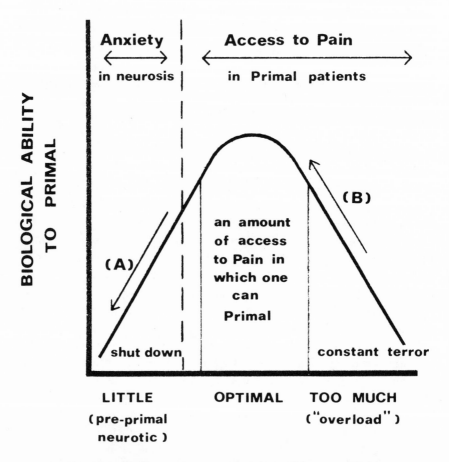

ACCESS TO PRIMAL PAIN

A neurotic uses tranquilizers, alcohol and/or cigarettes, and/or opiates and parasympathetic release forms to decrease anxiety (A).

A Primal patient who is truly overloaded needs to blunt Pain slightly, in order to Primal (B).

hypothalamus. The parasympathetic phase starts at precisely the moment one "drops into" the old feeling, often with a vivid memory from the past. Thus in a literal way "feeling the feeling" (totally) is the healing phase, the phase which delivers one from suffering.

Being overloaded with Primal Pain to the extent that one cannot Primal does occur in Primal patients. My impression is that it occurs less often than Primal patients think it does. That is, some people find the *pre-Primal* state so intensely unpleasant that they will use alcohol or seek tranquilizers for relief, not for helping them to Primal. *If one is truly overloaded*, then half a cigarette, half a glass of wine, a small amount to eat, etc., may be all one needs to Primal. Explicitly, with regard to gating of Pain, if one is overloaded, the valence or magnitude of the Pain is too great. A pain-blunter or a (parasympathetic) release (orgasm, urination), will decrease access to Pain. When that occurs the *gating of it will also decrease*, and one will enter the optimal zone of access to Pain: in which a Primal may occur. If one is overloaded and blunts Pain too much (4 drinks instead of half of one) then one will go to the left of the optimal zone of Pain access, and will not be able to Primal at all.

(The relationship discussed above can also be used to *determine* whether one is truly overloaded or not. If a pain-blunting maneuver leads to loss of the feeling and inability to Primal, one was probably not overloaded. If it makes it easier or more possible to Primal, then previous overload state is very likely).

Lastly, I would like to suggest that the process of Primal Therapy is one which gradually opens the sensory window of neurotic adults. The pre-Primal phase is one in which one is too sensitive; too sensitive to criticism, too sensitive to loud noises, too sensitive to bright light, too open to all sensory input. When the sensory window of a neurotic is opened, that individual suffers, and is close to Pain. Gradually, after being in Pain, in Primals, month after month, it becomes possible to have an open sensory window and *not suffer*. That is the gift of Primal Therapy. It makes people sensitive, and provides the mechanism for stopping human suffering.

The only neurobiological state which is truly comparable to the post-Primal state is that of infancy. One does not become an infant again, but the sensory window of a post-Primal person has the option of being wide open, as it was in infancy, before Pain. For most of us, "before Pain" means before birth, and that is why it takes quite a long time to become post-Primal. *People have been suffering all of their lives*. It takes a long time to feel most of that Pain.

REFERENCES

1. *The Primal Scream*
   Arthur Janov, Ph.D.
   G. P. Putnam's Sons, N.Y., 1970

2. Neurologic Mechanism Concerned in Epileptic Seizures.
   P. I. Yakovlev, M.D.
   Arch. Neurol. and Psych. *37*
   March, 1937, pp. 523-554

3. Mechanisms of Pathological Pain
   R. Melzack, Ph.D. in *Scientific Foundations of Neurology*
   Edited by Critchley, O'Leary and Jennet.
   F. A. Davis Co., Phila., 1972

CHAPTER SEVEN

The Nature of Pain and Its Relationship to Levels of Consciousness
Arthur Janov

Introduction

In a previous chapter, Dr. Holden has discussed our neuroembryologic development indicating that the brain is laid down sequentially in layers, the last and outermost layer being the one which is most advanced in man and which accounts for the higher thought processes.* The two lower layers, which consist of the spinal nerve-net system and the limbic system, are more primitive embryologically. There was a time in evolutionary history when the ancestors of man had only this primitive spinal nervous system. Later, the so-called reptilian or paleomammalian brain evolved which mediates affect, or what we now call feeling. This is the limbic system. Finally, in primate evolution, there appeared the typically human convoluted neocortex which has helped us to think, conceptualize and symbolize.

In some ways our ontogeny recapitulates our philogeny. The three key stages in the development of the brain correspond to the development of first, second and third-line consciousness. We start life with a relatively primitive nervous system with a large sensory component. This develops within the womb and continues to determine our responses for several months of social life. As I have explained in a previous chapter, the first level of consciousness corresponds to this phase of womb

---

* E. Michael Holden, M.D., "Levels of Consciousness" *Journal of Primal Therapy*, Vol. I, no. 2 (Fall 1973).

development. Though there is a second and third-line capacity for consciousness, it is not fully developed at that time and first-line consciousness predominates. The neonate registers his experiences organismically rather than being ideationally aware of events. His needs are largely biologic: to be touched, to be allowed to sleep peacefully, to nurse, to be kept dry, to be fed properly, to be adequately stimulated yet have a tranquil environment and so on. These needs are crucial; they must be fulfilled for the infant's proper development. When they are not fulfilled there is tremendous Pain, for the satisfaction of an infant's basic needs is a matter of life and death. Like a plant that is not watered, the infant is in danger of dying.

It should be noted that first-line Pain not only affects the first line. Because from the beginning there is an incipient second and third line interrelated with the first, they may be distorted in one way or another by that Pain.

As the infant develops, as he acquires a knowledge of words and begins to relate to a larger world than that of his mother's breast and the crib, he enters the second line of consciousness: at this time his limbic system predominates in his responses to his environment. He can now develop *emotional* attachments to his parents and relatives. He has the capacity to experience more than just physical discomfort and hurt; he can feel *emotional* suffering. This suffering occurs when his second-line needs are not attended to.

If he is not allowed the expression of his feelings, hostile or otherwise, to his parents, the general expression of feeling will be blunted as well as the consciousness of those feelings. If he senses early on that he is unsafe, that they do not care, and are not there to protect him, he will be forced to fend for himself and that will mean to defend against himself and his needs.

Later, third-line consciousness comes to predominate in the child's relations with his world. It is the third-line consciousness which can perceive, reflect, rationalize and symbolize Pain. It is the system of reason and logic, of full comprehension and external orientation. When there is too much Pain on the second line there is a "shut-off" so that the third line is pressed into service to help defend against and rationalize that Pain, rather than developing naturally as that integrating and coping system of higher consciousness.

As Pain (and I am using the upper case to denote Primal Pain, which may be from both physical and psychological origins) disconnected from the lower lines influences the third line, there is a symbolization of the Pain rather than a correct connection to it. So, instead of seeing the craziness in the parent's eyes, a realization that is catastrophic for a child, there is a blunted perception. With enough extra Pain later on, eyes may be hallucinated as "watching and dangerous." Those hallucinated eyes are a screened and symbolized memory; something registered on the second line barricaded away from the third.

It is continued Pain which produces more and more distortion until later the third line hasn't the slightest inkling of the Pain on the lower lines or even that there are such systems of consciousness operating below. The third line is simply impelled to become more and more symbolic as it becomes partially blocked away from the lower lines. The classifications of consciousness are not rigid categories; as Figure 1 reveals, there is extensive overlapping. At birth the first line is complete with level two partially functional. From then on levels two and three develop concurrently, level three continuing to develop for some twenty years before full maturity. The neocortex is functioning at birth. It may not be well developed enough to register all events in an organized way but there is some higher level of representation of first-line events even from the start of life.

Pain comes from not fulfilling the basic needs of the organism. We have lost touch with how catastrophic the Pain is because we have lost touch with those needs. Pain is the agency by which defenses are set in motion. It is the defense system which tries to maintain the integrity of the organism and its continuation.

I intend to show that there are levels of consciousness associated with the ontological (and phylogenetic) development of the brain and that these three levels process Pain, each in their specific ways. This means that there are three key Pain-processing systems associated with specific levels of consciousness. To block specific Pain is to be unconscious by that amount and to block on certain levels is to be rendered relatively unconscious on that level. The degree of Pain dictates the degree of consciousness.

The Pain of unfulfilled need is the central driving force in humans dictating how we feel, perceive, behave and think. The reason that Pain dictates consciousness is that it is not simply another experience. It is the key to survival. Those bereft of the faculty to perceive Pain are literally in danger of dying all the time. The whole development of man from the single cell amoeba has been to avoid painful stimuli and to seek fulfillment of need.

The problem in our field thus far has been that either consciousness or Pain was studied independently, not one as a function of the other. If, as I contend, Pain is the chief organizing principle of consciousness, it follows that the bringing of Primal Pain into full consciousness would liberate *a whole system of consciousness* rather than simply producing an awareness of one specific Pain or another. It is Pain which blocks the systems of consciousness and feeling it which unlocks those systems. There can be no fully mature human being without the participation of all three levels of consciousness.

The three systems of consciousness which I have proposed are: 1. The visceral-sensory: this deals with sensation and mediates bodily impulses and states. 2. The affective-expressive: this provides emotion and feeling. 3. The cognitive: this provides the discrimination and comprehension of feeling and deals with meaning. The three systems working together form an integrated feeling. When too much Pain occurs gates are activated to keep it on one level or another. Each system of consciousness has its own gating mechanism, and when an overload occurs the gates mercifully render us partially unconscious. Not only is the Pain blocked (or repressed) but the particular system of consciousness is affected preventing complete fluid access, in and out, of all other input. It is in this way that blockage of Pain renders us unconscious of nonpainful stimuli, affects general perception, reflection and introspection and also keeps us "split" from part of ourselves.

The aim of Primal Therapy is to open up the access among systems (or levels) of consciousness so that there is interconnection and full experience. The more that past Pain is given access the more the person lives in the immediate present, without old unconscious impulses driving him to do neurotic things.

Ronald Melzack is a key scientific investigator in the field of pain. A recent book of his called *The Puzzle of Pain*[1] cites much of the recent research on pain. He concludes that there are three central systems processing pain; and he numbers them, by chance, to correspond to my three levels of consciousness. They are: "1. The selection and modulation of the sensory input through the neospinothalamic projection system provides, in part at least, the neurological basis of the sensory-discriminative dimension of pain (Level One). 2. Activation of reticular and limbic structures through the paramedian ascending system underlies the powerful motivational drive and unpleasant affect that trigger the organism into action (Level Two). 3. Neocortical or higher central nervous

---

[1] R. Melzack, *The Puzzle of Pain*. Basic Books, New York, 1973.

system processes, [such as the evaluation of the input in terms of past experience] exert control over activity in both the discriminative and motivational systems. (Level Three)."

Melzack goes on to say that "It is assumed that these three categories interact with one another to provide *perceptual information* regarding the location, magnitude and spatiotemporal properties of the noxious (painful) stimulus, *motivational tendency* toward escape or attack, and *cognitive information* based on analysis of multimodal information, past experience and probability of outcome of different response strategies."[2]

Melzack gathers evidence indicating that the higher central nervous system processes exert a powerful influence on the Pain experience. This suppressing tendency exists all the way down the spinal column so that third-line consciousness can control sensory input and can influence nerve conductions at the earliest synaptic levels of the somesthetic system.[3]

The brainstem reticular formation (see Fig. 1) exerts a potentially powerful suppressive control over information projected from the spinal system. This formation has a descending inhibitory projection system which effectively gates upcoming information. And, on a higher level, the cortex has fibers leading to the reticular system which aids in the gating process.

Melzack has contributed to the understanding of the mechanisms by which gates open and close. He believes that the spinal gate system is influenced by the relative amount of activity in large-diameter fibers (which tend to inhibit transmission, and thereby close the gate) and small diameter fibers (which facilitate transmission upward and tend to open the gate). The small-diameter fibers open the gate, provide the basis of summation and cause, thereby, the spread of Pain to other areas of the body. What all this means is that input from the body can be gated before there is proper and complete apprehension of its meaning, rendering the person somewhat unconscious on the first line. Experience is organized on various levels of consciousness; and the only true, full human experience includes all of them.[4]

Melzack discusses a number of research studies dealing with the properties of nerve cells. He believes that there is a level of afferent barrage at which the cell responds, and a critical level at which there is silence due

---

[2] *Ibid.*, pp. 162-3.
[3] *Ibid.*, p. 160.
[4] For a technical and detailed description of precisely how each system gates another, the reader is referred to *The Puzzle of Pain*, pp. 102-3.

to inhibition. When we talk about the processing of Pain we are discussing whole systems of cells which function in unison to either facilitate or inhibit information from one level of consciousness to another.

There is no need to go over all the research leading to Melzack's conclusions since it is very complete on its own. What I want to point out is that the research seems to corroborate the notion of discrete levels of consciousness; something we have observed in hundreds of patients through thousands of Primals. Further, there are projecting fibers within each system of consciousness which interact with all other levels exerting both a facilitory and inhibiting action. In this way gates are either opened or closed.

Gating can be total or partial. Melzack points out that some central activities can close the gates for all inputs or can be selective and allow some information through while suppressing other inputs. What this means is that gating is not absolute. What is prevented egress is the *connection* to higher levels which makes the Pain a potentially overwhelming experience. It is connection which completes the experience of feeling and produces fully conscious Pain. What is allowed through, then, is *some* of the energy of the feeling which is felt as tension psychophysically.

The process is still a bit more complicated, unfortunately. For there are some first-line Pains, of being overstimulated by touch or noise, for example, which are barely tolerable; and the first-line gate may not shut off these experiences totally. But suppose later on the child is overstimulated by a constantly yakking parent, or constantly bickering family, then the *combined* load of first- and second-line Pains produces a shutdown on the second line.

If we can imagine that gate 1 can allow a Pain through with a charge value of 3 but not one with a value of 4; and if the limbic gate (gate 2) can allow Pains through with a charge of 4 but not 5, then when a Pain enters the second line with a charge value of 3 and combines with another subthreshold Pain on the second line with a charge value of 2, the second-line gate will shut down against both. We must keep in mind that the immature brain is less capable of integrating Pain than the mature one so that valences are high on the first line. Any kind of rejection may be catastrophic at two weeks but far less so at the age of ten. One major reason is simply that we have a more functioning brain with which to handle the load. That is why Primals on the first line are so intense and why they must not be experienced until much of higher levels of Pain have been resolved.

If we take the example above, the net result is that we have a person who cannot take excess stimulation; and the amount he can take on the third line as an adult will depend on the reservoir of blocked overstimulation seething on the lower lines. Thus, one neurotic who did not have that early experience may take a lot of input and handle it well, while another person may become totally frustrated, impatient and irritable with what seems to us to be slight input. We have all seen the person who blows up when asked one extra question. He may be still trying to integrate the first question. This can be expressed in the following equation: The greater the charge value of a particular repressed feeling, the less the charge value of the stimulus needed to set it off. The correlate of this is that the time distance between symbolic behavior and its connection to a real feeling is indicative of the degree of pathology. The degree of repression is what produces the time gap between a feeling and its ascent into consciousness. This time gap is a measurable quantity of repression. For instance, a new Primal patient may take hours to get to the root of his anxiety whereas in a more advanced patient it may be only a matter of seconds between the arousal of the feeling and its experience consciously. One patient who accidentally knocked his head against a door almost immediately found himself reliving a scene in which he had similarly hurt himself and been scolded for carelessness rather than comforted. The *macho* man would probably have reacted quite differently, denying any hurt at all, even in the present. An interconnected feeling person can be set off into feeling by almost any stimulation of the senses. The highly defended person is inured to most such stimuli and indeed something like a warm touch may only shut him down the more.

It takes very little to set off someone who is bristling with unfelt feelings, while it takes an exceptional amount of provocation to arouse someone who is deeply repressed. The nice person who never gets angry may simply be someone so well-defended that he is totally disconnected from his anger.

I want to clarify the equation above in terms of levels of consciousness. On the third line I may feel that Joe has not been friendly lately and I am mildly upset. I decide not to call him again but to wait for him to call me first. On the second line this becomes a feeling of abandonment of people close to me such as when I made the intolerable discovery at age four that my parents were not friendly any more and I ran away from home so as not to feel abandoned. On the first line this feeling turns into one of total abandonment and terror just after birth when I was placed in a plastic container away from the one person who could make

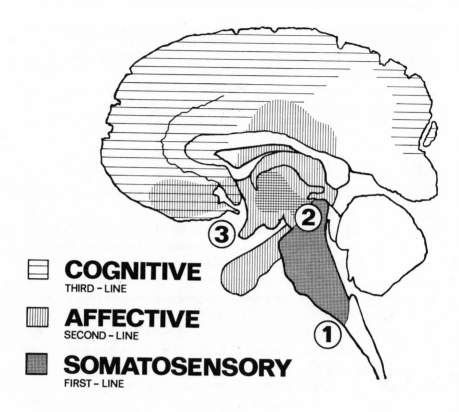

COGNITIVE
THIRD – LINE

AFFECTIVE
SECOND – LINE

SOMATOSENSORY
FIRST – LINE

Fig. 1   *The Three Levels of Consciousness in the Brain*

me feel safe. For there to be sequential access to that first-line feeling, there must have been a fully feeling consciousness on the higher levels. In neurotics the time gap between that lower-line feeling and consciousness is enormous whereas with the advanced Primal patient access is usually a matter of seconds. It is for the most part almost impossible for the neurotic to gain that kind of access unless he ingests some kind of mind-boggling hallucinogenic drug. This lack of access by the general population makes even the notion of the existence of that level of experience unacceptable to most of the intellectual scientific community.

Gating is a two-way process: ascending and descending. Not only do gates keep Pain away from the higher third-line consciousness, they also prevent external stimuli from overwhelming the system. That is one reason why we misperceive at a young age. We stop seeing what is too Painful to see, for example, that "they" don't love us. It is the function of gates to prevent incoming information (whether from inside or out) from overwhelming us. This is the way the integrity of the organism is preserved. Gates preserve our internal reality (the buried Pain) in its exact form. We never lose reality; we lose touch with it.

The misconception, however, can also compound our Pain. Once we suffer from deprivations early in life what happens is that we may misperceive events, which are ordinarily neutral, as harmful. Thus, no matter what our parents say, after a while we may misinterpret the meaning and make it into a hurt. So if a parent says, "Did you lose your glove?" the child may take it as a reprimand. Or if the parent says, "I'll help you find it," the child may take it as, "Why are you always treating me as an infant? I can find it myself." So the parent sooner or later can do no right, and the child's hurt becomes compounded.

Another reaction to early Pain is the almost total blocking out of reality, leaving the child and later the adult, insensitive to what is going on around him. Conscious awareness becomes very selective, allowing in only nonpainful stimuli. As consciousness narrows, unconsciousness expands so that the child becomes more and more unaware of his world. This lack of awareness begins under adverse conditions in the womb. As a result of tension in the mother which leads to smoking, drinking or taking drugs while pregnant, the fetus already begins to shut down his sensing apparatus and thus his awareness. We are born with a consciousness not an unconsciousness in the Freudian sense. However, we may have already had so many adverse experiences before birth that *in a sens*e we may be born partially unconscious.[5]

I want to underscore the Primal notion about perception. It is the third line which perceives and makes us aware of certain realities. Perception is an organic, holistic process which becomes blunted with Pain. When there is an overload of Primal Pain the *entire* perceptual function, both inner and outer, is impaired. Thus if certain inner realities cannot be perceived because of their load of Pain this will automatically blunt the perception of external realities related to that inner truth. In this way the system reflexively shuts out of awareness anything which can trigger off more Pain than can be integrated.

---

[5] See *The Feeling Child* for discussion of this.

The so-called blind spots of all of us are no more than these unconscious truths reflected in the outside world. *The truth is that we cannot
perceive beyond our needs and our Pains.* The deeper the Pain, the less
perceptive we become in those *related* areas. The more we are in touch
with ourselves, the more in touch with the world we become.

Naturally, neonates and infants can only gate with the cerebral equipment available. The cortex is not fully mature and the higher gates are
not going to be as well-functioning as later on. This means that since
there is an inadequate third line to integrate upcoming catastrophic
Pain such as being left alone for hours in the crib, the Pain must be
handled by the lower system. It is possible that a great overload of Pain
can overtax the systems of consciousness in an infant resulting in a
variety of effects from seizures to crib death.

First-line Pain is of the body and so are the defenses against it.
Bodily needs are the first to be shut down. As the infant buries his
needs (because they are unfulfilled and therefore painful) he creates
the first layer of unconsciousness. The suppression of bodily impulses
(crying, screaming) and the sensations (hunger) set up the deepest
(first-line) level of repression. Birth traumas and traumas which occur
even before birth are buried on this level; and they are largely inaccessible until one has descended in orderly fashion, as in Primal Therapy,
through the various systems of consciousness.

As the child grows older he becomes capable of fuller feelings and
emotions (the outward expression of feelings) on the second line. Brain
development allows him not only emotions but *emotional* Pain. He can
now feel, "My parents don't love me or care about me." When that
feeling is catastrophic the Pain produces a gating or shutdown and the
child becomes unconscious on that level of development; he becomes partially unconscious of his feelings. His emotional system is blunted, and
sooner or later he may no longer even feel, "I need my mommy or
daddy." Rather he begins his struggle to get them symbolically—high
grades, selling newspapers, doing the chores, and so on.

With even further development of the brain the third line predominates. The child can now rationalize both his needs (first line) and his
feelings (second line). In his teens he may go to a psychotherapist and
state that "My parents really loved me and I had a very happy childhood." If he can say that without any negative affect we might say that his
third line is functioning very well to block him from his feelings. If he
should sob or cry when he says that (and not know why), then there

would be evidence of some access to the second line. If the mention of his parents sets off a seizure we might hypothesize that there is first-line infiltration to the third line (more on this later). When someone is convinced that he was loved (and if he was indeed not loved) we can say that he is unconscious on all three levels. The gating of Pain has gated consciousness. He is becoming totally symbolic, living in his head instead of his feelings and needs. The intellectual defenses are being brought into action against the Pain. As Luria points out, the prefrontal cortex which mediates part of the third line (the site of intellectual defenses) does not really become fully functional until the age of four to seven.[6]

Here we see that defenses develop with the maturation of the brain and body system. The young child defends predominantly on a visceral and emotional level. The feelings, not yet absorbed into third-line symbols, are rerouted on a feeling level so that there may be temper tantrums, whining and constant crying or continuous fights with his peers. This emotional acting-out may give way later on to (third-line) fantasies of murder or revenge; or the person may live "in his head" reading and intellectualizing.

There is a point in time when the child *is* emotional, rerouted though it may be. But with enough punishment, scolding and spanking, this level of behavior is buried so that he is no longer an emotional human being. He now has lost touch with both his body and its sensations, and his feelings. He is becoming increasingly unconscious as well. So we see that being fully feeling is being fully conscious and vice versa. The loss of the necessary elements for feeling are progressive, just as is the process of losing consciousness in a physical sense (from *awake to comatose*).

Drugs and Consciousness

There are implications of what I am discussing for almost all of human behavior. It may be possible, for example, to classify drugs in terms of their predominant mode or site of action. Thus, alcohol might be considered a third-line drug because it acts on the highest levels of nervous activity, blocking acquired inhibitions and facilitating access to the second line where the person can laugh and cry perhaps for the first time.

---

[6] A. Luria, *The Working Brain* (Basic Books, New York, 1973), p. 87.

Certainly, small amounts of wine can put a Primal patient immediately into a second-line feeling and a subsequent Primal. Analgesics which act on peripheral receptors might be considered first-line drugs. They block Pain without the predominant influence of higher centers. First-line drugs may be those which activate in a most general way or inhibit in the same manner. Amphetamines certainly have higher (third-line) effects, but these may be due to their galvanizing first-line Pains causing their ascendance into the third-line; hence the insomnia and general, nonfocused agitation. All of this is not to say that drugs may not influence every part of the nervous system; rather, it is to wonder if there are certain systems over which they exert the *most* influence. Barbiturates, for example, affect much of the nervous system but one key function of them is to block or slow small-fiber (facilitation of transmission) action. This action reduces the afferent (incoming) barrage to a level below that necessary for the full appreciation of Pain. Barbiturates, then, are first-line drugs.

Tranquilizers, particularly the phenothiazine derivations, are intermediate in position, separating the first from the second lines. Their action is predominantly on the reticular system collaterals and they serve to hold down first-line Pain and prevent its full access to the second and third lines. They relax the face muscles, for example, and lower the voice. Those who need tranquilizers are those with "leakage" (partial painful access) from the second to third lines; those who feel emotionally overwrought yet know not why.

Sleep is a first-line activity. The sleeping pills which decrease REM sleep are, in my estimation, predominantly first line. However, drugs such as Chloral, Dalmane and Quaalude separate second from third lines. It is my observation that insomnia is often caused by partial access from the first line. This access is facilitated as a result of the use of drugs such as LSD. And those who have used LSD in the past often find it hard to fall asleep, sometimes for months afterwards. Enough marijuana can also produce that result. What has happened is that out-of-sequence first-line Pains have been shaken loose by the drugs which then constantly activate the third line. This does not mean that second-line Pain cannot also push the third line into hyperactivity when a person is on the verge of sleep, but I think that second-line Pain alone is usually not enough to cause chronic insomnia. It is the activation of the third line which keeps the mind racing and keeps us awake. Sleep means giving up third-line control; yet lower-line activation presses the third line into even greater service.

During the very early days of our lives, sleep patterns which tend to endure for decades are laid down. It is the first-line Pains which cause the system to be continually galvanized in a general way later on mostly because the Pains are nonfocusable and noncomprehensible, having been laid down before the existence of a viable third line which could delineate and circumscribe them.

The effect of caffeine (coffee) is paradoxic but I consider it first line since it activates our system in a general way often producing insomnia. Caffeine stimulates both the cortex and the medulla. What seems incredible is that some neurotics can drink large amounts of coffee at night and then go to sleep. Their gating systems are so locked in that even a strong stimulant like caffeine fails to stimulate the person enough to keep him alert. Primal Therapy, by lowering the gating action, produces dramatically different reactions in patients. Whereas before, patients could drink coffee and still fall asleep with ease, after therapy even one cup of coffee is sufficient to keep them awake at night. The neurotic's defense system is designed to keep him from feeling inordinately agitated by internal Pain so that it is no wonder that stimulation from without such as caffeine is likewise not felt. In other words the defense system does not differentiate between the sources of stimulation. It will gate with equal effectiveness stimulation by drugs or by internal Pain. In the advanced Primal patient where there is fluid inter-access there is no suppression or rerouting so that all stimulation whether by Pain or by drugs is felt immediately and directly.

LSD is exceptionally dangerous because it seems to open all gates flooding the cortex. It is my observation after treating many "acid freaks" that the continued use of LSD *permanently* alters the gating system producing a continuous (yet attenuated) flood state. Marijuana can reactivate a bad LSD trip by reopening a gate that is now weakened and functioning inadequately, at best. Marijuana does not blast open the gate system as LSD does but continued heavy use can result in the same effects. Evidence that LSD reduces third line functioning is the loss or serious reduction in the ability to abstract, to understand complex ideas or sentences and loss of very recent memory. Because the third line integrates lower line Pain, any loss in its integrity is serious for those who need all the third line they can get to keep from being overwhelmed by first and second line trauma. Marijuana does not affect the third line in such a serious way (except over time). Food, sex and music are much fuller experiences with marijuana because the person has fuller access to his body and its sensations, without the rigid third line cap. The reason that marijuana relaxes is the pressure is taken off the upsurging forces. This tells a good deal about the origin of tension because third line ideology, beliefs, attitudes, philosophies, religious notions, parental prohibitions and cultural mores all form an airtight hatch against feelings. The result of this clash between internalized third line belief systems and natural impulses and feelings is tension.

There are some therapeutic implications of all this; for if in a selected case there is too much first line Pain coming up it is possible to block it for a time with a first line drug such as codeine allowing the patient some rest and sleep. This would apply in a situation where the lower line gating was exceptionally inadequate.

It may also be true that second line drugs such as Valium can be used to quell overarching second line Pain allowing the patient to focus on one specific feeling or scene without being fragmented by a flood of ascending second line Pain. Again, this would only be indicated in exceptional cases where gating was weak. The drug must be specific, however, for codeine would not be as effective (if at all) in quelling second line Pain as Valium. In short, there are specific drugs for the Pains on each level of consciousness depending on whether the system mediating the Pain is visceral, body wall, or cognitive. We hope to learn more about this in the future.

These notions about drugs and levels of consciousness are more than academic. From our observations and information we can now distinguish which symptoms are associated with which level of consciousness; and therefore, which drugs might be appropriate. Headaches are a case in point. There are at least two broad categories of headache—tension and migraine (second and first line, respectively). For each kind of headache there is a specific category of drug to be used.

Migraine is essentially a problem of what happens to certain blood vessels under Pain. In order to understand migraine we need to view it as the result of changes in blood pressure. Blood pressure is largely in control of the hypothalamus—the structure which mediates many of our first line functions. What I think happens is that trauma on the first line, say of birth, leaves few response alternatives outside of the body. When the fetus cannot breathe or cannot get out of the canal tremendous pressure builds up in the head. The system quickly mobilizes its resources to ward off the Pain. The blood system constricts; and by that action may set up a prototypic response to later stress. Thus, later on, a great stress may trigger off the first line trauma and the result is vasoconstriction. But vasoconstriction is not enough to produce a migraine. The blood system can only constrict and clamp down for so long before its resources are overtaxed. At that point the constrictive process fails and a tremendous vasodilatation takes place. The blood coursing through the vessel stretches its walls and puts pressures on the nerve endings inside the vessels, resulting in the pain of migraine. (I have left out all of the complex mechanics involved in migraine for purposes of illustration of the main point. No discussion about the blood system's ability to dispose of its waste products under continued vasoconstriction, etc.)

When the migraine sets in, drugs are needed to help bolster the blood system's failing resources. Ergot (Caffergot) or caffeine would be the drugs of choice because they are cerebral vasoconstrictors, and in that sense are first line drugs. We must not forget that a prototypic organ such as the blood system develops a vulnerability, a certain weakness, when it is called upon time after time, year after year, to help sequester Pain. It is then that drugs must be used to aid the faltering system.

Tension headaches are quite another matter; I see them as second line involving problems around the body wall. Tension headaches usually result from tightness around the head, neck and shoulders. A drug such as Valium helps here because it eases that tightness. Tension headaches often feel like a band around the head or a tautness in the back of the neck. The tightness of the body wall is mediated by several brain structures, not the least of which is the limbic system which also mediates second line Pain. The tension headache is vastly different from the migraine; involves a different level of consciousness and requires drugs which operate differentially on those levels. Migraines are often devastating in their pain precisely because first line Pain is so excruciating. Migraine, therefore, *is* the feeling of that first line Pain only in derived, unconnected form.

It is not my intention to examine the biochemistry of drugs nor their particular sites of action. What I want to do is provide a new frame of reference for investigating drugs, and to try to reorient approaches to consider the levels of consciousness as they relate to drugs.

Part of this orientation includes an understanding of dosage; for it isn't simply that a certain drug, say caffeine, has this effect or that. Rather, one must consider the *amount* of the drug ingested. Small amounts of caffeine can galvanize the third line into greater function; helping the integrating process, enhancing third line suppression of lower line Pain. A much greater amount of caffeine, however, can be disintegrative of the third line, thrusting lower line Pains upward so that the third line is overtaxed and becomes fragmented . . . the amphetamine (speed) psychoses are a case in point. A little marijuana may feel good; lifting third line pressure enough to offer the person some surcease. (It is no accident that

marijuana is effective in glaucoma—high blood pressure of the eye.)*
By easing the third line lid off a bit the person has relief from inner pressure. But too much marijuana leaves the person bereft of sufficient third
line, lower line Pain comes up and the result is fright and a bad trip.

The clinical use that could be made of this scheme is considerable. For
example, in someone with a very tight musculature, who uses his body to
defend, muscle relaxants can attenuate those defenses while leaving the
"head" intact. This often permits a person to feel. In a person who cannot
experience Primals there may be a "paradoxical reaction" in that a weakened body defense may allow egress of Pain causing the head to race and
produce a feeling of mental agitation *even though* the muscle system has
a hard time tensing up. Second-line drugs such as Valium (a muscle relax-
ant) are dangerous in borderline psychotics who need every defense
possible including the body defenses. Valium acts on the limbic system and
the spinal cord. The use of alcohol by the near-psychotic is also exceedingly dangerous because it diminishes the third-line functions of cohesion and control. With too much liquor, the person either becomes violently paranoid or just generally bizarre in his ideation and behavior. You
can observe a person fragmenting and "loosening up" with the use of
alcohol. The use of LSD for the near-psychotic is the most highly dangerous of all as it drives up Pain beyond the system's ability to integrate
it. If any drug were to be used with the pre-psychotic and the psychotic,
for that matter, it would be the tranquilizer because what is needed is
something to suppress lower-line Pain, not liberate it. The function of
the tranquilizer is to permit the third line to gather its cohesive forces
by suppressing the second and first-line eruptions of Pain. In this way
the third line can focus upon a single feeling and integrate it.

Because we want a stronger third line in the pre-psychotic all of the
usual therapeutic techniques used with a neurotic to break down defenses are reversed. We do *not* isolate the pre-psychotic nor attack his
defenses. He is not busted and is initially allowed a good deal of dependence on the therapist. We encourage socializing during the initial treatment rather than discourage it. The aim however is still the same—to
get at the Pain. We strengthen third-line defenses in the seriously ill
patient not as an end in itself but as a means to integrate the Pain.

Some completely controlled third liners can be helped by general acti-

---

*Our preliminary research with the air tonometer indicates that Primal people (espe-
cially over the age of thirty-five) have significantly lower interocular pressure than
the general population. This will undoubtedly have implications for the treatment
of glaucoma.

vating drugs such as amphetamine or ritalin. The activation drives the Pain up through the gate system producing, in some cases, feeling. Too much speed produces the paradoxical reaction; it activates the whole gating system due to the overload causing a massive shut down. And, massive doses of amphetamines have been (and are being) used to quell epileptic seizures and calm hyperactive children. This is a dangerous treatment procedure, in my estimation, because it makes robots of the subjects, shutting them down completely, and later there is a price to pay for this massive artificial gating action. All that is being gated is the agitation from the lower lines. Gating doesn't eliminate the Pain; it only suppresses it until the drug wears off and the rebound (of Pain) begins. It is interesting to note that a dose of amphetamine which calms a child can seriously agitate an adult. It is my assumption that the child is more easily overloaded and shutdown, whereas the adult needs much more of a dose to create that state.

I want to reiterate that drugs are not usually part of the Primal process; which is a completely natural process. But I have received many letters from those outside this institute who have had experience of drugs besides reports from patients with pre-therapy drug encounters. What is obvious is that the effects of drugs depends in large part on the level of consciousness on which the individual operates. To activate a second-line hysteric who weeps and whines constantly with amphetamines is to run the risk of psychosis. To suppress a depressive runs the risk of suicide. To massively release lower-line Pain with the use of LSD runs the risk of either psychosis or suicide.

What is rather amazing about drugs such as alcohol is that people can drink for decades and never realize that they are in Pain. They delude themselves into thinking that they have a need for liquor rather than a need to kill Pain. Indeed, whenever Pain is on the rise a drink is automatically used to suppress it; and rarely is this a conscious process. A person who can "hold his liquor" is someone whose third line is so solidly defended and encased that even large amounts of alcohol cannot upset its control. The whole focus on drugs and alcohol seems to be third line—it is taken for what it seems to be rather than something related to events on the lower lines of consciousness.

I have a general rule of thumb in evaluating the action of drugs and it depends on how they affect our Pain. We know that in general anything which is noxious or painful tends to cause contraction or constriction in living forms away from that stimulus. Anything that is need-fulfilling (and therefore pleasant and non-noxious) tends to open up our systems causing relaxation, expansion and generally dilatation. Certainly this has been shown in experiments with pupillary reaction where even pictures of distasteful scenes cause pupillary constriction. It is also true of our blood system; I think that many problems of heart disease begin because of chronic vascular constriction due to Pain.

Our inner system cannot shrink away from a noxious inner stimulus (Primal Pain) as it can from outer stimuli which are harmful. What happens is that the system must use all of its resources to shut down against that internal stimulus. It galvanizes all subsystems, blood, muscle, respiratory, etc., to "lock up" the Pain and block it from overwhelming the organism. The brain shuts its gates and the vessels narrow or close their openings. If a drug tends to activate our Pain then the system will immediately compensate by constriction. And this is the wonder of the human body. For example, caffeine stimulates the Pain and can cause it to rise. (Enough stimulation—as, for example, large doses of amphetamines—can sometimes even produce psychoses.) The system, in order to guard against the rise in Pain, shuts down. In the case of caffeine all of the blood systems around the head and brain constrict; and caffeine is considered a cerebral vasconstrictor. Indeed, caffeine is sometimes prescribed for vascular headaches where there is too much vessel dilation. I believe that almost any drug can be understood in terms of how it affects Primal Pain. The body with all of its subsystems is an incredible monitor against threat and will find ingenious ways to compensate for alien intrusions.

A recent study was done by Dr. Wilbert Aronow on men with coronary conditions. He found that a small amount (ten puffs) of marijuana drastically reduced the amount of exercise that these men could endure before they developed severe chest pain. I think that there is an explanation for the University of California, Irvine, study, namely that marijuana tends to open gates liberating Primal Pain which in turn causes the body as a whole to shut down against Pain with the coronary artery constriction and angina as the result. We must remember that repression of Pain is not simply a brain function. The entire body functions in conjunction with the brain in the service of repression.

The perfect drug is the one which obliterates Pain effectively on all three levels; I believe that drug is heroin. The heroin "rush" is that state where all Pain is buried and the person feels relaxed as never before. The drug is so effective in blotting out consciousness, however, that soon the person is "on the nod;" he is out on his feet, either drowsy or asleep. The drug has done its job; it has reduced Pain by reducing consciousness.

For a drug to be fully addicting, in my opinion, it must be a good first line blocker. Any drug that cannot do that is not addicting. That is why marijuana and LSD are not addictive. Nor are the tranquilizers. Drug addicts, by and large, are constantly dealing with first line ascending Pain, and they have no other effective way to deal with it. They are addicted, not because of the drug, but because of the Pain. The after-effects of withdrawal are far less from any physiologic process as from the onrush of Pain which has previously been pushed down and compressed into a lurking, surging force. When the drugs are removed the Pain rushes to the surface with great force and then it takes even more drugs to keep it down. And so the cycle: compressed Pain by drugs, withdrawal of drugs, onrush of Pain and need for more drugs to push it back.

The final point I want to make is that it isn't simply Pain that one is suppressing with drugs, it is one's past history. Since suppressant drugs prevent access to our past they help to keep us very symbolic. The tranquilized neurotic may look and behave normally because his past is subdued but he is nonetheless totally disconnected from the source of his current symbolic notions. He becomes a kind of ahistoric auto-maton.

DRUGS AND LEVELS OF CONSCIOUSNESS
M. Holden

DRUGS	3rd LINE NEOCORTEX	2nd LINE LIMBIC SYSTEM	1st LINE MEDIAN ZONE OF BRAIN
Caffeine	Direct stimulation [makes 3rd line defenses more adequate in low doses; less adequate at higher doses].	Little effect on R.E.M. sleep. Stimulation, at moderate doses will cause tremor and increased muscle tension.	High doses increase access to Primal Pain. Stimulation of medulla and hypothalamus at higher doses. Huge doses lead to anxiety, panic, then seizures.
Methylphemidate [Ritalin, Meratran-diphenylmethanes]	Stimulates midline and intralaminar nuclei of thalamus with *secondary* cortical alerting.	Little effect on R.E.M. sleep. Increases speed of motor responses, slight increase in risk of seizures.	Little stimulation of hypothalamus. Rare tachycardia, rare hypertension. No "crash" as with amphetamines, after use.
Dextroamphetamine	Stimulates ponto-medullary reticular formation with *secondary* cortical alerting. Extreme anxiety at higher doses and impairment of 3rd line defenses.	Marked impairment of R.E.M. sleep. Stimulation, secondary to lower brainstem stimulation. External anxiety—psychosis, at higher doses.	Anxiety, adrenergic sweating. *Increased* access to Primal Pain. Tachycardia, hypertension, common.
Morphine	"Chemical frontal lobotomy." *Knowledge* of Pain not impaired. *Suffering* of Pain *not* appreciated. Frontal cortex opiate receptors known.*	Impairment of R.E.M. sleep. Opiate receptors in putamen, amygdala, and hippocampus. Tends to blunt second-line Pain, decreases muscle tension. Similarity, identity, with *dopamine* receptors, known.	Primary action on medial opiate receptor cells in medial midbrain, medial hypothalamus and medial thalamus. Markedly *decreases* access to first line Primal Pain. Withdrawal leads to *sudden* access to first-line Primal Pain: result may be psychosis. Opiate withdrawal in a Primal patient leads to a first line Primal.**
Benzodiazepines [Librium, Valium and analogs]	Anti-anxiety and anti-convulsant action secondary to inhibitory influence on second-line Primal Pain in limbic system. [Primal patients who were epileptic before therapy usually become seizure-free, off medications, later in Primal Therapy.]	Mild impairment of R.E.M. sleep. Inhibition of limbic system. Second-line Primal Pain-blunting effect.	No apparent blunting of first line Primal Pain, judging from experience of patients in Primal Therapy who have access to first-line Pain.

Chloral Hydrate	Thought to act on midline thalamus: blocks 3rd line access to Pain in lower levels of consciousness.	Does not impair R.E.M. sleep. Allows second line to function: does not appear to blunt second-line Pain.	No effect on first-line Primal Pain. [If a Primal patient is close to first-line Pain, chloral hydrate is little help for the insomnia, which is the clinical hallmark of increased access to first-line Primal Pain.]
Barbiturates	Increased EEG frequencies [beta] with low doses; slower EEG frequencies [theta, delta] with higher doses.	Marked impairment of R.E.M. sleep. Speed of movements decreased. Mild-moderate anti-convulsant action: [phenobarbital others].	Reticular core of brainstem probable major site of action. Sedation, not analgesia, results. Patients with access to first-line Primal Pain remain insomniac at 5-10 times usual therapeutic doses.
Cannabis, LSD	Moderate to high doses of cannabis produce effects similar to those of LSD. There is stimulation of the brainstem and impairment of cortical function. Access to Primal Pain is increased at a time when all gates to Pain are impaired. Thus one is exposed to catastrophic first-line Primal Pain which not uncommonly leads to psychosis, panics and nightmares. It is probable that the gates to Primal Pain are permanently opened by these drugs: more-so when there is long exposure to high doses.		
Ethyl Alcohol	Impairs third-line defenses, increases access to Primal Pain at low doses. Blunts Primal Pain at higher doses.	Marked impairment of R.E.M. sleep. Incoordination, clumsiness and relaxation of muscles: a second-line Pain blunter "decreases tension."	Very high doses, sedating doses, will blunt first-line Primal Pain, but specificity is low. At such doses, one risks systemic metabolic suppression.

We believe the Pain-blunting capacity of alcohol fully accounts for its widespread use in our society. Alcoholism is not a disease: it is a neurotic attempt to avoid Primal Pain. [Primal Therapy is a cure for alcoholism. Post-Primal people may drink socially or abstain, as they wish. There is no obligation to "achieve sobriety."]

*Snyder et al: Ann. Int. Med. 81, 534, 1974.
**An addicting drug in a Primal context is one which, when withdrawn, gives an individual sudden access to Primal Pain, no more, no less. Sudden access to Primal Pain will account for all features of the withdrawal syndrome.

Diagnostic Implications

I believe that a proper understanding of the levels of consciousness should reorient current diagnostic (and treatment) procedures. If my belief is right, then we can do away with the standard psychiatric nomenclature which has been with us for decades and which has been anything but precise. I think this lack of precision has something to do with the fact that it was not inextricably related to how the brain works. That is, nomenclature became an entity in itself largely unrelated to cerebral processes. My current proposal is that any diagnostic procedure should make *simultaneous statements about psychological and neurologic processes.* (A psychiatric diagnosis which does not accord with neurologic facts is inadequate.) This would include what we have observed in the Primal experiences of patients and what they report about their levels of consciousness during them; and also coalesce with what is known up to the present about neurophysiology. I should hasten to add that there is a problem in the other direction; namely, that neurological research has not had a frame of reference which includes the psychologic dimension. The result is unidimensional theories and the accumulation of facts unrelated to theoretical matrices. Melzack offers a theory of pain but not a theory of *people in pain.* He does not relate his concepts to an appropriate psychotherapeutic procedure except to make a plea at the end for "pain clinics." I submit that the Primal Institute has been a "Pain clinic" for many years. In addition, Melzack's approach does not relate to levels of consciousness per se; he wants to *control* Pain. He does not see the value or necessity of reliving and thereby resolving it. It is a most important step to understand that Pain exists as an unresolved memory which must be re-experienced.[7] Even though Melzack discusses "phantom limb" pain of amputees and notes that the pain may linger for years as a central memory process, he does not relate that phenomenon to psychological (Primal) Pain. The problem in pain research, as with any other investigation in medicine, is that it is *people* who are in pain, not neurons and it is people who must be studied in a holistic way. Having said that I want to turn the discussion to a new diagnostic procedure based on levels of consciousness.

My proposition is that there are first, second and third liners; individuals whose predominant mode of operation is on one level of consciousness

---

[7] "Re-experience" means to experience the Pain on all three levels rather than having it contained on one level as before.

or another. Within those levels are differences based on the differing experiences of people, not to mention differing physical systems. So, for example, the concept of "border-line psychotic" would have more meaning if we understand that the person is bordering on the Pain of the first line. Obviously, depending on the life history of the' person, he can be on the border of catatonia (unable to move, speak or emote) or of falling into a total hallucination pattern where first-line trauma erupts into the third line. There are many first-line traumas, and they are devilish because there is no way to consciously remember them as specific scenes. For example, a "loving" father can constantly be patting and rocking his infant to the point of overload. He may do this almost every time he picks the baby up, and there is nothing the infant can do about it. But that trauma may be hallucinated much later in life as a hand about to crush him or a general sense of vibration, etc. The current symbol in the hallucination is a direct reflection of an early first-line trauma which has no specific setting, no remembered time. It is a sensory memory and when reactivated comes out in sensory form via a hallucination. Delusions are ideational, not strictly sensory and therefore contain later Pain along with first line. First-line Pain is usually the result of life-and-death situations. It exists before we can conceptualize and tends to be catastrophic in its effects on the third line. One reason why it is catastrophic is that the range of possibilities for avoidance of the Pain during the time of its occurrence is extremely narrow; an infant can cry, sleep or squirm and not much else. The overload usually comes out within the body in the form of symptoms such as colic.

The classic Freudian hysteric, the one who is all emotion with no focus, can be thought of as a second liner. There are again, variations within this level; for example, one person may be in a constant rage (acting out in uncontrolled fashion rage at mother or father) while another may always be crying over one piece of trivia after another. These individuals find "excuses" to rationalize on the third-line eruptions from the second.

The characteristic of the second liner is continuous spillover from the second line to the third line. It can be in an artistic way, painting the feelings, or it can be in a destructive way, arguing and fighting with people. He is generally seen as an "emotional type."

The first liner is the impulse neurotic; the one who acts out without any control. The alcoholic is an example, and the rapist is another. The nymphomaniac is still another. These people act out with their bodies with few mental defenses (third line) to help them. Obviously, there are many second-line components to these impulse problems, but it is my

belief that severe acting out is caused by great Pain and tension which
existed before the mental apparatus existed to absorb and control it. Somatic complaints, like headaches, would be first-line ailments, particularly
those ailments which are close to the body midline (colitis, asthma,
ulcers, etc.) Here the body absorbs Pain. Instead of acting out physically,
we "act in" physically. The point, however, is that it is the visceral system
that is predominantly engaged, and that is the first line at work.

I want to emphasize that *all* levels of repressed Pain influence current
behavior. But there seems to be a predominant mode which characterizes each of us. Highly intellectualized individuals are what I call third
liners. They may have less control of their bodies, less coordination, less
sex drive (or highly symbolized sexual activity), and can only relate to
ideas or numbers rather than being able to relate in an emotional way to
other human beings. Many engineers, accountants, computer operators and
neurologists (to name a very few) are among the typical third liners we
see. And their choice of occupation already tells us what kind of patient
they might be. There is a Primal axiom that "if you scratch a third
liner you get a first liner. Generally, the implication is that there is so
much first-line damage that the second line doesn't develop adequately,
and you find a patient who cannot remember his childhood and the
Pains of his youth. Rather, they slip from the third line in therapy to
body action—writhing and thrashing without words or ideas about what
they are going through. In any case, the key to classifying a patient in
terms of his predominant system of consciousness is the word "access." If
a person has real access to his emotions he is considered, by and large,
a second liner. If his first line is but a hair away and is constantly pressing,
he is thought to be a first liner. If he has no access to emotions he is a
third liner. Obviously none of the categories are rigid and mutually exclusive. These are just shorthand methods of thinking about the problem.

Actors tend to be second liners. Their occupation (if they are good at
it) necessitates access to their feelings; and this too tells us how they
might do in Primal Therapy. Not only that, but in general we have an
idea as to what level of consciousness they will begin their therapy on;
assuming they want therapy. It is the third liner, by and large, who does
not. His defenses are working well protecting against the Pain on the
lower lines. Should there even be the slightest breakthrough, the chances
are that the third liner will choose the kind of therapy that will bolster his
temporarily inadequate defense system, not weaken it further. Thus, he
may want psychoanalysis so he can better *understand* his problems and
find ways to cope with them. Or he may choose conditioning therapy so as

to repress not only upcoming feelings but their symbols, as well. The second liner, by and large feels his suffering and wants surcease. There are first liners who are somewhat in the position of the third liner. They continue to act out and do not suffer until they are caught and punished. (The rapist is an example). They can be just as unconscious as the intellectual who uses his head to defend. It is possible to have elements of both first and third lines. What is missing is the all-important second line which provides the connecting emotional link which allows a person to relate to others in a meaningful way instead of as one body to another or one mind to another. A good "meeting of the minds" is not all of a relationship; nor is a seemingly adequate sexual relationship. A full, mature relationship includes all components of consciousness.

There are some who choose the pseudotherapies, embracing heuristic movements or East Indian philosophies, for example. These people look to a network of ideas and attitudes to cover their Pain. The paradox is that Pain *is* their central reality, whether they know it or not, and it is also Pain's defenses which separate them from the truth of life. To try to make other people's experiences and ideas one's own is to be in *more* Pain, not less, because they are no longer being themselves. They are trying to be one more person's (a guru's) idea of a good human being, and trying to live their life in terms of someone else's experience.

The paradox of Primal Therapy is that what might be termed the most highly disturbed patients with a history of failure in other therapies often do best with us. The reason is simple; other therapies, by and large attempt to control behavior, suppress "hysteria" and block the overt expression of free-floating anxiety. Those with Pain least defended are obviously the most difficult to control. They are therefore considered the toughest patients in other therapies. In Primal Therapy where we are after lower-line access, this turns out to be a benefit.

When a borderline psychotic or a person with free-floating anxiety goes to a mental hospital (and they are sent precisely because they cannot "control their emotions"), they are given drugs which help them defend against the very feelings which could make them whole. The drugs they are given help the gating process. The person who is hallucinating no longer may do so. The reason is, I believe, that hallucinations are a sign of breakthrough of first-line sensory traumas, now symbolized, and the drugs suppress that Pain. The person who is hallucinating seems to be in a state where first-line material is reactivated without the benefit of higher line rationalizations and interpretations. It is a more "pure" state, so to speak.

A late-blooming paranoia is the result of compounding; one plus two plus three. This means that the person holds himself together until some third-line stress or continued agony finally shatters his third-line cohesion resulting in paranoia. Given a quiet, later environment the person may never develop paranoia. So we might say that a predisposition toward psychosis occurs when the valence of one plus two is high. If the valence of one is high enough (if there were many compounded traumas on the first line—bad birth, sent away to an orphanage, etc.) it can be sufficiently predisposing to psychosis at an early age. But this does not mean that there is a "latent psychotic process" as we very often see in the psychiatric literature. Rather, it simply means that enough stress later in life weakens the third-line integrating mechanisms permitting access of lower-line Pain, resulting in bizarre psychotic symbolization. It is not psychosis that is latent; it is Pain. It only becomes psychosis when it cannot be integrated. For example, there are no crazy ideas floating around on the first line just waiting for the opportunity to come to the surface. Crazy ideas happen when too much Pain comes to the surface too fast.

What I want to underscore is that a Primal diagnosis, say of the second line, makes a statement about both the *brain and behavior,* not one or the other. This diagnosis may help determine the kind of therapy necessitated and also indicate what neurological processes are at work. Further, it leaves itself open to measurement both psychologically and neurologically. There should be certain EEG patterns shown with specific psychological changes, as indeed we have already found in our research.

Because a Primal diagnosis indicates certain things about the physical system the liberation of Pain should make differences in that system; as we have found in our research on vital signs of patients (lowered blood pressure, pulse, and body temperature). *When a diagnosis does not make a statement about the whole organism, then one is left to study only behavior, attitudes and other purely cerebral activity.* One is then to believe that the changes observed in those psychological parameters indicate profound changes in "personality." Moreover, it is also assumed that those psychologic changes corroborate the efficacy of the psychotherapeutic procedures employed. Thus, while the person is no longer drinking alcohol and may even say that he doesn't want it any longer (a sign of health in terms of those other therapeutic procedures) his physical system may be in great danger in terms of increases in vital signs such as higher blood pressure and pulse rate. So the psychologic diagnosis and prognosis look good while the person is in danger of a

premature death because the *outlets* of tension have been removed
without the accompanying elimination of Pain.

In Primal Therapy we would expect that someone who has facile access
to his first line (after a systematic journey through the higher lines) and
who has resolved many Pains on that level, would no longer suffer from
impulsive acting-out, from such physical symptoms as pressure headaches
or frigidity, for example. To successfully penetrate the second line means
to expand one's emotional range, to no longer suffer from "flattened affect," and to be able to relate to others in a more sustained way.

Perhaps now is the time to clarify some aspects of the third line. The
third line exists even in the neonate but in inchoate form. It becomes less
rudimentary as the child develops but is not totally adequate until after the
age of six or so. It is at about six and after that the child's emotional life
can be completely squashed resulting in the dampened affect we often
see. This does not mean that he does not gradually become dampened
from birth on with each trauma, but somehow in many of us the gate to

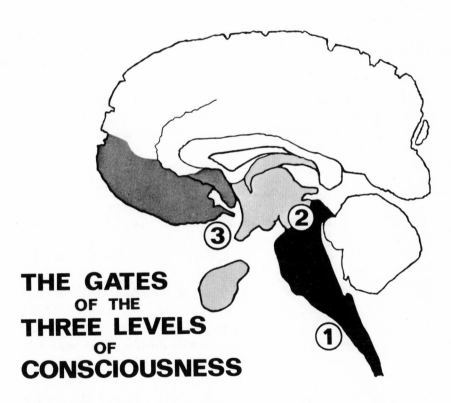

THE GATES
OF THE
THREE LEVELS
OF
CONSCIOUSNESS

feeling remains somewhat opened until we reach school age. What parents do not accomplish, schools and churches do. The age of six by the way is the time of development of the Freudian superego, an agency for repression of natural impulses.

Obviously, there are third-line traumas; to be mugged, raped, divorced are all current traumas. But whether those traumas will be responded to neurotically depends on whether the person can feel what is going on. If he is overloaded, if current events trigger off unresolved lower-line Pains, then he is going to shut down and respond neurotically. There are third-line traumas in our childhood. They existed in the "here-and-now" of our youth; failing in an important class, for example. But whether or not those Pains persist (and enter our dream life) in adulthood depends upon whether they were tied to unresolved second- and first-line Pains. My assumption is that a painful event will not persist if it was resolved back then. It will surely remain as a memory, but not a Primal Pain. It is the emotional traumas of our youth that could not be integrated that form the stuff of the second line. Having trouble learning geometry in the sixth grade is not going to be a trauma, even with failure, unless that failure has multiple Painful meanings besides learning geometry ("I am a failure and therefore not loved," for example). Wilder Penfield's work (discussed earlier) is significant in this respect because when his surgical patients were stimulated in the temporal lobe of the brain with an electronic probe they did not remember third-line events such as learning to solve problems, making decisions in the past, adding up a column of figures or writing a letter. Their memories were *emotional* (second line) and feeling (first line).

I consider the third line chiefly responsible for the integration of events on the other two lines. When reality is inordinately painful almost from birth, when there is no love, open rejection, abandonment, etc., the third line does not develop properly. Rather, it becomes fragmented, loses cohesion and tends to be easily submerged by any kind of subsequent trauma. Continuous trauma and harsh surroundings, then, produce *compounding*. The effect of compounding is to produce a fragile and delicate third-line system, the result of which is lack of coherence in speech, lack of continuity in thought, distractability, bizarre symbolization divorced from any reality, mystical notions, erratic behavior and a general fragmentation of thought patterns. A disrupted third line means that comprehension is limited, that insight is blocked, that bizarre meanings replace real ones. Psychosis is a "disturbance of thought" (as signified in the psychiatric literature) because lower-line Pain has been persistent

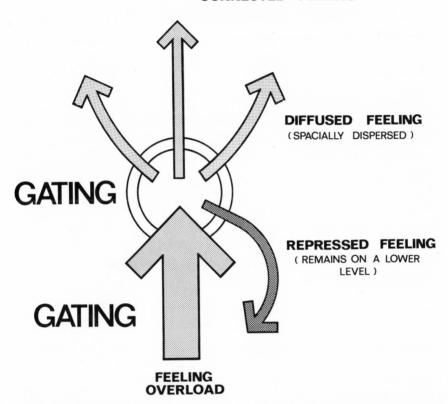

**STRAIGHT
CONNECTED FEELING**

DIFFUSED FEELING
(SPACIALLY DISPERSED)

GATING

REPRESSED FEELING
(REMAINS ON A LOWER
LEVEL)

GATING

**FEELING
OVERLOAD**

and harsh since inception preventing the development of a cohesive perceptual and conceptual structure. And, in a sense, yesterday's third line becomes tomorrow's second line; which means that traumas with an emotional component which existed in the here-and-now of our youth become stored on the second line (limbically). A non-trauma however such as learning to type at the age of twelve remains on the third line, easily recalled with facile access in the here-and-now.

I believe that it is too much Primal Pain which eventually disrupts and produces a split in the third line so that a person can be eminently rational in one area, say science, and totally irrational in another area, such as in the occult. In the totally well person I do not think such a split in the third line would exist. Any Pain coming up would be felt and *correctly* symbolized, therefore integrated. It would not, therefore, drive the third line into irrationality in order to keep the Pain away from conscious connection. It is an overload of Pain which drives the wedge into

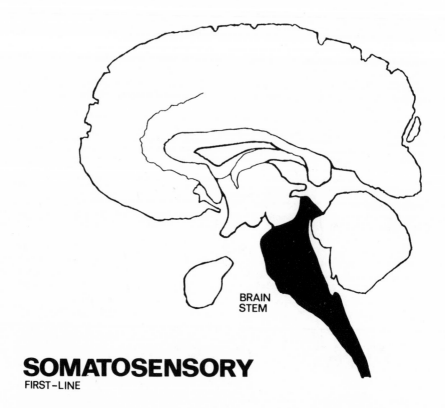

BRAIN
STEM

SOMATOSENSORY
FIRST-LINE

the third line; the deeper and more extensive the Pain the wider the gap between rational and irrational elements. This process may continue until the third line is almost totally engaged in dealing with Pain by (irrational) symbolization leaving little left to handle reality. At this point the person is no longer functional.

The split in the third line is something most of us are aware of while driving. We can daydream while shifting gears, stopping for signals, avoiding parked cars, etc. We are in the past and present, so to speak; symbolizing the past and perceiving the present. If the Pain is too great then daydreaming suffuses most of consciousness and a wreck is likely to ensue. The third line split has implications for sleep and dreams, and I shall discuss that in the appropriate chapter.*

---

*I have discussed in Chapter I the split-brain and its relationship to consciousness. It may well be that the split in the third line is related to the right-left hemispheric consciousness . . . the separation between a feeling consciousness and a thinking one. At this point it is conjecture, but the observational evidence points to a bifurcation in the third line.

Feeling, Insight and Change

The implication of what I am saying is that each system has its registration or kind of memory bank, and it is only when one relives first-line trauma that the truth of that statement is apparent. There is no way to remember being strangled on the cord except organismically—by reliving the experience physically just as it happened. There is no way to bring that event into third-line consciousness by any act of will. The event exists on its own level of consciousness and can only be resolved on that level; which is precisely why *understanding on the third line a problem which exists on a lower line is meaningless.* It certainly does not change that stored event and its effects on behavior. All that can happen is a better rationalization for it.

So we see that not only are there levels of Pain but there are levels of insights which exist on the same stratum of consciousness as the Pain. They are the understanding of the Pain, but they evolve *from* it. The action is from feeling to understanding, and not vice versa. Psychoanalysis offers third-line insights. They cannot possibly be as deep as someone who has a three-level Primal with insights which deepen and become more profound with each level of descent. What a patient may discover, for example, from a journey to the first line is how disparate current behavior is an attempt in some way to master an old trauma or fulfill an old need; so that he may find out that one reason he reads so much is that he must know what is going on around him, and that that need is prototypic of coming into this world drugged, handled roughly, removed from the warmth of a mother and not knowing what was happening to him. He uncovers the motivation behind his excessive need to know and devour trivia by reliving an event on the first line. What he may also understand is how each of us recreate our past symbolically in order to resolve it; whether it be to get father love out of men teachers or by reading everything as a way of knowing "what is going on around us." Once a feeling is felt the third-line change in acting-out in the present is automatic and needs no great effort to accomplish. Until it is felt the third line will be pressed into service to control the acting-out; and all that will be accomplished is that the acting-out will become more subtle. I want to make clear why it is that feeling feelings automatically makes changes in acting-out. I have said that repressed feelings drive behavior. But perhaps a better way of looking at it is that repressed feelings are interwoven into behavior. Contained in each piece of acting-out *is* the feeling. The neurotic does not feel it because he brings that old feeling into the present inside his behavior. He never sees the feeling as being from the past; so he cannot get angry at the garage man who just botched his repair job because the garage man *is daddy*. When the feeling of fear with daddy is felt completely, he can then express his anger in the present freely. Neurosis is indeed the generalized behavior in the present which derives from the repression of specific past experiences. The neurotic never knows that his behavior belongs to the past because the feeling attached to it has never reached his consciousness. From fear of a single man (father) there is a spread of that feeling and the subsequent acting-out (inability to get angry) spreads so that there is fear of almost every male adult.

This process of generalization is the key to understanding mental illness, for generalization occurs when there is disconnection from some specific feeling. It is very much like uncoupling a hose while the water is still running through. The energy of the water tends to spray in all directions. Similarly, the energy of a specific disconnected feeling spreads out and is generalized. Recently a young woman applicant for therapy informed me that she was afraid of being rejected because she was wearing her black slip. She said that black meant death and doom and therefore something bad was bound to happen. The idea that black no longer signified a color but had some elaborate and totally unrelated meaning indicates how far the generalization process had taken her. This was a psychotic leap. A neurotic generalization would be having homosexual relationships with men who had the physical characteristics of an adored older brother who left home early. In this case, a young man may still unconsciously generalize his need but the gap between the need-Pain and the subsequent behavior is not so bizarre. Nevertheless, not being able to specifically connect with the great loss the brother's leaving represented produced generalized behavior later on. Mental illness is the generalization of disconnected Primal Pain; and a Primal is transforming the general back to the specific.

In terms of levels of consciousness we may say that what is being generalized is lower line Pain which has been unhooked from the third line connection. It is continually acted out for a lifetime precisely because the third line is not linked specifically to those feelings. A man may try to get love out of *all* men now because he cannot fully feel (not just understand) his tremendous need for his father *back then*. The split in the third line allows someone at times to "understand" his need from the past but still have to focus on men in the present (to incorrectly symbolize) as desperately needed love objects. In neurosis the need is from the past (lower line) but the focus is in the present (third line).

It is the lower line Pains which make us unable to make accurate and *conscious* generalizations about what we are doing in the present. The homosexual cruiser does not see his new prey as "daddy." Each situation is treated de novo so that he needs one conquest after another, never truly satisfied because he really doesn't get what he needs. Or a man who needs "momma" may also want one sexual conquest after another, feeling dissatisfied but never knowing why. The past Pain makes us generalize but it is *"unconscious"* generalization: behavior based on a lower level of consciousness. A Primal which takes us back to specifics then allows us *conscious* generalizations so that we become aware of all the general *unconscious* behaviors produced by a specific feeling. This is what is truly meant by making the unconscious conscious. Nobody can do it for you. The unconscious has to be *felt,* not just understood.

We must keep in mind that it is not need which generalizes. Need, a specific need, remains forever the same. *What generalizes are the ways we go about satisfying that need. Primal Therapy is simple precisely because we never have to untangle the myriad ways we go about dealing with need.* The closer we are to our feelings and needs the healthier we are.

We can see how the generalization process affects our perception. If we are desperate not to feel alone then we will want to be with anyone who can help us quell that feeling. We may not accurately perceive the kind of people we are with simply because they are being used in the service of a need. Without the driving need we can be more perceptive, selective and specific about the kinds of friends we have. We can finally be objective.

The concept of generalization also helps us understand impulsive behavior. One patient recently felt the exact very early scene of standing before his mother waiting to be picked up and held. He wanted that touch and hug with every fiber of his being. Instead, he got the usual—rejection. Later, he became an impulse neurotic; he felt compelled to touch women and could not control himself. When that (old) impulse to be held was triggered, say by the sight of a woman, nothing he could say to himself would stop his acting out. His whole body was impelled to reach out and touch a strange woman's breast. *The strength of his impulse in the present was precisely the strength of that impulse from the past,* only the *focus* was different. As he began to experience that scene and the feelings it represented (which spanned years of his relationship with his mother) he could actually feel the impulse come upon him, transpose it back to its proper context and Primal instead of act out. It was a physical need back then and so it became a physical need in the present.

The need and its strength never changed; only the generalized object became different. We can understand, then, that someone who cannot control his impulses is just someone who cannot connect with his feelings.

The reason that a Primal patient is filled with insights during and after a Primal is that a single repressed feeling leads to that generalized behavior and, once felt, all that widespread activity based on the feeling is laid bare. So, for example, a sense that the parents could not be trusted, that they were unpredictable can summate into the feeling that "I'll never put myself in anyone else's hands again." That feeling begins very early and is not necessarily conceptualized. It is just an attitude that becomes interwoven into the way the child begins to meet his world. Later on, this can lead to acting-out in many ways. Once the patient feels that feeling, for example, he may say, "Now I know why I won't rent a house and must buy—I won't be in the control of a landlord. Now I know why I won't work for anyone else and must start my own business." That feeling (and others) led to many behaviors all of which rested on the need not to place his life in anyone else's hands. The patient then discovers why he would not take an apprenticeship leading to a top position in a company; he would not start at the bottom because that meant "people over you controlling your life just like parents." He then sees his history of failure because he would not place himself in a position to learn from others. Or he finds out why he must buy a house and live over his head instead of renting and living within his income.

Of course that is not all of it; for there are other feelings which join with that feeling of no one is to be trusted. For example, another Pain can be that they never kept their word—which not only meant that they could not be trusted but also produced a feeling in the child that he must have things "now"; for if someone makes a promise "they" are likely to change their minds later so better to get what one can now. This impatience joins with the other feeling of "no one is to be over my life controlling me." The result is impulsive behavior such as taking the first offer that comes along, or again, the inability to take a job from the bottom and have the *patience* to see it through until one reaches the higher ranks. So here are two contributing factors to a current life style; and there are many many more. It becomes infinitely complex, and we can see what a herculean task it would be to try to sort out mentally all the ramifications of an acting-out. That is why psychoanalysis takes so many years. One week of their therapy is concentrated on why buying instead of renting, another week on why this job and not another and so on ad infinitum. Whereas in Primal Therapy feeling feelings clarifies widely disparate behaviors in a single blow.

As each feeling is felt the defense structure is chipped away preparing for yet another feeling to be felt and more insights to be garnered. The deeper one goes the more profound the insights; the more feeling is clarified which underlies later neurotic acting-out. In this way Primal Therapy is a completely natural and orderly process. The patient who relives first-line material is discovering how those early traumas contributed to his later acting-out. A difficult birth, for example, may instill a feeling that no one can be trusted and this would be compounded by a later feeling of lack of trust; adding to it tremendous force because the force of the trauma was so great. He is having first-line insights. He is understanding the same behavior only on a deeper level. He sees how lack of trust was prototypic and started with birth, compounded later by parents who never kept their word and hurt him constantly, making him feel that "anyone over you hurts you," compounded again later when he is hurt by teachers, priests etc. Now we see what I mean when I say that feeling Pain unlocks whole areas of unconsciousness. So long as the old Primal feeling is intertwined with current behavior, the person remains unconscious of both the feeling and the motivation behind his acting out; and indeed he is unconscious that he is acting out. Buying a house may seem utterly sensible to the neurotic (of course it can be utterly realistic for the well person) yet his act is truly unconscious behavior.

Therapeutic Implications

The proper sequence of the therapeutic process is all-important. If a patient is forced to enter the first line too soon he cannot possibly have true integrating Primals. This is because there is nearly always a second- and third-line component of the feeling which remains to create tension. If the patient gradually works his way down to the first line he can integrate fully on that lowest level because the higher-level Pains have been experienced and resolved. It isn't as though the patient's tolerance for greater Pain increases as he reaches the first line. Rather, by chipping away on higher levels first there is an *overall* lessened load of Pain to deal with so that great first-line traumas can finally be felt and resolved.

In Primal Therapy what we try to do is reactivate an old feeling on its own terms; this means that if it is a preverbal trauma we use nonverbal means—a slight touch on the head, pressure on the back or chest, are examples. If a patient is into suffocation, a slight pressure on the mouth with a pillow may do it. If a patient is into a scene of being in Grand-father's arms then the therapist may cuddle the patient to reawaken the old feeling on the level it occurred.

If it is a second-line scene we may use props; a whip may be held over the patient if his father used to whip him. A teddy bear may be found just like the one the patient had as a child. Old photographs are used. If it is surgery a slight smell of ether may project the patient back to the hospital scene. Patients are encouraged to visit their old child-hood houses and schools to see their old chums—all in the service of feeling.

The patient with only third-line access needs to use words, to *talk* about his past, even the recent past if that is all he remembers. Perhaps a cur-rent scene will trigger off an old feeling that the patient is completely unaware of. The scene he is depicting is in the present; the feeling is in the past. Our job is to help him connect even to elements of the feeling in the past, and the way we do it is to use the present. Neurotics are, after all, having past feelings superimposed on the present; some know it and some patients do not. For those who do not the third line is the route we take.

Movies are good for Primal patients because they deal in images, in scenes and very often if it is a "Primal movie" those scenes may come very close to the patient's life. So we use the scenes that upset him and made him cry to gain access to lower-line levels, particularly the second line.

In Primal Therapy it is possible to enter a Primal feeling on almost any level. But the level chosen must be appropriate, timely and acces-sible. The sensitivity of a Primal Therapist is required to know on what line a patient is, what material he is ready for and what he is not. To touch a person too soon, in order to bring up the first-line Pain of not being touched soon after birth, may shut the patient down. He may only be able to talk about not being touched at first until some of the Pain is out of the way.

Generally, we begin a patient on the third line. He talks about his current life, then drops into second-line scenes and perhaps months later will connect the feeling in one of those scenes with first-line material. If the patient has second-line access we may begin with scenes from the past and bypass the present. If a patient only has slight access, it is pos-sible to catch him during REM period, wake him up while he is in the throes of a dream and get him into second line that way. Dreams occur when a person ascends from deep sleep to consciousness. He must pass through the second line on the way up and down and when he reaches that level from either direction he dreams.[8]

I have stated before that all three levels of consciousness are needed for the experiences of Pain and the reason we feel no Pain in sleep is that the third line which can interpret the painful sensations of the body is suppressed. This is very much the case in hypnosis where the subject feels no Pain because his third line has been systematically lulled.

As a patient opens up during the course of his therapy it takes smaller fragments of a past scene to get him into feeling. At first he may have to describe a scene with his father in his house when he was seven for over an hour before he can feel it. Later on, just the image in his mind can do it, or a single word, or a single sound can throw him into a Primal —the harsh sound of a voice like his father's, for example. What is happening is *connection;* thinking what you feel and feeling what you think. What is happening is that a direct line to feeling is occurring in this therapy; at that point it takes a conscious effort to *shut off* a feeling. A Primal Therapist must have mastered all the various techniques for gaining access to a particular level of consciousness. For example, in post-group he and another therapist may *recreate a scene* in the present that a particular patient is into from the past so that the patient can get back there. Two cotherapists may argue, or the man may dominate the woman therapist or whatever is appropriate. It takes an agile mind. The importance of the scheme of levels of consciousness is that it gives us a lever with which to approach a patient and understand where he is. The danger in this therapy is in violating the rules of consciousness so that the wrong level is entered into, or is infiltrated too soon; or in keeping the patient on the third when he can go to the second line. The ways of making errors are infinite and that is why the training of a Primal Therapist is so complicated and intense.

With an understanding of levels of consciousness we can see (and measure) progress in the patient. We can tell when he is ready for another level, and we can see his consciousness open up as he has three-level Primals, slipping from third to second to first line in a single session. That is our aim; to help a patient become a feeling, conscious person. And we usually don't have to guess as to where the patient is or how well he is doing. He knows as well as we do because he can feel his consciousness opening up and his symptoms based on a repressed con-

---

[8] Most dreams are second line and therefore we usually wake up on the second line, so that is a very good time to get someone into second-line material.

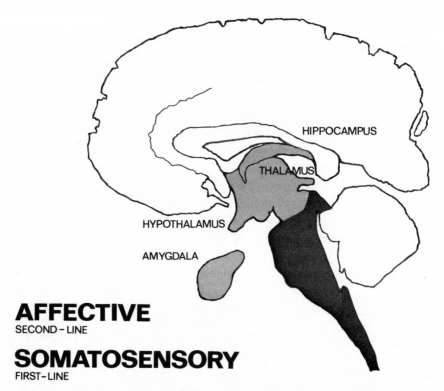

AFFECTIVE
SECOND – LINE

SOMATOSENSORY
FIRST – LINE

sciousness leave. He knows because he no longer has the compulsion to act out due to repressed unconscious forces.

The neurotic maintains his coherence through a system of well-functioning gates so that there is little intrusion of the Pain from one line to another. Primal cohesion is based on fluid interconnection which in turn is facilitated by the decrease in the shattering intensity of the Pain. There are those who manage to function and maintain coherence even with a weakened third-line system. There are essentially two ways that coherence can be shattered: either through those drugs which facilitate the ascendance of Pain; or through current trauma which overtaxes the system's ability to integrate what is happening. A severe business loss or losing a lover can do it. One of the ways that is commonly used to reconstitute the cohesion of the neurotic is electro-shock therapy. An electro-shock is a massive stimulus which results in overload and therefore shutdown. What we have neglected to understand is that a shock is a massive input to which there are no response possibilities for the organism except unconsciousness. It creates a constant state of defense—without current reason. Furthermore it ensures that there is a reservoir of *unacted reactions*. A Primal is the final connection, the conscious experience of a previously unacted reaction. In this sense we can view neurosis as a series of buried reactions; where there were stimuli without the possibility of proper response.

I want to reiterate one key point; namely, that each feeling we have has components from all three levels of consciousness. Each system adds its dimension. But there are feelings which have a predominate first-line element and others which are predominantly second line. For example, if the infant is not touched just after birth—if he is not placed near his mother in the first hours and days of life—he is being traumatized on the first line. If he is not held later on, not caressed sufficiently by his parents, he is traumatized on the second line. The first-line event is elaborated on a higher level of consciousness. The child not only is not being caressed, he begins to feel "unloved." It is not a new feeling which is occurring. The first-line Pain is being compounded. Later on, depending on life history, the person may act out sexually (trying to get touched, trying to feel held and loved) or, he may act out avoiding touch lest it reactivate Pain from the lower levels. He may later even believe that he does not need to be held or touched; that "men are sissies who need that kind

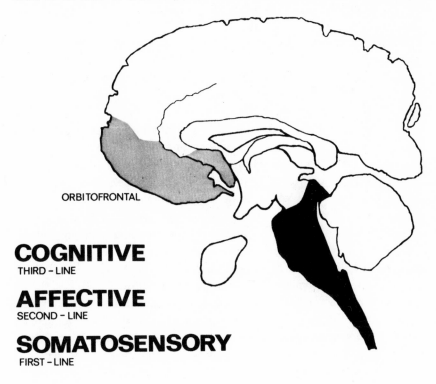

ORBITOFRONTAL

COGNITIVE
THIRD - LINE

AFFECTIVE
SECOND - LINE

SOMATOSENSORY
FIRST - LINE

of stuff." At that point his third line is sealed off from lower-line access in an almost complete way, and Pain did the job. The young child may have tried for years to reach out to his parents for some physical tenderness to no avail until one day he not only stops reaching out but forgets his need and develops an idea in his mind that he does not need. Such a notion is abetted when a father tells his son something like, "Men don't kiss, they shake hands." Then, in order to convince himself that he is loved, he tries to be that man and deny his first-line needs. He won't let himself be touched for fear of "loss of love" . . . and that, indeed, is a strange paradox. The third line deceives itself into feeling loved while the second and first lines are starving for it.

In Primal terms, the person who continues to act out his needs, who tries through nymphomania for example, to gain fulfillment, however symbolically, may be a much better candidate for treatment than someone who has decided against his need. What it means is that the former (the nymphomaniac, for example) is continuously operating on a lower line even without higher conscious comprehension of the fact. The third line does not have complete control and there is a constant eruption of the lower line feelings and needs. The problem is that there is not the fluid interconnection which permits the person to know what it is he or she is acting out. And it is that lack of connection which prevents higher-line control. There is simply too much need. We see this particularly in impulse neuroses such as exhibitionism where faced with a long jail term, the person, otherwise bright and understanding, continues to act out on the streets.

One final example of a three-level feeling and how defenses are organized, follows. A fetus may have a long and harsh birth finally making it safely out into the world. He may have been left with a first-line sense memory—that you have to "get out" to be safe. Later on, this person may have a bad home life with lots of fighting among the family. His only retreat is to run away—to get out. As an adult, when under stress, such as when having an argument with a girl friend, he may want to pack his bags and run away—to get out. The getting out becomes more sophisticated until he may take a jet somewhere whenever he is overloaded but the leitmotif would remain the same as it has since birth.

The defense was organized around the first line because it is a physical action rather than an introspective mental one. Most of us would have no idea that what we do now in response to stress began in the first minutes of life; and that is because we have not had the first-line access in any integrated way. The resolution of the irrational acting-out must be on

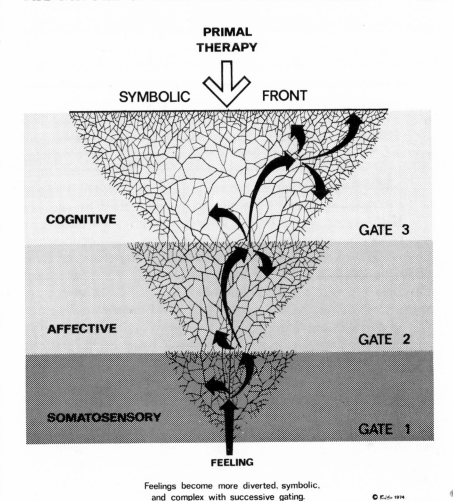

PRIMAL THERAPY

SYMBOLIC FRONT

COGNITIVE

GATE 3

AFFECTIVE

GATE 2

SOMATOSENSORY

GATE 1

FEELING

Feelings become more diverted, symbolic,
and complex with successive gating.

© KJ⟂ 1974

Fig. 2. *Gating Action Between the Levels of Consciousness*

all three levels; otherwise (assuming only level 2 is reached) there will always be a tendency or wish to run away, albeit in attenuated form. Running away isn't just something a person has to be "convinced" not to do. The memory from the first line is impelling him; and that memory says, "You've got to get out to save your life." Running away as a defense, then, is unconsciously a life-and-death matter.

Running away becomes either exacerbated or attenuated as a defense depending on life circumstances. Those circumstances on the second line may compound the defense, make it more complex and entangled, but the *impulse* has been given great initial force on the first line; and that is why impulse neurotics, those who cannot *mentally* control themselves, usually suffer from great first-line traumas.

When a feeling becomes disconnected from higher consciousness the energy still exerts a force; and that force grows in strength commensurate with the amount of Pain which is disconnected and repressed. As that force expands it produces more and more defensive reactions, and those defenses become so ramified and intricate that later on there is almost no telling what feelings gave rise to them. The complexity becomes inordinate when you consider that there are many powerful first-line traumas which are blocked and rerouted. As their energy is infused into the second line there is a compounding and again a blocking and rerouting so that the situation now is quite entangled; and there is no "mental" way to disentangle first from second lines when analyzing any piece of behavior. Only the gradual descent into, and resolution of, Pains on each line can accomplish that.

By the time a person is an adult any one of his actions such as impulsive eating or talking may have a myriad of repressed feelings driving them. There is no one-to-one cause. But the energy which causes a person to talk constantly or to talk loudly tells us something about the energy which impels the behavior. A person who talks to excess, and that can mean that he can fill you in with countless digressions and facts which have nothing to do with the point, is burning off that Primal energy. His talk has little to do with communication and more to do with personal release and catharsis; and that is why this person "turns you off". You sense he is not relating so much as releasing. And he will turn off his child (and create Pain in him) by his Pain because the energy of his constant talk won't allow the child to think for himself, to reflect and introspect. The child's focus must be constantly *outward* toward the parent. The nature of the digressions, how far afield his mind wanders, are other measures of how much buried pressure is driving him away from the central focus of what he wants to communicate. He has lost his simple needs and cannot speak them. His words are now outlets and defenses against need.

There is good neurologic evidence to support the notion of the energy of a feeling infiltrating other levels of consciousness while the specific *connection* remains disengaged. A. R. Luria in his new book points out that "every specific afferent or efferent (cortical) fiber is accompanied by a fiber of the nonspecific activating system, and the stimulation of individual areas of cortex brain structures."[9] So it is possible for there to

---

[9] Luria, p. 58.

be general activation of the system without specific connections being made. That is, the activating portions of the stimuli travel downward to galvanize the body while the specific connecting processes do not. So the person feels agitated in certain situations and doesn't know why.

The division of consciousness also helps explain the reason that some-one can be a genius in his field yet be totally irrational and mystical otherwise. A person can understand all the facts in his field, be logical

ENERGY FLOW CHART

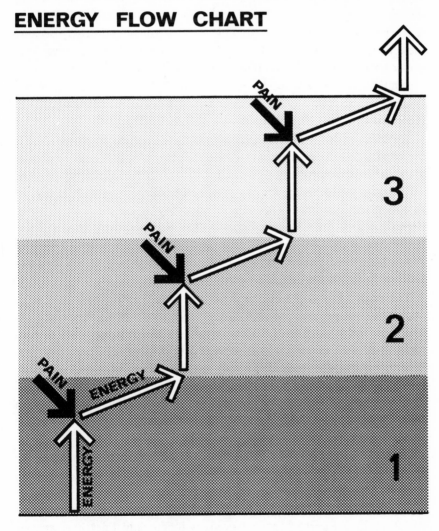

The compounding of PAIN continuously diverts the feeling and channels it into symbolic outlets.

and systematic, yet when lower-line Pain ascends it causes him to have a split third-line consciousness producing bizarre and illogical thoughts. There would be no relationship between his intelligence, the facts that he knows, and his ideas about life, marriage, outer space, drugs, blacks, and so on. A physician who watches his patient die on the operating table and can still believe that he lives on in different form, or who can believe that it "was meant to be," that some "higher force" was in control and willed it to happen, is another example. You fill in the blanks. The extent of man's capacity for irrationality boggles the mind—literally. One of the reasons some of us never discuss religion with others is precisely because these beliefs sit atop a volcano of feelings. If you never had a parent who was a friend, and you make God a friend (the one you never had and need) then no one is going to convince you that there is no God. When dealing with irrationality, in short, it is not a matter of changing minds; it is a matter of changing the Pain.

We can see from this discussion that the third line is plastic; it has the capacity for both logic and illogic. It can rationalize and symbolize Pain and try to make it logical; and it can keep that illogic apart from solving real problems in, for example, some scientific field. It is my assumption that our intelligence is predominantly logical at all times when lower-line Pain isn't leaking into it. That is why post-Primal patients become smart in a real way after therapy. They are not taken in by false values (one must achieve and be ambitious) once they have felt the basis for their false notions.

The second line is the link to the consciousness of the past. *It is most important that patients proceed through that level before they reach the first line.* Drugs such as LSD can throw up the first-line Pain prematurely; and with enough trips a groove develops between third and first lines bypassing the second. Second-line Pain then becomes encircled, forms an enclave which remains disconnected driving behavior and producing continued irrational thoughts. Incorrect therapy can accomplish the same thing. By driving a patient into first-line Pain too soon the same "groove" can occur encasing the second line.

If the present is too bad it can fixate the person so that he can never get back to his second line. If he has no money, no job, no wife and no prospects, he may be fully occupied and preoccupied in the present. If a person in Primal Therapy has nothing in the present, he may likewise get stuck in his past. A person needs a functioning third line, and we shouldn't imagine that living completely in the past is a Primal virtue.

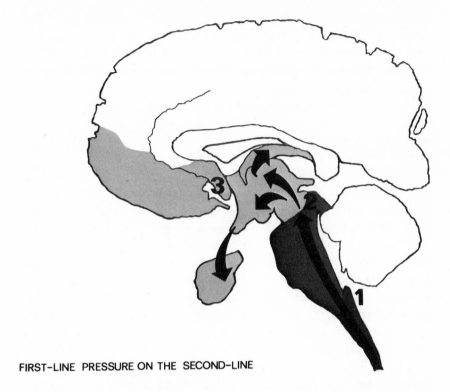

FIRST-LINE PRESSURE ON THE SECOND-LINE

Consciousness as Interconnection

When I discuss three systems of consciousness it must be remembered that those systems innervate the body; and that is why we can be suffering from Primal Pains, on one level, which finally produce an ulcer or diabetes and yet be completely unconscious of the fact that any Pain exists on another level. A recent discovery, for example, indicates that some diabetes is related to an excess of growth hormone secreted by the pituitary. A substance has been identified which improves the control of diabetes by influencing the output of the hormone. The drug has the apt name of *somatostatin*.* The aim is to control diabetes which is a worthwhile goal; but what is not discussed is *why* the pituitary (which is related to the hypothalamus and limbic system) is in a constant state of overproduction. It is my belief that we must look to some constant in the

---

* Somatostatin inhibits *glucagon* as well, a hormone which *raises* blood sugar. A recent article in *The Lancet* by Alford et al. (10/26/74) discusses the significance of this to diabetic control. (EMH)

nervous system (a continuous reverberating circuit of **Primal Pain**). There is evidence, for example, that a hormone factor in the hypothalamus is essential to tumor growth. The incidence of breast cancer in rats has been reduced by burning out a small section of the hypothalamus. The hypothalamus is intimately involved with the immune system. And there is evidence that cancer (and tumors) develop when there is a failure of the immune system to stop their growth.[10] *My point is that lower-line Pain when blocked from higher levels has access to the physical system producing a constant activation which may find its way into the hormonal system resulting in too much of a specific hormone; and the resultant disease is too often treated quite apart from any consideration of Pain and levels of consciousness.* The chronic headache is a good example of a symptom resulting from blockage of lower-line Pain. Third-line blockage means that lower-line feelings are disengaged from connection and that the energy pressure of those gated feelings disperses and is experienced as pressure as in a "pressure headache." Clearly, as connections are made there is no longer dispersion of feelings (the feelings are flowing smoothly through the gates) and no sensation of pressure. It becomes apparent why connection from lower to higher puts an end to chronic headaches; indicating why Primal Therapy has been successful with that symptom. When during therapy there is fluid access among levels one, two and three, symptoms leave. So long as there is two plus three or one plus three only, we can expect a continuation of the symptom but in attenuated form.

It is my assumption that the roots of mental illness including most of the psychoses originate from Primal Pains. Since Primal Pains affect the physical system there are bound to be biochemical changes. I think it would be an error to assume by measuring these changes that the roots of mental illness, therefore, are biochemical. It is my belief that most biochemical alterations are secondary to Primal Pain. We have reversed enough psychoses by now through natural means (Primal Therapy) to assume that many psychoses are not biochemical in origin. This does not obviate that possibility; but our experience indicates that if it exists it is not prevalent.

Psychosis, then, is how the brain organizes itself in response to insult.

---

[10] I have said elsewhere that cancer is the insanity of the cell and if we understand that consciousness is cellular and unconsciousness means pressure (by Pain) then first-line unconsciousness is indicative of tremendous cellular pressure. The more Pain, the greater the inaccessibility. That is one reason, I believe, why cancer has been refractory to treatment.

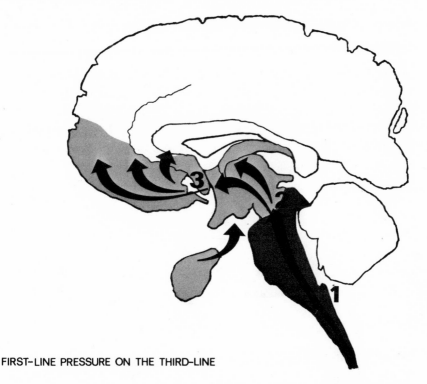

FIRST-LINE PRESSURE ON THE THIRD-LINE

That insult may be physical trauma, drug ingestion, toxicity, etc. I am indicating that the most prevalent of the insults in the psychoses is Primal. It is possible to use sophisticated equipment such as a spectrophotometer to measure the metabolites produced in a spinal tap of psychotics and find biochemical alterations. But to extrapolate from that and assume that those changes *cause* psychosis is unwarranted, in my opinion. Again, mental illness is truly a psychophysical illness. Naturally, there will be physical alterations in aberrant mental states.

It is because of the physical access of Pain that changes take place in the physical system as a result of experiencing Primal Therapy. When we talk about alterations in consciousness we must understand that those changes must be accompanied by physical changes one way or another, otherwise those alterations are spurious and only third line. We are altering, in short, levels of consciousness connected to a physical system. We are not just "changing minds," or altering awareness as do the conventional insight therapies. The changes are enduring; and it is that fact which is significant, for there are any number of psychotherapeutic approaches such as meditation, biofeedback, hypnosis, inter alia, which do produce some alterations but they do not endure. They do not touch the Pain which produces neurosis and its psychosomatic counterparts. They only rearrange the components of the third line.

As I discuss in "On Sleep and Dreams: Consciousness in Unconscious States," there are EEG patterns specific to certain levels

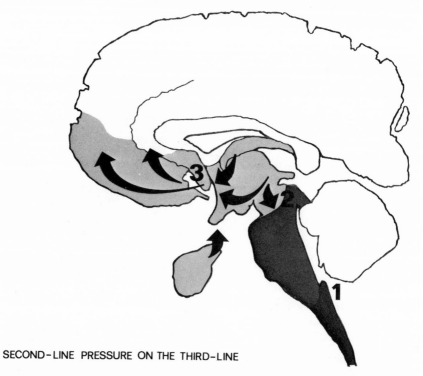

SECOND-LINE PRESSURE ON THE THIRD-LINE

of consciousness. For example, research indicates that a descent down the levels is accomplished by drop in frequency of brain waves. Deep sleep is related to slow delta waves. Elmer Green's work at the Gardner Murphy Research Center indicates that his subjects reported their most interesting dream-like images at a time when their alpha waves dropped from ten to eight cycles per second, and particularly when alpha shifted down into the theta range of slower than eight cycles per second. It is my belief that theta is a measure of feeling states; *alpha a measure of effective repression*. People feel relaxed in midrange alpha frequencies, I believe, due to the efficacy of their repression, which feels like relaxation. It is in the fast beta range that people feel agitated and anxious.

What is significant about all this is that it is possible to intercede on a certain level of consciousness and produce specific results. We can use strobe devices to pulse the brain activity down in frequency and the result is often a Primal in Primal patients; and a "spacy" reaction in non-Primal persons. (Strobes are not used in Primal Therapy now; they are unnecessary.) The work of T. H. Budzynski at the University of Colorado Medical Center is relevant in this regard. He is training patients with biofeedback to produce slow brain waves. Some of his patients fall asleep as a result of the relaxation. Others seem to have freer access to previously repressed thoughts . . . to feeling.

Dr. Jose Delgado has placed electrodes in the brains of some human patients. When the electrodes were stimulated, the patient acted in certain ways over which he had no (third-line) control. The subconscious electrical stimulation was stronger than any act of conscious will. And what is more the third line made up rationalizations for the electrically stimulated behavior to make it plausible. One patient when stimulated, for example, when asked what he was doing said, "I'm looking for my slippers." My point in regard to this is that Primal Pain *is* a strong electrical subconscious event which can at times suffuse third-line consciousness; we rationalize that Pain on the third line because we cannot connect with it. Connection dispels self-deceptions.

Dr. I. S. Cooper of New York has demonstrated that stimulation of the cerebellum markedly improves control in certain cases of epilepsy. Inhibition (or gating) *can occur without the conscious knowledge of the patient.* He and we can shutdown, in short, (and become neurotic) without the slightest hint of what is happening to us.

Related to the above is the use of acupuncture of late for treatment of narcotic addiction; particularly in suppressing withdrawal reactions. It makes sense (not Primal sense) if we understand that acupuncture affects at least one gate (blocking transmission of impulses up the spinal cord) and possibly more. What I think happens is an overload; a barrage of sensory input which helps shut down the gate so that Pain is no longer experienced. Obviously, this overload is going to help prevent the rebound of Pain which comes up when drugs are no longer used to suppress it. There is no magic. All the evidence, Primal and neurological shows that we store memories, particularly painful memories. If a treatment procedure dances around the periphery of the Pain it cannot be efficacious in a lasting way. It is truly unfortunate that all the recently hailed innovations for the treatment of addiction and other problems are little more than gate suppressants. I would accept them as necessary if we didn't already have a truly efficacious therapy.

I have discussed the work of Wilder Penfield in *The Anatomy of Mental Illness*. He did brain surgery on epileptics. Placing electrodes in the temporal lobe, closely related to the limbic system, he found that patients vividly reexperienced events of their youths. I wonder if the electrodes were to tap deeper levels of consciousness if the patient would not begin to relive first-line traumas such as the birth Pain. I want to quote from a book discussing Penfield's work because it is highly relevant to my discussion of levels of consciousness. The book is *The Brain Revolution*.[11] "One of Penfield's patients seemed to have a mental file for the concept of 'grabbing.' An event suggesting a boyhood experience in which something was yanked away from him would trigger a major epileptic attack. 'The actual memory of this incident brought on a fit; but so did seeing a child take a stick from the mouth of a dog (in the third line, my statement). Apparently, the same kind of filing system was used to evaluate both the present and. to tap into the stream of consciousness."

I think that the filing system is organized around *feeling*. It is a specific feeling which binds together various experiences; and the feeling has its lower-line elements which can be triggered by the events in the present. A normal person would connect to the feeling, but a neurotic might have seizures because of third-line repression which dams up the feeling creating enormous pressure which is released in a general non-connected way. Penfield was able to stimulate the brain and produce a specific hallucination or dream. In some cases it is the same hallucination or dream which always precedes an attack. Here again, I believe, is evidence of how lower-line feelings produce specific symbolic derivatives; and conversely how it may be possible by descending through those symbols to arrive at unconscious lower-line feeling.

Penfield's late writings (Sept. 1974) seem to be congruent with Primal formulations: "Thus we come to the conclusion that there are at least three functional units of gray matter involved in the act of scanning and recall of experience: (1) the interpretive cortex of the temporal lobe, (2) the hippocampi with their direct connections to the brain stem, and (3) the experiential recording within the higher brain stem . . . the proposition, then, is that neuronal potentials do pass from the hippocampi to the centrally placed experiential record, activating it selectively. . . . Thus,

---

[11] Marilyn Ferguson, *The Brain Revolution* Taplinger, New York, 1973.

the hippocampi play an essential role in the (conscious) recall of experience."[12]

What Penfield believes is that events are recorded in the brain which can be reactivated by stimulating the interpretive parts of the temporal cortex. The interpretive cortex seems to be the key to a "strange tape recorder" in the brain which can bring back past scenes, sounds, sights and thoughts. He goes on to talk about *keys to access* which seem to be formed in the hippocampus of each temporal lobe, and they are duplicate keys. These hippocampal keys can turn on the interpretive cortex allowing man to recall nearly everything that has happened to him. We talk about keys to access as well, and *it is precisely this access to the past that is the cornerstone of Primal Therapy.*

Again, let us listen to Penfield: "The tape recorder in the (upper) brain stem is unchangeable if one can judge by the experiential responses to stimulation." However that recorder is activated it seems to play the same tune. But the summarizing keys of access associated with the hippocampus changes. It can be enlarged and altered.

"Suppose now that the lines of *permanently facilitated connection* (my emphasis) from the hippocampus to the tape recorder *early in life* (again, my emphasis) are laid down at the posterior end of each hippocampus and more anteriorly later on." This would, in his opinion, explain retrograde amnesia as the inability to establish particular keys of access, for in order to have particular kinds of recall you need the anterior half of at least one hippocampus.

Penfield, through his brain surgery and his research, has now begun to pinpoint for us where some of the connections we have been discussing lie. He points to the hippocampus as all-important; something I hypothesized about some years ago in *The Anatomy of Mental Illness.* The hippocampus seems certain to be involved in recall of the past. It helps to scan that past. The past recordings are a continuous "pattern of neuron connections that have been permanently facilitated for the subsequent passage of neuronal currents. This continuous thread of facilitated passage is the experiential engram." It is my belief that this engram acts like a reverberating circuit stimulating the cortex and the body continuously in a general way because there is not the proper key of access which will produce conscious connection. It is possible for current related events to trigger off these reverberating circuits on lower levels of consciousness without the intercession of higher consciousness.

---

[12]Penfield, W. et al, "Memory" Archives of Neurology, Vol. 31, Sept. 1974, pages 152-54.

The ability to make a conscious recall and connection to early stored events requires the active help of certain portions of the hippocampus. It is my assumption that early events which carry a great load of Pain overload and block aspects of hippocampal functioning so that the keys of access are gated and diverted.

The Coding of Memory

I want to take the discussion a step further. I believe that it is not only the brain which codes memory; I think that the counterpart of certain memories are coded and stored in the body, as well. In *The Feeling Child* I showed photographs of bruises which occurred when a patient was reliving being bruised at birth. At a certain level of consciousness there was not only a mental memory but a physical one as well which accompanied that mental event. That is, memory was a *psychophysical* event, not just a cerebral one.

There is relevant research done with worms (planarians). Worms were trained to react to light. They were cut in half, and a month later they grew new heads. They remembered almost as well with an entirely new head.[13] The research investigator concluded that specific memories were stored chemically within individual cells and not only in the brain. What is true of the planarians may be true of all organic cellular life. This means, then, that consciousness has to be thought of in a new way—as a *total* system, mind and body. Its significance for Primal Therapy is that real psychophysical change in a human organism comes about only when there is a *psychophysical* experience (a Primal) as opposed to a strictly mental one such as in insight therapy. Memory, therefore, is a holistic state; and the body remembers in its own way and *on its own level*. Let me cite one more example to make the point clear. A patient recently came into his session with a memory; he remembered how his father used to sing to him when he was a young boy and how he rocked comfortingly to the music. One day his father was angry, no longer sang and told him to stop rocking like that. During the session he could clearly remember every aspect of that scene but he could not feel it. The therapist directed the patient to rock just as

---

[13] Maya Pines, *The Brain Changers* (Harcourt, Brace, Jovanovich, New York, 1973), p. 171.

he did when he was very young. Very soon the patient was writhing in agony over a Pain of being stopped from rocking and of not having his daddy sing to him any more. The memory remained in his "head" (third line) until he *physically* recreated the early scene. There was something about the sense of rocking that set him off, indicating to me a lower-line coding of that memory. It did not become a feeling until he got out of his head and into his body. This example also illustrates the split vividly.

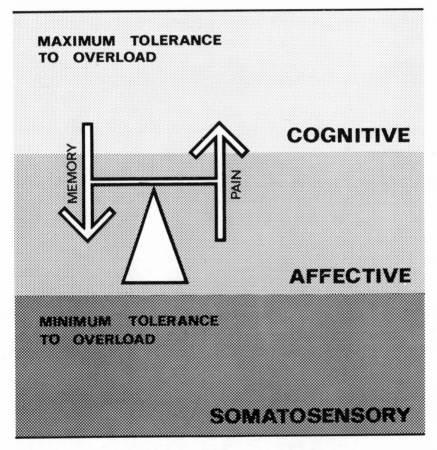

MAXIMUM TOLERANCE TO OVERLOAD

COGNITIVE

MEMORY

PAIN

AFFECTIVE

MINIMUM TOLERANCE TO OVERLOAD

SOMATOSENSORY

PAIN and MEMORY are reciprocal

I believe that an archaic consciousness begins with the first cell—a cellular consciousness, as it were. This cell can store information, react and avoid noxious stimuli. When billions of cells get together we have a most complex and intricate consciousness, but the dynamics of that consciousness lie in the plasticity and reactivity of that single cell. The fact that very primitive life forms made up of very few cells can be conditioned, means that it stores information and that information can be related to future behavior.

It is at the cellular level that we begin to make the connection between the electro-chemical activity of individual cells and so-called psychological phenomena. Reactivity, sensitivity and avoidance patterns are both psychological and physical. That is, they are psychophysical. *We as scientists have extracted the psychological from the physical for study, but in nature they are one.* The properties of reactivity and sensitivity are the elements of consciousness; those elements exist on every level of consciousness, whether there is awareness or not. The laws governing sensitivity and reactivity pertain to all cells no matter on what level of consciousness they exist (first or third lines). Though cellular function is differentiated, so that third line cortical cells have different functions than first line midline ones, the laws governing cellular life do not change. Cells can be overloaded and their functioning be permanently disrupted (as I believe occurs in some forms of cancer).

Each cell has its own state of equilibrium or normal resting state. An overload of Pain interrupts this equilibrium and interferes with the organization of the cell. This disorganization sets in motion a process which I believe is basic to all forms of organic life; namely, the move to homeostasis—the effort of the organism to reconstitute itself in original form. The way of nature is always toward unity. We can see this in literal form when a patient who has had corrective orthodontia in his teens will find after Primals that his teeth and jaw tend to move back to their original pre-orthodontia state.

When a collection of nerve cells has been disrupted by Primal Pain there is again this attempt at reconstitution. This process underlies neurotic behavior; for neurosis is the (symbolic) way we go about mastering old traumas and disruptions of normal functioning. The psychological name we give to this organic process is "hope." Hope is not a *different* phenomenon from reconstitution and homeostasis. It is the name we give to the psychological aspects of the organic process. Hope occurs when there is organic disruption in which the organism tries to reconstitute itself by mastering the trauma symbolically: "I hope I can find someone who can take care of me" is one example. Hope is what nerve cells offer up as their psychological counterpart but in the final analysis it is only an organismic process of reconstitution which takes place when cellular organization (intra- and inter-cellular) has had its unity and cohesion interfered with.

We can understand this when the noxious stimulus is external—when we put a probe against a cell and watch it move away. But we need to see that internal Primal Pain is also a stimulus which blocks the normal flow of events in the brain affecting cellular functioning.

Anatomical Structure		Analog	Consciousness		Function	Nº
Holden / Janov	Melzack		Stage	Level	Melzack	Janov
Spinal Reflex System and Median Zone of Forebrain	Neospinal Thalamic Projection System	Primitive Vertebrate (fish)	fetus → 6 months	Somatosensory (visceration)	Sensation	1
Basal Ganglia and Limbic System	Reticular & Limbic Structures & Paramedial Ascending System	Reptile & Primitive Mammal	6 months → 6 years	Affective	Emotion	2
Neocortex	Neocortical Processes	Higher Primate	6 years → present	Cognitive	Cognition	3

Fig. 3.   *Levels of Consciousness: Comparative Analysis*

The importance of all this is that *no level of consciousness can do another level's work.* If the trauma and disruption of functioning occurred very early to first line cells then *those cells and only those cells* can solve the problem and recreate unity. *The third line cannot, in short, master first line traumas. And that is why insight therapy never can solve early traumas.*

Perhaps now we can understand what Primal Pain is all about. What "hurts" in us is the disorganization of the cell—the disruption of our normal resting state on the lowest level of organization. We are literally "out of whack" on every level of our organism.

Pain "hurts" because there is a disruptive intrusion upon a balanced system rendering it askew. All the bodily systems must compensate for this intrusion and therefore can no longer function normally. The body cannot be itself, so to speak. When we keep an arm in an unnatural position it soon hurts. It stops hurting when we return it to its natural resting position. This is no less true of other systems even though the hurt is

less graphic and obvious. Primal Pain often produces continuous constriction of certain blood vessels. This in turn affects nerve and muscle
systems, and again the result is hurt. It "hurts" to be unnatural. The
system seems to have a need to be itself and Pain keeps that from happening. It is perhaps paradoxical that the neurotic often suffers from Pains
that do not hurt. That is, his body registers Primal Pain, his system
metabolizes it, yet he does not experience it consciously. Whether he is
aware of it or not seems to matter little since the system goes on dealing
with the Pain anyway. Eventually, the neurotic may become aware of
the systemic hurt in a system way; that is, he may develop an ulcer
because his system (unknown to him) has been secreting too much hydrochloric acid, and he then feels physical pain. But it is again no more than
the end product of Primal Pain.

Catastrophic Pain and the Arrest of Maturation

I have used the term "catastrophic" in describing Primal Pain, and
perhaps I have not been specific as to its meaning. In my view, it means
life threatening. The Pain not only hurts, it is a tremendous insult to
the system which can lead to death. For example, we have done experiments in our laboratory where a person will have a sustained pulse of
200 beats per minute in the pre-Primal phase. This pulse rate is in
response to *an early childhood or infancy Pain*. It is presumably the same
pulse rate that the child or infant would have were he not able to shut
down and keep the Pain away from consciousness. Clearly, a continuous
pulse of 200 is going to kill the child in short order. Thus, the Pain is
lethal if allowed into consciousness continuously. Mercifully, neurosis
intercedes and keeps that from happening. But if the Pain does not
change over decades as we have seen, then it is hardly likely that the
physiological response to that Pain would change either. The adult can
withstand a pulse of 200 for a time because he is stronger, but what is
more important *he can resolve* the Pain by feeling it, something the infant
could not do.

Perhaps we don't appreciate how vulnerable and undefended the infant
is. He doesn't have the fully operating neocortex that he will have as an
adult. He can't do fancy mental gyrations to fool himself. All that can
happen is repression, and that takes place *before* the full development of
the neocortex. He can feel Pain later on because he has that convoluted

mass of brain tissue. But imagine a Pain that makes his pulse go up to 240 beats per minute; he is six months old. What does he do? He represses. That is the survival mechanism. He becomes neurotic to save his life; and neurosis is the ultimate survival mechanism. It is an automatic involuntary process. Suppose there are Pains after Pains in his early life— growing up in a boarding home with no touch, no softness, no one to care. It is possible that the gates become overtaxed. They are overburdened and no longer function properly. First line Pains are always just a hair away because of the compounding of which I wrote elsewhere in this work. Neurosis is no longer working. When the gates crash under their burden psychosis is the result. It is the last mental defense. The gates work up to a point. They repress and repress until the person has all his affect and emotion cancelled out. But they too have a failure point, beyond which they no longer function. We see this clearly in patients who have used LSD many times. The body does everything it can to keep the Pain at bay, but all the fail-safe mechanisms have been contaminated by the drug and they give way.

When we take away the defenses in Primal Therapy we too are interfering with these fail-safe mechanisms. As we do so the individual goes into a panic state, a state which we see can lead to death. But fortunately we can direct what is happening; we can take the person to the source of his panic—the Pain. We can do the only rational thing—eliminate the *reason* for the gating.

Not only does a Pain that is catastrophic produce neurosis; it creates a certain kind of neurosis. In the case cited above a prototypic early Pain created a chronically fast pulse. What happens then is that the person grows up unconsciously matching his external environment to his inner one. This man with the fast pulse was always on the go. It determined the kinds of jobs he took and the kinds of interests he had. He remembered growing up in a tough neighborhood in Detroit. He didn't stay home and become a recluse to protect himself. He actively sought out fights. He put himself in positions where he had to run to save his life. Another person with a different prototypic physiologic response, say of high blood pressure, given the same environment might have acted much differently. Given to holding things in, his life style might be much more withdrawn and sedentary. What occurs from these prototypic Pains is a "physiotype." Not only is there a certain characteristic way the body handles stress (fast pulse, high blood pressure) but personality characteristics become interwoven with this kind of physiologic pattern: fast pulse, getting into fights and running for one's life, more need for fast pulse, etc. The physiologic and psychologic become intermingled into a unity until one cannot be extracted and distinguished from the other, and life becomes simply the unconscious denouement for one's physiotype.

It is consciousness which makes for Pain—the *experience* of Pain. The physiologic measures increase as the feelings become almost conscious. This means that it is connection which produces Pain and disconnection which suppresses it.

There is an important distinction between Pain and suffering. Almost all animal forms can suffer. But it takes a neocortex to fully experience Pain. That is because Pain is a fully conscious experience and suffering is not. Neurotics suffer because they are unconscious. They hurt in vague, nondelineated ways. *To feel Pain means an end to suffering.* Conversely, suffering is a disconnected state—a nonfeeling state. It is not suffering that makes us into feeling people; it is Pain.

A bellyache is suffering. Feeling the emptiness of life that makes for that suffering is Pain. As Dr. Holden has pointed out there are two distinct pain pathways, one for suffering and the other for pain. The oldest phylogenetically is the pathway for knowing the quality of pain suffering. These pathways were a much later development in accordance with how the brain and the spinal cord matured, embryologically and in evolution. For our purposes Pain is the uniquely human experience; it takes all the levels of consciousness to make Pain but only one level may produce suffering. The experience of Pain is an interconnected event. A patient can be writhing and thrashing and screaming—suffering horribly but not be fully in Pain. Because he is only suffering he will not resolve his misery and will continue to suffer thereafter from it. It is also possible to be suffering and not have the incredible rises in physiologic measures that we have seen in Primals.

When Pains are not felt they turn into suffering; they spread out in the system so that the person suffers from headaches, backaches and stomach aches. These symptoms are the result of disconnection. They disappear with connection. Fully feeling one's Pain is the only permanent way out of suffering. The reason this is true is that as adults we are *suffering from Pains* which may have occurred in the first days or weeks of our lives. We must go back in our personal history to be liberated.

The fact that there are two pain pathways, ancient and new, is critical in understanding the neurotic split.

The pathway closest to the midline of the nervous system transmits suffering. The newer pain pathway, further from the midline, transmits discriminative information about pain. The suffering system projects fibers *diffusely* to the entire cortex from the inner portions of the thalamus, whereas the discriminative pain pathway projects *selectively* to the primary sensory cortex, providing the *specific* connections to old, disconnected painful feelings.

Suffering can affect behavior globally because of its diffuse cortical representations, whereas the new pain system gives one a selective, particular *idea* of what the suffering is about. That is why connection dispels suffering, and why disconnection maintains it.

Where a number of therapies go astray is that they only deal with the disconnected aspects of a specific Pain: psychoanalysis handling the ideational, Reichian dealing with the somatic sequelae (physical tension). Conditioning therapy addresses itself to the disconnected *symbol* of underlying Pain; early fear of parents may later become transmuted into phobias of one kind or another. These phobias, then, become of the objects of Conditioning Therapy rather than the particular Pain. In this way Behaviorists concern themselves with the higher cortical representations of the suffering system, dealing with derivatives of the specific pain system. In Primal Therapy, the conversion from suffering to Pain converts phobias into specific fears from early life, and amorphous anxiety into Pain.

In terms of our maturation it must be emphasized there is no way to develop fully as a psychophysical being without this complete resolution of disconnected circuits. The therapeutic conversion from suffering into Pain is precisely the condition for new beard growth in male Primal patients and for new breast growth in female patients.

Again the dialectic; in the general (suffering) lies the particular, and in the particular (Pain system) lies the general (suffering). On the simplest level of neural organization it is the split between pain and suffering. We could suffer long before we could feel pain; and that means that we could suffer before we became feeling. Again we see how ontogeny recapitulates phylogeny. There are millions of years between the time of the worm (who can suffer) and the development of a human being who can feel. The same time gap exists in ontogenetic maturation. Only the gap between suffering (as a neonate) and feeling Pain (as an adult) is in a few years instead of millions. And in the adult the gap between suffering (as from a hammer blow in the finger) and pain may be in seconds. I often wonder, incidentally, if there isn't some fixed ratio between phylogeny and ontogeny—so many minutes or weeks in ontogeny for so many thousands of years of phylogeny.

In the adult human there is an interesting phenomenon in response to pain. He can hit himself on the finger with a hammer, say, "Oh my, I've really smashed myself," and then seconds later double up with the suffering of it. But in that time lag there is a chance to *block the suffering and attenuate the conscious experience of it.* The "mind," in short, can perceive pain and split from its affective body components in an instant. I have wondered if the major reason for the development of the neocortex was so that man could put an end to his suffering. What he has not been able to do until now is put an end to his Pain.

Perhaps if we had understood the relationship between phylogeny and ontogeny better we would have known that for man to mature he must pass through the earliest stages of his phylogenetic development from the moment he is conceived until birth; and that for man to mature during his lifetime he must pass through each stage of his life and master it before he can go on. This is the Primal premise. Man must master his birth as an adult if he did not master (integrate and resolve) the experience at the start of his life. And he cannot mature until he does. That mastering process takes place in reverse order, moving from the recent to the remote past.

Failure to integrate Pains at any level of development means an arrested maturation at that level. We must past through the early stages of life in an ordered sequential way both phylogenetically and ontogenetically. We must walk at certain times and be toilet trained at certain times and those times are genetically determined. To force those behaviors prematurely means to arrest development in some way. If that so-called mature behavior is forced it remains as a non-integrated trauma. To move on emotionally requires that those traumas must be resolved. Otherwise, to some extent the person is stuck on that level. He will be forevermore immature even though his intellect continues to develop. That is why there can be such a gap between emotional and intellectual development. The third line can learn the rules of emotional behavior and can act mature. But the lower lines cannot; and when you remove the mature act you find the child. The Freudians believe that when someone acts immature and childish he is in a "regressed state," and this is synonymous with mental illness. We now understand that there is no regression in the conventional sense as found in the psychiatric literature. When the act is removed we simply become what we are—children. We don't go back into the past, so to speak. We go to what is real, *now* inside of us; something that is everpresent. Regression is no more than being one's true emotional self.

The very existence of the phenomenon of regression as seen in hypnosis is testimony to the actual state of the organism, of arrested development. The Primal process is dialectic in the sense that going back to master one's arrested development which results in immaturity also results in freeing the organism to finally mature in a real way, not just on the third line.

There is a biological basis for this. A recent report by Dr. Graham Liggins of the University of Auckland indicates that it is the fetus which "decides" when to come into the world. When it senses that it is mature enough it releases certain hormones which act on the tissue of the lining of the uterus. This triggers off chemical changes in the mother and contractions begin.

The brain structure which mediates all of this is the hypothalamus, which we have discussed at length. So long as there are no significant traumas during gestation one might assume that birth will occur at the proper time. But if there are intrauterine traumas (the mother smoking a great deal, taking drugs or just being exceptionally tense) it is possible that the hypothalamus (the structure which mediates first line Pains) is already overburdened *before birth*. Signals then about the child's readiness for birth may occur out of sequence, with prematurity resulting.

The hypothalamus is one of the most ancient and least evolved brain structures. It is functioning long before birth and the possibility for its alteration due to Pain exists all that time. This structure represents the highest functioning level of neural organization during gestation. It integrates the outer and inner worlds with each other. When the fetus lives in an unstable neurotic world in the womb this can well have an effect on his later maturity. It is interesting that a recent finding showed that black welfare babies were born with a faster heart rate than white ones.

It is the hypothalamus which helps govern a great deal of our hormone output, and again if traumas occur during gestation a faulty hormone output may not only occur at birth but also afterwards. What may initially appear to be genetic or hereditary defects could be due to adverse conditions before birth; traumas which occur about the time that the output of thyroxine (20 weeks of gestation) is organized could possibly result in hypothyroidism from birth on, for example.

It is possible that the traumas which have to be relived in order to set the hypothalamus straight are those which occurred before birth. Certainly, the neural organization is there to register, code and store them. What all this means is that we can be neurotic before birth and neurosis in these terms means "altered hypothalamic functioning." We see now that neurosis is very much an internal affair and is not something between people. It is not a specific kind of behavior. And the treatment of neurosis does not involve having certain kinds of social interactions, whether it be having your transference or intellectual defenses analyzed by a psycho-analyst or in confronting someone in group therapy. The fetus behaves internally; his neurosis is internal and that neurosis lives on within him for a lifetime. No social confrontation in the world will solve that aspect of the neurosis.

The relationship of all this to regression is that neurosis affects the hypothalamus from the start of life and blocking of this structure in any way makes you systemically younger than you are chronologically. The neurotic, in short, is organized both brain and body as a child below the neocortical level. It is the frightened child who lives inside of each of us and makes the heart race and stomach acid flow excessively even in a tranquil environment. It is the infant traumatized at birth who still resides in our systems. That is what we really are because that is what we have never mastered or resolved.

It is no wonder that many women suffer sexual problems; their bodies are still that of children (and often look like child's bodies—with almost no breasts—another development governed by the hypothalamus) and they have not yet grown up internally as sexual human beings. That is why a number of men in their twenties come to us with almost no beard growth; and why after resolving early Pain their beards become that of men. As neurotics they are in a continuous regressed state, so to speak; or better put, they are in a state of arrested development.

What Is Curative?

We may now ask, "How is it that feeling a feeling is curative?" If we think of "feeling a feeling" as simple abreaction then the answer is that it is not curative. It is but momentarily relieving. Abreaction as the out-pouring of the energy of an old feeling does not involve reliving and connection across the levels of consciousness. Reliving birth is something more than just abreaction; when the bruises from a harsh birth reappear on some patient during a Primal in their exact early form we can hardly call that abreaction. Primals extend the concept of memory far beyond consciously remembered events. Memory for the abreactionists means third line *awareness,* sometimes accompanied by second line affect. But Primal Therapy considers that there are levels of consciousness and levels of experience so that a consciously remembered event can be a first-line memory registered and "remembered" physically.

There are different kinds of memory and those differences are all important in understanding what exactly is curative about memory. There is the *memory of a feeling*. This is a third line event. It tends to be dim and not lucid or immediate. There is the *feeling of a memory*; that is known as a Primal. One is a total experience, the other is a psychological event. True memory uses the language of feeling in recalling the past. Third line memory uses the language of intellect in that service. Primal memory is always vivid; it is a presence.

A child who is taught to address his parents in formal ways may on the 3rd line ("I remember that mother insisted we call her 'mother'") recall an early event within the structure of that formality. But it all vanishes under the impact of Primal memory and the language is the real language of a child to his parents, not the acquired one. ("Mommy, I want my bottie.") Same scene, different memory experience . . . and different therapeutic result.

But why is it that reliving an old experience is curative? If we understand that a feeling is represented on its particular level of consciousness with representations of the feeling located on other levels, we see that "feeling a feeling" means a total three-level experience. It is Pain which produces gating, thereby disrupting the circuit of representations involved in a feeling. The result is tension which is the energy of the feeling unable to pass through the gate to complete its circuit. This produces a disconnected experience where a segment of the circuit becomes reverberating thus activating the system in random ways. It is like a body of water coursing fluidly in its channels passing through a dam. When the dam is suddenly shut, the water and its great built-up energy is deflected in all directions.

Opening the dam to permit reconnection is the key. For a patient can discharge his anger at other group members, against the wall or pounding a pillow and solve nothing. The reason is that nothing has been done to reconnect the *original* disrupted circuits which produced the anger in the first place. Those early circuits are the cause of the anger and anything which bypasses dealing with them cannot be curative; simply abreaction and palliative. The circuit must be made complete for there to be liberation.

Primals are curative because they reconnect disconnected circuits so that old events are resolved and the system returned to a normal resting state. Primals create unity and cohesion. They correct the system and allow proper intra- and inter-organization of cellular life.

The unity created by Primals seems to be what Dr. Gardiner has found in his research. For the advanced Primal brain seems to have a greater harmony: in terms of electrophysiology there is a greater congruence of brain wave patterns between back to front and side to side of the brain.

We can take the hypothesis further, for it may be that very deep early Pain is more disorganizing to cells than later second-line Pain. Further, that the deeper the Pain the more disorganizing it is, so that there would be a continuum on a cellular level from mild disruption to total disorganization. The deeper the Pain the more life-endangering its effects on cells. And the concept of "life endangering" is something we might use as a criterion for the kind of Pain involved. Thus, cancer would be the result of severe first-line Pain, colitis would be somewhat less severe, ulcers still less, and so on. Cancer as a cellular disease would be on a first-line disease resulting from first-line pressure on certain cells. Indeed, cancer is most often associated with the viscera and the midline affecting precisely those organs and areas mediating the first line. No non-Primal person can begin to understand the kinds of pressure in our bodies which ultimately cause the cells to become totally disorganized until he sees a patient writhing and thrashing in Pain almost continuously for one or two years during Primals related to one event at birth that lasted possibly only minutes. To see that pressure liberated day after day for months indicates to us the kind of tremendous compacted inner force constantly at work against the cells. In some cases of vulnerability the cell gives way and disease results. Perhaps certain kinds of latent viruses are liberated producing disease. But the cause, I submit, is in first-line Primal pressure; and cancer would be the insanity of the cell. That same pressure when liberated against a weak third-line consciousness could result in another kind of insanity—the kind we are used to seeing—the insanity of the mind.

Perhaps we can correlate body and mind phenomena in terms of levels of consciousness, there being psychoses, severe neuroses, mild neuroses—of the body and the mind. Cancer and psychoses being the most severe and most life endangering (a psychotic cannot conduct himself safely in life), while mild neuroses and mild headaches could be equated. Asthma would be first line and can easily be life endangering. Gastritis would not. In short, I believe that there are body psychoses and neuroses; but those terms really don't add much to our understanding except that they are shorthand terms indicating degrees of pathology.

The criterion for that physical pathology is the degree to which the disease is life endangering or potentially life endangering.

Cells are specialized, it is true, so that brain cells are not the same as stomach cells. But when we discuss psychoses or neuroses whether of the mind or body we are still talking about cells; and cells are governed by certain biologic laws. All of us understand that the "mind" becomes disorganized under severe social pressure. What we may not realize is that the mind is but an aggregate of cells working in unison. Mind, in short, is not something ex machina but a cellular function. The disorganization of the mind *indicates* a cellular disorganization of some kind. I am assuming that there is some basic life process that propels us to overcome disorganizing influences and return to our normal resting or homeostatic state. We act out symbolically in order to fulfill *old* needs in order to finally achieve unity and cohesion. The aim of neurosis, then, is to be well.

The pressure of the first formed (and I believe more delicate) brain cells associated with the first line perhaps may explain the process of brain deterioration, ultimate senility and possibly aging itself. For the brain cells which first deteriorate are of the first line, the second group to deteriorate are second line, and lastly it is the third line cells which wither. I would speculate here that this aging and deterioration process may be associated with the severity of the Primal pressure on certain kinds of cells. If we concede that inner pressure can have a disrupting and disorganizing effect on cells, the greater the Pain the greater the pressure on those cells, then cellular deterioration which follows in sequence from first to third line should be a logical denouement.

I think that research investigators and philosophers alike have gone astray by trying to isolate consciousness in the brain. They failed to recognize that the brain is encased in a body; and the pattern of neuronal firing, the specific interconnections made, the frequency and amplitude of neuronal action, all are influenced by the state of *organic consciousness,* not just by cells in the brain. It is the dialectic interchange of brain and body and effects of each on the other, a state of being, which produces a consciousness. Part of the error made by those interested in the nature of consciousness is equating awareness (a "mental state") with consciousness. To reiterate, there is but one consciousness embracing many separate awarenesses: acoustic, visual, visceral etc.

Consciousness is a brain phenomenon and dialectically the brain is a phenomenon of consciousness. Consciousness has changed throughout evolution with the evolutionary changes in the structure of the brain and the structure of the brain has changed in evolution because of alterations in consciousness.

If we see it in this light then we understand that consciousness shapes the flow of specific cerebral activity. It isn't that consciousness is the psychological result of neuronal action—a "leakage" of brain cells— it is a dynamic interactory state of neuronal activity being a function of a state of being. The miracle of human beings, to me, is how a conglomeration of cells packed together in a certain way can grow in such a way as to be able to make an exact copy of the outside world inside, and then relate itself to that image just as if it were outside. And what is even more miraculous is how those pieces of matter can offer up pictures in the mind with color and sound.

The Dialectic

I have used the term "dialectic" a good deal, stating that Primal Therapy is a dialectic process. Perhaps its meaning should be clarified. The dialectic means the interpenetration of opposites forming ever-new syntheses. This is not simply an academic distinction. It is the basis of life and is, I believe, the key law of motion of living things. Man and woman come together sexually and produce a new human being. That new being comes together later on with someone else and produces another human being, and so on. This dialectic is how life comes into being. I do not believe that dialectical laws can be overlooked when dealing with the maturation, neurotogenesis and treatment of neurosis in man, for the dialectic is the very basis of life. Thus, feeling one's Pain dispels it; not feeling Pain keeps it intact. Feeling little helps one grow up; not feeling little makes one act it out, and remain immature. Feeling alone helps one be alone. Not feeling it makes one flee into sociability. Feeling fearful helps one develop courage. Not feeling it causes one to be forever fearful. And so on, ad infinitum. It is when we neglect the dialectic that our therapy goes awry. When a patient feels powerless we help him into that feeling completely. Not to do so means that there will be unconscious feelings of powerlessness which will force the person to act-out being powerful, for example, for a lifetime. It will be part of the basis of his lifetime neurotic behavior. And the only way out of acting-out being powerful is to feel powerless; nothing else will do. Nothing else will cure. I want to reiterate the point with another example even at the risk of repetition, as I think the point is crucial. If we understand that all critical life experiences are registered in the system then the feeling of helplessness in the womb during a harsh birth remains for a lifetime. But there is no God in the womb, nothing to lean on mentally to make the trauma easier. Later, however, when the brain is further developed we can manufacture an all powerful God to help us with our early, undelineated feelings of helplessness and powerlessness. The strength of that need for a helpful and powerful God will be in some measure (but not at all solely) determined by the strength of the residual feeling of helplessness from birth. To dispel that symbol means that we must in some way deal with those feelings which gave rise to it, and that is the dialectic. The symptom or symbol is the synthesis resulting from the contradiction between a trauma and the necessity to repress it. To deal with the symptom or symbol *in any way* without regard to the dialectical interplay underlying it means to do incorrect therapy. No ahistoric therapy, therefore, biofeedback, conditioning, meditation, encounter, Reality Therapy, Rational-Emotive, etc., can be curative, for the historical dialectic has been overlooked. The dialectic is obdurate and intransigent. It dictates that nothing else can work, for no progressive development takes place without it. It is undialectic to think that social problems can be solved without regard to the inner states of the individuals who live in society. And it is equally undialectic to think that internal problems can be completely resolved without regard to the social structure we live in. Life begins with the dialectic and develops dialectically.

The base of the dialectic process is materialism—which means that there is a material basis for mental events; and of course there was matter in the universe long before there were minds and mental processes. This leaves no room in our theoretical schema for a mystical force such as the id or an elan. Each construct is tied to something concrete. The basis for mental illness is that something concrete happened to us in our early youth that had an effect on the material system; nerve pathways were rerouted and energy was bound to disconnected circuits. The treatment for that affliction is again the dialectic—a neurosis in reverse . . . going back over those early events with a different resolution, freeing the bound energy by connecting the circuits. Blocking the Pain produced neurosis and feeling the Pain undoes it. The treatment process is a *process*—a constant dialectic interplay between repressive and expressive forces with continuous new resolutions bringing the person to ever-new syntheses— new levels of consciousness and functioning. And, as with all dialectic processes, the therapy has the seeds of its own undoing. The more Pain one feels the less one needs therapy; the more that need is met in society the less overall need for any psychotherapy. The further the patient goes along in treatment the less he needs a therapist—and this is a key point since it is not true with any other form of therapy. One has to meditate constantly, for example, or one can remain in psychoanalysis for many years and still need more treatment. It is not a self concluding process. So long as one does not deal directly with underlying forces then one must beat back and repress those forces and the result is the continual danger of their breakthrough again. And again therapy will be needed for control and repression. This will continue to happen until we recognize the dialectic—that there are forces at work producing neurosis and it is those forces that must be dealt with.

Even if we recognize those forces, however, we must again keep the dialectic in mind in the treatment process. For the therapy is *neurosis in reverse*. This means that we proceed from late events to early ones in the exact opposite manner in which they were laid down. In the brain it means that we proceed from the perimeter to the deep interior in a most literal way. We don't defy neuroembryology; we work with it. We don't plunge into first line early material (as do some therapists who work with LSD) but regard the whole matter of therapy as a slow and inevitable and ordered process. We are not looking for mystical events such as death and rebirth, destruction of the ego, or whatever; we are seeking after concrete events that happened to us in our lives at particular times which left concrete effects on our neurophysiology.

Nor are we helping a patient toward some mystical or idealistic notion such as "peak events" or "bliss states." We are helping him make a journey into himself in a very real way, not to achieve peak states but to create new resolutions of the forces at work inside of him. Those forces are knowable, they are physical and are timeless and everlasting until resolution. So long as any idealistic notion remains in a psychologic theory it will have that much of a weak link. Freud, despite his brilliance and his perception still had an unknowable, unchangeable, almost non-material force at work creating neurosis—the id. He was right about repression but the question was what was being repressed. If he said "Pain," instead of incestuous forces or libidinous impulses, then his treatment would have taken a much different turn. It would not have relied on building defenses against seething impulses. Rather, those impulses would have been dealt with and resolved. His dream theory would not have been about wishes which come out in an unconscious made up of mystical forces, but would have been about repressed early events which emerge when consciousness is not strongly at work.

If Freud had kept in mind that all things are knowable then there would have been no unfathomable id creating all that havoc. And the superego would not have been some strange mental force which suddenly appears at the age of six. There would be no Jungian shadow forces nor any special "will to meaning" as in the Frankl schema.

Once one has left the dialectic then any matter of theoretical deviations from reality is possible and all deviations will be equally ineffective. For example, there are the pep talk schools of therapy—"You can do it; you've got to have a better attitude. You are taller than Napoleon. You are capable if you want to be. Don't let negative thoughts defeat you, etc." All of these haranguing, exhorting, essentially dictatorial therapies with a chief guru simply overlook a lifetime of experience of the people they are encouraging which has a concrete basis in their physiology; we do not overcome our physiology and change rerouted neuronal circuits by simply having a better attitude. The patients, disconnected from their inner forces, accept idealistic notions precisely because of that disconnection from what is real. They search after unreal solutions; they seek out the mystical because disengaged from internal reality they need to believe in magic causes and therefore magic cures. So of course then there would be strange shadow forces emerging in dreams, and of course the results of their so-called therapies will be mystical with peak states, bliss, cosmic consciousness and the like. The results of their therapies will be as spurious as the causes they posit for their problems. They will either be convinced of profound change or they will convince themselves of it; they will imagine profound internal change without ever resolving *those forces which alone can make that change possible.* If you don't recognize the Pain then you must rise above it in some way into some specious state of being. And that is the legacy of idealistic nondialectic therapies. The dialectic is all.

The dialectic dictates that something does not come into existence without cause or reason. Nor does it exist alone. Each new entity brings with it its opposite; Pain ushers in repressing agencies, and repression maintains the force of Pain. They are ubiquitous cocompanions and form a unity. The strength of repression indicates the strength of the underlying Pain, and conversely, the amount of buried Pain will dictate the amount of repression. A law of physics states that for each action there is an equal and opposite reaction, and that is why we must always keep the dialectic in mind when considering psychotherapy. We do not treat repression with more repression and hope to solve anything. We understand that a repressed person is in Pain and we come to know his Pain not by what he says (since he can often feel nothing and deny the existence of Pain) but by the degree of his repressed state. If he is affect-less we know that his affect is buried with the Pain.

The interplay of forces between Pain and repression gives rise to a resolution—a neurotic resolution resulting in symptoms or other appearances. The resolution is neurotic because catastrophic Pain prohibits a non-neurotic resolution. In every neurosis, therefore, there are two elements—the essence and the appearance. The appearance is a manifestation of the internal dialectic interplay. It is an overt sign of covert content. Obviously, the appearance should not be treated as though it were a viable and discrete entity. But this is precisely the state of psychology and psychotherapy today; dealing with appearances rather than essences. It is still in the Aristotelean, classificatory mode.

Thus, there is acupuncture, dream analysis and sex therapies all treatment forms unrelated to specific causes. They are therefore the therapies of appearances and their cures must be couched in terms of what happens to those appearances. If the symptom disappears the treatment is a success.

Sometimes the appearances are quite subtle; as for example the increased brain wave frequency and amplitude in certain mental states. It is possible through biofeedback techniques (discussed elsewhere) to reduce those appearances but it surely is an undynamic nondialectic approach. The point is that when the dialectic is neglected one becomes unanchored in reality and one then enters the realm of the mystical, and any therapeutic approach is mystical which posits states of being which are eternal, nonverifiable and unrelated to causation. Anything goes in nondialectic approaches because appearances are the focus; and there are many ways to beat back appearances—even beating someone with a stick can drive away many so-called neurotic behaviors.

The rejoinder of the nondialecticians is that their therapy "works." And, in a pragmatic society the phrase "it works" becomes the apotheosis where pragmatism is exalted and superficiality enshrined . . . all because the professionals have neglected a very small word—"Why?"

Other Evidence

Perhaps this is a good time for further discussion on memory as a holistic state and how this relates to the Jungian collective unconscious. I have said thus far that the unconscious is made up of the Pains we have repressed; but that may not be all. There may be a "genetic unconscious" which also shapes our general adult consciousness and helps determine how we react to life. All of us would probably agree that we inherit features from our parents, grandparents and ancestors. We have the same nose, curly hair, teeth, color of eyes and so on, as they do. Sometimes we look just like our father and other times we resemble our mothers. Why would an inherited nervous system escape this process? Why couldn't we have a general nervous system which tends to function like one or another or like an ancestor? Certainly, nature didn't decide to stop with hair, eyes and teeth and mark a line against the central nervous system. My assumption is that part of the unconscious is genetic, not in the way of content but in general neuronal firing patterns (fast firing, vs. slow firing, for example) and in general predispositions. It may be possible that a generally fearful predisposition forms part of the first-line system. If the mother was a fearful person, constantly anxious during the time of pregnancy, why could this not be transmitted into our physical structure? Nor is this simply wild speculation.

A peptide has been isolated and synthesized from rats called scotophobin. Extracts from the brains of rats who were trained to avoid the dark (be afraid of the dark) were injected into untrained rats. It produced dark-avoidance behavior. The implication is that there is a "transfer of training" produced chemically. My belief is that this transfer may occur subtly between mother and fetus. The Darwinian approach indicates that changes in structure and function brought about with evolution are species-specific rather than individual. My assumption is that there are not only species-specific changes over the millennia but individual changes, as well. It may be, for example, that the quality of thinking predominantly in images is a "family trait." We have seen families like that. They are the artists and the poets. A son may not turn out to be a poet, he may become an architect or engineer; but the quality of seeing things spatially or in images may be a genetic factor inherent in the unconscious of both mother and son. Musical ability may be another example. Songs aren't coded in the memory store so that we know songs mother knew as a child just by inheritance. But the quality of pitch, meter and rhythm may be inherited and this genetic factor may unconsciously help determine how the child reacts to his environment. Given even a slightly musical environment he might become a musician, while someone else might not.

There has been a controversy about the natural rhythm of blacks.

Without delving into this question in depth at this time I would like to suggest that there are indications that the black African babies in particular develop motor skills much earlier than do whites. One wonders if natural childbirth (producing less catastrophic first-line Pain) among blacks, does not permit them greater access to their bodies than do the artificial conditions under which most white children are born.

The brain is not a *tabula rasa* upon which life plays its song. It has qualities which help to determine how life will be responded to. There are qualities inherited by the species; or else we would still have a Neanderthal brain, and qualities which are inherited on an individual basis. Our whole brain structure has changed during evolution and we must assume that this structure became altered slowly due to man's interaction with his environment—by experience. Even the way the brain is split has changed with evolution because the very lowermost portion of the brain (the brainstem), something we have in common with birds and fish, is not split.

I have discussed split-brain research in "The Nature of Consciousness." (Chapter I). I have indicated that one hemisphere deals mainly with intellectual matters while the other (right) predominantly mediates feeling. The significance of this in terms of present discussion is that the connecting-link, the corpus callosum, between the two hemispheres is not fully functional until the age of two. At that time everything which occurs on one side (such as a feeling) becomes available immediately to the other side. The importance of this is that the child is beginning to be able to make sense out of his experience. He can start to reflect on it, and on his feelings; he can suffer emotionally.

There is some interesting research on split-brain by Gazzaniga which relates to systems of consciousness.[14] Gazzaniga tested patients who were being examined for brain tumors. Small doses of an anesthetic were injected into their left hemispheres putting that half to sleep. The result is a paralysis on the right side, even while the other half remains awake. "We put an object, say a cigarette, in his left hand. He feels it. We remove the cigarette. Then the effects of the amytal wear off and the left hemisphere wakes up. We ask the patient how he feels. 'Fine,' he replies. 'What did I put in your hand?' 'I don't know', says the patient. Then we show him a series of objects and ask him, 'Which one was it?' In spite of what he has said, his left hand immediately points to the cigarette." Gazzaniga says it is a psychiatrist's dream because

---

[14] Pines, p. 157.

there is something which influences behavior that the person cannot get at. *"It may explain why memories formed in earliest childhood are inaccessible."* They may control future behavior. But since they were formed before the child learned to speak, they cannot be recalled through the *language system.*

All of this again indicates that there are levels of experience organized independently. Split-brain research is only one dimension of the problem, since the split in consciousness is not only horizontal but vertical, as well. It appears that first-, second- and third-line systems embrace aspects of both the horizontal and vertical in a most complicated way. We shall leave it to neurologists to solve that problem. For my purposes, I only want to cite relevant research which corroborates what we in Primal Therapy know many times over—there are levels of Pain, levels of consciousness, and the two are related to produce either neurosis or health.

Conclusion

I have said above that it is my belief that one of the major factors in the evolution of the third line, of man's neocortex, is Pain. It is by no means the only factor, since a changing environment is paramount; but very often those changes produced Pain. And if we look at any other form of life, even that of plants, we see that development takes place *around* adverse events. If you block a plant's growth it will tend to grow around that barrier; and if we didn't see other plants of its species we might believe that the odd growth pattern was its natural state. I believe that man grew "around" his inevitable Pain; that he developed a higher cortex to handle that Pain and symbolize it. This enabled him to continue his life fairly much intact. The price has been neurosis.

It is Pain which has caused convoluted behavior in a man's life, which, over time, may have literally convoluted the brain. I am suggesting that we have needed much of that neocortex to handle overloads; and because the lower-line systems are quite vulnerable we seem to have produced a higher cortex to reroute all that inner pressure. In that sense, it takes much more to overload the third line because it expanded literally to handle (symbolize, rationalize etc.) and cope with life.

We have to ask why it is that man "preserves" his Pain in its exact form throughout his lifetime. Why doesn't he just grow "bent" and not have those memories reverberating around his system? I think that one reason is that it is the exact means left for man to "right himself," and so continue his evolution as a stable form. It is the cortex which has allowed man to journey back in time—not only personal time but geologic time. When a patient descends the Primal chain and Primals on the first line, he is, in a sense, reaching back to make contact with his prehistoric ancestors; making contact with a brain system which existed millions of years ago in his vertebrate ancestry. He is tapping a storage and mediating system which lay millions of years of history away from the language system used to explain those events. No wonder it can be incomprehensible to modern man with his giant neocortex that he can be in touch with an ancient legacy in his brain. No wonder we never believed that first-line events stay stamped in that brain. We have relied on language, the language of the neocortex to explain events which lie far far below that capacity.

That something of our species' history remains inside us throughout our individual lives should not be so surprising when we consider that the very new fetus develops gill slits common to our ancient fish ancestry. The human being seems to have this remarkable capacity to retain aspects of both his personal and anthropologic history. Gill slits are but another indication that we do not transcend our history but evolve from it. There is always an element of the past in us. Not only do we preserve aspects of the historic organism but also its *environment* as well. The new fetus is in a liquid milieu, and that milieu is a saline solution not unlike the ocean. As we develop personally we "preserve" our early milieu as a physiologic memory. The scene in our mind is a duplicate of that early environment with all its original sights, smells and sounds. ·

Everything we go through psychologically and in evolution stays with us. The memory of the sixth grade classroom is *physiologic*. It is not something in space; it is part of our bodies, just like gill slits. The body becomes distorted through psychological events because those events belong to the body.

What we must understand is the necessity of Pain (and the neocortex it produced) for health; for if it didn't stay with us we could not *solve our history* and undo the neurosis. It is again the dialectic. Pain helped evolve a neocortex; and that neocortex is the precise mechanism by which Pain is resolved. So Pain helped produce the exact mechanism it needed for its resolution. The brain, after all, is the only matter in the universe that can be conscious of itself. When I visualize the neocortex I see an intricately convoluted series of folds encased in a narrow box. It seems "unnatural" to me to have such a great amount of structure for so little space; and I believe that it is largely Pain which has constantly activated the brain to develop more and more cortex to handle it. That neocortex sits over the other two historical systems of consciousness like the lid on a kettle; only in man's history the lid has swallowed up and overshadowed that kettle. It is clear to me that Pain is a survival agent and one major reason why it is stored is so we will have an inbuilt memory system which tells us what to avoid in the future.

What brought on all that Pain for man? Adversity, scarcity, social organization, changes in the earth's structure and climate; many, many factors. The very fact of social organization means to defer one's self for the good of the whole. It means hierarchies, control and authority. It means specialization and narrowing of one's interest and sphere of influence. It means exploitation. Organisms which invaded man meant that some would die before their time leaving children parentless. Cataclysmic events, floods and earthquakes produced the same effects, as well. And our brain had to become equal to the task. And it did. It stored all those childhood cataclysmic events, postponing the time when they had to be dealt with so that later on they could be trotted out in adulthood one at a time when there was sufficient strength and independence to be relived and experienced.

I think that the Primal unconscious is different from almost every major previous concept of the unconscious; it is not a "given." It is not evil and destructive; and it is not inviolable, everlasting, immutable. We are born with a *consciousness,* not an unconsciousness in the Freudian, Jungian and Adlerian manner. Man is a truly conscious, potentially rational being to start with. It is Pain and repression which make him both unconscious and irrational. It is Pain which makes the Freudian unconscious timeless because it is Pain which endures everlasting until felt and resolved.

CHAPTER EIGHT

The Nature of Defenses in Neurosis
E. Michael Holden and Arthur Janov

PART ONE—E. MICHAEL HOLDEN

1. Historical Background

In ancient times, and even to the present, people have considered themselves to be dualistic, of mind and body. The subjective experience of mind as separate from body encourages such a viewpoint. In the early 1800's, crazy or troubled people were considered to be possessed by spirits or demons. Under the influence of physicians such as J. M. Charcot a medical model for "mental illness" slowly emerged, and, though full of internal inconsistencies, persists to the present. The observation that brain tumors, rabies, encephalitis, nervous system syphilis and other brain disorders could make people crazy reinforced the brain-body duality for theoreticians and gave support to the medical model of mental illness. At the same time, early work in embryology made it clear that the brain and body are an integrated unit but this insight was largely overlooked.

Sigmund Freud was trained as a physician and was well aware of the medical model for mental illness, although the theories of psychoanalysis are only obliquely related to it.* Freud postulated the existence of internal libidinous drives and an id of primitive drives against which one had to defend with mental defenses. This point of view not only reinforced a mind-body duality, it also proposed divisions of the mind.

---

*Articulately discussed by Dr. E. Fuller Torrey in his recent book, *The Death of Psychiatry*, Chilton Press.

Anna Freud formalized the viewpoint and categorized the defenses in her book *Ego and Mechanisms of Defense*.

The *application* of this theoretical model gave patients other *words* for their feelings (in psychoanalysis) but had little overall effect on them. They left therapy with the therapist's views of their problems, "under-' standing" more but usually *feeling* the same way.

2. A Biological Model for Neurosis

a) The Primal viewpoint is that people are not born neurotic or driven by mystical forces, they are just born. Biologically, it is certain that the brain and body function as a single integrated unit, so there is no reason to propose that people defend against Pain with a mental process only. On the contrary, one would predict that the entire organism participates in the defense against Pain. We have found this to be so in our research. The observations and their interpretation are presented below.

b) The Primal premise is that neurosis evolves in relation to physical and "psychic" pains at birth, in infancy and in early childhood. This is not a theoretical abstraction about "mind." It is based on observations of hundreds of patients who have undergone Primal Therapy at the Primal Institute in Los Angeles. Another articulate indicator that neurotics are people in Pain are the consistent increases in the use of pain blunters by neurotics. Alcohol, nicotine, opiates and benzodiazepine tranquilizers (Valium, Librium, Serax) are being used and abused with steadily increasing frequency. *What is conventionally called "repression" is not a mental operation against psychic "forces" but is more accurately a group of physiologic responses which oppose the re-emergence of Primal Pain.* Implicit in the Primal premise is that the brain and body (as a unit) can register pains for later potential emergence and recall. This also is not a theoretical abstraction, but is a biological, verifiable viewpoint, based on observations of Primal patients.

3. The Nature of Defenses

The physiology of the defense system can be measured and quantitated, as one gains access to Primal Pain, during a Primal.

Methods:

We are measuring pulse, blood pressure, core body temperature and the integral of the occipital alpha (8-13 cps) activity of the electroencephalogram (EEG), before, during, and after Primals.* Primal patients are men and women between the ages of 23 and 50. Control patients in the same age range have also been studied (doing "mock Primals"). Measurements are made with the patient's eyes closed.

Observations:

The physiological changes observed in Primals are remarkably uniform in kind, and distinguish Primals, as one response pattern, from abreactions, as another. We are publishing two graphs which are representative of the physiologic changes in Primals.

The first graph depicts a Primal session of a 36 year old, previously hypertensive man, 16 months after starting Primal Therapy. (Before starting Primal therapy he had well-documented systolic hypertension with systolic blood pressures as high as 215 mm mercury, recorded.) He had been hospitalized in mental hospitals three times in the past for acute psychotic episodes and had received high doses of Thorazine and several electroshock treatments. Throughout the recording session he cried repeatedly like a newborn child.

Initially, as he gained access to Pain he experienced the feeling of terror which invariably accompanies the pre-Primal phase. The conventional term for the pre-Primal phase of access to an old, painful feeling, is an "acute anxiety attack." This is the outward manifestation of a sympathetic nervous system "crisis" analogous to the "fight or flight" response first described by W. B. Cannon. (see below) It is significant that this occurs, in a Primal context, at a time when an individual is lying down, comfortably. The "crisis" is personal, in relation to old Pain. As seen in the first patient's graph, the physiological response to Primal Pain access, is elevation of pulse, blood pressure, and the amplitude of the EEG alpha activity. For this patient, it was only possible to measure core body temperature before and after the session. It fell from 99.8°F. before, to 99.0°F. after. [As seen in the second graph, core body temperature is elevated in the pre-Primal phase just before full access to the Pain is reached].

The portion of the nervous system which concerns itself with internal, visceral regulation is called the autonomic nervous system. It has two major divisions, "sympathetic" and "parasympathetic," each with specific functions. The hypothalamus is the main control center for both divisions.

---

*Polygraph: "Physiograph Six"—Narco BioSystems
Electronic Sphygmomanometer—PE 300—Narco BioSystems
Electronic Thermometer—Yellow Springs Instr. Co., Model 43TA
EEG Filter: Model NB-121—Narco BioSystems
EEG Integrator: Model GPA-10—Narco BioSystems
Gold Disc Electrodes: Grass Instrument Co.
    (Held on with collodion and gauze)

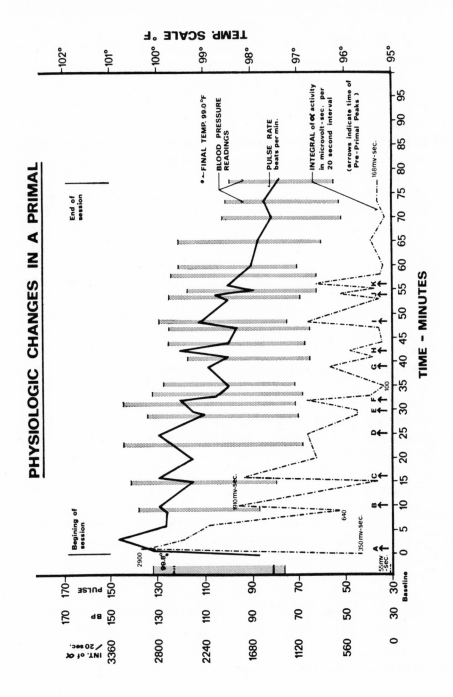

PHYSIOLOGIC CHANGES IN A PRIMAL

Sympathetic nervous system responses mobilize the organism for "fight or flight" and predominate in stressful situations. Parasympathetic nervous system responses tend to mediate a reparative or recovery phase, and typically predominate during rest and sleep, when the organism is less stressed. Sympathetic responses are high energy responses which rapidly utilize energy stores and "push" the organism to high levels of performance, often to the very limits of endurance. By contrast, parasympathetic responses are energy conserving and by their action, increase the energy stores of the body and repair tissues following phases of stress. Parasympathetic responses are healing and rejuvenative. In mammals there is continuous alternation between these modes although seldom to the limits of each system. We suddenly pass into sympathetic dominance in emergency or life-threatening situations. The sympathetic nervous system mediates the alarm reaction, with sudden increases in heart rate, blood pressure, body temperature and blood supply to body muscles. More sugar is mobilized from the liver to fuel the required high energy "crisis". When this occurs, the parasympathetic division is temporarily subjugated and reparative and digestive activities are markedly curtailed. Mammals can perform extraordinary tasks when so mobilized. It is a time when the performance becomes as good as it can be: the body resources are utilized to their limits. The alarm reaction utilizes so much energy that it is typically a short-lived event, lasting only minutes. The sympathetic crisis occurs in all life-or-death situations and other major emergencies. The mobilization of body resources is for "fight or flight" and its goal is the preservation of the organism, by virtue of a huge short term output of energy, for the sake of survival. Often, it succeeds, as in rescuing someone from a flaming building, but sometimes it will fail, as in trying to outrun a tiger or a train. When it fails, in an overwhelming circumstance one screams in agony, and not uncommonly one then loses consciousness before the peak of the crisis. This "failure" is merciful and represents a way in which one is spared being a "witness" to death or overwhelming agony. If the sympathetic crisis is successful, however, in mediating a survival response, in time it passes and is replaced by a *para*-sympathetic recovery phase. In the recovery phase one often cries, and experiences extreme fatigue and exhaustion. The nasal, lacrimal (tears), bronchial and digestive secretions are all increased in amount. Blood is once again allocated to the "conservative" tasks of digestion and other visceration. Often there is a strong desire to sleep. Less extreme but clearcut alternations between the predominance of first sympathetic then parasympathetic responses, are seen: 1. before, then after an epileptic seizure,[4] 2. before sexual relations, then after orgasm, and 3. just before extreme pain, then after, with resolution of it.

When we record individuals' vital signs during and after a Primal we observe this *same* cycle of sympathetic crisis followed by parasympathetic recovery phase in response to the old Pain, then to its resolution, as described below. Re-experiencing the old painful feeling occurs at the instant the parasympathetic phase begins. It is the phase of healing and repair.

Gradually, over months of Primal Therapy there is a consistent decrease in the vital sign values[1,2] and in the amplitude of one's EEG.[3] We interpret this to mean that neurosis is a state of inappropriately great sympathetic predominance in response to old Pain, and that Primal Therapy is healing and reparative by resolving the early Pain, and brings the sympathetic and parasympathetic modes back into appropriate metabolic balance.

When the pre-Primal (sympathetic) phase reaches its maximum, quite suddenly a patient starts to re-experience and old Painful event with a vivid memory of it. At this moment also, *the subjective feeling of terror and panic ends*, as does the sympathetic crisis, and abruptly, one enters a phase of parasympathetic (and cholinergic) predominance. The latter is characterized by sudden decreases in pulse, blood pressure and EEG alpha amplitude, also by bronchorrhea, increased salivation, hard tearful crying, decreased pupil size and sudden profuse sweating. This "cycle" of sympathetic crisis followed by parasympathetic recovery phase is similar in kind, and presumably mechanism, to that seen in relation to a seizure.[4] Primals and seizures share certain physiological mechanisms but are not the same. A comparison is discussed later. During a single Primal session, a patient may have several-to-many pre-Primal peaks, about each of which the alternation from sympathetic to parasympathetic predominance always occurs. Over the course of a Primal session the absolute values of the vital signs gradually decrease or in some sessions undergo periodic increases, with a dramatic fall in the values toward the end of the session. Either way, we typically see lower than baseline values at the end of the session. For the first patient whose graph is shown, all of the parameters measured were lower at the end of the session than the starting values. Pulse decreased from 87 to 78 beats per minute. Blood pressure changed from 125/66 to 99/54 at the end of the session. Core body temperature decreased from 99.8°F. before, to 99.0°F. afterwards. The integral of the alpha activity decreased from 350 to 168 microvolt-sec. per 20 second interval. Thus, as a result of this man's Primal session, he became profoundly relaxed and free of tension, and this is manifest in the decreased values of his vital signs at the end of his session. It is of considerable theoretical importance that the EEG correlate of the profoundly relaxed state following a Primal is *low* amplitude alpha activity, not high amplitude alpha activity.

Graph #2 is that of a 25-year-old woman, one year after starting Primal Therapy. As a young child she had abnormal structure and function of her kidneys (3 kidneys, abnormal ureters) and from age 18 mo. to seven years had many operations, with months of hospitalization. In her Primal session with monitoring of her vital signs, she vividly re-experienced Painful events related to early life hospitalization. The relationship of her vital sign changes to pre-Primal peaks is clearly shown. With access to Pain there are sudden increases in pulse, blood pressure and the integral of alpha activity in her EEG. Traditionally, when attentive *cognition*, not Pain, is the variable, then students of EEG are accustomed to associate alertness with a *decreased* amplitude of alpha activity, and inattentive drowsiness with *increased* alpha amplitude. Clearly demonstrated here however are the EEG changes associated with access to pain; changes which are the "reverse" of those associated with cognitive tasks. In the pre-Primal phase of terror one is maximally alert, and the EEG correlate of terror is a striking increase in alpha amplitude, often to values five times the resting value, or more. The amplitude of one's EEG activity increases rapidly until the parasympathetic recovery phase begins, at which moment there is a sudden decrease, clinically associated with the moment a person starts to vividly re-experience an old, Painful feeling.

Interpretation:

We interpret the sudden rise in alpha amplitude with terror to mean the brain is electrochemically working harder in opposition to the Pain. Thus we believe the increased EEG amplitude of the pre-Primal phase is a manifestation of defense against fuller access to Pain. The mechanism of sudden change from sympathetic crisis to parasympathetic recovery phase is not known with certainty, but by analogy to the same sequence in seizures is mediated by the hypothalamus.[4] We propose as hypothesis that when one's "defense system" *fails* to keep the old Pain at bay is when one vividly, totally re-experiences the old feeling state. Short of the failpoint of the defenses, one remains in the over-mobilized terror state, mediated by the sympathetic crisis; clinically *an acute anxiety attack.*

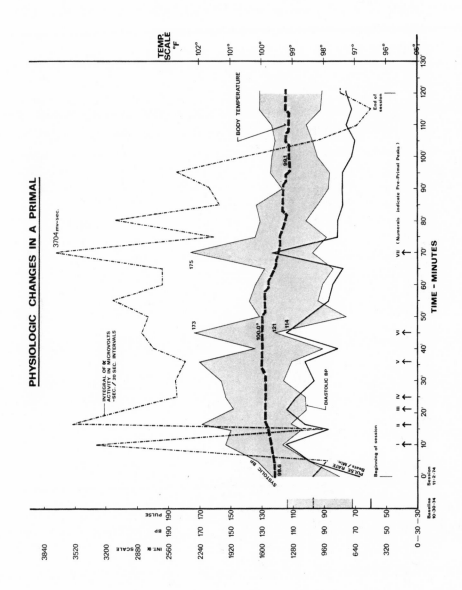

PHYSIOLOGIC CHANGES IN A PRIMAL

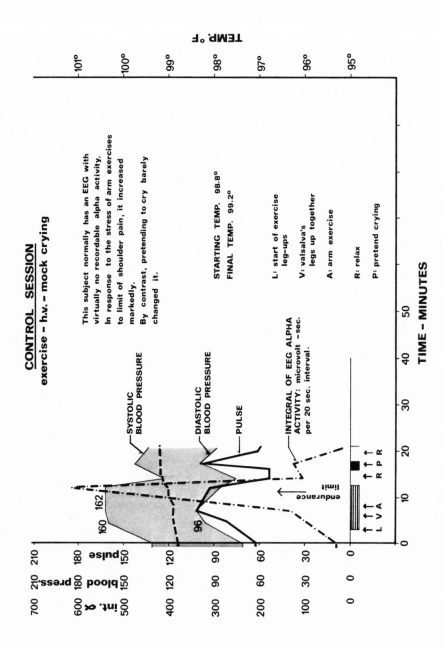

CONTROL SESSION
exercise – h.v. – mock crying

This subject normally has an EEG with
virtually no recordable alpha activity.
In response to the stress of arm exercises
to limit of shoulder pain, it increased
markedly.
By contrast, pretending to cry barely
changed it.

STARTING TEMP. 98.8°
FINAL TEMP. 99.2°

L: start of exercise
   leg-ups

V: valsalva's
   legs up together

A: arm exercise

R: relax

P: pretend crying

SYSTOLIC
BLOOD PRESSURE

DIASTOLIC
BLOOD PRESSURE

PULSE

INTEGRAL OF EEG ALPHA
ACTIVITY: microvolt –sec.
per 20 sec. interval.

endurance
limit

TEMP. °F

TIME – MINUTES

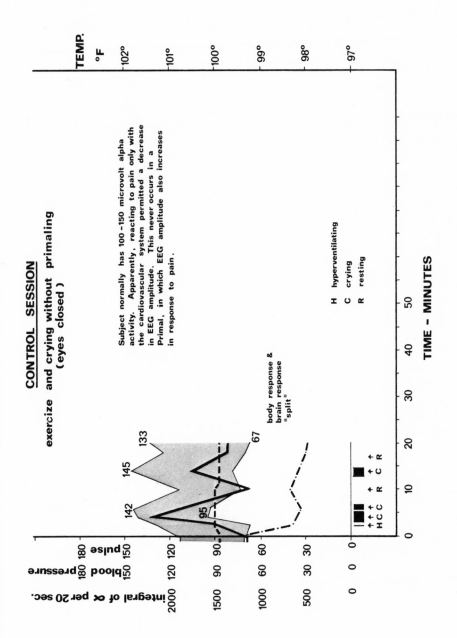

CONTROL SESSION

exercize and crying without primaling
(eyes closed)

Subject normally has 100 -150 microvolt alpha activity. Apparently, reacting to pain only with the cardiovascular system permitted a decrease in EEG amplitude. This never occurs in a Primal, in which EEG amplitude also increases in response to pain.

H   hyperventilating
C   crying
R   resting

body response &
brain response
"split"

TIME - MINUTES

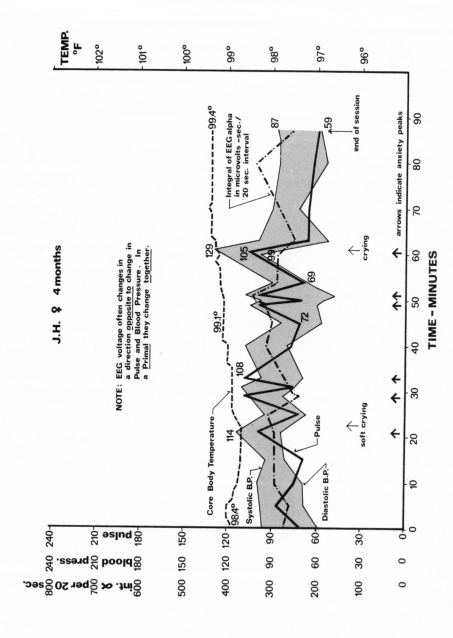

J.H. ♀ 4 months

NOTE: EEG voltage often changes in a direction opposite to change in Pulse and Blood Pressure. In a Primal they change together.

This attack suddenly resolves itself if one's defenses are sufficiently weakened, so that there is resolution through re-experience of the early life Pain. With resolution there is a parasympathetic recovery phase. In Primal Therapy, an effective therapist helps a patient resolve neurosis by repeatedly helping the patient gain access to Pain *beyond* the limit of the defense. Anything short of that point is an overwhelming stress on an individual, *without resolution.* In everyday life, one with an acute anxiety attack may approach the limits of defense but seldom reaches these limits, and thus the Pain and terror is experienced amorphously, but without ultimate resolution.

Discussion:

The point to emphasize is that a "defense system" evolves only in relation to Pain. What was originally a "life support" system is forced to become a "life salvaging" one. The higher vital sign values in neurotics are articulate indicators of a "re-routing" operation occurring in the brain. A person's response system is brought into the service of the body to oppose Pain, and becomes a defense system. I have previously noted that the brain of an infant possesses the sufficient but not the necessary capability to determine neurosis.[5] We respond to the circumstances of our lives. If the circumstances are painful, we defend against them. There is no *a priori* reason for an infant to anticipate pain in the environment, (although brain function may have done so in eons of evolution), so one can see that neurosis is an *option* for an infant, not a predestined certainty.

Body Temperature:

Mammals regulate their internal temperature within narrow limits, independent of temperature fluctuations in the external environment. Failure to do this leads to illness and/or death. For mammals, the enzyme systems which determine their biochemistry have an optimal temperature for functioning. Below that, enzyme reactions proceed more slowly, and above that, they proceed more rapidly than normal. Factors which raise the body temperature also raise the requirement for basic foodstuffs, substrate, and require more physico-chemical work from the organism. Hyperthyroidism or febrile (fever) illnesses illustrate this principle well: one needs more food, tends to become thin, tends to lose

fat and muscle tissue, have a faster heart rate and an increased requirement for oxygen. The mild elevations in temperature occurring in Primals
reflect a regulation of body temperature even within the old Painful access.
If the core body temperature rose 10 or 15 degrees, one would die in a
Primal, in hyperthermia. Such excesses are not observed, and at the end
of a Primal session, the temperature is typically lower than baseline.

Pulse and Blood Pressure:

The work of the heart is vital for survival: it supplies food and
oxygen to all tissues and, ultimately, also effects disposal of metabolic
waste products. The vascular system is a life support system which
becomes a prominent part of one's neurotic defense system when an
individual is exposed to pain. This is true in chronic hypertension and in
those with rapid heart rate as continuous responses to severe pain. It is
also true, in an acute reaction to the ascent of old Pain, via increases in
pulse and blood pressure. We can recognize as yet another manifestation
of the wisdom of the body the failure of the cardiovascular system to
defend against pain, occurring *when it does*. If the blood pressure rose to
300/160, or the pulse rose to 280/min., the risk of dying in a Primal
would be great. *Such excesses are not observed*, however; in its wisdom,
the vascular response to Pain cuts out before seriously high pulse rates
and blood pressures occur. One may think of the safety valve on a pressure cooker, by analogy: when the pressure is too high the valve-top
blows off, preventing a pressure buildup which would, if continued, turn
the pressure cooker into a grenade. If an individual in everyday life
ruptures a cerebral blood vessel when the blood pressure reaches extreme
values like 250/160, this represents a failure of the "fail mechanism" in
the vascular defense system. If, at a lower blood pressure than such a
high value, one were able to enter a *parasympathetic recovery phase*, this
variety of stroke would be prevented. In short, a Primal would prevent
the excesses leading to such a rupture.

EEG Alpha Amplitude:

Is there a clinical disorder of EEG activity in which a massive rise in
the amplitude of the EEG is followed by a failure of this system? Yes, the
disorder is idiopathic epilepsy. A seizure is preceded by an alarm reaction
of the whole organism, mediated by a sympathetic nervous system crisis

(with increases in pulse, blood pressure and body temperature).[4] The event rises to a peak of a sort different from that seen in a Primal only in *degree*.* Instead of an amplitude increase to 150-200 microvolts as typically occurs in a Primal, one sees much greater amplitude "spike and wave" activity, characteristic of a seizure. In a Primal, moment by moment, cortical brain function is preserved. A Primal is a conscious experience. In a seizure, cortical brain function is impaired and partial or complete stupor occurs. A seizure is usually not a conscious experience. After a Primal, one experiences post-Primal lucidity and clarity of thought. After a seizure one experiences confusion and impaired thought. Both Primals and seizures demonstrate a sympathetic crisis followed by a parasympathetic recovery phase. Profound muscle relaxation follows both types of event. When a Primal patient re-experiences an old feeling, there is no reason to propose that this is very different from the re-experiencing of an old feeling which occurs commonly as the aura of temporal lobe epilepsy and during temporal lobe stimulation at neurosurgery, in awake patients.

The other point to make is that we are only measuring four of the "vital signs". What about blood glucose level, electrolyte balance (sodium, potassium, etc.) and levels of insulin and other hormones? For emphasis it is likely that all the "life support systems" are components of the "defense system" in neurotics, in relation to Pain. We see Primal patients lose their allergies permanently in Primal therapy. Does this mean that immune lymphocytes also participate in the defense against Pain? We believe this is probable.

We are studying some of the most vital signs during Primals at this time. In the future we may study other vital signs as well such as hormone levels, liver enzyme levels, salt balance, etc. It should be possible to eventually define the defense system with some precision, *entirely in physiologic terms*. Neurosis is a disorder of the entire body which evolves in relation to early Pain. The systems of life support become recruited as systems of defense against that Pain. Only pressing those defenses to their limits will allow one to vividly re-experience old Pain. As that repeatedly occurs, neurosis dissolves.

---

*It is probably true that a Primal is a partial seizure, of unique type, characterized by widespread subcortical depolarization (electrical activation) but sparing much involvement of the cortex, during the pre-Primal phase. When one is vividly re-experiencing the old Painful feeling, however, there is almost surely activation of the sensory and association cortex as well, where memories have their topographical, neural representation.

PART TWO—ARTHUR JANOV

It is no accident that the type of treatment a disease receives depends in great measure on the concept of the disease. Since the days of Freud we have imagined that mental illness is "mental" and that an aberrant defense system which characterized an abnormal state was a problem of *mental* deviation. Thus the defense system outlined by Sigmund and Anna Freud included only mental mechanisms—rationalization, projection, denial, and so on. The treatment, then, had to be a manipulation of these systems and the method of doing so was also mental; i.e., psychotherapy. We have found out differently. We see that neurosis is psychophysiologic and that all the mental manipulations in the world are not enough to change it. Our treatment must match our concept; Primal Therapy, therefore, is a *psychophysiologic* one. It is not as though we "decided" that neurosis was also of the body. It was obvious in many ways and our biologic measurements verified it for us. If the early therapists had done careful measurements of their patients they too would have known that neurosis was psychophysiologic and they would have not only developed Freud further in terms of advancing his theories into the biologic area but would have then been forced to find a therapy to accommodate itself to this new concept of neurosis. Instead, a cycle developed in which mental illness was defined as mental, theories of defenses were advanced which were mental and therapeutic techniques were detailed which were mental or psychologic. Progress was then measured in terms of changes in mental outlook which then validated the theory and technique, and so it went. Hard data would have saved everyone a lot of trouble. Wilhelm Reich certainly knew better and for his pains he was ostracized from the therapeutic community. He compensated so much against the mentalistic notions that he became solely body oriented and then developed most of his techniques to deal with the body armor. His schema overlooked the brain, a not insignificant organ. But he was trying to tell the profession something—something so obvious that it was amazing how it had been overlooked—namely, that there was a body attached to our brains and it also reacted to what was going on in our lives.

What was even a worse error was to imagine that defenses were somehow viable psychologic entities with their own special properties unrelated to what was going on in the brain that carried them. And so the manifestations of mental defenses were studied and tested. Psychological tests were developed to measure such things as projection via the

Rorschach test. And these projections were supposed to lay bare the inner structure of the person's neurosis. These projections were then interpreted within a theoretical framework—usually Jungian, sometimes Freudian. But in any case projections were mixed with projections—the patient's with the therapist's, and then some valid result was supposed to ensue. What happened then was a self-fulfilling prophecy. The patient's projections were made to fit into the projections of a therapist via his theory (and a "psychological" theory is just mental notions about someone's behavior). If the subject found softness in certain Rorschach cards it "meant" dependency, for example. This finding validated the test, it was thought, but really had no measureable effect on the ultimate treatment of the person. Since we are all dependent, finding it in a test was a safe bet. But the *why* of dependency, the deep motivation was not discovered by the test, nor could it be. It could not look into one's history—it was "present-bound." The test results had to be as superficial as a mental diagnosis by a psychiatrist because both were based on the belief of a *mental* illness. The body was always left out of the calculations. And so was the brain! Almost nowhere are neurologic processes related to psychologic events. Certainly, none of the major psychologic theories takes neurology strongly into account. The brain is just going along for the ride, so to speak . . . a kind of nuisance that must be tolerated when one expounds a theory of behavior. And so when the brain and body are eliminated one is left with a disembodied theory and technique to be applied to disembodied psychological processes. If one continues to leave out the brain and body in calculations of progress in therapy, for example, it is possible to imagine all sorts of changes and progress which really do not occur in reality. To put it another way, if one simply takes verbal changes (I feel terrific, I've decided to get a divorce, I'm going to college and get my degree, I've beat back my depressions) as gospel or reality one is bound to be deceived. For words and ideas are ephemeral and change back and forth with facility. Not so with brain waves or blood pressure. They testify to deep thorough change as ideas alone cannot. Another way of putting it is that in psychotherapy one can change awareness but in Primal Therapy we alter the structure of consciousness, and that is defined as the way the brain and body operate structurally.

Dr. Holden makes several key points. First, we are not born with a defense system. We are simply born with a functioning biologic system which becomes converted into a defense structure in response to Pain. Under the influence of Primal Pain the system stops developing fluidly and becomes instead one of compensating maneuvers in order to keep us shut down and repressed. In the therapeutic situation we know both that there are defenses and we know that we effectively and economically dismantle defenses because in a matter of minutes with the use of special techniques we can bring a patient beyond his defenses into his early Pain. When we begin to do that every part of the defense system is strained to the utmost. Every part of the patient is galvanized to maintain repression and to keep the experience of Pain away. This, by the way, also keeps the ability to fully experience anything away, as well.

The defense system begins life as a protective one. Later on, surprisingly enough, the body does not differentiate past from present. The adult patient in our research laboratory reacts as though he were going to die as the Pain comes up. He doesn't decide to do that. It just happens. It is an *involuntary* process. It is an infantile feeling that may be ascending and so far as the system is concerned that feeling is catastrophic and maybe even fatal. So all systems are "go" in an attempt to drive it back. At a certain critical level *the defense system fails*, and the person drops into the feeling. The defense system failure is in itself another back-up defense system, as it were. For if the body kept up its pace, its heart rate and blood pressure increases, death could easily result. Before that happens, feelings occur, and feeling marks the end of the defensive efforts. It is no longer a theory—it is a biologic fact! We see the incredible strain of the defense system at work and the equally incredible relaxation after feeling (a pulse of forty or fifty is not uncommon). Feeling is the end of defenses, and if we could feel from the beginning of our lives, if there were no catastrophic Pain to contend with, there would have been no defenses in the first place.

The shift from the defense system to a feeling, relaxed one is essentially a shift from a sympathetic nervous system dominance to a parasympathetic one. Dr. Holden has explained what that means. But the implication is that over the millennia particular aspects of the nervous system developed to regulate both defenses and feeling; and these two aspects or systems work in conjunction with one another as part of the autonomic nervous system. They control the automatic functions of the body, both for defense and for feeling. The results of sympathetic nervous system dominance can be measured and these measurements can tell us, by and large, how defensive (as opposed to how feeling) a person may be. There is a fine balance between the two systems and Pain is the upsetting factor which makes one predominate over the other. It is Pain which makes one of the systems (sympathetic) work too hard, ultimately causing various systems of the body which are involved in the defense system to break down. Instead of the system being life supporting it becomes neurosis supporting. It is used in the service of repression instead of expression. This upsets the relationhip between neurotransmitters and the hormone system. The adrenaline-noradrenaline balance changes and can be measured. Those with the inability to express their anger show a different relationship from those who can (anger in v. anger out). Nothing escapes, for neurosis is a total state of being; that is the point of this discussion. Repression is not a psychologic state. It is as surely biochemical and neurologic, as psychologic. Indeed, the psychological manifestations simply reflect the great internal changes going on. A repressed person does not perceive well psychologically because his *brain* is being gated; and there are neurochemical accompaniments, as well. His serotonin levels may be different from normal (although this has yet to be measured in our patients because no one is anxious to do spinal taps for the sake of research).

There is little question that the brain is part of the defense system. It too responds to Pain in measurable ways. And it too changes with feeling. It is obvious that neurologic processes cannot be eliminated from consideration in psychologic theories and techniques. The brain goes to work against Pain and that work is reflected to all the systems controlled by that brain. Blood pressure is not only a measure of a blood circulating system, it is a reflection of brain processes. They are an integrated unit. To make a statement about blood pressure or heart rate is to make a statement about the brain. To make a statement about psychological processes means that one is discussing the brain and body. It is perfectly legitimate to make psychological evaluations so long as one remains anchored in the biological. To pull up that anchor means to leave the shore of reality permanently.

None of the foregoing discussion is meant to imply that there is no such thing as psychological defenses. I am sure there are, but they are not isolated entities. It is my assumption that each level of consciousness has its own defense system. The first line defends with the viscera, and first line pressure is handled by the internal organ system. Second line defenses would be of the body wall; thus an immobile face in which no one can tell what you are feeling is a second line defense. Eye tics would be second line defenses in that as a feeling begins to rise tics begin instead of feeling. Third line defenses would be the so-called psychological ones. Here is where we rationalize or blame someone else for our errors. Here is where we deny the mistakes and explain them so elaborately that they no longer seem like mistakes. It is the third line which uses elaborate language to defend.

We usually use all three systems of defenses in one way or another, but some may predominate. An immobile face and rigid body structure may be part of an overall bodily defense system where under pressure the person tightens down his musculature. Others are the psychosomatic type; they defend with the inner system and internally somatize the Pain.

Defenses develop with the development of the brain. A newborn cannot project his Pain on someone else; he just does not have the cerebral equipment to do so. The three year old can, however. He can blame his kindergarten friend, and he will if he has already been blamed by his parents so much that he cannot accept any mistakes on his own part. The young child who still has second line access will tend to use second line defenses. He will divert his emotions, beating up on his sister instead of his parents or cry over the least occurrence. As his third line develops he will have the capacity to act out. After the age of five or six he may begin to wear dresses secretly. Or, before the age of twelve he will begin to smoke or masturbate. Later on his acting out will become more complex just as his brain has become. He will be more symbolic and subtle so that even he does not become aware that he is acting out a *feeling*. The acting out becomes automatic.

Under ordinary circumstances the body gates and defends quite well. But given a certain stimulus which gives rise to repressed Pain, new defenses are required. That is, as the curve rises, as the Pain ascends, it becomes more necessary to employ new defenses. As one reaches the pre-Primal peak (experienced as an acute anxiety attack) every defense system is in full operation. The person may begin talking endlessly, eating, smoking and drinking almost all at the same time. The stomach is churning, the neck muscles are taut, and the ways one acts out are myriad. One person may get on the phone and explain his problem to everyone he can. Another may escape in reading books. Still another may act sexually. Indeed, everything a neurotic does under the impetus of Primal Pain can truly be considered a defense. Just how loudly he talks can be defensive. If we take that away and force a person to speak softly he may drop into a feeling.

Compulsive anything, whether of reading or masturbating, is defensive. Some defenses are obvious and some are not. Working hard every day may seem like a necessity (and it may be) and not considered a defense.

But when a patient has a feeling which tells him that he overworks for certain defensive reasons then we understand the problem more clearly.

As a rule the situation or stimulus which brings up Pain will also bring up a defense. The charge value of the Pain and the time of occurrence in our lives will determine the kind of defenses to be employed, by and large. Very early in life we may use sleep as a defense. If we are left very often to cry it out (in the crib) then sleep is one of the few alternatives available. This defense may become prototypic and may be used throughout the rest of our lives. As we mature many other defenses become available. It all depends on the early life situation. Being in a repressive household and being sent to a repressive school such as a military boarding school may dampen opportunities for acting out; the result is a pattern of acting in—of keeping things to oneself, of withdrawing socially and learning to take care of oneself completely. If approval is given by rejecting parents who really don't want to take care of their children for all this self reliance on the part of their children then "self-reliance" may well become a solidified defense.

The meaning of "defense" is "defense against Pain." Defenses are used to keep us from feeling; so a well defended person feels no Pain but he feels very little else. He is effectively dead and no matter what he does his life seems drab, gray and dull. Yet he continues to do exactly those things which keep him from feeling. And he does not usually know he is defending. Feelings rise, say because of a hostile confrontation, or being forced to make a report in public or because of an argument with a boyfriend, and they are squelched in every way possible. The ways become characteristic for each of us and become interwoven into a "personality type." So one of us may use humor as a defense—laughing off the Pain, so to speak. This defense may become so polished that the person becomes a professional, a comic. Now the defense is used to make a living in addition to holding back feelings. It becomes a way of life. The person is then praised for his personality or defense and it gets reinforced. Indeed, he may imagine that he is loved for his defense—being the life of a party, being entertaining, and the like. And so now instead of being loved for being himself, his feeling self, he is loved for his polished defense system. When we treat a comic in Primal Therapy we are forced to take away his humor and his gift of gab. We don't let him make jokes and the result is always the same—Pain.

In Primal Therapy we take away a person's defenses; and this takes a good deal of skill, first to know what they are and secondly to know how to remove them skillfully. If we are dealing with second line body wall defenses we may make the person move a lot or make faces, in this way showing expression. We may stop him from talking too much or, conversely, make the patient talk more than he is used to. We watch the breathing for shallow breathing is one more of thousands of automatic defenses. But the removal of a defense is carefully timed and is always in accord with where the patient is at the time. There are times when he needs certain defenses, especially if he is being overwhelmed by Pain. Then he is encouraged to sit up and discuss his life in detail, to describe things and understand himself. For the third liner who is well defended this would only compound the problem.

As a person goes on feeling he comes to know exactly when he is defending and he knows what to do about it. The point of no return is reached in this therapy when the defense structure, the characteristic personality reactions, are no longer automatic; feeling is.

Until there is feeling, no matter how aware we are of our defenses we are forced to defend and act out. If we are taught to control our defenses, such as smoking, drinking and promiscuity, then we just have one more defense—control of the acting out. This compounds the problem; it doesn't solve it. The failure of insight therapy is the delusion that control of acting out is the same as solution. Nothing could be further from the truth. Solution of a defense means to resolve the Pain which gave it life.

REFERENCES

1. Research with Primal Patients—Vital Signs
   B. P. McInerny, Ph.D.
   J. of Primal Therapy II, #1, p. 51, 1974
2. Neurophysiological Measurements of Patients Undergoing Primal Therapy.
   R. Corriere and W. Karle
   The Anatomy of Mental Illness
   A. Janov, Ph.D.
   G. P. Putnam's Sons, 1971, p. 215
3. EEG Activity and Primal Therapy—I
   Martin Gardiner, Ph.D. 9/74 (not yet published)
   (EEG study performed at UCLA Brain Research Institute.
   Dr. Gardiner is not a Primal person and is employed by UCLA). Study is
   summarized in ref. #3A, pp. 106-109
3A. Primal Pain and Aging.
   E. Michael Holden, M.D.
   J. of Primal Therapy II, #2, p. 97, 1974
4. Neurologic Mechanism Concerned in Epileptic Seizures
   Paul I. Yakovlev, M.D.
   Arch. Neurol. and Psych. *37*, p. 523, 1937
5. Levels of Consciousness
   E. Michael Holden, M.D.
   J. of Primal Therapy I, #2, 1973

CHAPTER NINE

Toward a Meaningful Psychotherapy
E. Michael Holden and Arthur Janov

PART ONE—E. MICHAEL HOLDEN

It is widely held as a premise for much present-day research that inter-
ventions such as biofeedback and meditation which increase alpha amplitude in the EEG are producing a more relaxed individual with a more
relaxed brain. Barbara Brown has recently written, "Alpha waves are the
giant rhythmic brain wave companions of relaxed states of feeling."
(*Psychology Today*, August 1974). We present data below which are
directly contradictory to that notion. An individual who increases the
amplitude of his/her alpha activity often experiences a subjective sensation of relaxation. We believe, however, that such a sensation results from
a neurophysiological change which is "defensive" and repressive in nature. As indicated below, an increase in alpha amplitude is actually a
surface manifestation of *increased* brain work. We have learned that
increased alpha amplitude is a component of one's defenses, defenses
against the rise of Primal Pain. One experiences the subjective sensation
of relaxation when *access* to Primal Pain is *decreased*. One experiences a
progressive increase in tension, anxiety and fear as access to Primal Pain
increases. The characteristic *clinical* presentation of one with increasing
access to Primal Pain is *an acute anxiety attack,* with or without related
"psychosomatic" symptoms.

Recently, at The Primal Institute in Los Angeles, we have been monitoring some physiological parameters in patients undergoing Primal Therapy. As previously reported and subsequently twice confirmed in separate
studies done at UCLA[2,3] there is a progressive *decrease* in the alpha

amplitude of one's awake EEG with each succeeding month in Primal Therapy. This important physiological change accompanies the progressive decreases in pulse, blood pressure, and core body temperature which also, predictably, occur during Primal Therapy.

The emphasis of the present study is on the physiology of a Primal itself. We are continuously measuring pulse, blood pressure, core body temperature and the integral of the occipital alpha activity during Primals. The psychology of Primals has been well discussed previously[1,4] the physiology of Primals is currently being studied.

Since Primals are foreign to the experience of most physicians, psychiatrists, and psychologists it may be helpful to draw the following analogy. Dr. W. Penfield and others have documented that temporal lobe stimulation (during surgery) in an awake individual causes one to vividly re-experience the feeling state, the emotional (outward expression) state and the cognition associated with a previous memory. Typically the recall represents a small fragment of a total experience in the past. In a *Primal,* a very similar if not identical phenomenon occurs (without any surgery, however) only the "sample" of one's prior experience is much *larger.* The re-experience is total, organismic and completely vivid. Primals are typically involved only with *Painful* past memories, (which at the time of origin were physically painful, psychically painful or both).

The methods of study of Primal patients has been discussed in the previous chapter.

Results:

We are publishing two graphs at this time; one depicting a recording session of a young woman (23) after 3 weeks of Primal Therapy—the other a session of a woman (26) done after one year of Primal Therapy. The first patient had a sixty-six minute session with 2 pre-Primal peaks, the second patient had a 120 session with 7 pre-Primal peaks. In principle, the graphs are quite similar. (The subjective experience of old memories always occurs immediately following a peak of anxiety.)

As defenses become ineffective, there is increased access to Primal Pain and a crescendo increase in pulse, blood pressure *and integrated alpha activity* occurs. The core body temperature rises in response to the Pain but far more slowly than the other parameters. It should be kept in mind that these changes occur within several minutes, in individuals lying com-

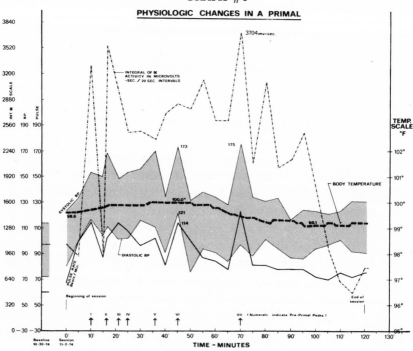

GRAPH #1

PHYSIOLOGIC CHANGES IN A PRIMAL

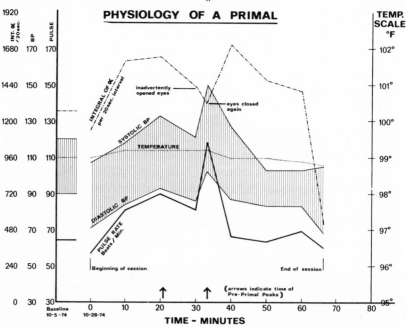

GRAPH #2

PHYSIOLOGY OF A PRIMAL

fortably on their backs. As seen in these graphs, the blood pressure often rises into the hypertensive range and the pulse rate may quickly become twice or three times its resting, "before" value. It is also characteristic of this pre-Primal phase that the *alpha amplitude increases markedly, often to values 5 to 10 times higher than its resting value and it reaches its maximum at the peak of access to Pain* (at the anxiety maximum of the Primal). We know of no historical precedent for this finding. The significance of this elevation in alpha voltage can be appreciated further in a comparison with pulse and blood pressure. *If* the percent increases were the *same*, the pulse would be between over 250 beats per minute and blood pressure would rise to a value greater than 350/200. Immediately after the pre-Primal peak, the pulse, blood pressure and alpha amplitude fall to lower value. In graph #2, there is approximately a 33% drop in systolic blood pressure from peak to end, about a 1% drop in body temperature, a 40% drop in pulse from peak to end. These results indicate clearly to us the relationship of Pain and its resolution to elevations and decreases in the vital signs. We submit that brain voltage must be considered one of the vital signs. The temperature typically stays elevated until the last minutes of the session, usually until one's last pre-Primal peak in the session. After the last Primal (in a session) there is a decrease in all the physiologic parameters being measured, to typically lower than baseline values. After a Primal, a *total organismic feeling-response to Pain*, one's brain and body are *truly* relaxed and the *physiological correlate of this truly relaxed state is an alpha activity amplitude which is lower than baseline* (in graph #2, at 115 min., 670% lower than the pre-Primal peak), clearly demonstrating the relationship between alpha activity in the EEG and Primal Pain.

Discussion:

There are three very important conclusions derived from this study:

1. The "defenses" of mental illness are total, organismic defenses, not simply "mental" as so many believe, and they form an integrated unit. The defenses act as "governors" to dampen our access to Primal Pain.

2. One of the major defenses is *increased brain work* which defends against access to Primal Pain.

3. In biofeedback studies or in studies of meditation, an *increase in alpha amplitude does not represent a physiological correlate of relaxation and freedom from Pain, it represents the mobilization of increased brain work* to maintain an *outward appearance* of relaxation only, and the subjective self-deception of relaxation. Therapies which lead to body relaxation via increased brain work have simply shifted defenses around;

a shuffling which we believe is accomplished by selective gating of Pain at a cerebral hemispheric level. A post-Primal person is defense-less, is not gated to old Pain and is truly tension-free. The pulse is 50-60, the blood pressure in the vicinity of 100/60, the core body temperature 2 to 3 degrees F. lower than "normal" and the EEG is *low* amplitude alpha activity.

One may reasonably ask: "Why does a complete re-experience of early Pain have a curative effect?" The answer is that partially felt Pain in infancy and childhood is "partial" because of blocking, a gating (higher threshold) to protect the organism from excessive Pain. *The energy of that Pain does not go away*. It remains sequestered in the system, and is the origin for acting out in neurosis, and acting in, in neurosis; the latter represented by increased EEG amplitude and (all) psychosomatic symptoms. When the Pain is felt in its entirety, in Primals, blocking is no longer necessary, and neurosis dissolves. Non-Primal controls, doing mock or pseudo-Primals, increase the values for the parameters measured, including alpha amplitude, and at the end of the session, all values are *higher* than baseline values.

To our knowledge, only Primal Therapy permanently lowers all the vital signs *and* the *power of the* EEG, over time.

PART TWO—ARTHUR JANOV

The results of our studies, particularly our long term studies, indicate that we are making profound alterations in *consciousness* rather than simply changing awareness. The structure of consciousness is organic and does not change from moment to moment depending on sensory input. It is neurosis which interrupts the organic integrity of consciousness and produces an "unconscious." In the Primal context there is no unconscious as we have been used to thinking. There is only blocked consciousness. And there are really three separate consciousnesses—or three discrete levels of consciousness. What Pain does is sever the consciousness and produce an unconscious *on each particular level*. This unconsciousness, however, does not take on certain properties and functions of an "unconscious" as the Freudians and Jungians believe. It is still part of a system of consciousness disengaged from its connection.

That is why connection produces a resolution and a plethora of insights, for it brings with it consciousness . . . on the level on which it existed. We can be conscious on different levels, and this is precisely the point about why patients undergoing surgery can later remember the surgeon's conversation with colleagues even though the patient was heavily anesthetized and "unconscious."

Recently (February, 1975) Dr. David Cheek reported on research done with anesthesia and hypnosis (UCLA neurosciences lecture). He discussed a case of surgery on a woman who was suspected of having a carcinoma. During the operation the surgeon at one point exclaimed, "Oh my! it's a malignancy," a fact not borne out later on. This woman did not do well afterwards and the healing process was exceptionally slow. To discover why, she was hypnotized. The first result was a recall of a surgery done some time before. The second session of hypnosis brought out the memory of what the surgeon had said during the operation. "Once she had access to this unconscious information and it was made conscious for her the healing process began immediately" (Dr. Cheek).

Here again from information remote from Primal Theory we see confirmation of the fact that unconscious factors affect somatic ailments and in particular the healing process. Something inserted on the second line affected this woman's state of being enough to keep her from getting well. And of course it is the Primal position that in neurosis there is a constant lower level activation going on which affects not only whether one falls ill but also how fast one will recover. Disconnection perpetuated an ailment, and connection healed.

The results we are observing indicate a significant point: it is not just screaming which produces drops in all of the physiological parameters; it is the *connection* that does it. Control groups who have simulated Primals without connection do not achieve the lower values of Primal patients. There is a difference between abreactive release and a Primal. Indeed, we can scrutinize before and after values of patients and predict who has had a Primal and who has not; who has had a completed Primal and who has not.

Connection is the key to Primal Therapy. By connection I mean *access* . . . the precise link to an early event or feeling which I call a Primal. The connection produces insights which is no more than an understanding of all the behaviors based on the unconscious feeling. The insights become deeper as the access dips lower. Feeling the feeling is self explanatory and no one has to provide insights for a feeling person.

If all our thousands of observations are correct about the existence of stored Pain, if all the neurological evidence of coded memory by Penfield and others is true, if all the hypnosis studies of age regression can be accepted then one would be hard pressed to deny the existence of repressed Pain. How then can we deny the need to deal with that Pain? Primal Pain obviously isn't some idea that was picked out of the air and dressed up into a sophisticated theory. It is a reality; and any approach which ignores it circumvents reality.

What happens to a heart patient who has his pulse lowered and his blood pressure reduced (temporarily) through biofeedback techniques? Where did the Pain go which made those elevations necessary?

First, we need to understand that biofeedback is simply an electronic form of conditioning dealing with presenting symptoms. Indeed, it was through parental conditioning that most of us became neurotic, and biofeedback is just a more refined way of tampering with the body again. It "dictates" how we shall respond to certain situations. It's aim is to distort the way the body functions under the notion that the therapist is doing something for the patient's good. Any method that involves control and redirection of the system tends to drive it further from its natural state. In that sense, conditioning and biofeedback may help reinforce or even worsen neurosis rather than alleviate it. The patient may learn to control his pulse and blood pressure so that a certain colored light comes on (blue) when he voluntarily lowers those values. Later on, in response to blue light, both pulse and blood pressure may automatically become lower, with the conclusion that one has made inroads on the problem of heart disease or hypertension. But what has happened to the Pain which drove those values higher in the first place and kept them high over a long period of time? *It is still there.* What has happened is that it finds another avenue for release for the moment. Remember that the whole body and brain form a unified defense system. This means that to artificially change a part of that system, either through conditioning, biofeedback, meditating, drugs, etc., will cause other aspects of the defense system to take up the slack and compensate for the intrusion into its (neurotic) integrity. So while we lower blood pressure the alpha power of the EEG may rise; or if we slow the pulse the body temperature may go up. There is no escape; *once the Pain is there it must be dealt with.*

What actually happens in biofeedback or conditioning therapy when the therapist produces vasoconstriction by turning on a certain colored light or sounding a certain kind of bell? The precise mechanisms for all that must be complex and are not as yet known. But what we do know is that somehow the operation is "speaking" directly to a lower level of consciousness. He has found a technique, in the case of vasoconstriction (or vasodilatation) for altering first line functions on a temporary basis. He is, in effect, conditioning the hypothalamus which mediates these functions. The reason that his results are ephemeral is that there is no interlevel connection. Since the Pain cannot be conditioned (or hypnotized, or drugged, or analyzed) away results are always transient.

It is possible to condition or alter any level of consciousness. Biofeedback techniques, for example, can alter second line functions so that patients can be taught to become attuned to certain muscles of the neck which tense up leading to headaches. By learning to relax those muscles in response to certain cues (a buzzer or light) headaches can be temporarily avoided. The therapist might believe that he is altering the patient's unconscious—an unconscious with special properties—when in fact he is simply addressing himself to a different level of consciousness, which, were there no gating going on, would not be unconscious at all, and therefore would not need to be conditioned in the first place. It is neurosis which transforms a lower level of consciousness into "unconsciousness." Lower levels of consciousness are not unconscious states. They are conscious states with simply different functions and mediate different aspects of our systems. Without Pain and gating these lower levels would be knowable in the fullest sense of the term. It is neurosis that makes us see them as unconscious states.

When one conditions any level of consciousness we are making it lie. If we suppress muscle tension it is tantamount to the body's artificially saying, "there is no Pain." Since those muscles are usually tense in response to old Pain in the neurotic we have forced a lie on the patient's system. This makes the patient hurt more, not less, even when that hurt is not immediately evident. The truth endures, and so long as Pain is our inner truth and the cause of our symptoms, there will always be a part of us dealing with it, producing new symptoms no matter what. It may well be that conditioning a higher level of consciousness forces the outlet or symptom down into another level. Thus, altering muscle tension through biofeedback may well drive the symptom down into the lowest level of consciousness (first line) where symptoms develop which are even more inaccessible. In this real sense, these techniques are making the patient worse in the name of getting him well.

Our research shows quite clearly that vital sign values *plus EEG alpha* respond to Pain. They rise in its anticipation and fall with its resolutions: and those changes are not transient. They endure.

What we see is that Pain increases brain activity . . . tremendously so. Since activity has something to do with brain growth it might be assumed that Pain has been a double agent; it helped develop our humanity—our neocortex and higher thought processes—and at certain critical levels took that humanity away by preventing us from feeling. But the ability to deal with Pain is not only extensive throughout the brain it is phylogenetically ancient. Thus, almost from the beginning of time, cells have had this survival capacity to deal with and turn away from pain. Perhaps man would not be man today and would not have developed all those higher mental capacities if it had not been for pain.

It is possible to be in pain but not to suffer. This is the situation of the patient with a frontal lobotomy. He feels pain but does not suffer. His attitude is, "I know it is there but so what?" *This is also the situation in neurosis.* Only in neurosis, depending upon the degree of gating, the person can feel neither pain nor suffering. His face can show misery but he may be unaware of it; his body can be highly tense yet without any comprehension of why. Nevertheless, we find that the *brain structures mediating alpha also mediate Pain: and that is a significant finding.* Among other things, it would indicate that, apart from our research findings, *high amplitude alpha is not associated with a relaxed, feeling state as has been assumed.*

The differentiation between Pain and suffering is important when it comes to understanding what a feeling is. The lobotomy patient can have the *sensations* of pain and yet not be *feeling* suffering. He cannot feel because he no longer has the interlevel fluidity that produces a total human feeling. He is forevermore bound to his sensations. Feeling means to have a totally open system; not in the growth center concept of being verbally open to say whatever is on one's mind, but to have interlevel access that opens up one's whole system of brain and body so that all experience is experienced, and not blocked and diverted. If you can feel you can learn from experience. If you cannot feel you cannot experience and therefore cannot learn in any real way. You will go on making the same kinds of neurotic choices, have the same kind of neurotic compulsions and no amount of punishment and education will change it.

We are developing an accurate index of repression based upon the parameters discussed by Dr. Holden. By taking all the measures together we have a profile and a numerical inndicator of the amount of Pain and repression present. We can use that index to then predict a number of factors—progress in therapy, ease of access to feelings, plus many other factors such as amount of dream sleep to be expected on a certain night. We have had encouraging results in our as yet preliminary work. We believe we can tell when someone has had a completed Primal and when one has only abreacted.* We can roughly predict the sleep and dream patterns; an incomplete Primal is followed by more REM sleep. We hope to be able to pick out certain psychosomatic groups based on their repression values; and we also hope to learn about those diseases which are heavily related to repression, for example, how high the index is among diabetics as compared with epileptics, etc. We will have an objective measure of how the patient is doing in therapy. The index can be used in comparative studies of Primal Therapy with other therapeutic methods. We hope to know when an improvement in a condition is transient so that in drug addiction, for example, we may have a good idea when to expect a return to drugs again. We may have now an objective measurement for the criminal who wants parole; and we can find out with some degree of accuracy what kind of risk he will be. The same is true for those in mental hospitals who request leave or dismissal.

We have already been able to judge with some accuracy the ease with which a new patient will get to his feelings based on blind judgments of pre-therapy records. The uses of the index will be multifold. Finally, we do not have to guess about the relationship of the experience of Pain to therapeutic efficacy. I reiterate the original Primal premise: repression of Pain leads to neurosis and the experience of Pain is curative.

---

*Abreaction is an emotional release without Primal connection. It can in itself be a powerful (often disintegrating) experience. Because it can look like a Primal, both a patient and therapist can be deceived into thinking that Primals are taking place when it is not the case. There are patients of mock therapists who believe that the therapy doesn't work, and for them it really *doesn't* because they are abreacting not Primalling. Too often, this can go on for months without the person being aware of the difference. Our measurements tell us soon enough what is going on; and when joined with our clinical judgment we have an accurate picture of the patient's state in regard to therapy and feelings. A Primal is a total feeling with a memory. An abreaction is a memory about a feeling, without connection.

REFERENCES

1. *The Anatomy of Mental Ilness*, Arthur Janov, Ph.D., G. P. Putnam's Sons, New York, 1971.

2. A Study of the Neurologic and Biochemical Changes of Patients Undergoing Primal Therapy, B. P. McInerney, L. A. Pam, Submitted in partial fulfilment of the requirements for the degree of Doctor of Philosophy, 1973. (Copies available from authors.)

2A. Research with Primal Patients: Vital Signs, B. P. McInerny, Ph.D., Journal of Primal Therapy, Vol. II, #1, p. 51, 1974.

3. EEG Activity and Primal Therapy Initial Tests for Possible Changes During Therapy, Martin Gardiner, Ph.D., UCLA Brain Research Institute, (not yet published).

4. *The Primal Scream*, Arthur Janov, Ph.D., G. P. Putnam's Sons, New York, 1970.

CHAPTER TEN

Further Implications of Levels of Consciousness
Arthur Janov

A. ON MORALITY

> Out-worn heart, in a time out worn,
> Come clear of the nets of wrong and right;
> Laugh, heart, again in the grey twilight,
> Sigh, heart, again in the dew of the morn.
>
> WILLIAM BUTLER YEATS

My basic hypothesis is that morality does not exist on the deeper levels of human existence. Morality is a third-line concept involving the "shoulds" and exists when individuals have lost their internal access. On the feeling level of existence there is no morality, no notion of right and wrong, only what is. Feelings, unlike morality, are never judgments; they are states of being. Morality is what fills the gap when people leave their feelings behind. Because it is only third-line deep, moral principles must be invoked time and again to have any effect. They must be drilled into people, accompanied by a variety of real and imagined punishments in order to counteract natural feelings and impulses. Thus, when one is allowed his feelings, morality vanishes. *Feelings are the only moral principles for natural man.* They direct him to be honest, considerate, kind, thoughtful, generous, etc. When neurosis prevents feeling, when man is frustrated and angry and cannot trust what he feels, then he needs to be kept in check by morality. Neurotic man cannot be kind or considerate, and have all the virtues we usually extol in any *real* way.

When people cannot live by feelings they must live by categories: right and wrong. For them, all behavior must be so classified. When

Grandma says the children are "bad" because they never call or see her, she isn't considering their desires. Their feelings never enter the picture; only her needs count. Indeed, it is the moralist who creates "sin," not only in the semantic sense that it takes a moralist to conceive of a notion of sin, but because it is the moral principles themselves which counteract feelings and produce aberrant "sinful" behavior later in life. Those principles block natural, pure impulses and transmute them into immoral acts. Consider the man who drinks, comes home to beat the children and then goes to confession to be "forgiven." If he could feel his Pain he wouldn't have to drink it away. If he could feel his old rage at his parents he wouldn't have to take it out on his children. And after beating them he certainly wouldn't have to go somewhere to have his behavior labelled "sin" in order to be forgiven. Indeed, the notion of "forgiveness" changes nothing, erases nothing. It allows a person temporary relief for his behavior until later or until he again acts out in the same way. Feelings nullify morality and make it an extraneous concept; classifying a behavior does not automatically help us to understand it.

Feeling people cannot harm others or even harm animals. Because they can feel, they experience the impact of their every act. They can feel the Pain of others and would not do anything to hurt them. Feeling people have no need to be immoral in the societal sense. They don't want more than they need; therefore they require no outside exhortations *not* to be greedy. Of course the whole notion of morality is based on the premise that we are inherently evil and must be exhorted against natural "evil" impulses. We have been observing neurosis with its attendant immoral behaviors for so long that we have come to accept base living as the nature of things. It is only when we finally get man to his feelings that we see what a pure, honest and moral soul he is. And the strange dialectic is that the most moral of institutions—the church—spreads the kind of antifeeling ideology which produces "immoral" behavior—drunkenness, homosexuality, etc.

When you cannot offer people what they need you must give them morality. Morality is the enemy of the people; as the suppressor of feeling it makes us act immorally to one another. In countries where religion has the strongest hold we often find rampant starvation. Where society is acting most immorally against its people, morality is powerful. The whole notion of a future reward serves to keep people from fulfilling themselves in the present. It keeps them working under exploitation, producing profits for others. For without the future reward in heaven the populace might decide to make a better life for itself in the "now." The more needs are denied to the people the greater the need to inculcate in them moral principles which will make them tolerate that denial. Morality is truly the opiate of the people. The superstructure of morality is built into a society in inverse proportion to how feeling it is.

Morality is basically a totalitarian notion since it involves an outside power coercing people into certain modes of behavior. It contravenes the principle of self-determination. The less a society attends to need, the more suppressive it must be. The fewer feelings allowed, the more external guidelines must be offered. Suppression and moralism go hand in hand. Moralism is the way suppression is carried out, and suppression is the wellspring for moralism. It is nearly always the church-dominated moralistic societies which permit the most immoral of acts, which perpetrate wars and develop the vigilante mentality of punishing those who feel and wish to act on their feelings instead of on moral principles. For a feeling person the notion of morality would scarcely enter his mind. By fiat of his feelings he is continually acting morally; thus morality is not an external force that merits ritualistic devotion. Morality is his way of life, not something superimposed on him against his will.

Right and wrong are obviously abstractions, not realities. We refrain from cruelty to our children not because to hurt them is "wrong," but because a feeling person cannot hurt anyone else. We don't avoid beating them because someone gives the act a symbolic label, "bad," but because feeling people are intrinsically moral in the real sense of the term. If we have to tell people not to be cruel it is only because we expect that without some kind of restriction they will be—thus, morality is based on a basic distrust of human intentions. We have yet to learn that the only meaningful discipline is feelings. They negate impulsive, antisocial behavior.

The logical question which arises from this discussion is, "Won't the absence of moral principles in a society lead to anarchy?" The answer is "yes," but we must hasten to explain the meaning of anarchy. It is my assumption that the need to be governed, to be told what to do and how to act, declines with the ascendance of feeling. We always need some ground rules in order to make social intercourse work more smoothly but to be submissive to the rule of law instead of the rule of feeling is another matter. To be governed by feelings lessens the need for law as an external force. It is our current unfeeling society which produces anarchy —an "every man for himself" attitude. Society produces a proliferation of laws because people cannot be trusted. In a feeling society each person is doing "his own thing." That "thing" does not involve exploiting others because no one has excess buried need. In a neurotic society each person "doing his own thing" means true anarchy.

When I say that we must be governed by feelings I must explain that neurotics *think* they feel. Until they experience deep Primal Pain they cannot know that they have never felt deeply. The neurotic may think of himself as moral because he has "risen above" anger, but that attitude does not eradicate his anger; it only keeps it buried. To "sink into" one's deep rage eradicates it and truly makes us unaggressive moral beings. Otherwise, what one gets is superficial piety and unctious behavior which is never real. It is specious morality. Obviously, if one grows up frustrated and deprived there is going to be real anger and perhaps vengeful thoughts inside. If we rise above these feelings we are only pretending to be moral and it is all a sham. Thus, for neurotics, *Pain is the avenue to true morality, and neurotic morality is the road to Pain.*

Once we understand how neurotic behaviors such as perversions are driven by past Pain, there is no need to moralize and create "sin." We can never transcend sin until we get beyond morality. It is first- and second-line Pain which leads to third-line immorality; and it is the experience of that Pain which leads to true morality. Pain is the price we pay for the truth, and sin is the failure to feel that truth—the failure to be ourselves. So long as people have no inner access to the painful truth they must operate from the third line alone. It is at this level that both morality and sin occur. Once into feelings there is neither.

I consider the Primal Institute a moral institution precisely because it invokes no morality. There is no judgment and no blame. Relationships between staff and patients are based on feelings, not rules. There is a hierarchy of expertise, not a chain of command. There is no higher morality to which we appeal to settle our difficulties; feelings take care of that. In the outer society the entire superstructure has a moral bent because of the absence of feeling-dominance. Each social institution is designed, however unconsciously, to deal with a failure of feeling in one area or another. Even in the mental hospitals there are "bad" behaviors which must be conditioned out. Imposed morality is so absorbed into therapeutic ideology that it is not even noticed. Schools are every bit as moralistic as churches; here too feelings are considered extraneous matters that interfere with the rules. For some reason it never occurs to school authorities that to allow feelings fully is to diminish the need for rules. When feelings predominate there is no need for external forces. Contrarily, for each abrogation there is even stricter enforcement—a treadmill and a web in which the real lesson is never learned.

The appeal to feeling is the only real moral principle to be found. It is no doubt a terrorizing and lonely thought to realize that no one is "up there" judging, ready to even the score for all our previous suffering. It is scary to think that we must be guided only by feeling, because this means an end to our "safety." No more can we calculate our actions on formulas of social approval or disapproval. No more guidelines and advice from others. No more "how to" books, eternal truths, Eastern philosophies to guide us. No leaning on family tradition, etiquette, etc. It is just a matter of being honest with oneself. Agony is the price of a moral life.

B. ON SUICIDE

It seems like an incredible idea that people attempt suicide because something went wrong with their birth process, but I hope to show how this may be so.

I shall introduce only one new term, "commensuration," to explain my thesis. All the term means is that symptoms are commensurate in quality and extent with the original Pain underlying them. Thus, a very large Pain early in life becomes disconnected from consciousness and reverberates in the system as tension; the *amount* of tension is commensurate with the amount of Pain experienced at the time. Further, the kind of symptom which follows is often directly related to the original Pain. With specific regard to the problem of suicide, I believe that, by and large, death as a solution to current Pain stems from a prototypic trauma— usually around the time of birth—in which death *was* the only solution. The notion of death as the *only* way out then becomes fixated in the system as an unconscious memory, shaping the way a person thinks about solutions to overwhelming problems later on. Thus, commensuration in the case of suicide means that death is the underlying theme which unites past Primal Pain with current Pain. The reason that it involves first-line rather than later Pain is that first-line Pain almost always involves near-death situations, and death is nearly always the result if that Pain is carried to its extreme. Strangulation at birth is an example. Being left totally alone without warmth or human touch immediately after birth is another.

There are occasions when second-line Pain sets up a prototype death-thought syndrome, but I think that those situations are possible-death events. One girl who attempted suicide on several occasions was brutally raped by her father at the age of three. Such a catastrophic event happened at a time when there was no other way to end the Pain but death. Thus, any later stress or hurt would tend to reactivate that *second-line* Pain and suicidal thoughts would arise reflexively.

Generally, Pains on the second line are not strictly life-and-death events. Being ridiculed or hurried at the age of four does not lead to death. What is important to bear in mind is that the child can hurry himself along, or offer to apologise for his acts. That is, he can construct a set of viable defenses against the Pain. By comparison, the alternative responses are extremely limited on the first line.

People attempt suicide for many different reasons. One person might do it for revenge, another to show "them" his misery. Whatever the reasons, the lengths they will go to to achieve their end will depend upon the nature of their Pain. By and large, first-line events are necessary but not sufficient conditions for suicidal preoccupation. What is also needed is a very repressive early atmosphere, or religious home, military school, parochial school, etc. These environments limit or stifle the outward expression of Pain so that the only place a person can go when he is hurt is "in." The crushing weight of all the inverted Pain can eventually lead to suicide.

Even the method chosen for suicide is largely symbolic and commensurate with Primal Pain. One girl characteristically chose razor blades to slash her wrists with. She wanted to see the blood ooze out. In a Primal she relived a forgotten memory of when she was six years old and was being smashed in the nose by a father completely out of control. Her nose bled profusely, and she took the blood and smeared it on the walls to show them she hurt. "Blood" became the symbol of making her hurt known, and razor blades were the way to get the blood out. When this woman hurt so much that she could no longer take the Pain, she began to hallucinate blood and, before therapy, never knew why. One patient would think about hanging himself whenever he was upset. The Primal in which he resolved his obsession was one of being strangled at birth. Somehow he was unconsciously trying to return to a very early situation in order to master it. The fantasy he had was of hanging himself and of being discovered and cut down at the last moment. We can see from these cases that to feel the underlying unconscious feelings is to dispel the symbolic behavior based upon it.

There is almost never just one reason why someone wants to kill himself. Symbolic reasons proliferate as the Pain becomes compounded so that we get an "overdetermination" (to use a Freudian notion) in a single piece of behavior.

What is important for Primal patients to understand is that during therapy suicidal thoughts may persist for many months or even for a year or two simply because the first-line prototypic Pain has either not been reached or has not been totally experienced or resolved; it takes dozens of Primals to relive and resolve the usual first-line Pain. However the patient now knows what to do with his suicidal impulse: feel it, rather than act it out. Before therapy there was no way for him to handle his ascending Pain. There was truly no way out for him.

In some instances suicidal thoughts do not persist for a long time in therapy. In such a case the person has generally resolved an underlying prototypic second-line Pain. The woman who was raped by her father at a young age was able to relive that event many times early in her therapy and, as that Pain was resolved, so were her thoughts about death. Before this resolution she had been constantly on the verge of suicide, and there was nothing she could do about it. She had no lever with which to understand her obsession and, even if she could have known about early Pain, there was no way for her to connect to it until Primal Therapy.

If there is a leitmotif to suicide, I think it lies in hopelessness—in there being no way out, no way to get love any more, no way to succeed, no way to fight back. One solution remains—death. This thought can be symbolic of an early Pain such as: "If they won't love me I'll die." Turned around this means, "I cannot live without their love," or "I don't want to live without their love," or "the only way I can be loved is if I die." These feelings usually occur because the parents really hate the child, who, in the end, has no way to please them except by removing himself from the world.

How do we know how accurate this hypothesis is? After all, it is quite an extrapolation to say that suicide is based on birth trauma. It is observation that solidifies our position and removes it from the realm of wild theorizing. My extrapolation comes from the study of patients who suddenly become suicidal in therapy and immediately plunge into birth Primals. When they come out of the Primal they have many insights which explain the whys of their suicidal thoughts. So, by observation of the process of commensuration we can make some statements about the connection of past to present Pain. A person who becomes totally preoccupied with death in therapy will usually go to his first line and feel for perhaps hours. It may take many Primals to resolve the death-thought impulses completely. What tends to corroborate my hypothesis is that suicidal thoughts often do not get intense until a person has advanced in his therapy, until he has dismantled his defenses sufficiently to allow access to his first line. This state of being may trigger either hallucinations or suicidal thoughts and this helps us relate both responses to the first line. When we see this phenomenon crop up repeatedly in many patients the hypothesis is reinforced.

There follows the transcript of a seminar on suicide which was held recently at the Primal Institute.

WHY SUICIDE?

A number of patients with a history of suicidal tendencies were asked what they felt about their attempts, and if they had made any connections as a result of their therapy.

*   *   *   *   *

GWEN: I was eighteen the first time I tried to kill myself. I was away at college and had gotten involved with a boyfriend who was a lot like my daddy. My parents weren't talking to me at the time, and when my boyfriend rejected me as well, it just brought up all my pain. I was numb. I went back to my dorm and started to cut my wrists. My roommate came in and I got under the covers. Eventually—it seemed like years—it began to hurt because I kept going into the same vein; finally it stopped bleeding. I couldn't keep it bleeding but the feeling remained.

I tried again two years ago. The night before that attempt, my best girl friend and I had gone to see this guy; I guess he was about forty-five. What happened was a scene that just mimicked what had happened with my father when I was fourteen. The guy made a pass at me, and my girl friend didn't protect me from him. It just brought all that pain up. My boyfriend didn't want to see me at the time and I ended up staying up all night doing mescaline and trying to kill myself with it. The next day I was moving around; there was no land, nothing for me to step on any more. The feeling was that there was so much pain and just no place to feel it, no way to feel it. I couldn't put on my little mask anymore and be a good little girl and I couldn't get up in the morning. Living for me has always been minute by minute. How do I get through the next minute? I was just falling apart.

I didn't see any point; I mean I just couldn't feel it. So I took a lot of pills and I guess they take you down. I was lying there . . . thinking. I was living in a girls' residence and my best friend was in the room next to me. I knew she'd come in and find me dead—and she was into such heavy shit herself. She was the only one to stay by me in my daily life and that's what really mattered. I'd said good-bye to my parents a long time ago; there was nobody else. So I went next door and told her I'd taken the pills and she took me to the hospital.

ART: How many?

GWEN: I think I took fifteen sedatives and a lot of uppers.

ART: Uppers! You were trying to kill yourself with uppers?

GWEN: I just took all the pills I had. I was on the critical list. I mean I almost did die and the whole point of the difference now that I'm in Therapy is that I really don't want to die. I mean attempting it is just bullshit for me and I've felt enough of my pain now that for the first time in my whole life I don't wake up thinking about it all the time. That is as much as I've gotten out of Therapy: I don't want to die all the time.

ALICE: Previous to Therapy, it was all the time?

GWEN: Not all the time.

ALICE: Every crisis?

GWEN: It was very strange because a lot of the time it was in the middle of something very ordinary and I'd just feel "Gee, I want to die." I was always planning it . . . where I would go, like a motel and all this kind of stuff.

ALICE: Once it was razors, once it was pills. Is there anything to that? What makes you think of a different method?

GWEN: Well, the first time was when I was eighteen years old and I didn't know anything about anything. There was just no other way. I didn't have any pills and I was already in the crisis and a razor was the only thing I had. I could never cut myself again after doing it that time.

MARY: I'd be interested to know how many people have attempted suicide while on drugs. I know when I did it I was on acid and speed and a thousand other things.

LILLIAN: I did it on heroin. I don't know how serious it was . . . I mean I tried to stab myself: I tried to stab my boyfriend.

ART: Serious?

LILLIAN: It's hard to say how serious that time was because I was just so stoned. I really did want to die but I was just so out of it. During that whole period I had also shot up with a needle that I knew had been used by a person who had hepatitis and was on the critical list in the hospital. So I was really into not giving a fuck about it. I feel like I have had one really serious attempt and others that were different degrees of less serious. That was because I was so stoned. The first time I ever really, really wanted to commit suicide was when I was fourteen and I got drunk for the first time. I really felt like I wanted to. But that, I think, was just not knowing what to do when the pain came up and also wanting sympathy because I was at a party with all these people. It ended up with me just cutting myself, which is this thing I have about me cutting myself, and they had to take me to the hospital where I got stitches. I didn't even cut myself on my wrists so that was kind of ridiculous.

About a year and a half ago I tried again. I had this really bad period when I put myself in a psychiatric ward for four days until I found out what that was about and left. Everybody walked around with purple circles under their eyes and they just kept sticking tranquilizers into me and I refused to take them. I ended up just leaving. Every single day after that I felt like walking out in front of a car and killing myself. I was living with my girl friend and her boyfriend and they were kind of taking care of me. Then I moved in with this guy and I got to where I'd just lie around. He'd leave for work in the morning and seven hours later I would be in the same position as he had left me. I'd get totally spaced out and he didn't understand what it was, and I just felt like I couldn't move. I couldn't even get up to go to the bathroom. He was saying I was lazy; he wanted me to go out shopping and cook for him and do all this stuff that I just couldn't get together. So we were just going to have to part. He said he was going to go out to eat and go to a friend's house and that I could take my stuff out of the closet. I started doing that but realized that I just didn't know what to do, so I took twelve downers. I was so totally irrational that I still kept packing.

ART: Twelve downers? What kind?

LILLIAN: Quaaludes. I guess it was only in my system about two hours before I had my stomach pumped.

ALICE: What happened when you took them?

LILLIAN: I took them and I was still packing my clothes, because I couldn't figure out what to do. I wanted to go out and sit on the door and I just didn't know what to do. My boyfriend finally came home about two hours later and I was sitting there laughing. He called up the poison center because I kept saying they wouldn't kill me. I did really want to die. I just didn't care. No, it's not that I wanted to die; it's that there was no other choice. It was death or . . . I don't know. I do feel that as soon as you start to get off the pills it brings the pain level down a little bit. So then I had second thoughts, like, "Wow, what am I doing?" The pills would numb the pain.

I've had the feeling so many times since I've been here that I want to die. Once, in my three weeks, I went to a session in which I felt I didn't feel anything; so I went home. I fell asleep for fifteen minutes. I woke up in a daze, picked up the razor blade, and started cutting myself. As soon as I started going over it in the same place the physical pain started to get really bad. I feel that cutting in the same place really does something. It enables you to start feeling the pain. Then I wasn't concerned with dying as much as I was with feeling the feeling.

ART: What made you want to die at that point?

LILLIAN: It's just hopelessness. I wake up in the morning with the same feeling, that I want to die. Sometimes it's worse than others. With me I feel that the reason is that I'm not feeling or that I'm not getting anywhere with the Therapy, and with me that's a really big feeling. Or I feel so bad that I don't even want to come in here and feel it. It seems ridiculous—crying for the rest of my life.

ALICE: Do you know what that thing is about cutting yourself?

LILLIAN: Well, it got to be like I would cut myself; but then after I'd done it, it had nothing to do with killing myself any more. Before I came to group I would cut myself whenever the pain would start to come up.

MARY: Gwen, you said that since you've been in Therapy that feeling doesn't come up for you. Did you ever get to a specific time in your life when you felt like you were dying or that you wanted to die? Do you know if that feeling goes back to anything in the past which would be the reason why you want to kill yourself in the present?

GWEN: Oh, do you mean one specific scene? I think it was what my father did to me. It just seems impossible to ever feel all of that. It's so fucking real and intense now.

ART: What's that?

GWEN: My father raped me when I was three and it just seems like it will never end. I would rather bang my head open on the floor than feel it. So, I'm sure a lot of it goes back to then.

LILLIAN: I haven't felt this yet, but I've had the feeling that since I've been here whatever I do or whatever I say leads me back to crying like a little baby. So I feel that when I was really, really little, I vaguely felt I had the feeling that I wanted to die . . . just crying and crying and crying and crying, and nothing happened, and nobody coming, and I sort of occasionally feel in that, that I want to die.

ART: Death was the only way out.

LILLIAN: That's right. Also, when I feel like I'm being strangled or being choked that feeling is like I am dying and at that time I don't care. I would just as soon die; it hurts so bad.

JOYCE: I want to say where I am. These days I'm right in the middle of feeling I want to die and it's the first time I've ever had it come up. The thing that's scary about it is that I know it's an old feeling but when I get in it it's awfully hard for me to realize that. When I'm feeling suicidal, I'm in a place that's really hard for me to say I'm not going to do it. It's ever since I've gotten back into one period of my life, and it's tied in with a lot of things that I used to do. It's like with all attempts I've made I've never called them suicide. This is the first time since I've been here that I've admitted to the fact that I wanted to die. I used to cut myself with razor blades all the time when I was a kid and I never knew why. I did know that I didn't want to die after somebody touched me. That is, somebody would usually touch me if I cut myself. The feelings of really wanting to die come from reliving a period of my life when I slept next to my parents for about five years. The feeling was like my daddy attacked my mommy every night. I was between nine and fifteen and I had forgotten about it when I came here. I have remembered it purely through feelings, not knowing at all the feeling was going to go there. It's really laying me out; it's really awful. That's when I started cutting myself. It was absolutely pure hopelessness that nobody was ever going to touch me, and they had each other. The thing is that I also felt the feeling as birth. I had an operation when I was a week old to remove a birthmark. I had a big scar on my head. I used to tell people that I was operated on by a doctor who didn't use any anaesthetics. I don't know why I said that but it meant something really big to me. I have been having feelings lately that could really be that surgery and the thing is that when I cut myself it was a reminder of that first thing too, like I was trying to solve my problems.

ART: Make that clear.

JOYCE: Well I hurt. I get completely hopeless, just completely hopeless. When I was at college away from home I thought I was being forced to go home. It was near Christmas vacation. I took a razor blade and cut my wrists and I just walked up and down the streets with my arms bleeding; at night with nobody around and the feeling of hopelessness came over me. That kind of solved . . . it kind of relieved the pain.

ART: What's it got to do with your head?

JOYCE: There's something about getting near my mama or nearer my Pain; I don't know. I rub my head and everything when I'm in these things. Before I started cutting myself I used to get hung up if I had an indentation on my skin. I can rub my scars and have a feeling, so there is some kind of a tie-in with a big trauma, a big horrible pain and I keep trying to get it back. If I could ever solve that I would be okay. And there is no way to solve it.

GWEN: I used to feel that if I could just suffer enough, if I could just make the suffering complete, then I wouldn't have to kill myself. But I could never make it complete so I felt like I'd have to die. Also, I've been getting to the feeling of being really dirty; after my father raped me I just felt really dirty. I used to feel that there was something evil, something really evil in me and the only way I could get at it was to kill my entire self.

FAYE: My feeling was to live, but I wanted to get rid of the body. In my fantasy I was split from my body and I couldn't connect; I couldn't pull *me* back into the body so I had to get rid of the body.

MARY: Why the body?

FAYE: What was in me was out of me and I couldn't bring me back and I couldn't stand the split. I couldn't bear it and I didn't tell anybody; it was a secret. Nobody knew. So I had to get rid of the body. It felt like sanity to me. It also felt like that when I attempted suicide. Nobody even knew about it then. I just did it with such rationality. I cooked some oleander leaves in a hamburger and I ate it. I just sat very calmly and quietly waiting for the split to stop. Waiting for the body to go.

ART: You were going to kill the body so the other could . . .

FAYE: So the other could stand it, you know, you can't stand being split. For me there is no worse hell than being split. And I'm really shaky about it now because I haven't done this for a long time and it's just started again last weekend; that I started splitting again.

Art: How long has this been happening?

FAYE: I started splitting deliberately when I was five. It was my trick, my way of escaping, and I had a ritual that I went through. Part of it was taking a little tiny piece of my hair and twisting it and that was the final thing. And still I get a weird feeling when I work on this little tiny piece of hair. It was a long ritual and I split and then my body couldn't feel and I couldn't be hurt and I would be down there and, you know, she couldn't hurt me up there. Nothing could happen to me and I would do it out of a sense of control; I was in charge.

MARY: What happened the night you took the oleander?

FAYE: Nothing. I waited patiently and nothing happened. I just got violently sick, but nothing happened. I got some strange heart reaction.

ART: Was it Japanese oleander?

FAYE: It was the kind that was supposed to be poisonous. I mean I did get good and sick. I didn't tell my husband until we were going to adopt a child and then I thought I should tell. I married him and I'd been splitting but I never told him I split. But the difference now I'm in Therapy is that when I'm split it feels terrible to me. On Wednesday I split and I had to call a therapist. I mean I've never been in a position where I could ask for help and I'd never want to let anyone know that I was that vulnerable or that desperate. So, now it feels different. But the thing with knives is this: I'd get a numbness when I wasn't splitting and I'd hear a voice say, "If you just put the knife there, you'll feel." I can't stand to be numb.

MARY: Did you actually hear a voice?

FAYE: Yeah, it would be so real to me. I couldn't believe that other people couldn't hear it too. It would say, "Push until you feel," and then I would push until I would feel; and then I would feel better. I would even have orgasms. It would feel so good to feel.

ART: Orgasms? When?

FAYE: When I'd push the knife into my abdomen.

ART: Did you draw blood?

FAYE: It was just pressure, just pressure. And, there was a spot on my face that I had when I was fifteen or even younger, where I would want to put scissors and I would go around rubbing it. It was just a place to feel. I'd go around and rub and rub and rub until it would be all sore and I'd have a huge pimple or boil there. I'd just think about putting the scissors through there and the feeling was if I could get the scissors through, the Pain would come.

MARY: Is that anything like what you were saying, Joyce, about rubbing?

JOYCE: Yeah, the numbness, the wanting to feel. That's it; anything when you're feeling hopeless, when there is nothing anywhere. That's what I'd do to feel and it was hope too, hope that I'd get someone to touch me. So, it was a lot of those things.

BURT: About a week ago I had the feeling of wanting to take a knife and just slash myself all over my body. I was talking to my therapist about it because I thought someone should know about it. As I was talking to her I realized that the reason I wanted to slash myself was that there is so much Pain in my body that it was tearing my body apart in my muscles. I wanted to take a knife and dig down to where that Pain was to get back at it because it was hurting me so much. It's acting out getting to the Pain. The thing that brought on this business about suicide for me was going to college. Living a life that was totally at odds with who I was, it's like I had life and society and circumstances pulling me one way and my Pain pulling me the opposite way. I could either live up to what society demanded of me—being a good boy—or I could sink into total despair, which was myself. Incredibly enough, it seemed that it was getting away from my real self that brought me to so much Pain and so much hopelessness that I bought a gun. I finally had to quit college. It wasn't sinking into my Pain that made me suicidal, it was having to stay away from it.

PHYLLIS: It's not being able to feel that does it. That reminds me of when I was drinking a whole lot, before I came out here. I drank because then I could feel. I couldn't feel without the liquor, and I would have chosen the Pain any day, rather than go on feeling like there was no life inside my body.

What just struck me is that I've always had the impulse to kill myself. It seems to recur throughout my life. I can remember that the first time I thought about suicide was when I was eleven or twelve. I was sitting in my living room chair, looking out over the fields and I just felt like I wanted to commit suicide. I just sat there trying to decide whether or not to do it. I still haven't got back to those feelings; they were so terrible. I just thought, "No, there are certain things in this world that are just too beautiful for me to leave." One of them was my piano. The piano really made me feel that I could express myself. So I didn't do anything then.

MIKE: I have never tried as an adult or a teenager but I really did try as a three-year-old.

ART: As a what?

MIKE: As a three-year-old, I tried three separate times.

ART: What did you do?

MIKE: I ran my tricycle . . . I timed it just right from behind a parked car and ran it across the street into a car coming down. I've been able to remember that but I've never been able to remember what happened after I got beyond the grill of that car. I could see the grill of the car but I can't remember what happened in the street. It's been coming back and, you know, I trust this because it's my way. I recall things visually first. Like I see this little boy get in the street in front of the car and the grill of the car is coming right up to him, and I think I turn at the last minute. I keep expecting to hear the brakes screech but I just haven't got to that yet. My grandmother told me years later that I did that. It has to do with being around that house, so silent and so alone or else having to play outside, alone with no physical touch from my mother at all. But my feeling is that I could just feel it and feel it . . .

PHYLLIS: I don't remember feeling suicidal again—after that time when I was twelve—until I got to college, and it was like all the pressures were on. I felt such severe anxiety I just thought that if this is the way I had to live, I didn't even want to live. Then I started to see a shrink there, and I guess he fucked me over, but all I can say is he kept me alive until I heard about this place. That's really true. He gave me hope and that's what the piano meant to me too; hope. But it's a constant impulse. I always live with suicidal thoughts. It was like that all the time during my first three weeks of Therapy. I called my therapist twice and told her I felt like killing myself. It's just like that's where I automatically end up, regardless of what's going on. And even during my three weeks I'd just go through those fancy schemes. I was disappointed that there were only two floors in the motel because if I jumped out of the window then I wouldn't kill myself. For the next month I just lived on. When waking up, the first thing on my mind would be taking a death walk; putting my clothes on and walking until I died. I've had feelings where I'm on a kind of treadmill, and the feeling is I'll never make it to the end. I've also had feelings where I'm going down in a whirlpool. I know these are symbolic expressions of the real feeling. I've been having birth feelings lately and there is some connection there.

The feeling that drives me to it is hopelessness, despair and hopelessness. I feel like I only just glimpsed a bit of all that bleakness when I felt it with a therapist. There's lots more of it inside. I'm not saying it's gone away. I still think suicidal thoughts all the time.

ART: Let me just say something here about the death wish, the Freudian death wish. It's prototypic thought. Some people will wake up and say, "God, I gotta have a cock" or "I gotta have a cigarette" or "I gotta have a drink." You guys wake up and say, "God, I gotta kill myself." Usually it's the Pain that could not be shut off in infancy; when you couldn't go out and smoke cigarettes, eat meals or jack off. You know, when you are one month old or at birth, the only solution is death. That solution is a locked-in memory circuit. So, whenever you are near that same first-line Pain, you get that fix or that thought. It's symbolic. It's your way out.

GWEN: Well, when my father raped me I was three so that's first line?

ART: No, second line.

GWEN: In the feeling I feel that he's going right through my body.

ART: But that's such catastrophic Pain. You see second-line Pain, in general, is not life-and-death. It's being made to talk too early or whatever it is, stuttering etc. But your Pain on the second line was catastrophic life-and-death which is rare. With life-and-death, death becomes the solution. It's the only thing you can do. That becomes your fix and you will have that just like other people have recurring headaches, almost for as long as you're in this therapy. It's nothing to worry about. It does get better.

LILLIAN: I can see why it gets better for you, Gwen. It's because you connected yours to the rape. For me, I don't know where exactly it is, but I recognize that it's early Pain. When I wake up in the morning I have gotten to where I can recognize the old feeling. It starts in my stomach and in my heart, like from the way my heart hammers I know that that feeling is probably an early feeling.

ART: Yes, you know best. That's why this is such a unique clinic; it isn't the staff having seminars about suicide, it's the patients.

MARY: The staff are just patients too.

ART: Yes, but what I mean is, the only idea we will ever have is from the patients. If you don't know about your own suicide attempts better than we do, then we are all in trouble.

C. ON SLEEP AND DREAMS:
CONSCIOUSNESS IN UNCONSCIOUS STATES

There are levels of consciousness which operate in all of us and those levels exist in both the awake and sleep states. What I want to discuss in this chapter are the kinds of mental activity associated with each level of consciousness and how these activities are manifested while asleep as well as awake.

Buried and frozen events do not disappear in sleep; they exert a force, a force which shapes the nature and content of our dreams, and provides the energy of our dreams—the terror and apprehension, the anger and rage. They also dictate our awake behavior. The symbols of our daily conduct are usually not so condensed and obvious as in our dreams because there the range of possible symbolic behavior is condensed, but when observed closely we see that they are very much alike.

I am suggesting that the levels of consciousness which I have described correspond to the levels of sleep as described in the scientific literature. The stage of dream sleep, also known as Rapid Eye Movement (REM) sleep would correspond to second-line consciousness. Deep sleep, also called Stage 4 sleep, would lie on the first line. During REM sleep we dream the unresolved Pains of our early childhood. Stage 4 dreams involve the needs and traumas occurring in and around the neonatal period. Dreams on this level would involve the most traumatic of events because the traumas on the first line are nearly always life-and-death struggles—strangling on the cord during birth, being starved in the crib, etc. Therefore it would follow that the Stage 4 first-line dreams would be nightmares, and as it turns out, that is true. Nightmares do not occur predominantly during REM sleep as one might imagine.* There are several reasons for this. We must keep in mind that the repression of Pain produces an unconsciousness to some degree and this repressing process is very much like what happens in sleep when certain aspects of consciousness are repressed. In order to achieve unconsciousness, then, we must block the action of brain processes which attend sharply to the outside world: in the case of Pain we must shut out anything which might trigger it, and in the case of sleep we must focus away from what is happening around us as well. Repression is the key process, for complete represssion brings on deep sleep, meaning that the person is operating on first-line consciousness oblivious to the world—all of his automatic functions take over; he continues to breathe and move, however.

I believe that the process of repression utilizes the same brain functions whether dealing with sleep or Pain. Both require a gating and/ or blocking of third-line consciousness, and, depending on the depth of repression, a blocking of second-line consciousness as well.

There are investigators who differentiate between nightmares and night terrors, the latter being a more severe and frightening dream. The night terror would be what I call a nightmare (as opposed to second-line "scary" dreams) and is first line. For example, a study of night terrors was done by Charles Fisher, et al.** Here is what he has to say: "The night terror is ushered in by sudden loud piercing screams, the subject

---

*Ferguson, M. *The Brain Revolution*, Taplinger, 1973, N.Y., p. 145.

** Charles Fisher, Edwin Kahn, Adele Edwards and David Davis. "A Psychophysio-logical Study of Nightmares and Night Terrors." *The Journal of Nervous and Mental Disease*, 157, No. 2, August 1973, pp. 75-97.

passing into an aroused state characterized by motility, intense autonomic discharge (precipitous doubling or even tripling of heart rate,
great increase in respiratory amplitude, marked decrease in skin resistance), brief duration (1 to 3 minutes), varying degrees of amnesia for
the episode and rapid return to sleep. The night terror is a much more
severe phenomenon than the REM nightmare although the latter is more
frequent." The description above, when taken out of the sleep context,
describes a Primal. Just because it occurs at night doesn't change its
reality; it doesn't alter the fact that there is something inside us that is
explosive and terrifying that can erupt without warning when our conscious defenses are lulled. To be succinct: Primal is a daytime night terror,
connected; and a night terror is a nighttime Primal, disconnected.

An inchoate awareness of two levels of consciousness associated with
sleep is found in *The Brain Revolution* (op. cit., page 154), which states:
"Paradoxical (REM) sleep and slow-wave sleep (Stages 1-4) apparently
involve *two interrelated but somewhat autonomous brain systems*. Either
kind of sleep can be eliminated by surgical interference." You are not
just eliminating sleep by such a procedure, but are interfering with
the action of *a system of consciousness*. To be operating on the first
line alone during waking means to be psychotic; and that is why I have
often called psychosis the "waking nightmare." Whether awake or asleep,
anything which causes access to unintegrated Pains of the first line will
be highly disturbing. Sleepwalking, for example, occurs during Stage
4 sleep (first line). Sleepwalking offers a good illustration of the point
because it is strikingly similar to psychotic states in which the person
wanders around the world totally oblivious of what is going on outside
him. He is completely directed from the inside. The sleepwalker often has
his eyes closed, but that seems to me to be the major difference between
him and the psychotic. The psychotic's third-line, reality-oriented consciousness seems to be completely suffused by the lower lines, and in
particular, the first line. The reason for this is that the first line contains
the kinds of Pains which are most difficult to integrate, which are so
horrendous as to be fragmenting of consciousness and which cannot
be integrated until much of the second line has been absorbed and
resolved.

So both the sleepwalker and the psychotic wander around the house,
do chores, open windows and doors and are unconscious of their acts.
Obviously, the impulses must be terribly strong that can move a person
out of a bed and around his neighborhood all without the intercession
of the third line. It may be that nearly every impulse neurosis which in-

volves physical acting out is indicative of early physical trauma and the third line is powerless to stop the impulse. It can neither rationalize nor control it.

There are several physiologic factors which help produce nightmares. One may be due to what happens to a chemical substance known to mediate repression (serotonin). It seems that with continued repression serotonin gets used up.* This occurs in both sleep and in severe mental illness. As it is depleted, the barrier against first-line Pain is diminished allowing an ascendance of terror. As the first-line terror rises into consciousness there is the nightmare. The terror has caused the third line to make up a story to explain it; and the dream story is bizarre because there is no logical rationale for such a fright. And so the crocodiles come out of the water to get us.

The nightmare means that the first-line Pain has caused the third line to make up a "crazy" story, which is exactly what psychosis is. If there were no third line to rationalize the Pain, I believe the Pain and terror would be catastrophic. Indeed, the infant who suffers from first-line Pain is exactly in this fix. He has all that Pain, no third line to make sense (even unreal sense) out of it, and so must bear the total brunt of it. Crib death may be one result of that helpless situation.

There is a report by Dr. Elliot Weitzman of Albert Einstein College of Medicine (in the book *Sleep Disorders*, Vol. #1, by Halstead) which pinpoints the cause of crib death as due to a functional abnormality of the respiratory center in the brainstem. He suggests that babies often lose their breath during sleep but that certain ones suffer from this condition more than others, and these latter ones may have a brain dysfunction. Dr. William Dement, the well-known sleep investigator, studied sleep disorders at Stanford University. He found when monitoring sleeping patients that many of them stop breathing during their sleep and often had to literally wake up to catch their breath. He termed this syndrome "sleep apnea." What I think both investigators may be dealing with is individuals who are very close to first line traumas such as losing breath for a sustained period during birth. In sleep these persons (infants included) come close to this trauma resulting in the loss of breath. The infant may die when this occurs because he simply has not yet developed the defenses necessary to shut down against the Pain.

Obviously there are very heavy Pains which occur on the second line but without severe first-line Pains I believe they are neurotogenic,

---

* As reported in the Stanford University study on agitated depression.

not psychotogenic. Dreams on the second line, then, are neurotic-style dreams; and though they are scary, they have neither the form nor the content of first-line dreams. Generally, they are not catastrophic in terms of the underlying feeling of the dream and further, they do not wake us up with a jolt as the first-line dreams can do. There are some critical differences between the two levels of dreams and I want to explore them now.

First-line (stage four) sleep is characterized by slow brain waves (one to three cycles per second) with very high amplitude. (And very high amplitude is evident in waking states in persons struggling to repress. See research section) Ordinarily the higher voltage (amplitude) serves, in my opinion, to keep first-line traumas on the first line, preventing access to higher lines. Since I view brain wave frequency as part of the defense system, the slowing of brain waves during first-line sleep may leave the person open to those first-line traumas. The increase in amplitude may take up the slack to keep the Pain at bay. When the Pain has too great a charge value there is likely to be a breakthrough into higher level of consciousness, and the result is a nightmare. We not only become awake but also aware of the existence of some tremendous feeling; we may charge it off as meaningless only because we don't understand the existence of lower levels of conscious activity.

It is interesting that the frequency of brain waves in deep sleep very much resembles the awake pattern of an infant. In any case, I see amplitude and frequency as reciprocals whose absolute values are raised with neurosis. It is our research observation that very repressed individuals have high alpha amplitude and very fast alpha frequency, and that this frequency and high amplitude tend to diminish as Primal Pains are felt and resolved. While a slowing of brain wave activity (through the use of strobes, for example) into the theta range may produce second-line Primals in a Primal patient, it is likely to produce only amorphous terror in a non-Primal neurotic. As the brain slows its activity in sleep that terror becomes a nightmare.

It may be that the large categories of brain wave activity—delta, theta, alpha and beta—reflect levels of consciousness: beta activity (13-28 cycles per second) indicating the state of highest Pain and repression; delta corresponding to first line (as it does in sleep) with slow wave activity; theta being associated with second line (4-8 cycles per second and alpha indicating activity of the third line (8-12 cycles per second). This is speculation but discrete sleep stages have been observed again and again and in some way these stages must correspond to differing levels of consciousness. That is, *what has been observed are not simply stages of sleep but larger categories of consciousness*. These stages are each more highly attuned to their own levels of reality. Thus, phenomena which involve feeling are more quickly and accurately perceived on the second line than the third; and during sleep the second line is processing feelings via dreams. A good example of the independent perceptions associated with each level of consciousness is found in research on the electrical conductivity of the skin. It has been found that the subconscious is more in touch with feelings than the so-called conscious mind (which I call third line). Experiments where "dirty" words are flashed on a screen too fast to be consciously perceived are reacted to by the skin in terms of changes in electrical conductance.*

Experiments were designed to fool the conscious mind, as for example telling subjects that they would receive light electric shocks of varying and diminished intensity when, indeed, all shocks in the series were exactly the same.* Though the subject would report less and less discomfort the skin reported more accurately that the shocks were of the same intensity. This kind of experiment is important because it means that in a variety of ways the third line could be deceived and made to misperceive either through suggestion or education. But the truth is still being processed on a different level of consciousness; during sleep when we are in touch with that consciousness, that truth is apt to appear in our dreams. So though we might believe consciously that nothing bad happened in our childhood (just as we come to believe that the continuing series of shocks are less intense), the truth remains on a different level of consciousness.

The reason that the simple experiments with skin conductance are important does not have to do with what they tell us about the skin; rather, it is the same nervous system (autonomic) which innervates both the skin and the internal organs affecting heart rate and blood pressure, so change in the skin conductance is also an indicator of changes internally. So though we may think that nothing is bothering us our hearts are pumping faster over events in our past which have only been accurately perceived on lower lines. It is no wonder, then, that during sleep when we operate on those lower lines we can have nightmares with our heart racing. The problem is that we tend to think that the heart races because of *the dream*, instead of a past reality.

Psychology Today, August 1974, p. 54.

** *op. cit.*, p. 54.

The facility with which we can forget those dreams depends upon the strength of our gating systems. With less facile access to lower lines any temporary intrusion into the third line can be quickly forgotten. That is, the more defended we are the more quickly we can put feelings back into the lines where they belong and keep them unconscious. We are, after all, not forgetting a "dream"; we are forgetting a *feeling* of which the dream was only the vehicle for its ride to consciousness. We *must* forget the dream in some way because it is the symbolic lever by which we can gain access to the feeling. We push all of the symbolic reminders aside in the same way that consciously we maneuver our lives so as to avoid old painful feelings; we marry the person, for example, who will not bring up certain kinds of Pains.

We have to ask ourselves, "Why would the heart rate go up to 170 during certain kinds of nightmares (as reported by Fisher, et al., op cit. page 92)? After all, the *dream* isn't real. There really isn't a crocodile coming out of the sea to get us. Clearly it is the feeling that is real; we do not fool our bodies. The heart must be responding to a real event. If ever there were proof that the past lives on and affects our behavior it can be found in dream life. We do not border on a heart attack during sleep because of some fantasied crocodile. We are on the verge of dying (and may eventually die from the strain) because there is a true past horror that lower levels of consciousness recognize and deal with continuously in their own way—elevated blood pressure and heart rate being just one example. It is no accident that in our own research the heart rate and blood pressure can easily double just before a Primal. I want to reiterate a most crucial point: *we do not deceive the lower levels of consciousness.* All of our observations and all of the experimental evidence indicate that they respond to reality in real ways (as, for example, the skin conductance experiments). It is the third line with its emminent plasticity which can be deceived and made to believe almost anything.

Though it is the third line which mediates external reality while awake, there are aspects of the third line which operate even in sleep. Thus the noise of a garbage truck is incorporated into sleep consciousness by the third line. It is not perceived for what it is, however; rather it is mixed with lower-line dream material and fused into the story line. Nevertheless the third line is in charge of handling sensory input. Previously, we have schematized levels of consciousness as (3) the here-and-now—externally oriented; (2) the emotional—feeling component; and (1) the internally directed, bodily oriented.

I have discussed how Pain produces a split in the third line (see "The

Nature of Pain and Levels of Consciousness"). This split allows part of the third line to symbolize feelings during a dream while the other aspects of that level are quiescent and no longer alertly attend to the outside world. My assumption is that in a well person this division would not exist so that feelings during sleep would net be automatically symbolized; rather, they would be felt for what they were. The hypothesis is that the well person would not have old Pains coming up during REM sleep. REM sleep would simply be another stage of sleep, less deep than first-line sleep. Again, it is the job of the third line to correctly symbolize sensory input from both external and internal sources. During REM sleep a good part of the third line is inactive; nevertheless, whatever sensory input occurs should be correctly interpreted. In other words, it isn't sleep which makes for incorrect third line interpretation. It is Primal Pain which does it. Sleep doesn't distort the third line. It just puts it to rest. Or rather, third line rest helps produce the state of sleep.

We have observed Primal patients for seven years now and their dreams do have a continually reduced symbolism. We assume that this is directly due to lessened Pain in the system. We symbolically dream our Pain in the same way that we symbolically act it out while awake. With-

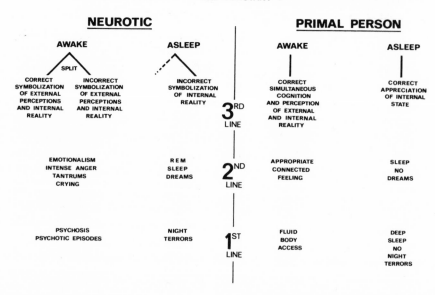

THE LEVELS OF CONSCIOUSNESS
ARE CONSTANT

NEUROTIC			PRIMAL PERSON	
AWAKE	**ASLEEP**		**AWAKE**	**ASLEEP**
CORRECT SYMBOLIZATION OF EXTERNAL PERCEPTIONS AND INTERNAL REALITY	INCORRECT SYMBOLIZATION OF EXTERNAL PERCEPTIONS AND INTERNAL REALITY	INCORRECT SYMBOLIZATION OF INTERNAL REALITY 3RD LINE	CORRECT SIMULTANEOUS COGNITION AND PERCEPTION OF EXTERNAL AND INTERNAL REALITY	CORRECT APPRECIATION OF INTERNAL STATE
	EMOTIONALISM INTENSE ANGER TANTRUMS CRYING	REM SLEEP DREAMS 2ND LINE	APPROPRIATE CONNECTED FEELING	SLEEP NO DREAMS
	PSYCHOSIS PSYCHOTIC EPISODES	NIGHT TERRORS 1ST LINE	FLUID BODY ACCESS	DEEP SLEEP NO NIGHT TERRORS

out Pain we would only feel, not symbolize (incorrectly), awake and asleep. To feel means to *correctly* symbolize.

Once we understand that a level of consciousness exists with its specific kind of stored history of Pain, irrespective of whether we are awake or asleep, we can easily see the relationship of Primals and dreams. The more complete the Primal the less the need for REM dreams. Our beginning research already indicates that after a complete Primal REM dreams may diminish by seventy-five percent on the following night. Conversely, interrupted or incomplete Primals produce an extraordinary amount of dreams on the following night. That is because both the Primal and the dream may be dealing with *exactly the same feeling*, on the same level of consciousness. *To resolve the feeling during the day in a Primal means that we do not have to deal with it at night during sleep.*

The first thing to understand about dreams is that the feeling is always "right." That is, the feeling during the dream is the exact buried feeling stemming from specific events in our early life, only the feeling is unconnected. If it were a connected feeling it would be called a Primal and we would be feeling it. Indeed, Primal Therapy takes our dreams and nightmares, sifts out the feelings inside them and helps us make the proper connections. What I am saying is, we don't invent feelings during sleep. What we invent is the story to make the feeling plausible. And that story involves the various strands of our past life interwoven into an image which may compose itself from elements of our current life. The story is one aspect of the way the third-line consciousness deals with second- and first-line Pains. Part of the function of the third line is to symbolize external and internal input (our feelings). So, the noise of a siren during sleep might become a phone ringing during a dream story; and the Pain of suffocation during birth an episode of drowning during a nightmare.

One wonders about the miracle of a dream in which a whole story is run off without any conscious direction. How does the brain know what to do next, what turn to take, who should show up in the dream and what the outcome of the encounter should be? The answer is that the mind does not direct; it is *directed*, and it is directed by feelings ... the scenario run off in a dream is precisely that run off in waking life only it is more subtle and less condensed than in a dream. In short, the scenario *has already taken place*—in our early life—leaving a residue of feelings which are unresolved and which then later produce dreams as a symbolic recapitulation of those early life events. That is, the feelings constantly surge for connection and resolution and thus produce recurring scenarios which constantly end with the same lack of resolution as occurred in early life; the reason is that because there has been no conscious connection the feeling (and the symbolic acting in and out) remains unresolved. The dream makes a statement about our lives.

This is no different than playing out one's feelings in music or in painting. The source for the *content* of one's productions (be they dreams or art) is usually second line unresolved events. It is often true that an artist will be stuck in the same theme in the same way many of us are stuck in a recurring dream. The real way to grow, then, is to be able to connect and finalize feelings which keep us stuck. Primal Therapy does not alter creativity (since that is usually an innate talent which no therapy can undo—such as a perfect sense of pitch and timing for the musician) but it will change the form that the creativity takes. We have noticed, for example, that some artists who painted abstract pieces only when they started therapy were also the ones with fragmented noncohesive dreams. As cohesion took place it was reflected in both dreams and art.

Fragmented individuals usually "prefer" their fragmentation. They want to hear music that is free form, often nonmelodic and abstract, in the same way that very rigid people cannot stand it. They can't bear deviations from the norm and so prefer very predictable music. Non-feeling people "prefer" nonfeeling music since they want nothing in their lives to trigger off any emotion. But we can see that when we say that art or music is a matter of taste, what we are really saying is that most of us arrange our lives in terms of past scenarios which have left an unconscious legacy; and this legacy very much dictates our behavior including our interests and preferences.

We see this in the movies. We go to a dark place where there are no third line distractions—that is, the third line is lulled so as to permit second line access. A dream sequence is run off for us and we can cry, laugh or scream depending upon the emotion evoked. The fascination of the terror movie is that it reawakens in the viewer old fears in which the outcome is resolved favorably.

In Primal Therapy we can often tell where a patient is in terms of his level of consciousness by observing his dreams; those dreams foreshadow the material he is ready to feel because they are the first indication of the lower-line seepage into higher consciousness. They are an inchoate, as yet unconscious awareness of Primal Pain. Unconscious awareness is not a contradiction in terms; it means awareness on the second-line level of consciousness but without the full participation of the third.

An example of the point above: recently a patient had a dream where she meets an old friend who supposedly likes her a lot. Suddenly he flies into a rage and seems to hate her for no apparent reason. She wakes up full of anxiety over the strange behavior of her close friend.

The next day she had a Primal about her parents: people who were supposed to love her, she suddenly feels, really hate her; she has an agonizing Primal over the realization. The dream foreshadowed that conscious realization. The insights she had as a result of the feeling were how she remained a partial recluse from people whom she even suspected weren't completely friendly. She protected herself against that *old* feeling of hatred by this behavior. Isolation became her protection. Another insight she had was that she automatically expected hatred (unconsciously) from others and shrank into the background with any new social encounter. Until the dream and later the Primal she had no idea what propelled her behavior. It is rarely a symbolic dream which provides insight, interestingly enough. It is only a *connection* with a feeling which does it. And the insight is commensurate with the level of the feeling experienced.

For example, later on this patient had a Primal where she was immobilized in the canal at birth. She immediately understood that feeling immobilized under stress was the prototypic forerunner from shrinking back (and feeling unable to "go out") at birth. This was a first line insight. The Primal following her dream produced a second line insight. If she were in psychoanalysis she would be filled with third line intellectual insights (usually provided by the analyst).

The dream, the Primal and the insights all are indications that the patient was ready for the feeling. The third line was ready to accept lower line trauma; and the dream was our first indication of that readiness. If the first line trauma erupted without that readiness there would have been no insights, just more flooding and symbolization.

There was a second part of the dream described above: "A strange foreign little girl is on a street corner. I meet her and we fall in love immediately. I take care of her, help her across the street, buy her ice creams and even take her to my house. Her parents don't seem to care about all this. In the dream I feel, 'How strange that we seem closer to each other than the parents are to their own child.' "

The following day's Primal: "Mommy, just because I'm little I still have a soul. I need to be taken in your arms and be held and loved." She screams then, "It doesn't matter, Mommy, I'll take care of that little girl. She needs to be loved." Suddenly the insight: "*I'm* the little girl and I've always taken care of myself so I wouldn't feel that there was no one to take care of me. I wouldn't allow myself to get into any dependent situation where I had to rely on someone else. I would never work for anyone else. In short, *I took care of me* (that little girl) because no one else would. This is again related to feeling hated, trying to please them all the time so I wouldn't feel hated, but somehow knowing that I would have to fend for myself." The underlying feeling was that she always expected that little girl to be hated and that is why no one would take care of her; and, secondly, feeling there must be something radically wrong with her to be so hated. She shrank away from others before they found out what that secret was.

Here again the dream foreshadowed the emergence into third line consciousness of important feelings which had driven her behavior for a lifetime. The way the Pain was symbolized in the dream was an exact reflection of how she acted out symbolically in life . . . taking care of that "little girl." It is a crucial point since the symbolic activity on that level of consciousness is the same awake or asleep. Sleep does not change anything except reduce the range of possibilities for acting out the feeling. If she resolves the feeling she will neither act out during the day *nor symbolize it during sleep*. In short, she will sleep, not symbolically dream.

There are many of us who get stuck in the third line and believe that we cannot rely on others to give us what we need because we are genuinely disappointed by their conduct. We become fiercely independent without ever being able to reach back and feel why. One reason for this is that there is truly so much current disappointment from others that our independent behavior seems justified. And what is more, we create dreams in which others let us down all the time so that our independence *even while asleep* also seems justified. In other words, awake or asleep we *make* the conditions for our neurotic behavior.

After some months of therapy a patient may remember how he was left alone at the age of eight. His dreams before the session might involve stories of being forgotten or lost. He is getting ready to feel the rejection of him by his parents. As he begins his rejection Primals he may initially have nightmares of being left behind or lost somewhere; he is beginning to feel his true lifetime feelings. He no longer has to look lost or get others to make him feel wanted—in short, he no longer has to act out the feeling.

What is happening is a descent down the levels of consciousness, and dreams will reflect that descent. They are the barometer. We must remember that each of our feelings exists on all three levels, extending down the chain of consciousness. Neurosis (repressed Pain) erects barriers between those levels, compartmentalizing them from one another. It can happen that catastrophic current events can so shake the defense structure that first-line material is shaken loose, resulting in first-line dreams which occur out of sequence. The person will still have to feel on the second line in order to have an interconnected Primal consciousness.

Many of us have had the experience of waking from a nightmare and being temporarily "psychotic." We are so caught up in the terror of the dream that when we awake we still do not know what is real and what is not for a few moments. It may take several minutes until we get oriented; until we can shake off the *reality* of the dream and reconstitute our defenses. We can see from this momentary state the powerful impact of the first-line Pain and what it can do to us. The psychotic differs from the neurotic in that he is nearly always close to the first line and must find ways to deal with it.

I have stated that in a dream the feeling is always "right," so the first way we differentiate second and first-line feelings is by the nature and intensity of the Pain. If it is life and death then there is usually an element of the first line present. There are rare circumstances, however, when second-line Pain is life and death. In that event the second-line dream will have a life-and-death intensity. This is not the usual case, however.

The second key difference is in the way the feeling is handled in the dream. By and large, there are *no* coping mechanisms on the first line and this is reflected in the kind of dream where the person is totally helpless and where there is nothing he can do about the situation. One of my first-line dreams involved being inside a washing machine, winding around the central core in a thick fluid. There was nothing I could do except let the current take me. I shall go into other examples later.

The second-line dream has a more complex story and more often than not the person is trying to cope in one way or another. Maybe he is leading an army up a hill or he is fixing a broken machine or he has a rope to pull himself up a cliff. Coping mechanisms really do not develop in any profound way until the advent of the second line and that is why when in our dreams we are coping, however inadequately, we tend to think that the time of the frozen cerebral event we are dealing with took place after we became able to manipulate our environment.

There are more people in second-line dreams and the focus is not solely on physical events happening to us. There can be words (feeling-related words exist on the second line), arguing and complaining. There are more people because the events on the second line are more apt to be interpersonal rather than intrapersonal. Second-line dreams are apt to be more directly related to early interpersonal contact with our parents and relatives. If the first line is pushing, if the person is not well defended, then the quality of the Pain will intrude on the second line and we have a complex situation, with second-line symbols rationalizing a first-line Pain. Generally, there are *no words* in the first line dreams.

The bizarreness of the story helps differentiate the two levels of dreams. First-line Pains "strain" the third line into making up bizarre stories to cover and explain the horror; particularly since there is no access and no understanding that the Pain being dealt with comes from the.first second of life in this world or just before. Second-line dreams hold together better. They are more related to our everyday life and there is a cohesion about the stories. The people in them may well be people from our early life; whereas first-line dreams tend to be peopled with shadowy figures (less real), monsters and strange and forbidding animals.

First-line dreams have a directness about them which makes them easier to understand once we understand that they are related to events in and around birth or soon after. Being in a tunnel trying to find one's way out is one example. Being hung by a rope and choking to death is another. Drowning is a frequent first-line dream. Of course, there are embellishments to the story but the underlying feeling is usually very intense and quite clear, which may not be so with second-line dreams.

I want to reiterate: *all* feelings in neurotics descend to the first line. It is the defense system which bifurcates them and keeps them disconnected from the various levels of consciousness. A fully interconnected person (a hypothetical notion) would not have nightmares; if he had resolved most of his Pains then the kind of sleep he had would be different from neurotics. I think that he would be very much like an infant who spends most of his time in deep sleep where the most rest can be had. I believe that he would have little or no second-line dreams and that the amount of sleep he needed would be far less than what we have believed to be necessary. He would sleep the four or five hours of deep sleep which all of us sleep each night and that would be that. He would not have to deal with a lifetime of unresolved second-line feelings during REM sleep. This is not to say that there is no cycle during sleep in which we would not sleep on Stage 2; rather, that REM sleep would not be a dream stage, since many feelings on that level would be resolved. It would simply be a stage of sleep that is less deep. The well person would have much less of this stage of sleep.

I am going to give some examples of different kinds of dreams to illustrate the levels of consciousness they are associated with. I will not spend much time on examples as I find the endless exposition of dream material tedious and unnecessary. One patient had a recurrent dream in which he is being sent in a space capsule to another planet that is completely "strange and weird," and lit with strange and blinding lights. He is breathing painfully in this capsule and is feeling nauseous. He feels totally alone and afraid of this new experience. He feels, "This is the end of me." He steps out of the space capsule and tries to breathe voluntarily. There is a sense that strange gases are filling his lungs. The feeling of breathing on this new planet is "painfully different." There is a terrifying aloneness on the barren earth; no one to help or direct him.

This is a first-line dream, and the way we know is that it was a recurrent dream which ended with first-line Primals that finally made sense of it. "The strange planet was the world (and still is) I was being sent into. I split before I could 'feeling-wise' make the air transfer from the cord to my lungs." The aloneness is exactly that terrifying feeling infants have being on a new planet with new sounds, lights and sensations, strange voices and no one to comfort or hold them and make this new experience bearable.

Not so coincidentally this patient had been preoccupied for years with life on other planets. He wrote poems and had waking fantasies about outer space all the time. He was literally "spaced out," as he put it. The feeling during the Primal was, "I have never been able to make this world my world since my inception." We see here the correspondence of symbols between awake and asleep life. The feeling frozen in time produced circumscribed symbols frozen in time. Analysis of the symbols of the dream would hardly touch that stored memory of the first seconds of life. We may note about the above dream that the dreamer felt helpless in his situation. There was nothing he could do; he was being transported beyond his will into a new place—mirroring exactly what happened to him decades before. That is the key—the dream is an exact reflection of the experience: if there were nothing he could do during the birth sequence then that would be reflected in the later dream material. The feeling and form of the dream does not lie. *The symbols may become complex and deceptive, but so long as we understand that analysis of the symbols is unnecessary our job is made easier. All we have to do is to use the symbols to get to the underlying Pains.*

A second-line dream: A patient whose father died early in her life dreamed that she saw him in the supermarket. They had a conversation but she had the funny feeling that he shouldn't be there. She felt also how nice it was that he really wasn't dead. She had a Primal in which for the first time she felt how she never accepted the death, how somewhere in the back of her mind she expected him to come back some day and even thought for fleeting moments that people she saw on the street might be him. In the Primal she at last felt the finality of it all and how her needs for him would never be fulfilled. She realized that during her awake life she wanted older men to replace her father. She acted out symbolically wanting that daddy, wanting to be cared for and directed. The dream reflected her feelings which she had been acting out unconsciously for years. It wasn't the dream and its analysis which cleared up her acting out. It was resolving the feeling. The fact that she dreamed about her father indicated to us a readiness to come to terms with the finality of his loss; the feeling was reaching consciousness, albeit in slightly marked form.

Are there third-line dreams? I rather doubt it; or at least only in the sense that there are third-line symbols for lower-line feelings. For example, there are patients who dream about what they will do tomorrow: how they will handle their boss, tell him off, complain about the way he handles employees, etc. Generally, these occur just before sleep in some in-between state where third line is merging into second. Perhaps we might label it "quasi-sleep." The feelings in these dreams, however, are usually old second-line feelings—such as being crushed by authority (parents) and the need to strike back in some way. If the feelings behind the symbols were truly third line I would suppose that the person would be awake since his thoughts and feelings would be completely about current reality. One patient had dreams in which she was begging her boyfriend not to leave her. When she Primalled, she knew that the inordinate fear of his loss was an old second-line feeling related to her parents. If she were just afraid of the boyfriend's loss then she would feel it for what it was during the day and not have to dream about it. She dreamed about it because there was a Primal anlage influencing the situation. Having this dream helped her realize how she clung to her boyfriend out of an *old* anxiety and was conducting herself in exactly the way that would make him leave.

Another clue we have to the time of the trauma being relived in a dream is simply the age and situation of the dreamer. For example, if the dreamer is back in his old house in Brooklyn, if he is going to grammar school, if he is riding the same bike he had when he was ten, there is an indication of the period of the feeling involved.

If there is a timeless quality to a dream then we have to think about it as preverbal and first line in origin. Indeed, the loss of orientation to time, asleep or awake, makes me think of first line. One test of psychosis is called "reality testing"—does the patient know where he is and what day and hour it is? What causes the timelessness? I believe it is caused by being plunged into feelings which occurred before the infant could distinguish between thought and feeling; before he could form abstract concepts. Time, after all, is a concept [although awareness of time passage is a percept]. Feelings, then, become the total reality. There is no organized thought at that stage which can tell time and place. The feeling seems boundless and timeless; indeed, a fetus struggling to be born certainly has no concept about when his agonizing journey into life will end. He only senses relief when it is finally accomplished.

We often note the sense of timelessness of those on LSD, and this happens, I believe, precisely because out-of-sequence first-line Pains are starting to enter consciousness. These Pains are terrifying and fragmenting because they have no remembered times or social settings. They are only amorphous, nonconceptualized agonies which suffuse all third-line consciousness.

Being plunged into the time when thought and feeling were not distinguishable often results in an "out-of-space-and-time" experience. The person is catapulted into symbolism so that he imagines he is in a past life (living in ancient Egypt for example) or perhaps that he is a sperm. He might believe that he has finally transcended time and space and achieved "cosmic unity" or an out-of-body astral projection. Obviously, there is going to be more cohesion to a dream or idea which stems from a buried feeling related to an event which took place at the age of eight years than at two weeks. A two-week-old hardly has a cohesive mental structure.

A current reaction in a dream is only the symbolized form of the early real one. The feeling is terrifying and fragmenting *now* because it it was *then*. *If the event was first line, in which the infant could do nothing to stop the Pain, then the dream or nightmare will reflect that passivity and helplessness; in the dream the person will be helpless, as well.*

Here are a few other examples of dreams: "I am sitting in a public dining room somewhere. My girlfriend is at another table and I know she is going to leave (and she does) but she won't come over and talk to me about it. She sends a note saying that she is leaving but the explanation is about half a page of unintelligible hieroglyphics." The subsequent Primal this young man had was about his mother dying when he was only two. The hieroglyphics related to there being no understandable reason for her dying, no way he could understand it at that age. Of course, each element of a dream has some special meaning and I suppose we could spend days analyzing each separate element. But it is the leitmotif which is important; the general meaning it has for the person, his key repressed feelings and his life. This was an example of a second-line dream. It was organized, held no terror but was somewhat anxiety-producing. (Remember that dreams are our special creations, which leads me to think that creativity is largely a second-line phenomenon.) The dreamer in this case "made" his girlfriend not come over to him and created that half-page of hieroglyphics. I assume he could have made an intelligible letter while he was at it, but *feelings* dictated the characters, the plot and the scenario.

What is nearly always the case in frightening recurrent dreams is that the struggle never ends; because the feeling is not yet resolved. You have to battle an elephant and once he is slain there is a bear and then once he is done away with there is a tiger, and so on. There is usually the feeling of not quite making it about the dream: the sisyphean battle, which occurs because it is an attempt during sleep to conquer the feeling, which cannot be done until it is consciously felt and resolved. You never get away from the Nazis or the criminals who are after you no matter what; but once you *feel* how your parents never got off your back, how they never let up, for example, the Nazis will evaporate.

Here is an example of a dream with both third and second-line elements: "I am looking after two abandoned infants in a wood on the edge of a village. I go to a health-food store and buy them lots of nourishing food, but in doing so I face threats and hostility from the villagers. The person in the store is the only sympathetic character."

The feeling in this man was that he was really looking after himself and that produced hostility in others—specifically, as it turned out, he was troubled because coming to the Primal Institute to save his life had met with hostility from his family who were terribly upset by his choice. It seems that they were always upset by any of his attempts not to act in accordance with their dictates, which usually meant he had to act neurotically. The health-food store in this instance was the Institute.

Thomas De Quincey's *Confessions of an English Opium Eater* is replete with examples of drug dreams: "I was buried for a thousand years, in stone coffins, with mummies and sphinxes, in narrow chambers at the heart of the eternal pyramids. I was kissed with cancerous kisses, by crocodiles and laid, confounded with all unutterable slimy things, amongst reeds and Nilotic muds."* This seems to me to be classic first-line Pain. I am sure that to the neonate who has no real concept of time or when his birth struggle will end, it must seem like a thousand years. De Quincey says that crocodiles were always his special horror. He escaped from them sometimes but all of the feet of tables soon became crocodiles, their leering eyes staring at him. Here is a description of a birth feeling in another of his dreams: "Somewhere, I knew not where, somehow, I knew not how—by some beings, I knew not whom—a battle, a strife, an agony was conducting, was evolving like a great drama or piece of music, with which my sympathy was the more insupportable from my confusion as to its place, its cause, its nature, and its possible issue. I, as is usual in dreams, had the power, and yet had not the power to decide it. I had the power, if I could raise myself to will it; and yet again not the power, for the weight of twenty Atlantics was upon me . . . I lay inactive. Some greater interest was at stake; some mightier cause than ever yet the sword had pleaded or trumpet had proclaimed. Then came sudden alarms. I knew not whether from the good cause or from the bad; darkness and lights; tempests and human faces; and at last, with the sense that all was lost, female forms and the features that were worth all the world to me. And then everlasting farewells . . . and again and again reverberated everlasting farewells. And I awoke in struggles, and cried aloud, 'I will sleep no more!' " I can't think of a more eloquent description.

It is the function of both the dream and hallucination (as symbols) to attempt to make rational old nonrational stored events. Yes, hallucinations are attempts at rationality, even though they seem so irrational. They are attempts to explain incomprehensible, nonfocusable unconscious experiences which are bombarding the third line. If we understand the underlying feelings, the symbols of dreams and hallucinations make very good sense. They are only irrational because they are out of context.

It must be obvious that there can be no universal symbol which has the same meaning for each of us. Symbols are offered up as masks for feelings. The same dream symbol in two different people will have two different meanings depending upon the past experience of those individuals and the feelings which gave rise to the symbols. A stick can

---

*John E. George and John A. Goodson, *Great Essays* (Dell Publishing, New York, 1969), pp. 89 and 92.

mean a phallic symbol to one person who used sex as a defense and yet can simply be an object of fear to someone who was frequently beaten with sticks by a parent.

One must ask the question: Why is it that in a certain stage of sleep the body regularly goes into an alarm reaction with the heart pumping faster, the blood pressure rising, temperatures increasing and respiration more rapid? I believe it is for precisely the same reason that those phenomena occur when a person is about to Primal—because painful feelings are on the rise which threaten the organism, and that threat occurs unconsciously. This is a most important point because the system is galvanized automatically against unconscious Pain without any outside triggering stimulus. Somehow, our systems unconsciously recognize the danger of old Primal Pain and mobilize resources against it. During the day the constant threat may be manifest in a chronically elevated blood pressure or fast pulse. It isn't a natural function of REM sleep to have all our vital functions exacerbated; rather, it is because REM sleep permits second-line consciousness and its Pains to ascend. It is no accident that coronaries during sleep occur with greatest frequency during the long early morning REM period. They occur, I submit, because repression is at an ebb and the person is least defended against his Primal Pain. It is the very long REM period which also produces the most complex and symbolically entangled dreams. Again, I think that this is because the cortex must exert itself to cover Pain which is very near.

Another name for REM sleep is "paradoxical sleep"; meaning that the EEG pattern is similar to one who is awake. I think that the reasons are clear—REM sleep is not a true state of restful sleep but is only second-line consciousness operating without the help of the third-line orienting consciousness.

There have been many experiments indicating that there is a "rebound" when subjects are deprived of REM sleep. If a person is constantly awakened during REM sleep or if he is given drugs which block that stage then on the next sleep cycle he will have much more REM sleep, as though the body is trying to make up for its loss. He can also suffer from severe upset and transient psychosis. I do not think that the person is trying to make up for REM loss, however; it would seem that deprivation of REM produces a blockage of feeling outlets and the rebound we see derives from the suppression of *feelings,* not REM sleep per se. Failure to sleep well (insomnia) is a failure to repress certain cerebral functions.

I have not yet discussed the opposite of insomnia—sleep as defense. There are those who in times of stress just "conk out." And they report that their sleep is like that of someone drugged. It is not, in short, a regular sleep state. To explain this we must talk about prototypic situations, since sleep is one of the very few things an infant can do when he is in Pain. When he has cried his heart out for an hour in the crib for milk there is nothing much more he can do except sleep. But why that pattern persists may be due to even earlier events; namely, a birth process where the neonate was rendered helpless, passive and immobile. That passivity may become translated later on into a sleep defense given certain other conditions. Sleep is the most effective way to become unconscious of what is going on. Some people can just "tune out"; others may get themselves so busy and preoccupied that they are effectively unconscious. But others need a more total state—sleep.

We have treated cases of narcolepsy, the sudden falling asleep for inexplicable reasons. The treatment was successful. More than one patient has learned that sleep as a defense is prototypic. As they get close to a feeling of death at or around birth they "fall away." It is a total dysfunction of the second and third lines. Some say they sleep like death, not moving a muscle, and that sleep is analogous to the death state; while at the same time sleep is the most significant defense available against catastrophic Pain at birth. One person who actually died at birth (and many of us come very close to that in birth; far greater numbers of us than we had imagined) believes that his death-like sleep was a recreation of that early trauma *and its original response.* Many of us "go dead" in times of great stress. We became immobile, lifeless and completely passive. Sleep is a "remembered" prototypic reaction to early Pain. Some of us have to be totally unconscious to keep from being conscious of that early trauma. In the same way that some suicides use death as a defense against Pain, so on a lesser level do compulsive sleepers use sleep. Indeed, one seems to be an extension of the other—shutting oneself off totally against Pain.

Elsewhere I have cited experiments which indicate that patients under anesthesia are able to reproduce conversations they overheard while unconscious, if they are later hypnotized. This means to me that the anesthetic put them on a second-line level of consciousness. They felt no pain because the third line was not there to interpret the meaning of the bodily experience. These experiments are important in aiding the understanding of dream states and levels of consciousness, for they show that there is a level of consciousness which exists, attends to stimuli and comprehends those stimuli without the help of higher levels of consciousness. There is Pain on that level but it is not experienced as such since the Pain is disconnected from other levels of consciousness—and it is *connection* which makes a complete feeling painful. So long as it is disconnected it is registered unconsciously as a painful sensation but it is not experienced as a total feeling. What is unconscious, then, is simply a different level of consciousness disconnected. I suspect that with deeper levels of anesthesia the patient would not understand what the doctor was saying during surgery but still the cutting of the skin would be registered. The deeper anesthesia would put the patient on the first line where there is no mental comprehension, only the registering of physical events.

The surgical experiments also indicate that unconscious experiences remain and exert an unconscious force. It wasn't until someone thought of hypnosis that we could retrieve those experiences. We in Primal Therapy have known for years about those phenomena because any number of Primal patients have relived aspects of their surgery. Primalling is the conscious way we have found to penetrate levels of consciousness down to the first line. But hypnosis and chemical anesthesia do show us that there are levels of consciousness below the third line which register experience and influence higher levels of consciousness. For example, if certain suggestions are given to a patient under hypnosis about what he will later dream that night, there is a good chance that he will indeed dream about what has been suggested—all on an unconscious level. There is usually a symbolic wrapping to disguise the material but the symbolism tends to be obvious and quite related to the hypnotically suggested material.

In hypnosis a subject can be brought down to his second line by lulling the third-line here-and-now consciousness and he can recall in detail events which took place in his schoolroom at the age of six. Because of the dysfunction of the third line the hypnotic subject is totally inside that memory and is not aware of his present surroundings, *even though he is talking to the hypnotist.* Both he and the neurotic can seem to be quite aware, aware enough to carry on a conversation with someone else, yet be almost completely unconscious. So we must not be deceived; what looks like "awake" activity can be its opposite. Here again is a good example of the close relationship between the unconsciousness of sleep and the unconsciousness of awake activity. The hypnotic subject is operating on a lower level of consciousness and could just as well be in a dream.

The neurotic also operates on a disconnected level of consciousness but that level may be the third line, in which case he is stimulus-bound, responding only to current stimuli without internal reflection. The hypnotic subject may be operating from the second and part of the third line, but he has no separate (third line) awareness of what he is doing. Even though he is on the second line he cannot reflect, judge, analyze, or truly understand his behavior. Obviously, there are many neurotics in that position, as well.

If the subject is taken into a deeper trance (by suggesting something similar to sleep—"You are getting more relaxed, more drowsy," etc.) then he can be placed on the first line. Here there are no words nor conscious memory. Rather, the subject can be made totally rigid so that he can be stretched between two chairs with only his head and ankles being supported.

The hypnotist tacitly recognizes discrete levels of consciousness even though he may not label them as such. What the hypnotist is doing is knocking out the third line, and dealing with the second line, by and large, funneling in input on that second level, then putting the subject back on third line with a new unconscious experience which will be acted out on cue in the post-hypnotic state. I doubt if that could be done with truly interconnected people. Hypnosis is an excellent example of split consciousness and unconscious motivation.

Dramatic evidence of the lower levels of consciousness is found when female labor patients coming out of anesthesia begin to scream their real feelings. Without anesthesia, those feelings might surface in the person's dream life. "I'll never let you touch me again," is one example offered by a patient.

The therapeutic implications of the above should be clear. There are levels of consciousness which lie below conscious awareness which exert a force on all behavior, awake and asleep. Bad dreams are the neuroses of sleep, just as nightmares tend to be the transient psychoses. In Primal Therapy we sometimes use dreams to get the patient back into his feelings. *A Primal is the translation of the dream back into its original form.* In therapy we have the patient tell the dream as though it were happening "now." Doing this helps him sink into the feeling of the dream and then down into the early connection to the feeling. Later on in therapy dreams are not dealt with extensively because patients can get to their feelings straightforwardly without any deviations. Advanced patients can dream, sink into the feeling while asleep, Primal and make the connections—all on the sleep level of consciousness.

One of the more significant facts about Primal Therapy is that as the new patient is put into isolation before his therapy begins, as his usual defenses are removed, he begins to dream and nightmare as never before —indication to us that his feelings are on the rise and further corroboration of the relationship between buried feelings and dreams. When a patient has an incomplete Primal for one reason or another (if he is interrupted) we can be sure that the excess Pain will find its way into a dream later that night. Here again we see how dreams absorb excess Pain and what an important function they play. They are the symbolic "acting in," counterparts to the awake symbolic "acting out" of Primal Pain. They are, in short, release forms, and of course when they are dammed up artificially, say by drugs, there will be a serious rebound. It is not an accident that the same drugs which prevent REM sleep also prevent seizures—massive doses of amphetamines produce an overload and a complete shutdown. Barbiturates also shut down the gates holding back Pain. These drugs are used to clamp the lid on lower levels of conscious activity; obviously they are only temporary solutions, and there is always going to be a rebound of feelings—feelings which create all the REM activity and the cerebral activity resulting in (psychogenic) seizures. All this activity takes place because of the divergence of feeling and symbol. The further apart they are (first-line feeling, third-line symbol), the more cerebral symbolic activity required.

It is interesting to note that several applicants for therapy have noted on their autobiographies that after taking certain tranquilizing drugs such as Valium or Librax they are apt to have severe dreams. What is happening, I believe, is that these drugs are depressing limbic activity; since it would appear that the limbic gate is instrumental in holding back first-line Pain the result seems to be the rise of first-line traumas symbolized in dreams—suffocation, strangulation, etc.

There are those who claim not to dream. Evidence indicates that we all dream whether we are aware of it or not. Those who do not recall any dreams are generally walled off from even the symbols of their feelings—the compartmentalization in these cases seems complete. These individuals seem to have no access even to their second line. We expect these highly repressed individuals to be more difficult patients. For them, we may use other techniques to get them to their feelings—first-line approaches such as with smells, music or photographs reminiscent of early experiences.

We must remember that symbols are derivatives of feelings and are therefore appropriate once we find the feeling. This holds true of both awake and asleep activity. Mental illness is inappropriate symbolization. The point of Primal Therapy is to match the symbol to the Pain through feeling so that the person becomes real. A Primal connects a second-line symbol to a second-line Pain, or a first-line symbol to a first-line Pain. *Connection* is the point. Once the Pain driving it is felt, the symbol becomes redundant, and in this way we are able to face reality clearly. That is why patients have less symbolic dreams in Primal Therapy as their treatment proceeds; and this lessened symbolism is a good index of therapeutic improvement because it indicates that the person is *feeling* and is connected. He therefore has less need to be symbolic in a neurotic way. This is true for both waking and sleeping states. Lessened symbolism is a total, organic state and not something confined to sleep, therefore nonsymbolic dreams make a simultaneous statement about a person's sleeping and waking behavior. Advanced patients with first-line access no longer have nightmares and also no longer have sudden bursts of temper or other irrational behavior while awake. It is all of a piece.

The integration of old feelings (meaning interconnection on all lines) not only means lessened symbolism but that lessened symbolism means greater longevity. There is less Pain constantly activating and enervating the system. It is not an accident that advanced Primal patients show an overall lessened brain-wave frequency and amplitude. I think this is a result of integration of feelings so that as the person matches the feeling with the appropriate symbol or thought there is less overall cerebral activity to mask and repress those feelings. In short, there should be a correlation between dream symbolism and the nature of cerebral activity shown on an electroencephalograph. We shall attempt to investigate this later on.

Freud thought that the analysis of dreams was the via regia to the unconscious. It turns out that dreams are a good road to the unconscious; but it is not their *analysis* that provides the access—analysis is only staying on the top level of the interchange. Feelings are what is unconscious, and feelings are the end of the road.

D. ON PSYCHOSIS

Recently, at the Primal Institute, a woman was "freaking out" on the floor of the waiting room while I was working in my office. She was thrashing about, screaming and wailing. After about half an hour of this, I interrupted the dictation of a letter to ask my secretary who the patient was. She did not know and nor did anyone else. It turned out that she was not a patient at all but merely someone who had dropped in. She failed to make any sense when we questioned her and continued intermittently with her mumbling and wailing. It was then that we decided that she was having a psychotic episode and, for her own protection, called to have her taken to a psychiatric ward.

Had this woman been our patient no one would have bothered to stop and question her as it is common for our patients to Primal almost anywhere in the Institute. The significance of this account is that it shows how similar are the outward manifestations of a Primal and a psychotic episode. In a sense, a Primal is a kind of psychotic episode in that the person is not "here" but rather is living a scene completely out of the past. Both the person in a Primal and the psychotic have lost their third-line orientation, the former temporarily and the latter almost permanently. The psychotic has no third line to tell him that he is in the past reliving old feelings and scenes, whereas the person in a Primal can bring himself out of that state and back into the here and now at will. Let me illustrate this by reference to a patient who had a difficult experience while Primalling at home. The noise of his crying carried to the neighbors who summoned the police in the belief that something dire was happening next door. When the police knocked on the door and demanded to know what was going on, the patient, from reliving a painful scene that had taken place when he was only a few years old, returned to the present, as he put it, "in a flash." His third-line consciousness was suddenly brought back into play and, though he had been completely immersed in the terrors of the past but a second before, he was able to take immediate stock of what was happening and offer the two policemen a very calm and rational explanation. Had his feeling in fact been a psychotic experience he would probably not have been able to do this.

In a sense a Primal is a controlled episode, since a patient knows that it is not something that you do in a supermarket, for instance. A psychotic, on the other hand, is not selective as to where he has his so-called Primal. On those rare occasions when a patient has a Primal in public, he becomes an immediate candidate for the funny farm. A policeman once stopped a patient who was on his way to the Institute to give him a speeding ticket. He was unusually harsh and the patient began Primalling. The logical assumption was that the person was psychotic and he was promptly delivered to the local psychiatric hospital.

It took many phone calls to get him released. The point here is that feelings are such an anathema in this society that when a person is seen having his feelings in public, the assumption is that he is insane. The supposedly sane thing we all do is to keep our feelings buried. When feelings get very much out of control, we hospitalize the person and pump him full of drugs until they are squashed again.

A distinction can be made between neurosis and psychosis on the basis of the ability or inability of the person to reconstitute the third line. For example, let us suppose one patient has the feeling in bed at night that there are robbers in the closet coming to get him. He makes a wide track around the closet door when he goes to the bathroom and has the impulse to nail the closet door shut. This would seem like a psychotic delusion . . . someone who acts on a total fantasy. Yet when asked about the delusion the person will say, "I know my ideas are crazy and irrational but I can't help myself." This means that he has a third-line consciousness which appraises his false beliefs and reaffirms reality for him. He is neurotic. The psychotic does not. He *believes* there are robbers in the closet, does not think his ideas are bizarre or wrong, nails up the closet and buys a gun to shoot "them." He has no separate third-line consciousness to differentiate reality from unreality. For a psychotic there is nothing to help him separate one reality—the past, from another reality—the present. One conclusion we can draw about psychotics, then, is that they cannot properly "time" their episodes. They cannot march to the Institute to feel and fall into the past. They are in the past all the time. What they need is to climb into the present. Because they have too much Pain to feel one specific feeling at a time, their Pain level needs to be brought down in some way at first. It is my understanding that patients on the verge of a psychotic break are being flooded by catastrophic first-line Pain. They need to be helped to hold back that material, and to be allowed to focus on and feel more specific, later-developing, lesser Pains. The psychotic must continually deal with out-of-sequence Pain. He is the one who comes in and has birth Primals in the first week because his gating mechanisms are overtaxed and thereby rendered inoperative. The neurotic, on the other hand, seems to go to his Pain in an ordered, sequential way; lesser Pains first, catastrophic earlier Pains last.

The reasons that the psychotic cannot properly gate are complex. First, the sine qua non, is horrible birth trauma; anoxia at birth, for example, affects the hippocampus of the limbic system so that the pain-dampening system may have been weakened in a permanent way. Then there is what I call compounding, where there is catastrophic Pain at each step of the developmental ladder. Drunken fathers, beatings, poverty, divorce and boarding school, rejection by peers and teachers, being left alone very early while both parents work; the reader can fill in the blanks. All of this overburdens the gating system so that Pain cannot be held in its proper silo. Rather, lower-line Pain invades current consciousness, blotting out perception, causing hallucinations and delusions. Thus, the past blots out the present.

An hallucination involving images such as seeing blood or "visions" is usually the past perception of a preverbal first-line trauma superimposed on the present. One patient, for example, heard a constant scratching noise in her head. This symptom indicated to us the possibility that a very early trauma was pressing itself into third-line consciousness. This would be an unlikely symptom for the neurotic whose consciousness tends to be infiltrated more by second-line feelings, with the result that his ideas and perceptions are not as bizarre as an hallucination. The gates are working in the neurotic so that catastrophic perinatal traumas stay effectively buried.

The patient who heard the constant scratching and who had been previously diagnosed as an hallucinating psychotic had a birth Primal on her second day of therapy in which she felt the forceps scraping harshly across her ears during birth—the origin of her hallucinations. It might take a solid neurotic more than a year to arrive at the point she arrived at in two days. The fact that she had that symptom and the fact that she could get to it immediately in therapy was due to a weakened gating system. We can see that there is a very close resemblance to the hallucinated symptom and the real early trauma. The patient in the case above was still hearing the scratching—only now it was out of context. There was little abstract symbolism because the Pain was not totally blocked and rerouted by a series of well-functioning gates.

I have already indicated that usually being on the verge of a "nervous breakdown" means that defenses are broken down and the person is open to his Pain. For the prepsychotic this often means open to first-line Pain. We may all have first line Pain but the prepsychotic has inadequate gating so that his very early Pains are no longer compartmentalized and are constantly ready to burst through. In the fairly well integrated neurotic it is the second line Pains which are threatening to rise into consciousness. One reason for the inadequate gating in the prepsychotic is compounding, the effects of which I have already discussed. Another reason may be catastrophic later trauma—death of both parents in a violent way, for example. Still another cause is the previous constant use of marijuana or LSD which has permanently altered the gating system.

The prepsychotic or psychotic has partial access in some ways to his first line, bypassing the second. We see this in patients in various forms. One is the evidence of bruising as discussed in the Appendix. That is, as the patient gets into feelings of being beaten as a child bruises suddenly erupt on the skin in the exact place where the child was beaten. This means there is facile access to the first line. It is a sign to us of both great Pain and fragile gating system. One person, for example, started to have a "nervous breakdown" before therapy. Two red spots appeared on his forehead and he immediately assumed that he was the devil with horns. He became "the devil." He began to damn everyone and everything. His role took on bizarre proportions and he truly became psychotic. Much later he had a Primal in which he relived his delivery and the two red marks reappeared. They were the marks of forceps. What had happened was that horrible birth Pains were coming up which he could not deal with at the time which ultimately drove him crazy. All that happened was that the *physical access*, via the forcep marks, became apparent. The Pain itself did not rise to consciousness to become connected but the concomitants did. He focused on the red marks and became the devil because he was also into feelings of being unloved and being a terrible person because he was so unloved. He damned everyone except his parents in his psychotic state. He was hospitalized and given shock treatment, which of course bolstered his weak gating system and drove back the early Pains. The shock made his past inaccessible for the time being, meanwhile creating more catastrophic Pain which had to be felt later on ... the Pain of many severe electrical jolts. The shock did help drive away his bizarre ideation, however. Here is what he said later: "After a series of electric shocks I was numb, flat and cold. I went home with everything delicate and recent in my mind blotted out. Psychotic ideas, trivia and important memories were lost. Behavior modification had its day."

Some time later this man began working in a chemical plant. The fumes were quite noxious. He began to have another psychotic episode and refused to drink milk. He was convinced that the milk was poisoned. This became an elaborate delusion in which people were trying to poison him. More shock and more hospitalization. Years later he had the Primal ... he was sucking at his mother's breast at the age of three months and her milk was sour. The experience was very unpleasant and he could not eat nor could he communicate the problem. He kept getting sick everytime she fed him and no one knew what was the matter since she had enough milk and just assumed that the child was being cranky and spoiled.

What triggered the episode? Clearly, it just wasn't noxious fumes in the chemical plant. Let's hear how he explains it: "I was thirty-five years old. Easy credit plans and unbelievable medical expenses from my daughter's auto accident (also a major trauma) were forcing me into bankruptcy. I was totally absorbed in an extremely difficult chemical pollution problem which had created a crisis for the company. Acid fumes in the plant soured my taste and smell. Tears flowed sour; my skin itched and noisy equipment bombarded my ears as I dug into the bowels of the plant."

He cracked up, and the sour fumes triggered off the early breast feeding trauma which, because it was not connected, became elaborated into the poisoning delusion. A few years later he had a heart attack which he calls the "psychosis of the body." I think that shock therapy which drove the Pains back deep into the system may have contributed to that heart attack. The shock permitted no other outlet and was a great trauma in itself. This man is Primalling on his own and has recently written: "I am no longer afraid of psychosis. It is only a symptom of Pain which can be eliminated with Primals."

We need to keep in mind that psychotic ideation stems from repressed feelings. One person who broke down before therapy became obsessed by license plates. She always looked for the number "4" on the plate and believed that it was a secret message to her from some hidden force. She kept saying it meant, "What's it all for? What's it all for?" The hidden force was those hidden feelings, and those feelings were, "I've tried and tried and nothing happens. I can't get them to love me so what's it all for?" "Four" became the trigger stimulus for the old feeling. In psychosis the person is so vulnerable that almost any stimulus can set off an old feeling because the gates are lowered and feeling is constantly near the surface. Only Primals could dissipate the false notion about the license plates and their message. This person finally felt the early hopelessness that she had blocked very early in her life.

A patient who has the delusion each night that his father is sitting on his bed talking to him is very close to his real need, but again, out of context. The underlying feeling may well be, "Stay with me, Daddy," a feeling resulting from being abandoned at a tender age by his father. The "delusion" is an out-of-sequence reality. If he could have felt it "back then," he might not be thinking in this way now in the closed ward of a psychiatric hospital. What he now gets for his ill-timed Primal (called a delusion) is a drug to suppress his truth, his Pain and his chance to get well.

He suffered from a so-called "thought disorder" because his thinking was unfortunately in accord with a past reality, not the psychiatrist's current one. When Pain is suppressed by drugs, the "thought disorder" clears up because that thinking is only an outgrowth of ascending Pain. Here again we see how close to reality a current, bizarre thought might be. This is not to say that psychotic symbolism cannot get very complex. It can and does. When it does, the person has less chance of health only because the amount of underlying Pain has produced inordinately convoluted symbolism. It is the specific connections that ultimately dissipate psychotic symptoms; the feelings are not complex and are relatively few. Thus, no matter how convoluted the symbolism, it all evaporates once the feeling underlying it can be felt and connected. The woman who heard the scratching in her head would have continued to hallucinate perhaps for a lifetime if she had never been able to make that specific connection to her birth experience.

One of the reasons that people start to feel like they are going crazy when early Pains come up is that they cannot imagine that what happened to them as a child, "ordinary" things when viewed from the perspective of adulthood, could be so catastrophic. It is difficult for us as adults to imagine that when father yelled at us as a child it meant disaster. Or that when mother refused to speak to us for a whole day at age six the Pain was enormous and catastrophic. We forget that then they were our whole world and their rejection was a matter of life and death for us. We tend to discount the enormity of those experiences. What happens when those Pains arise is a tendency to place "out of space," "out of time" meanings on them, instead of feeling how commonplace were those terrifying events.

When a first-line trauma is triggered, the exact early reaction to that trauma also comes up. So, when a second-line Pain triggers off something else which took place very early, before the child had a proper conception of space and time, there would be a tendency to imagine that he is undergoing an "out of space and time" event. Because he cannot connect and feel the Pain of a trauma that happened at the age of three months, he has indeed "transcended" his own reality. The result may be psychotic ideation or the feeling of going crazy.

There is often an underlying symbolic theme in psychotics, namely, that there is some unseen, intangible force "out there" which is going to destroy them. It used frequently to be the Communists, while now it is often the Mafia. Both these groups are symbols to the psychotic precisely because they are unseen and their power is not measurable. The psychotic feels overwhelmed by an overpowering force; what he does not realize is that it is his feelings which constitute that force, not an outside enemy. The symbolism can get fancy—"There are yellow men about to throw a switch to destroy my brain"—but the underlying theme is usually that "they" are going to "hurt me" or "blow my mind." He is right in many ways; he is about to feel hurt and his mind is about to be blown by that hurt—only the battle is inside him.

Let us examine the complexity of paranoid ideation to see psychotic thinking at work. A patient who had recently entered Primal Therapy became very suspicious of his therapist; suspicious to the point of paranoia. In his application and pre-therapy interview there had been no sign of this. But on the second day of treatment, he was convinced that the therapist was trying to trick him. He wanted to know why a chair was placed in a certain position; why a doll was moved into a corner. He was convinced that there was some special significance to the fact that a black pillow was placed for his head. "Black" meant certain ominous things. All of this had a paranoid quality. Yet after the session his ideation left. What happened in that session to make him appear to be psychotic? The therapist was bringing him close to his feelings but, as his gating system was inadequate, the feelings he was about to drop into were the overwhelming Pain of being left alone just after birth. He was not going to feel being criticized at the age of eight as some neurotic might have done. Rather he sensed that he was going to be overwhelmed and his mind called on all its resources for protection. What the patient was doing was testing the therapist to make absolutely sure that he could be trusted so that he could then feel safe enough to fall into that black, nameless void. Everything he did and said at that point seemed bizarre because great Pain was pushing his behavior. He conjured up all sorts of strange questions to make sure that the therapist knew what he was doing. We would never have known about this if we had not helped the patient to know about such feelings and their effects and then helped him into them ever so gradually. In the usual psychiatric setting, the patient would be considered a paranoid and drugs would have been administered to help him suppress his Pain and thereby his chance at ultimate recovery.

The reason that I characterize the patient above as showing a "paranoid reaction" rather than as being a "paranoid schizophrenic" is due to his ability to reconstitute the third line. He is able to stop after a feeling and reorient himself in the present. Under stress he reacts in a bizarre way but that reaction is not indicative of a permanent state. The therapeutic implication of this is that with severely disturbed patients it is necessary at times to steer them away from early feelings and help them reconstitute their third line. Discussions in the present about current problems are helpful; having them discuss the feelings they have just had in a session to analyze and integrate them is likewise helpful. There are a number of specific techniques used by Primal Therapists to keep first-line Pain from becoming disintegrating to the patient. Unlike the neurotic whose gates must be systematically dismantled in order to help him descend into feeling, the psychotic or pre-psychotic needs to have his defense system bolstered so that instead of being flooded by Pain, he can focus on specific hurts and experience them in a Primal. To blow open the deep gates too early produces psychosis. Once that is allowed to happen it will take a much longer time to get the patient strong enough to experience Primals sequentially. This is precisely what happens with the use of LSD, but it also happens when a pre-psychotic (someone with a great load of Pain and an inadequate gating system) is isolated for a long period, when he is removed from friends and family, when he is abruptly stopped from taking tranquilizers, alcohol or cigarettes. For all these reasons the preparation for the Primal treatment of a pre-psychotic (someone who usually has a mental hospital history) is often the opposite of the neurotic. He is not isolated nor is he stopped from smoking. A great deal of discussion is had with these patients all along the way to strengthen their intellectual, third-line defenses. It has occurred to me that what the heroin addict, psychogenic epileptic and pre-psychotic all have in common is that they are continually dealing in their own way with ascending first-line Pain; thus the usual neurotic defenses cannot work for them. If the epileptic and pre-psychotic were on heroin, I doubt if they would suffer their mental and physical symptoms. But if the heroin addict were forced to kick the habit suddenly, he might develop either convulsions (as they often do) or bizarre mental ideation.

The substrate for prototypic paranoid reaction may occur very early in life. If there is trauma at birth where the fetus is harshly handled or cannot easily get himself born, he may consider the world unsafe and threatening. The world becomes hurtful and something he must protect himself against. There are no words as yet for such a feeling, simply a general sense that the world is potentially threatening. Later, when there are words, the child may be able to conceptualize his feeling. If his parents really don't like him and are really out to hurt him, then his prototypic orientation is reinforced. With enough hurt he may become paranoid, feeling that people in general are out to hurt him. They really were: he is just forgetting what year it is. The paranoid reaction to life, however, may have begun long before he could think and say, "They are out to hurt me." He was hurt from the start.

When I state that the psychotic has forgotten what year it is I am being quite literal, for one of the functions of third-line consciousness is to orient us in time. Pure feeling has no notion of time. Dreams as an outgrowth of feeling do not contain abstractions such as time. There may be a sense of waiting in a dream but not of exact time. This is probably why there are seldom if ever causal notions in a dream, rather just a continuous series of events, one after another, with no third-line connecting links to explain the transition for us. When the psychotic operates below the third line, he is bereft of those functions that separate past time from present time for him and therefore the present is only symbolic of the past. The paranoid must disregard all reality that contradicts his delusion because his old feeling *is* his overarching present reality.

I have stated that symbolism in psychosis can be inordinately complex. For example, a patient can hallucinate seeing death wherever he turns, or he can see death masks where they don't exist, or perhaps he sees skeletons on the wall. The Pain he may be dealing with is indeed death—that is, the near-death events around birth which cannot be kept at bay, for one reason or another. Somehow life circumstances might have challenged his defenses. A long illness might force someone who is constantly on the move to finally sit still so that all he has left to do is feel. Loss of a child or a spouse can also precipitate psychosis. But in any case, the person becomes preoccupied with seemingly strange notions. The severity of his condition can usually be judged by the amount of generalization involved. If he sometimes sees skeletons in the faces of his friends he is apt to be less sick than if he sees death masks on the walls or the rugs. That is, if he is not merely misperceiving but hallucinating everywhere, the Pain is greater and the defenses are weaker. If the ideation is still more bizarre, he might have the notion that someone in the next apartment is ready to throw a switch to kill him. He may still be dealing with the death event and the feeling of impending death (ultimately, the Primal feeling of impending death at birth) but he has stretched the story into full-blown paranoia. The preoccupation with death is coming from an unknown source—

the unconscious. However, because he has no idea that early death events continue on in mental life, he has no choice but to imagine that the source is outside himself. Sometimes it is reassuring for a patient just to understand that those early Pains remain in the brain as reverberating circuits.

When a person is reliving first-line Pains in his Primals, then all stimuli take on first-line meanings. This is also true on the second line. For example, when a patient holds onto the therapist's legs during a session, he may feel for the moment that he is holding onto the daddy who kicked him away when he was first learning to crawl and wanted to approach his father. Once the Pain is felt, however, the patient sits up and talks and then he can hold onto the therapist's legs without any such meaning entering the situation. The psychotic, however, is stuck in his first-line meanings. Events in the now *continually* have first- and second-line meanings to him and that is why his notions seem bizarre to someone like a therapist who is only operating on the third line. The psychotic cannot sit up later and detach himself from the first line and view those feelings objectively; that is what makes him psychotic. Primal patients who feel they are going crazy generally know that they are dealing with very early Pains and that it is possible to feel them. Even when for the moment they cannot connect to those Pains they can be reassured and have less anxiety through the knowledge of what is the source of their tension and Pain.

One of the hallmarks of the psychotic state is the inability to concentrate and the general distractability. Both result from a loss of cohesion and are pretty much the same thing. If we can imagine the third line as a puzzle put together (which is cohesive), and if we can imagine lower-lines Pain thrusting upward against the puzzle to disrupt its organization and cohesion, we may get an idea of what the problem is in psychosis. What happens from that force or thrust is that the puzzle fragments (the third line integrates the Pain) and you are now left with many pieces which are just separate entities and do not fit into a whole picture any longer. In psychosis when there is that lack of cohesion the person then attends to each separate stimulus or idea apart from any overall cohesive structure. He may start out with a perfectly straight notion and then say something bizarre which is a complete non sequitur. The reason that happens is that lower Pain is constantly pressing upward and there is just no adequate defense system to buffer it. The psychotic and borderline psychotic do not know that it is Pain erupting or often even that there is a pressure coming up from below; rather he only experiences the *results* of that pressure in the form of a scattering of thoughts. He cannot keep his mind on one thing because that pressure intrudes and drives his mind elsewhere again. And where the mind goes may be toward a direct symbolic derivative of an old feeling. "I know why you are wearing glasses today. So I won't spit in your eye," is an example.

The third line is so weak in the psychotic (and borderline) that when they first wake up in the morning they often do not know where or who they are for a few moments; whereas the neurotic wake up only feeling slightly apprehensive or fearful.

Psychosis (and the borderline states) can be treated in many ways. A third-line treatment is removal to a quiet, stable environment away from all stress—usually a sanitarium or mental hospital. Occupational therapy (keeping their minds away from the Pain) is still another third-line therapy. The problem with removal to a place where third-line pressure is removed (sometimes, therefore, allowing the development of third-line defenses to handle the Pain) is that the person is also removed from his loved ones (or his family who may be unloving but are still his family). If any of us can imagine what it feels like to be removed from all of our familiar surroundings and our families and put away in a building or dormitory that is not built for human scale (but for mass scale) we can get some idea of the tremendous pressure on the patient (even if he is not aware of it in his psychotic state) and why he often becomes "institutionalized" and worse. The psychotic is still human with human needs.

The second-line (and first-line) treatment can be drugs, as I have discussed elsewhere, or a variety of cathartic techniques which include yelling and screaming in a group encounter (provided they can make some contact), music therapy (having catatonics move to music) or exercise programs. I believe that exercise is very important therapy for the psychotic. It is a first-line release form and can help to drain a substantial amount of tension. It may be possible for the psychotic and pre-psychotic to work off enough tension through jogging to stop the enormous pressure on his third line. It may help him to sleep which is very important for his overall strength and it allows the third line some respite to organize itself. One of the reasons that megavitamins seem to help is that they strengthen the general physical ability of the person so that he can better cope with Pain. None of the release forms discussed, however, deal with the causes; none exorcise the Pain. The Pain will be there for a lifetime without Primals. That is why they are always vulnerable to further breakdown even if they should recover for the moment and make a satisfactory social adjustment.

A psychotic break is a breakdown of the gating system. The difference between it and a Primal is that in the latter the gates are opened slowly and systematically. Nevertheless, once the gate is open both the Primal person and the psychotic are in the past. The psychotic is in a permanent, disconnected Primal state. The Primal person connects first and second line to third. He has integrated the past with the present. The psychotic's present is disintegrated by his past. The slow integration of Pain is the necessary and sufficient treatment for psychosis.

E. ON SEXUALITY AND PERVERSIONS

Sexuality and sexual behavior do not always go hand in hand. Sexuality is a matter of feeling, but sexual *behavior* can take place with or without feeling. Sexuality is only part of a general ability to feel in our bodies. It is something *of* the body, not an activity apart from it. We can, therefore, see how shutting off any experience of Pain in the body affects sexuality in the same way, for to shut off Pain is to shut off feeling.

By definition, every neurotic has a sex problem, overt or not, because every neurotic has repressed Pain and thus a diminished ability to feel. The degree of repression will determine how deeply sexuality is affected. Thus, there are degrees of frigidity and impotence ranging from having no sexual desire and no ability to function sexually; to some sexual desire but no orgasm; to some sexual activity with occasional orgasm; to orgasm brought on only by masturbation but not by penetration of the penis; to orgasm with the aid of specific fantasies and finally, to full orgasm with penetration. To compound the problem there are many men and women who have orgasms during sexual intercourse who are unaware that those orgasms are not the result of fully sexual experiences. They are tension releases—tension which has been eroticized. Rather than encompassing the whole body, these orgasms are generally localized.

Even though someone has a particular sex problem such as premature ejaculation, the real root of the problem may not lie in the area of sex at all. For the most part the problem is the result of a welter of Painful experiences which predate any sexuality. As I have said elsewhere,* there can be no sexuality until there *is* sexuality; in other words not until puberty is reached and the sex glands have been activated.

The idea that sexual functioning is directly affected by an ability to feel is not an esoteric theory; it is the result of observing hundreds of patients with all kinds of sexual problems. We have seen how, through Primals that seem to bear no direct relationship to sex, those problems can be solved. One patient had Primals about her inability to have an orgasm when having intercourse with a man despite the fact that she could easily come when masturbating alone. The connections that she made showed that the original Pain had nothing to do with sex. It had been very unsafe for her to ever lose control or be spontaneous in her parents' presence, so that when she grew up she was unable to "let go" enough to have an orgasm in the presence of another person. To think of sexuality as something apart from the body's ability to feel, and to imagine that the sexual experience can transcend the body and achieve a viability of its own are mystical and unsound notions.

In mature sex all three levels of consciousness are involved and the body functions without inhibition. There is proper hormone output and balance (level 1), there is an emotional involvement with another person (level 2), and there are the techniques of love-making (level 3). Rather than having the levels integrated with each other, neurotics usually have one level predominant over the others so that their sex life is idiosyncratically lopsided.

The person with the predominant first line is commonly known as an "animal." He engages in indiscriminate sex with anyone at any time because his sexuality is totally inner-oriented. He does not relate to people except insofar as they relieve his need. He relates to himself. Compulsive masturbation is another example of this. It is purely tension relief, not sexuality. The penis is merely the valve through which tension from a wide variety of sources is discharged. One patient explained how sometimes when masturbating he felt an urge to vomit, defecate and urinate almost simultaneously. In his own words, he wanted "everything to flow out of him" in the same way that he had always wanted his feelings to come out of him throughout his life and in the same way that, originally, he had wanted to "flow" from his mother's womb. His supposedly sexual activity had very little to do with sex.

The "second-liner" is into symbolic sex: indulging in perversions

---

The Feeling Child (Simon and Schuster, New York, 1973), p. 161.

which allow him to act out second-line Pains. He may "dress up," exhibit himself, make obscene phone calls, whip his sexual partners and so on. He is acting out his childhood in the present, but he needs a certain set of circumstances in order to get aroused and "get off." He needs his dress, or to show his penis on the street. In putting on the clothes of a woman, a man may in some cases be trying to get close to a woman (his mother) but, because his mother was cold and forbidding (causing an inability to make friendships with women in adult life), he has to turn himself into the warm, touching mother he never had.

The person with a predominant third line is generally into symbols. Like the "second-liner" only more so, he has split sexuality—the split of the body and the mind—so that he requires images and symbols in his head to help him gain access to his body. So, he or she must hear certain stories and perhaps "dirty" words or look at "dirty" pictures. One may have to envisage the other as a movie star or some other similar figure. In these cases, the relationship is mainly to symbols and mental fantasies with only a minimal sex drive. When the third-liner has sex it is mostly intellectualized and the relationship he has with his partner can be termed a "third-line relationship," a "meeting of the minds." The third liner often needs drugs or alcohol to become sexual.

The loss of sexuality begins at birth and probably before. A mother's tension adversely affects her fetus and alters its hormone balance. This imbalance can affect the general way the newborn meets life; thus it is possible that because male-female hormone output is altered (even imperceptibly) a male neonate is "feminized" so that later trauma produces a "soft" feminine reaction to life. Or the imbalance can later suppress the sex drive (given additional second-line deprivations and repressions) leaving the person asexual.* It is my belief that a whole person has a sexual "aura" to him or her; that he or she is very much masculine or feminine, and it shows. Neurosis desexualizes an individual. "Coming on sexy" (using it as a defense) is not the same as being truly sexual.

With each shutdown of Pain in our early lives, we lose that much of our feeling and therefore of our sexuality. When the well person performs sex, it is a purely *sexual* act because there is no past, Primal anlage to give it any other meaning. In the neurotic each sex act is contaminated by that anlage of Pain. For example, many women patients

---

*See *The Feeling Child*, for a full explanation of the hormone changes during gestation.

have discovered that they used sex in their lives chiefly in order to be held and caressed. Sex was the way they went about getting what they needed (but did not get) as children. Because the areas of social intercourse are fairly limited for them (they usually cannot use business as an outlet as men do) they often focus on sex to satisfy old needs. Obviously, men use sex neurotically as well, but they can conduct their struggles for love in a greater number of other areas as well. In a male-dominated society, where a woman stays home and waits for her husband to come home at night, she is quite dependent on him to fulfill her needs.

The problem is that while a woman may want to feel loved and to be held, she must accede to penetration of the penis. Many women who can achieve orgasm "outside" by manipulation of the clitoris cannot do so when there is penetration. There are many reasons for this but patients believe that it is essentially because something has penetrated inside to where the Pain lies. There is an invasion of the body beyond the perimeter defenses. A tight, unlubricated vagina is one such defense causing a total shutdown of feeling and the resultant frigidity.

Parents do not pervert us sexually except in rare instances (by incest, for example). By and large, they pervert *our expression of love* and how we go about getting it. We can see how interwoven sex and love are when that perversion of love by our parents later causes *sexual* aberrations.

If we understand that the neurotic tries to master the past by symbolically manipulating the present, then we see that his sexual behavior is no exception. A man may be impotent because he unconsciously married a "mother." The old need is for protection, being taken care of, being told what to do, etc. The need which is prepotent is for "Momma." Sex, to be successful, however, must be performed with someone who is not "Momma." Almost every sexual problem, in my view, is a Primal one. If the organs are not functioning well it is because the sex act is being used symbolically.

Let us examine the process by which a Primal feeling becomes sexual and symbolic. First is the basic need of the infant for touch caress, hugs and body warmth. This need is rarely fulfilled. Neurotic mothers rarely can give of themselves and their bodies wholly and freely. Not having all of themselves they cannot give of themselves. Most often they give symbolic love: money, presents, food, etc. The young child latches onto the symbol because it is all he can get. But he needs true affection and that early need is overpowering. For the deprived child even the notion that

mother will come over and pick him up is arousing. When he reaches out
to her it is with every fiber of his being. His arousal is not sexual because
he is not as yet sexual. It is simply a generalized state of activation.
When the need is not fulfilled it remains in force. *The need and its
energy never change.* All that changes is the ways the child and then the
adult goes about trying to fulfill it. If he can't fulfill it in a real way then he
will have to fulfill it in unreal ways.

The infant cannot smoke and drink or turn on TV. When his needs
are frustrated the best he can do is shut down his feelings and needs, the
energy of which is funneled automatically into first line channels—throw-
ing up, colic, enuresis, thumb sucking, head-banging (the forerunner to
masturbation), or falling asleep. With the shutdown he stops fully experiencing his needs and that is a key point, for thereafter he can only
approach them symbolically. They are still there, however, exerting a
great pressure.

As the young child begins to move around he will still try to approach
his mother and hold her. She is usually too busy cleaning house or cooking and what he holds on to, perhaps, are her stockings. The stockings
come to represent mother. They may in some instances become the symbols of love. In the first years of life he may want to go to his mother's
drawers and hold her stockings when she has left for work. Later on in
adolescence he may begin to fantasize about women in stockings and
masturbate to his fantasies. His symbolic activity is becoming second and
third line. Still later he may have a continuous overpowering impulse to
dress up in stockings (and often women's panties) while masturbating.
That ritual may come to dominate his sex life. There can scarcely be any
sex without it. He may now be decades away from that very early need
and he has no idea that such a need even exists. He *thinks* he needs
stockings. *Because he cannot feel his needs he must think them.* He
becomes as excited over his ritual as that little infant was over the need
and prospect of love. Indeed, the excitement and arousal are precisely
those past feelings; only the focus is now in the present. The excitement
has become sexual because the person is now grown up into a sexual
being. Sex is obviously one of the best ways to release tension. It can be
the most explosive and convulsive of any relief form; and lacking the
means by which to attain true relief the neurotic must find it symbolically. And so stockings become tremendously exciting.

Obviously the symbolic outlet is different in some way from person to
person; but the *process* by which a simple need becomes transmuted into
a sexual ritual can be understood. What is overpowering about a ritual is

the early need which impels it, not the necessity for stockings on one's legs. The need is overwhelming because it has to do with survival. And that is why neither the threat of punishment, jail, loss of wife or husband can stop the ritual once it is set in motion. The true impulse is for love, not for dressing up. *Treating the perversion is to miss the point entirely.* It is treating the wrong impulse. This is a key point. For the need to wear women's stockings cannot be an overpowering need in and of itself. It has nothing to do with basic needs of life as such. It is only when we understand that it is derivative of real survival needs that we can comprehend its strength.

To treat a symbolic ritual as a discrete pathologic entity usually makes matters worse. For what therapies such as conditioning therapy usually do is take away the outlet without resolving the need-force underlying it. This creates more pressure, not less, and sooner or later the person is forced to act out again.

I am concentrating on one example, but the possibilities for perversion of need are endless. We must always keep in mind that when we speak of perversion it is a perversion (and diversion symbolically) of basic need. The reason that stockings and panties are so arousing to some men is that it unconsciously represents fulfillment and release from need. Since it truly isn't going to relieve the need the ritual is sexualized and the release is sexual. He gives himself the satisfaction his parents could never give. The person can then rest for a while until some life circumstance sets off the old need again (losing a girlfriend, for example) and then the ritual begins again in full force. The person is rarely aware that it is a very early feeling which is behind his compulsion. But even when he is it won't matter. Unless he can experience that need on the first or second line, knowing won't help at all. One patient before therapy, for example, knew about a scene in his early life where he was sitting on a floor playing a game when his mother stood over him with no panties on. When he tried to look up her legs she slapped him. She seduced him and then slapped him for his interest time and time again. As an adult he was mostly aroused by having women stand and straddle him while he looked at their crotch. He knew the origin of his compulsion. But it didn't change anything; it continued to be overpowering and was the key way he had to have sex. This is another way of saying that third line insights do not alter lower line traumas and Pain. *The reason why rituals continue in force for so long is that they are constantly relieving need symbolically.* Frustration grows and the impulse can no longer be contained in the head as a simple fantasy. It was physical and all powerful in infancy and it remains so. The trauma occurred *before* there was an organized mental apparatus to handle it, and later rationales, therefore, do little good. The person can tell himself how dangerous it is to carry out his ritual and still do it despite his (third line) knowledge. He continues to be fixated on a symbol for a lifetime and what is worse comes to find *sole satisfaction* in his ritual—unable to accept the real thing any more. He cannot take real love when it is offered; rather, he will take a loving person and even may insist that she take part in the ritual. He entangles her in his neurosis and cannot disengage himself enough to accept real love.

So that is what has happened to simple need. It has been blocked because it was not fulfilled and thereafter constantly nudges the third line into its ritual whenever the need is triggered. There is no stopping that compulsion, or any compulsion, without *connection* among the lines of consciousness. The impulsive act is compelling because it is *survival*—the person must feel that survival threat and need in all its intensity *in context*.

We can begin to understand the strength of our early needs by interpolating the force of a compulsion into the body of the infant. Or another way of understanding his agony is to remember when we were in some needing situation such as waiting for final grades, acceptance into graduate school, sale of a house, or getting that key job. We could scarcely concentrate on anything else. That matter dominated our lives for those moments. And those issues were not even survival as it is with the infant!

It is unavoidable that sex will be acted out symbolically in the neurotic. Everything he does—the way he eats, talks and walks are reflections of his past history. His need lies in his muscle system, his blood stream and his hormone system. It is everywhere just because that need is total and systemic. Sexual conduct, then, is just one more way the neurotic acts out his Pain and need. The man who orders around his secretary in order to feel important (to his parents) is not acting qualitatively different from the pervert. Indeed, ordering around a secretary *is* a perversion of need but it just doesn't have a sexual cast. In bed he may "get off" by beating or spanking women. The feeling is the same in or out of bed; the way it is acted out changes with the social circumstance.

Spanking and being spanked during the sex act is very common among neurotics and its symbolism is highly obvious. Many young girls only got attention when they were bad and the only physical contact they had from their fathers was when it came to physical spankings. When they grow up and become sexual they find spanking arousing and usually never know why. The man who wants to spank women likewise may never see the relationship between wanting revenge on mother and his current sexual practices.

The symbolic ritual is not only a derivative from early need but is also the way into that need. It is the means by which the neurotic can make contact with his body (where the need and sexuality reside). *For the neurotic to feel he must feel his need; since he cannot contact that need directly (as he can with a Primal) he does so indirectly.* His ritual, in short, galvanizes feeling which is immediately and automatically re-channeled into sexuality and he then ejaculates the tension set up by that ascending need—all the while thinking he has been sexual. Indeed, he may pride himself on his sexuality since the need is so strong that he must ejaculate every day or even several times a day. That early arousal which I spoke of earlier has now been completely transformed into a sexual arousal.

The strength of the impulse is the strength of the need. Need is what is overpowering, *not* the ritual or perversion. Sexual rituals only twist the need but *do not augment or reduce its strength.* It is rather amazing how many neurotics never understand that though the perversion is focused in the present, the feeling is from the past. Even when they do under-stand that it is a past feeling they have no idea where or when in the past. They can hardly conceive that they are dressing up in stockings and panties because of events which took place in the first few weeks of life. *Feelings are so automatically eroticized in adulthood that the neurotic never knows that his sexual conduct is* not *really sexual.*

What seems to happen to that deprived infant is that his need, once repressed, is rechanneled into at least one key area of the brain mediating sexuality—the hypothalamus. The hypothalamus is a key first-line struc-ture in the brain active at birth which aids in the general arousal pattern of the organism—hormone output, blood pressure changes, heart rate increase, etc. Arousal by need becomes translated by the hypothalamus and later becomes sexualized. All of the need arousal is the same from the infant to the adult, but in adulthood it is experienced only as a sex need (which the third line then twists into symbolic form appropriate to the early unresolved trauma).

It must be clear that if a person did not have his ritual he would be feeling his Pain. The ritual is an excellent defense; the only way it can or should be removed is by experiencing the feelings it represents. "Experi-ence" means to bring a Pain registered on a lower level of consciousness into connection with the third line. It is that connection which completes the circuit and alters a *registered* event into a totally *experienced* one. It is the *experience* that makes for the great Primal Pain, not simply its registration. And it is experience that makes the unconscious (lower levels of consciousness) conscious. At that point there is no longer diversion of feelings into perverted symbolic channels. *Having experienced the Pain means to no longer be driven by it or forced to ritualize it.*

My premise is a simple one: when affection cannot be given or received as a child then its expression becomes perverted; and when affection later is tied to sex, then sex will also be perverted. If a child had no opportunity to give his love to his parents, the object of his love becomes transmuted; to his dog, his mother's clothes (symbols of her) or whatever. This transmutation takes place often before the age of sexuality. So it isn't that the child becomes sexually perverted in adolescence; *rather, his already existing perversion becomes sexualized.* At that point he may masturbate in his mother's panties. His struggle for love is perpetuated possibly for a lifetime on this symbolic level. And this is little different from those who use sex to be held and touched. Being held and caressed certainly eases tension and feels good but it is not to be confused with sexuality. This is why I think that homosexuality is not a sexual act except incidentally. It is sexual *behavior* but not sexuality, in the primal sense. The male homosexual's perversion exists long before he is sexual. When he tries to get male love out of his male teachers or older schoolmates because he cannot get it from his father, it is a sign that perversion of need already exists. In adolescence he may use sex to try to get that love. He wants a man (his father) to make him feel good, to make him feel wanted, attractive and admired. He needs a man to ease his tension because originally it was a man who set up that Pain by failing to be the loving parent he should have been.

Obviously there are about as many reasons for homosexuality as there are homosexuals . . . seeing daddy give all his love to mother and trying to be a "woman" for him is but one example among many. There are homosexuals who are predominantly first line, just wanting physical relief; in males it is wanting one penis after another. These individuals are involved in trading sensations for feelings. The sensation of having the penis fondled is a symbol for having Daddy being loving and making his son feel good. There are other homosexuals who can sustain a homosexual relationship. The problem is that because the lover is a "stand-in" there is often dissatisfaction and these relationships tend to be stormy. This is because in any neurotic love relationship, old unfulfilled Primal needs become translated into the person's fantasy of love. A loving person, then, is someone who takes care of you, is considerate and indulgent, listens to you, and so on. However, no one in the "now" can stand in and fulfill what neurotic parents did not do, so the relationship will have its storms. Trying to make that someone into a loving parent (as of course also happens in heterosexual relationships) is to not let him be what he is; rather he must become what the person needs. In this sense, current third-line disappointments are simply rerouted second-line Pains. It is Pain and hopelessness not felt; and it is this unresolved Pain which makes relationships difficult.

There are any number of homosexuals who do not see their activity as the expression of a need for a daddy. They believe that their deprivation was suffered totally at the hands of "Mother" and that they tried with "Daddy" simply because there was some small ray of hope there. Perhaps the father was just passive and weak yet kind and gentle. Even though he might have been removed emotionally, the young boy's needs were funneled toward him. So the needs, as it turns out, may be first for a loving mother, but no real mother existed nor did even the *possibility* of one.

Other homosexuals feel that homosexuality is a first-line disease in that there was total denial and Pain from the very beginning. If there had been a loving mother from the start, a warm, tender, nursing mother, then no matter what a father did later, no matter how tyrannical he might have been, there would have been no homosexuality.

Nowhere is the symbolism of deviant sexuality more apparent than in the homosexual's need to suck a penis. One homosexual had the insight (after a Primal in which he felt the need to nurse) that the nipple and breast stand in the same proportion to the mouth of the infant as the erect penis does to the mouth of the adult. That is, it "feels" the same and is clearly a substitute activity.

Needs are like plants seeking sunlight. They grow toward any kind of fulfillment. If an older brother were the only love object in the home and if he left home early, then the younger brother may symbolically act out finding that brother in later homosexual contacts.

In neurosis there is always a need for symbols. Either the person himself is symbolic (as in the case of homosexuality where the lover stands in for "Daddy" no matter how unconsciously), or the lovers use symbols (pictures of nudes, of sadistic scenes, etc.) to get aroused.

One can see the progression of sexual liberation in Primal Therapy. Women who are completely frigid at the start of treatment begin to have some sexual feeling as they feel more and more early Pain. As they become more feeling, sexual stimulation will tend to drive their underlying Pain to the surface so that upon orgasm there will also be screams of Pain or just simply a great deal of deep crying. Or, in many cases, as the stimulation grows there will be a release, not of sex but of Pain. Men have complained that during this phase of their therapy ejaculation was painful, as though they were "shooting out Pain instead of pleasure."

The relationship of sexual feeling to the general repression of Pain is brought home when a woman, after reliving a catastrophic birth trauma, finds her vagina totally lubricated, and then reports later that her first free orgasm was experienced as a result of that Primal. Second-line Primals, even when they deal directly with sex, for example "Mommy spanked me when I touched my vagina," may not produce spontaneous lubrication as the first-line "non-sexual" Primals may do. Primalling on the second line about sexual and non-sexual traumas prepares the way for the first line which will finally offer the person back his or her body. In short, frigidity and impotence are essentially first-line (body-functioning) problems. Generally, full access to the first line helps give a person back his sexuality. But as in all generalizations there are exceptions. There are certainly plenty of traumas on the second line, both sexual and non-sexual, which take their toll. If the weight of these traumas is extraordinary then their resolution is going to go a long way toward liberating a person sexually. If a person is beaten frequently, as in the case of one young woman who was frigid, that is certain to shut down the body. In her case, reliving all the beatings helped immeasurably in opening up her body. Another girl had to offer her hands to her mother daily who then inspected and smelled them to make sure her daughter hadn't masturbated. Obviously, this takes a toll. This girl not only never masturbated but was terrified to have orgasm. There is no need to labor the point. Sexuality is of the body. When the body is shut down so is sexuality. There is no escape from that law. Nevertheless, no matter how much second-line trauma there is, it is a general rule that whenever there is a good deal of first-line trauma (as there exists in almost everyone), *full* sexuality does not return until significant resolution takes place on the first line. That is precisely why we have heretofore had no idea about real sexuality and what it was. We simply had no fully sexual individuals. Surely, one might counter by offering numerous examples of women who reach orgasm easily. But having an orgasm and achieving the quality of sexuality which encompasses the whole body are two different matters. Sexuality is not just a matter of vaginal or penile release. It is a matter of *feeling* in a total way. Certainly, any number of men, for example, achieve orgasm when they dress up in women's clothes. Are they sexual? No. They have sexualized orgasm but not sexual feeling.

If a person has repressions then, at the point of sexual release, part of the body is going to be engaged in *suppression* instead of in full *expression*. The orgasm must be partial because to fully feel during sex would mean to fully feel all the unconscious Pain. As the level of excitement rises during sex, so also does Pain since feeling is a unified experience. The screams and cries that people utter at the point of sexual release may not, in short, be so much sexual as Primal.

Partial orgasm in men may be incomplete ejaculation and, unless the man had at some time experienced full ejaculation, he would not know that he had a problem. Indeed, he may turn it around and feel more masculine for being able to come twice in a short period of time. In women, partial orgasm may simply be a strong but localized release around the vagina; not having access to the total body would mean lack of full-body orgasm. There would be a sensation, not a feeling; and that sensation is a transmuted sensation—from Pain to pleasure, from tension to release. It becomes pleasure because there is a focus for release. It is unfortunate that in neurotics the state of pleasure is confused with the release of tension, so that true pleasure is unrecognized. Most neurotics have had their feelings blunted long before they even knew there was such a thing as feelings, so it is no wonder that later in life they have no concept of what sex should be.

Since most neurotics are only familiar with the type of orgasm they have customarily had since adolescence, they cannot know what kind of orgasm is normal. Therefore they tend to think that they are normal. It is very much like never knowing how much we have been unloved until we get it in the present. This is probably why surveys fail to elicit the true scope of sexual neurosis in our society. The only person who knows true sexuality is the one whose body is no longer engaged in repressions. All the ideas, then, as to what constitutes normal sexual behavior can only be found by studying him or her. Anything else is a study in neurosis. Thus, the frequency of sex—two or three times per week as shown in several surveys—may not be normal at all. Once tension is excised from sex, the frequency tends to drop though the quality may rise.

To return to the initial question about sexual behavior, it is entirely possible for a man to block his Pain and become hypersexual. To all appearances he would be behaving sexually. But on closer examination we see that it is similar to frigidity where Pain is blocked and the woman becomes unsexual. *Neither behavior is sexual.* The only difference is in how each acts out the Pain and tension. The man may be releasing generalized tension resulting from a mélange of early Pains which have been eroticized. The sex centers are overworked because they are carrying the load of a lifetime of Pain. It is no different from the person who eats away his tension.

There are no doubt many reasons why men go "out" with their sexual behavior and women "act in." One reason may simply be the fact of differing biologic equipment. Under the stress of Pain the body contracts: the muscles, blood vessels, pupils, etc. For a woman this may mean constriction of the vagina resulting in vaginismus (painful and tight vagina during intercourse). But for the man this same constriction may be a factor in ejaculation, particularly premature ejaculation. This is speculation, but the fact that sexual behavior tends to be the cultural mode for men and not women must include the biologic facts.

In addition to the repression of sexuality in this society there is the almost as frequent suppression of hostility; children are usually not allowed to get angry at their parents, tell them off or even complain. Thus in the storehouse of buried feelings is all that leftover hostility. As feelings rise in sexual situations it is entirely likely that hostile feelings will also come to the surface; a man may, for example, want to beat his woman in order to "get off." This tends to be particularly true if he has suppressed rage toward his mother. In order to feel anything, then, his true feelings must ascend. What he is feeling in the sex act are his true feelings, only out of context. He is "beating his mother" through his girlfriend and is finding tension relief in doing so. The entire sequence is nearly always unconscious, but that changes nothing.

Murder is not all that different dynamically from sexual sadism. A man finds pleasure in the pain of women. In murder there is simply a total loss of the third line, which is what makes a person "know" he is acting out a controlled ritual. In sexual sadism the symbolism is confined to a specific area of functioning and the person is aware of what he is doing, even though he may be completely unaware of the second-line Pain and deprivation which makes him act out this ritual year after year. In murder there is a total fusion of the past with the present so that there is literally no distinction. Likewise, in many cases of exhibitionism, for example, there is an almost total loss of the third line during the act. The person appears as though he is in a coma because he is "back there" acting out symbolically a message to his parents; he is not "here."

It is the strongest need which arises first in sexual behavior. So, even while a woman is making it with a man, if there is great mother deprivation she may have to fantasize breasts or other symbols of mother's love during sex. Just as many female infants were deprived of breasts as male babies. In order for a woman to suck on breasts later in life she must engage in homosexual acts and bear that stigma. There is no safe way for her to act out that simple need as men do. I suppose the reason that we think that so many women are bisexual is that they also want a woman's love (their mother's) just as men do, if they have not had it as a child. In Primal Therapy, during group, women may sometimes act out that need with other women and patients begin to feel the real feeling, knowing finally that it is not sex they want. There is no stigma attached to their fondling other patients, because it is understood that they are using it to get to their need and Pain. It is often true that it takes a year or more of Primal Therapy for women to discover the need and acknowledge it.

The fact that a feeling is buried and unconscious means that it will, in some unconscious way, influence sexual behavior inasmuch as it influences all behavior. A woman who never had a kind and warm mother carries that need with her no matter how she rationalizes to the contrary. Her need for a woman may be so strong but unacknowledged that during sex with a man she will simply feel nothing; she has to feel nothing because she must suppress her strongest need. She may be so removed from her need (and thus from her body) that she doesn't even recognize it in the form of fantasy. If she can acknowledge it she may well fantasize going down on a woman or sucking her breasts while having intercourse with a man. In other words, in order to feel with a man she must accede to her real needs and feelings. Even though she has a penis inside her, the *experience* in her head (which is where part of our experience lies) is with a woman. She would be having some feeling in sex with a man because she has access to some real feeling even though that feeling is diverted into fantasy. A woman with this kind of unconscious need may prefer cunnilingus because it is an undifferentiated sex act; either a man or a woman can do it. Also, while a man is doing it, it is still possible for her to fantasize about women. Likewise a man who fears full heterosexuality may prefer fellatio because it is an undifferentiated sex act. He may also prefer to give cunnilingus out of the same fear. The person who neither dreams nor has sexual fantasies is usually more removed than the one who does because it means that he cannot even come close to the feeling symbolically—even symbols derived from the feeling are suppressed.

In Primal Therapy we may encourage women to face their fantasies in order to get them into the feelings which lie below. They are not encouraged to change those fantasies or their behavior because those fantasies are signifying something real in them. The symbols are never manipulated in the name of therapy.

The whole notion of reconditioning therapy, for example, is the manipulation of symbols: substituting a more acceptable symbol for an unacceptable one. Shocking a homosexual male while presenting him with pictures of nude males is one example which is similar to shocking the smoker who sees pictures of cigarettes and their effects. Where does the need and tension go after that? In the case of the homosexual, the conditioning therapist has neglected the fact that a nude male is a symbol. The symbol arose out of need. You cannot remove the symbol and expect the need to disappear unless you are inclined to believe in magic.

Any approach to sexual problems, such as that of Masters and Johnson, which treats sexual difficulties apart from a person's history must ultimately fail. It neglects the whole area of non-sexual traumas which influence sexuality. It does not deal with early need and deprivation but instead views sex in isolation as a viable entity which can be changed with a few proper lessons. This is not to say that some new information about technique could not be helpful to the well-adjusted, but it is useless in dealing with serious sexual problems. A person who has resolved the old feelings behind his neurotic sexual behavior will do what is natural, free and instinctive in sex and usually not need any kind of sexual instruction. Experimentation with a person at the same point as himself will take care of that.

When I see someone struggling with a birth trauma (a trauma that shuts down the body in the first minutes of life) for more than a year in almost constant first-line Primals, I realize how complex the treatment of sexual difficulties is and how impossible is any other approach than that taken in Primal Therapy. Neurotic sexual behavior is historic and cannot be solved by any approach which is firmly rooted in tackling the here and now. The Gestalt technique of caressing and hugging and sometimes sexually fondling each other in group therapy is an example of the ahistoric approach. There is no way to neglect a lifetime of experience and yet hope to profoundly alter present behavior. The resolution of a problem with a history means the resolution of that history. What should be obvious in the treatment of sexual problems is that they are not just "sexual problems." There is no way to cure homosexuality by encouraging the person to have heterosexual erotic encounters, as if the problem of homosexuality were just parts such as the penis, testicles and vagina. Sexual divergence is a reflection of a lifetime of warping events which simply do not warp the use of the penis and leave the rest of us intact. It is not a problem of where and into whom one inserts his penis. It is more that the penis is part of our total psycho-physiology, and how it is used depends on the body in which it is encased and the history which gave it shape. It is no different than a stuttering or stammering problem. We don't call it a mouth problem and treat the tongue and lips (and if we do we usually stamp out the *expression* of the problem, not the problem itself). We usually understand that early events shaped the problem and we deal with those events.

SOME INSIGHTS ON MY HOMOSEXUAL SADO-MASOCHISM
Gilbert

I feel that what happens to each patient teaches the staff something new and what happened to me may be instructive in terms of handling similar cases in the future.

Trusting my body against the advice of the therapists could be a risky business because I may have been trusting my defenses rather than my real feelings; however, in one particular area of my therapy I followed my body toward some significant and curative insights.

When I entered the therapy six months ago, I was a "conventional" homosexual—that is, my ritual was basically hugging, kissing, sucking, holding, fucking. I had come to L.A. from a situation where I was a "closet" case. I rarely acted-out at all for years before therapy and when the obsession became overwhelming, I would go to public men's rooms, to the baths, or come to L.A. and act out to the point of exhaustion. Then I'd return home satiated but depressed.

Moving to West Hollywood was a totally new experience for me. After my three weeks, I found it impossibe to ignore the constant cruis-ing and propositions and I became very promiscuous. Therapists were against it; I was busted, hassled and advised, but just like in life outside the Institute, the best advice couldn't stop the urges—the need.

For the first five months of therapy, I rarely ever cried. I didn't have to struggle to feel, but the feelings always stopped at the rage or anger or frustration and never quite dropped into the deep hurt and I never really cried from the depths of my body. This was due, according to the staff, to my constant acting-out. At this point, I was aware that the therapists were probably right, that my acting-out probably *was* stopping the feelings. I knew it was a defense and that I was running from Pain, but struggle as I did, I couldn't give it up. (And it was a struggle against where my body was at.) Every time I would abstain for a week or so and get myself unbearably horny, I would go to group and feel: "Daddy, hold me. Please touch me . . . etc." but it just never connected to the Pain. Those feelings always seemed very unreal to me because I didn't want MY daddy for anything. The most I could connect to was that I wanted some other daddy, a good daddy to hold me. Anyhow, time passed.

As I wallowed in the candystore atmosphere of West Hollywood, something began to happen. I began to feel that no matter how many guys I went with, no matter how handsome they were, no matter how big their cocks were, it just didn't make the Pain, the need, go away. And I began to get bored with my "conventional" ritual.

I noticed a new direction in my fantasies and my ritual. As I began to be more open to my feelings and in touch with my body's needs, I deviated into some sado-masochistic scenes. I started looking for big, mean-looking stud types who would stand over me and "make me" do things to them. I got into wanting to drink their piss and have them come all over my face and yell at me and hit me across the face and humiliate me. I let myself go with this a couple of times and it felt like I had never been so excited, never enjoyed sex as much as I did acting-out this crazy new ritual. I got to a place where this was all I wanted to do, and I was no longer turned on by just hugging and kissing and touching. All I wanted to do was jerk off while these guys did anything they wanted to me.

I only had to act-out this new ritual a couple of times before the feelings started to come up. I would go to group and have a therapist stand over me and I would beg him to piss on me, etc. and then I would beg my daddy, but the feeling would instantly change to: "No! Don't hurt me anymore." Still, it didn't quite seem real, didn't connect. I would stand up in post-group and describe the whole scene and wind up on the floor screaming anger: "See what you did to me. I'm so damaged . . ." but again, the feelings never really connected and I had no insight into WHY I needed to do what I was doing. I still had the urges.

Finally a therapist sat for me one afternoon in a private session and I again described my wildest sexual fantasies. She helped me by making

me describe each thing in explicit detail and really beg the guy to do it. I
began to scream: "Please, piss on me . . . hit me . . . hurt me . . . Come
on. Do it. It's the only way I can get off. I have to do it this way. It's the
only way I can feel anything. It's the contact. It's the only way I feel like
I'm getting anything." And it was that statement: "It's the only way I
feel like I'm getting anything" that finally connected. As I screamed out
and Primaled suddenly I *knew*. It all made sense.

I had to be hurt and humiliated to get off sexually because the only
real contact I ever had with my father was when he was hurting or
humiliating me. The only times I felt as if I was getting anything from
him, getting his attention, was when he was yelling at me, hurting me or
degrading me. Then the real Pain started rushing up and I began to
realize that this wasn't one or two or ten scenes to feel but my hour-by-
hour, day-by-day relationship with him. I saw that he had hurt me so
consistently that the only way it made sense to act-out the need for him
was to symbolically reenact this constant daily relationship.

I also realized that I had never been able to respond to a man's kindly
attention, sexually or otherwise. I realized that I simply didn't have any
experience from which to react to kindness and it either made me uncomfortable or I was just dead to it. I saw that my most successful relationships with men in non-sexual situations had been unfeeling, competitive and struggling. In sexual settings, I could only be really attracted to
men who were not interested in me and made me struggle for every
shred of attention. In no way could I be or had I been attracted to someone who was nice to me, who wanted me or who acted like they liked
me. When I realized all of this, when I connected to it, I began to really
cry from the depths of my feelings. This was what he had left me with.
This was how he had damaged me.

(The Primal was huge and curative as I'll describe below. I know that
there may be other feelings under these, that some of my new ritual
must have to do with my mother, etc., but the Primal described above
seemed to "clear me out" for a while so it seems like it must have been
real.)

*   *   *

I began this article with the statement that I had trusted my body over
the advice of the therapists. I don't say this to be Primally smart because
it didn't occur as a conscious effort to defy them and do what I thought
best. It just happened that I couldn't or didn't stop acting-out as soon as

they told me I should. In retrospect, I feel that it was mandatory for my therapy that I go through what I went through; a kind of natural progression of sinking into the depths, kind of sexually "hitting-bottom" in order to start up again. Secondly, that hitting bottom was also discovering my REAL ritual. I had been so shut down before that I didn't even know that's what I wanted to do! (When Art said, "Let yourself have your ritual," that must be what he meant.) By letting my body take the lead, it found the feeling for me as I described above. *And it was only after having that Primal and making those important connections that there was any behavioral change.* Since having those feelings, I haven't had the urge to act out much at all. The need is greatly diminished. Everything has changed, the obsession is almost gone. I can go feel it now instead of doing it. I see it as a feeling, a defense, etc.

I know now that my homosexuality has little or nothing to do with needing anything from a man in the present and has nothing to do with love or tenderness. Getting to that "bottom-line" ritual has shown me that my homosexuality is the symbolic recreation of the system that my father set up in order for me to get anything from him. (And reading that in *The Primal Scream* doesn't mean shit until you've felt it.)

It certainly seems likely that I could have gotten to the same connections by just feeling and not acting-out at all. But at the time it would have been a huge struggle not to do what my body wanted to do. (It was a huge struggle anyhow, just not to act out any more than I did.) It also seems to me that the progression toward the connections was rapid, only a couple of months.

Another thing, since that huge Primal, the urge to act-out has, as I said, been substantially reduced. And since I haven't been acting out, I've been getting to the deep hurt feelings that I couldn't get to before. But it was only three days ago, after six full months of therapy, that I finally touched on feelings of the *real Pain* of how much my father had hurt me. The Pain was so overwhelming that my body shut down after only a few minutes but as a therapist said, I have a handle into that Pain and I know it's there. My feeling is that I wasn't *ready* to feel *that* Pain until now. It seems to be coming up now as part of the natural progression into deeper and deeper levels of Pain. I feel very strongly that had I not had that sexual Primal and the accompanying connections, I wouldn't be able to properly integrate the Pain I'm feeling now; the Pain of how much and how he hurt me.

As it is, everything is falling into place now and my feelings are coming up in a sort of progression and everything gets integrated properly (at least so far). I cannot stress how important it seems to have been to just follow my body through the therapy, let myself be where I was at, and how by doing that I've arrived where I'm supposed to be on schedule (such as it is): open, crying and feeling at six months.

There follows the transcript of a seminar on homosexuality which was held recently at the Primal Foundation.

WHY HOMOSEXUALITY?

A number of homosexual patients were asked what they felt about their homosexuality and if they had had any insights or connections as a result of their therapy.

*   *   *   *   *

GWEN: Let me tell you a little about myself. I spent about four years living with two different girls. Living a homosexual life, not having anything to do with men at all. Before that I was heterosexual. I haven't acted out that way for about six years and I've been here for three.

ART: Weren't you a prostitute?

GWEN: No, I first became a prostitute and then I started going to gay bars and then having three-way scenes with the guys and then the thing snowballed. I would say that the two relate to each other.

ART: Did you hate men?

GWEN: Well no, I hated men all along. That just amplified it. There was a time in my life when I would walk down the street and if a man said anything to me I would challenge him to fight. If I went into a store and there was a man or a woman that could wait on me, I would always take the woman. I went to a psychiatrist and got things "worked out" and started doing the "right thing." I think that homosexual men are totally different in society from the way women are.

ART: How are they different?

GWEN: Well, I don't think that there is such a stigma put on females. I think that men are very curious about girls going to bed with each other and they accept that more. In fact probably join in on it. I don't think they feel that way about men.

MIKE: Years ago I read an article by a psychiatrist in New York who claimed to have a great amount of success with homosexuality. I think it was called "A Thousand Homosexuals" or something. He said it was one of the really big problems and he was really condemning the Kinsey Report as contributive to the male homosexual problem. There were two factors in it: women were much more arcane in their activities but society condoned it, in that society accepts women touching and kissing each other. By the same token the threat to the female being exposed is much greater because the wife can be staying home with the children and making it with the lady next door and nobody knows about it. But when the Kinsey man comes and says "Have you ever had a homosexual relationship?" they always say "No," whereas guys usually tend to say "Yes," and are usually proud of it. I think in an anonymous report men tend to be more honest about it. I've been a homosexual all my life. I feel I still am one. Like Gwen, I began to do the "right things" too. About fifteen years ago I tried to free myself of it. I went into psychoanalysis which did absolutely nothing for me. Then I went into Christian Science for about ten years and that helped me in other ways but not in the homosexuality. I was leading what looked like a very successful life in New York: I was successful on the stage, I made a lot of money, I had a fine social life, nice people, nice parties. I just became more secretive, hiding out in toilets until I read *The Primal Scream,* and here I am.

ART: How do they find each other, the butch girl and the kind of nellie guy? How do they get together and marry?

GWEN: For me, I'm terribly afraid of men so I go after someone that's meek and faggy.

GEOFF: I always had a lot of girls who were just friends, who liked me because I was never aggressive. They'd want to be my friend as opposed to a lover.

MIKE: Were you married, Geoff?

GEOFF: Yes.

GWEN: Why did you get married?

GEOFF: I was trying to push the homosexuality under, and during that time I met Pamela and married her. She is in the therapy too now.

GWEN: Did you have a sexual relationship with her?

GEOFF: Yes, in fact on a physical level it's much more satisfying.

ART: That's why homosexuality is not a sexual thing.

MIKE: Yeah, I think a lot of my homosexuality has to do with the affection I got from my brother. I was deprived of both parents really, but I did have a brother for about six months when I was a baby. Later on he was the one person in my family who was affectionate. He was like that with everybody, we used to call him cry-baby, he'd hug and kiss everybody in the family. In all of my Primals the Pain goes to him and the loss of him when he went away. I might not have been a homosexual had my sister been there or some other female that I "got" from, because I got nothing from my mother, ever.

ANDREW: I think that neither of my parents ever touched me. My mother only touched me aggressively, sexually, like she wanted me. That's what I've felt so far. I like girls, but sexually I'm terrified of them. My whole genital area just contracts when girls come near me. All my life I've been attracted to guys since the day I started puberty. There has never been any sexual attraction toward girls.

ART: How did your mother seduce you?

ANDREW: Just touching me and wanting me. Saying things like "I'd like to eat you up" and rubbing me and stuff like that. She was cuddling me, but it felt like she wanted me.

GWEN: Sounds like you've got an extra factor in there, it's not like your mother and father not touching you, it's like they were actively doing something else to turn you off.

ART: That is a very good point.

ANDREW: Yeah, I've felt that in a couple of Primals.

BEN: When I first found out about the facts of life, I would lay in bed and think about fucking girls. This was when I was twelve. Then when I was thirteen my friend and I would talk a little bit about girls and sex, and we tried it with each other. I just put my cock between his legs and pretended I was fucking. I came and I was very upset. Then I went home and told my mother what had happened and I was very worried. She said, "Don't worry about it, it's part of growing up." I stopped fantasizing about girls and just sort of put it off and began to say things like, "People don't have sex with girls until they are twenty-one." I wanted to do it again with my friend and I kept looking for guys who I wanted to do that thing again with. It would be a tall guy with a good build and I would fantasize it. That's when I became homosexual. But before that something else happened. It was the same summer after I was thirteen. My mother had a friend who had a daughter who stayed with us. One night I was sleeping and she came into my room in her nightgown. I looked at her standing there and I began to get a hard-on. I said, "What do you want?" Then my mother started coming up the steps and she ran away and I went to the bathroom. I saw my mother chasing her into my sister's room and she ran in and slammed the door in my mother's face. I was very scared by this and I said, "Mom, what's the matter?" She turned toward me and she said, "Now look, I'll send her right home, she came here to stay out of trouble . . . " She was screaming at me in absolute hatred, and I

was terrified. I never had an attraction to a girl again. It just faded away.
ART: That's called one-trial conditioning, by the way. You can shock
a rat when it's a baby and that shock will last a lifetime. You can do that
with humans too. If you terrorize them enough, that one thing can do it.
TED: I've been married for five years and I really like fucking women
a lot. I haven't acted out sexually with a man for many years. I even
wonder if I'm homosexual at all. I started when I was ten. I met a young
guy who started feeling me up and I liked it and I started feeling him.
I used to hitchhike a lot and I would be in a car and these guys would
start touching me. I couldn't say no, and it would go on from there.
Another time I ran away from home and I met a homosexual in the
park and he said if you come home with me I'll give you five dollars.
I did it but I hated it. I got in a lot of trouble with the police and was in
jail. Then I met a guy about five years older than me and we went fishing
and camping together. I really loved that but when we had sex together
I did nothing at all. I was passive. Sometimes I liked it but most of the
time I didn't. I had no desire to touch him at all, and yet I did this for
five years.
MIKE: How long has it been since you've acted out with a man?
TED: Seven years.
GWEN: Ted, do you see men on the street who you are attracted to?
TED: No, not at all. But women I am. A woman just has to touch me,
or sometimes just talk to me sexually, and I'll get an erection. But at the
same time I'm absolutely terrified of women. Like the first time I'm with a
woman I usually never make the first move.
GWEN: That's another reason why they are attracted to each other, the
weak man and the dyke woman.
TED: Yeah, right, and I like being fucked by a woman too.
ANDREW: In the last six months I have made an attempt to become heterosexual, but the women I am attracted to are not dykes. They are usually
very full, voluptuous women. Let me tell you some of the insights I have
had in this therapy about my homosexuality. My mother said mine was an
easy birth. She wanted me. She nursed me for three days, and then they
took me away from her and did not allow her to see me for ten days.
It was something in the milk which they said was not good for me. My
mother cried for ten days. She told me recently that she vowed when she
got me back she would never let me go again. That's one of the reasons
I am homosexual. She wanted me to be either for her or for no woman.
To this day she still has my balls and I'm fighting to get them back.
Then when I was small my father came home from the service, and

the air around him was constantly anger. He was a terrifying, aggressive man, and my homosexuality is also wrapped up with my anger at him. I have never been fucked, all I wanted to do was fuck, acting out trying to be in control of my father. Every male I'm with, I'm in control, and as long as he wants me I'm still in control. Another thing is, almost exclusively my fantasies include a certain type of male. That male is almost always blond, and part of my homosexuality is to want to take care of him. The second day of my therapy I brought in a picture to show my therapist of the first little blond boy I wanted to take care of, and it was me. So it's three things: Mommy, all that possessive sexual thing she did to me, which made me withdraw from women; the anger in my fucking, and the trying to be big, which is against my daddy; and taking care of this little blond boy, which is me. I have my package deal!

ART: The first thing that is obvious about that is that there is no "homosexual." Each of you is different from anybody else. Isn't that true? If you analyze everything you do in your homosexuality, the way you fuck, what you do or what you prefer, each part is a separate feeling, like Andrew has just shown. But homosexuality is still the condensed symbolic ritual that describes your life.

GEOFF: I had an insight last night. My therapist held me and I started Primalling and felt the need for a man to hold me and touch me, and the thing that struck me was it wasn't a sexual need.

ART: You're forced into homosexuality in a way because there is such a tremendous social taboo on male touching and tenderness. If you're in a conditioning therapy they shock you every time you get a hard-on thinking about a man. Instead of letting you feel what you need straight, hugging and kissing, they blast it out of you in a million ways.

JAMES: Recently I've been allowing myself to feel men tenderly, like be with them instead of that sex stuff like jerking off. I never feel homosexual when I'm with a guy just feeling his body. I've never allowed myself that before. I've always kept them out there, I'd never let men close. I was almost as afraid of men as I was of women. I am sexually a man. I was born a man but I was denied my sexuality by my parents. My maleness is not there. By not being able to feel me I was not able to feel my maleness. Every time I get in touch with my body through feeling I feel manly.

ROBERT: I have acted out homosexually only twice in my life. Basically my sexual outlet since I was nine has been to dress up in women's clothes or to fantasize being dressed up in women's clothes. Being dominated or punished goes along with the fantasy. I'm always a boy being forced into the situation. I never got from either of my parents. My brother started going out with girls very early. He always had girlfriends. When he got a car he was gone all the time. I knew he would be with girls and there would be big fights around the house. My father would scream and yell and one time I remember he beat my brother with a horsewhip. For years all I heard from my parents was how rotten it was of him to go out with these girls.

ART: People often equate transvestism with homosexuality. If you dress up in a dress they think you're queer. It has nothing to do with it as you can see. Robert's ritual, his acting out, is being forced to be a girl. It's the exact symbolic replica of what happened to you in your life—your parents didn't want you to be a boy. And that is what all perversions are about. They are the precise condensation of what happened in your life.

MIKE: I've felt an affinity with Robert because that's exactly what happened to me. My mother forced me to be a girl. She wanted me to be born a girl, and when she found out I was a boy she tried to kill me. When I get near those mother feelings it becomes a life-or-death situation for me. My mother hated me and she never told me because she couldn't. Now any unstraightness from women around me makes me want to go act out.

STUART: I would say that sex is my main-line defense. In my previous therapy where you were supposed to reprogram yourself by not doing things and doing the "right" sort of things and all that sort of shit, I couldn't make myself stop acting out. We'd try to figure out ways to make me stop but it's like something comes over me and after it's over it is like it happened to somebody else. It's a complete dream, I'm not there at all. I had the same problem when I first came here, I just couldn't stop acting out. I always feel like there is this unspoken condemnation of my homosexuality.

ART: See, at the Institute, there is condemnation of your acting out, but not on moral grounds. It's because when you act out you are symbolizing a feeling that if you felt you wouldn't act out. It's not condemnatory, it's just telling you that what you do then is rob yourself of the feeling. You're the one who loses.

MIKE: I always knew that if I'd come down here and feel, instead of just trying to force myself to stop when I had the urge to act out, I'd get to the feeling.

WILL: My experience here has been a searching down through the years of my life. Each time I have a Primal I seem to find another facet of my sexuality. There are a number of things that happened to me in my childhood, some of which were bad, some alright. The equilibrium seems to have enabled me to marry. I've been married thirteen years with four children. It's been reasonably successful, but I'm still homosexual at times. It's as if there is no one specific trauma for me. There is a little bit here, and it is added to by this and that, and if I get a particular set of phenomena in a present-day situation, I get the urge to act out homosexually. One of the events that caused this was being weaned at four months overnight. I was then propped with a bottle. I had a Primal two days ago about it. I never got picked up after that either. So that day I lost the breast and I lost touch. This deprived me of the ability to explore. I remember going mad watching my wife feed both of the babies. When either of the kids would be sucking at the breast their hands would be exploring her face or her breast. Finding out about their little world. I couldn't do that because I had to hold the fucking bottle.

ART: The sudden cut-off from sucking, that's important.

GEOFF: But why is the life-long need of a homosexual to suck a penis instead of a woman's breast?

ART: That's my point again. It isn't just the need to suck, you understand. If there is a need to suck and then you don't have a daddy, then it becomes a need to suck Daddy. You have to disengage every aspect of your losses to solve your homosexuality. To the baby's mouth the nipple stands in the same relation, in size and feel, as the cock to the adult's mouth. I think it's a direct displacement. It also gives "milk."

WILL: That's true, because yesterday I Primalled after I looked at a picture of a man's prick. I wanted for the man to put his arms around my waist and for me to suck. I went down into this Primal and I felt something go into my mouth, and it was my mother ramming the bottle into my mouth. So I decided, "If that's all I'm going to get, I'll fucking get it alright." In sucking pricks I was saying, "I don't really want a breast." But I did, and yesterday after I'd felt some of that it was different.

ART: How different?

WILL: Well, I looked at my wife when she was having a shower and I thought, "That really is nice—her body." It didn't last long and I didn't feel sexual, but it was different from any way I've felt about it before.

GEOFF: What's happening in this therapy? How many homosexuals are getting cured?

ART: Well here you are. How many of you are cured? The point is, can Primal Therapy cure homosexuality, so that you no longer need to act out with members of your own sex?

BEN: You can cure that.

GEOFF: I didn't come here to be cured of my homosexuality, I was just tense and in pain. Now I'm starting to get in touch with my homosexuality, and I see it as a wall that has got to be torn down and it can be. I don't think I'm crippled for life.

ART: Does your tendency to act out homosexually get less? You've been here a long time, Mike, so has Gwen. I'm interested to see what happens after years of Primalling.

CLARE: I used to act out sexually as well, but when I talk about "acting out" with a woman I'm talking about a whole neurotic relationship where I was constantly trying to get her to like me and always not quite making it. It was my whole life, it would take precedence over everything. I haven't had that now for months, that kind of relationship went away.

ART: Do you still want it?

CLARE: No. Now I've started to really like being with my husband. I'm getting to some of the really horrible feelings that I have about men. In January when Gwen's friend Cathy came, all the feelings of wanting came back up. She came on to me and she was ready to give me everything I've always wanted from a woman. I really didn't want to be crazy so I got away from her. It took a while, and I hurt a lot for a long time. That will happen again, some Cathy will come along and I'll be right back in it. But now I can say no. I could see what was happening and I didn't have to be crazy. That's just wonderful, it makes me so free.

MARK: When I first came here I was going to porno places and sucking guys off and getting fucked and doing all these things. And then just lately I went to this guy's house who had fucked me and I just got violently sick, the idea of sex was intolerable to my body. I realized that being fucked for me was pushing the anger up and fucking was shooting it out of my cock. I don't go to the bathrooms any more and I don't cruise. When I was on the street I used to find men attractive, and look at their crotch to see how much of their cock was showing. I don't do that any more, but just recently I put up a picture of a male nude on my wall, and I have masturbated to that once in a while. I never used to put up pictures of men or women.

ART: What's happening is that your symbolism is diminishing and becoming more refined. Instead of going out on the street and acting out, what happens is it becomes a mental fantasy. Mental fantasy is a way station to acting out. It's the first step to acting out, but now you are doing it in reverse. That's a very important point.

ANDREW: I came into this therapy not wanting to be homosexual, but I am and I feel now that I may always have the urge at times. My homosexuality it not just the symbol of some surface pain, it represents the core of my need. The only thing I believe I can do about it is the daily vigilance. When I have feelings about men now I can either lay down and feel that or act it out.

CLARE: I want to say something. I know that there are dozens of women that I see in here that I would have gone after before, but I don't want to any more. So I don't feel it's true that the urge will be there forever.

ART: I'll tell you what my idea is and you tell me if I'm right or wrong. I think that you will never get the old need fulfilled, but you get over the Pain of not having had that need fulfilled. It's the Pain that blocks the need that deforms you. In other words you are deformed because the need is blocked and you go around acting it out instead of being straight. The point about a symbolic ritual is that it is blocked Pain. If you remove the block what you've got left is the direct need, for instance to suck your mother's breast rather than a man's penis.

ANDREW: I agree that the need will always be there, the Pain perhaps will lessen. I believe there will be constant choices made. Right now I am involved with a girl. We just had the most devastating moment of our lives. She just went right to the guts of my Pain. When I lay down to begin feeling it, my first impulse was to run away into a homosexual thing. That was my choice: either find some guy and fuck, or feel the pain of what she said. I made the choice, and that's why I've been here all day!

ART: You are able to make that choice when your third line is not overwhelmed by second- and first-line catastrophic Pain. As you go into the Pain your third line operates so that you can make the choice rationally.

MIKE: Fred used to say something that I thought was so fucking cynical of him. He would say, "The tendency will always come up," and that was counter to every piece of hope that had ever kept me alive. I thought that the day would come when I would get up and would never have the inclination at all, any homosexual inclination. Finally I began to see that what he said was true. The inclination does come up and he said wait until you hit a crisis, then you'll know how far you've come. I think the thing becomes more refined as you go along. As you feel more and more, the pressure of that tremendous need is gone. The compulsion is gone.

GWEN: You have a choice after you've been feeling a while. You aren't compelled to act out, you can choose to do it and stay crazy, or face the feeling behind it.

ART: The other end of it is this. Not only must you feel, you must get other satisfaction in your present life. If you don't, when you get those

tendencies, you're going to act out. If you have other things in your life, if you do something consciously on the third line, that's the point. Socialize with people after group, for example. Do things that you enjoy.
ANDREW: I have some friends from therapy whom I am coming to love, to really feel for. When I feel sexual about them, I tell them, I come down here and I feel it. But I have some kind of life back home as well and I know that I have to go home. I have to face my parents and my roommate and my lovers and my life back there. I'll be directing a show this summer. We have a little theatre back there. I'm frightened to go back, but I know I have to face my life in Maryland, not in this room. The thing that is helping me as much as the therapy is the friends in my present. If I had not got involved with Susan I would not have felt the panic, the fear and the hatred that being with a woman meant to me. If I did not get involved with Joe I would not know it was possible to love a male and not need to fuck him.
MIKE: Make sure you have a place to feel when you go back. I went to London a year ago and I had nowhere to feel. I was in a hotel room and then a flat. I got really sick with flu. That should all have been feelings!

CHAPTER ELEVEN

The Prolongation of Life
Arthur Janov

The brain and body do not just "grow old." They age because of certain conditions, internal and external; and they age in rather orderly ways. They age faster, obviously, under the influence of disease, and I am going to show that neurosis is a disease, a disease which markedly affects aging of the brain and body. This aging process ultimately determines our longevity—how long we can expect to be on this earth; the more severe the neurosis the shorter the longevity.

I believe that there is a way to slow the aging process, reduce catastrophic disease which hastens it, and significantly increase our chances of living much longer than we imagined possible. Further, it is my belief that man's longevity has been vastly underestimated. I think that the average human today, even given all the stresses in his environment, should live beyond one hundred years.

The way to achieve all this, I submit, is Primal Therapy. This is neither esoteric theorizing, Utopian daydreaming nor guess work. Our research at the Primal Laboratory appears to make increased longevity quite possible, not on theoretical man, but on the very people in Primal Therapy today. To understand this I shall discuss the factors which make us age and die and how they can be altered. Let us first briefly review the Primal viewpoint.

As I have noted, all the things which happen to us in life, including those events just before and during birth, do not just roll off us like rainwater. They are registered and coded in the brain and body. If the event is too painful it is registered as a trauma. Traumas mean that there is more pain, either physical or psychological, than the system can integrate.

The system is overloaded and it automatically tries to shut down against the pain. Fortunately, there are a series of gates operating in the brain which aid us to shut down or repress pain. When the gates shut down against a trauma there is a split or disconnection between the affect or feeling of the painful experience and a knowledge of it. The disconnected or unhooked pain continues on as a reverberating circuit constantly affecting the system in one way or another. *It will do so for the rest of our lives until it is resolved*, which means appropriate linkage to its cognitive counterpart.

It takes a constant flow of energy to keep that pain sequestered. The more pain and the higher its charge value or valence, the greater the amount of energy needed for its repression. When you consider all the possible pains in our lives, traumatic birth, early surgery, childhood illnesses, plus all of the day to day psychological traumas we suffer with our parents, the amount of Primal Pain grows almost geometrically. Each time in our childhood when our needs are left unattended the weight of repression grows. If we are ignored, left to cry it out in the crib, forced to walk or talk too soon, not touched tenderly by our parents, not allowed to express our feelings, not permitted to speak during dinner, humiliated and ridiculed, constantly criticized, etc., we are forcing the system to expend more energy in the service of repression.

So long as we are young the body seems to meet this extra energy demand. The child doesn't experience his pain; rather, he just seems to have "boundless energy." In fact, he can hardly sit still. That "energy" he has is usually no more than the body being energized by Primal Pain; but because of gating, it remains an unconscious process.

There are physiologic signs of this high energy state, or hypermetabolic state, as we call it. Since the system is working harder it usually creates more heat and the basal body temperature rises slightly. Too, the blood pressure goes up a bit, not so much as to be medically treatable, but it is higher than it should be. To meet more of its energy demands the heart works a little harder and the pulse is somewhat elevated. Rarely, early in our lives, would a physician consider that slight elevation serious enough to warrant treatment or even comment. Indeed, having seen so many of us with these readings he might believe that it was a normal state. Thus, ninety eight point six has become the standard for the "normal" body temperature. We are learning that this may not be so at all. What seems to have happened is that neurosis has become so all pervasive that neurotic norms of the vital signs have become the standard for normal.

Pulse, blood pressure, body temperature are called the vital signs, because you are not going to be very vital (literally, have life) if they go astray. They are the usual measures by which physicians test our physical state to determine if disease is present.

Now suppose that a body temperature of ninety eight point six were not normal, which I believe is the case. A physician reading his thermometer would have to assume that a patient of his with that reading is sick. How could it be proved since the patient claims to feel fine and to be in perfect health? The job of convincing both of them that indeed disease is quite present would be a formidable task.

That disease is called neurosis. It is subtle, and insidious. It has no discernible smell or taste. It can hardly be seen, and what is worse, the carrier is often totally unaware that he is sick. Neurosis happens when the load of Primal Pains reaches a certain critical point so that the system can no longer handle them. The system is overtaxed and beginning in subtle fashion fails to do its job properly. The neurotic then goes to a doctor to be treated for what he thinks is his "real disease." It can be a kidney problem, migraine, ulcer, asthma, allergy or whatever; but the real disease is neurosis. That is why the treatment of the apparent disease usually goes on for a lifetime. It is the treatment of an "apparent" disease, not the real one. The best that one can do with this ostensible ailment is treat it symptomatically—pills, medication and more pills, all designed to suppress the appearance of the *symptom*; not to treat its causes. Those *causes*, however, are constantly churning below the surface, hasten our aging and eventually our deaths.

How do we know that? How do we know that there are Primal Pains churning away below the surface? And even if there are now can we be sure that they have anything to do with disease, aging and death? Aside from the fact that we at the Primal Institute in Los Angeles have treated many hundreds of patients from every walk of life and from almost every country in the world and have consistently found those traumas residing in each one of them, there is a good deal of collaborative research, as well; and this research is quoted throughout this book. There are the famous experiments of the neurosurgeon Wilder Penfield, who used an electronic probe on certain brain cells and produced an instant re-experience of an early childhood event in his patient with tremendous clarity and absolute recall. As soon as the probe was removed the experience stopped. That is, he could actually electronically stimulate an old coded memory in the brain.

There are literally thousands of studies of hypnotic age regression where subjects are brought back to the earliest months of life to re-experience events with complete lucidity. We now know that there is a form of "memory" that does not conform with previous notions we have grown up with, and "memory" is no longer synonymous with "conscious" recall. This new concept of memory is important because it means that events early in life can be registered in the system and "remembered" systemically; further, those "memories" exert a constant force on the system. Thus, we see in the Appendix pictures of bruises reappearing on a woman who was Primalling about a scene of being beaten by her father. The body cells "remembered" the bruises and exhibited them just as if the experience were happening in the present; again pointing out how the body does not differentiate past from present in the handling of Primal Pain. The memory of those beatings, it seems, were not simply inert engrams. They had a vitality, a life force which must have had some kind of continuous effect on the system. This is the force which devitalizes the system over the years.

We have indicated how the vital signs of our patients are changing with their therapy. To review; we have found a drop, at times, of up to three degrees in body temperature from just before a Primal to just after —a period of some two hours. One might demur, "All that screaming and thrashing could cause those changes," but quite the contrary, activity usually pushes up the vital signs, not down. Also, control groups who have simulated Primals without having connections do not achieve lower values. The brain has its own pulse, so to speak, and a quantity of activity called its amplitude. Amplitude is generally a measure of how many neurons in the brain are active at any given epoch of time, and this measure tells us how hard the brain is working. In this sense, it can be considered one more key vital sign. The brain has an optimum work output and excesses indicate that it is overworked. Since it is hooked up to every system of the body, a hyperactive brain means that other parts of us are working under stress, as well. For the first time we are developing what the average workload of the brain is, and we are developing norms which tell us when a brain is working too hard. Because we have not had a truly normal, relaxed population to work on before, such standards could not have been made. We are now beginning to get a good idea about when and how neurosis is present in the brain.

We have done several one year studies with patients and have also measured those who started their therapy more than five years before. The results have a particular import for increased longevity.

The Primal is a unique event physiologically. There seems to be no phenomenon like it in the annals of medicine. The patient lies in the research laboratory with his therapist, usually oblivious to the variety of wires streaming from the various parts of his body. His therapist is there to help him experience an early Primal feeling. In each case the research subject is also a clinical patient. As the patient approaches the feeling he is in obvious Pain. His pulse may rise by seventy percent or more, blood pressure can reach far into the hypertensive range (200/110 being not uncommon), body temperature will become elevated and the alpha amplitude of the brain can increase to 1000% higher than its resting value. If we were to compare the increase in another vital sign such as pulse it would mean that the pulse would be over 250 beats per minute, while blood pressure would be 400/200.

I call these rises "pre-Primal peaks," for they are evidence that the entire defense system of the body is straining to hold down the Pain. At a certain critical point the defense system becomes overtaxed and fails; the patient drops into the feeling and becomes locked-into the past, so to speak. There is a dramatic shift now from a sympathetic nervous system predominance to a parasympathetic one. All of the vital signs start to change and continue to do so right through until the end of the feeling, perhaps an hour later. What happens then is as dramatic as what happened before the pre-Primal peak. The body temperature can drop as much as three degrees. The pulse may fall off ninety percent from the peak, there may be a forty to fifty percent drop in systolic blood pressure from the peak and a fall of more than 1500% in alpha amplitude from the peak to the end of the Primal. These changes are not isolated to one patient. They are a commonplace (though the drop in body temperatures is more likely to be one degree on the average).

What does all this mean? First that *Pain and neurosis can be measured.* That neurosis has a profound affect on nearly all systems of the body and that the vital signs and systems they represent respond to Pain. They increase in its presence and drop with its resolution. It means that there is something inside of us that is tremendously threatening; and that something is no more than an old feeling or event. The rise in vital signs as feelings approach is strong evidence for the fact that early Pains remain coded in our systems for a lifetime. The chronic elevations in vital signs in the average population mean to me that the average neurotic is not living as long as he should; that he is aging far too rapidly, and that Primal people should live a very long time.

We know now that the vitality of the human system is linked to the amount of pain stored and unresolved. The alarm reactions we see during the pre-Primal peaks tell us that there is a defense system which ordinarily shields us from Pain, but leaves unanswered the question, "What happens to the Pain each day of our lives when we are *not* feeling it?" Where does it go and what does it do? What it does is kill us much too soon. Where it goes is in circles, as it were. That is, once disconnected it becomes a reverberating circuit cycling through the lower brain centers innervating the body, overstimulating the hormones, using up vital energy, creating pressure against organ systems, inhibiting the proper secretion of vital fluids within the endocrine system; all the while wearing us down, aging us and draining us. What is more, we think we have an idea about what structures in the brain are the key culprits for all this, and I shall have more to say about that shortly.

What we see is that Pain uses up tremendous amounts of energy. In the ordinary course of events we don't notice it because there is a governor system which modulates and equalizes all the vital signs and the expenditure of energy so that each system takes up a bit of the strain; the only way we can notice it is by the slight elevations in vital signs which unfortunately medicine has come to take as normal. It isn't as though the body is just using energy when the feelings start their ascent. Energy is being expended silently and unconsciously all of the time to keep the feeling well repressed. It is a totally automatic process. It is that chronic expenditure of energy, however, that does us in; for it is basic to the aging process.

I have not as yet spoken about the fact that Primal Pains produce the kinds of diseases which also hasten our demise, or cause us to develop habits such as smoking and drinking (to quell the Pain) which eventually produce fatal diseases. The linkage between smoking and lung cancer is too well known to repeat, as is the relationship of drinking to cirrhosis of the liver. Compulsive eating and obesity is still another route to early death. When the Pain doesn't get us directly it will kill us indirectly through the various habits we pick up in order to quell it. Almost everyone knows that smoking and heavy drinking will lead to early death. Is everyone masochistic with a death instinct? I think not. They simply would rather not be in Pain. They have made an unconscious pact with themselves; death in the long run to avoid Pain in the short run.

Not only is there a drop in the vital signs just after a Primal but our research indicates that after eight months of Primal Therapy there is a continuous drop in those measures among our advanced patients. The whole system seems to be "cooling down," using less energy, metabolizing more slowly with a far less busy brain. If we examine the questionnaire chapter we see that the ailments mentioned before plus dozens more seem to disappear and do not return. The gamut is from hemmorhoids to asthma.

The weakest systems will be the most vulnerable and they will give way soonest; but every system is constantly operating under stress so long as Primal Pains are left unresolved in the system. The resolution of these Pains, then, is a matter of life and death; and any therapeutic system which hopes to be effective against disease, either psychological or physiological, must address itself to the matter of Pain.

Not only does Pain hasten the aging and deterioration process but it does so in highly selective ways. For instance, the brain does not age uniformly. It ages from inside out; the inner portions deteriorating sooner, the middle section next and the outer core last.* This is important for many reasons as we shall see; but one encouraging note is that the outer and topmost portion of the brain, the neocortex, has a very slow deterioration rate; so that our higher thought processes are relatively untouched even in the years beyond one hundred. You *can* teach an old dog new tricks!

This is crucial; for if Primal Man lives beyond one hundred there is little reason for him to do so if he cannot steer himself around a complex world. If his thought processes are dimmed, if he can no longer read books or comprehend a story on television life wouldn't be much fun. But fortunately none of this is lost. What is lost? Why does the brain age from inside out? Could that aging process be reversed? We believe that it can.

The valence or charge value of first line Pain is high and the residual tension it leaves in the system for a lifetime is enormous. Because all later Pains are laid on top of this substrate, accessibility to these traumas is difficult. Gating works immediately, even before birth, so that the earliest Pains are gated and disconnected from awareness. The newborn with a harsh birth may suffer from a variety of derived ailments such as colic or excema but he certainly has no awareness of what he has been through. He simply doesn't have enough third line consciousness yet to make any distinctions about the source of his Pains. But because he does not recognize them and is unaware of them doesn't mean that they are not there. They are there and their Pain is intense. We know because when a patient finally has access to his first line Pains and begins to resolve traumas on that level the drops we see in vital signs are tremendous. This is one way we know about the existence of very early trauma, their veracity and their

---

*A more technical and neurological discussion of brain aging is presented in "Primal Pain and Aging" by Dr. M. Holden. J. Of Primal Therapy II, #2, 1974.

charge value. Obviously, with large rises in vital signs just before a first line Primal, and with tremendous drops in those signs after the resolution of the Primal we know that we are dealing with high valence events. This is to say nothing about the subjective relief that the patient experiences afterwards. He knows as no one else can what the charge value of the trauma was and how it feels to begin to resolve it. It is not unusual for the patient to come in with his symptom in full force just before a giant first line Primal. With resolution and connection he does not leave with it. Connection means that the trauma finally is no longer gated but has access to the highest level of consciousness which can now acknowledge and integrate it. That connection can be observed and can now be measured. If there is little or no vital sign change afterwards the patient will usually continue to suffer his symptom.

It is clear to us that first line pressure is often the greatest and that first line Pain rarely has a match. It is also evident that those Pains reside for a lifetime in *precisely that section of the brain which ages first.* Our assumption is that aging of the brain's inner core is in large measure due to first line trauma and the great pressure it exerts on the delicate cells of the inner brain. Certainly, rises and falls of hundreds of percent in the alpha activity of the brain before and after and Primal do indicate the enormous effects Pain has on the brain.

It is not just Pain which resides on the first line. Each level of consciousness mediates certain activities of the body. When a newborn has a trauma he is going to respond in terms of what brain and body systems are adequate at that point. The newborn isn't going to walk around to shut off his tension. He isn't going to rationalize and explain it and he isn't going to go to the refrigerator for a beer. He is largely adequate in the viscera and so he will have more secretions in his stomach perhaps; or he may develop respiratory problems. Generally, the responses he has will be internal and will be along the midline of the body which is mediated by the inner brain. If he is tied down to his crib by a blanket which is much too tight for hours before any one comes there is not much else he can do but cry and respond internally. That response, say of increased hydrochloric acid to the stomach, may become prototypic. This means that with all later stress situations he will be prone to gastric hypersecretion. He is, at his tender age, working on an ulcer. All that he needs is years of stress and wear and tear until the stomach lining finally develops a lesion. He will not undo that prototypic response until he resolves the prototypic trauma on the particular level of consciousness in which it occurred.

One of the most frequent response patterns on the first line is of course increased heart activity. The heart speeds up in response to Pain and this speed-up can also be prototypic. What again matters is that rapid heart rate, later palpitations and skipped beats all are prototypic responses to specific early events in our lives which *still live* in the system. Those events continuously innervate the system causing it to expend energy in the service of its repression. We don't know about it because it has been repressed or gated away long before we had a fully adequate neocortex to make sense of it for us. No wonder then that we find it hard to believe that there is such a thing as birth trauma which stays with us for a lifetime. But it does, and it takes its toll on our lives. It makes the heart beat a bit harder all the time, and under even slight stress it tends to speed up considerably. This is because later stress events tend to trigger off the prototypic buried one, setting off the prototypic reaction. So we might say that many of us are working on our heart attack almost from the moment of birth, or even before.

Not all of us tend toward higher heart rate and blood pressure under stress. There are prototypic events which tend to drop the heart rate. One patient was placed in ice water in order to be revived just after birth when he came out dead. His prototypic response was a lowered pulse and blood pressure and that is how he responded to stress throughout his life. In his case, lowered vital sign values were not a sign of health or longevity. His brain was quite hyperactive and other systems became involved in the hyperactivity other than the heart and blood system. Those systems would eventually fail resulting first in rapid aging and then premature death.

It is difficult to comprehend the tremendous pressure of first line Pain for until now we have not had the techniques for opening up people to that level of consciousness. We simply have had no idea about the magnitude of internal pressure until we let it out, and now we find that a person may have hundreds of Primals over one or two years about one single event which lasted for a matter of a few minutes at the start of his life. He will scream, drool, writhe and thrash for hours per day over that trauma; and by doing so he is releasing forevermore that much unresolved Pain and pressure. No one could fake that kind of Pain month after month; no one would want to. And no one would enter into that kind of process no matter what any expert told him unless he himself were convinced that something very beneficial were going on inside him. That beneficial process prolongs life.

It is tempting to imagine that only so-called hysterics have that kind of experience. But this is hardly the case. We have had scientists including a number of experienced psychiatrists relive first line events and all of them are quite convinced about it. Many of these professionals have had years of psychoanalysis previously and felt fairly well integrated, hardly hysterics, before they reached us. It would be pushing logic to the extreme to imagine that some seven hundred patients all were hysterics or were particularly suggestible to having a certain kind of experience. What we have found cannot be faked: the drop in the vital signs after such a Primal experience. This is the sine qua non of the resolution of Pain. These physiologic measures tell us how a patient is doing; if he is truly feeling and resolving as opposed to abreacting. There are any number of those outside the Primal Institute who imagine that they are Primalling only to discover in our laboratory later on that they were abreacting. And abreaction is not resolving of Pain; it is palliative, and temporarily alleviating. Without resolution of Pain all the crying and screaming in the world will not change the aging process one scintilla. Aside from subjective reports we now have objective measures for checking progress in therapy. This is important because patients or anyone can easily delude themselves. Subjective reports are only important in conjunction with objective ones. For example, subjects who meditate claim to achieve relaxed bliss. Research indicates, however, that brain amplitude *rises* with meditation. Our conclusion, therefore, is that the state of bliss is a delusion, a self deception which occurs because meditation *increases* the amount of brain activity involved in gating and repression; the result of more effective repression is a subjective feeling of relaxation. That kind of relaxation can only *hasten* death. There is no magic. In every therapeutic approach we must ask the question, "What happened to the Pain?" If the approach, medical or psychiatric, neglects that question it may well be neglecting the root source of the affliction. It will suppress the symptom leaving the disease intact. "The operation was a success but the patient died" is a literal statement of the case. The death has just been somewhat delayed. There are many neurotics·who find life so rotten that the last thing they would want to do is prolong life. But they must understand that resolving Pains also resolves one's misery so that life becomes terribly precious and important.

I do not wish to deny the obvious value of living in a stress-free environment. Certainly, there are factors which can prolong life even with neurosis. Proper diet, pollution free environment, less competitive society, less demanding job are all important. But with neurosis present they only constitute a delaying action.

Perhaps it is time to be more precise about life and death; for when one discusses death one should also have some concept of life. The essence of life is organization; and the essence of dying is disorganization. Everything about us is organization—of systems functioning in unison. We are vital when the organization is efficient and the distribution of life systems functions fluidly. The maximum rate at which energy is used to restore efficient organization is called the vitality of the system. Deterioration occurs when the demand on a system exceeds its capacity to meet it. When this occurs over time the system loses its ability to recover. This is precisely what happens in neurosis—constant demand on the system to keep the Pains at bay until the system can no longer hold up.

Pain is disorganizing. It causes a massive rerouting process in the brain so that thoughts and feelings are no longer unified. We see it manifested in psychosis where cohesion is lost, fragmentation of thought occurs and the person is generally inattentive and distractible. We are observing a disorganized mind; what we may overlook is that the "mind" is no more than a collection of nerve cells with a particular kind of organization. I am introducing the notion of cellular disorganization because generally there are two major ways out of this life for us all: heart disease and cancer. I shall discuss heart disease later. Cancer is a clear example of cellular disorganization, and years of studies by eminent researchers have not solved the riddle of why it takes place. I am suggesting the possibility that cancer (many cancers) is psychosomatic. It may be that the reason that we have not found a solution before is that we neglected this option. Instead of only studying cells under a microscope we should be studying the *people* who carry those cells around; *for those cells are ultimately a reflection of an internal state.* If that state is hypermetabolic, if the inner pressure is gigantic, it is bound to be reflected in the cells.

In cancer the structure of the cell loses its integrity and there follows a wild proliferation of abnormal cells. In Primal terms, I would call this the insanity of the cell. It has lost its organization and cohesion.

It is no accident that a recent study by a team at Northwestern University Medical School (as reported in the Medical Tribune Report) found a high correlation between hypertension (high blood pressure) and cancer; both are first line disease states. But if blood pressure is so clearly related to Pain why shouldn't cancer be? Could it be that such a high correlation is meaningless? I rather doubt it. They are correlated, in my opinion, because they *both* are reflective of internal Pain. And it is not by some mere chance that the highest correlation is between high blood pressure and cancer of the colon . . . exactly in the midline where the deepest Pain and repression lie.

High blood pressure indicates a pressure inside the body. We have observed cancer patients in Primal Therapy. When they arrive at the key Pains of their lives there is no mistake about how gigantic the pressure is. Those with stomach cancer feel incredible pressure in the stomach during Primals; and that makes them aware of how they have been grinding down there for years, day in and day out. It is only when the grinding of the stomach stopped that they could appreciate what they had been doing to themselves. I am not stating outright that Primal Pain caused their cancers. I am saying that the focus of the Pain seems to be in key areas, and after decades of that focus there must be cellular and tissue breakdown. It is certainly worthy of investigation; particularly now that we have access to the deepest levels of Pain and have a chance to see what kind of relationships there are.

If we go on studying the cell alone as a discrete and viable entity then all we can hope to discover may be the *result* of Primal Pain, and we won't even know it is a result. If we disengage man from his cells then we have neglected a very important factor in the reasons for cellular breakdown. This will leave us in the position of studying the many ways cells break down without touching upon the causes for the disorganization. The recognition of the influence of Primal Pain has eluded us for all these years not only because we had no means for gaining access to the deeper recesses of the mind, but because the effects of Pain are systemic and cannot be localized in one spot. There is nothing to put your finger on. We haven't studied whole man before because we had no way to do it and we could not find "whole man" anywhere, in any case. Now that we have found a way to make man whole, body and mind, we can gain some appreciation of what it means to be integrated.

To return to the problem of cancer. There was a recent research study from the University of Chicago in which rats with leukemia were cured by taking out the pituitary. The pituitary in humans is a closely related glandular structure to the hypothalamus. Together they regulate the hormone output and the vital signs. Because the hypothalamus regulates blood pressure and blood pressure is correlated with cancer we might look to this structure for some clues to the disease. That is, maybe there is something about the hypothalamus which affects both blood pressure and cancer. The hypothalamus does affect the immune system of the body, and there is evidence that cancer occurs with a breakdown in the immune system. It is the immune system which can inhibit the proliferation of cancer cells.

The hypothalamus is an important structure for it is one of the central mediators for Pain. It relays it, reroutes and funnels it into the various organ systems. It is pretty much the visceral regulator for the body and translates Pain into symptoms or changes in the vital signs. It is a first line structure, and traumas on this line are mediated by it. Overstimulation or inhibition of hormones takes place here along with the pituitary. It is a key structure because it regulates all of the automatic functions which keep us alive—breathing, blood circulation, temperature and heart beat.

We ought to take a hint from rat and mice studies and understand that if the structures mediating Pain are removed from animals, and leukemia is reversed, there may be some important connection between Pain and cancer. Fortunately, we don't have to do surgery on humans to cut out the Pain. We have a way of relieving the heavy burden of Pain the hypothalamus carries. I won't say it isn't Painful, but our discoveries indicate that feelings are not Painful in and of themselves. It is the blockage of them that hurts. That is why all the vital signs drop when a person starts into feeling. The system is no longer under stress or threat. It is simply reacting. Let us put it another way. Feelings are blocked because they are Painful . . . back then. They can be finally felt by the adult for he no longer is going to die if his mother doesn't come to his crib.

There is a very good reason why we haven't seen first line Pain in evidence (although some psychotic episodes are evidence of it, albeit unrecognized). They have the least accessibility. The reason for this is, inter alia, that our survival depends on proper first line functioning. If first line Pains could be easily triggered so that they ascended quickly then almost any event could completely upset our systems causing radical swings in the vital signs. We wouldn't want that to happen too often and fortunately it doesn't. What we may get instead from that deep unconscious repression is cancer. Primals are something extraordinary to observe; for they are catastrophic in appearance and in their experience. Any patient Primalling on the first line, for example, knows he is going through something profound. He also knows for the first time that there lies deep inside his brain forces previously beyond the scope of his imagination. He is certain as never before that those Pains would have killed him in one way or another and he begins to worship at the tabernacle of his body for the miraculous way it hides the ugly truth from us and keeps us functioning.

It is the hormone system which is usually considered the chemical mediator of feelings. Hormones affect everything from how tall we grow to how much milk a mother will have for her baby. They largely determine our sex life and how large a woman's breasts will grow. Hormone interaction makes up a system known as the endocrine system. This system is most sensitive to feelings, and feelings can alter it radically. Hormone-related diseases such as hypoglycemia and diabetes are also feeling-related afflictions. Emotional upsets often adversely affect them. Through an understanding of prototypic trauma and prototypic response we can now begin to see how hormone related diseases, often fatal in the later decades of life, get their start. Severe trauma very early in life when the body and brain are organizing the hormone output can seriously disrupt the endocrine (hormone) system. It can alter the setpoint of something such as thyroid output so that later stress can either inhibit proper output or cause a hypersecretion. Primal trauma can affect the system in the same way that excessive weather conditions can overtax the thermostat in your house. Eventually, with continuous overwork the heat system is going to break down. This may be the case with hypothyroidism for example. Trauma causes there to be insufficient circulating thyroid hormone in the system. The person becomes easily fatigued and enervated and doesn't know why. He may feel chronically depressed, may rationalize his inactivity and general lifelessness in one way or another because he doesn't understand what is wrong. Even if he has tests and is finally treated for his thyroid condition, *he is still not being treated for the cause of it*. I may hasten to add that any number of thyroid cases have been successfully treated with Primal Therapy, along with many other of the hormone-related diseases. We have seen cases where a patient who has been on five grains of thyroid a day can leave her pills after four months of therapy without any of the previous symptoms of hypothyroidism appearing. Laboratory tests confirm the changes we observe.

Hypothyroidism is not usually considered a fatal disease, but I think that any Primal disease is fatal in the sense that we become fatalities in life much sooner than we should. It is a sign that the system is not working properly—that it is askew, and after decades of malfunction the system eventually "caves in." I have observed that this generally happens in the late fifties and early sixties to most neurotics. It is as if this wonderful human system can take almost any abuse for that length of time. It can absorb malfunctions in systems for five decades with equanimity. But that is about the extent of it, then the ravages of "old age" seem to set in; but they are not the afflictions of age at all. They are the end results of carrying a burden of Pains around in our systems all that time.

It is a general law of the body that it shuts down against Pain. The blood system constricts, the muscles tighten and even the pupils narrow in the face of something painful or unpleasant. So it is no wonder that with a constant burden of buried Pains many of us are eventually going to have circulatory problems. Indeed, neurotics do show a gradual increase in blood pressure with age (not the case in Primal people studied to date). The results of this continuous constriction process place a burden on the heart; and malfunction of the heart is the way out of this world for most of us. Having an open and fluid blood system, then, is paramount to longevity. We have seen several cases of angina in men in their fifties. Angina is a most common heart ailment characterized by a urgent, intense, squeezing pain in the chest. One of the factors involved in angina is constriction of the coronary blood supply. During an angina attack there is a spasm of the vessel and the flow of oxygen is cut off to certain cells of the heart. When the cut off lasts long enough there is cell death (this is commonly experienced as a "heart attack.") "Cell death." It sounds so clinical, but that means part of us is dying. We are no more than an organized collection of cells. And that part is dying because it did not have enough oxygen. I am suggesting that this may be because the system is trying to ward off Pain through the constriction process.

We have produced cessation of angina in men who have come to us and have indeed headed off angina attacks that had already begun. The Pain, instead of being funneled off into the blood system arrived into full consciousness instead. Here, clearly we can see the relationship of Pain to disease, and what is more important the relationship of Pain to death.

Long Range Studies

There are less dramatic ways to die other than coronary attacks but the end result is just as permanent. For example, there is a theory in comparative anatomy that each species is alloted just so many heart beats and when the supply is used up that is the end. The mouse which has a lifespan of three years has a normal heartrate of 2-300. The elephant which lives 60 or more years has a heartrate of 60-70. In other words, what seems to be the case is that a slower heartrate is correlated with a longer life, even considering differences in body size. It is of some great consequence that in our long range studies of Primal patients the average reduction in heart rate is ten beats per minute. Further, blood pressure is considerably lower; in some cases of hypertension before therapy, there has been a fifty percent drop in blood pressure after treatment.

A USC biologist believes that if man could lower his body temperature by some three degrees he could add several decades onto his life. While we have not as yet done that, long term patients do average one degree less than the ninety eight point six in the average population. We must add into these calculations the fact that Primal people do not smoke. What this means is that aside from avoiding lung cancer their hearts are not working as hard; for smoking and nicotine in particular tends to constrict blood vessels causing the heart to work much harder to supply its blood and oxygen.

And there is another important factor in this prolongation of life. I have indicated that disconnected Pain keeps the system mobilized. Now the reason many neurotics do not feel that mobilization is that they organize their lives to meet that activation. They continuously find new projects and struggles so that they never have to rest and relax. Their life, in one way, is one large rationale for their unconscious Primal activation. They might imagine that all those work and deadline pressures are external but that is because life has been maneuvered and contrived in that way in the first place. The end result is that the person is dashing around using up his heartbeats and his energy. It is not overwork that kills. It is the cause of overwork which is fatal. The tragedy of this is that there is nothing he can do to reverse the process. Primal Pain is exactly like having your motor turned on and accelerated for life. *Nothing in this world will turn it off except resolution of Pain.*

That is why having one heart attack or cancerous affliction makes another likely. The activation by Pain never changes and never loses its force. We have seen new patients sometimes struggling to get to a feeling for an hour or more; and we know they haven't because in the end there is no change in the vital signs. Screaming and hollering never make real changes in and of themselves; and that is why it is not called Primal Scream Therapy. Screaming is what we do when we are in Pain; but Pain is the goal, not the scream.

There are several ways that the heart can be damaged. Perhaps the most common affliction is atherosclerosis. This is characterized by the development of fatty deposits along the vessel wall. There is enough research now to indicate that stress leads to increase blood fats (lipids), and many investigators believe that this is a major determinant of atherosclerosis. What is significant for our discussion is that it is the hypothalamus which may again play a key role in the development of atherosclerosis. There have been experiments with rabbits fed on a high cholesterol diet. They were then separated into two groups; one group received chronic hypothalamic electronic stimulation and the other group did not. At the end of three months the first group who were stimulated developed much high serum lipid levels and at death showed far more severe atherosclerosis of their aortas.* It is my assumption that sequestered Primal Pain acts exactly as an electronic stimulator to the hypothalamus; and those who die from atherosclerosis may well do so not because they had a high fat diet over the years but because of what the body did with that diet. To put it another way, many of us have to watch our diets later in life because Pain is causing the hypothalamus to stimulate the production of blood lipids. The diet is a counterbalancing measure to internal stress. And indeed much of internal medicine is exactly this counterbalancing approach. We have to cut down on too much excitement, too much exercise, too much of this or that because there is already too much going on inside.

Let me make myself clear. Primal Pains do not cause all disease. But they most certainly do create a lifetime metabolic burden: and this burden leads to any number of diseases eventually when the system weakens. This metabolic burden, in my opinion, radically shortens the life span. We don't need sophisticated instruments to measure this burden; we can see it in people's faces. People in Pain do not look well and they do not age well. Starting in the forties** they begin to look ravaged even though they still cannot feel it. Though we tend to think that this is the inevitable result of growing old, it is more the product of carrying around a load of Pain. It is my belief that we can grow old gracefully and beautifully without Primal Pain, and this is more than guesswork. We have seen our older patients grow younger and look better as their therapy proceeds. The vital sign changes do show on their faces for a simple reason; they are more vital.

There is a way to take the Pains out of our systems; and we do not need to do surgery to accomplish it. Stored Pain means repressed feeling and disconnected circuits. The solution is feeling and reconnection. Feeling gives us back our unity and organization and makes us come alive in a most literal sense, both physiologically and psychologically. That is surely the way to beat death; the death of our feelings which makes life not worth living, and the death of our bodies which has used up all of its energy in the struggle against Pain.

---

*Gunn Friedmann and Boyers ref. J. Clin. Inv. 1960.
**While psychosomatic illnesses and cancers do certainly occur in young people they are more common in middle life because, we believe, it is in middle life that our bodies begin to fail under the burden of constant stress.

CHAPTER TWELVE

Feelings and Survival:
An Evolutionary Perspective
Bernard Campbell

For many years I have been interested, as a professional anthropologist, in communication among both animals and men. I have been especially concerned with so-called non-verbal communication and its close similarity in man and those animals most closely related to us, the monkeys and apes.

The insights that we gain from a study of animal behavior (some of which I have briefly attempted to set out in this chapter) should show us, if nothing else does, that a failure in non-verbal communication, or to be more precise, a failure to express our emotions, may be not only socially disruptive but lies at the very root of the present human condition. If men are alien to one another, and if as a result society is fragmented, it is for this profound reason: that we have failed to be ourselves in the expression of our feelings—our pains, sorrows, anxiety and joy. We have failed to convey to each other the truth about our nature or the extent of our need.

Emotional honesty is the social bond, and if honesty is lost the bond will wither, and society will die as its members destroy it and so themselves. That is why I see the expression of the emotions, not merely as a road to mental health in Primal Therapy, but as a matter of concern to us all.

The Nature and Function of Feelings

What are feelings for? Why do we have emotions? It is a surprising fact that emotions have only recently been thoroughly investigated by scientists. Typically, it was Charles Darwin who made the pioneering study just one hundred years ago in his book *On the Expression of the Emotions in Man and Animals* (1872), in which he documented the similarities which existed in the expression of the emotions in man and a number of animal species, especially monkeys and apes. The similarities were so striking that it was a short step to suppose that the emotions of men and animals had a common underlying physiological basis which was a response to a certain recognizable range of experience.

However, it was not until the 1920's that further work was done on the emotions by Walter Cannon, who made detailed investigations of their physiological basis and showed how the adrenal glands operate as the body's danger alarm system (*The Wisdom of the Body,* 1932). Following this, Hans Selye began work on the hormones produced by the adrenal cortex, including cortisone, and over many years studied the part played by hormones in the body's response to stress—work which is summarized in his book *The Stress of Life* (1956). Here he showed, from a medical viewpoint, that many diseases which until then were believed to have a simple physical cause, such as certain cancers, heart failure and asthma, were at least in part the product of stress. This research has been developed much further since then by many others. [Also, it is increasingly evident that physical illness often occurs in relation to one's burden of Primal Pain.]

All this work has demonstrated a number of important points for the subject of this essay: that the response to stress is deep-seated and produces very wide-ranging physiological effects in the body; that it involves lower brain centers including the limbic system as well as the endocrine system (especially the adrenal hormones); that for this reason it certainly evolved many millions of years ago and is shared in common by all mammals. Therefore the function of emotion is surely extremely important and biologically profound, and has been maintained throughout time by natural selection.

For purposes of discussion we can now divide the emotional response into several components:

1. A sensory component—the input stimulus.
2. A physiological component—the neurophysiological basis of the response.

3. A subjective component—the consciousness of that response which we call a feeling.

4. An expressive component—the motor response, or emotion.

The physiological and subjective components form the motivational aspect of emotion which brings about the expressive and motor response. Evidently, natural selection has brought into existence motivational-emotional responses to certain stimuli which prove effective in getting done the adaptive tasks required for survival, such as finding food and water, avoiding predators, achieving fertile copulation, caring for the young, and training them to cope effectively with the requirements of a given environment.

We can best understand the adaptive function of the motivational process by considering the part played by it in a highly evolved social animal such as a higher primate. Baboons are well-studied in the wild, and have a highly integrated social structure. One important reason for this is that in the presence of dangerous predators such as the lion or leopard, a lone baboon is unable to defend itself: his survival depends on co-operative defenses. Any baboon that falls behind during troop movement and becomes separated from the troop is as good as dead. Troop solidarity and integration is therefore an adaptation of the greatest importance to these animals, and troop solidarity ultimately depends on the maintenance of a series of inter-individual bonds. Motivational patterns have evolved which make bond maintenance pleasurable, and bond disruption painful. The bonds are varied from those which cause adult males to be solicitous of the welfare of the young, to the mother-infant bonds which are very strong indeed. So strong is the maternal motivation that a mother baboon will carry a dead infant around for 3 or 4 days, until it begins to disintegrate. In contrast, a human mother would rapidly lose interest in a totally unresponsive infant. The child's response to mothering in the form of smiles, chuckles and so on, is an important, indeed essential, reinforcement to the motivation of proper maternal behavior on the human mother's part. Such reinforcement by the infant is evidently less essential to the appropriate behavior of the baboon mother. Thus the expression of pleasurable satisfaction on the part of the human infant is important in its survival.

Responses to pain and pleasure are present in both baboon and human; they find their origin in the same lower brain centers of the limbic system. The difference between monkey and man lies in the flexibility of the expression of emotion, and in the inhibitory mechanisms which are available to block the subjective component of emotion from consciousness.

Feelings and Communication

We see then that while the oldest and perhaps the most important function of emotion is to direct essential behavior, it also serves as a vital means of communication, at least in mammals. The expressions of fear and rage, for example, are manifold. The hormone adrenalin, as is well known, brings about many bodily changes, some of which are invisible (increases in blood sugar level and rate of heartbeat) while others are visible: hair standing on end, blanching of skin, sweating and changes in facial expression. During the process of evolution, the visible changes have come to serve an important role in social communication. The evolution of a highly socialized group such as we find among the primates (our nearest relatives, the monkeys and apes) depends on a very sophisticated means of communication to maintain the integrity of the group. Primates communicate by a number of means: by bodily gesture and touch, by facial expression, by vocalization, by scents, and by locomotor activity. Those who have studied primate communication have come to realize that none of these means of communication is equivalent to human language, and that even the vocalizations have an entirely different genesis; they are in fact no more nor less than the expression of the individual's emotion at a given moment. What we find in a noisy, active group of social monkeys is that each animal is transmitting a continuous account of its emotional state, and that all other members of the troop who can do so are monitoring it. Monkeys that live in close proximity and can see each other easily (such as the terrestrial baboons) express their emotions by gesture and expression rather more than by vocalization. Those which live more scattered in dense forest have to rely on vocalizations for this purpose. But one thing is clear, animal "language" is not language at all, but an expression of their emotional-motivational state generated by the limbic system.

It is not quite true to say that all emotions are immediately and directly expressed, however, since in the presence of an autocratic alpha male a more junior male may inhibit his feeling of rage. But the inhibition of expression is usually short-lived, and in most cases may appear as a displaced response. In this case anger which is properly due to a senior member of the hierarchy may be redirected to a lower member, and then passed on down the ladder of seniority. This redirection seems to be a common product of emotion and inhibition.

In both animals and man repressed emotions can obviously result in physiological disturbances such as might affect the digestive process, heartbeat or blood pressure. Changes in hormone levels can also be measured as a result of repression. A monkey which has been rejected in a sexual context by a high-ranking male will show a lowering of testosterone level, just as a human child in a hopeless institutional setting will show a drop in level of growth hormones.

Similarly, a monkey or a child will also show displacement activity of the kind described above. In a caged monkey troop such displaced response can be passed right down a hierarchy to the lowest ranking member (who in this way gets it in the neck for every aggressive action that occurs among his superiors). Yet this displacement is in a sense adaptive because it reduces overt conflict in the group at the price of putting terrible stress on the most junior member, who has literally nowhere to go with his feelings. In wild primates the lower ranking individuals soon learn to run away so that the need to act out by the first victim is discharged in a short chase. Here the social rejection of the low ranking animal can put him outside the breeding group, and castrate him psychologically. This indeed may be at the root of the mechanism by which the size of animal populations is controlled. These individuals may leave the breeding population, and as Seligman has recently shown, animals in hopeless situations may literally drop dead from what has been labelled parasympathetic death (a lethal response to hopelessness by the parasympathetic nervous system). In this way it appears that repression and its metabolic expression may be ancient and highly adaptive as a species survival mechanism. We may expect to find it in all social animals and indeed in any vertebrate species in which competition occurs over sexual partners.

Besides noting the antiquity of the response, however, it is worth stressing that non-human primates usually act out their feelings immediately, even if they are displaced. At the same time, the extent to which their response can be said to be symbolized is very limited. If monkey B is attacked by monkey A and then turns upon monkey C, there is a sense in which C could be said to be symbolic for A, but the symbol (C) is not far removed from its referent (A), and the symbolic options available are strictly limited. A monkey at the bottom of the hierarchy who cannot act out in this way is more likely to become catatonic than he is to find a more remote symbol to attack, such as a tree.

The fact that emotions are generally "out front" means that each member of the troop knows the feelings of all members: there can be no emotional dishonesty. As far as our non-human cousins are concerned, this is the key to social survival, the key to community life. The free expression of the emotions of group members is a profound and vital ingredient of their social stability and evolutionary success. In contrast it is characteristic of man that he can to a great extent hide his emotions from his fellows. (The lie detector measures pulse rate, respiratory rate, blood pressure and skin response: it is designed to detect those physiological changes which result from the production of adrenalin, produced under stress and fear. In so far as it is effective it is so because man has not learned how to control his emotions as fully as he believes he has, and the physiological component remains to be monitored by scientists.)

To return to non-human primates: it is clear that in a social animal the communicative function of emotional expression is very important to survival, and for this reason it has been evolved in great complexity. The complexity of facial musculature and the variety of vocalization in primates is a correlate of the importance of the precise expression of the emotions in their social life.

A third function and effect of emotion is to highlight and order certain memories. Ease of recall of previous experience will depend on the amount and nature of the feelings associated with the original experience. This is an important phenomenon, which directs and accelerates the learning experience in all animals. Biologically important experience—which is that which may threaten or secure an individual's survival—is accompanied by feelings: fear, pain or pleasure. Biologically important memories are associated and recorded with that emotional context: the neuronal record is more deeply impressed. Thus the learning of biologically useful behavior which is concerned with the survival of both the individual and the species is facilitated at the expense of biologically useless behavior, and memory of it carries a feeling component which is adaptive. This may be one important function of the subjective component of emotion, feeling. When I refer to behavior concerned with the survival of the *species,* I am thinking not only of maternal behavior, but of all reproductive behavior, and especially sexual behavior. Such behavior always carries a high emotional tone because it is essential to survival in this sense.

Feelings and Man's Evolution

Under the heading of emotion man differs from the non-human primates in a number of ways (some of which have been mentioned) which are of great significance to a proper understanding of human behavior.

These may be summarized as follows:

1. First and foremost, a new means of communication called language has evolved to supplement emotion. Feelings can now be communicated verbally: a new option is available.

2. Emotion can be readily repressed and redirected and this can become a stereotyped process. The redirection may be symbolic and so increasingly inappropriate and maladaptive. *In other words, symbolic options are available for the expression of emotion, which may be false.*

The evolution of language is probably man's most remarkable characteristic: it is certainly unique among living organisms. It allows communication to operate in an entirely new way. While previously communication was almost entirely confined to the expression of the emotions, it can now include reference to objects in the environment including other individuals, classes of objects, and even abstract ideas and functions. This highly significant character of mankind brought with it a vast number of correlates which have profoundly altered man's behavior from that of his primate ancestors.

In the first place, the spontaneous expression of the emotions is no longer the only means available to communicate feelings. Men can talk about their feelings, their joys and their pain, without expressing them from the limbic system. Language is generated in an entirely different part of the brain, the neocortex, and some parts of this structure, essential to language, have only evolved in the last two million years or so. The fact that this means of conscious expression has arisen in evolution suggests that it must have become adaptive under certain conditions. Just what these are we do not know, but my own idea is that where a social group is living in a confined space, the stress on individuals created by monitoring the intensive emotional expressions of the whole group might be maladaptive. The history of man's evolution is suggestive in this respect. Early man, until nearly a million years ago, had lived in the open, as many hunting and gathering tribes do today in parts of the world where the climate is warm and dry. As man began to explore the northern hemisphere where protection was needed from the elements as well as dangerous predators, he took to living in caves and building shelters and huts. He began to create circumstances in which the social groups were far more crowded than they had ever been before, and from which it was not always possible to move away, especially at night when protection was needed from cold and danger. Under these circumstances, the power of emotional expression to evoke emotional responses could have become exhausting: if a child cried, all mothers would respond; and if a woman wept, all the males would feel the pull of her need. When a baby cries in a limited space, the sound has a very intense effect on the adults present. The cry is designed quite precisely to get a response from a neighboring adult, especially the mother, and that is why continuous crying "gets on people's nerves." The sound has been selected in evolution to do just that. [Also, it is not by accident that "wailing" sirens are for "emergencies" on our city streets]. Thus it seems plausible at least, that in confined spaces the use of speech to convey adult feelings would change what was previously a widespread transmission into a "tight-beam" signal—that is, one intended for only one person, rather than the whole group. In this way we can perhaps see some possible advantages of lowering the intensity of a range of limbic expression by inhibition and eventually more permanent repression. With language available to override emotion the social group could in this way retain its cohesion through communication. In all these ways I see the evolution of repression as a *socially adaptive neurologic response*.

A further advantage of effective emotional repression may have come with the development of technology. The mental processes involved in manufacturing skills and intellectual activity may operate optimally when the cortex is free of limbic inputs. Certainly anyone who has to smoke in order to concentrate on his work is demonstrating this thesis. But this cortical inhibition would presumably be employed *after* the build-up of repressed pain reached the point when its expression could be maladaptive.

This essay, however, is designed to emphasize the many long-term disadvantages of this important development. Both the characteristics of a species' behavior and its anatomy and physiology are in practice compromises between the differing demands (expressed as natural selection) of the environment. Survival of a species depends on its being able to maintain a balance between opposing responses. It looks from the story of human evolution as though a little repression became a good thing, but from our present position we can see that too much is very dangerous. One way of looking at the repressive process is to state that emotional dishonesty became possible for the first time. Men can say one thing while they feel another, and can often mislead other people about their emotional state. As de Talleyrand cynically put it: "Speech was given to man to disguise his thoughts." The surprising thing is that human beings can even mislead themselves. Such emotional dishonesty immediately endangers the integrity of the group. I believe that those modern ideals of western man of living in close communities in social harmony are bound to fail as long as the repression of emotion permits emotional dishonesty. Survival of the fully integrated group (and the integrated marriage) depends, like a primate troop, on the full expression of the emotions, not through language, but through the paths proper to them. It is important to realize that while in our society we do not use primate vocalizations very extensively, we do still retain the full range of vocalizations and bodily and facial expressions which we have inherited from our non-human ancestors, and it is in our power to be as open in our emotional life as they always were.

But the inhibition of emotional expression is more serious in its consequences than that. The inhibition of juvenile and infantile feelings, as the reader will be well aware, causes neurosis—a state of tension with far-reaching deleterious effects. In older people the effects are less obvious but nearly as dangerous. If the active, motor response to the production of adrenal hormones is inhibited, over and over again, even in adults, the result can be serious hypertension of the circulatory system, ulceration of the stomach and arteriosclerosis. Heart attacks were very rare until recently. Today, the straightjacketed lives which we lead are literally crippling us. If the body is not allowed to respond in an appropriate way to the production of adrenal hormones, then the effect of these hormones can be dangerous.

From this it is clear that both the communicative and the physiological function of emotional expression is still of vital importance in human society. The baby's cry is a signal to its mother that some need requires satisfaction. Most animals possess such signals, and their proper functioning is an essential part of the child-rearing process, indeed an essential step in the survival of the species. Monkeys and apes have a further insurance against child neglect which we do not have. In times of need or danger, the infant is strong enough (after only the first few days) to run and cling to the mother's fur, and get its own nourishment at the breast. Ape and monkey infants are born with a well developed motor system which allows them to take the initiative in seeking and clinging to their mothers very shortly after birth. Thus the infant monkey initiates the satisfaction of its needs, and indeed does everything that is necessary for itself. The mother's fur allows it to cling to its mother's underside even if the mother is running full speed to safety in a high tree.

While in man the baby still initiates the satisfaction of its need by crying, it depends absolutely on its mother to act in response and pick it up. Even at the breast it has to be held by the mother, as she has no fur to which it can cling. The human infant is at its mother's mercy in a way that no monkey infant is (after the first three days). Thus the behavior of the human mother has a far more critical effect on the behavior of its child than that of the monkey or ape mother. If the mother herself cannot empathize with the expressed feelings of her infant she may fail to give it satisfaction and so cause the dangerous repression of painful feelings.

The Generation of Neurosis

From this we can see that mankind is uniquely vulnerable to failure in child-rearing, even in the absence of special stress due to crowding, or misleading books which purport to instruct women in motherhood. At a basic level, maternal response to the emotional expressions of children is innate, but the appropriate motor pattern of response is learned and can be repressed. The greatest danger arises from the child's ability, under stress of deprivation, to repress the whole emotional-motivational mechanism which could have led it in later life to respond to its own child correctly.

It is because of the important emotional determinant of memory that I have referred to above that repression of a painful memory implies the repression of a painful emotion, and finally the repression of the subjective, feeling component of our emotional life. As Freud realized, those repressed feelings and memories are the generating force behind most of our much vaunted civilization—they timelessly propel the neurotic creature that is western man.

The function of the repressive mechanism in childhood deprivation is not difficult to envisage. It is a means of reducing the pain level in infants who would otherwise die from neglect. The mechanism is not by any means perfect since, as we know, many babies do still die of neglect (crib death) especially in foundling homes. Réné Spitz in his book *The First Year of Life* (1965) and John Bowlby in his book *Attachment and Loss* (2 vols. 1971 and 1973) have recorded how children react to the absence of a mother, and how they seek out an alternative person to give them the security that they need from a mother. We can see from this that if the mother is lost the baby has the ability to transfer his affection to another —clearly an adaptive reaction to stress. Only when a succession of women fail to supply that security does the infant completely withdraw from any attempt to associate itself with an adult, and become more or less schizophrenic or autistic. *That a proper relationship with an adult is literally vital to the well-being of a child has been well known for centuries. Only recently do we seem to have forgotten how to bring up our children.*

There is much evidence of disturbed,behavior in domesticated and zoo-bred animals, but very little evidence that this kind of thing ever happens in the wild state. It is of especial interest therefore that Jane Van Lawick-Goodall in her fascinating book, *In the Shadow of Man* (1971), described how neurosis was generated in a young chimpanzee. The infant in question, whom she called Pom, had an accident to its hand when it was young which made it impossible for it to cling to its mother's fur, in the way which is normal for young chimpanzees. As a result it became necessary for its mother to support her infant against her chest and belly at all times, and run about on three legs. This is the usual pattern for the first few days of the infant's life but would not be necessary in a normal situation after that time. Pom's mother, who was called Passion, was not a good mother, and clearly became tired of this extra demand made on her. Instead of supporting the infant in the appropriate way she therefore pushed it up onto her back so that it could ride astride her. This position is normal for young who have reached the age of 6 to 8 months, but quite inappropriate for a small infant. As a result Pom kept slipping back beneath her mother, to a more comfortable and less exposed position and in order to reach her nipples. Each time, Passion pushed her up again onto her back. Pom's life was a continual, strained battle to find the security she needed, and her mother continually thwarted her attempts to do so. As Pom grew up, she stayed close to her mother, and later, at the time when other young chimps were romping freely together some distance from their mothers, Pom still stayed close to the mother who had never given her the security that she needed. Pom always remained a frightened creature, and never strayed far. Cast too early from the security of her mother's breast, she never lost the need for it, and never felt safe without it.

This account of the development of neurotic behavior in a chimpanzee is an exact parallel to the process in a human infant. In the case of the chimp, although the disturbance was considerable, it was nowhere near as bad as that which not uncommonly develops in human children. The story shows us that the higher primates do possess the possibility of developing neurosis, even in the wild, and that the neurotic response is in a certain sense an appropriate reaction to the stress that caused it. What the infant lacks, it seeks, ever more intently. The trouble with this response is that it may prove a very inappropriate behavior pattern if it becomes symbolic and continues, as it may, into adult life. The other point which comes out of this observation of Jane Goodall's is that any further deviation in the mother's response would probably have resulted in the death of the infant. Thus it happens that the process of natural selection will weed out deviant and inappropriate behavior from a wild population rather than allow its perpetuation as a chain of neuroses, from generation to generation. An infant mortality rate of 50% has been estimated for chimpanzees.

Of course, captive animals are well known to respond neurotically to childhood stress. Observation of zoo behavior shows that they develop many behavioral abnormalities that we usually associate with humans. Sexual perversions, masturbation to excess, facial and bodily tics, catatonia, stereotyped activity, rocking and tooth-grinding are a few of the many kinds of neurotic and psychotic behavior which we share with other mammals. In the zoo, as in human groups, human ingenuity and medical advances in pharmacology allow the survival and perpetuation of behavior patterns which are completely maladaptive to the individuals carrying them and to the society as a whole. The main difference between ourselves and wild animals is that we, like creatures confined to zoos, go mad yet survive the process well enough to pass the madness on to our children, and indeed throughout society at large.

While humans display all these behavior patterns characteristic of animals, they do differ in one important way. They have options not available to primates in the way they act out, and these options are a direct result of the way that the human cortex functions. The evolution of a capacity for language has placed at man's disposal the facile symbolization of any neurological input which gains consciousness, sensory or emotional. It is therefore possible for mankind to act out repressed emotion symbolically with a complexity far beyond that available to nonhuman primates in ways which are inappropriate and totally maladaptive. It also offers them an alternative, after the first few weeks of life, to parasympathetic death.

Conclusions

It is clear that emotion and feelings are not so much an annoying and disruptive human characteristic as an important biological attribute of all higher animals. Emotional expression finds its apogee in the higher primates such as monkeys and apes. The emotional response appears to have three important functions: motivation, communication and memorization. It is very surprising that psychologists and doctors have until recently so neglected the part played by emotion and feeling in human life. In such low esteem is emotion held that "emotional" has become a term of disdain, and "hysterical" a term of abuse.

I have described how his evolutionary history has enabled man to reduce the overt expression of his feelings by repression and how through the neocortical structures associated with language, he has come to be able to act out his pain symbolically as well as use a verbal response to disguise it. *He can now talk about his feelings instead of feeling them* [as in psychoanalysis]. Repression in children is a necessary defense against intolerable pain, but it has also made possible a degree of unconsciousness in human beings which has deeply disturbed the development of human nature. Human society is now threatened not only by problems arising from its size and density, but by the by-products of this unconsciousness, this emotional dishonesty, which divides man from his nature and allows him to lie to himself and so to others. Shakespeare understood this when he put these profound words into the mouth of Polonius:

> This above all: to thine own self be true,
> And it must follow, as the night the day
> Thou canst not then be false to any man.

The idea that truthfulness is a product of integration has been stressed throughout this chapter. It can be put in yet another way, when we consider the hopeless search by science for true objectivity. So long as man carries repressed pain, an obscuring mist rises from it to distort his view of the world and his fellow men: his observations are not reliable and true objectivity will escape him. Only when his feelings have been felt instead of reasoned over, when his life's experience is integrated into consciousness, can he come to see the world as it really is. Thus it follows that true objectivity, true detachment, is only possible as a consequence of the experience of subjectivity—the experience of what has been repressed. And what has been repressed is determined to a great extent by the culture in which we live.

In this chapter I have tried to show, by taking a look at some of the behavior of monkeys and chimpanzees, how important is the part played by emotion in our lives. I have attempted to show the very close relationship between emotion and communication, and to stress the importance of such communication both for a pre-verbal infant, and for an adult member of a social group, be it an expedition to Antarctica or a regular marriage. When it comes to the experience of a lack of response to such communications, we are dealing with what is regularly a matter of life and death. While a baby may actually die of crib death, an older person may die on his feet, and never come alive to feel the joy he never knew, the joy of reciprocity and togetherness. Emotion and feelings constitute the life-force, the *élan vital*.

One day, perhaps, we shall travel the full circle. Our pre-human ancestors were integrated, emotional creatures, like the other higher primates, the baboons and chimpanzees. They lived in the open, openly, their responses immediate and direct. In time the rigors of man's adaptations to confined spaces, cold climates, demanding technology, have put a premium on dissociation as an adaptive trend. But the trend has now gone too far, the disease called man has become a commonplace: from Inquisition to concentration camp, cruelty and heartlessness have flourished. The survival of *Homo sapiens* is at stake. If man does not rediscover his emotional life, the very root of his existence, he will wither as a species, his fruit shed and his growth at an end.

CHAPTER THIRTEEN

The Primal Questionnaire: Patients' Reports on Changes During Primal Therapy
E. Michael Holden

Periodically, at the Primal Institute, individuals undergoing **Primal** Therapy have completed a questionnaire regarding physical and physiological changes which occur during therapy. A simple earlier questionnaire and the responses it elicited were received and discussed in 1971 by Dr. Janov in *The Anatomy of Mental Illness.*

Starting in late March 1973, a second questionnaire was given to Primal patients, introduced as follows:

> Enclosed is a questionnaire which concerns the physical changes that you may have undergone as a result of Primal Therapy. To date, we have received a lot of anecdotal reports and verbal heresay about changes in body function that have occurred during therapy; however, we have never conducted an actual written survey. This questionnaire, which is being distributed to all our patients, will help us to clarify the range and extent of physical changes that arise during therapy.

Patients were asked to comment on physical changes regarding the following body parts or functions:

Body weight
Height
Stature/Posture

Eyes/Vision
Ears/Hearing
Nose/Sinuses/Sense of smell
Throat
Mouth (teeth, tongue, lips, taste, mouth sores, etc.)
Chest/Quality of Breathing/Chest colds/Pain
Heart-rate/Rhythm/Blood pressure/Palpitations
Abdomen/Appetite/Pain or discomfort
    (Bloating, nausea, cramps, constipation or diarrhea) also, if applicable, ulcers, colitis, hepatitis, hemorrhoids, etc.
Urinary tract/frequency/discomfort/infections
Genitals/size
    sexual performance
    menses
Sex life (Sex practices/attitudes)
Breasts/Size/Shape/Cysts/Discharge
Nervous system
    Headaches/migraine headaches
    Blackout spells
    Tremors/Tics
    Epilepsy, Narcolepsy
    Paralysis, including sleep paralysis
Musculo-skeletal
    Muscle Tension
    Muscle spasms, cramps
Skin
    Color
    Texture
    Moistness
    Warmth
    Lesions/Rashes/Moles/Marks
    Hair/Quality/Distribution
    Nails
Sleep
    Quality
    Dreams (symbolism/nightmares/topics)
    Length of sleep
    "Do you feel rested in the morning?"
Exercise
    "Do you exercise regularly?"

Diet

"Has there been any change in your diet or eating habits?"

and Miscellaneous Comments.

83 men and women between the ages of 25 and 50, who had completed three months of Primal Therapy or more, responded to the questionnaire. Not all questionnaire topics elicited responses. Some responses were brief, others quite detailed.

The intent of presenting the questionnaire chapter is to further document that Primal Therapy leads to profound physiological changes in neurotic people. It also supports our view that consciousness represents the total sensory reactivity of all body tissues; the skin, muscles and viscera no less than the brain. In some instances, not only tissue function changes in Primal Therapy but also tissue *structure*.

The responses given on this questionnaire support the assertion that virtually any body structure, organ or function may participate in the substitutive responses characteristic of neurosis. Changes in hearing, vision, taste, hair distribution, jaw structure and spinal curvature are not uncommon in patients undergoing Primal Therapy. The general principle that neurosis is a disorder of the entire body is supported repeatedly by the changes in Primal patients. This in turn is a corollary of the more general principle that all living cells have "feeling," are sensitive, and can register Pain. Each cell in the human body contributes to the total consciousness. If an individual has had a Painful life then each cell contributes to a neurotic (or if extreme, a psychotic) consciousness. At this time it appears that only the Primal response can affect individuals in totality, literally to the cellular level. When we see birthmarks, bruises from delivery and forceps' marks on people during deep Primals, we have no reason to doubt that individual cells can register Pain for a lifetime. The changes during the course of Primal Therapy indicate further that the Pains are reversible, at least in the sense that they can become fully integrated into a larger consciousness, instead of causing disease in the substitutive patterns characteristic of neurosis.

The physical, physiological and endocrine changes reported by Primal patients have different "value" in support of the notion that each cell can register Pain. It is not unusual or surprising for a psychotherapy, virtually any one, to change one's appetite or a woman's menstrual periods or the quality of one's dreams. We consider it differentially important and much more unique, however, when adults tell us of phenomena like growing an inch or more, of having new hair distribution, no longer requiring eyeglasses or no longer having impotence/frigidity. Similarly, one is more impressed when a lifelong condition like asthma or constant allergy disappears in three to four weeks of Primal Therapy. We believe the larger issue is one of *access:* that psychoanalysis and other therapies only have limited access, and that Primal Therapy has complete access to the disordered physiologic manifestations characteristic of neurosis. Disorders such as alcoholism, drug addiction, ulcerative colitis, asthma and stuttering (only symptomatically, palliatively treated by medicine or conventional psychotherapies) are readily *cured* in Primal Therapy. This occurs because Primals have access to even the deepest portions of the brain (most notably the *hypothalamus,* regulator of visceral homeostasis and the vital signs of pulse, respiration, blood pressure and temperature).

One's physiology changes during Primal Therapy but the direction and amount of change is quite individual and also is quite different depending on how many months one has been in the therapy. Some changes occur in nearly everyone. others are more specific to individuals. One generalization which emerges, especially regarding hunger and sexuality, is that these needs become *actual* after they are no longer linked to tension. People no longer eat food unless they are *actually* hungry, and intercourse or masturbation are no longer used to release tension, but are enjoyed when people are feeling *actually* sexual.

It is also true that during the course of Primal Therapy *new* symptoms appear, presenting themselves for resolution by Primals. They appear in a sequence which is logical *only in terms of an individual's particular personal life history.* Thus, skin rash in the groin (diaper rash) is only associated with Primals and feelings concerning infancy, whereas the return of facial acne (transiently) refers to feelings and Primals from puberty. Forceps' marks on the head and birth marks which reappear during Primals are ancient memories for individuals (near birth). Not always, but generally, one Primals in a sequence from the more recent past to earlier and earlier events. The symptoms and physiological changes during Primal Therapy reflect a re-emergence of body memories within that sequence, but an individual's chronology determines each particular sequence. The same outwardly expressed symptoms may have very different personal meanings for different people. Thus there are relatively few generalizations which can be made (and those apparent will be noted later). A stuffed-up nose or sinusitis may reflect nearly drowning at birth for one person and require birth Primals for resolution, but for another may be a manifestation of held-back tears at age 3, requiring resolution by age-appropriate Primals. The quality of sleep and feeling rested in the morning seem related to time in therapy. Earlier, after 3-6 months in therapy, people sleep poorly, have many nightmares and wake up *not* feeling rested. Later, after 6-24 or more months in therapy, people judge their sleep quality as improved, their sleep requirement as slightly less, and report feeling rested in the morning, having had fewer, less symbolic dreams.

The purpose of sharing the questionnaire responses with the reader is not to prove something in particular, which would be poorly done by subjective questionnaire responses. Rather, these responses indicate the wide range of symptoms and functions which became component parts of a neurotic physiology and consciousness. There has been no attempt made to delete negative responses because *for individuals* the functions or changes described are either neurotic or normal, and need not conform rigidly to any desirable/undesirable spectrum. An example would be change in jaw configuration and re-alignment of teeth. This changes a person's appearance and dental occlusion but it is neither good nor bad in terms of the individual's normal self; there has been a return to one's actual biology, leaving a disordered (neurotic) one behind . . . similarly . . . if a woman's breasts become larger or smaller, if weight is gained or lost, if hair distribution changes, if a person stands straighter but has a pot belly, or if sleep requirement changes. Objectively, it is neither good nor bad if one has intercourse twice a week or twice a month. Primal patients reach an internal regulation which is right for each person and they feel it that way. There is an intrinsic logic, then, to having *patients* make the before/after comparisons because only they have lived through the profound changes and feel the difference; they are in the best position to describe the changes. By the amount that these changes are outwardly manifest (vital signs, EEG, weight change, skin appearance, etc.) they can be measured, and reported as data. It would be foolhardy, however, to try measuring internal feeling states, per se, for the methods and understanding of these are too primitive to do so accurately.

The questionnaire responses also indicate that the list of psychosomatic (neurotic) illnesses is larger than most people realize. We see patients who stutter only between Primals but speak normally within Primals. We see that patients with ulcerative colitis achieve permanent remission after sufficient time in therapy, even though flare-ups early in therapy are not uncommon. We need not consider *alcoholism* an illness as if that gave it some medical rationalization; it appears to be just *another subcategory of neurosis*. The queston of total versus partial abstinence from alcohol, so important to Alcoholics Anonymous, is an irrelevancy for Primal

patients who were alcoholics; after Primal Therapy they may drink socially if they wish or abstain if they wish. They don't participate in the
spiral of drinking more and more and more, after Primal Therapy, because they have *felt their Pain in Primals* and no longer need alcohol to
suppress Pain. A similar dialectic exists for heavy cigarette smokers:
after Primal Therapy people no longer want to smoke cigarettes, feeling
naturally that it is poisonous to their systems, and no longer needing the
substitutive oral gratification smoking provides for neurotics.

Also, although it was not requested, many Primal patients made interesting observations relating symptoms to Primal Pain and to Primals
themselves. The importance of these observations is the demonstrated
linkage between *symptoms* and *Primal Pain*. One of the more common
responses to the emergence of Primal Pain into awareness is the development of a tension (or more severely a migraine) headache, which goes
away after Primalling. In general, once a person knows how to Primal,
doing so will minimize, improve, or eradicate physical symptoms. Conversely, however, if one is close to his Pain and *postpones* having a Primal too long, then: 1. previous symptoms will re-appear, or 2. those
symptoms present will worsen, and/or 3. simple, less symbolic dreams
will become more bizarre, with more nightmares and fitful, anxious sleep.

To a neurotic, the sudden appearance of asthma, a migraine attack, a
skin rash or a bowel disturbance often makes no sense. For Primal patients they are easily understood in relation to the emergence of early
Pain, which requires Primalling for its resolution. Sometimes, many Primals may be required before a symptom resolves completely (one index
of extreme repression). Viewed conversely, one's symptoms may derive
from a great deal of Primal Pain or from very *early* Pain such as nearly
dying at birth, in which case resolution takes longer. Another variable to
keep in mind is that some people have *much more Pain to feel* than
others, so that after two years of Primalling, a less neurotic individual
may feel well, sleep well and be symptom-free, whereas a very neurotic
person may intermittently feel tense, have restless sleep, have severe
symptoms and still be having long and frequent Primals. It is understood,
and acknowledged, that for some very neurotic (or some psychotic) individuals, several years of Primalling will be necessary to achieve resolution of their Primal Pain and the numerous symptoms it engenders. It
is interesting, and of theoretical importance, that most patients who still
have severe symptoms after one or two years of Primalling feel that they
"have a long way to go" or "have a lot more to feel," acknowledging thereby the effectiveness of Primals in helping their symptoms and decreasing
their Pain.

In this series the patients were their own controls, before versus during therapy (up until the time questionnaire was answered). Relatively slight changes like a change in skin rash or dream quality are the sort of variable requiring external controls (patients in other therapies) more so than more striking physical changes such as loss of allergies, or no further need to wear eyeglasses, radical shifts in sexual attitudes, teeth re-alignment or the cure of alcoholism. Most patients undergoing Primal Therapy experience such profound subjective and objective changes in physiology that we feel it unnecessary to use external controls for comparison. This point of view applies particularly to the consistent lowering of background EEG amplitude, pulse, blood pressure and core body temperature. (People are not used to considering neurosis as a hypermetabolic state with increased physiologic work required of the organism each hour, each day, but the changes in the vital signs during Primal Therapy indicate that this is indeed the case.) When a therapeutic intervention obviously works, there is little need for external controls. One requires that a new analgesic be compared against aspirin, morphine and placebo, but no one required controls for penicillin and B-strep. throat, or for morphine itself as an analgesic, or for digitalis for failing hearts. *Primal Therapy is a profoundly, incisively effective treatment for neurosis and the physiologic disorders (diseases) of neurosis.* If one believes that Primal Therapy is "just another therapy" for neurosis, then our point of view appears arrogant. However, our point of view is generated directly from observations of profound psychophysiologic reorganization produced in all patients undergoing Primal Therapy and our point of view is consistent with those observations. Our continuing studies of the vital signs and EEG's of Primal patients provide the objective support for our belief that Primal Therapy is an effective, actual cure for neurosis. The questionnaire responses which follow provide subjective support which is informative and often quite interesting. When the actual responses are cited (rather than a summary statement as in yes/no questions), it will be noted in parentheses how long that individual had been in therapy, for it makes an obvious difference in the interpretation of the responses (as noted for sleep quality, previously).

(It should be noted that the noun and verb usage of the word "feeling" is used somewhat differently by Primal patients than conventionally. Being "close to feeling" means a person needs to Primal and experience the Pain and meaning of that feeling. Also, to "feel the feeling" means to *Primal;* distinct from simply being "aware of" the feeling as occurs in abreaction).

Weight Changes

Number responding 28
Number who gained 11
Number who lost 12
Number who varied up or down 5

gained	time in therapy	changed up or down	lost	time in therapy
15 lbs. —	8 mo.	140 118 140: 19 mo.	36 lbs. —	5 mo.
20 lbs. —	5 mo.		6 lbs. —	18 mo.
8 lbs. —	9 mo.		8 lbs. —	5½ mo.
5 lbs. —	3½ mo.	195 173 185: 10 mo.	5 lbs. —	5½ mo.
7 lbs. —	15 mo.		10 lbs. —	36 mo.
20 lbs. —	5½ mo.		30 lbs. —	15 mo.
25 lbs. —	25 mo.		10 lbs. —	13 mo.
6 lbs. —	4 mo.	down 15 lbs./2 mo., up 35 lbs./yr.	7 lbs. —	6 mo.
7 lbs. —	9 mo.	down 20 lbs. next 9 mo.	5 lbs. —	9 mo.
10 lbs. —	36 mo.		•10 lbs. —	9 mo.
10 lbs. —	24 mo.		30 lbs. —	18 mo.
			50 lbs. —	19 mo.

up 15 lbs. in 1st yr.
down 9 lbs. next 4 mo.
up 50 lbs. in 1st 8 mo.
down 37 lbs. in 17 mo.

Height Changes

up ½″ — 30 mo.
up 1″ — 36 mo.
up 1¾″ — 13 mo.
up 1″ — 10 mo.
up 1½″ — 36 mo.
up 1″ — 15 mo.
down 1″ — 6½ mo.

Questionnaire Responses About Posture

	Time in Therapy
1. "Much improved"	30 mo.
2. "Shoulders no longer rounded, posture more erect"	26 mo.
3. "Less rigid, more flexible"	36 mo.

4. "Previous slouch posture, now no slouch"   23 mo.
5. "Feel more solid, move as a unit"   9 mo.
6. "Developed a pot belly 'like a baby'"   4 mo.
7. "Posture more upright, head no longer down"   18 mo.
8. "Pelvis more forward"   16 mo.
9. "Walk with legs apart 'like a toddler'"   3 mo.
10. "Slightly improved posture"   20 mo.
11. "Straighter posture"   14 mo.
12. "Feel straighter now"   19 mo.
13. "Straighter"   18 mo.
14. "Instead of my legs carrying a separate rigid torso, everything moves together"   10 mo.
15. "No more round shoulders"   25 mo.
16. "Right shoulder droops less"   6 mo.
17. "Posture like a baby's, abdomen protrudes"   9 mo.
18. "Hard to stand up when tense, now, back gets bent"   3 mo.
19. "Collarbones are coming into more horizontal alignment; letting down shoulders"   6 mo.
20. "Back alignment altered, hip portion changed—better balance, hence relief of chronic lower back pain"   9 mo.
21. "I've been able to lose much of the real fat on my body that I've never been able to lose before. Posture much improved"   28 mo.
22. "From childhood I've been round-shouldered. No conscious effort has been able to improve my poor posture. At one time even tried a back brace but without success. After only a few weeks of therapy I began feeling my body straightening out. I don't really know what correct posture should be but I can feel that my shoulders are back from where they used to be and my head and spine are in a more erect position"   4½ mo.
23. "Not hunched anymore. I walk straight and tall and carry myself totally upright"   9 mo.
24. "Think my posture is better—stand up straighter"   3 mo.
25. "Slightly less curvature of back, and much greater freedom of movement of back and left leg which were in a very stiff condition before therapy"   36 mo.
26. "From a hunched posture to a more straight stance"   18 mo.
27. "Better posture except when Pain is rising . . . then I slouch again"   5 mo.

28. "Recent medical check-up showed a correction in the spine curvature I had (I was slightly swayback prior to therapy)"   25 mo.
29. "No longer have a dropped shoulder, straighter spine"   15 mo.

Questionnaire Responses About Eyes/Vision	*Time in Therapy*
1. "Eyes less tense"	35 mo.
2. "Improved vision"	30 mo.
3. "Slight farsightedness (since therapy)"	26 mo.
4. "Red eyes often before, now gone"	23 mo.
5. "Can't see well when in Pain"	9 mo.
6. "Eyes more open"	18 mo.
7. "More blinking, more eye rolling"	16 mo.
8. "Eyes more sensitive to light"	3 mo.
9. "Eyes more sensitive to light"	5½ mo.
10. "Eyes more wide open now"	20 mo.
11. "Eyes seem to be getting weaker"	5½ mo.
12. "Two diopters less myopia, no more astigmatism"	36 mo.
13. "No more pressure behind eyes"*	15 mo.
14. "Vision worse—pains behind eyeballs that I used to get only when hung over"	6 mo.
15. "Very great tension in my eyes now.* This also blurs my vision; eyesight changes from day to day and from hour to hour"	9½ mo.
16. "Both vision and hearing seem less linear, more whole, often reminding me of drug states (psychedelic)"	18 mo.
17. "Eyes and ears more sensitive"	5 mo.
18. "I wore glasses before therapy. I do not wear glasses at all now, with no eyestrain whatsoever"	6½ mo.
19. "Nose and eyes become quite itchy when I'm in early birth feelings"	15 mo.
20. "Contact lenses don't fit when I'm into baby feelings (I've worn them 11 years)"	5 mo.
21. "Vision becomes occasionally blurred when feelings are coming up"	4½ mo.
22. "Vision has improved; sometimes I don't need my glasses"	15 mo.

*[Recently, we have been measuring *intra-ocular* pressure in Primal patients with a modern air-tonometer. We have found that those in therapy several years have much *lower* intraocular pressure than those just starting therapy. These observations generate the hypothesis that *glaucoma* is a neurotic disorder.]

Questionnaire Responses About Ears/Hearing

		Time in Therapy
1.	"Ears waxier"	3 mo.
2.	"Better hearing"	14 mo.
3.	"Used to get blocked eustacian tubes; no more"	19 mo.
4.	"Hearing improved"	10 mo.
5.	"Hearing more acute"	36 mo.
6.	"I now notice very high frequency sounds at times"	8 mo.
7.	"More sensitive to sound"	15 mo.

Questionnaire Responses About Nose/Sinuses/Smell/Allergies and Colds

		Time in Therapy
1.	"Nose clearer"	35 mo.
2.	"Clearer"	30 mo.
3.	"Colds rare now, frequent before, nose much more sensitive to smog"	26 mo.
4.	"Nose was chronically clogged, now clear. Goodbye Dristan"	23 mo.
5.	"Colds only with stress"	18 mo.
6.	"Nose no longer blocked"	18 mo.
7.	"No more post-nasal drip"	5½ mo.
8.	"Can smell better, nose not clogged"	5 mo.
9.	"Nose gets clogged up more"	6 mo.
10.	"Rare colds now"	20 mo.
11.	"Nose clear for the first time in my life"	14½ mo.
12.	"Nose no longer runs constantly"	13 mo.
13.	"Fewer colds"	36 mo.
14.	"Nose no longer clogged (breathed through mouth all my life)"	10 mo.
15.	"More colds"	25 mo.
16.	"10 years of hay fever—gone"	3½ mo.
17.	"Nose no longer stuffed up, rarely ever have colds"	15 mo.
18.	"Used to pick nose incessantly—stopped"	13 mo.
19.	"No more sinus congestion"	13 mo.
20.	"Allergies seem worse, and more closely associated to emotionally upsetting incidents and periods"*	16 mo.
21.	"Nose: much discharge during Primals"	9 mo.
22.	"For 5 years prior to therapy I suffered from sinusitis all	

the time. I had been to many different doctors. I had severe
sinus headaches (and infections frequently) 2-3 times a
week. Finally they had me on steroid sprays because they
thought it was an allergy. This 'worked' and I had to use it
about two times a week, for the past year. I have used it
only once since therapy because I had a bad cold. I don't
have sinusitis anymore"   4 mo.

23. "Nasal passage fills completely during birth Primals"   6 mo.

24. "I used to have a recurrent hay fever when I was little. The
    same hay fever has recurred in my therapy, and with it, all
    the feelings I'd been into at that time. Feeling the feelings
    has stopped the hay fever"   28 mo.

25. "Severe sinus congestion for four years. Had to use nasal
    spray once a day. Since therapy the congestion began clearing
    up and has not returned"   4½ mo.

26. "Had sinusitis often—not any more"   9 mo.

27. "I have had allergies* with continual nasal stuffiness, itching
    and sneezing since high school. In therapy I notice that when
    I am unable to cry the symptoms return, and disappear (only)
    when I feel the feelings and cry"   10 mo.

28. "After heavy feelings (Primals) my sensation in eyes, ears,
    nose and throat is heightened, very similar to a marijuana
    high. I have felt my internal nasal passages open up like
    they've never done in my whole life"   3 mo.

29. "Used to get fairly frequent colds which would always go to
    my chest. Have had only one since I've been in therapy"   6 mo.

30. "Had chronic nasal congestion—addicted to Afrin spray,
    nose clear now"   18 mo.

31. "Asthma and hay fever still, but much less intense"   16 mo.

32. "I've had hay fever since age 11 or 12, it used to get so bad
    I could hardly catch my breath when sneezing·continually.
    I was always on some kind of medication for it. Now it only
    comes once or twice a year"   48 mo.

33. "Occasionally but seldom, apparently at times of stress when
    I'm unable to feel, there is a return of a symptom from high
    school years, of deep sinus congestion and post-nasal drip.
    This can cause a sore throat. It is not nearly as severe as

---

*"Allergies" may simply result when cells of the immune system carry a metabolic
burden of Primal Pain.

when I was in high school. A good Primal will usually clear
the condition"   24 mo.

34. "No longer have any allergies (hay fever, etc.)"   15 mo.

Questionnaire Responses About
Throat/Voice/Mouth/Lips/Taste

		Time in Therapy
1.	"Lower voice, neck muscles relaxed"	35 mo.
2.	"Lips were dry (before), no longer need lipstick"	36 mo.
3.	"No more sore throats"	23 mo.
4.	"Voice lower"	9 mo.
5.	"Jaw further forward, more mobile"	16 mo.
6.	"Used to get cold sores (on lips) several times a year, now none since starting Primal Therapy"	18 mo.
7.	"Voice deeper and stronger, no more mouth sores"	5½ mo.
8.	"Face bones changed" (not further specified)	20 mo.
9.	"Much improved sense of taste"	19 mo.
10.	"Don't grind teeth anymore—before always woke up with swollen gums, no more since therapy started"	18 mo.
11.	"No 'lump in throat,' feels better, food tastes better"	13 mo.
12.	"Grind teeth since therapy started"	25 mo.
13.	"No more canker sores"	5½ mo.
14.	"Taste more acute"	12 mo.
15.	"Tongue was sore for 4 years—less so since therapy"	12 mo.
16.	"My case of leukoplakia buccalis has diminished in severity; my dental occlusion has been shifting around"	6 mo.
17.	"I ground my teeth in my sleep so badly that my gums were receding from my teeth. Dentist fitted me with a bite block which I put in my mouth at bedtime. I used this for 10 years. When I would forget to use it my husband would wake me up to remind me. I have not used it since start of therapy—my husband says I do not grind my teeth and dentist says there is no sign of further damage"	7 mo.
18.	"Throat sore a lot now"	3 mo.
19.	"Taste has been heightened"	9 mo.
20.	"Can now taste foods—unbelievable"	57 mo.
21.	"Tension in mouth, especially lips, which often feel like concrete—has been relieved for short periods by Primalling"	4½ mo.
22.	"Voice is characteristically lower now than before"	36 mo.

23. "Taste is better, lips more sensitive, jaw seems to be re-
    forming—teeth change positions according to length of time
    in therapy"   18 mo.
24. "Less mucus in mouth"   4 mo.
25. "The back vertical bones of my jaw have grown (they were
    undersized proportionately) since I began Primaling pushing
    my jaw more forward. This was verified by my orthodontist
    2 months ago"   5 mo.
26. "I used to grind my teeth. This went away after I had some
    feelings of being born"   36 mo.
27. "Sense of taste improved"   25 mo.
28. "Last 6 months, I've had general sore throats. Before that,
    none for two years"   36 mo.
29. "I clamp my teeth together at night"   5 mo.
30. "Sometimes get mouth sores when in early feelings. Mouth
    generally is and looks more relaxed"   15 mo.
31. "Teeth have re-aligned, badly. However I was clamping my
    jaws in my sleep before therapy. This has disappeared except
    re-occurs occasionally"   18 mo.
32. "My voice is raw and hoarse—is lower pitched—I can no
    longer sing"   5 mo.
33. "Teeth have gotten worse. Taste improved. My mouth's shape
    is completely changed"   15 mo.
34. "Voice is deeper—and is lower than before Primalling—
    (singing: reaching low notes I couldn't before)"

Questionnaire Responses About
Chest and Breathing

	Time in Therapy
1. "No longer choke or cough"	8 mo.
2. "Easier, less tense"	30 mo.
3. "Deeper"	26 mo.
4. "Deeper, few colds"	36 mo.
5. "Deeper, freer"	23 mo.
6. "Chest tight, not yet liberated"	4 mo.
7. "Breathing slower, more shallow, more efficient"	18 mo.
8. "Easier breathing"	18 mo.
9. "Much deeper breathing"	5½ mo.
10. "Breathing repression—trouble inhaling"	3 mo.

11. "More even—less tense—fuller"   5 mo.
12. "Hard to breathe during feeling period"   6 mo.
13. "Chest more open"   20 mo.
14. "Asthma has returned since beginning therapy, but generally
    occurs only during Primals"   14½ mo.
15. "Breathing 'deeper' more satisfying"   19 mo.
16. "Normal breathing—wasn't possible before"   13 mo.
17. "Breathing deeper"   10 mo.
18. "Breathing free and deep"   3½ mo.
19. "Looser, more abdominal breathing"   36 mo.
20. "Breathing easier"   15 mo.
21. "Breathing deeply, from belly"   13 mo.
22. "Deeper and more spontaneous"   8 mo.
23. "Breathing deeper and more relaxed after a Primal"   13 mo.
24. "Breathing slower, more relaxed"   9 mo.
25. "Have had trouble breathing deeply since end of first month
    of therapy"   6 mo.
26. "Improved diaphragm moves more"   3 mo.
27. "Much better—chest is enlarging. Chest still fills with mucus
    in birth Primals—it subsides soon after (each)"   6 mo.
28. "Asthma has diminished considerably—haven't required a
    shot of adrenalin since therapy started—occasionally flares
    up when I get close to big feelings, i.e. the oxygen tent, or
    daddy"   3 mo.
29. "Breathing much fuller"   28 mo.
30. "Breathing has become deeper"   4½ mo.
31. "Breathing deeper and easier for approximately the last 7
    or 8 years, I've had a pain in my chest just under my left
    breast which often subsides lately, or is much less painful"   9 mo.
32. "Fuller, slower (before therapy, used to sigh a lot—do very
    little now)"   3 mo.
33. "Although my breathing is still tight and unnatural, I don't
    have to fight for breath as much as before therapy, when I
    had to sigh deeply to get a good breath"   4½ mo.
34. "Breathing much better—not as tight or labored—no
    longer smoking"   18 mo.
35. "I'm breathing from below the belt now. Before, up in
    my chest"   5 mo.
36. "Breathing from below the belt now. Before, up in chest"
37. "Frequent shortness of breath. Find myself holding my

breath frequently and I experience the feeling of being
smothered"   5 mo.

38. "I think I breathe abdominally more often, though not when
under stress"   4 mo.

39. "Deeper and much less effort in breathing. My body is
doing it my 'myself'—coming from the belly"   15 mo.

40. "Went from size 32 to 34 bra (before weight gain). Rib
cage expanded"   18 mo.

41. "Deeper and more even"   3 mo.

42. "I sigh a lot, and have to take occasional deep breaths to
make up for lack of air and lack of normal breathing"   4½ mo.

43. "Constant weight on my chest. Momentary relief after
feelings"   15 mo.

44. "Breathing deeper"   25 mo.

45. "I don't hold my breath nearly as much and I breathe
from the right place now"   4 mo.

Questionnaire Responses About
Pulse, Blood Pressure, Cardiac Changes

		Sex	Time in Therapy
1.	BP change: 120/55—105/55 Pulse Change: 55—65/min	M	30 mo.
2.	Pulse: "slower rate, less frantic"	M	23 mo.
3.	"Tachycardia and skipped beats when Pain rises"	F	9 mo.
4.	"No more palpitations"	F	18 mo.
5.	"Pain in heart—intense when afraid of physical abuse"	M	6 mo.
6.	"No more palpitations"	F	5½ mo.
7.	"Hypertensive before, on med's (Aldoril) from 3rd to 5th month was normotensive, off med's—: required again in 6th month: BP 150/100"	M	6 mo.
8.	"Pulse and blood pressure lower"	M	10 mo.
9.	"Pulse from 60 to 70/min., at rest"	M	5½ mo.
10.	"Pulse decreased by 10/min."	M	36 mo.
11.	"Lower blood pressure, lower pulse, less awareness of heart"		15 mo.
12.	"Pulse change 64-80/min."		16 mo.
13.	"Blood pressure from 160/100 to 138/70"		9 mo.
14.	"Blood pressure is labile, it goes down (100/60) after		

Primals, and is as high as 145/95 between Primals" M 7 mo.
15. "Pulse was 80 to 100/min. now is 56 to 72/min." M 9 mo.
16. "Pulse is down, to approximately 60/min" M 3 mo.
17. "Pulse is in the 50's—has been in the 40's after
     Primalling in group" M 36 mo.
18. "Pulse and B.P. lower" · M 3 mo.
19. "Heart rate slower, less heavy—usually in the low
     or middle 60's. Smoother transitions from
     fast to slow" M 18 mo.
20. "No more palpitations" F 25 mo.
21. "My blood pressure has gone down" F 48 mo.
22. "Had severe palpitations from sensitivity to noise.
     This has decreased" M 4 mo.
23. "Pulse down from 72 to 58/min. B. P. also down,
     now 105/60" M 15 mo.
24. "I used to have incredible palpitations and pains
     in chest that would almost black me out. I've had
     some since, but I feel they're gone now (it's pre-
     natal Pain—since I began feeling it, they're gone)" M 15 mo.

Hypertension and angina pectoris are common disorders so the general importance of Primal Therapy to heart patients cannot be underestimated. It is becoming clear also that it is safe for patients with angina and/or hypertension to Primal. One patient evaluated recently had severe angina pectoris sometimes occurring even at rest. At the end of his first three weeks of Primal Therapy, he had a Primal which included 10½ minutes of a pulse of 132/min. and a blood pressure of 156/110, *without* experiencing angina. The experience of another man with angina, following a heart attack, is recorded in *The Journal of Primal Therapy* I, No. 3, p. 213-222, and also as an Appendix in this volume.

More cases are needed to evaluate this extraordinary relationship of rapid heart rate in an angina patient, without pain, during a Primal. The implication of the early observations is that angina pectoris is related more to coronary artery vaspospasm in relation to stress and Primal Pain, and less to coronary artery narrowing, per se, than most physicians realize.

While we have relatively few cases upon which this conclusion is based, we must keep in mind that Primal Therapy is a *pre*dictive rather than a *post*dictive process. Therefore, the power of its predictions increases rapidly, with a smaller number of cases. Postdictive processes require, as a rule, large numbers of cases to justify conclusions. Postdictive therapies usually involve elaborate statistical manipulations because they deal with statistical rather than biological truths.

Questionnaire Responses About Appetite/Abdomen

		Time in Therapy
1.	"Less constitpation, less bloating after meals"	35 mo.
2.	"Normal, no more compulsive eating, colitis flared up, then went away"	5 mo.
3.	"No more excessive gastric acid. No more farting, belching or anal itching"	30 mo.
4.	"Spastic colon much improved"	26 mo.
5.	"Need less food—bloating rare (often before), no more flank pains."	36 mo.
6.	"Used to talk myself out of food—can't do so now."	10 mo.
7.	"No change"	23 mo.
8.	"Appetite less—not eating to painful fullness anymore. Colitis cured"	9 mo.
9.	"Pain with bowel movements"	4 mo.
10.	"Eat less, enjoy food more, started belching (not able to before)"	18 mo.
11.	"Increased flatulence—eat too much and too fast"	3½ mo.
12.	"Unchanged, still vomit periodically"	15 mo.
13.	"Appetite decreased, no more binges—milk intolerance and bloating, no change with Primal Therapy"	18 mo.
14.	"No more compulsive eating. Decreased appetite, much less constipation. Colitis of nine years' duration gone"	5½ mo.
15.	"Almost unaware of appetite"	3 mo.
16.	"Stomach cramps after feeling a lot"	6 mo.
17.	"Used to have hemorrhoids—they went away"	20 mo.
18.	"Foods taste better, enjoy food more, and no more constipation"	19 min.
19.	"Marked increase in appetite"	5½ mo.
20.	"Less appetite"	13 mo.
21.	"Cramps and diarrhea when Pain rises"	10 mo.

22. "Voracious appetite—much increased, still have bloating, farting and anal itching"   25 mo.
23. "Appetite is still poor . . . I shit a lot (scared shit) but it's improving"   15 mo.
24. "Ulcer symptoms (actual ulcer) almost gone—rarely need meds. Hemorrhoids have disappeared"   3½ mo.
25. "Eat less"   36 mo.
26. "Much less interest in food. Used to fart a lot, rarely now. No longer have colitis"   15 mo.
27. "Appetite increased a little. Gave up coffee but constipation worse now"   12 mo.
28. "Appetite increased a little."   12 mo.
29. "Heartburn for about a week's total elapsed time since therapy began, I've never had this before."   6 mo.
30. "Still have stomach bloating"   6 mo.
31. "No constipation when I've felt deeply"   13 mo.
32. "Hemorrhoids more constantly irritating"   16 mo.
33. "Decrease in appetite. Marked decrease in constipation. Before therapy, was using 200-300 mgm. of Colace/day and Dulcolax suppository every 2-3 days. Now, no problem at all. Bleeding hemorrhoids prior to therapy; no problem at all now, using no medication at all"   9 mo.
34. "Appetite decreased. I'm getting less and less constipated as therapy progresses"   6 mo.
35. "I see my appetite as having normalized. I used to have a craving for cookies and would keep eating them even though my stomach was full. I like to eat but food is just food to me now, not something to make me feel better"   7 mo.
36. "Appetite has decreased markedly—increases when feelings are coming up"   34 mo.
37. "Improved bowel functioning"   3 mo.
38. "Now appetite varies widely—generally I don't eat as much"   4 mo.
39. "Appetite has dropped off—I eat two meals a day"   3 mo.
40. "Appetite—ravenous. Hemorrhoids much less of a problem"   9 mo.
41. "Appetite has really been an incredible change. I know when I'm hungry now—for real, and when I'd just like to eat to keep Pain from coming up. Food doesn't mean something good to have that I need—it's just food"   28 mo.
42. "I eat less food—I'm just not hungry"   9 mo.
43. "Starvation has been a pattern for me when I was in Pain,

presently I am into feelings which have caused me to lose
my appetite again"   5 mo.
44. "Appetite gone down—less capacity for very sweet things"   23 mo.
45. "Sharp pains presently in lower abdomen. Intestines and
stomach muscles often sore"   9½ mo.
46. "Not much overeating, easier to diet when necessary"   3 mo.
47. "Food tastes great—like foods now, I didn't before—
used to take Rolaids for excess stomach acid all the time
for 27 years; haven't needed to since 3 weeks after therapy
started"   36 mo.
48. "No longer overeating—get really hungry"   18 mo.
49. "Had ulcers (duodenal) from ages 17 to 21. They
disappeared and I developed a chronic dermatitis on my
hands. Before therapy I had a chronic contact dermatitis
on the palms of both my hands for seven years. It was
difficult and very painful to use my hands at all. I went
to a total of 5 different doctors and nothing worked. Here,
I've felt my hands break out as a feeling rises. When I
can feel my hands are better. Overall, they're much better"   16 mo.
[Included in this category to illustrate the symptom transition
from ulcers to dermatitis, the relationship to feelings and the
approaching resolution with successive Primals—EMH.]
50. "Bloating and gas pains—relieved by burping after
Primalling in group"   4 mo.
51. "I feel no desire to snack anymore"   5 mo.
52. "Always feel like eating something. History of severe
(ulcerative) colitis 10-15 times a day, mostly water with
considerable blood and a lot of gas. This lasted till
about the fifth week of therapy and then totally
disappeared. Started up again in 10th week—much milder,
no bleeding and not so severe"   3 mo.
53. "Severe constipation before therapy. Sometimes when I
can't feel I get constipated, but as soon as I have the feeling
I can have a bowel movement"   36 mo.
54. "No longer constipated. No more problems with
hemorrhoids"   25 mo.
55. "My appetite is excellent, however I am unable to eat
large portions"   6½ mo.
56. "There is considerably less tension in my gut. I don't
hold my belly in very much anymore"   15 mo.

57. "I used to feel I had to eat everything on my plate. Now
I stop eating when I'm full"   6½ mo.
58. "Monstrous appetite—markedly increased. Hemorrhoids
were there before therapy but not painful. Became horribly
painful and increased in number until I began 'need'
feelings—then they disappeared in one session"   18 mo.
59. "Appetite varies from none to ravenously hungry"   5 mo.

Questionnaire Responses About Urinary
Tract and Genitals

	Time in Therapy
1. "Urination more frequent at night"	26 mo.
2. "Used to urinate about once a day—now more often"	23 mo.
3. "Urinate less"	23 mo.
4. "Less aware of need to urinate—little warning"	3 mo.
5. "Used to urinate often, with urgency; no more"	19 mo.
6. "Urinary frequency before—ceased with Primalling"	6 mo.
7. "Genitals larger" (male)	18 mo.
8. "Vaginal discharge with birth Primals, with same musky odor as when my two children were born"	13 mo.
9. "Change in pubic hair, from silky and smooth to kinky and coarse"	25 mo.
10. "Increased urinary frequency"	5½ mo.
11. "Urination easier, penis more relaxed"	3½ mo.
12. "More aware of urinary need"	36 mo.
13. "Urinate a lot less: frequency from 10-12 times/day to 5 to 6 times day"	13 mo.
14. "Urination discomfort"	6 mo.
15. "Urinary frequency from 10-12 times/day to 5-6 times/day"	9 mo.
16. "It wasn't unusual for me to urinate 12-15 times a day before therapy—urination is now less frequent. Penis more relaxed"	4½ mo.
17. "Increase in testicles and penis size"	18 mo.
18. "Was developing chronic urinary tract infections before therapy—have had no trouble since therapy started" (female)	16 mo.
19. "Frequent urination before therapy still persists"	4 mo.
20. "Now my erected penis is longer and wider"	5 mo.

21. "Occasional tightness in penis while urinating"   5 mo.
22. "I urinate much less frequently"   5 mo.
23. "Urinate more often, especially at night. What it feels like
    is just that when I need to pee, my body says 'now.' I can't
    save it up and if I try to, usually the tension I need to do it
    becomes a headache"   15 mo.
24. "Genitals increase in external size apparent visually. Also,
    on previous pelvic exam, doctor said uterus was abnormally
    small. On recent exam, doctor said it was of normal size"   18 mo.
25. "When I am changing levels (in a Primal) or just letting
    go of a feeling and loosening my body, I will urinate more
    frequently. This is particularly significant because I used to
    be able to go 8-9 hours without urinating at all"   5 mo.
26. "Very frequent urination"   4½ mo.
27. "Genitals' size increased very noticeably—partially from
    growth, partially from decreased tension" (male)   15 mo.

Questionnaire Responses About
Breasts and Menstrual Periods

		Time in Therapy
1.	"Breast cysts softer, smaller"	36 mo.
2.	"Used to have severe dysmenorrhea with a 21 day cycle, now much milder and have a 24-27 day cycle"	18 mo.
3.	"Breasts 'dormant' not quite attached"	3 mo.
4.	"Continuous bleeding (menstrual) for the previous 3 years; stopped in the past 2 months"	15 mo.
5.	"Breasts larger. Less blood loss during menses"	13 mo.
6.	"Breasts larger, no more dysmenorrhea"	25 mo.
7.	"Menstrual flow used to be very heavy, now is small to moderate"	34 mo.
8.	"Stopped taking birth control pills one month ago. This time my period started on time for the second time in my life. In my 3rd week in therapy my breasts hurt very much. This lasted about a month. They seemed to grow a little but now I'm back where I was before"	4 mo.
9.	"Breasts larger, and I no longer need to hide them"	28 mo.
10.	"Hips wider, breasts fuller (clothes' sizes changed from teens' to women's)"	16 mo.

11. "Used to suffer during menstruation with severe cramps, nausea and bloating. Now cycle is more regular, bleeding less and for a shorter time, and other symptoms much milder"   48 mo.
12. "Breasts larger now"   18 mo.
13. "Menstrual cramps less severe. Periods still irregular but there is less spotting. Breasts are fuller. I've had a vaginal discharge since puberty and this has now almost completely disappeared"   5 mo.
14. "No more cramps before periods"   13 mo.
15. "My period is still a terrible ordeal. Before therapy I had incredible pain—inability to function—always since the first period. Since therapy, the physical pain can be brought up somewhat into Primal Pain and felt. The first 6 months of therapy this happened and after Primalling, my menstrual pain subsided"   16 mo.
16. "Had cramps when very young. In mid 20's, went away. Returned during therapy. However, now they last about 30 minutes. In my youth they would last 6-7 hours"   18 mo.

Questionnaire Response About Sexuality		*Time in Therapy*
1. "Decreased desire"	F	8 mo.
2. "Decreased desire, less masturbation, much less promiscuous"	M	35 mo.
3. "No libido"	F	5 mo.
4. "Decreased frequency of intercourse and masturbation"	M	30 mo.
5. "Less driven. Orgasms physical and energetic"	M	26 mo.
6. "Decreased frequency, increased pleasure"	F	36 mo.
7. "Talking, touching, much more meaningful than screwing"	F	10 mo.
8. "Before therapy, had an almost constant erection. Masturbation or intercourse about 5 times a day. Now, masturbation or intercourse about once a day. Found *Deep Throat* boring"	M	23 mo.
9. "I don't perform at all, very afraid of intercourse, want touching more"	F	9 mo.
10. "Rare masturbation, no confidence in sexual ability"	M	4 mo.
11. "Improvement: more sustained sex—masturbate less"		18 mo.

12. "Sexual preoccupation diminished—ok to go without
    for a while"   M   16 mo.
13. "Diminished from two times a week to once a week" M   3½ mo.
14. "Variable, but proportional to feelings 1:1"   F   18 mo.
15. "No desire for intercourse—the idea scares me"   F   5½ mo.
16. "No sex since the start of therapy—fearful"   F   3 mo.
17. "Much more sex enjoyment. Masturbate much less.
    No more loss of erection"   M   5 mo.
18. "Used to be impotent with girls—am no longer
    satisfied by acting out sexually with men. I need more
    than that"   M   20 mo.
19. "Sex has become less mechanical, more enjoyable.
    Orgasms more powerful. Masturbate less"   M   14½ mo.
20. "Much better, fuller orgasms. Masturbate less"   M   14 mo.
21. "Much more pleasure. Loss of sexual compulsions"   M   19 mo.
22. "Prefer sex only in a warm relationship—not for its
    own sake"   M   18 mo.
23. "Marked decrease in sexual desire"   M   5½ mo.
24. "Less sex"   F   13 mo.
25. "More of my body responds during intercourse.
    Homosexual practices decreased from 3 times a week
    to 3 times in past year"   F   25 mo.
26. "Marked decrease in desire"   M   5½ mo.
27. "Desire sex about once a week. Sex more enjoyable"   3½ mo.
28. "No sex before—sporadic now"   M   36 mo.
29. "Less interest (frequency), more enjoyment"   M   15 mo.
30. "I used to need many different women constantly and
    be very promiscuous. I have been able to drop that
    struggle completely"   M   12 mo.
31. "Need and sex are getting separate. Seek intercourse
    much less (1-2 times/month)"   M   8 mo.
32. "Better at times. Impotent at times"   M   13 mo.
33. "Much less—not used compulsively very much"   M   16 mo.
34. "Sexuality decreased"   M   9 mo.
35. "I had the first 'good' heterosexual dream in my life
    a few months ago"   M   6 mo.
36. "I rarely have sexual feelings since being in therapy.
    Have intercourse about once a month"   F   7 mo.
37. "Sexuality is changing slowly—I am much more often
    interested in sex with husband than with a woman.

My sexual attractions to women only arises as clearly part
of a feeling (before a Primal) and feels very different
than what I want with my husband" F 34 mo.

38. "Decreased frequency" M 3 mo.

39. "For the most part I'm just not interested, and rarely
think about it" F 4 mo.

40. "Performance is fine when it happens. I just don't
perform much (very often) any more. Haven't acted
out with a man since entering therapy. Still masturbate
though. Started having heterosexual fantasies" M 6 mo.

41. "More staying power. Feelings much more intense.
Climax often sets off a Primal" M 9 mo.

42. "Used to be totally frigid. Can now enjoy sex and
reach orgasm" F 28 mo.

43. "Less frequently, more intense, more real. Other sex
just a prelude to intercourse rather than using sex
(fellatio, etc.) for symbolic acting out and tension
release" M 57 mo.

44. "Tremendous decrease in my sex drive. Still a great
attraction for other men" M 4½ mo.

45. "I almost never masturbate nor do I even have the
urge to do so. I feel a lot more during sex than ever
before" F 9 mo.

46. "The most significant change has been the disappearance
of premature ejaculation—more specifically, being
unable to maintain penetration, and coitus without
orgasm. I had been unable to have sex relations from
approximately 2½ mo. ago to 1 week ago. Any contact
with a woman produced such intense Pain, and
therefore was unable to 'make' any woman. After
Primalling those feelings I was able to have sexual
intercourse. What I noticed was that I was no longer so
tense that I was continually contracting the muscles
of my buttocks and perineum. As a result, I was able
to continue intercourse pleasurefully as long as I wished
and have orgasm when I was ready—amazing" M 5 mo.

47. "I don't ejaculate nearly as soon as before—much more
able to build sensation" M 23 mo.

48. "Sex life greatly improved. I feel much more relaxed
and natural in a sexual context now. Intercourse lasts

longer and is generally more pleasant"   M   9½ mo.

49. "With only one exception I can think of I had never
been able to masturbate to orgasm. This changed in
about my third month. The only time I seem to have
trouble now is when I'm close to feelings"   M   3 mo.

50. "Sex urge has been almost nil since beginning of
therapy"   M   3 mo.

51. "Since therapy, frequency of masturbation has
decreased from about once/day to 1-3 times/wk"   M   4½ mo.

52. "More easy and casual. Much less tense.
Less frequent, more satisfying"   M   36 mo.

53. "Less sex, less need for sex"   M   18 mo.

54. "Was frigid before therapy. Am just beginning in the
last few months to feel any natural sexual urges
at all"   F   16 mo.

55. "My desire is much less than usual"   F   4 mo.

56. "I used to come quickly and as I'd begin to, my
body would go limp and the semen would just squirt
out of my penis. I had absolutely no control of my body.
Now, I don't come as quickly and my body is in
rhythm as I ejaculate. (It's beautiful!)"   M   5 mo.

57. "I had intercourse twice daily before therapy. Now
frequency varies. I want sex most a week after I
menstruate"   F   36 mo.

58. "Reduced sex life but much stronger orgasms"   F   10 mo.

59. "No sexual relations for the past year"   M   6½ mo.

60. "Like sex much more—now, able to reach orgasm"   F   36 mo.

61. "I could never have an orgasm before therapy. I
usually had to drink alcohol (a lot) before I could
relax enough. I was never free about my body in any
way. I could never walk around nude in front of
anyone. Now I can, and do frequently. My attitude is
much more free and open"   F   48 mo.

62. "My sexual orientation still remains fixated on
transvestite fantasies. Was recently able to have
intercourse with a girl but was unable to reach
orgasm . . . lack of gain in this area"   M   24 mo.

63. "Had sexual intercourse only twice in the last
5 months"   M   5 mo.

64. "I still have very little sex because I'm so scared of

women. But my desire is much stronger. I used to
block my need for sex with drugs and rationalization.
I've become attracted to some men too since
therapy—though I would occasionally notice homosexual feelings before therapy I would run from them.
However, my attraction to men, physically, is nowhere
near as constant and obsessive as my attraction to
women"   M   25 mo.

65. "Generally, screwing is becoming more and more just
screwing. When I do it I am more in the present than
ever, but still aware of not being altogether in my body
in the here and now"   M   15 mo.

66. "I haven't had intercourse since I've been here—I vary
in the desire to do so. Often, I have no sex drive for a
week or more. I masturbate less because of tension.
I don't any longer struggle to get someone to bed. I
used to a lot"   M   6½ mo.

67. "Intercourse much less frequently now. Have always
enjoyed, so that hasn't changed. I move more now"   F   18 mo.

68. "About a month ago I lost my desire"   M   3 mo.

69 "Less frequent intercourse"   F   5 mo.

70. "Masturbate about twice a week, sexuality
is decreasing"   M   4½ mo.

Questionnaire Responses About Neurological
and/or Psychophysiologic Symptoms

		Time in Therapy
1.	"Right hand tremor when anxious"	35 mo.
2.	"No more tension headaches"	30 mo.
3.	"First migraine (ever) occurred with 'nameless baby' feeling"	26 mo.
4.	"Headaches now—with hyperventilation"	9 mo.
5.	"No more headaches"	18 mo.
6.	"No headaches, but feel continuous pressure inside head, ears and base of skull"	15 mo.
7.	"Many fewer headaches than before therapy"	5½ mo.
8.	"Get severe headaches when feelings rise"	3 mo.
9.	"Still tremble sometimes"	5 mo.

10. "Severe headaches in post-group when can't tell people
    what I want to"   6 mo.
11. "History and EEG evidence of grand mal seizures, stopped,
    while off dilantin. (EEG focus in the left front-temporal
    region apparently became normal). Used to have migraine
    headaches daily. Stopped after Primal therapy"   19 mo.
12. "Feel stronger—able to work for myself. Don't need to
    be 'taken care of' as before"   18 mo.
13. "Previously, had trembling of hands and voice, now
    gone. No more episodes of sleep paralysis"*   10 mo.
14. "Occasional migraine"   25 mo.
15. "No migraine since started Primal Therapy"   5½ mo.
16. "Sometimes almost black out when birth feelings
    are pushing"   15 mo.
17. "Some paralysis during deep Primals"   12 mo.
18. I blacked out once when physical pain got intense and
    woke up in a Primal with convulsions"   8 mo.
19. "Migraine headaches, only when struggling"   10 mo.
20. "One episode of sleep paralysis—was unable to answer
    the phone" (see note on sleep paralysis)   6 mo.
21. "Headaches—fewer and shorter"   3 mo.
22. "All residual (Primal) Pain is signalled immediately
    by a small dull headache"   6 mo.
23. "Occasional headaches"   3 mo.
24. "I seldom had headaches before therapy; now I occasionally
    get one when I'm holding back feelings"   9 mo.
25. "Used to faint under stress—no longer occurs. Used to have
    total body tremors when physically close to guys—
    no longer occurs" (female)   28 mo.
26. "Very bad pain in right shoulder during first month of
    therapy—has been gone since then"   3 mo.
27. "After a very deep Primal last December I began to regain
    my body rhythm (improved coordination)"   5 mo.
28. "No headaches before therapy—Now I have them when
    certain feelings are pushing"   36 mo.

---

*Sleep paralysis is a neurological syndrome in which people "wake up" mentally, after sleeping,
but find that they are totally paralyzed. This may last a few seconds to many minutes. It occasionally occurs as one is going to sleep as well. Traditionally, neurologists have considered sleep
paralysis a component of narcolepsy, with which it is often associated. The causes of both
syndromes are unknown; but suggesting to us that they are components of neurosis, was a recent
case of narcolepsy (in a physician), markedly improved by Primal Therapy.

29. "Very seldom have headaches now. Used to faint due to
    hyperventilation, no longer do so"   25 mo.
30. "More headaches, starting after 9 mo. in therapy"   10 mo.
31. "I had persistent migraine headaches for 10 years. I have
    had one migraine since starting therapy—in my second
    month—none since"   6½ mo.
32. "Used to have severe headaches requiring much
    medication—no longer occur"   48 mo.
33. "Return of tension headaches: less severe now than
    in high school"   24 mo.
34. "I used to get frequent headaches behind my eyes along
    the sides of my head, back to my neck, usually when I'd
    had insufficient dream time the night before. This has
    happened only once so far, since therapy started"   4 mo.
35. "Instant headaches when feelings needing to be felt are
    not felt (Primalled)"   15 mo.
36. "I still sometimes get bad headaches when at work"   6½ mo.
37. "I used to have bad hammer toes—they straightened
    out in one Primal"   18 mo.
38. "Some severe headaches"   3 mo.
39. "I've never had headaches, but now I do if I'm holding
    back a feeling"   5 mo.
40. "Used to have (rare) blackout spells but don't anymore"   15 mo.

QUESTIONNAIRE RESPONSES ABOUT SLEEP/DIET

	Time in Therapy	SLEEP				DIET
		Quality	Amount	Dreams	Feel Rested?	
1.	8 mo.	good	8 hours	recalled, about Pain	yes	avoid sweets
2.	35 mo.	better	was 10-12, now 8-9 less	———	———	more salads, less sweets
3.	5 mo.	anxiety attacks		———	yes	———
4.	30 mo.	lighter sleep	much less	less symbolism	yes	much improved, don't eat sugar
5.	26 mo.	good	9 hours	less symbolism	yes	can't eat grease or spices
6.	36 mo.	much improved	6-7 hours	less symbolism	yes	need less food
7.	10 mo.	———	7 hours	dream more, less symbolic	no	———
8.	23 mo.	———	was 12-14 hrs. to 8 hrs.	———	yes	amount the same; better food
9.	9 mo.	better but not good	5-6 hours	less symbolism	not sure	don't like chewy foods, like liquids
10.	4 mo.	improved	6-7 hours	seldom recall dreams	yes	eating more—nervous about no job
11.	18 mo.	———	8 hours	symbolism more related to feeling	yes	eat better food—no synthetic food
12.	16 mo.	———	6-9 hours	seldom recalled	yes	no change
13.	3½ mo.	———	7-8 hours			eating more
14.	15 mo.	poor	9 hours	heavy dreams	rarely	eat better food
15.	18 mo.	good	8-9 hours	many	yes	less, nibble a lot
16.	5½ mo.	sleep less "dead"	7 hours	recall seldom	seldom	craving for meat, avoid starch
17.	3 mo.	improved	7-10 hours	seldom recall	yes	
18.	5 mo.	poor	7 hours	less symbolism	no	eat more fruit

QUESTIONNAIRE RESPONSES ABOUT SLEEP/DIET (Continued)

	Time in Therapy	SLEEP				DIET
		Quality	Amount	Dreams	Feel Rested?	
19.	6 mo.	poor	———	many struggle dreams with me losing	no	stopped health food, went back to "shit" food
20.	20 mo.	poor	7-8 hours	many nightmares	no	no changes
21.	14½ mo.	get to sleep quicker	fewer hours		yes	———
22.	14 mo.	———	1-2 hrs. less	struggles are milder and I win more	yes	
23.	19 mo.	better	5-19 hours		yes	high protein diet, gives me more energy
24.	6 mo.		7-8 hours	unchanged, many dreams	yes	no changes
25.	18 mo.			vivid detail, little symbolism	no, because often need to Primal in sleep	eat more fruit, eggs, salad
26.	5½ mo.	no changes	———		yes	no changes
27.	13 mo.	very restful sleep	———	very real dreams	yes	no longer craving sweets
28.	10 mo.	sounder	———	less symbolism	yes	no change, always ate well
29.	25 mo.	sounder	9-10 hours	less symbolism	yes	new foods, more fruit
30.	5½ mo.	———	less	much symbolism	very seldom	enjoy eating, enjoy more chewy foods
31.	3½ mo.	———		less symbolism	yes	
32.	36 mo.	———	4-6 hours	nightmares still	sometimes	———
33.	15 mo.	need less	4-7 hours	———	yes	less meat, more fruit and vegetables

QUESTIONNAIRE RESPONSES ABOUT SLEEP/DIET (Continued)

	Time in Therapy	SLEEP Quality	SLEEP Amount	Dreams	Feel Rested?	DIET
34.	13 mo.	same	need less	—	—	I eat less "crap"
35.	12 mo.	poor, still tense	8-9 hours	struggle dreams	no	more sweets but I am so thin that I can't get too concerned
36.	8 mo.	more fitful	7 hours	—	sometimes yes, sometimes no	—
37.	6 mo.	—	—	nightmares almost every night	yes	—
38.	13 mo.	sometimes better, sometimes worse	8 hours	often, not usually	no	—
39.	16 mo.	generally okay	10 hours	some symbolic	yes	no changes
40.	9 mo.	poor, still full of dreams and tension	5-8 hours		no	eating very little meat
41.	6 mo.	poor, still tense	8-11 hours	rarely symbolic	yes	no change
42.	7 mo.	unchanged	6-8 hours	symbolic dreams	no	I eat what I want now. I really don't have to maintain a struggle to keep my weight down.
43.	34 mo.	better, need less	5-9 hours		yes	no change
44.	3 mo.	rotten	6-8 hours	very symbolic and scary	no	no change
45.	4 mo.	variable	7-8 hours	very plain symbols	no	eat a lot less
46.	6 mo.	good	8 hours		yes	vegetarian for 10 years, enjoy food more now
47.	3 mo.	poor	3-8 hours	—	no	
48.	9 mo.	improved		no nightmares	yes	less snacking
49.	28 mo.	more restful	need less	less symbols	variable	

QUESTIONNAIRE RESPONSES ABOUT SLEEP/DIET (Continued)

	Time in Therapy	SLEEP				DIET
		Quality	Amount	Dreams	Feel Rested?	
50.	57 mo.	no change	7½ hours	rare symbols	yes	less regular—2 meals
51.	4½ mo.	more restless	8-10 hours	seldom recalled	sometimes yes, sometimes no	no change
52.	9 mo.	——	7-8 hours	more often	yes	I want to eat more kinds of natural foods such as fruit and vegetables
53.	5 mo.	more	same	not symbolic	variable	no change
54.	23 mo.	better relaxed	6-8 hours	more vivid, less symbolic	variable	fewer sugars
55.	9½ mo.	lighter	8 hours	more real, less symbolic	rarely	no change
56.	3 mo.	same	same	dreams seldom recalled	yes	no change
57.	6 mo.	better	8 hours	dreams symbolic in simple ways	yes	eating more when I want to, I think I can tell my body what it needs now
58.	3 mo.	——	——	simple symbolism	yes	eating less bread
59.	4½ mo.	better	6-8 hours	bizarre dreams and nightmares	not much	——
60.	36 mo.	good, satisfying	6-7 hours	——		——
61.	18 mo.	better	5-9 hours	——	my sleep has been the slowest thing to improve. I have never felt rested and still don't	I eat healthy food now
62.	16 mo.	poor	6-10 hours	cry a lot in sleep	rarely	no change

Questionnaire Response About Exercise

72 of the 83 Primal patients questioned about exercise replied. 24 individuals still exercised regularly and 48 individuals no longer exercised for its own sake, but in the latter group some felt their change in life style made exercise unnecessary.

Questionnaire Responses About
Muscles/Tics/Muscle Tension

		Time in Therapy
1.	"Rare left eye tic. Decrease in tension of right side"	30 mo.
2.	"Some body tics—no more eye tics"	26 mo.
3.	"Less muscle tension. Pre-Primal Therapy shoes no longer fit because toes aren't tense."	23 mo.
4.	"Fewer leg and foot cramps"	9 mo.
5.	"Muscle tension diminishing"	18 mo.
6.	"Diminished muscle tension"	16 mo.
7.	"Used to have back muscle spasms—now gone. Much less tense."	18 mo.
8.	"Intermittent tremors"	3½ mo.
9.	"Muscles still ache"	15 mo.
10.	"Much less tense"	18 mo.
11.	"Much looser, less tense"	5½ mo.
12.	"Still tense"	3 mo.
13.	"Less tension"	5 mo.
14.	"Muscles much less tense"	14 mo.
15.	"Still have body spasms"	19 mo.
16.	"Muscle tension markedly reduced"	10 mo.
17.	"Very loose, tension-free"	25 mo.
18.	"Less tense after Primals"	5½ mo.
19.	"Much looser"	3½ mo.
20.	"Tension varies with Pain"	36 mo.
21.	"Much less muscle tension"	15 mo.
22.	"Less muscle tension"	13 mo.
23.	"Muscle tension variable"	8 mo.
24.	"Much less tension at times"	13 mo.
25.	"Fantastic tension build up in back of neck, shoulders and down both sides of spinal column—This is certainly birth stuff—relieved after Primals"	16 mo.
26.	"Tension decreased"	9 mo.

27. "Muscles tense in sleep"   6 mo.
28. "Muscle tension greatly lessened to the point of feeling
    like there is no tension at times"   9 mo.
29. "Severe muscle spasms and cramps in birth Primals—much
    more relaxed between Primals"   28 mo.
30. "Feel really relaxed after a Primal"   23 mo.
31. "Very great tension at night during sleep. Overall though,
    my body seems more relaxed. My walk especially seems
    to have loosened up greatly"   9½ mo.
32. "Facial musculature in particular more relaxed, mouth
    especially"   3 mo.
33. "Not much if any muscle tension"   36 mo.
34. "Decrease in muscle tension"   18 mo.
35. "Muscle tension variable according to how I feel"   16 mo.
36. "Before tension would build in my neck muscles while
    driving till they would burn so I could scarcely stand it.
    After the first two months of therapy that tension is gone"   5 mo.
37. "Much more relaxed since therapy"   36 mo.
38. "Jaw used to ache in AM from clenching teeth at night—
    no longer happens"   25 mo.
39. "My body is not as tense as it always was. I used to get
    severe neck muscle spasms, have them rarely since therapy" 48 mo.
40. "Still have neck and muscle tension but is slowly
    decreasing"   24 mo.
41. "Still have considerable muscle tension in sleep and
    while awake"   5 mo.
42. "Still have tension in back, neck and shoulders"   25 mo.
43. "My chronic back condition and pain turns out to be one
    of my main target areas based in prototypic Pain in
    getting out of the birth canal. All my birth Primals involve
    a lot of work taking place mainly in my back and neck. I've
    felt that my head was not supported immediately after birth.
    As a result of therapy I can have my back pain—feel my
    feelings (Primal) and the pain goes away. Before, it would
    stay for days or weeks. Much less muscle tension, especially
    in the abdomen. Less tension all around and I'm a better
    athlete now"   15 mo.
44. "Still tense most of the time"   15 mo.
45. "Less tension generally, especially in neck, but still a great
    deal in head at times"   3 mo.

46. "I now get muscle aches but my neck and shoulders
    are more relaxed"   5 mo..
47. "I am definitely less tense"   6½ mo.
48. "My body is so soft now. There's not a hard muscle in it.
    I used to have a slightly tense stomach" (female)   18 mo.

Questionnaire Responses About
Hair, Skin and Nails

		Time in Therapy
1. "No more lichen planus, more hair on chest"	M	30 mo.
2. "No more cold hands. Skin warmer, drier"	M	23 mo.
3. "Feet and hands no longer cold. No more flaking, scaling. Hair grows faster"	F	36 mo.
4. "Used to have many lumps in skin, now all gone"	F	10 mo.
5. "Dry, pimply skin gone from arms, hands and feet"	M	23 mo.
6. "Psoriasis and unfelt feelings vary together, gets better after effective Primal. Still have nail fungus"	F	9 mo.
7. "Much less hair loss than before, thicker hair. Nails no longer break. Skin feels more alive"	F	18 mo.
8. "Much less forehead perspiration (before, occurred with stress)"	M	16 mo.
9. "Skin more moist, and have more hair"	F	15 mo.
10. "Before always had freezing feet—now they are warm. Nail problems also gone"	F	18 mo.
11. "Palms drier—used to be wet all the time. Feet and hands no longer cold"	F	5½ mo.
12. "Hands and feet warmer"	F	3 mo.
13. "Less acne on face"	M	6 mo.
14. "Bite nails a lot now"	M	6 mo.
15. "Had warts on hands and arms, now they are gone"	M	20 mo.
16. "Pores on face seem smaller. Face skin less oily. Baldness still progressing"	M	19 mo.
17. "Skin is gray and wrinkled when Pain is rising; is pink and less wrinkled after a Primal"	F	18 mo.

[The above comment is pertinent to the subject of *aging*. It is generally true that Primal people look 10-15 years younger than their actual ages, and we frequently observe the change in skin and facial expression referred to above in relation to individual Primals. We believe, as hypothesis, that the changes of the vital signs (inwardly expressed) and the changes in appearance (outwardly expressed) actually indicate that Primal Therapy slows down the aging process.—EMH]

18. "Skin not sensitive to stray hair on back . . . used to drive me crazy. Skin not dry anymore" F 13 mo.
19. "Hand rash returned" M 10 mo.
20. "Changed from oily to dry skin. Hair color darker" F 25 mo.
21. "More sensitive to cold, or decreased temperature of skin" M 5½ mo.
22. "Nails grow faster, skin warmer, more moist" M 3½ mo.
23. "Smoother skin. Less burning or tanning from the sun. Receding hairline returned to normal" M 36 mo.
24. "Used to feel hot all the time—normal now" M 15 mo.
25. "Sweating decreased except when tense" M 9 mo.
26. "Mild psoriasis still present" M 6 mo.
27. "I have always had cold clammy hands. I have noticed that if I'm into a feeling, my hands will be wet and frequently cold. When I'm out of a feeling my hands become warm and dry" F 7 mo.
28. "Skin softer, losing my warts" M 7 mo.
29. "I had a rash on my face for a year before therapy. It's gone now, but since therapy I have had one on palms of both hands" F 4 mo.
30. "Skin—better—feet stay warm now. Herpes condition on penis has come back only once. Before therapy, I had cyclical Herpes (virus) eruptions for 11 years" M 6 mo.
31. "I've got pimples on my shoulders, neck and back and face (started just recently)" M 3 mo.
32. "Pubic hair used to be in male pattern, up on abdomen. In therapy has gone back to female triangle shape" F 38 mo.
33. "More moisture on hands. Scaling skin on knuckles gone. More hair on legs and abdomen" M 9 mo.
34. "Shortly after beginning therapy, my scalp broke out terribly with pimples. I've had this thing for a month and every week could have written something different. Things (symptoms) come and go" M 4½ mo.
35. "My hands and feet used to be very cold, but they are much warmer now, much more often" F 9 mo.
36. "Just before entering therapy and for approximately the first month, I have noticed large hives on various

parts of my body whenever I blocked feelings. This
has been completely cleared"   M   5 mo.

37. "Scalp has been extremely tense and sore for almost
9 years now. I wish I could report that this has
changed, but it hasn't"   M   9½ mo.

38. "A mole in the center of my left cheek has faded
though not quite disappeared. My beard has grown a
lot fuller also the appearance of hairs down the
middle of my chest which were not there before
therapy"   M   6 mo.

39. "Do not mutilate my nails anymore"   M   3 mo.

40. "Used to be cold all the time, more heavy clothing—
no longer present. Bit nails and cuticles badly to the
point of bleeding. No longer biting nails or cuticles" M   18 mo.

41. "Return of facial acne"   F   4 mo.

42. "On the 4th day of therapy I noticed my hands and feet
were warm for the first time in ages. They are constantly
warm now, which they never had been, all my life"   F   4 mo.

43. "Although I don't feel differently, I've noticed for the
first time that when I push those elevator buttons
activated by body heat, they sometimes won't light
up when I touch them"   M   3 mo.

44. "Skin was paste white before therapy. I could never
tan, only burn and peel. Now I usually have some
color in my face and when I am in the sun, I tan"   F   36 mo.

45. "Softer skin. No longer always cold. Had Herpes (viral
skin infections), no more problems"   F   25 mo.

46. "I seem to be much more sensitive to cold"   M   6½ mo.

47. "Hair grows much faster. Nails grow much faster"   F   36 mo.

48. "After a Primal, 2 months ago, I got a rash on my
elbows that I used to get when I was little, in the
late springtime for some reason"   M   4 mo.

49. "I missed out on pimples during adolescence but I
get tons of them now. I've noticed a lot more hair
on my chest since I started therapy"   M   25 mo.

50. "Faint scar appearing on the upper lip (for 1st time)
Both toe- and finger-nails grow much faster now.
Seem to be getting slightly hairier—especially on
my right side, which has always been noticeably
less hairy than my left side"   M   15 mo.

51. "Face not as white except when sudden Pain
    comes up"   F   18 mo.
52. "Hives for the past 3 weeks, on and off. Increased
    beard growth"   M   15 mo.

Questionnaire Responses About New or Unusual
Phenomena or Perceptions   Time in
                                                     Therapy

1. "Women seem smaller . . . like girls"   26 mo.
2. "Used to have arthritis of my jaw, now gone"   23 mo.
3. "White spots on arm and breast went away— the one
   on the neck stayed"   9 mo.
4. "All senses more acute"   18 mo.
5. "Librax *threw* me into Primals and I had to stop it"   18 mo.
   [This response is of great theoretical interest. The benzodiazepine
   drugs are known to markedly inhibit the limbic (2nd line) system.
   This patient's experience is typical among Primal patients who try
   Librium or Valium. Among those who do, a paradoxical *increase* in
   access to very early Primal Pain may occur. From these reports we
   believe these drugs tend to open the gate to first-line Pains. Neurotics
   are calmed by benzodiazepine drugs which partially disconnect *external* stresses to *internal* visceral responses. But, as noted, Primal patients are brought closer to Pain with these drugs.—EMH]
6. "During birth Primals I developed spots of dry skin
   where I used to cross myself (Catholic) with holy water"   13 mo.
7. "Sensitivity to all stimuli keener"   3½ mo.
8. "I feel that my entire metabolic rate has slowed down,
   for longer and longer periods of time"   8 mo.
9. "For 25 years I have taken thyroid medication—for the
   last 10 years: cytomel 50 mcg and Prednisone 5 mgm
   (daily)—Main signs and symptoms of thyroid deficiency
   were irregular menses, lethargy, feeling cold, and
   tendency toward depression. I have taken no meds since
   starting therapy. My periods have been every 27-28
   days, completely normal flow. I no longer feel deficient in
   thyroid" (taken for 8 years—had produced remission
   of mild stein-levinthal Syndrome)
10. "My spine used to have a huge indentation from my middle
    back to my butt. Because of all my birth Primals and

other feelings, it's just about straight. (Most of my birth
Primals—over the past two years—have been
excruciatingly painful, physically, with deep muscular
spasms radiating from my stomach throughout my legs
to the tips of my toes.) My shoulders have lowered and
straightened out (from all the intense muscular pain and
terror at birth)"   28 mo.

11. "Up until recently I could not burp. Recently, however,
I've been burping which for me is amazing. Before
therapy, I used to get severe abdominal cramps from excess
gas, to the point of having to be hospitalized for six days
once, to try to discover the source of my pain. That's
when they discovered it was trapped gas. There was
so much gas in me at times that x-rays were totally black.
I haven't had a gas pain since therapy started"   9 mo.
(The following is a clearcut description of the pattern of sensing
Primal Pain: Starting in the lower body and *ascending*. See chapter
6).

12. "During the first four months of my therapy, I suffered
very few physical problems. However, within the month,
since I have been more active socially, my physical
problems are returning. It seems that the further I get
from the Painful mental feelings of therapy, either
psychologically or geographically, the more my body starts
to hurt. It begins with my feet becoming cold and numb,
then pressure builds up in my solar plexus or around my
heart—and then, if I continue to stay away from feelings
(don't Primal) the pressure goes to my head, resulting in a
severe headache and high blood pressure, leaving me
with a death-like feeling"   5 mo.

13. "Before Primal Therapy, I took 1500-7000 mgms of
Chloral Hydrate per night to sleep. Now—none"   14 mo.

Miscellaneous   *Time in*
                                                           Therapy

1. "I haven't touched a drop of alcohol in 6 months. I was
up to a quart of whiskey/day before therapy. I haven't
smoked, whereas I was chain smoking non-filter cigarettes
before therapy"   6 mo.

2. "Since entering therapy I decided I want to live, and
   since I've found life can really be great, I want to live as
   long as possible. So I've become interested in nutrition:
   take some vitamins, avoid foods with many chemicals,
   etc. I'm not compulsive about this, though"   14½ mo.

3. "Most significant for me is a new consciousness of my
   own health—what I feel like, how it changes, what my
   body needs, what its damage is. Before therapy I was not
   aware of my health, or the severe damage I was living
   with each day"   18 mo.

4. "I have a long way to go. I still get horrible sneezing and
   sinus attacks and have no real idea why. The biggest change
   for me has been in a simplification of my life. My energy
   goes into trying to take care of myself and get the work
   money sphere settled. I always avoided facing this before
   therapy"   6½ mo.

5. "Basically what I feel about the physical changes in my
   body is that my sickness inhibited and twisted and distorted
   natural body functions and growth. The more I feel and the
   more of me I get back and connect up to the more my
   body approximates what it might have been without
   neurotic interference. Tension that works itself out in
   many days reduces and my body is left more to do what it
   needs and wants cleanly. A blessing, this therapy"   15 mo.

6. "Am straightforward with doctors. Can now tell the
   difference between physical pain and Primal Pain"   9 mo.

*Summary Comment*s

The patterns of physiological and psychological change in Primal
patients, first reported by Dr. Janov in *The Anatomy of Mental Illness,*
are certainly evident in this series of questionnaire responses. The phenomena which were experienced by a majority of Primal patients in this
series included:

1. Straightening of posture
3. Clearing of sinuses and nose
3. Fuller, deeper respiration
4. Normalization of appetite and food intake

5. Marked decrease in sex urge with increased enjoyment
   of sex (less often, but more enjoyable)
6. Marked decrease in muscle tension
7. Recognition of relationship between symptoms of
   illness and Primal Pain.

One of the long term goals of Primal Therapy research is to do followup studies of patients over many years: the most direct test of the hypotheses that Primal Therapy reduces the incidence of diseases and prolongs lifespan. As results of these studies become available, they will be reported.

CHAPTER FOURTEEN

Therapeutic Implications of the Levels of Consciousness: Dangers in the Misuse of Primal Therapy

Arthur Janov

Primal Therapy is a therapy for Pain. There are specific Pains for each of us and therefore a specific Primal Therapy for each individual. But there is not a different Primal Theory for each case. The theory ties together all of the disparate facts and observations into a single cohesive structure and then is *applied individually*. A cohesive structure does not mean a rigid one, for a dynamic theoretical structure should have the flexibility to include a variety of techniques peculiar to each patient.

The concept of levels of consciousness has sharpened our thinking about patients—their diagnoses, treatment and prognoses. It helps orient us as to where the patient is at any given moment and where he is heading. A solid grasp of the patient's predominant mode of consciousness is a shorthand way of knowing a great deal about him and the kind of therapy he should receive. We can observe the levels at work in patients daily. For example, an advanced patient will spend an hour or two on second-line material, and when he has resolved a particular second-line scene or feeling he may automatically drop into the first-line connection to the feeling. Though it will be a different kind of Primal from the one he began, the relationship of the two is apparent both to the patient and therapist. Should the patient drop too quickly into the first line, we can spot it as a defense rather than a true connected feeling. Levels of consciousness is a structure which gives us a constant overview of the patient and his therapy.

The purpose of having Primal Therapy is to get to early Painful feelings, and relive and resolve them so that they no longer drive symbolic behavior. Any failure to do that is a failure of the therapy and will leave the patient neurotic to some degree. Thus, it is crucial that the major Pains are experienced and not left unattended inside. Without an over-view and without a cohesive theoretical structure it is likely that major Pains which impel neurosis will not be reached; I shall discuss in this chapter why this is so. *Primal Therapy is not simply a matter of thrash-ing, writhing and screaming, or punching pillows or yelling one's rage.* It is a matter of *integration:* that is the key term, and I shall be discussing this at length. Each and every feeling must be connected and integrated or else the person is not Primalling. I am suggesting that there are many ways to go wrong in doing this therapy and they usually boil down to the lack of integration.

Further, it is not just a matter of third-line connections, for that is not true integration. It is a matter of a systematic integration of the Pains on each level of consciousness. That is, each Pain must be integrated on the level where it resides. To *explain* a first-line Pain is not integration; nor is it integration when one uses words for a feeling which had no words. Each feeling must be integrated in its own terms. *The lack of integration is precisely how symbolic behavior got its start, for when a certain feeling was blocked its energy had to take devious routes.* Integration automat-ically dispels symbolic behavior; that is one way we can check on whether Primals are taking place.

Integration can be defeated in several ways; essentially, it is either therapist or patient error. By patient error I mean the conscious violation of the rules of the therapy which were set up to help people to get to feel-ings. Thus, if the patient takes drugs, smokes, and drinks he is not going to have Primal Therapy. But therapist error is far more serious because it means that not only is the current patient going to suffer but possibly all later patients will also not receive true Primal Therapy. I shall discuss therapist error at some length and indicate how Primal Therapy can go wrong. I shall also investigate how an understanding of levels of con-sciousness helps therapeutic integration. Further, I shall discuss other techniques used by non-Primal therapists who believe that they are doing a form of Primal Therapy (I call that "mock Primal Therapy") in order to show how those techniques bypass integration. First, let us begin with therapist error.

There are many ways that a therapist can defeat the Primal process and rob the patient of his feelings. There is the so-called "hard" approach in which a hard "bust" so overloads the patient that he is stopped in his tracks. Being busted in this way usually means that something is said to the patient in a cruel way and is brought up long before the patient is ready to hear it. This means that the patient cannot possibly feel and integrate the Pain, and if he cannot feel then the Primal process is defeated. A premature bust means that defenses are assaulted too quickly leaving the patient open to too much Pain. The result is an overload and shutdown, rather than an opening up. A bust doesn't mean that the therapist says to the patient, "I hate you, you're disgusting; your nose is too big and you are the kind of person I could never like." That is simply cruelty masquerading as therapy. A bust is simply telling the patient the truth about himself: "You talk too much. You're always talking about yourself," for example. If the patient has been rattling on to flee a feeling, he might stop and start to get underneath his defense. As the defense is stopped and as he starts to feel he may say, "I always talked to hold their attention because I always felt they wanted to get away from me." From there he will soon be into his Pain, something underlying his defense. The bust will aid integration.

Busts are sometimes necessary. Patients do not often know when they are defending and it is the therapist's job to know about defenses and to point them out to the patient—properly timed and administered. But it is not only patients who do not know when they are defending. Every Primal Therapist is also a patient and therapists are not exempt from reality. They need to know when they are blocking, defending and developing inappropriate ideation. The best situation for this to happen is a heterogeneous staff who are not all like-minded, who do not have similar personalities and who are open and honest enough to be straight with each other.

If a therapist has serious unresolved feelings of his own, especially feelings which coincide or clash with the patient's, then there are going to be problems. For example, if the patient is a talker, and the therapist had a mother who was a constant talker, then the therapist may have some hostility to the patient and bust him hard about his talking when such a bust is not appropriate at that time. If the patient pushes the therapist's "Primal button," challenging his competence, sincerity, love, intelligence, etc., and the therapist has unresolved feelings in those areas, then the patient is going to suffer. If a therapist was made to feel stupid at home, then when his patient challenges his intelligence, the therapist may come down on the patient, be defensive and not allow the patient an aggressive act so necessary for his health. In short, the therapist may treat the patient just as his father and mother did, reinforcing the neurosis. If a therapist always had his motives challenged in his early home life then any challenge to his motives by the patient may likewise set off a myriad of defenses; in that way the patient who may be seeing a reality in the therapist is shuttled away from that reality and nudged into unreality. All this is to say that no therapist is perfect, but that to be a Primal Therapist one must have a lot of old Painful feelings out of the way.

There is another way to rob the patient of his feelings, a way so subtle and deceptive that the patient never perceives what is happening to him. After all, he can see the hard bust and if he has any resources there may be some things he can do about it. That subtle way is excessive softness and protection by the therapist of his patient. The reason that it is not perceived is that *it feels good,* not bad, as in the case of the hard bust. This approach can be rationalized by the therapist as "letting the patient be where he is," a nice sounding phrase which can be a rationalization for an inability to confront the patient when necessary. Too often, letting the patient be means *letting him be neurotic.* The patient gets love and acceptance from the therapist instead of his Pain, and really, who wants Pain when he's got a chance to get what he never got . . . an all permissive, loving, authority figure. A patient is apt to wallow far too long in his apparent safe therapeutic atmosphere instead of feeling how in his whole life there *never was any safety. Therapists who use the so-called soft approach are in reality doing psychoanalysis, not Primal Therapy.* They give to the patient out of their own unconscious needs (giving to others what they never got and need) so that patient never feels his lifetime deprivation in all its agony. This kind of therapist is encouraging transference, to use a Freudian term. *The psychoanalyst is usually warm, permissive, kind and understanding, and patients never truly get well precisely because he is all that, never penetrating the defense system of his patient.* The so-called soft approach is done by the passive therapist who has trouble in confrontation. He never confronted his parents, has not confronted his peers and is afraid to confront the patient out of a deep Primal fear of evoking hostility. What this therapist is often afraid of is triggering off anything in the present that will bring up the overload of parental rage against him. He becomes the "good guy" therapist (and son or daughter) who never takes a chance on feeling hated (not the present hate but the hatred from his parents that he could never dare feel). And because he was forced to be "nice and good" to mollify (and avoid the feeling of) parental hatred he really does become a nice person—too nice, because it is unreal. But he is seductive because he seems and acts like a very good person. His charm and kindness are eminently seductive but he has never resolved a very deep layer of fear and hostility—handmaidens which arose from a family full of hatred, arguments and a general air of distrust and bitterness. What makes the soft approach subtle and therefore doubly dangerous is the therapist has taken a technique which is obviously necessary at times and *abstracted* it to the level of a principle. That principle is then superimposed *generally* on a wide class of situations rather than being used when appropriate. It blankets reality, rather than uncovers it. The philosophy is an invention of the therapist as a way of avoiding his own feeling. Instead of feeling, "I could never get mad at my father," or, "Mother terrified me so I could never feel angry," a philosophy is devised that makes it all unnecessary.

Now obviously both the premature hard bust and the continual soft approach are neurotic and unreal, simply because there are no "eternal truths" in this therapy—it changes with the needs of the patients and the reality at the time. If a therapist has one continual approach it means he is frozen into a certain response pattern—frozen by unresolved old feelings that keep him from being flexible and changing with the needs of his patient. There are times to bust and times to be soft and errors in either direction can seriously rob the patient of his feelings.

When a therapist has no stake in being the "nice, warm guy" with his patient the patient can feel safe with him and that is a very important factor. It is most necessary for patients to feel safe with their therapists. But there are two kinds of safety: one is real and the other is quite unreal. Real safety means to be in the hands of someone who is straight, who does not have many old unresolved feelings which will be quietly shunted onto the patient. Unreal safety means to be in the hands of someone who inadvertently perpetuates the patient's neurosis because he (the therapist) has not come to terms with his own early Pain. Unreal safety can feel very safe to the neophyte patient precisely because his defenses are tolerated, sometimes even reinforced, his tension and anxiety are reduced thereby and what has happened is that an atmosphere has been created where the *patient is safe to be neurotic. We must make it safe for the real person, not his neurosis.* The greatest protection a patient can have is to have a therapist who is honest about himself and his feelings, someone who levels with the patient when he has made a mistake, someone who will tell the patient about his own weaknesses and occasional blind spots —someone, in short, who is not defended.

All of this does not mean that the therapist should not be warm, permissive, tolerant and kind with his patient. It is essential that the patient feel truly safe in his therapy, but I am trying to point out that it is easy to be seduced into a false safety by the saccharine pseudowarmth of someone who himself was never allowed to be anything else but that in his own early life. Thus, there may be an unconscious pact between therapist and patient to *make it safe for each other:* "I'll be kind and never busting if you agree never to get mad at me." Here we see what I mean by a therapist carrying out his exact early life with his patient. The danger here is that such neurotic acting-out is often *elevated to the level of a principle,* then that principle is labeled a philosophic belief by the person, who then claims to have philosophic differences with his associates. These philosophic notions may then include the need to let the patient be where he is, which implicitly means never confronting him, and confronting is exactly what the therapist could not do, was not allowed to do with his own parents. So his neurosis becomes a matter of principle. He has rationalized his inabilities and weaknesses, and has developed unreal ideation out of repressed Pain, calling that ideation a philosophy. Thus the passive therapist who has blocked the feeling of being hated by his parents by always being terribly nice, someone who has blocked out all his aggression so as not to rile hating parents, comes to believe in the passive approach as something objective and outside himself. The problem is that the rationale for such an approach can become so elegant, so refined and intellectual that it is almost impossible to extricate the feeling which lies below it. The person may take an implacable philosophical stand on the basis of not wishing to compromise his principles when in reality he is defending against those underlying feelings which would have to be faced if the philosophic cover were removed.

You cannot have a philosophical difference from reality. And it is reality we are discussing, not philosophies. For example, someone may say that it is his philosophy that birth Primals are essential to getting well and that patients must have them to have a successful therapy. The fact is that it is possible for some of us to have had a good birth, and the real first-line trauma may lie elsewhere. That philosophical difference may cause the therapist to drive the patient where he does not have to go, but he may try and try to do it to please a therapist who is stuck in that Pain himself. Or another difference: someone may think that patients need lessons in how to conduct their current life because Primals are disintegrating. The fact is that Primals *integrate* Pain when the patient is not pushed and allowed to proceed naturally in his therapy. There are no philosophical differences from the fact that the grass is green and the sky is blue.

The greatest danger is to get to a certain point in therapy where the Pain is horrific and to be encouraged, subtly or not, to retreat from that

Pain by a mothering therapist who fears that place himself. The danger is that the patient will be left neurotic, with the delusion that he is getting well. It is easy for the therapist to psychologically seduce his patient at this point: keeping him "safe," convincing the patient that he alone knows where he's at, etc. It is easy because none of us really get down deep without a little help and sometimes a little gentle pushing. We neurotically prefer that so-called safety because we are neurotic. If we were totally real then we'd know better.

I started this chapter with a discussion of integration, and I want to detail that now. Too much Pain cannot be integrated. There is an overload and the patient symbolizes the excess. It can come out in a dream where the patient dreams about great fear or murder or whatever. Or the patient can fixate on the therapist, develop inordinate fears or hostility and perhaps never overcome them without careful help. Likewise there is no integration when the patient is robbed of his feelings, a robbery of the most silent kind—something which takes place in front of him of which he is totally unaware—as, for example, hugging and mothering a patient who needs to confront someone in the chair in post-group, rushing to a patient who stands up to say his feelings so that the patient does not have to take that step for himself. The patient who does not confront is left with unresolved feelings and he cannot integrate them because he did not get a chance to experience them.

Integration means that consciousness is ready to accept and absorb an upcoming feeling. The feeling must be allowed to come up, not be squelched by a too hard or too soft approach, both of which bury the feeling.

What is disintegrating is to be overloaded with feelings so that they cannot be fully experienced. When Primal Therapy is done slowly and methodically there is no reason why *any* feeling the patient arrives at on his own has to be disintegrating. But we must remember that we cannot integrate feelings we are deprived of, so to arbitrarily decide that there are certain feelings patients must avoid is to seriously rob him of crucial experiences. It means that he will forevermore be driven by feelings never reached because someone decided he knew more than the patient and his reality. To experience a Primal feeling whose time has come *means* to integrate that feeling and that thereafter there will be that much less neurosis. There is no need for integration exercises, particularly if we understand that neurotic behavior is driven by *feelings,* not by lessons. *Changes in behavior depend on changes in feelings, not on third-line lessons.*

There is no way to take lessons in how to live. Each of us has to find his own way to do that. It is not simply arrogance to presume to tell any person how to lead his life, it is incorrect therapy. A therapist who has blocked his own early powerlessness and helplessness may act-out on his patient by taking power over the patient, directing his life and in this way continuing the underlying helplessness of the patient. The patient does not learn out of his own feelings and experience; what he learns (often unconsciously) is how to please one more parental figure—and deny himself. If the patient's neurosis is exactly this passivity and helplessness, he may even (neurotically) welcome being told what to do. If the therapist has this old need to avoid his own helplessness and powerlessness by gaining control over others (which is symbolically gaining control over his parents) then he will miss the entire interaction between himself and his patient, will not spot the patient's defenses (because it coincides exactly with his own needs) and will keep the patient sick, which means keeping the patient from *feeling* helpless and powerless. Instead, the patient will continue to act out those feelings.

One way that this kind of therapist rationalizes, and thereby avoids his feeling, is to invent the notion that Primals are disintegrating and therefore the patient needs help and direction in integration with his current life. A program is arranged for the patient in which he must do certain things—date, throw a party, take a certain kind of job, and so on. What the therapist is doing is arranging one more program for the patient (just as the parents did) under the slogan we have all heard in our childhood, "We know what is best for you."

Patients will function in their own way out of their own reality when allowed to if the therapist is straight with himself and has faith in the Primal process. It is the neurotic who lives out of the past continuously; it is in reliving the past step by step which brings him into the present. When one leaves this dialectic notion behind, one is apt to go astray. Indeed, to stray from the basic dialectic in any situation is to miss reality because it is the central law of life.

It is precisely those so-called integration exercises which keep a patient in the past. By focusing on present behavior (when in reality the patient is behaving out of his history) is to keep the past alive to drive *current* behavior. If the patient behaves counter to his feelings at the direction of someone else he is *de facto* burying his reality. There are times in this therapy when the patient should not function (particularly if his neurosis has been to function at a high rate), and we must trust the patient (and his body) to sense when that is. By feeling he will be in tune with his own rhythms; letting a patient be means not to tamper with those rhythms.

There is still another kind of philosophic error, and it harkens back to Otto Rank's disagreement with Freud; that is, to believe that birth Primals are the *sine qua non* of Primal Therapy. Birth Primals are so dramatic that it can appeal to many as the essence of the therapy—the rock bottom of what we do, so to speak. But such is not the case. Those who focus almost exclusively on the first line make the opposite error of those who believe that the patient must stay on the third line and function well in the present. The first-liners don't mind it if the patient is constantly in a state of disintegration, usually because he is dealing with too much Pain that he is not ready for. Some mock therapists begin each session with patients curled up in a fetal position and start the therapy from there. Sometimes a birth Primal occurs; this is particularly dangerous.

This kind of error is made for several reasons—and we have seen it at times occur within our own clinic. Usually it happens to therapists who are stuck on the first line themselves or who are close to it; they push the patient to go where they (the therapists) need to go. They encourage the patient to act-out symbolically the therapist's Pain. This kind of patient does not have a sufficient third-line reality because he is awash in very early Pain which has not been integrated. Here is where careful supervision is required, for the results of this problem are both subtle and serious for the patient. These therapists are fixated on a single line of consciousness to the exclusion of the interconnecting links. They may develop a philosophy (as Rank did) that birth Primals are the aim of the therapy and that no therapy is complete without them. The ideology becomes an encased structure and is deceptive because others are forced to deal with the ideology rather than the therapist's feelings which gave rise to it. It would be serious if a supervisor missed the feelings of the therapist and concentrated on convincing him of the errors in his ideology. He would be dealing with a third-line defense of the therapist against first-line flooding, and *there is no way to talk someone out of his Pain.* There is a stake in the misperception by the therapist and that stake is to avoid having to go into the Pain himself. Rather, he drives the patient there and, as can happen, the patient starts to use the first line as a defense against feeling later Pains because first-line Primals are familiar or now comfortable.

Nearly every therapist on our staff has Primalled on the first line many times. By now, most have come out of that level and have three-line interconnected Primals. This means that they are fully feeling people. It is this interconnection which allows them to see clearly when someone gets stuck on a certain level. They have been there. They are perceptive precisely because they have been there and *back*. They have a third-line reality.

It is the rare patient who goes to the first-line during his first three weeks of therapy. The ones who do are generally highly disturbed and obviously have almost no second or third-line defenses left. They may be borderline psychotic (meaning on the border of experiencing the first line) or previous acid freaks.

There are serious consequences of being kept on one line or another. To stay on third or second line means that the first line is still driving behavior. To be kept on the first line usually means that the patient has unresolving Primals, keeping him in so much Pain and turmoil that he cannot cope with everyday life.

Most patients start in the third line (immediate present or just recent past) and go back in graduated steps, integrating a bit at a time. But sometimes the patient's body is Primalling on the first line during the first three weeks while his head is not there yet. That is, the patient can talk about something in the present or at age nine and begin gagging, spitting up, thrashing, shaking, etc. It is very easy at that point to imagine that the patient is on the first line and either push his head down into a pillow, stuff a pillow over his mouth, tell him to go with his body, etc. After a few days of this the patient may indeed find his way into the first line . . . *long before he is ready to do so.* He has been pushed through his normal defenses and *not allowed* to be where he is by a therapist who may convince the patient that *he* knows where he should go. The patient thereby becomes overloaded and fragments. He is not ready to integrate that first line and should be kept on the second or third line until his consciousness (not just his body) is ready. Because the patient is so open and vulnerable during the first three weeks when his defenses are becoming dismantled, he is most susceptible to errors of this kind by a therapist. The patient then becomes immersed in first line and does not develop a third-line reality to deal with his current life as he should. Naturally the body shrinks up and curls up against all kinds of Pain, and that curl-up looks fetal and it may be. But it is often a defense against current or second line Pain and it is that Pain which must be faced and felt—not have the fetal position be reinforced. Obviously, there are some patients who are fully on the first line and need to be there. But after many months of unresolved tension, general lack of progress and inability to deal with one's current life, something is very suspect. And it is our job to do the suspecting. I want to remind the reader of the chain of Pain which I have discussed earlier, which links all three levels of consciousness.

Each "now" feeling is connected to experiences throughout our life which relate to that feeling; thus feeling alone in the present can be related to feeling alone throughout one's youth (a giant second-line feeling) and that can be connected to the prototypic feeling of being alone just after birth when the newborn is placed in a container away from his mother. Each time a patient feels his aloneness or any other feeling in the present it can set off the entire chain of feeling including the prototypic feeling. Thus the patient may gag, thrash, spit up, shake, choke, curl-up, convulse or whatever when he gets into any feeling. It is an easy error for the therapist to decide therefore that the patient is ready for the first line. Simply watching a scary movie can bring up first-line terror (and symptoms) if the person is close to it. But to be able to Primal there may take months; this is what a skilled therapist must know. This is especially true of highly disturbed or prepsychotic patients who are in touch with their first-line terror all the time. It is so pervasive that any current fear can trigger it. But what they need initially is bolstering of the integrating third-line, not to be disintegrated on the first.

If after months of therapy a patient is not beginning to do some integrating, if he has very few insights, then I believe he was not ready for the first line. Or if he was, there was still too much emphasis on it to the neglect of third-line reality by the therapist. The patient becomes enmeshed in his first line, confused and instead of being pulled out of it so he can rest and get his head together, first-line oriented therapists continuously drive the patient back there producing ongoing fragmentation and a constant state of free-floating, non-connected anxiety. This approach drives patients *beyond* feeling.

It is not a matter of philosophic differences. Simply to call an unreal idea a philosophy and thereby grace it with some kind of intellectual cover doesn't make it real.

The hysteric patient (to use a Freudian nomenclature), one with tension and Pain constantly bursting through, the one who is very near his first and second line all the time, is just the one who needs some here-and-now defenses—the one who does not need to shatter himself on the first line. He needs to talk about his current reality a great deal. There is no good going to the first line if you cannot *integrate* it. Insights are one very important index of integration.

What is important to realize is the vulnerability of a patient who is losing his defenses. In the first weeks of his therapy the therapist is all-important, and it is then that the patient can be subtly moved away from a proper course. For the patient is learning a *Primal style* in the first weeks of treatment and that style may stay with him a long time. So long as it is *his* style all is well. If it is the therapist's, then there is trouble. For example, to continue from the previous discussion, it is possible to encourage the patient to go with his body during each session so that the first line is encouraged. The patient may go there at the first sign of *any* feeling and what happens is that other level feelings are rerouted into that line. The body movement becomes a defense and the patient is no longer integrating, therefore no longer Primalling. He has the *appearance* of spectacular Primals because he is thrashing around or spitting up, screaming and crying, and he can do that for hours at a time since all levels are compressed into the first line. When he finishes, however, he may still feel bad, just as bad as when he started. He has integrated nothing and resolved nothing; he has had a catharsis. And even if he feels better later it is only due to release of tension.

This incorrect Primal style is actually overloading the patient so that when he finishes for the day he is in danger of acting-out on the street or with friends. He will have bad dreams and nightmares from the left-over unresolved Pain. It is also possible that a patient can have nightmares after having real Primals, particularly when those Primals are catastrophic and can only be felt a piece at a time. It is again up to the skilled therapist to know the difference.

The danger in keeping patients on the first line is that when it is arrived at prematurely it truly is disintegrating; the patient feels worse or feels that the therapy is too much and wants to run away. He may become convinced that he is a special case—that the therapy is too much for him—that he is too sick for it, and so on. All of this therapist error may drive the patient out of therapy and leave him neurotic forever; for this therapy is truly a one-way street that must be entered into with full understanding of the implications. Once a person has been opened up it is not so easy to close him up again. Should he leave therapy too soon he may really be sicker than before in the sense that he is more anxious than ever, more acting-out, less in control and less able to function. He may well blame the therapy instead of the therapist since he usually doesn't know what has happened to him; that is the true danger of going to those who are untrained in this therapy. It is not like other treatment forms which one may leave with impunity almost at will.

It is the first-line patient who often has skipped over the second line, which is the connecting link between present and past, a link which aids the integration process. I have discussed (in the chapter on the Nature of Pain) how valences of Pain grow larger as one descends the chain of consciousness because there is less brain (cortex) to handle the load in our early weeks of life. Therefore, it is clear that one would naturally go the lesser valences (all else being equal) in the initial phases of therapy. This means a progression of three-to-two-to-one. The average neurotic will do that when he is left alone to follow the body's natural course of experiencing Pain.

There are even more complications to driving the patient into an overload. As the patient becomes more shattered, upset and vulnerable, the one he must place all of his trust and hope onto is his therapist. The transference onto the therapist becomes impenetrable precisely because the patient is overwhelmed by Pain he cannot integrate and the therapist therefore can brainwash him even more. The patient fails to make significant progress in therapy even though he seems to Primal twice as much as anyone else. He does not become Primally smart.

Primal Therapy is a *natural* process. *Feeling will find the appropriate level* if someone isn't diverting the patient in one direction or another. If a patient is not continuously having his mouth stuffed with a pillow, if he isn't having his head crammed onto the floor, if he isn't incorrectly made to talk out his feelings, if he isn't being held too much by a well-meaning therapist, then his feelings will tell him where to go. Feelings are the only authority.

The first line as defense can get quite subtle so that for instance in post-group as a patient starts to confront someone in the chair, suddenly the whole chain of Pain starts coming up and the patient falls to the floor gagging and convulsing instead of finishing with his necessary confrontation. Or if he does finish, he may still reroute a second- or third-line feeling into the first. He isn't consciously using the first line as a defense; rather, he has learned in his therapy to go there at the sign of any Pain. So the patient no longer confronts his co-patients, his therapists or others and instead hides behind his style, and that is what keeps him sick. He is forever in the past.

As I said before, many of us have felt alone all of our lives, beginning with just after birth. But there are levels of that feeling and levels of Pain associated with the feeling. The more we descend down the chain of Pain, the more we experience the Pain of that feeling. One day we can descend the entire chain and back up again and it is then that we have a fully Primal consciousness. We cannot expect to get to the giant prototypic aloneness in the first weeks of therapy.

The great danger for all of us, of course, is to stop feeling; to abort the therapy before there is a fully integrated three-level consciousness. Because defenses tend to be all or none, that residual unintegrated Pain is liable to keep us just as neurotic as before therapy. We can go along for a long time in therapy and imagine we are just as sick as before precisely because of residual unfelt Pain. It isn't that the therapy is failing; it is that Pain has great depths, and we are just now appreciating those depths and how long it takes to get there. So all of us will want to act out along the way and that is when we need to stay and feel. For defenses that we have built up over a lifetime become encased and grooved so that Pain from *any source* is funneled into them. So even after two years of therapy homosexuals may want sex with other men, or transvestites may want to dress up, not because they have gotten nowhere but because defenses do not differentiate out special kinds of Pain. *Any Pain can drive them.* Safety is coming to feel. *Safety is in the feeling; not in someone outside yourself.*

This is why I might encourage individuals who cannot get into Primal Therapy at our Institute to help each other Primal informally. The danger is self-styled experts who do mock Primal Therapy with their patients and call it "Primal." I do not know why it is that others do not do what I call proper Primal Therapy. We have taken into treatment therapists from many countries of the world who claim to have done Primal Therapy on their own before. It is clear to us that they did not have a proper understanding of Primal Theory, and it soon becomes clear to them that what they were doing bore little relation to the kind of skilled therapy they get at the Institute. We have no desire to keep Primal Therapy contained, but we do understand how very dangerous it is in untrained hands and we shall make every effort to protect the public from those dangers. I think incorrect Primal Therapy can be more dangerous than no therapy. A person may be anxious but he still may be able to function without this therapy. But we have seen improper therapy produce psychotic states, suicides and create "basket cases" who could no longer function in the here-and-now. It can be dangerous because you are opening up Pandora's box of Pain and unless that Pain can be safely integrated the result is an overload and worse shutdown together with physical and mental symptoms.

We all want to get what we didn't get. We all want good loving parents, and we all can be seduced when it seems as though we get a smidgeon of it in the present. We all want a safe place. And I submit that the ultimate safety is to be in a real place so that you don't leave the therapy half-done. If I had a choice today between a loving therapist and one who forced me into my Pain I'm sure I'd try to avoid the latter, even though I

knew that he is the one who could help get me well. We've all had so
much Pain in our lives we don't want any more. We got the double
whammy. We had all that Pain and then to get rid of it we have to go
through it all over again. It is totally unfair. But we didn't put the Pain
there. "They" did. It is not a matter of soft and hard in one's approach.
It is a matter of being real and doing what is appropriate for the patient
at the time. If one can only be one way, something is wrong. If the therapist is always hard he's got old feelings to get to. He is blocking his
tenderness and softness. If he is too soft, he is blocking his hardness, his
aggression.

When therapists have an overview, when they see the ultimate objec-
tives of the therapy, they will make all the changes necessary. We stay
open to change, which is precisely why when there is a crisis regarding
staff in this therapy we bring the *patients* in for a meeting: the only psychiatric clinic in the world to operate that way. We want the patients'
thoughts and feelings and we have changed radically over the years depending on what they say.

The real danger in Primal Therapy is when patients stop being individuals—stop being themselves. When overloaded they want to band
together with others who are in a similar place and develop mass ideas
which are really symbolic. Let me give you an example. One trainee
who was into birth Primals started having strange ideas at a certain point.
"We need openness here! It is all closed down. There is *no room* for us
to express ourselves." Many of us knew where he was symbolizing his
first-line Pain onto the staff. We tried to disabuse him of his paranoid
notions but we were fighting the Primal tide. He then found two others
in the same place and they developed an interlocking neurotic framework
which became impervious. They reinforced each other's unreality and it
became encased. Instead of having third-line reality they had first-line
reality projected onto the present. And they became convinced that they
needed to get out; unfortunately, they needed to get out of the wrong
thing. It wasn't the clinic, it was the womb. But if you are overloaded in
the past, the present only becomes symbolic of it—and that is the danger
in Primal Therapy.

Thus, the patient error is to become cliqueish. It doesn't matter what
feeling he is running from; if he bands together with others who are in
the same place, they might develop a mutually reinforced defense. If it is
hostility they cannot come to terms with, they will want to run to a "safe
place." They may want to join others in finding a tranquil country environment or a therapy that does not deal in Pain. It doesn't matter where

they escape to; they are escaping from feelings. What they really want is to preserve the last vestiges of their neuroses because it is so Painful to go into hostile feelings, feelings which would have brought the wrath of their parents down on them if they expressed it in their childhood. *To get into hostility means to feel overwhelming rejection early in life,* so it is *natural for the neurotic* to want to flee, and the skilled therapist must help him not to.

To say that there is a specific way to do Primal Therapy is no different than to say that there is a specific way to do heart surgery. Obviously we do not have the precision of the surgeon's knife, but Primal Therapy in the proper hands is precise. It is not precise in the sense of a rigid set of mechanical rules to follow; rather, there are precise clues which differ with each patient which dictate the use of specific techniques and those techniques evolve from a carefully worked-out theory, based on previous observations.

I bring up this point because I want to indicate that it is not possible to join other approaches and theories with Primal Therapy in order to make some kind of enhanced Primal Therapy. We thought for a time that it was possible to use a variety of techniques to get patients into feelings, particularly Rolfing and bioenergetics since we had therapists on our staff who had previously practiced both. Some patients were Rolfed during their Primal Therapy and the results were mixed and occasionally dangerous. We have since abandoned the other techniques as unnecessary. The natural way, it seems, is best. No way of hurrying the process along really accomplishes anything. The body gets to feelings in its own time, and that is the way it should be.

One patient had ten Rolfing sessions outside the Institute after his fifth month of therapy. He was becoming open and what happened was that the physical manipulation interfered with bodily defenses and he opened up too much resulting in an overload and an almost constant state of Pain. His Rolfing therapist had understood Primal Therapy but because he was untrained he was at a loss as to how to handle the situation. We have been open to all suggestions precisely because we have had therapists from almost every persuasion join our ranks. They soon discover themselves that anything unnatural is useless.

We have found over the past half-dozen years that there is little necessity for drugs, breathing techniques, inter alia, not because we oppose them philosophically, but because they either did not work or were superfluous, or worse, dangerous. Drugs particularly, of almost any kind, are not needed and either retard the patient by blocking feeling or cause him to skip over one level of consciousness or another. They nearly always prevent full connections.

There are those who imagine that it is *Primal Scream* Therapy; that all patients have to do is scream or let out their anger or tears. Crying is not necessarily feeling; it can often just mean release or catharsis. Screaming is hardly Primal Therapy. There are months that go by in some patient's therapy when there is no screaming, just plenty of feeling and crying, or just gagging and spitting up, or just writhing and pleading, or whatever. The scream is what *some* people do when in Pain; others react differently to Pain. In any case it works from the inside out, not the outside in; so a patient must scream as a result of felt Pain, not scream as an exercise to get to feeling. He must not scream or do anything like that as a result of some dictum of a therapist. Indeed, the hallmark of mock Primal Therapy is the authoritarian structure in which therapists in some way manipulate, order and control the patient. They may open the patient up and then tell him that he is really angry and must express his rage. Or they will have him lie down and scream, "I hurt," until he cries, or perhaps they will have him call out to "Mommy" with ideas of the therapist ("Tell her you want her or need her help"). The point has been made; anything mechanical which does not evolve from the patient is wrong. It is a subtle point, of course, because a patient who is ready to cry will cry and scream in Pain when he talks to his mother during a session; but that is not systematic Primal Therapy. And it is entirely possible that the Pain for the patient is "Daddy," not "Mommy," or it may be neither. The patient may be into something physical, such as surgery, or a beating administered by a sadistic brother. He is being led astray by his therapist.

Once a patient is feeling (usually after several months of treatment), he will be able to keep the therapist and his own therapy straight. And that is the safety for him and the therapy. *It is self-regulating.* The more he feels the more he can feel it when improper therapy is being done; he simply would not allow it. And if the therapist is open he will take the correction and feel what it is for him to have made a mistake of a particular kind with the patient. Special kinds of mistakes mean special kinds of blocked feelings, as a rule.

It is important that the therapist not get defensive and attack the patient and his criticism. For this will only confuse the patient who did see reality; it will place the patient in the same position he had with his parents during his childhood when he had honest feelings and tried to express them only to be met with disapproval and attack.

What I have discovered in patients who have been therapists previously is a tendency to use their old techniques initially when they become therapists. More than one of them has asked why he cannot combine his old ideas and techniques with the new, taking what is best from both. After a good deal of therapy (and the therapy trainees have their own groups which are powerful tools for growth and change) they no longer hold onto those ideas; they discover that old ideas and techniques were adopted by a neurotic (they were previously neurotic) and were part of their defensive structure. They held onto them (the ideas and techniques) as they would cling to any part of their old defenses, until they are fully feeling. Once they are completely open they only want to use the most refined skills available to get the patient into feeling and will discard everything else. So we have refined and honed the techniques to eliminate waste. We have dropped the extraneous precisely because it is extraneous. When a person doesn't drop his old style he is usually still clinging to part of his neurosis.

The ways that someone can interrupt the orderly process by which the body rids itself of Pain can be subtle. For example, when the bioenergetic therapist puts his fingers on a muscle group he is also placing them on a *memory*. And it is more than likely that the memory of the body he is dealing with is not the one that is ready for consciousness at the moment. Keep in mind that there are usually physical counterparts to our memories, particularly first-line material. This is another way of saying that the body is hooked up to the brain and is not an entity unto itself. So it is not *body* manipulation we are doing. It is *brain* manipulation. In any of the body manipulation therapies it is the *therapist* who decides what muscle group to work on next; this again is deciding for the patient where he must go. It is likely that the patient should not be into anything physical for months, if ever. The physical approach may place the patient on the first line too soon and keep him there too long. Touching and caressing a patient too soon can also build defenses if the patient has great Pain over never being touched.

A more subtle form of the above is any interpretation that a therapist offers to the patient for his feeling. First of all, it can be quite wrong since it always must come from the patient, but secondly what it might do is transform the experience onto the third-line explanatory level instead of allowing the patient to keep his experience on the lower lines. In this way, the third-line defense is bolstered, allowing less access to the lower lines.

There are those who believe that every approach has something to offer. I disagree. *If we are talking about just changing behavior,* then yes, every approach can do that in some way. Conditioning therapy can do it, beating someone with a stick can do it, and psychoanalysis can do it.* But if we are speaking about profound change that is another matter.

How would we possibly combine psychoanalysis with Primal Therapy, for example? If we know that the former *strengthens* defenses in some cases why would we use it with an approach such as ours which dismantles them? This is to say nothing about the profound differences we have in the notion of the necessity for defenses and the nature of the unconscious. The analysts, by and large, believe that getting into the Pain is completely disintegrating, and we think it is completely integrating. Or what about Gestalt? In Gestalt Therapy confrontation is often a central technique, particularly in the group setting. People are encouraged to express themselves vehemently to each other; they ventilate and agitate under the guise of showing their true feelings. But it nearly always stops there. The true source of the anger, fear, etc., is not reached. The patient is not taken back in time to the *causes* of his feelings; thus he is just having a catharsis, not feeling. He is having a disconnected experience in which old feelings are displaced onto the immediate present. He is encouraged, in short, to act out, and usually his behavior (even if he starts into a Primal) is dealt with. It is either interpreted or reacted to by the other members of a group. The patient is not left alone to drop into his feelings all the way.

In Primal Therapy we know that confrontation in and of itself solves nothing; *neurosis is internal, not between people.* If there is confrontation it is for the purpose of getting in touch with an *old* feeling. So, again, why would one use Gestalt with Primal Therapy if Gestalt falls short? Certainly, there are times when a person in Gestalt Therapy has a Primal but these are accidents, not a direct function of the aim of the therapy.

Nor does play-acting as in psychodrama have anything in common with Primal Therapy. Why spend time taking roles when the patient has been taking a role all his life, which is precisely why he is neurotic? He has never been himself. So why not use precisely those techniques which help him get to himself, not to his father, mother or sister?

It is not my intention to take up every approach and discuss its shortcomings; a book on that subject is being prepared by one of our thera-

---

*In this electronic age there seems to be some mystique about hooking someone up electronically so that the person feels that something scientific is really happening to him. They do not see that electric shock administered to a patient while being presented with a certain stimulus in conditioning therapy is no different from being beaten with a stick each time, and is just another form of what neurotic parents have done to their child; they are both doing it for his good. The only difference is the definition of what that "good" is.

pists. I only want to point out the illogic of trying to use approaches which in the past have failed to get to Primal Pain, and which often do not recognize the necessity of doing so. Or, if they do agree that reliving Pain cures, then their arriving at Pain is only a by-product of whatever else they are doing. Of course if a therapist does not agree that experiencing Pain is crucial then why even use Primal Therapy which is precisely designed for it?

I think that there has been a proliferation of mock Primal Therapies in which many individuals, often without any professional training or license, set up a practice because there has been a tacit recognition by the public that psychotherapy has *not* been a science; and that what one person does is as good as another. Thus it follows that "anyone with good intuition can do it." Someone could read a few books, become conversant with major theories of psychology and believe that he was as ready as the next person to treat psychological afflictions. The fact of the existence of so many schools of psychotherapy is another indication that there are many opinions about what proper psychotherapy is; there are about as many schools as there are opinions. And who was to say that one opinion was better than another since few of those schools were systematic and generated testable hypotheses? All schools claim their successes (usually based on changes in *behavior*) so it was perfectly natural for a young therapist to choose one as he might items in a supermarket. If the eclectic approach were to be applied to any other field we would see its folly immediately. Suppose a chemist wanted to use a different formula for making salt from the established one. Or suppose a physician decided to treat an infection with tetracycline *plus* several other previous remedies that were already known to be ineffective. Why on earth would he want to use what was inefficacious when he had the precise and most efficient tools for producing the desired effect?

Electicism has a good deal of appeal since it argues for an "open mind." But sometimes an open mind becomes a sieve, in which the significant is drained away because the mind has no closure, no ability to focus and organize. Lack of cohesion, then, becomes elevated to the level of the principle of being open. Very often, it isn't as though the searchers disagree with the Primal approach, they simply want to retain what they used to do as well. And when you are not thoroughly conversant with the Primal technique it would make sense to want to hold onto something else. So this kind of therapist appears to be quite catholic, when it may come from a real inability to form a total commitment to anything.

One of the ways Primal Therapy is misused is again what I call the "bag of tricks" syndrome, in which someone will latch onto a few selected techniques and imagine he is now doing "The Therapy." Two examples: I just received a letter from a mock therapist (who formerly led encounter groups) who tells me that he had been using the breathing techniques (which we use most rarely) on a borderline psychotic in order to "break open" his defense system and get him into feelings. He did, and the result was an overt and now untreatable (by him) psychosis. This mock therapist used breathing indiscriminately, did not know when to use and when not to use it, and a patient suffered. A man in England has focused on isolation; he isolated a delicate young girl in her late teens for six days and again the result was overt psychosis. It is always necessary to understand the profound before using specific techniques; otherwise those techniques become fragmented and are not used systematically within a larger theoretical structure. They are not used in terms of the patient's needs so much as the therapist's.

Primal Therapy believes that everyone of us is different; therefore techniques must be applied differentially. And this is what makes the therapy so difficult to learn. In conditioning therapy, for example, each patient is not seen as different. The techniques may be applied in a similar manner to a whole host of different kinds of people. They do not evolve out of the shifting structure of the patient; they are superimposed out of a theoretical structure which largely eliminates the psyche in its considerations. It takes a feeling person with trained skill to know when to breathe a person and just what kind of person should be breathed. It takes fragmented people to use techniques in a fragmented, isolated way; and they cannot see the whole because they are usually so well compartmentalized internally.

The techniques of Primal Therapy have not been published for a number of reasons: the paramount consideration is that unfeeling people cannot do feeling therapy. One can know all about levels of consciousness and still be unable to put them to use with patients. I believe that any techniques made public will inevitably be incorporated into the neurotic structure of the therapist; I have indicated just how this took place by indicating how some of our techniques in *The Primal Scream* have been misused (the indiscriminate use of breathing, screaming and isolation, to name a few examples). Sometimes the therapist may get lucky with a few patients using the techniques. But sooner or later one patient is going to be overloaded and then there will be more trouble than the therapist can handle. We receive letters daily relating suicide attempts by patients who get into severe Pain with a mock therapist who did not know how to stop it.

It would be irresponsible for us to shorten our training period (it takes no less than two years to learn to do the therapy, irrespective of the professional background of the trainee) for the sake of expediency. We know the work it takes to make a responsible, competent therapist, and even though we would like to have many more therapists available to treat the patients who are waiting for treatment, we know the folly of that compromise. *Primal Therapy cannot be faked.* That is the reason we do not give workshops; it cannot be learned in a weekend or two.

What drives us at the Primal Institute and the Primal Foundation is the quest for reality. We have created an atmosphere where each therapist is his brother's keeper; it is our mutual pact—to keep each other feeling. It is the only insurance we have against going astray and harming patients. We are safe here because no one is free to be neurotic.

CHAPTER FIFTEEN

Summary Comment
E. Michael Holden

In this book we have indicated that the Primal Formulation is not an abstraction separate from the development and the functioning of the human brain. Embryologically and anatomically the brain is tripartite.[1] The phenomena observed in Primal Therapy indicate that consciousness is also tripartite. Feeling, expressing emotion and cognition are the three fundamental operations of the brain and each of these matures in an orderly sequence with development of the three neuropils of the brain, from within outward. These three operations of the brain integrate the functions of the body and expressed behavior. Pain leads to disorders of feeling, expressing emotion and cognition, respectively. *Primal Therapy is an approach to mental illness meaningfully related to brain functioning.* For decades there have been two disciplines, neurology and psychiatry, and heretofore they have not been meaningfully integrated into a combination of both disciplines, *neuropsychology.* We believe that this volume is the start of an actual *neuropsychology,* in which the casual factors for both physical and mental illness may be viewed as having common origins, related to suffering in early life.

The following comments summarize in general terms the pertinent features relating phenomena of Primal Therapy to those in neurology.

In clinical neurology, with structural brain lesions, especially *cortical* lesions, we recognize that behavior becomes organized in a more primitive way as its highest representation is at a basal ganglia, thalamic, or brainstem level. Such patients perceive the world and themselves in

---

[1]Penfield, W., et al.: "Memory" *Archives of Neurology* 31, Sept. 1974, pages 152-54.

a simpler way, a way quite analogous to the perceptions of children, and both demonstrate simpler, less abstract, less symbolic ways of responding to the world. This is seen after strokes to a noticeable degree, but is mostly clearly evident with the gradual cortical neuron loss in Alzheimers' disease. Not by accident did the early neurologists speak of dementia as the second childhood. Also, the release of primitive reflexes—sucking, snouting, grasping, Myerson's glabellar sign, upgoing toes, and the bias into flexion—are manifestations of a simpler, more child-like behavior.

During a Primal, an adult looks like a child, sounds like a child, responds like a child and perceives like a child. It must be then, that with an intact adult brain, it is possible to transiently organize brain function and concommitant behaviors in a simpler, more child-like way. Observationally, and by measurement of core body temperature, heart rate, breathing rate, and EEG, the brain function during a Primal is different than during meditation. Not unexpected then is that a person's behavior while meditating is different from a person's behavior when Primalling. Also, whereas meditation reveals to one a *non-ordinary* reality with size, shape, form, color and light distortions, the subjective perception of one Primalling is ordinary reality, intensely Painful and intensely personal, with a real content from one's own personal past memories. If we acknowledge then that during a Primal, brain function changes and becomes more primitive and childlike, the next question is: How primitive? how childlike? In principle, clearly evident in clinical neurology, the brain can organize behavior, *still compatible with life,* at extremely primitive levels. One can survive large strokes of both hemispheres, profound metabolic disarray with uremia or hepatic failure, and hemorrhage into the thalamus or upper brainstem. The quality of survival is impoverished with these disorders but even in deep coma, one may breathe, maintain cardiac output, maintain normal body temperatures and maintain a blood pressure compatible with biological existence. And in a different but analogous way a person in coma has awareness restricted to self, oblivious of stimuli in extrapersonal space except for exceedingly painful ones. But even to those, the response options are profoundly limited and primitive in form, such as a groan in response to a forceful knuckle on the sternum. If the insult is great enough then biological homeostatic life fails and death ensues.

In Primals we see transient increases in the values of the vital signs, followed by decreases *below* the baseline values (after Primals). These changes in homeostatic regulation tell us that the transient change in brain function during a Primal reflects neurophysiological organization at a more primitive level. There is a transient change of hypothalamic function, change in the ability to regulate the vital signs within narrower limits. Indirectly at least, in relation to the hypothalamic change is a related change of brainstem function, evidenced by gagging, choking, change in the quality of vocalization, gasping, sobbing, changes in respiration and, in the deepest Primals (birth Primals), transient brief paralysis of respiration, sometimes to the point of cyanosis and the start of asphyxiation.

Behaviorally, then, it appears that the entire brain, from the cortex to the medulla, participates or may participate in a Primal. Primals are organized and predominately mediated by different portions of the brain. The brain and body are a single integrated unit and rather than saying that the trachea remembers birth asphyxia, or saying that the medulla remembers birth asphyxia, it is more meaningful to say that the entire organism registers that Pain, although the engrams for such registration may be predominantly in certain brain and body structures. We have no reason to doubt that every significantly Painful event in one's entire life is permanently registered by our consciousness. Dr. W. Penfield and his associates demonstrated that temporal lobe stimulation in awake patients led to vivid recall of feelings, emotional expressions and cognitive memories from a person's past. *The point to emphasize is that the exact same phenomena occur in Primals.* Primals have *access* to one's earliest feelings, emotional expressions and ideas. Dr. Penfield recently speculated with regard to the memory mechanism: "There must also be summarizing keys of access in (or associated with) the hippocampus. Such keys become summarizing units and so correspond with nonverbal concepts."[1] Primal Therapy indicates daily that the scanning mechanism of memory is influenced by the Pains of one's early life, as are the keys of access. With regard to our earliest experiences and memories, it is the Pain associated with them that appears to limit their access to the full consciousness. If we have felt that Pain completely then we have a larger consciousness than if we have not. Though one may remember the ideas of Pain, its poignancy, suffering and agony are mercifully sequestered from subsequent waking awareness.

Dr. Penfield proposed that the scanning units for memory retrieval, for memories of different ages, were topographically localized in the hippocampus with older memories retrievable by neurons further back than for the more recent memories. The hypothesis seems reasonable

---

[1] Op. Cit. page 152.

from the clinical-pathological correlations presented.

It seems probable to us that the scanning mechanism for *Pains* of different ages are similarly organized. When a person is Primalling in reference to a given Painful memory, and suddenly drops into a much *older* (earlier) Painful memory, the neurophysiological implication is that he has reached keys of access to hippocampal neurons more posterior in location than was true at the start of the Primal.

If the burden of Pain in totality which we sequester out of awareness is small, then we are conscious and well. If it is large, then we are partially unconscious and prone to illness.

Primal Therapy is a mechanism for removing the defenses, for unsequestering and re-experiencing the Pain and for attaining mental, emotional and physical health.

We do not doubt as hypothesis, and hope to eventually demonstrate, that a wide variety of illnesses including all psychosomatic ailments, alcoholism, drug addiction, hypertension and many cancers will rarely or never occur in Primal individuals. The hypothesis is that physical illness results when the Pain of a lifetime stays registered in one's brain and body, and that it rarely or never occurs in the body of one who has rid himself of those Pains in sequestration. A Primal is not a pseudo-phenomenon: it is a profound, all-encompassing total reorganization of one's biology, from the psychotic or neurotic state to the post-Primal state.

CHAPTER SIXTEEN

Primal Man: The New Consciousness — Conclusions

Arthur Janov

All of the observations, theory and research cited herein lead us to one central conclusion: there is a new quality of consciousness available to man, a consciousness not possible to attain heretofore in the thousands of years of man's recorded history. It is not that man has not been previously capable of this consciousness. Rather, the Pains of his everyday life have sealed his normal consciousness and left him with a false consciousness. I believe this new Primal consciousness is the only hope if mankind is to survive, for it is out of neurotic consciousness that social institutions are erected—and it is those institutions which suppress feeling, keep man neurotic and cause his societies to self-destruct.

Primal consciousness means an end to neurotic tension and the numerous ailments that issue from it. It means a society with far fewer needs for drugs, physicians and hospitals, and a greatly reduced need for prisons. Not only does it mean less crime but the elimination of the need for narcotics upon which a great deal of crime is based. It means an end to alcoholism and all the results of it: traffic fatalities, marital breakup, cruelty to children, violent crimes and failure in school and on the job.

Primal consciousness certainly means an end to war, for no one who recognizes that his body belongs to him is going to allow some abstract force to ship that body thousands of miles away to be maimed or killed. And Primal Man is incapable of doing violence upon another human being. Having experienced Pain he feels it when others hurt and therefore cannot inflict it on others. It is neurotic man who automatically inflicts Pain on those around him, particularly his children, because *he needs* and those needs supersede anyone else's.

Primal consciousness is the sole property of Primal Man; indeed, one is the condition for the other. And Primal Man is now free, not in the sense of having many choices outside of himself, but free from the tyranny of his neurosis, free from the Pains which have caused him to act in ways beyond his control, free from inexplicable symptoms that have kept him in bed with headaches, allergies, ulcers, asthma and all the rest of the psychologically-induced physical symptoms. Primal consciousness is the only freedom, for without that any external freedom has little meaning. And with that, Primal Man will create institutions which aid and abet free choice, institutions to fulfill need rather than exploit it. Real freedom no longer means the fight to make symbolic choices (the freedom to make more and more money) but the ability to feel what one needs and the latitude to know how to go about fulfilling them.

Primal consciousness means greatly enhanced social relations, for Primal people are not imposing their problems on others. They are not exploding over the most minute and insignificant of events, nor are they displacing old hostilities and fears from the past onto the present. Primal Man does not have unreal expectations (Daddy and Mommy) from his spouse and friends and so is not crushed and disappointed when those neurotic expectations are not fulfilled. He enjoys sex in a mutual feeling way and not as a symbol for conquest, masculinity, virility and the like. Primal Man, now experiencing his feelings, can feel joy and love simply because he can feel. There is a new dimension to his life—the key dimension that makes life worth living—feeling. He can feel it when he is loved and can truly care about others. It is the neurotic who cares symbolically—who projects his needs and Pain onto others and then cares about that, really caring about himself in a roundabout way.

Primal Woman, having ejected old Pains from her body, gives the best possible chance in life to her offspring, for they are born naturally, free of drugs (a woman who wants to experience her life wouldn't allow herself to be drugged) in the proper rhythm and at the time they are supposed to be born. She has a healthy body to nourish the fetus, having inhaled no smoke, eaten the proper foods, taken no drugs and being free from chronic anxiety. She has enough milk to nurse her offspring for as long as he needs, and tension will not interfere to shut off her supply and dry up the infant's source of nourishment. She is automatically gentle and quiet with her newborn because she will not be harassed by tension. Having felt her own needs she does not have to run from the child in an effort to fulfill those old needs. She has the baby *consciously,* when she is ready and not by accident, which is usually a result of neurosis. Having gotten her body back she is fully sexual which means a better marital adjustment, less infidelity, jealousy and endless arguments over sex. There is no way to put on paper what the true joy of sex is; few women have had it, and when they (and men) discover it, their lives become much richer for it. And the implications of enhanced sexual relations mean an end to promiscuity, trying somehow in that way to get something out of sex. There is now the ability to choose someone who can really be satisfying.

Having a Primal consciousness means to be able to choose a partner who is a companion, not a mother or father substitute; there can therefore be true satisfaction, not the constant struggle to remake the partner into something one truly needs. Neurotics choose what fits their neuroses and they are bound, therefore, to be unfulfilled. Knowing oneself completely leaves one free to choose someone who truly fits himself or herself.

Primal Man sleeps better and is more rested. He is therefore going to be healthier and more productive and efficient in what he does. He is also therefore less cranky with his spouse and children. He doesn't suffer from recurrent nightmares and Pain which finally puts him into an early grave. He isn't doing the things that hasten his demise such as drinking, smoking and endless pills of one kind or another. He doesn't suffer for years with lung and throat cancer because he smoked and could not stop no matter how hard he tried; nor does he suffer and be bedridden with cirrhosis of the liver due to too much drinking. He does not suffer a lifetime of humiliation over his obesity because he could not stop eating. *He is free at last from his compulsions because he is free from Primal Pain.* Primal Man is finally going to give us insight into our true longevity. We will know how long man should live, and my guess is that our patients, all else being equal, will live beyond one hundred years. I do not believe that any of this is Utopian. We have the means by which to produce Primal Man. He is not some idealistic notion in someone's head. He is real. With a greatly reduced metabolic rate, with less excess cerebral activity, Primal Man is not burning up the energy he otherwise might. His hormone system, working in harmony at last, is no longer producing hormone related diseases which often lead to an early death (diabetes being but one of many examples).

Primal Man, no longer acting out of suppression, is no longer moralistic. He can let others be, and when others misbehave or act antisocially he doesn't reflexively yell for the death sentence or long prison terms. He seeks for understanding, and most of the antisocial behavior he observes is readily understandable to him. He has only to read some of the details of crimes, such as bizarre murder, to understand what is wrong and what must be done. Having deep access to himself, he is no longer taken in by superficialities. He is not satisfied with pat cliches, slogans, empty political promises or personal assurances from psychopaths. Because he has no importuning old needs his main desire is to be left alone and not be exploited. Nor would he want to exploit anyone else.

I believe that Primal Man is essentially anarchic. Very few that I have observed become involved with politics. Even among those who used to be quite involved, none any longer are. They do not want to control anyone else's life, and therefore have no political ambitions, indeed, very few ambitions except to live a life in peace. I don't believe that anarchy means chaos except for neurotics, who left to their own desires will ultimately do what is neurotic and contrary to the social best interest. So again the dialectic: those who are quite individualistic act for the social good; they want what is best for themselves and humanity—because they are now fully conscious and human. To act for the social good means to no longer have to dominate anyone—to lord one's power over children, or to conquer women as a means of showing one's manhood—or having too many children as a way of proving one's virility. And what the latter means eventually is a lessened population with an attenuation of all the social problems we see today resulting from too many people—the pollution, lack of food, consumption of natural resources.

Primal Man, who enjoys beauty and reflection, is not going to chop down forests for profit, nor pollute the seas with his garbage. He has learned through his experience in therapy to respect what is natural and to revere nature. He will not have too many children out of his neurosis and more importantly, the inability to give love to so many children will be gone. He won't allow anyone to dictate his life and tell him how many children he should have.

If we consider that there is survival of the fittest, then Primal Man ought to have the best chance at that survival since his system can best withstand stress. He is not easily overloaded any longer and will not crack under strain. His consciousness is organismic, and that is more than semantics. For he not only has a new awareness but a new bodily system in which that organismic state of consciousness reflects itself. *He hasn't just "changed his mind" about things,* in other words, he has changed his whole system; we see this in the alterations in the vital signs, in his posture, gait, speech, coordination and physical freedom. That new consciousness reaches down into every cell; it is my guess that Primal Man will not be afflicted by catastrophic ailments, such as cancer, which to me indicate incredible Pain at the cellular level.

Man must do more than just change his *attitudes,* which is why articles beseeching him to change his priorities if we are to survive are largely useless. Attitudes are a *reflection* of a state of being or a state of consciousness; *that* change is the priority.

With the discovery of our ability to relive events in and around birth we have greatly expanded the traditional view of consciousness for we now see that consciousness exists on levels and that it is possible to expand our consciousness into the innermost depths of the brain and mind. A consciousness without that access is only partial. We can no longer speak about a consciousness that is solely neocortical. For we now know that kind of consciousness is only the tip of the iceberg and that man's thoughts and behavior are influenced and directed by events which exist within systems of consciousness far below the neocortex. By changing his attitudes he is but changing that top level of consciousness; that has little to do with making profound changes in his behavior and general outlook.

One of the great deficits in the Marxian literature, which is so profound on the social level, is a discussion of consciousness—or even feeling, for that matter. The Marxian view has been that man's consciousness has been the result of the material conditions of his life, particularly as those conditions reflect his relationship to the means of production—whether he is exploiter or exploited. But it is my view that man also *creates* the conditions of his life, his social systems and its institutions; and man literally alters his physical environment by bulldozing mountains, rechanneling the seas, chopping down forests and creating a floor of cement everywhere which obliterates nature. Neurotic man will do this, I believe, irrespective of the social system in which he exists. And no matter how equitable the social system created by the cognoscenti for him, he still will tend to create a reflection of that neurosis outside himself. He still will be unwilling to give up individual prerogative for the social good because he *needs.* The environment that neurotic man creates, the kind of houses and buildings he builds for example, affects his consciousness. And so he is caught in a vicious cycle where he creates the very conditions that perpetuate his neurosis and do not fulfill his needs—because he had lost touch with his needs.

In a complex society it is no longer either/or. It is not that consciousness produces social institutions or that social structures produce a consciousness. They are in a constant dialectic state of interaction—inter-
penetrating one another, creating together continuously new syntheses. I
lectured recently at a university in a foreign country and found the university to be a direct reflection of the personalities I had met there—
sterile and rigid. The buildings were all glass and white gleaming walls,
not a plant around, no soft textures, nothing really human. It was a
totally efficient structure devoid of any humanity. And the students live
in that environment; their consciousness produced it and their consciousness is affected by it. That interaction maintains the neurotic structure.

I think the most significant thing about this work is the coalescence of
our observations of Primal patients with the latest work in neurology.
Consider for example, the notion of specific and non-specific systems in
the brain. We know from our observations that the energy of disconnected
feelings gets through in order to produce the sensation of tension in our
bodies while the connection is blocked—the direct means by which the
split is maintained. But the notion of a dual tract system helps explain
how the system can be mobilized in a general way while the specific connections are inhibited. So we feel tense and don't know why. Or take the
original Primal hypothesis about a split: we now are much more sophisticated about the mechanisms of that split. We know that Pain is gated; and
further, that Pain is gated on different levels or within different systems.
*Our observations likewise indicate that patients feel on three distinct
levels* and it is crucial that neurology tends to confirm our observations.
The fact that three distinct systems of Pain gating seem to exist helps
corroborate our notion of the three levels of consciousness. Not that we
"decided" there were three levels as a result of reading some research.
Rather, our observations time and again have led us to this conclusion
and research sharpens our thinking on the matter.

I believe that for the first time we have been able to open man up to
his primordial depths in order to discover his true nature. And what we
have found is that he is basically neither angry, aggressive, fearful or full
of demons and devils ready to spring out. We have been able to put man
in touch with a part of his brain which existed millennia ago, placed him
in contact with his animal or instinctive self, and learned that he is not
really a killer needing social control. He is neither rapacious nor acquisi-
tive. He is not basically competitive. We have probed man into depths
beyond comprehension a few short years ago and have discovered that

Primal Man is a very simple soul, neither ambitious nor burning with productivity. He is not basically tense or driven. His wants are few. He is someone who loves beauty and nature, and can cooperate with his fellow man, respects animal life and is highly individual; he does not join clubs, belong to political groups, or constantly attend meetings of one sort or another. He is efficient and does what needs to be done without flourish or turmoil. He will not place himself within any rigid system which dictates his life. He or she will not be told when to use the pill or when not to. He will not be governed by religious dictates, what to eat on which day—*he will be governed by his feelings.* He is certainly not a good company man. And all of this takes place, I might emphasize, without any ideas being inculcated into him. He loses his religious ideas without one word about religion being discussed in his therapy. And here we see what true education is about—we learn from the inside out, and not vice versa. And this experience leads Primal Man to create the kind of educational environment where this kind of real learning takes place.

Primal consciousness means an end to the proliferation of rules and laws and the need to be constantly governed, for Primal people cannot cheat anyone because they are not split and cannot be duplicitous. They do not need to be told how to live, how to cooperate and get along with their fellow man. Primal consciousness means to have a built-in conscience and a special kind of morality that is not derived from the outside. To feel is to have consideration for mankind. There is no need for the notion of a superego which must be inculcated into nihilistic man. Rather, growing up feeling obviates that; feelings dictate naturally moral behavior, just as repressed feeling inevitably lead to immoral behavior. Primal Man needs no masters nor religion upon which to place his faith. He has himself, which is sufficient.

Having now observed hundreds of human beings who have journeyed into the "antipodes of the mind" (to quote Aldous Huxley) we can say with some assurance what "man" is like. And he is nothing like we expected. He is not evil or wickedly lustful, or selfish. When he has felt his early needs he no longer has to acquire symbolically for a denied baby self. He is not basically feeling inferior or superior. That notion is anathema to him. It is not in the lexicon of Primal Man. Those are not true feelings. He just feels himself—not a relationship to others by which to measure that self.

Primal Man certainly has no power needs as Alfred Adler imagined. Quite the opposite. Our observations of advanced patients is that power over anything but themselves is the last thing they want. It is the power-less who need power, and once someone has deeply felt his early help-lessness and powerlessness against his parents there is no need for a symbolic power over others. *What is significant about all this is that we are not theorizing or philosophizing about some Utopian concept of man.* We are not inferring as the early psychologic theorists had to do. We have made close observations and patients have observed themselves and we have come to our conclusions based on our and their experience.

We don't have to theorize about man's inner shadow which springs up in dreams to bedevil him. We see that once feelings are felt dreams are pure and do not contain all the demons that we imagined to be travelling around the "unconscious."

What we have previously tended to think about man's basic nature has come from an examination of neurosis—a phenomenon so widespread as to indicate something basic about man himself. And when we see a whole country of individuals competing with one another we tend to believe that it must be something endogenous. Or when someone goes crazy and becomes violent we have tended to think that without proper social con-trol we could all be capable of that, when in reality it is *control* of feel-ings which have damned up early anger and caused it to spillover in adulthood. When people lose control what comes out is not what is basic. What erupts is the acting out of specific feelings *which cannot be gotten to*: the basic hurts never felt and fully experienced. And if anything is basic about man's unconscious it is the reservoir of hurts residing there. Because we have not led man below his acting out (fearful of the demons that lurk below) we have mistaken his neurotic behavior as indigenous. We have covered it over with drugs, reassurances, restraints and distractions.

True human consciousness has tremendous power. It can know all, so to speak, so that nearly all of one's behavior is understandable to oneself —how one relates, why one eats or drinks to excess, why one dreams this or that, why one has a headache or stomachache, etc. It enables man to perceive realities outside himself clearly so that he has an instinctive grasp of politics, religion and its function in society, education and what it should be, and child care and how one should go about it. Conscious-ness produces a new kind of taste; an ability to see harmony, so that one dresses in new ways or understands art for what it is. Primal conscious-ness produces an integration of the body so that finally one can play sports with some facility and enjoy it. I am always amazed at staff parties, for example, that every one of the staff dances very well; many did not when they entered therapy. Not a major contribution, one might think, but it all adds up to a more enjoyable, participatory life.

The true power of full consciousness is in leading a consciously-directed intelligent life, so that one doesn't marry the first boy or girl one meets, or doesn't get involved with someone based on old unconscious needs who is not really suitable. It is the power that keeps one from getting in over one's head, tackling jobs that are too much or taking positions over one's level of competence. Full consciousness is what prevents man from driving himself into an early grave trying to fulfill his old needs in the present, such as for prestige, fame or success.

The true power of full Primal consciousness is in having access into oneself so that when one is upset or feeling very anxious there is something one can do. No longer does a Primal person have to wring his hands in anguish because he is filled with inexplicable anxiety. When the child of a Primal person is having trouble or is upset the parent is no longer at a loss as to what to do. Generally, he can understand the problem and know what to do about it. He can truly help his child. In this sense Primal Man is truly in control of his life; life is not ruling him.

Primal Man recognizes his inherent solitude. He is not frantically trying to connect socially as an escape from himself. He no longer has to flee the self he is totally familiar and comfortable with. No Pain keeps him on the move unnecessarily. And he is not trying to get; he knows that there is little to get in this world other than love and pleasure, and he is not trying symbolically to achieve success, fortune, fame, prestige, and all of the other symbolic goals. He is also not searching for meaning to his life; he is not involved in deep philosophical search to really explain his own misery (as neurotics do) because his misery is at an end. If there is anything that Primal Man is not interested in it is philosophy and ideology. He is no longer the intellectual; rather, he is intelligent. And that intelligence helps him survive in an unreal world, for Primal Man cannot possibly be complete in today's world; but it is the world that he lives in and he makes the best of it, knowing how difficult it is to make profound changes in society. He does what he can to change himself, for that he can do. He does not succumb to the society, take up its values and goals; rather, he takes whatever he can from it wherever he can without compromising himself—something he can no longer do. His interest is mostly to seek out beauty and enjoy it.

Primal consciousness means to no longer be plagued by irrational fears and phobias which often constrict one's life drastically. Some patients could never leave the house before therapy. And the lack of irrational ideas extends to the rest of his life so that he is not spending countless hours contemplating mystical phenomena or out-in-space events. He is content to know what is real. He recognizes that the time here on earth in the now is the only time in life and he wants to make the most of it, so he is not preoccupied with an afterlife or reincarnation. Having felt his early brush with death at birth he is not plagued by irrational fears of death. Not that he wants to die or that he doesn't care if he dies tomorrow, as many neurotics feel; he reveres life and wants to stay around a long time. Life is no longer one constant agony as it used to be. Having the ability to experience fully he knows the depths of joy as never before, and having this inner access means an end to periodic bouts of depression, which is just repression of many inexplicable Pains. So we see the broad scope of full consciousness. It isn't simply enhanced perception or cognition. It is access internally; I think this is an important point because it has been thought previously that one could have a broader consciousness and still be depressed or anxious without the two being related. But they are very much related, and if consciousness cannot prevent depression and anxiety, then what good is it? To broaden one's knowledge of the universe? Toward what end?

Primal consciousness means the power to save one's own life. I remember thinking recently how important this was when I read about the death by heart failure of a fifty-eight year old philosopher, a "free thinker" who wrote books on consciousness, who seemed liberated in terms of his world outlook, who acted relaxed and free and who seemed to have broken loose from the academic mold. All that was missing was true consciousness that would have saved his life. He "overcame" his early environment mentally, it is true; he could think in new ways but he did not have the power to save his life—the most important power of all.

What all of the above means to me is that the third-line of consciousness is eminently plastic. It can be rearranged, changed radically, yet without making a dent in the lower lines, the constant activation of which eventually kills us prematurely. It is unfortunate that we have come to believe that the proliferation of the third line is somehow consciousness expanding. This is particularly true in the writings on the psychedelic drugs.

Another key point we have tried to make is that consciousness and unconsciousness begin even before birth; that the fetus lives in an environment and reacts to that environment long before he meets or sees another human being. Consciousness, in short, is not just a matter of learning. Nor is unconsciousness a matter of unlearning. I reiterate: it is

a *state of being*. It includes the functioning of the body in its interrelationships with the brain. It includes what the *whole system* has experienced and not just what facts or perceptions have been piped into the
brain. Thus, in order to recapture our full consciousness we must experience those events back into the earliest minutes of our lives.

It must seem to be an inordinate extrapolation to relate consciousness
to sexuality and sexual functioning, particularly when we say that the
retrieval of a certain level of consciousness during the time of birth and
just before is essential to sexual liberation, but our observations lead us
to no other conclusion. To be conscious means to be sexual and vice
versa. To be conscious in the Primal sense means to have retrieved a
level of consciousness which mediates bodily functions thus giving us
control of our body. In this way a whole host of sexual problems are
solved from frigidity to premature ejaculation. And Primal consciousness
means an end to sexual perversions, which are only thinly disguised
Primal symbols—acting out symbolically in the present events from the
past. It is a great relief to be oneself so that one is not impelled to im-
pulsively attend pornographic movies, read dirty books, masturbate in
public, etc., or indeed to be compelled to do anything.

When someone has achieved a high position in society and then finds
himself acting in criminal ways beyond his comprehension or control it is
most degrading. This is particularly true of the homosexuals who often
are compelled to cruise toilets to find penises to suck. An arrest by a
vice officer can destroy the homosexual's career and sometimes his life.
That is the power of Primal consciousness; it means that one no longer
has to act in ways so as to endanger one's life. Or, if the impulse to act
out is there, there is an option—one can lie down and feel what is
behind it.

When I say that one no longer has to act in ways to endanger one's
life, I mean it literally; since one no longer has to drive cars at break-
neck speed or even race cars professionally. One race driver discovered
that he came close to death at birth and drove races at top speed in
order to feel alive—that is, he unconsciously needed to recreate that
early death scene, to brush death, so to speak, only to insure a different
ending. After feeling the near-death at birth the need to drive at life-
endangering speeds evaporated. *Feeling dissipates symbolic acting out.*
That sentence or paradigm is a truism that has remained since the discovery of Primal Therapy. Feeling is the antithesis of neurotic tension
and behavior. I suppose that life will seem duller to outsiders when they
consider that there will be no more death defying auto races, no highs

on drugs or alcohol in a Primal society, but they forget that life will be qualitatively much richer.

Our concepts about consciousness mean that we can now do something with prisoners in jails besides have them rot while waiting to get out and perform their next crime. *They can be effectively treated,* and since a great deal of the criminal population is made up of drug addicts, there is something concrete that can be done. Prison is an almost ideal place (if we ever really need prisons) to do Primal Therapy since there is no real productive functioning required of the inmate. He only has to serve his time; he might as well get well in the bargain. There would be no need to follow and control a post-release inmate since if he had done Primal Therapy and were measured, observed and tested as he went along, we could rest assured that after his release he would act in social rather than anti-social ways. The cost of recidivism alone must be enormous, particularly in the alcoholic cells where a ten-time offender is commonplace. And we must consider the safety of society. To release a killer or a previously violent person into society endangers us all. This is patently immoral when we now know what to do with criminals. *The tools are at the disposal of the powers that be; they have only to use them.*

The same is true of the mental hospitals. It is criminal for authorities to keep people sometimes for a lifetime rotting in mental hospitals, pushing pills down their throats in order to control them when the means of getting them out of the hospital and back into society are available. I believe that it is the duty and moral obligation of the psychiatric profession to seriously investigate Primal Therapy as the means of treating their patients. When a proper treatment exists for certain disease entities, it is the obligation of the doctor to familiarize himself with that treatment or at least to seriously investigate its possibilities.

We have observed those who came to us from jail as well as those who came directly out of mental hospitals. We have seen the profound changes in these patients and believe that *every person* now in a hospital or in jail has this right as a citizen and human being. It is unavoidable that Primal Therapy seems like a panacea but in truth it does cure a whole host of diseases, both psychological and physical, because Primal Pain is their substrate.

It is clear to me that the Pain and stress which causes a heart attack doesn't disappear after the attack. It will continuously assault the body where it is weakest. *The only insurance against future attacks is to get rid of the Pain.* The only other alternative is what happens now in medicine—drugs to control and subdue the Pain—drugs to open up a blood circulation system which is constricted against Pain—drugs to quiet the anxiety over having a weak heart, and drugs for the person who now cannot sleep out of fear that it will be his last night on earth.

It doesn't matter whether it is the heart which finally gives way or an ulcer or colitis which appear in later life. If one cannot eliminate the activation by Pain one has no other recourse but to control it, and that means a lifetime of watchfulness, anxiety, medicines and restriction of activities. It is only consciousness which can stop the flow of unconscious activation, because consciousness means that the unconscious is now conscious—and that is the *only* meaning of consciousness for me.

I have said elsewhere that it is a life sentence to be neurotic, and the thought comes home to me whenever I hear about a non-Primal person having to go to bed for days at a time because of migraine headaches, and they have to do this year after year because they have no idea what is behind their headaches or what they can do about it. They are truly helpless and powerless; perhaps even worse is having to be hospitalized because of seizures year after year, not being able to work or attend school regularly, not being able to relate to the opposite sex sexually because of the malady. It is truly a life sentence to have to go through that for a lifetime. Or stuttering: having a lifetime of humiliation because one cannot relate socially without stuttering and grimacing. The tales of woe are endless and they all devolve to one central point—the lack of full consciousness.

I believe we have made giant leaps in demysticizing the basic nature of man. *We finally know a great deal about what makes him sick, both physically and psychologically,* and better yet, we have found a method which can resolve that sickness. Even if our theory were perfect about what causes neurosis it would be a terrible deficit if we could do nothing about it. Luckily, we have both: an understanding of cause, and treatment. Not that we know everything; no one would say that. But I think we have made a qualitative leap in terms of diagnosis, understanding and cure. Primal Man is amazing not because he is superman but because he is simply human.

APPENDIXES

Research with Primal Patients: Vital Signs
Bernard McInerny

The purpose of this study is to explore and measure any biochemical and neurological changes that take place during the process of Primal Therapy. In Primal Therapy, as in other therapies, the state of "feeling better," as reported verbally by patients, has never been a measurable quality. Indeed, psychotherapy has not been considered a science because it has been little more than chance endeavor in the curing of mental aberration. The alarming rise in mental illness and crime, and our full institutions and prisons will attest to this fact.

This study was prompted by the verbal reports of patients in Primal Therapy that certain physiological changes were taking place as their therapy progressed, as well as reports that they were feeling better. These subjective indications of change, if true, must have some basis in objective, measurable fact.

Tension has always been the enemy of a restful life. Also, tension has long been the target of studies attempting to find its effect on body processes. Certain bodily manifestations, such as rapid heart-rate, higher temperature, confused mental activity and chemical imbalance have been equated to tension. But in most studies just one aspect of the human body has been isolated and examined separately. This is especially true of the studies that have been done of the changes in the human system brought about by psychotherapy. Indeed the literature reveals only a few isolated examinations of changes in some aspects of human anatomy during psychotherapy. We have, for the first time, examined patients for total bodily function as they underwent a systematic psychotherapy. We have examined these patients both over short-term and long-term therapy conditions. The results, we feel, are very encouraging, not only in terms of changes observed but in terms of providing impetus to new research with revised methods.

Here, in the first of a series of reports, we will examine our findings on two "vital signs". The "vital signs" of pulse, body temperature and blood pressure are the most fundamental of all physiologic measurements. They are called vital because they measure the elements most necessary to sustain life—they are generally the first things a physician measures in his patients. Therefore, pulse and core body temperature were chosen as the measurements to be taken for this study.

The subjects measured in this study were patients undergoing Primal Therapy. A total of twenty-two subjects were included, selected from the more than one hundred new patients entering therapy from May 1972 to January 1973. There were fourteen men and eight women, with an average of 33.4 years. The subjects were measured three days prior to starting therapy, after three weeks, three months and six months. Eight subjects also have one-year measurements. All measurements were taken and recorded at the Primal Foundation Laboratory by the same doctor. The measurements were taken in the morning, before breakfast, and each subject was instructed not to ingest any stimulants or medication prior to the tests. The pulse was taken while the subject was in a sitting position. The prone position was necessary for recording temperature as it was a rectal reading.

Each subject was permitted to accommodate to the laboratory environment and rest for five minutes prior to each reading. After five minutes it was assumed that a resting physiologic level had been attained. The right radial pulse was monitored manually for a full two minutes and the number of beats was divided by two to obtain the mean pulse.

Core body temperature was derived using an electronic thermistor probe which was inserted two inches into the rectum. The readings were taken after two minutes. The thermistor is a sensitive device and can measure temperature to the first decimal place more accurately than a glass thermometer.

The T statistic

$$T = \frac{(\overline{X}_1 - \overline{X}_2)}{\sqrt{\dfrac{SX_1}{N-1} + \dfrac{SX_2}{N-1}}}$$

was utilized to test for significance in both the analysis of pulse and core body temperature. This treatment was used because of the smaller amounts of variables.

Pulse

Pulse is the record of heartbeats per minute. It is usually measured at the wrist as the number of beats per minute of the radial artery. The average value of the young adult (20-30 years old) is 72 beats per minute.

In measuring and recording the pulse of the twenty-two Primal patients (Table 1), the mean change was found for each series of tests following the initial or baseline measurement. The measurements over a six-month period show an interesting trend as illustrated in Figure A. The average pulse rate of 74 had dropped to 70 after three weeks of therapy. This gives a T score of 0.08, not statistically significant. The range for the baseline tests show a +6 in subject 10 and a −18 in subject 16. After three months of therapy the mean score has dropped to 69 and is now significant at the 0.05 level. The range has changed also showing a high of +12 in subject 9 and a −22 in subject 15. The six-month test has a mean change of −8 from the base of 74 to 66. This change is significant at the 0.01 level. The range has again changed from a high of +7 in subject 19 to −24 in subject 15. The comparison of the baseline record to the six-month record shows that 68.18% of the patients showed a reduction in pulse after therapy, while 18.18% increased and 13.63% had no change. Of the increases in pulse rate only one (subject 12) had an increase (+4) above the average value of the young adult.

In reviewing the eight patients who had recordings for a full year (Table 2)[1] this downward trend is continued (Figure B). When comparing the baseline mean score of the eight subjects with the one-year mean scores, the decrease from −0.8 to −8.3 is not statistically significant. However, this may be attributed to the sample size. The percentage of patients decreasing in pulse rate is higher for the first eight subjects (75% vs. 68.18%) over one year than for the twenty-two over six months. Both the percentage of increases (12.5% vs. 18.18%) and no changes (12.5% vs. 13.63%) have diminished for the eight one-year patients.

---

[1] The eight subjects in the one-year studies do not correspond to the first eight subjects in the six-month studies.

Body Temperature

Body temperature is regulated by a substantial brain structure called the hypothalamus. The cells of warm-blooded animals like man function best at an optimum temperature. The temperature reflects the rate of cellular activity. A one degree centigrade rise in temperature can raise the cellular metabolic rate ten times. Therefore it is incumbent upon the body to maintain a homeostasis in regard to its temperature. To accomplish homeostasis the body can quickly undergo sweating and vasodilation (flushing, perfusion of the skin with blood) in order to lose heat, and shivering, with vasoconstriction (the sequestering of blood internally) to maintain its heat.

Body temperature follows a diurnal variation with a range of about 1° F., being lowest in the early morning and highest at night. Body temperature is usually measured orally—underneath the tongue—and rectally. Rectal temperature is one degree higher than oral temperature and reflects the internal temperature. It is therefore called the "core" temperature. The temperature norm in the United States for young adults is 98.6° F. This is where an arrow is placed on many commercial thermometers. For this study the temperature was recorded from rectal readings only.

In examining the recording of core body temperature (Table 3), a trend of continual decline from the baseline can be observed (Figure C). The mean difference from baseline to three weeks is −0.43°, which is statistically significant. The range of mean change was from a high of +1.5° for subject 3 to a low of −1.1° for subject 5. At the three-month test interval there is a mean change of −0.45° which is significant at the 0.01 level. The range of mean change was from a high of +0.4° in subjects 3 and 4, and a low of −1.8° in subject 8. The six-month test shows a mean change of −0.54°, which is again significant at the 0.01 level. The range has gone to a high of +0.5° in subject 19 to a low of −1.7° in subject 18. The percentages of baseline score compared with the six-month recording shows that 81.81% of the patients had a decrease in temperature while 4.66% had no change and 13.63% had an increase in temperature.

The continuation of temperature recording for the eight subjects over one year (Table 4), shows that the first measured trends continue (Figure D). The mean change after one year of therapy was −0.6°. This is not statistically significant, again probably due to the sample size. In comparing the eight subjects' one-year temperature recording with their baseline scores, 75% show a decrease in temperature. The range for the eight subjects after one year is 0.0° to −1.3°.

Covariance

In examining the two vital signs of pulse and core body temperature together, a picture of covariance (Table 5) is available. After six months of therapy 63.8% (14) of the patients show a decline in both pulse and temperature. Only 9% (2) of the patients show an increase in both pulse and temperature. Additionally, 13% (3) had no change in one reading while the other reading showed a downward change, whereas just one subject showed a no change in one reading which was accompanied by an increase in the other. There were two who showed an increase in one measurement while the other decreased. When covariants are reviewed for the twenty-two patients over the six-month period, a continual decline from baseline test to the six-month test is shown (Table 6).

The trend of decline in both pulse rate and core body temperature is continued in the one-year study of eight patients (Tables 7 and 8). A decline in pulse rate shows generally an accompanying decline in temperature.

In examining the two vital signs of pulse and core body temperature for Primal patients we see that a general decline in both signs accompanies the therapy. This decline has proved to be statistically significant for the larger population (n=22) as the time in therapy increases. The smaller sample (n=8) gives additional support to the findings. The interesting aspect of the general declines in both pulse rate and temperature is the high percentage of covariance (63.8% in n=22, 75% in n=8) between the two signs over the tested time in therapy. There appears to be little doubt that these changes in vital signs are due to the influence of the therapy.

Summary

It is not difficult to produce a temporary change in pulse, since it responds rapidly to outside stimuli. Studies of persons on exercise programs also reveal a lower pulse rate than the given norm. However, although Primals are usually active events they are not a daily routine and they decrease in number as the length of time in therapy increases. Whereas the three-month measurement decrease may be argued as an "exercise effect" this is not the case in the six-month and one-year measurements.

The reduction of core body temperatures is also very meaningful. Recent studies (U. S. Department of Health, Education and Welfare)[2] reveal that a significant change in body temperature is 0.5° F. or more during a two-hour span. We see, then, that what might appear as a slight change (−0.54° for six months and −0.6° for one year) is a significant one. A high temperature often denotes a rapid circulation so that white blood cells are speeded to the site of some disease. Our six-month and one-year measurements showed an overall decline, which we view as a reduction of tension—a reduction in the defense system which keeps a patient constantly under stress.

When we viewed the results of the two vital signs together, the covariance was remarkable. The overall trend was a reduction in both pulse and core body temperature, suggesting that the changes go beyond those of mere chance. But the general trend obscures the remarkable individual changes. For example, we see in patients 3, 11, and 15 (Table 5), a drop in pulse rate of very unusual proportions. For the same patients a corresponding drop in temperature or no change is observed. In patients 6, 7, 8, 10, and 22 the corresponding drop in both pulse and temperature after six months of therapy is followed by the one-year study (Table 7) where patients 3, 4, 7, and 8 have maintained the same lowered readings.

Conclusions

Before compiling and analyzing the research data we made certain assumptions leading to a central hypothesis. These assumptions were part of the general theory of Primal Therapy as developed by Arthur Janov. The first assumption was that neurosis is a total state affecting man's total psychophysiological makeup, that neurosis develops from the pain of deprivation of infant and childhood needs, and that this pain is manifested in the psychophysiological makeup by tension. The next assumption was that the neurotic relieves himself of the ravages of tension by developing a series of traits which are only symbols of the underlying unfulfilled needs. The final assumption was that in a psychotherapeutic cure a physiological change would accompany the disappearance of the symbolic traits. In other words, the psychotherapy must eradicate the underlying source of tension, the original pain, in order to be curative: a mere changing of

---

[2] *Biological Rhythms in Psychiatry and Medicine.* Public Health Service Publication No. 2088.

symbols would not produce bodily changes. The general hypothesis, therefore, was that repressed pain produces permanent tension, that the experiencing of this pain eradicates tension, and that the eradication of tension produces changes in bodily functions and operations.

In terms of vital sign changes, we have concluded that the therapy has produced measurable changes in bodily functions that correspond with the patients' claims of remarkable reduction in neurotic tension. The changes in pulse over six months and one year are conclusive enough, but when the picture of covariance with temperature change is reviewed the changes are even more convincing. The reduction in both pulse and temperature means that a patient's bodily pace has slowed without lethargic effects. The patients are living their normal lives without the grinding crush of the neurotic pace, the pace that makes people of forty to fifty drop dead at the peak of life.

TABLE 1
Pulse: N = 22, 0-6 months

Subject	Baseline	3 Weeks	3 Months	6 Months
1	62	60	66	68
2	66	68	72	72
3	88	86	68	66
4	80	80	84	76
5	64	52	74	64
6	76	60	62	60
7	68	72	66	52
8	72	72	58	62
9	70	68	82	70
10	70	76	58	62
11	94	88	77	72
12	73	73	73	76
13	76	75	67	72
14	81	74	76	76
15	82	60	60	58
16	66	48	48	48
17	72	66	67	68
18	88	82	75	70
19	65	62	72	72
20	62	64	62	60
21	80	80	82	80
22	76	80	76	64
N = 22	74*	70*	69*	66*
		−4**	−5**	−8**
* Mean pulse ** Mean change from baseline				

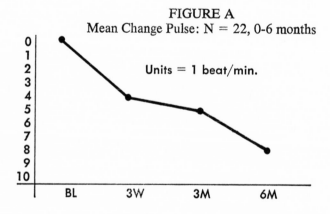

FIGURE A
Mean Change Pulse: N = 22, 0-6 months

Units = 1 beat/min.

TABLE 2
Pulse: N=8, 0-1 year

Subject	Baseline	3 Weeks	3 Months	6 Months	1 Year
1	62	60	66	68	68
2	66	68	72	72	64
3	88	86	68	66	64
4	80	80	84	76	64
5	80	80	82	80	76
6	64	52	74	64	64
7	68	72	66	62	52
8	72	72	58	60	62
N=8	72.5*	71.7*	71.2*	68.7*	64.2*
		−0.8**	−1.3**	−3.8**	−8.3**
* Mean pulse ** Mean change from baseline					

FIGURE B
Mean Change Pulse: N=8, 0-1 year

Units = 1 beat/min.

BL 3W 3M 6M 1 YR.

TABLE 3
Core Body Temperature: N=22, 0-6 months

Subject	Baseline	3 Weeks	3 Months	6 Months
1	99.0	98.4	98.7	99.2
2	99.0	98.9	98.3	98.6
3	99.0	99.5	99.4	99.0
4	99.4	99.2	99.8	99.2
5	99.0	97.9	98.9	98.7
6	99.0	98.5	98.5	98.5
7	99.4	99.0	99.3	98.2
8	99.9	99.0	98.1	98.4
9	99.0	98.9	98.6	99.3
10	99.6	98.7	98.5	98.5
11	99.2	98.8	99.0	98.6
12	99.3	98.8	99.0	98.6
13	99.5	99.4	99.1	98.6
14	100.0	99.3	99.3	99.4
15	99.3	98.4	98.5	98.5
16	98.8	98.8	98.6	98.4
17	99.1	98.1	98.9	98.8
18	99.8	99.1	98.3	98.1
19	99.0	98.4	98.7	99.5
20	98.9	98.7	98.5	98.5
21	99.6	99.8	99.6	99.5
22	99.5	99.2	99.0	98.1
N=22	99.2*	98.8*	98.8*	98.7*
		−0.43*	−0.45**	−0.54**
* Mean temperature		** Mean change from baseline		

FIGURE C
Mean Change Temperature: N=22, 0-6 months

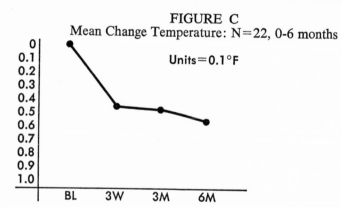

Units=0.1°F

TABLE 4
Core Body Temperature: N=8, 0-1 year

Subject	Baseline	3 Weeks	3 Months	6 Months	1 Year
1	99.0	98.4	98.7	99.2	99.0
2	99.0	98.9	98.3	98.6	98.5
3	99.0	99.5	99.4	99.0	98.6
4	99.4	99.2	99.8	99.2	98.6
5	99.6	99.8	99.6	99.5	99.5
6	99.0	97.9	98.9	98.7	98.5
7	99.4	99.0	99.3	98.2	98.2
8	99.9	99.0	98.1	98.4	98.6
N=8	99.3*	99.0*	99.0*	98.9*	98.7*
		−0.3**	−0.3**	−0.4**	−0.6**
* Mean temperature ** Mean change from baseline				

FIGURE D
Mean Change Temperature: N=8, 0-1 year

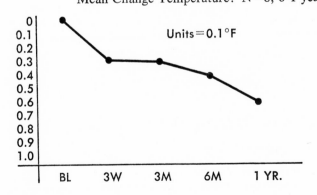

TABLE 5
Covariants, Pulse and Temperature: N=22, 0-6 months

Subject	Pulse	Temperature
1	+ 6	+0.2
2	+ 6	−0.4
3	−22	0
4	− 4	−0.2
5	0	−0.3
6	−16	−0.5
7	−16	−1.2
8	−10	−1.5
9	0	+0.3
10	− 8	−1.1
11	−22	−0.6
12	+ 3	−0.7
13	− 4	−0.9
14	− 5	−0.6
15	−24	−0.8
16	−18	−0.4
17	− 4	−0.3
18	−18	−1.7
19	+ 7	+0.5
20	− 2	−0.4
21	0	−0.1
22	−12	−1.4
Values of Baseline vs. 6 months		

TABLE 6
Covariants, Mean Changes: N=22, 0-6 months

	3 Weeks	3 Months	6 Months
Pulse	−4	−5	−8
Temperature	−0.43	−0.45	−0.54

TABLE 7

Covariants, Pulse and Temperature: N=8, 0-1 year

Subject	Pulse	Temperature
1	+ 6	0
2	− 2	−0.5
3	−24	−0.4
4	−16	−0.8
5	− 4	−0.1
6	− 0	−0.5
7	−16	−1.2
8	−10	−1.3

TABLE 8

Covariants, Mean Changes: N=8, 0-1 year

	3 Weeks	3 Months	6 Months	1 Year
Pulse	−0.8	−1.3	−3.8	−8.3
Temperature	−0.3	−0.3	−0.4	−0.6

The Significance of Research on Vital Signs in Primal Therapy
E. Michael Holden

The research data on patients undergoing Primal Therapy presented by Dr. McInerny in the preceding issue of this Journal are of considerable physiological interest.

Primal Therapy is associated with the gradual attainment of a tension-free condition which may be termed the "post-Primal state," as there are no precedents for terming this condition otherwise. Because several parameters of the basal metabolic rate decrease in numerical value from a (neurotic) pre-Primal Therapy baseline, it is reasonable to propose that neurosis is a high-energy or *hypermetabolic* state of the body. Behaviorally, post-Primal patients struggle less than their neurotic selves before therapy. Post-Primal patients achieve a heightened sense of well-being and alertness in association with a lower-amplitude, slower EEG. This is indeed an unusual and probably unique phenomenon in human physiology. In clinical neurology it is widely recognized that a slower, lower-amplitude EEG (in neurotics) is found to be associated with lethargy, drowsiness, metabolic encephalopathy or diffuse cortical disorders such as Alzheimer's disease (senility). In hypothyroidism there is a lower amplitude, slower EEG[1,2] which is associated with the lethargy and hypothermia of that disorder. It is also known (Scott[3]—cited in note 2) that artificially induced hypothermia decreases the amplitude and frequency of the EEG. These changes in hypothyroidism respond, with return to higher-

---

1 Kooi, Kenneth A.: *Fundamentals of Electroencephalography.* Harper and Row, 1971.

2 Kilch, L. C. and Osselton, J. W.: *Clinical Electroencephalography.* Butterworths, London. Second Edition, Reprinted 1970.

3 Scott, J. W.: "The EEG During Hypothermia." *Electroenceph. Clin. Neurophysiol.,* 1:466 1966.

amplitude faster EEG rhythms, with administration of thyroid extract or tri-iodothyronine.[2] Conversely, the EEG frequency is increased in cases of hyperthyroidism[1,2] and this background activity returns to pre-hyperthyroid frequencies with effective treatment of the hyperthyroidism.[1] Thus, there exists in the non-Primal population a model which may help to understand the EEG changes in Primal patients; i.e. neurosis probably represents a hypermetabolic state, when compared with the post-Primal state. What is quite remarkable is that the post-Primal state is characterized by alertness and a sense of well-being; for if one used *only non-Primal criteria*, one would predict that a slower, lower-amplitude EEG and lower pulse and body temperature would correlate with lethargy or stupor, which, by observation, is *not* found in the post-Primal state. It will be of interest to systematically study thyroid metabolism and basal metabolic rate before and during Primal Therapy, in the future.

Of the lower vital sign values characteristically seen in the post-Primal state, the most noteworthy is the lowered core body temperature. While a critical view could submit that the slower pulse rate is an exercise effect (the "athlete's heart") related to a therapy which often contains strenuous physical exertion, such an explanation will not account for a lowering of core body temperature. *The implication of the temperature decrease is that the central control of body temperature in the hypothalamus is affected by Primal Therapy.*

Destruction of the anterior hypothalamus, in animals, leads to hyperthermia (over-heating), and stimulation of the anterior-preoptic region leads to hypothermia (cooling).[4] A simple way to say this is that the "thermostat" of the body is in the *anterior* hypothalamus. It is also the anterior hypothalamus which regulates the adrenal and thyroid gland secretions.[4] Also, it has been shown that the dorsomedial posterior hypothalamus is essential for shivering, whereas the ventrolateral part is responsible for inhibiting heat production.[4] The *posterior* hypothalamus functions as a center for visceromotor control to bring about the actual thermoregulation.[4]

We are confronted by the fact that Primal Therapy lowers core body temperature in humans, presumably by altering the intrinsic physiological mechanisms in the hypothalamus. The mechanism for this is not yet known. The fact that this does occur challenges the notion that 37°

---

[4] Myers, Robert D.: "Temperature Regulation: Neurochemical Systems in the Hypothalamus." Chapter 14 in *The Hypothalamus*, Edited by Haymaker, Anderson and Nanta. Charles Thomas, Publisher, 1969.

[1,2] See footnotes, page 479.

centigrade is truly the normal body temperature, genetically determined, for human beings. The vital sign changes during and after Primal Therapy support the assertion that the post-Primal state is physiologically unique, and the decreased values of these physiologic parameters are part of the definition of that state. This provides one with objective physiologic parameters to follow as an index of the therapeutic process and frees one from the obligation of following behavioral changes only.

If subsequent research on Primal patients discloses that the blood pressure lowering with Primal Therapy persists into old age, then as with the temperature change, *the notion that systolic blood pressure "must" increase with age will also need revision.*

As Dr. Janov has previously noted, one of the concomitants of a long-term lowering of body temperature will be a probable increase of life span, considering the relationship between body temperature and the speed of biochemical processes. Fever increases metabolic rate and increases requirements for substrates. It seems probable that the slight hypothermia produced by Primal Therapy will be associated with a lowered metabolic rate and a decreased requirement for substrates and may then be viewed as a means of conserving biological energy (when compared with the metabolism of non-Primal individuals).

The data reported in Dr. McInerny's study supports the assertion that neurosis is a hypermetabolic state. During Primal Therapy the core body temperature is decreased as the *non-neurotic state* is gradually achieved, and is an essential part of its definition. *To our knowledge, Primal Therapy is the first process in the history of medicine capable of permanently lowering the vital sign values.*

Primals are physiologically unique and demonstrate paradoxical changes in the vital signs, when completed. Strenuous muscular exertion and a high level of alertness occur in a Primal, yet characteristically, the core body temperature, blood pressure, pulse rate and EEG power are *lower* following a Primal than they were before it. The implication is that Primal Pain exerts a force or a "pressure" *against which one exerts energy in opposition to the Pain.* We do not yet know the metabolic definition of Pain "registered in cells," but one can be sure that this occurs, via the observed changes in energy relationships following a Primal. The lowering of vital sign values is thus an indirect measure of Pain's effects on cells. There is a practical aspect to consider here as well. Primal patients are familiar with the difference between Primals with "connection" and abreacted feelings, without connection. Connected Primals are followed by (Primal) insights and a drop in vital sign values, whereas abreacted feelings are not. Thus it is possible for one to be close to feelings for several hours without changing the vital signs at all. The magnitude of one's Primal Pain, the effectiveness of one's defenses, and one's Primal "style" all contribute in determining how often one has connected Primals. The practical point is that therapy for some individuals will proceed more rapidly than for others, and the rate at which one becomes well will be reflected in a more consistent decrease in the vital sign values, over time. One's own biological regulation and particular past seem to determine the rate at which one benefits from Primal Therapy. This rate can be increased somewhat in the setting of Primal group sessions or during individual weeks with a therapist (contrasted to Primalling on one's own). It was implicit in the discussion of stroboscopic light frequencies, in Dr. Janov's *The Anatomy of Mental Illness*, that the rate of one's therapy could perhaps be increased with the aid of certain strobe-light frequencies. The hypothesis is that greater depths of feeling can be quickly reached with lower strobe-light frequencies. This intriguing hypothesis hasn't yet been specifically tested. In the near future we will be testing this hypothesis: to see if the number of connected Primals can be increased, using a strobe-light "stimulus." It should be possible to objectively test this relationship by following the vital signs before, during and after Primals. Thus, following vital signs in Primal Therapy provides objective evidence that this therapy changes brain function, and also provides a way to evaluate the mechanisms and speed of the therapy itself. Is there a faster or "more productive" way to have Primal Therapy? Following vital signs in Primal patients will permit us to evaluate future hypotheses seeking to answer that question.

An additional significance of the vital sign changes in Primal patients is that *other therapies* can be evaluated, using *physiological* rather than only *behavioral* criteria to evaluate therapeutic effectiveness. We believe at present that only Primal Therapy produces the vital sign changes characteristic of the non-neurotic state. The issue has not been explored very much however. (We hope to compare Primal Therapy with other therapies in the future. To "compare therapies" unavoidably is seen as threatening or at least as a challenge, however, and a comparison could only be made in an arena of genuine curiosity about neurosis, with relative disregard of the politics involved. Suffice it to say here, those approached to date have shown little interest in comparing therapies, using physiological criteria as the "yardstick" of effectiveness.) For the present we will continue to document vital sign decreases in Primal patients as an objective support of the Primal formulation, and as a way to evaluate the therapy itself.

Lastly, the significance of following vital signs in Primal patients is in relation to internal medicine. There are disorders in which *prognosis* of one's illness is closely related to the vital signs. Examples are found in all forms of heart disease especially *angina pectoris* (coronary artery insufficiency leading to chest pain), and in the disorders which occur in people with *hypertension* (high blood pressure). Strokes, heart attacks, a severe kidney disease and vascular insufficiency in limbs (from atherosclerosis), are all more common in hypertensive people. There are theoretical reasons for believing that Primal Therapy either stops or slows down the insidious process of atherosclerosis (see "Primal Pain and Aging," this issue), but beyond the theory, there is huge practical significance in a process which slows down pulse and lowers blood pressure. Changing these two vital signs to lower values will slow down the atherosclerotic process and markedly reduce the work of the heart. This combination is literally life-saving for an individual with severe hypertension or with angina pectoris.

Hypertension and angina pectoris are common disorders so the general importance of Primal Therapy to "heart patients" cannot be underestimated. It is becoming clear also that it is safe for patients with angina and/or hypertension, to Primal. One patient evaluated recently had severe angina pectoris, sometimes occurring even at rest. At the end of his first three weeks of Primal Therapy, he had a Primal which included 10½ minutes of a pulse of 132/min. and a blood pressure of 156/110, without experiencing angina. The experience of another man with angina, following a heart attack, is recorded in *The Journal of Primal Therapy,* Vol. I, No. 3, pp. 213-222.

More cases are needed to evaluate this extraordinary relationship of rapid heart rate in an angina patient, without pain, during a Primal. The implication of the early observations is that angina pectoris is related more to coronary artery vasospasm in relation to stress and Primal Pain, and less to coronary artery narrowing, per se, than most physicians realize.[5]

While we have relatively few cases upon which this conclusion is based, we must keep in mind that Primal Therapy is a *pre*dictive rather than a

---

[5] Angina pectoris has been documented in patients with normal coronary arteries. See *The Lancet*, Sept. 21, 1974.

*post*dictive process. Therefore, the power of its predictions increases rapidly with a smaller number of cases. Postdictive processes require, as a rule, large numbers of cases to justify conclusions. Postdictive therapies usually involve elaborate statistical manipulations because they deal with statistical rather than biological truths.

Angina pectoris is a transient phenomenon and thus our focus must be on transient precipitating causes. We have seen that during a Primal, a patient with previous bouts of angina can have a rapid heart rate, and *not* have chest pain. This directs our attention then to the relationships between Primal Pain and the work of the heart.

Patients with respiratory diseases, especially asthma, also benefit markedly from Primal Therapy. Recently, 83 questionnaires from Primal patients were reviewed and a large majority reported deeper, fuller breathing as a consequence of the therapy, and some noted a slower respiratory rate than prior to therapy. This emphasizes for our consideration that the trachea and bronchioles of the lungs are common "targets" for Primal Pain, no less than the heart. For patients with respiratory diseases, a slower respiratory rate and dilation of the trachea and bronchioles markedly improves overall prognosis.

The interrelationships between disease states and Primal Pain are many, and will be discussed at length in later publications. The vital sign changes in Primal patients are themselves potentially life-saving for patients with certain cardio-respiratory disorders.

In summary, we believe that the vital sign changes in Primal patients are important, and provide us with invaluable measures of an individual's progress in therapy and ultimately, document a steady improvement in health, as therapy continues.

APPENDIX A / PART THREE

EEG Study of Primal Patients
Bernard McInerny

In the following pages are the results of a study, the purpose of which was to explore and measure any neurological changes that take place in patients undergoing Primal therapy. This is a report of EEG changes in Primal patients and is condensed from a much more extensive study reported elsewhere. The details of methodology, data collection and analysis have been shortened.

Fifteen subjects were selected for this measurement. Of this group nine were men and six were women. The average age was 33.2 years.

Two analyses of EEG data will be reported. In the first study, EEG from six patients were compared for recordings made on the Saturday preceding the start of therapy and for the Saturday which followed the completion of the initial three weeks of intensive therapy. As the initial three weeks is daily intensive therapy, we sought to test for changes after this period. In this longitudinal test for changes each individual in this period was measured twice.

The second study sought to test for longer-term effects. The EEG from the same set of six patients before therapy was compared with a second group of four patients who had had six months of therapy, a third group which contained five patients who had had one year of therapy or more, and a control group.

All measurements recorded for this study reflect the resting EEG and only the alpha activity has been examined.

For measurement, gold disc electrodes (Grass Instrument Co.) were attached by means of water soluble past (Grass FC-2) at the following locations according to the 10-20 system: F_3, F_4, C_5, C_6, 0_1, and 0_2.

Additional electrodes were placed at a dominant hemisphere location over Wernicke's speech area and at a symmetric location on the opposite side of the head. The electrodes were also placed above the eyes to monitor eye movement. EEG from each electrode was recorded monopolar against a linked mastoid reference, and also in some bipolar derivations. The study presented will deal only with recordings made from F_3, F_4 and O_1 and O_2 locations. The recording was made with the subject seated in a comfortable chair, in a dark sound-attenuated chamber, with eyes closed. The EEG signals were amplified using a Grass 6 electroencephalograph, and were recorded on FM analog tape by means of a tape recorder, along with a timing code that is used by the computer during analysis.

The first study was that of six patients measured before therapy started and again after three weeks of individual daily therapy. The EEGs were first examined and the first four twenty-second epochs free from artifacts were selected for each of the six subjects (in a few subjects it was necessary to make use of some ten-second epochs where insufficient twenty-second epochs were available, but in all cases the length of record analyzed added up to eighty seconds). After digitizing by computer and submitting the tape for epoch analysis by spectral analysis, a resolution of 1/4 cycle over the frequency range of 0-16Hz was obtained. The results of the epoch analysis, properly weighted to allow for the length of epoch on which they were based, were averaged together to produce a single average spectrum for each channel based on the full eighty seconds of record. This averaging was first compiled individually for each subject's base line and three-week test, and then each individual averaged together, until the grand averages were compiled.

After averaging, various parameters were calculated to describe the spectra averaged. The analysis in this study was based on the parameters limited to the spectra from channels O_1, O_2 (from the back of the head), and F_3, F_4 (from the front of the head). The parameters describing the spectra (29 in all) are listed in Table 1.*

The analysis of the study is limited to a detailed description of the alpha band (8.00 to 12.25 Hz) in the various channels and the interrelationships of alpha properties between the channels (Table 1). The 1/4Hz band showing the maximum power within the alpha band in each channel was first found (var. 1-4) and the relative power in these bands recorded (var. 5-8). The average peak power for occipital (var. 9) and frontal (var. 10) were calculated. The average power across the alpha band was next computed for each channel (var. 11-14) and used to give average power for occipital (var. 15) and frontal (var. 16) areas. The

*Tables follow part 4.

alpha sharpness parameter (the ratio of peak power to average power in the band) was next calculated for each channel (var. 17-20) and averaged for occipital as a whole (var. 21) and frontal as a whole (var. 22). The ratio of occipital to frontal peak power (var. 23) average power (var. 24) and sharpness (var. 25) were all calculated. Finally, ratios of peak power and average power between the sides (var. 26-29) were calculated.

The wish to examine the frequency at the alpha peak in occipital areas to 1/4 Hz resolution and the intensity of alpha activity is motivated by Dr. Arthur Janov's earlier studies (Janov, 1972). The parallel studies of frontal alpha, and the calculation of parameters expressing the ratios of alpha power and sharpness over different regions of the scalp are motivated by results that are appearing in a more extensive study of Primal patients.

The mean values and standard deviations for the twenty-nine variables for the group of before and after three weeks of therapy are tabulated in Tables 2 and 3. The F statistic was used to test observed changes in group means.

When this process was applied to all twenty-nine variables, note that two parameters, the occipital laterality indexes, variables 26 and 27, showed a significant change in mean value, both variables relating to changes in the relative strengths of alpha between the two hemispheres in the occipital regions. There was also evidence of a shift from a situation where alpha was relatively weaker on the left side compared to the right to a situation of greater equality.

There are other changes in mean values which are of interest even though they do not appear to reach a level of significance with the amount of data. The occipital alpha shows a slight decrease of mean frequency in 01 and a decrease in mean peak and average band power in directions conforming to earlier reports by Janov (1972). The frontal alpha on the other hand shows evidence of a slight increase in frequency with no apparent change in amplitude. There is also evidence of a decrease in the ratio of frontal to occipital alpha which approaches significance in both amplitude and average power (variables 23 and 24).

The fact that none of the actual alpha power parameters show significant mean change (for this sample size) are in part a reflection of the high degree of variability between subjects. This can be seen, for example, in peak power in 0, (variable 6) where a drop in power of a factor of 2.78 is still far from significant. The ratios (variables 17-29) meet this problem of using each subject as his own control. In a sense it is perhaps, in part, that the changes shown in these parameters show less variability, and some reach significance even for this small sample size.

The within-group standard deviations were also treated by F statistic (Table 3).

The within-group standard deviations show many changes. Power in the occipital region is significant (var. 5 at the .05 level and var. 6 at the .01 level) as well as the average of these two variables (var. 9). Additionally, variables 11 to 15, 23 and 28 and 29 are all significant. In all the variables the changes indicate decrease in variance for the group after the three weeks of therapy as compared to before therapy.

This data, in summary, seems to support a picture of a trend towards *a decrease in peak alpha power* within the group and trends toward *greater uniformity of alpha distribution between the hemispheres* and *between the front and back (occipital) parts of the brain as therapy progresses.* These mean changes appear to be parallelled by decreases in the variability of alpha characteristics between subjects after the three-week period.

The second evaluation of EEG was a comparative study to test the trends appearing in the longitudinal study. Three more groups of subjects were selected. A "6 month" group contained four subjects who had had six months of therapy. A "1 to 4 year" group contained two subjects who had had one year of therapy, and three subjects who had started therapy four or more years ago. A control group consisted of four subjects drawn from the UCLA community. EEGs in all three subjects were measured and quantified in a manner identical to that described in the preceding section. The collected data was used to test for differences between the "before" group of the preceding section and each of the comparison groups plus a comparison between the control group and the "1 to 4 year" group. The mean data analysis was identical to that used in the preceding section. The results of the mean data for this comparative group are listed in Table 6.

The results from the "before" versus "six month" study (Table 4) appear to support the first study ("before" versus "three weeks") and in fact gives indication of a maintenance of some of the trends observed there. *The occipital alpha shows evidence of a drop in power between "before" and "six months," and a maintenance or slight rise in the frontal alpha. The occipital power changes are in the same direction as "before" versus "three weeks," but larger.* The occipital peak in the six-month group now shows a decrease in sharpness compared to the "before," but there is a net increase in sharpness in the frontal areas, maintaining a trend suggested by the "before" to "three week" study. Thus the ratio of sharpness between occipital and frontal (var. 25) shows a decrease which is large, and in fact reaches the 1 per cent level of significance. The laterality ratios change in the same direction in the "before" to "six-month" group as that observed in the "before" to "three-week" study but not quite as slowly. Note also that the change in variable 27 is still significant at the .05 level but the change in variable 26 is now below the level of significance. The average frequency of the alpha peak now shows an increase for "before" versus "six-month" in both occipital and frontal which reaches a 5 per cent level of significance for both areas.

The within-group standard deviations (Table 5) again show general decreases for the "six month" group as compared to the "before" group. The decreases for variable 2 (O_2 frequency) is significant and for variable 1 (O_1 frequency) is large but not significant. The changes in variance for occipital peak power are again significant and in the same direction and slightly larger than for "before" versus "three weeks." Other changes in alpha power parameters are in the same direction, but the frontal changes do not reach a level of significance. Among the ratios there are only two significant changes in variance, variable 18 (sharpness in O_2) and variable 21 (sharpness in O_1 average) both representing a decrease similar to the "before" to "three week" group.

The trends observed with the "before" versus "three weeks" and the "before" versus "six months" group are again largely supported by the data in the one to four year group (Table 6). *The mean alpha power in occipital areas now show a substantial decrease for "one to four years" compared to "before" in both variable 1 (O_1) and variable 2 (O_2).* Although the decrease is still not significant by the F statistic, the fact that the alpha power in these leads for "one to four years" is only about half that in the "six-month" group is very striking. The frontal alpha, on the other hand, shows a slight increase for "one to four years" versus the "before" group. The frontal alpha peak at "one to four years" again shows an increase in sharpness as compared to both the "before" and "six-month groups." The occipital sharpness peak decreases in variable 1 (O_1) but increases in variable 2 (O_2). The sharpness ratio, back to front, now drops below 1.0, a change from the "before" condition which is significant well above the 0.1 level. The ratio of peak power, forward to back, is much lower for "one to four years" as compared to the control group but is not quite significant. The laterality ratios are again different in the same direction as in the previous data, though the difference is no longer significant. The mean peak alpha frequencies have again dropped and are now below the frequency of the before group.

The standard deviations for the frequencies and for the alpha power measurements are again uniformly lower for "one to four years" (Table 7) than for control and in most cases they are also lower for the six month group. *The occipital alpha changes are much more significant, often at the 5 per cent level or approaching it.* Some of the frontal changes are also significant. Among the ratios the decrease in sharpness of 0_1 (Var. 17) is seen as a trend in the six month data, reaches the 5 per cent level of significance, but the greatest difference is seen in variable 23 and 24 *back to front variables for peak power and average power where the variability now shows a decrease in the one to four year group as compared to the before group that is significant at the .01 level.*

Further insight can be gained by breaking down the data from the one to four year group into two subgroups, one containing the two subjects who had one year of therapy starting over four years ago (Table 8). The average alpha power at four years is far smaller in the four year group as compared to the one year group but the back to front ratio in sharpness does not show a substantial difference. The back to front ratios in alpha power do, however, show a substantial difference when the combined one and four year group is compared with the four year group. The laterality ratios are near 1.0 in the one-year group maintaining approximately the same general laterality as for three-week and six-month groups but the *four-year group shows a decrease from this situation toward lower amplitude for left than for right hemispheres.*

The standard deviations (Table 9) are often lower for the four-year group than when compared with the one-year group. This is particularly true for the frequency variable. In the amplitude variable the variances are often within order of magnitude of each other, and drops appear no more probable than increases, suggesting that it is possible that there may no longer be any systematic difference between the two groups.

To summarize, the one-to four-year group data compared to the before group data shows a continuation of trends visible in data at the three week and at the six-month levels. These trends receive, in most cases, further support when the one- to four-year group data is broken into one- and four-year groups.

Given natural variability among individuals, selection of a control group is both difficult and somewhat arbitrary. It appeared useful, however, to attempt to do so to see, for example, how individuals in Primal Therapy compare to individuals of the same age who were not in Primal Therapy. The control group consisted of four individuals from the UCLA community: one a professor, one a graduate student, one a mathematician working as a bartender, and one a housewife.

The control versus before group is shown in Table 10. The control group shows a similar occipital frequency but a somewhat higher frontal frequency, a lower amount of alpha power, but a higher amount of frontal alpha power when compared with the before group. Continuing the comparison the alpha peak is somewhat sharper, the frontal less sharp, the back to front ratios somewhat lower, the occipital laterality ratios somewhat higher and the frontal ratios somewhat lower. In most respects the controls differ from the before group in mean values in the same direction as do groups after some therapy when compared to before therapy. The principal exception is the frontal areas, where the alpha power is higher and the peak less sharp in controls while groups after therapy were found to not show substantially higher power in frontal alpha, but to show increase in alpha peak sharpness. Note, however, that most of the differences do not adhere to a level of statistical significance but are rather noticeable trends. The only mean difference found significant at the .5 level is the change in occipital laterality indexes.

The standard deviations support the same picture (Table 11). Controls show an occipital alpha with less variability but a frontal alpha with more variability in power when compared with the before group. The occipital changes are shown to be significant. There are also significant reductions in the back to front ratio variability in control versus before groups. Controls differ from before mostly in the same direction as do individuals who have had some therapy; however, the picture in the frontal areas is somewhat different.

Control versus one-to four-year tables are shown in Table 12. There are no longer any significant mean differences although the difference that appears most significant is in variable 25 (average sharpness). Note, however, that in general the one-to-four year group show longer alpha power in both frontal and occipital areas and a lower alpha frequency, as compared to the control. The occipital sharpness is lower, but frontal sharpness is higher for the one-to four-year group. This accounts for the relatively higher significance for variable 25. Thus it appears that the controls are more like the one-to-four year group than the "before" group. In some respects, *the one-to-four year group show greater differences than the control group, namely in decrease of occipital power.* Many of the differences are in the same direction, with the main contrast being that Primal patient changes are in the direction of a large change in sharpness of frontal peak in the alpha while a much smaller change exists when comparing the controls and before therapy groups. The breakdown of one-to-four year groups into one and four year subgroups points up this contrast even more strongly.

The standard deviations (Table 13) are generally smaller in the one-to-four year group than the controls and in some cases these differences are significant though for variables 24, 27, and 28 the variance situation is actually greater for the one-to-four year group than for the controls. Note that when the one-to four-year group is subdivided there is still, generally, smaller standard deviations for the four-year as opposed to the one-year patients.

The "before" versus three weeks study gives evidence of trends. These supported by the "before" versus six months and "before versus one-to-four year comparison giving further evidence of some progressive changes with therapy. The controls are more like the one-to-four year group than the before group. The overall picture of the control group looks most like the six-months group. As noted in the chapter on Primal Pain and Aging, the decreasing EEG power as Primal Therapy progresses argues that Primal Therapy changes brain function. The change appears to be toward a brain metabolism performing less physical-chemical work per unit time (ultimately, the power of the EEG is related to the biochemistry of neurons).

The brain wave changes were revealing. The direction was generally downward in both frequency and amplitude after entering therapy. This downward shift continued after one year of therapy, and it was also observed in three people whose major therapy had taken place some four or more years before.

In terms of the EEG we have concluded that the general *diminishing of both frequency and amplitude in alpha rhythm shows the eradication of tension through therapy*. Because the brain is a necessary part of the neurotic's defense system, it *must remain hyperactive* to repress the Pain of past deprivation. This is even true for the alpha state. We have concluded that *as the therapy continues, the frequency and amplitude of brain waves diminish, allowing for a much less busy brain*. This is brought about by the connection of present Pain to past memories, a direct path so to speak, which eliminates the need for larger areas of the cortex to be active in suppressing the past Pain.

Another conclusion is that as tension is eradicated, a shift of electrical activity occurs. This change in laterality means that the patients are more influenced by the feeling side of their brains (right side) than the task or abstract side (left side). This shift has taken place, by the way, *without apparent loss of previous abilities in abstract reasoning*. It is speculated that the abstract abilities will increase, although this has not been tested yet.

EEG Changes in Primal Therapy
E. Michael Holden

A detailed and sophisticated study of EEG's in a small number of Primal patients and controls was carried out by Dr. Martin Gardiner, a biophysicist working at UCLA Brain Research Institute in Los Angeles.[7] This study was performed at UCLA using modern techniques of data retrieval and analysis. The analysis of data from that study is still underway. The study design, methods and approach used in analyzing the data will be reported later. The salient findings are summarized here:

(a) There were no changes in the EEG's of Primal patients which reached statistical significance in those having had Primal Therapy for eight months or less.

(b) From eight months to five years in Primal Therapy, patients demonstrated a trend of gradual decrease in alpha power (EEG activity between 8-13 cycles per second). This trend approached the 0.05 level of statistical significance.

(c) From eight months to five years in Primal Therapy a similar EEG trend was noted for "non-alpha" power, in the frequency range from 2 cps to 8 cps. This trend was significant at the 0.05 level of statistical significance.

(d) When the anterior quadrants of the brain were compared with the posterior quadrants, there was a consistent trend toward decreased alpha

---

7 Gardiner, Martin: "EEG Activity and Primal Therapy—I: Initial Tests for Possible Changes During Therapy." First draft, 9/13/74 (not yet published). Dr. Gardiner is not a Primal person and is employed by UCLA.

power (8-13 cps) in the posterior quadrants and a simultaneous increased alpha power in the anterior quadrants: a shift then of alpha power from back to front. Stated differently, all quadrants demonstrated a tendency to generate alpha power approaching the mean alpha power of the entire brain. ("Normal" EEG's show more alpha power posteriorly and less alpha power anteriorly. Primal Therapy decreases this front-to-back asymmetry.)

(e) Also, from eight months to five years in Primal Therapy there was a definite trend toward an increased amount of non-alpha power (2-8 cps) in the left anterior quadrant of the brain, more striking in that location than for the right anterior quadrant.

(f) Dr. Gardiner writes: "The paper records typically showed lower amplitude alpha activity in individuals who were extensively into their therapy."

Dr. Gardiner and his colleagues have searched the EEG literature for a study of EEG's, done with modern and sophisticated equipment, which demonstrates a statistically significant EEG change related to any other therapy for mental illness (neurosis or psychosis), and were unable to find one. We therefore believe that his study of Primal patients is the first of its kind to demonstrate a significant EEG change accompanying a therapy for mental illness; in this case, Primal Therapy.

This indicates for the first time that a psychotherapeutic procedure has been shown to change brain function. The other definite indicators of this are the *permanent* decreases in the values of the vital signs, which occur in Primal Therapy; (in contrast to meditation states which are reported to transiently slow pulse and decrease blood pressure). The decrease in alpha and non-alpha power in the EEG's of long-term Primal patients is an important finding. It suggests that after one or more years of Primal Therapy the physico-chemical work of the brain is decreased, which if physiologically true is congruent with our hypothesis that Primal Therapy slows the rate of aging. The exact *meaning* of the decreased EEG power is not known. It may simply be the EEG correlate of a lowered core body temperature. What is apparent however is that the energy relationships within the body change, as one proceeds in Primal Therapy, a change in which *less energy is being required* for homeostatic regulation than was the case before Primal Therapy. In the course of an individual single Primal, as noted previously, one consistently finds a *lower* core body temperature *after* the Primal than *before* the Primal. Control patients have been studied during extreme voluntary exertion (mock Primals) and show not a fall but a slight rise in body temperature right after the exertion. What has happened? The details are still unknown. However, it appears that having *re-experienced an early-life Pain* in a connected Primal, the body's *energy utilization transiently decreases.* The drop in temperature may be as little as one or two tenths of a degree or as much as 3-4 degrees. We interpret this to mean that as long as the Pain was within the body, *energy was required to oppose it,* much as additional metabolic energy is required to oppose a common cold virus or a staphylococcal abscess (conditions which *raise* temperature). Early Pains, as noted, are very severe and the remarkable fact is that the temperature falls as *little* as it does, after a Primal. The slight fall in temperature is, however, itself subject to a cybernetic type of feedback regulation. Were it not so then the entire organism would be at risk of dying as a result of re-experiencing Primal Pain. We are fortunate that the temperature fall is slight rather than say, 10 or 15 degrees. The central point to emphasize here is that Primal Pain seems to exert a "pressure" or "force" against which the body must expend energy, to keep it in check. Just as the release of Primal Pain is accompanied by a slight fall in temperature so it is, in the opposite polarity, that neurosis is accompanied by a slight rise in body temperature. (What is presently considered normal body temperature is the normal value for neurotics. The lower values after Primal Therapy tend toward a lower mean value which is *biologically* more actually "normal.") Neurotic people are slightly hypermetabolic in relation to their content of Primal Pain. As they release that Pain in Primals, the metabolic burden lessens, the core body temperature decreases and *the power of the EEG decreases.* The trend toward a less active metabolism is very gradual but very consistent, and the low values may not have yet been witnessed; i.e. does a person who Primals for 10 years have an even lower temperature and EEG power than one who has Primalled for 5 years? We do not yet know where in time the trend ceases to progress. Additionally, if it were later shown that the decrease in EEG power occurred relatively *independently* of a drop in temperature (for instance if one occurred months before the other), then the hypothesis would emerge that the "force" or "pressure" or "insult" of Primal Pain expressed itself metabolically in a direct way, increasing the power of the EEG.

In summary, a decrease in EEG power over time, in Primal patients, is entirely consonant with the view that neurosis is a hypermetabolic state, and that Primal Therapy reverses that; and *probably thereby slows down the rate of aging.*

TABLE 1

Spectra Parameters

Variables		Location
1	Power in 1/4 Hz band	O_1
2	showing highest power frequency	O_2
3	of alpha range	F_3
4		F_4
5	Power in 1/4 Hz band	O_1
6	showing highest power within	O_2
7	alpha range	F_3
8		F_4
9	average of variable 5 and 6	O_1
10	average of variable 7 and 8	O_2
11	average power in	F_3
12	alpha band (8.00-12.25 Hz)	F_4
13		
14		
15	average of variable 11 and 12	
16	average of variable 13 and 14	
17	sharpness parameter for 01 (var. 1, 5, 11)	
18	sharpness parameter for 02 (var. 2, 6, 12)	
19	sharpness parameter for F_3 (var. 3, 7, 13)	
20	sharpness parameter for F_4 (var. 4, 8, 14)	
21	average of variable 17 and 18	
22	average of variable 19 and 20	
23	Forward to back ratio for highest band (var. 9, 10)	
24	Variable for average power (var. 15, 16)	
25	Variable for average sharpness (var. 21, 22)	
26	Laterality index (Gardiner, et al, 1972) Peak power (var. 5, 6)	
27	Laterality index (Gardiner, et al, 1972) Ave. Alpha Power (var. 11, 12)	
28	Laterality index (Gardiner, et al, 1972) Peak power (var. 7, 8)	
29	Laterality index (Gardiner, et al, 1972) Ave. Alpha Power (var. 13, 14)	

TABLE 2

Means and F statistic of six patients before and after three weeks

Variable	Before	3 Weeks	Grand Mean	F.
1	9.16667	8.66667	8.91667	0.0646
2	8.50000	8.83333	8.66667	0.0297
3	7.00000	8.83333	7.91667	0.5397
4	7.50000	7.83333	7.66667	0.0147
5	1297.16650	1012.66650	1154.91650	0.0815
6	2674.83325	966.00000	1820.41650	1.6009
7	393.00000	343.50000	368.25000	0.0642
8	348.33325	372.33325	360.33325	0.0126
9	1985.66650	989.00000	487.33325	0.7629
10	370.33325	357.66650	364.00000	0.0039
11	286.83335	183.33333	235.08333	0.2557
12	570.00000	204.00000	387.00000	1.3745
13	141.50000	98.50000	120.00000	0.3631
14	115.33333	102.16666	108.75000	0.0450
15	428.00000	154.50000	291.25000	1.1622
16	128.16666	146.66666	137.4166	0.0445
17	3.59166	4.81333	4.20250	1.1669
18	4.13833	4.55000	4.34416	0.1373
19	2.79166	3.44666	3.11916	0.5818
20	2.85666	3.42999	3.14333	0.4772
21	3.86166	4.67833	4.26999	0.5612
22	2.82333	3.43499	3.12916	0.5321
23	4.17333	2.65667	3.41500	3.2808
24	2.92833	1.94833	2.43833	2.3034
25	1.39833	1.39000	1.39417	0.0024
26	0.42000	1.10000	0.76000	8.3768*
27	0.44000	1.02500	0.73250	6.7618*
28	1.14500	1.01667	1.08083	0.4317
29	1.15667	0.99833	1.07750	1.2716

df=1.10
*significance: 4.96=.05

TABLE 3

Standard deviation and F statistic
of six patients before and after three weeks

Variable	Before	3 Weeks	F.
1	3.37145	3.44480	.94
2	3.44964	3.25064	1.12
3	4.04969	4.57894	.77
4	5.08920	4.40076	1.27
5	274.59888	885.66235	6.55*
6	189.98071	876.38647	13.24**
7	434.05371	201.11548	4.62
8	445.41675	273.61670	2.65
9	654.26196	875.71362	9.18*
10	434.49023	234.13628	3.42
11	491.52954	98.83655	25.10**
12	755.61475	117.4733	41.60**
13	168.40508	46.85614	13.32**
14	141.28923	56.16907	6.30*
15	614.56519	92.04942	44.62**
16	154.22498	149.69250	1.06
17	1.15840	2.51632	.20
18	1.90557	1.94207	.94
19	1.41675	1.55476	.81
20	1.35351	1.51699	.79
21	1.48761	2.21742	.43
22	1.37727	1.52366	.81
23	1.92019	0.72082	7.07*
24	1.42457	0.68724	4.32
25	0.16678	0.38341	.17
26	0.37030	0.44054	.70
27	0.34957	0.42599	.68
28	0.43785	0.19284	5.10*
29	0.32197	0.12090	7.07*

df=5.5
*significance: 5.05=.05
**significance: 11.0=.01

TABLE 4

Mean and F statistic for before to six month patients

Variable	Before	6 Month	Grand Mean	F.
1	9.16667	12.25000	10.40000	2.96
2	8.50000	12.50000	10.10000	4.91
3	7.00000	9.75000	8.10000	0.77
4	7.50000	10.00000	8.50000	0.60
5	1297.16650	884.00000	1131.89990	0.12
6	2674.83325	920.25000	1973.00000	0.14
7	393.00000	386.25000	390.29980	0.00
8	348.33335	399.25000	368.69995	0.03
9	1986.00000	902.12500	1552.44995	0.62
10	370.66650	392.75000	379.50000	0.00
11	286.83325	247.00000	270.89990	0.02
12	570.00000	249.25000	441.69995	0.67
13	141.50000	96.25000	123.39999	0.26
14	115.33333	96.50000	107.79999	0.06
15	428.41650	248.12500	356.29980	0.31
16	128.41666	96.37500	115.59999	0.15
17	3.59436	3.36936	3.50436	0.11
18	4.14178	3.70453	3.96688	0.20
19	2.79723	3.70374	3.15984	1.10
20	2.85979	3.74786	3.21502	1.05
21	4.01383	3.55743	3.83127	0.28
22	2.83363	3.72278	3.18929	0.07
23	3.65309	2.88786	3.34700	0.21
24	2.52206	2.67014	2.57329	0.01
25	1.44382	1.00509	1.26833	11.54**
26	0.42474	0.84782	0.59397	3.80
27	0.44543	0.92225	0.63616	6.38*
28	1.14835	1.00616	1.09147	0.36
29	1.16109	1.01177	1.10136	0.67

df=1.8
*significance: 5.32=.05
**significance: 11.3=.01

TABLE 5

Standard Deviations and F statistic for before to six month patients

Variable	Before	6 Month	F.
1	3.37145	1.25830	6.51
2	3.44964	1.00000	9.30*
3	4.04969	4.90903	.99
4	5.08920	4.83046	11.99*
5	2274.59888	662.37573	31.43**
6	3189.98071	539.44531	1.97
7	434.05371	292.16577	1.52
8	445.41675	342.03516	17.74
9	2654.14697	596.89038	1.71
10	434.47266	313.97778	7.93
11	491.52954	165.18063	23.22*
12	755.61475	148.63678	8.48
13	168.40508	54.85759	6.13
14	141.28923	54.11404	13.82*
15	614.37183	154.71164	7.51
16	154.06073	53.23276	1.76
17	1.15935	0.82193	51.98**
18	1.90532	0.25368	1.27
19	1.41840	1.18515	.95
20	1.35324	1.30856	10.77*
21	1.63594	0.47966	1.06
22	1.37730	1.25014	I 1.22
23	2.48936	2.61211	.90
24	1.78952	1.77280	I 1.21
25	0.18970	0.21612	1.59
26	0.36974	0.27026	4.59
27	0.34924	0.15654	6.46
28	0.43919	0.16823	2.54
29	0.32168	0.19392	1.89

df = 5.3
*significance: 9.01 = .05
**significance: 28.2 = .01
I = inversion

TABLE 6

Means and F statistic for before to 1 to 4 year patients

Variable	Before	1-4 Year	Grand Mean	F.
1	9.16667	6.80000	8.09091	1.56
2	8.50000	7.00000	7.818118	.67
3	7.00000	6.60000	6.81818	.03
4	7.50000	6.60000	7.09091	.11
5	1297.16650	481.59985	926.45435	.61
6	2674.83325	542.59985	1705.63623	2.71
7	393.00000	442.39990	415.45435	.04
8	348.33325	394.59985	369.36353	.04
9	1986.00000	512.09985	1316.04541	.48
10	370.66650	418.50000	392.40894	.04
11	286.83325	138.00000	219.18181	.42
12	570.00000	138.79999	374.00000	1.57
13	141.50000	103.79999	124.36363	.21
14	115.33333	96.20000	106.63635	.07
15	428.41650	138.39999	296.59082	.06
16	128.41666	100.00000	115.50000	.14
17	3.59436	3.47060	3.53811	.05
18	4.14178	4.25764	4.19444	.01
19	2.79723	4.38370	3.51835	2.65
20	2.85979	4.27762	3.50426	2.28
21	4.01383	3.94537	3.98271	.00
22	2.83363	4.33508	3.51611	2.47
23	3.67309	1.26993	2.56984	4.36
24	2.52206	1.30072	1.96691	2.21
25	1.44382	0.95718	1.22262	18.45**
26	0.42474	0.74754	0.57146	1.98
27	0.44543	0.83766	0.62371	3.79
28	1.14835	1.07259	1.11391	.12
29	1.16109	1.04379	1.10778	.54

df=1.9
*significance: 5.12=.05
**significance: 10.6=.01

TABLE 7

Standard Deviation and F statistic for before to 1 to 4 year patients

Variable	Before	1 to 4 Years	F.
1	3.37145	2.77489	1.40
2	3.44964	2.34521	2.07
3	4.04969	3.04959	1.67
4	5.08920	3.04959	2.67
5	2274.59888	447.05151	24.77**
6	3189.98071	361.10181	74.85**
7	434.05371	302.35107	1.96
8	445.41675	219.75945	3.91
9	2654.14697	398.40479	42.58**
10	434.47266	259.20752	2.67
11	491.52954	127.23206	14.30*
12	755.61475	100.82507	53.85**
13	168.40508	72.39264	6.16
14	141.28923	58.35835	5.62
15	614.37183	113.98976	27.89**
16	154.06073	64.88544	5.39
17	1.15935	0.44453	6.53*
18	1.90532	1.46531	1.62
19	1.41840	1.81952	I 1.57
20	1.35324	1.76566	I 1.76
21	1.63594	0.98942	2.64
22	1.37730	1.79152	I 1.76
23	2.48936	0.49671	24.57**
24	1.78952	0.34879	26.25**
25	0.18970	0.18375	1.01
26	0.36974	0.38871	I 1.14
27	0.34924	0.31001	1.14
28	0.43919	0.19211	4.90
29	0.32168	0.16212	3.84

df=5.4
*significance: 6.26=.05
**significance: 15.5=.01
I=inversion

TABLE 8

Means and F statistic for before to one and four year patients

Var.	Before	One Year	Four Year	Grand Mean	F.
1	9.16667	5.00000	8.00000	6.8000	1.62
2	8.50000	5.50000	8.00000	7.00000	1.55
3	7.00000	5.50000	7.33333	6.60000	.36
4	7.50000	5.50000	7.33333	6.60000	.36
5	1297.16650	965.00000	159.33333	481.59985	113.97**
6	2674.83325	915.00000	294.33325	542.59985	23.38*
7	393.00000	734.00000	248.00000	442.39990	10.34*
8	348.33325	591.50000	263.33325	394.59985	6.06
9	1986.00000	940.00000	226.83333	512.09985	74.49**
10	370.66650	662.75000	255.66666	418.50000	8.53
11	286.83325	274.00000	47.33333	138.00000	59.69**
12	570.00000	247.50000	66.33333	138.79999	92.51**
13	141.50000	179.50000	53.33333	103.79999	30.78*
14	115.33333	152.00000	59.00000	96.20000	9.59
15	428.41650	260.75000	56.83333	138.39999	72.09**
16	128.41666	165.75000	56.16666	100.00000	17.78**
17	3.59436	3.54468	3.42123	3.47060	.07
18	4.14178	3.67844	4.64379	4.25765	.44
19	2.79723	4.07350	4.59050	4.38370	.07
20	2.85979	3.90704	4.52468	4.27762	.11
21	4.01383	3.60297	4.17364	3.94537	.33
22	2.83363	3.99774	4.55998	4.33508	.09
23	3.65309	1.45397	1.14724	1.26993	.38
24	2.52206	1.57330	1.11900	1.30072	3.10
25	1.44382	0.91638	0.98439	0.95718	.12
26	0.42474	1.08150	0.52489	0.74754	4.79
27	0.44543	1.10551	0.65908	0.83766	4.93
28	1.14835	1.23352	0.96530	1.07259	4.22
29	1.16109	1.18339	0.95073	1.04379	4.85

df=1.3   *significance: .05=10.1
             **significance: .01=34.1

TABLE 9

Standard Deviations and F statistic
for before to one and four year patients

Variable	Before	1 Year	4 Year		F.
1	3.37145	4.24264	1.00000		23.91*
2	3.44964	3.53553	1.00000		16.57
3	4.04969	4.94975	2.08167		7.47
4	5.08920	4.94975	2.08167		7.47
5	2274.59888	9.89949	101.00659	I	78.18
6	3189.98071	199.40411	98.85504		5.37
7	434.05371	161.22034	167.68721	I	.81
8	445.41675	74.24620	170.92775	I	3.96
9	2654.14697	94.75230	88.31807		1.52
10	434.47266	117.73328	167.38147	I	1.51
11	491.52954	29.69847	33.29163	I	.94
12	755.61475	.16.26344	22.50183	I	1.42
13	168.40508	7.77817	30.00554	I	11.17
14	141.28923	7.07107	39.96248	I	23.94
15	614.37183	22.98096	27.82234	I	10.98
16	154.06073	0.35355	34.85803	I	7,435.63**
17	1.15935	0.42033	0.54565	I	1.22
18	1.90532	0.56396	1.89107	I	8.51
19	1.41840	0.72165	2.49009	I	8.92
20	1.35324	0.67022	2.40450	I	9.61
21	1.63594	0.04584	1.32720	I	816.75*
22	1.37730	0.70178	2.44605	I	9.08
23	2.48936	0.40126	0.59706	I	1.62
24	1.78952	0.14200	0.33074	I	4.14
25	0.18970	0.17233	0.22339	I	1.24
26	0.36974	0.24652	0.29311	I	1.08
27	0.34924	0.04735	0.26741	I	31.68
28	0.43919	0.11773	0.15400	I	1.38
29	0.32168	0.10622	0.12020	I	1.08

df=2.3
*significance: .05=19.2
**significance: .01=99.2
I=inversion

TABLE 10

Means and F statistic for Control to before groups

Variable	Group Control	Before		F.
1	9.25000	9.16667	9.20000	.00
2	9.50000	8.50000	8.90000	.21
3	9.25000	7.00000	7.90000	.53
4	9.50000	7.50000	8.30000	.31
5	643.50000	1297.16650	1035.69995	.29
6	696.25000	2674.83325	1883.39990	1.42
7	524.00000	393.00000	445.39990	.11
8	708.75000	348.33325	492.50000	.53
9	669.87500	1986.00000	1459.54980	.89
10	616.37500	370.66650	468.94995	.32
11	136.75000	286.83325	226.79999	.34
12	164.25000	570.00000	407.69995	1.07
13	111.50000	141.50000	129.50000	.09
14	137.75000	115.33333	124.29999	.05
15	150.50000	428.41650	317.25000	.76
16	124.62500	128.41666	126.89999	.00
17	3.74846	3.59436	3.65600	.03
18	3.43140	4.14178	3.85773	.13
19	3.19349	2.79723	2.95573	.13
20	3.38334	2.85979	3.06921	.24
21	3.57038	4.01383	3.83645	.20
22	3.29336	2.83363	3.01752	.18
23	1.58215	3.65309	2.82472	2.52
24	1.28292	2.52206	2.02640	1.80
25	1.19134	1.44382	1.34283	2.65
26	0.96296	0.42474	0.64003	7.42*
27	0.89757	0.44543	0.62628	5.37*
28	0.89401	1.14835	1.04661	1.14
29	0.95024	1.16109	1.07675	1.40

df=1.8
*significance: 5.32=.05
**significance: 11.3=.01

TABLE 11

Standard Deviations and F statistic for control to before group

Variable	Group Control	Before	F.
1	6.02080	3.37145	3.52
2	5.74456	3.44964	3.06
3	5.73730	4.04969	2.20
4	6.13732	5.08920	1.60
5	726.65063	2274.59888	I 8.81*
6	827.10425	3189.98071	I 16.46*
7	782.50195	434.05371	3.60
8	1102.81445	445.41675	6.77*
9	776.48242	2654.14697	I 10.46*
10	942.63721	434.47266	5.18
11	120.89215	491.52954	I 14.83*
12	159.75259	755.61475	20.05**
13	110.26178	168.40508	2.07
14	158.99960	141.28923	1.39
15	140.00175	614.37183	17.26**
16	134.60577	154.06073	1.14
17	1.46983	1.15935	1.76
18	1.19385	1.90532	I 2.27
19	2.04978	1.41840	2.30
20	2.03932	1.35324	2.25
21	1.31223	1.63594	I 1.38
22	2.04410	1.37730	2.43
23	0.72378	2.48936	I 10.65*
24	0.32918	1.78952	I 27.82**
25	0.30650	0.18970	3.06
26	0.14755	0.36974	I 5.94
27	0.20013	0.34924	I 2.60
28	0.20332	0.43919	I 4.16
29	0.17265	0.32168	I 3.18

df=3.5
*significance: 5.41=.05
**significance: 12.1=.01
I=inversion

TABLE 12

Means and F statistic for Control to 1 to 4 year group

				F.
1	9.25000	6.80000	7.88889	.66
2	9.50000	7.00000	8.11111	.80
3	9.25000	6.60000	7.77778	.80
4	9.50000	6.60000	7.88889	.87
5	643.50000	481.59985	553.55542	.17
6	696.25000	542.59985	610.88867	.14
7	524.00000	442.39990	478.66650	.04
8	708.75000	394.59985	534.22217	.39
9	669.87500	512.09985	582.22217	.15
10	616.37500	418.50000	506.44434	.20
11	136.75000	138.00000	137.44444	.00
12	164.25000	138.79999	150.11110	.08
13	111.50000	103.79999	107.22221	.01
14	137.75000	96.20000	114.66666	.30
15	150.50000	138.39999	143.77777	.02
16	124.62500	100.00000	110.94444	.13
17	3.74846	3.47060	3.59410	.16
18	3.43140	4.25764	3.89042	.82
19	3.19349	4.38370	3.85471	.85
20	3.38334	4.27762	3.88016	.49
21	3.57038	3.94537	3.77870	.24
22	3.29336	4.33508	3.87209	.66
23	1.58215	1.26993	1.40870	.59
24	1.28292	1.30072	1.29281	.00
25	1.19134	0.95718	1.06125	2.04
26	0.96296	0.74754	0.84328	1.07
27	0.89757	0.83766	0.86429	.11
28	0.89401	1.07259	0.99322	1.82
29	0.95024	1.04379	1.00221	.69

df=1.7
*significance: 5.59=.05
**significance: 12.2=.01

TABLE 13

Standard Deviations and F statistic
for control to 1 to 4 year group

Variable		1-4 Year		F.
1	6.02080	2.77489		4.99
2	5.74456	2.34521		6.36
3	5.73730	3.04959		3.74
4	6.13732	3.04959		4.28
5	726.65063	447.05151		2.78
6	827.10425	361.10181		5.55
7	782.50195	302.35107		7.05*
8	1102.81445	219.75945		26.60**
9	776.48242	398.40479		3.98
10	942.63721	259.20752		13.96*
11	120.89215	127.23206	I	1.04
12	159.75259	100.82507		2.64
13	110.26178	72.39264		2.44
14	158.99960	58.35835		7.84*
15	140.00175	113.98976		1.57
16	134.60577	64.88544		4.54
17	1.46983	0.44453		11.61*
18	1.19385	1.46531	I	1.40
19	2.04978	1.81952		1.32
20	2.03932	1.76566		1.40
21	1.31223	0.98942		1.87
22	2.04410	1.79152		1.35
23	0.72378	0.49671		2.25
24	0.32918	0.34879	I	1.06
25	0.30650	0.18375		2.95
26	0.14755	0.38871	I	6.52
27	0.20013	0.31001	I	2.26
28	0.20332	0.19211		1.16
29	0.17265	0.16212		1.19

df $= 3.4$
*significance: $6.59 = .05$
**significance: $16.7 = .01$
I $=$ inversion

APPENDIX B

Letter from a Self-Primaler
Introduced by Arthur Janov

The following letter may profoundly affect our thinking about certain classes of patients, namely, those with heart conditions. It is the policy of The Primal Institute not to accept anyone with even a hint of a heart condition. Primaling is such an obvious physical strain that it seemed to us that it could seriously aggravate an existing heart condition. Mark, however, has found otherwise and probably saved his life in the bargain.

We did not adopt the "no heart condition" policy lightly. Some acute studies at the UCLA Brain Research Institute (not an official UCLA study) on Primal patients showed that just before getting into a Primal, the blood pressure and pulse rate could easily double, the blood pressure going over 200. But the relief afterwards was equally dramatic. I, too, was hooked up to a variety of electronic instruments during these studies and after my Primal my heart rate dropped to forty. The importance of these acute studies should not be overlooked, for it corroborates my notion that Pain remains locked in the system exerting a continual force. Because we have internal governors which dampen the Pain and keep our pulse and blood pressure (usually) only mildly elevated, we don't realize the amount of energy our system is using to keep the Pain down. But as soon as we rearrange the situation and remove top-layer defenses, up comes the Pain and the alarm reaction of the body. If the Pain were not there, clearly there would be no such reaction. In one case the normal heart rate went up to 225 as the Pain began its ascent. That Pain is a danger to the system and the system galvanizes itself for survival. The Pain was more than a young child could take but it can be absorbed slowly and systematically by an adult; evidently, something the system has not entirely realized, judging by its alarm reaction.

Once into a feeling there is no more cause for alarm and the system is just experiencing. It is not the feeling itself which produces all those exacerbated effects; it is the *anticipation* of it. The dramatic drops we see in those post-Primal readings say something about survival. For the average person with a heart condition there is nothing he can do to stop the constant Pain activation which makes him a sitting target for attacks. The best that he can do is use drugs to dampen the *effects* of the Pain on the heart (and on his blood pressure) but he cannot alter the Pain an iota. And, as I have stated a number of times before, he is in a double bind, for there is a price to be paid for that dampening by drugs. That is the Primal rebound. Symptoms such as an increased pulse and elevated blood pressure are necessary outlets for Primal Pain. To shut off those outlets only means an increase of internal pressure which will eventually come out one way or another. Generally, other things go wrong. The tension moves against other organ systems and so one may, for example, find oneself saddled with arthritis or ulcers and stomach trouble. For others the pressure finds its way out during sleep when conscious defenses are slackened. Though the story in a nightmare may not correspond to any apparent reality of the dreamer, the *feelings* inside the nightmare are very real—they are the result of the built-up pressure produced by daytime drugs. Most heart attacks, not so surprisingly, occur during the dream periods when the repression of deep sleep has eased off, and feelings begin ascending. They are particularly evident in the final period of REM sleep (dream sleep) which occurs in the early morning hours when the person has the longest period of dream time and when serotonin, a key chemical agent for repression, is at its lowest ebb (having worked all night to keep up a deep sleep).

One of the central repositories for serotonin is the limbic system which is the storage center for emotional memories and the regulating system for their egress to higher consciousness. One of the reasons for the alarm reaction in a person about to Primal is, I think, the depletion of serotonin and the consequent partial opening of the limbic gate of stored Pain. It is when Pain threatens to become conscious—when the upcoming memories start to hook up to consciousness and make a connected experience of Pain—that the system goes into an alarm reaction. It is then that the whole system, brain included, gets busy to push the Pain back into its bin. The brain is flooded with thoughts and the body is in a highly agitated state. More cortex is recruited for repression resulting, I believe, in a higher frequency of brain activity and a higher amplitude, as well. We are just finding out that if one pulses the brain of epileptic children to a higher pace one can manage to hold down seizures.* That is, we can artificially soup up brain activity to hold Pain down. Acupuncture is a case in point: an overload of Pain certainly seems to tranquilize.

It is quite possible that a person with only a slightly chronically elevated pulse and blood pressure is heading for a heart attack. We would not be aware of it, however, as long as we do not measure other parameters involved in the repression of Pain. It is brain-wave frequency and amplitude that help keep the lid on, and so long as we neglect these factors, we cannot have a rounded picture of the attack-prone individual. The neurotic's generally busier brain is the automatic way he represses. Conversely, one might say that the more internal pressure the more the brain must do to handle it.

The problem up to now is that we really have not had norms as to how busy the brain should be. We have had no normal people on whom to measure frequency and amplitude.

Therefore, we have taken our neurotic norms for what is normal. Most of

---

*Controlling seizures by stimulating the *cerebellum* is related to this topic. This is analogous to mild electroshock treatment at a positive level: the gate to first line Pain is closed. (EMH)

our brains are working overtime in the service of repression, but because this tendency is so prevalent most of us remain unaware of it. What we are finding in our research, for instance, is that the pulse drops an average of ten beats per minute as a result of Primal Therapy. This means that the norm for pulse rate established by medical men is in error, even though that norm has been predicted on the results of studying tens of thousands of individuals over many decades.

There is a correlation between core body temperature and heart rate. For every degree of temperature rise there is a corresponding increase in heart rate. Conversely, we have found that Primal patients have an average drop in body temperature of approximately one degree. This finding, together with that of lower blood pressure, corroborates our hypotheses about lower rates of metabolism and, I assume, increased years of life in these patients. It has been, and still is, gospel that ninety-eight-point-six is normal body temperature. We are finding that that is not necessarily the case; again, the so-called "normal" temperature we all carry around may be imperceptibly killing us. It is my position that until the advent of Primal Therapy we have never had a normal group to measure norms by.

One never understands psychosomatic medicine so clearly as in observing the acute studies of Primal patients. When the Pain arises it is often accompanied by somatic counterparts in highly exaggerated form. I believe that even the slightest elevation in the key measures discussed above is serious, for it does not mean that the problem is slight—rather, that the internal governor is doing its job well. We should look to the brain-wave activity for further important signs about how serious those "slight" elevations are.

It is the job of the brain to absorb and smooth out those wide swings in vital signs and keep us in homeostasis. It has occurred to me that the swings transfer from the body to the brain; instead of a blood pressure that goes up and down fifty points the brainwave amplitude increases. So long as we isolate the brain from the body and study them separately we are not going to solve the problem of heart disease. A busy brain, one that cannot easily fall asleep, is again a symptom of stored Pain. That activity can also be suppressed by certain drugs. But no drug can make *permanent* alterations, simply because no drug can alter a stored history which has become an inextricable part of our physiology. And so if we sleep better because of drugs we will be more agitated during the day due to rebound. More tranquilizers will put the person on the merry-go-round which eventually must end in premature death. Heart disease is indeed a disease of the heart, but not the way we usually think about it. It is a disease of the feelings that heart activity reflects. It is only dealing with feelings that can offer the final resolution.

About electroshock, what is clear again is the rebound from such treatment. The results of shock often look good for a while. The person functions and he seems more at ease for some months. He will come back, as most do after a time, for more shock; he, too, is on the merry-go-round. What is evident from the following article is that appearances deceive. Electroshock is one more severe trauma to the system and produces an overload so that nothing is felt, at least for a time. The gating produced offers the delusion of health and functioning since the person seems to be out of Pain. The person is in neutral. The so-called health-giving shock therapy is making the person sicker, piling up more trauma to be dealt with by the system. Certainly, it will shorten the person's life by adding to residual tension and making it less accessible. And it is this Pain and trauma which must be felt if the person is ever to gain full access to his lower levels of consciousness. Research indicates time and again that one major function of electroshock is to make early memory irretrievable. It is that fact that makes health also irretrievable. Fortunately, with the advent of Primal Therapy it is not a permanent condition. Here we see someone reliving the skull-cracking feeling of electroshock therapy. How could we know that each experience registers in our systems and not imagine that electroshock also registers? We have been taken in by appearances and have therefore been superficial. People who have had shock therapy often do function better; the only price to be paid is an earlier death. Shock therapy need not *immediately* affect the heart adversely, but eventually it packs down the Pain more firmly so that the person is even less aware that his body is dying.

December 1, 1973

Dear Art,

Thanks for your prompt and gratifying reply to Carol's and my letters. I'm sorry about the lateness of this report on my heart attack and Primalling. Every time I started to work on it, I got into feelings that started me Primalling, and I've just been through another fairly intensive three week period.

On January 23rd this year [1973] I suffered a heart attack with typical symptoms of pain in the left shoulder, vise-like grip around my heart, nauseous feelings, and shortness of breath. In the grip of that vise of pain I felt the truth that I might really die. I vowed that if I survived, I would end my self-destructive life and somehow get Primal Therapy.

I guess I needed an ultimate crisis to get to real feelings and take heed of my intuition which had been hinting to me that this was coming. (It just came to me—writing this—that intuition is simply unconscious feeling trying to become conscious.)

I was hospitalized in an intensive coronary care unit where my condition was diagnosed as a moderately severe myocardial infarction. I spent a week in the intensive unit and two weeks in the normal recuperative section. My recovery was good, and I was released from the hospital and continued to convalesce at home with my wife and three daughters. I carefully followed the prescribed regime of tranquilizers, anti-coagulants, low cholesterol diet, and gradually increasing exercise program.

The end of conventional convalescence came on my forty-third birthday, March 11th. This also would have been my father's birthday were he not dead of a heart attack. I now know what powerful Primal triggers were pulled that day. Anyway, after a very nice birthday party with my family and friends, I was suddenly seized with terrible feelings that I was undeserving, and with unbelievable swiftness, plunged into psychosis. All my efforts to avoid emotional stress for the sake of my heart collapsed. The stasis of rigid neurotic tension broke, and I became a dynamo driven by pure pain for twenty-one hours a day for three weeks and then sixteen hours a day for two weeks. The feeling I have about that period is that it was an ultimate explosion of primitive (Primal) life energy rather than an implosion of self-destructive energy.

After my birthday party, I flew into many rages. Carol had the sense to begin directing me into Primals. Everything got very messy. I got caught up in all kinds of symbolic acting out and even poked out your eyes on the cover of *The Primal Revolution*. Rather than feel my outrageous pain, I behaved outrageously toward Carol. By sheer terrorism just short of physical violence, I pushed her into Primalling within two days.

During this hectic period we shared feelings from the very best to the very worst in rapid-fire succession. Because they were real feelings, we grew ever closer to each other and somehow learned how to help each other into and through Primals. Your books, of course, were very helpful. We would like to suggest that perhaps the Primal Institute might set up an emergency "hot-line" for people caught without guidance in spontaneous Primalling. Several times in sheer desperation, we called the Institute. From just brief conversations, we received that vital reassurance that Primalling is *actually real*! And that's so necessary during those critical life-death moments.

Our three daughters (Lorraine, 16—Jane, 17—and Karen, 20) were marvelous. They acted instinctively—listened to us when we were able to explain what was happening, read your books, and graciously allowed us our privacy by staying with friends or with Karen who had her own apartment. They would check in on us now and then with comments like, "How are my four-year-old parents doing?" We are still amazed that at all times one of us remained in contact with the realities of the external world. Somehow, the laundry got done, meals cooked, shopping done, etc.

I'd like to insert here that psychosis is no stranger to me. I was hospitalized from November 1965 to July 1966 for a mental breakdown. During the initial stages of that breakdown, I was hyperactive, screamed for Mommy, and switched from being left-handed to being right-handed. For a while I was totally symbolic, but then I began to develop what I now recognize as dual consciousness. I remember feeling that I was an infant and growing day by day to four years of age. At that point, I was given sixteen electroshock treatments, and I went dead and flat. When I tried to return to work as an industrial research chemist, I couldn't even understand my own research notes. I felt the utter despair that my intellect and my feelings had been robbed. I was rehospitalized and given insulin treatment. This returned me to a shaky neurotic existence. From then until my heart attack, my technical performance was excellent, but I was very much out of touch with my personal feelings. In essence, I had been split even further much to my own and my family's detriment.

A few days after my birthday, I found that I was picking up exactly where I had left off prior to the electroshock. I had long agonizing Primals during which I felt each and every electroshock. The feeling was that my head was made of cast iron and was being broken apart.

At that time, I also experienced all the pain of breaking my neck in a diving accident when I was twenty-three. I writhed for hours on end with the feeling that wire cutters were cutting steel bands of tension in my neck. My head would flap and twist in terrible contortions. During this Primal, I simultaneously experienced the day that my father cut off the head of my pet chicken—and I faced the horrible feeling that he could kill me at any second. I came to know why I had walked around all my life expecting an axe to fall on my head.

Immersed in a sea of pain, a single pain would come into sharp focus demanding total concentration. The pain would slowly begin to move and I would experience scenes and feelings and move automatically with them. All sense of clock time was lost, and the eternity of a pain interval was my sole measure of time. Total terror of dying was mixed with total determination to live, and I concentrated on the moving pain as one would concentrate on every movement of a treacherous mountain climb. At the end of some pain sequences, I was able to discern and remember the location of tension release of specific muscles in my neck. In a following Primal, my neck would twist or snap as if an expert chiropractor had yanked my head. There was a momentary feeling of fatal pain. Then I would feel that the snap had been smooth and was non-fatal because specific tensions which would have interfered with that precise movement had been removed in previous Primals.

With this repeating itself over and over, I was awed by the relentless power and subtle logic of this natural healing. The same rigorous logic that requires breaking an old, badly healed bone injury and realignment to proper position for natural healing was breaking down all the deformities in my mind. Although all kinds of Primals occurred at every stage of this intensive period, the overall pattern was from head to neck to heart, gut and respiratory, if they can be categorized. I had to feel the inhuman pain of electroshock first to get any access to human feeling. Then, in order to feel pain from my heart, my neck had to be sufficiently loose to writhe safely with the rest of my body.

The heaviest Primalling related to my heart occurred between two and four weeks into the intensive period. I would writhe for hours feeling like seam after seam of a straightjacket was being ripped open in my chest, back, shoulders and arms. Often I felt that vise of total tension around my heart at the beginning of a Primal, but as with my neck, a single pain would focus and move. Often a climactic pain would stab to the center of my heart. Needless to say, it was very scary to feel on the edge of death so much.

Many Primals began with the same pain in the left shoulder as that of a heart attack, radiated to my heart and down my arms to my fingertips as I experienced feelings of murderous rage and the desire to strangle, hit and scratch mixed right in with the desire to reach out and hug Mommy and Daddy. Doubled up in pain, arms folded over my head, feeling, "Please don't beat me anymore," I would hear my father's constant reprimands to sit or stand up straight, and I would arch back, feeling murdered with a knife stabbing through my back.

The tension release from these Primals was tremendous. Often I would experience pure euphoria. My arms were able to straighten completely for the first time in my memory. Previously, my elbows had felt as if I had a bone deformity in them, preventing complete straightening. My chest felt expanded and breathing became easier and deeper.

In April, I developed continual pain in my chest, suggestive of a heart attack. I wasn't exactly following the conventional rules of getting proper rest and avoiding emotional stress. Also, I had stopped taking tranquilizers without consulting my doctor. (I had stopped the anticoagulant at that time on his advice.)

I went to the doctor again, and he diagnosed the pain I was having as "Tse Tse syndrome," an inflammation of the breastbone which simulates some of the pain of a heart attack. I realized this had been caused by Primalling where my breastbone and a point in my back behind my heart were the center points or fulcrums of much strenuous exertion. The doctor ran an EKG, and we were delighted that his report showed an excellent healing pattern, far beyond his expectations.

My feeling about the healing process of my heart is that I was very tuned in to my limitations and only exerted myself safely. I think Primal theory explains that the exertion was free of emotional stress by conventional definition, and the motor activity was healthy exercise in the fullest meaning of the term. I felt also that I really was getting proper rest, since I slept well and woke up refreshed.

My Primalling tapered off gradually after the intensive period, pretty much as described in your books by other Primal patients. I have gradually gone deeper and deeper into pains that I couldn't face before, and I have felt further symptoms of a heart attack—nausea and shortness of breath—as part of the whole repressive swallowing, choking-down pattern. In many Primals I have felt a lump-in-my-throat (or my-heart-in-my-mouth) feeling which relates to single episodes. My mother used to cover my mouth to stop me crying when I was an infant in the crib. I'm currently having Primals centered around these feelings.

When I am free of tension, I feel in excellent health. I have done some fairly strenuous bicycling and mountain climbing. When tension builds now, I feel it and get to my feelings in a Primal.

I had a checkup two weeks ago, and the cardiologist reported my EKG pattern as normal and the evidence of a heart attack "virtually nonexistent." This puts me in a fortunate 30% statistical group. My own truth is that I no longer have a "heart condition." Having felt the bulk of the whole syndrome of a heart attack, the heart condition disappeared, and I am just not that uptight anymore.

Carol and I have adopted a quiet life-style and have become very, very close to each other. There are no secrets separating us; nothing inhibits us from being what we feel. It all feels very natural which is what it's all about.

Looking forward to meeting you and my best regards.

Mark

APPENDIX C

Comment on Physiological Changes Accompanying Meditation

E. Michael Holden

Neither Dr. Janov nor I agree that the physiological changes *during* a period of transcendental meditation are related to those which occur *over time* in months of Primal Therapy, or to those which occur following an individual Primal.

1. The confusion arises largely from an incorrect premise, a premise upon which a lot of current research is being based. While it is true that a relaxed individual with eyes closed has more alpha activity in the EEG, the converse is not necessarily true. Specifically, one can have alpha activity in the EEG while tense, while attentive to specific mental tasks and with the eyes open. It is simply erroneous to equate alpha activity with total relaxation.

2. References on the physiology of meditation repeatedly comment on physiological changes *during meditation*. There is scarcely mention of changes in the long run, day after day, at times when one is *not* meditating.

3. At the start of a Primal, there is an abrupt increase in heart rate, blood pressure and core body temperature. At the "peak" of a Primal these values start to fall, and at the end of a Primal are all *lower than* (before Primal) baseline values. The EEG amplitude and frequency is markedly reduced at the end of a Primal, compared with the EEG activity before a Primal. Over time (months) in Primal Therapy there is a permanent lowering of the vital signs values, greater as therapy progresses. Over time in Primal Therapy there is a consistent trend toward *less alpha power* from the entire brain, with relatively more seen frontally, and relatively less seen occipitally. Thus we view the amplitude and frequency of the EEG as a component part of one's defense system. As Primal Pain is felt, the EEG changes permanently in a way that argues persuasively for a decrease in brain *work* per unit time.

It follows then that *during meditation*, the *INCREASE* in alpha power seen is an outward manifestation of a *more defended* system, not a more relaxed one. To be sure, one is apparently relaxed in an external behavioral way, but the outer appearance is purchased at the expense of a tighter brain defense, or more accurately, by a higher gate to Primal Pain, which is metabolically costly, not metabolically conserving. We have another important reason to hold these beliefs. Those patients in Primal Therapy who *previously* practiced transcendental meditation have come to recognize that meditating is a subtle but quite effective *defense* which makes feeling more difficult. Because they want to feel their early Pain they abandon meditating, just as others abandon other tranquilizing release forms, such as drugs, alcohol, cigarettes and acting out, as Primal Therapy progresses.

4. Thus, meditating produces a transient change in the EEG which is a manifestation of *increased* brain work. Primal Therapy produces a gradual onset, but permanent, change in the EEG, which is a manifestation of *decreased* brain work.

5. We believe that meditating alters the gating of Pain in the brain which allows for outward calm at the expense of inner blocking. Unless it can be shown that transcendental meditation permanently decreases core body temperature, blood pressure, heart rate and mean alpha power in the EEG, we will have no reason to change our impression about meditating. We don't believe it has total brain access, as Primal Therapy clearly does.

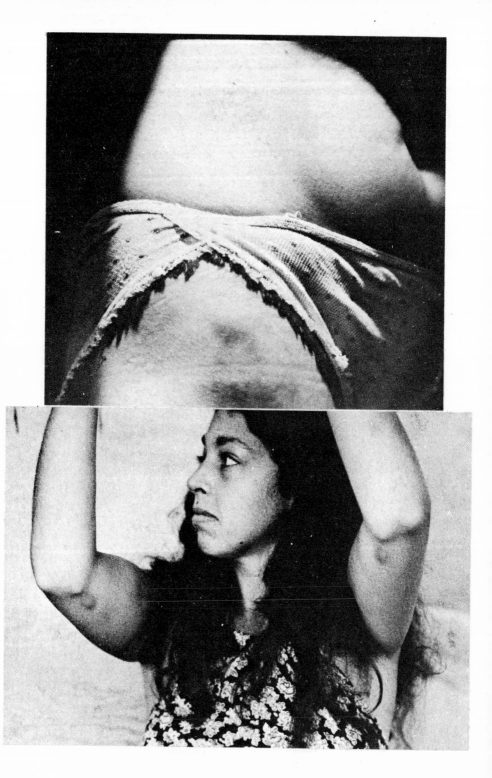

APPENDIX D

Primal Pain and Cellular Experience
E. Michael Holden and Arthur Janov

The first photograph on the preceding page shows the bruises on the thigh of a 56 year old woman, who has been re-experiencing (in Primals) being periodically beaten with a riding crop, from the age of 5 to age 13, in her childhood. Each bruise which re-appears during a Primal on her skin is specific to each beating she received, nearly half a century ago. The second photograph shows the bruises on the arms of a young woman that appeared after a birth Primal in which she re-experienced being pulled out (of her mother's uterus) by her arms. The bruises lasted for 3 days following that Primal.

Such phenomena vividly illustrate the principle that each body cell can feel and register pain and thereby contribute to the totality of consciousness. Pain of such magnitude cannot be fully integrated and experienced by a child, for whom it is overwhelming. Primals have full *access* to these early overwhelming Pains, and allow adults to re-experience and finally integrate them. If such Pain is *not* re-experienced in Primals then the individual must exert a constant metabolic effort in opposition to the Pain. The hypermetabolic state created in response to many childhood Pains is neurosis. Only Primals can reverse the neurotic state.

Previously,* Dr. Janov discussed another woman's leg bruises, which appeared originally when she was born and roughly held upside-down, bruises which re-appeared in her birth Primals. Part of that discussion is included below.

"The most obvious fact is that Pain (physical pain, in this case) which cannot be integrated early in life remains imprinted into the system for a lifetime. When an organism is unable to assimilate what is happening to it due to an overload of Pain there is an automatic separation of the mind from its experience. That disconnecting process preserves and perpetuates the event as an unresolved, unconscious force. The body is a memory bank which preserves all of its experience, forgetting nothing, even when the conscious mind is unable to recall certain events.

*From *The Feeling Child* by Dr. Arthur Janov, published by Simon and Schuster, 1974.

"It is not only the 'mind' which preserves or 'remembers' experience; it is the entire body. Because the body and mind are a unit, the body constantly reacts to experience which has been disconnected, coded, and stored. In other words, Pains (and unfulfilled needs become transmuted into Pains) are tissue states; the tissues 'remember' in a physical way. It is the kind of 'memory' similar to what happens when our systems 'remember' that we have taken a great deal of a certain drug and produce an immunity to it.

"Experience is not an encapsulated entity preserved in the brain alone. An unintegrated early experience sets up a reverberating circuit in the brain innervating the body as an inextricable counterpart of that experience; the site of innervation depends on the nature of Pain. If the early Pain was a physical bruise, then bruising may become a tendency of the organism, as it was with this woman, who often developed bruises which were inexplicable. If, for example, the trauma was of coming out of the womb into a very cold delivery room, then the blood system responded to that trauma by constriction. That constriction process may become a fixed one, so that there is an inordinate cardiovascular response to any stress reminiscent of the early one. Later in life, due to the reverberating circuit of early unresolved Pain, cardiovascular disease may be the result.

"Here we learn something about the healing process as well. In the case being discussed, without those critical early connections there was a continuous inadequate healing of the bruises which appeared on her body. We have found with other patients who were bruise-prone that making early connections during Primals not only immeasurably affected later tendencies to bruise, but also greatly enhanced the healing process when a rare bruise appeared.

"There are target organs of the body which are vulnerable not only because of the genetic endowment (which should not be discounted) but also because of the nature of early trauma. An obvious example would be having been schedule-fed, often starved in the crib, and later having gastrointestinal problems. Those symptoms are the way the body 'remembers.' They are 'translated' memories.

"We must ask ourselves, 'Where was that bruise all those intervening forty-eight years?' Clearly, it was coded somewhere in the system, was always a latent tendency.

"When that bruise occurred there may not have been an adequate cortex to properly interpret the event. Later it would take an 'adult' brain to conceptualize for the 'baby brain' and tell it what had happened to it. That is the connection: knowing the source of the Pain—*making it specific so that it does not have to be generalized neurotically.*

"We can make one general statement from our observations about early Pain: physical trauma seems to be generalized physically, and psychological trauma may be generalized psychologically. Obviously, because of the unity of body and mind there is an overlap.

"In order for that early bruise to be resolved it had to show itself again. Simply to have 'remembered' it in the mind, apart from the body, would have done nothing. It is total psychophysiologic experience which alone is curative. Thus, insight or awareness or vivid remembering does not stop unconscious tendencies of whatever origin. None of them can control the body in any real way.

"The preceding discussion should clarify the distinction between a Primal and an abreaction or catharsis. Abreaction is usually considered to be an emotional outpouring accompanying a memory. One would have to stretch the term beyond its usual meaning to include such a phenomena as bruises at birth. The difference is one between remembering and reliving. Having bruises suddenly appear during a reliving event is not an abreaction; it is a *Primal*."

LETTER   April 14, 1975

Dear Dr. Janov,

I would like to elaborate on your statements about Primal Therapy, the relationship between it and narcotics abuse. During the latter part of 1972 and most of 1973 I was employed as a physician in the Philadelphia prison system. This gave me an opportunity to observe individuals in an acute state of narcotic withdrawal. I was struck with the intense emotion exhibited by these individuals. That they were in pain I had no doubt. Facial configuration, body posture, crying, respiratory patterns and other physiologic responses bore close resemblance to what I have read describing the Primal state.

My observations, which I have been unable to confirm in the literature, are as follows: Physically traumatizing experiences that an individual had while under the influence of a narcotic are not experienced as painful at that given moment. Examples are sprains, lacerations and surgical incisions, which may have occurred days, months or years prior—at the time of acute narcotic withdrawal many of these prior traumas are experienced as pain for the first time. Striking was a case of an individual who had received a skin test for Tuberculosis (PPD) months prior to my seeing him in acute withdrawal. While he was using large amounts of intravenous narcotics it is my hypothesis that there was a suppression of the physiologic response to the skin test. During the state of withdrawal, however, a classical positive skin test developed in the exact spot on his left arm where the material was inserted months prior.

I, therefore, submit that my observations are consistent with the Primal hypothesis and I firmly believe that the acute narcotic withdrawal state facilitates expression of both psychological and physiological concomitants of a pre-primal experience.   R. A. Lippin, M.D.

COMMENT BY DR. JANOV

What this physician found again bears on our findings. It is our assumption that neurotics are often in catastrophic Pain and do not feel it because the bodily system is automatically narcotized both chemically and by the gating system which we have discussed. The addict usually has an inadequate gating system and needs assistance from outside—drugs. The drugs help the body do what it should do naturally. The fact that a skin test mark shows up months after the test was given when an individual is in withdrawal (and is therefore open to his Pain and its concomitants) is exactly the point we have made about birth marks which show up decades after the birth trauma has occurred when a person is open to his Pain in a Primal. A person in a Primal is in a state of withdrawal, so to speak. His automatic gating functions have been interfered with so that he no longer is narcotized, in exactly the same manner as the addict is when his drugs are removed.

Whether the withdrawal is from drugs or not, the subsequent experience is exactly the same; the person is partially defenseless and is open to old Pain. It is then that the stigmata appear . . . the physical concomitants of Pains which could not be experienced totally before.

APPENDIX E

Due to publication deadlines the most recent physiological studies of Primals could not be included in this volume.

These studies indicate precise distinctions between Primals, abreactions and incompleted Primals. In a Primal, the vital signs change *together* and fall below baseline at the end of the session. In an abreaction, the vital signs do not change together, or reach the extreme values seen in Primals, and the vital signs do not fall below baseline values. An incompleted Primal starts with the physiologic pattern of a Primal, but changes to the pattern of abreaction toward the end of the session, and only some of the vital signs fall below baseline.

Those interested may refer to the article "Primals vs. Non-Primals" in the winter 1975 issue of *The Journal of Primal Therapy*.

E.M.H.
September 1975

WARNING!

Primal Therapy should not be practiced by anyone who is not qualified to do so. The only person qualified to practice Primal Therapy is someone with a certificate as a Primal Therapist from The Primal Institute in Los Angeles, California, and who has the approval of that Institute. "Primal Therapy" is service marked in the United States of America and many foreign countries. It may not be used by unauthorized persons.

INDEX

ablation studies, on limbic system and temporal lobes, 146

abreaction, 141, 222, 223, 267 and *n.*, 359, 481–482, 520–521

acne, facial, 384, 416, 418

acting out, 148, 171, 184, 185, 191, 193, 194, 199, 200, 226, 254, 256, 262, 336, 337, 434, 456

acupuncture, 209, 230, 510

acute anxiety attack, 155, 238, 242, 247, 258

acute psychotic episode, 150, 152

Adler, Alfred, 235, 455

adrenaline, 370, 372

adrenaline-noradrenaline balance, 253

age-regression, 33, 35, 105, 220, 264, 352–353

aging process, 350, 354, 355, 356, 357, 359, 363, 364, 366, 417, 494, 495; *see also* longevity

alarm reaction, 156, 240, 248, 304, 354, 509, 510

alcohol, 156, 157, 158, 159, 171, 176, 177, 181, 237, 323, 420

alcoholism, 61, 147, 157, 181, 183, 384, 385, 448, 449

allergy, 352, 384, 391, 392, 393, 450

alpha waves, 20, 38, 49, 208, 237, 242, 258–259, 261, 262, 265, 266, 289, 354, 485, 487, 516; and analyses of data on Primal patients, 485–494 *passim*, 496–508 (tables)

Alzheimer's disease, 73, 446, 479

amnesia: automatism with, 127, 128; retrograde, 211

amphetamine, 153, 172, 177, 178, 180, 308

amphetamine psychosis, 152, 154, 175, 178

amygdala, 19, 21, 131, 143, 180, 198

anabolic visceration (Yakovlev), 63, 67, 69, 114, 118

analgesia, 121, 152, 172; hypnotic, 134

anarchy, 271, 272, 452

anatomic midline, 62, 70, 71, 72, 79

Anatomy of Mental Illness, The (Janov), 4, 27, 65, 109, 210, 211, 381, 421, 482

anesthesia, 50, 115, 153, 263, 305, 306, 307

anger, 5, 8, 32, 156, 167, 192, 223, 253, 272, 285, 370, 441

angina pectoris, 150, 178, 364, 397, 483 and *n.*, 484

anorexia nervosa, 61, 87

anoxia at birth, 114

anxiety, 107, 149, 150, 155, 158, 180, 185, 258, 457, 458

apraxia, 70

Archives of Neurology, 211*n.*, 445*n.*

Aronow, Wilbert, 178

arrhythmia, cardiac, 72, 118

asthma, 71, 72, 81, 91, 93, 118, 125, 128, 143, 145, 152, 157, 184, 224, 352, 356, 368, 384, 386, 395, 484

atherosclerosis, 365, 366, 375, 483

Attachment and Loss (Bowlby), 376

attention, neurophysiology of, 129–130

autism, infantile, 376

automatic talking, 106

automatic writing, 126

automatism with amnesia, 127, 128

autonomic nervous system, 238, 290

awareness: consciousness differentiated from, 1, 2, 3, 7, 39, 225; definition of, 2

barbiturates, 172, 181, 308

Bard, P., 140

basal metabolic rate, 480

behaviorists, 41, 42, 44, 219

benzodiazepines, 147, 180, 237, 419

beta waves, 38, 208, 289

bioenergetics, 438, 440

biofeedback techniques, 42, 207, 209, 230, 258, 261, 264, 265

birth trauma, 71, 79, 81, 82, 83, 88, 89, 90, 98, 106, 110, 114, 170, 210, 222, 227, 286, 295, 305, 311, 313, 317, 331, 335, 358, 431, 521; *see also* trauma, first-line

Birth Without Violence (Leboyer), 47, 155*n.*

blacks, natural childbirth among, 232

blood pressure, 125, 138, 145, 156, 186, 248, 249, 253, 259, 261, 262, 264,